User-Centered
Design Stories

The Morgan Kaufmann Series in Interactive Technologies

Series Editors:

- Stuart Card, PARC
- Jonathan Grudin, Microsoft
- Jakob Nielsen, Nielsen Norman Group

User-Centered Design Stories: Real-World UCD Case Studies
Carol Righi and Janice James

Sketching User Experience: Getting the Design Right and the Right Design
Bill Buxton

Text Entry Systems: Mobility, Accessibility, Universality
Scott MacKenzie and Kumiko Tanaka-ishi

Letting Go of the Words: Writing Web Content that Works
Janice "Ginny" Redish

Personas and User Archetypes: A Field Guide for Interaction Designers
Jonathan Pruitt and Tamara Adlin

Cost-Justifying Usability
Edited by Randolph Bias and Deborah Mayhew

User Interface Design and Evaluation
Debbie Stone, Caroline Jarrett, Mark Woodroffe, Shailey Minocha

Rapid Contextual Design
Karen Holtzblatt, Jessamyn Burns Wendell, and Shelley Wood

Voice Interaction Design: Crafting the New Conversational Speech Systems
Randy Allen Harris

Understanding Users: A Practical Guide to User Requirements: Methods, Tools, and Techniques
Catherine Courage and Kathy Baxter

The Web Application Design Handbook: Best Practices for Web-Based Software
Susan Fowler and Victor Stanwick

The Mobile Connection: The Cell Phone's Impact on Society
Richard Ling

Information Visualization: Perception for Design, 2nd Edition
Colin Ware

Interaction Design for Complex Problem Solving: Developing Useful and Usable Software
Barbara Mirel

The Craft of Information Visualization: Readings and Reflections
Written and edited by Ben Bederson and Ben Shneiderman

HCI Models, Theories, and Frameworks: Towards a Multidisciplinary Science
Edited by John M. Carroll

Web Bloopers: 60 Common Web Design Mistakes, and How to Avoid Them
Jeff Johnson

Observing the User Experience: A Practitioner's Guide to User Research
Mike Kuniavsky

Paper Prototyping: The Fast and Easy Way to Design and Refine User Interfaces
Carolyn Snyder

User-Centered Design Stories

Real-World UCD Case Files

Edited by

Carol Righi

and

Janice James

Amsterdam · Boston · Heidelberg · London
New York · Oxford · Paris · San Diego
San Francisco · Singapore · Sydney · Tokyo

Morgan Kaufmann Publishers is an imprint of Elsevier

Publisher	Diane Cerra
Acquisitions Editor	Asma Palmeiro
Publishing Services Manager	George Morrison
Senior Project Manager	Brandy Lilly
Assistant Editor	Mary James
Composition	SNP Best-set Typesetter Ltd., Hong Kong
Copyeditor	Graphic World
Proofreader	Graphic World
Indexer	Graphic World
Interior printer	Sheridan Books, Inc.
Cover printer	Phoenix Color

Morgan Kaufmann Publishers is an imprint of Elsevier.
500 Sansome Street, Suite 400, San Francisco, CA 94111

This book is printed on acid-free paper.

Library of Congress Cataloging-in-Publication Data

User-centered design stories: real-world UCD case files / edited by Carol Righi and Janice James.
    p. cm. — (The Morgan Kaufmann series in interactive technologies)
  Includes bibliographical references and index.
  ISBN-13: 978-0-12-370608-9 ((hardcover))
  ISBN-10: 0-12-370608-4 ((hardcover))
  1. New products—Management–Case studies. 2. Customer relations—Case studies. 3. User interfaces (Computer systems)–Case studies. 4. Reengineering (Management)–Case studies. 5. Management information systems—Case studies. I. Righi, Carol. II. James, Janice (Janice Sue)
  HF5415.15.U74 2007
  658.5′038—dc22

                                                                                    2007007430

ISBN-13: 978-0-12-370608-9
ISBN-10: 0-12-370608-4

Contents

PART II
Research, Evaluation, and Design 121

Foreword

There once was a young man who wanted to become a jade merchant. He approached a master craftsman and asked if he could become an apprentice to learn about the semi-precious stone. The master agreed. On the apprentice's first day, the master gave him a piece of jade to hold and then told him stories for an hour. None of the stories had anything to do with jade. The apprentice was puzzled but returned the next day to a different piece of jade and more stories. Each day it was the same. After several days the apprentice's impatience was mounting. He arrived at the master's shop that morning intending to confront the old man and demand to be taught about jade. But the moment the master put the piece into his hand, he immediately cried out, "This isn't jade!"

We instinctively recognize the power of stories when teaching children about the world. But stories are relevant for adults as well. Kevin Brooks, the only person I've ever met with the title of "Technology Storyteller," sums it up: "The human animal is a narrative animal. We are made of stories." Unfortunately, as our formal education progresses, we often lose touch with storytelling in favor of methods that are sometimes more efficient, but lack contextual richness.

I assume that everyone with an interest in this book already understands the importance of user-centered design (UCD) methods, so I won't preach to the choir. Instead, let's talk about *how* to learn a new skill. There are many ways. One way is to just try doing it, make mistakes, and figure out what works. Often a memorable way to learn, but perhaps too time-consuming or impractical in the business world. Another way is to seek advice from people who have done it—hear them describe what worked well and what they would do differently. Professional meetings and conferences are good venues for this, but opportunities to attend them may be few and far between.

Textbooks are also a fine way to learn, but they have their drawbacks. As my friend Jared Spool is fond of saying, "In theory, theory and practice are the same. But in practice, they're not." Most books describe theory—the way a process is supposed to work. The practice is often quite different, full of distractions and detours. The schedule slips by a month. Legislation is passed that affects your industry. Your new manager walked straight out of a Dilbert™ cartoon. As Dwight Eisenhower said, "Planning is essential, but plans are useless." The challenge for usability practitioners is to be ever-prepared to come up with a Plan B, because what actually happens to your project will never quite match the way it was supposed to work.

And then there are stories. This book is about the practice of user-centered design, and it's written in a unique way. Each chapter is a case study about a situation where a user-centered design method or process was used (or, in some cases, mis-used). Some chapters are about particular methods—card sorting, personas, remote evaluations, etc. Others discuss various challenges of running a UCD program—promoting it, estimating projects, outsourcing, etc. All the case studies are set in a realistic context of politics, tensions, and ambiguity, because these stories are real. They describe real events that happened to real people, though some details have been disguised. Not every story has a happy ending, but there are lessons aplenty.

A dozen years ago, a friend recommended a book about management. *The Goal: A Process of Ongoing Improvement* by Eliyahu Goldratt and Jeff Cox is actually about the theory of constraints. But it's told as a story about Alex Rogo, the manager of a manufacturing plant. Both the plant and his marriage are foundering, the former despite his overtime hours and the latter because of them. With the help of an enigmatic former professor, he discovers something called the theory of constraints and applies this knowledge to their manufacturing process. Each time Alex finds a bottleneck and fixes it, new and more subtle problems emerge. But in the end he saves both the manufacturing plant and his marriage.

As a novel, *The Goal* would never make the best-seller list—a manufacturing process doesn't make for compelling drama. But it works quite well as a story about how the theory of constraints can be used to analyze and improve a process. It's certainly much more engaging than the theory of constraints served up in a vacuum. Years later, I daresay that I recall more of what I learned from *The Goal* than from any class I took in business school.

Here's an example closer to home. In 2005 I participated in a Usability Professional Association workshop on "Reporting Formative Test Results." The goal of the workshop, which was part of a larger ongoing effort, was to develop a template, guidelines, and best practices for reports of usability tests. A bunch of us sat in a room and described how we wrote our reports. And there was plenty of controversy—I think the only report element we all agreed on was page numbers. Each time one person tossed out a statement like, "Surely you wouldn't write a report without including recommendations," three others would pipe up with real situations where recommendations hadn't been appropriate.

Those discussions were valuable because people explained not just what they put in their reports, but also *why*. Often it had to do with the composition of the project team and the relationships the usability practitioner had with them. For instance, one person might say, "I'm an integral part of the team, and they 'get' usability testing. I don't have to explain it in my report." Someone else might say, "I'm an external consultant. I never know who might be reading my report down the road, so I always document my methods in writing." Those are two very different situations, each with many implications about the "right" way to write a report. By comparing my situation to other people's, I could decide whether it made sense for me to do the same thing they did. Stories hold the kind of contextual richness that helps us make these decisions.

There are several ways you might use this book. One is to be like the apprentice and simply read it cover to cover as a collection of stories, trusting that your subconscious is absorbing wisdom that will appear when you need it. Another way is to consider each chapter an extended example of how a particular method works in practice, and read the ones that are most relevant to you.

A third way is to put yourself in the shoes of each protagonist and consider what *you* would do, before you read what they actually did. There are questions embedded in each chapter to help you to do this. It's OK if your answers are different than the authors', because part of your brain will engage in interpreting the situations based on your own unique experiences. In other words, you'll naturally start thinking about how to apply the lessons to your own life. You might even want to take this a step further and have a colleague read the book along with you, especially if you are planning a similar project.

One way or another, this book lets you vicariously relive the experiences of others and assimilate their lessons sans the first-hand pain. The authors are professionals of stellar reputation, with collectively about a gazillion years of experience. The editors are cut from the same cloth, plus they had the vision and drive to make this book a reality. Thanks to all for sharing your stories. What you've given us is not your typical textbook, but a learning process that is much more memorable, thought-provoking, and enjoyable!

Carolyn Snyder
Usability Consultant, Snyder Consulting

Preface

Those of us who have been in the Usability Engineering industry for more years than we wish to count, have learned many valuable lessons from the real-world stories that professionals both inside and outside our industry have shared with us. The ancient art of story telling is an essential vehicle to communicate what's really happening—both in our world and in our minds as we work through our real-world problems.

In this book, the authors have used the art of story telling, drawing from the tradition of the Harvard Business School case studies, to provide a glimpse of the various real-world situations in which usability engineering and user-centered design meet business and bottom line reality. The purpose of the case studies is to involve the reader at a more personal level by drawing them into the story and details of the various players as they are driven by their corporate roles, project needs, and other influences, including of course, the users. We hope this more personalized approach allows the reader to come away with a more practical perspective on the real-world challenges we commonly face as UCD professionals.

All of the case studies are based on real events, real people, real companies, and real UCD challenges. Of course the names of people and companies have been changed to protect ourselves, as well as the innocent.

Is This Book for You?

If you are a current, or aspiring, UCD professional responsible for developing or enhancing products to enable end users to accomplish their tasks more effectively, more efficiently, and without undue pain, and even pleasantly, then we are confident you will benefit from a thoughtful reading of this book. Where else can you be a "fly on the wall" at such a wide variety of real life UCD experiences without leaving the comfort of your living room?

The case studies in this book assume a basic level of knowledge about UCD, whether derived from a few college courses or a year or so of work experience in the UCD field. The more seasoned UCD practitioner will no doubt recognize many of the scenarios and possibly benefit even more so by reinforcing his or her own experience, and by learning alternative ways to approach and solve commonly experienced problems.

A few of the case stories are didactic in nature, containing a good deal of "how to" guidance, while others are oriented more toward exploration and discovery, requiring the reader to examine the specific facts, understand the motivations and roles of the characters, and search for creative solutions.

How This Book Came to Be

This book is the brain-child of Carol Righi. She envisioned a book of user-centered design case studies that would provide even the most experienced practitioner with insight into the problem solving required for the everyday practice of UCD. She was also smart enough to know that the production and creation of such a book would be a lot of hard work, so she cleverly invited me to join her.

The authors we successfully enlisted to contribute to this book are some of the most knowledgeable, skilled, and well-known usability engineering practitioners in the industry. Their corporate, university, non-profit, and independent consulting UCD stories are, like real-life, sprinkled with both positive and negative events. There are no simple answers to every problem that is posed. But in every case, there are valuable real-life lessons to be learned and insights to be gained that no standard textbook can teach. These lessons are, in effect, the teachings of experts from the field.

We hope this book is one that you will return to time and again as a reference to gain insight, or inspiration when facing the more difficult challenges of UCD.

Because all of these case studies are based on actual projects, the problems posed had actual solutions. We encourage readers to provide their own answers—think through how you would analyze the problem, and posit what you would do if the situation presented itself to you. Not everyone would solve all the problems the same way; in fact multiple solutions are possible. Then, once you have worked through the problems, you can find the solutions provided by the authors by downloading the file at www.mkp .com/UCDcasebook.

Janice James

Acknowledgments

Creating a book such as this could not have been done without the support of many people.

UCD is iterative by nature; we wouldn't expect that writing a book about UCD would be any different. We would like to thank our chapter authors for agreeing to take part in this venture, and for taking the time, care, and attention to endure several rounds of edits and reviews. Their desire to share their stories, and to do so with high quality and good humor, helped make this task much less daunting and much more fun. We are indeed fortunate to be associated with such a talented group of professionals.

A special thanks goes to Carolyn Snyder, Deborah Mayhew, and also, Catherine Courage and Susan Weinschenk, for lending their time and considerable talent to help review these chapters. Their insights and recommendations were extremely valuable and most welcome by all.

An extra Thank You goes to Carolyn Snyder, who was kind enough to contribute a wonderful Foreword.

We'd like to thank our colleagues at Perficient for their help and support, especially Danielle Arvanitis, Jan Arvanetes, John Sulivan, Naresh Tammineni, Jake Truemper, and Suvit Nopachai.

Thanks to our friends at Morgan Kaufmann, especially Asma Palmeiro and Diane Cerra for supporting our vision, and for keeping us as on track as humanly possible.

Finally, a personal and huge Thank You goes to our friends and our families, especially Philip Marlow and Sarah and Ethan Righi Ripperdan for their unending love and limitless support through a very long and focused process.

Carol Righi and Janice James

PART I

Promoting, Establishing, and Administering a User-Centered Design Program

These six chapters provide case studies about introducing user-centered design (UCD) into an organization, how to manage the politics within an organization, raising the awareness of and understanding of the UCD process, and expanding the acceptance of UCD through successful work.

CASE 1

Changing Products Means Changing Behaviors

Jon Innes, Intuit

> *Senior staff and management recognized that they needed to differentiate themselves in the market space by becoming better at designing usable products. They needed someone who could help justify a UCD mission within a company totally unfamiliar with the concept.*

A group of very smart and talented engineers founded JMC Technology. They had designed an elegant and powerful solution to integrate the various enterprise software packages used by midsize to large businesses. The solution kept things like sales orders and accounting packages synchronized in real time, allowing companies to better manage their money. Their software was scalable and could be adapted to work with almost any enterprise software package to streamline business processes. At the time this was a quite a feat, and JMC initially had few competitors. The company grew quickly and held a successful initial public offering.

Soon competitors began to copy JMC's ideas and make similar software. At first the founders mocked these cheap imitations, but alarmingly the competitors soon started gaining market share. What was happening? Debate raged, but one thing management agreed on was that users believed JMC's products were overly complex and hard to use. Feedback from win/loss analyses and market analysts showed a clear trend. JMC's competition was perceived as being more user-friendly. The sales and marketing teams, as well as prospective customers, raised complaints that JMC's UI (user interface) looked sloppy or it "lacked flash."

3

In addition to addressing the direct competitive threat, JMC wanted to expand their business and develop new applications that leveraged their middleware to further differentiate themselves in the market space. Senior staff and management recognized that this would require becoming better at designing usable products, as they would be starting to compete against "GUI (graphical user interface) companies." Management began searching for a solution. They needed someone who could understand their complex technology and make it easy to use. They decided to hire a full time "UI guru."

The Advocate

Jack Chu, the senior vice-president in charge of engineering, had recently hired Mark Ashby as vice-president of applications at JMC. Mark's task was to execute a new strategy to help fend off the emerging competition. Mark was to develop a series of applications that would leverage their existing technology and serve as demonstrations of the "unique capabilities of their core technology." Mark had many years of experience managing software projects and had worked with user-experience professionals before. He quickly realized after starting at JMC that they had a problem with usability. Mark could see that products were not designed with the end user in mind. It was clear from casual observation that the UIs used inconsistent layouts and terminology. This made the products overly complicated and hard to learn. He was one of the strongest advocates of hiring professional help in this area because he viewed effective UIs as key to his team's success. Mark knew there was no way the new line of applications he was charged with building would be successful without the help of a professional. Mark convinced Jack that this effort would align closely with Jack's initiative to drive more rigor and discipline into the overall engineering process at the company. As the key advocate for the position, Mark was chartered with finding and hiring the UI guru.

Mark asked members of the user experience team at his prior company if they knew of a good candidate. He wanted someone who could relate to the development teams. Otherwise, the candidate would never be accepted at the company. After some searching he found Jim. Jim was working at a large software company managing a user experience team working on applications design. He seemed like a good match, because he had worked on very technical products and had experience starting teams and designing first-release products. Mark listed the skills he believed Jim should have to be a good fit for the job.

> **Questions**
> 1. What skills and experiences does Jim need to be a good fit for the job?
> 2. What should Jim do to determine the organizational needs for user experience after he starts?

Analyzing the Situation

After some discussion and several rounds of interviews, Jim agreed to join JMC and lead a company-wide initiative to improve the product design process. From his prior experience, Jim knew one of the first things to do when starting a new job was to analyze the organization. Product designs are often reflections of the organizations that create them (Christensen, 2000), and changing the products requires changing the behaviors of the people involved in the product design. Very few managers hiring user-experience professionals realize that the person they hire will need to change the process of producing the product to have a true impact. Mark understood the job was largely a change management challenge, which was one key factor in Jim's decision to join JMC. After joining, Jim began his analysis of what needed to be changed, promising Mark he would come up with a high-level plan for how to improve the usability of the products within the first month.

Jim started his analysis by getting introductions to the key people working in the various functional areas of the company (e.g., marketing, product management, sales, support, professional services, etc.) and getting their perspectives on what was wrong with the current processes. He also asked them what was working well. Mark and his boss, Jack, were very helpful with the introductions because they had regular interactions with everyone and knew most of the key people well. At first, Jim started drawing traditional organization charts to help him keep track of who did what, but he soon realized that a crucial dimension was missing: level of influence. The official structure did not matter as much as the ability of the group to influence the way products got developed. Not surprisingly, the size of a group was highly related to its influence on the company culture. Although this may not always

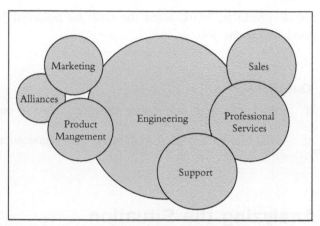

Figure 1.1. Relationships of the functional groups influencing product design.

be the case, most often the largest teams are usually the most influential. Jim sketched out the diagram shown in Figure 1.1, using differently sized circles to indicate each group's ability to influence the quality of the product design.

By looking at the diagram, it was clear JMC was a classic example of an engineering-oriented culture. The engineers were definitely in charge. Jim noted that due to this strong engineering culture, product management was a bit unusual. At other companies where Jim had worked, product management was often responsible for project planning and managing the engineer's interactions with others in the company. This was not the case at JMC. The product management team was struggling because of the historically fuzzy relationships among product management, marketing, and engineering roles. Many of the product managers had a development or IT (Information Technology) consulting background, but few had been product managers elsewhere. They spent a fair amount of time helping the alliances group (the team responsible for developing business relationships) form partnerships with other companies related to new technologies and not much time defining requirements to guide product development efforts.

Jim began setting up meetings to talk to individuals in each of the functional areas. His plan was to interview someone from each team, conducting interviews in the same order that the teams were involved in creating a new product or defining the features of a new release. He wanted to begin with marketing and product management, because in many companies these teams decide what to build before anyone else is involved. Jim set up his first meeting with Larry, the head of marketing.

A short time later, Jim found himself in Larry's office. Larry was a smart guy who knew a lot about the competitors and the overall market in which the company competed. His team produced a lot of material extolling the virtues of the products and gathered analysts' reports for internal use. Larry began explaining the company's situation to Jim: "Analysts who study our market clearly recognize that JMC was the first to market in the space we compete in, but newer competitors keep gaining market share. One thing that keeps coming up is that the product is complicated to use compared to our competitors. Our product does more and is better in many ways, but we keep losing sales to simpler competitors." Of course, Larry was probably partly to blame for this situation. Just like other companies, marketing focused on "keeping up with the Jones's" by adding new features and thereby adding to complexity of the UIs. From what Jim could tell, in the past most features were added based on the reports of industry analysts or reviews of competitors without much additional analysis. Because of inadequate data on existing customers' needs or untapped market segments, the teams lacked a clear vision to guide future product development. Jim could plainly see that this short-sighted race to add features (combined with a lack of usability metrics to assess the impact of these additional features) had caused the company's products to become bloated with features and thus unusable.

A few days later Jim talked to Laura, the vice-president in charge of product management. Laura was a tough take-charge woman who was comfortable working with difficult engineers. She often got involved personally when her staff disagreed with the engineering managers over feature prioritization. Laura reviewed the situation with Jim. She said, "I'm very supportive of the user-experience initiative, but some members of my staff are unclear of how we will separate requirements from UI design."

Jim speculated, "Seems like some of your team cannot differentiate between requirements and design, from what I can tell, and this doesn't seem to be limited to UI design. Some of the requirement documents include ideas for screen designs but there are no accompanying explanations of who the user is, or what task the proposed design might address. I've also observed your staff having long arguments with the engineers about how the product should be built from a technology standpoint. We need to help them define their roles in relation to the engineering and user-experience functions. They need to stick to the 'what' so we can solve the 'how' based on their direction."

Laura seemed to agree, at least at a superficial level. She ended the conversation by saying, "In principle I agree, but keep in mind that the members of product management are very technical and have a lot of good ideas about the technology as well as the design, both technically and from a UI standpoint." Jim left wondering whether Laura was going to be a help or a hindrance. He would need to convince her team to play the role of defining and prioritizing requirements rather than trying to design the products directly.

Next on the list was Jim's own functional leader, the head of engineering. Jack Chu was officially the senior vice-president of engineering but really functioned as JMC's chief operating officer. Jack was ex-army: a tough logical man who prided himself on running a tight ship and getting things done. Jack made things happen and was the source of discipline and order, not only in engineering but also in many cases throughout the company.

Jack made the following comments when Jim talked to him: "My engineers are constantly working on patch releases for problems found in prior releases so they never have enough time to focus on the next major release." Jim knew from his other discussions that Jack didn't like "UI-related stuff" because it caused him trouble in the past. Jack continued, "It seems like UI bugs or usability issues are always causing delays." Jim knew that Jack prided himself on meeting deadlines. Jack explained, "I can't stand the fact that my staff is always wasting time in meetings debating UI design related details." Jim also knew that Jack had been convinced to hire him because of a recent delay in shipping a key product when the founder and CTO (Chief Technology Officer) did not believe it was ready. During the project review the CTO indicated that he was unhappy with the product's usability and overall quality. Jack was frustrated by the CTOs comments; he had delivered on time but believed he was the victim of a poorly defined goal. The engineers had constantly been asked to change what they were building while they were building it. As a result it had led to the engineers cutting corners to meet the schedule.

When he was not meeting with people in the various functional areas, Jim spent the rest of his time reviewing the existing product offerings. One of the key products for the company was a development environment designed to allow customers to create IT applications by modeling their business systems graphically. A small group of developers who had a lot of experience coding GUIs worked on this product. They reported to Michael, an experienced manager, but because the engineers working on the GUI were very senior, Michael took a very hands-off approach.

Michael's team had carved out a niche for themselves over several years and wanted to preserve it. Their product had been the focus of many of the complaints about the UI, and deservedly so. In the past they had tried to respond to these complaints by hiring UI consultants, usability engineers, and graphic designers to help them improve it. They had experienced mixed results with these prior attempts. Also, because of downsizing they had just recently laid off their dedicated graphics designer and a junior usability engineer, who had only started less than a year earlier. When Jim asked several of the engineers for copies of the design specifications and usability test reports, they said they didn't have much formal documentation but might be able to dig up notes of some kind. They promised to look for these and forward whatever they had. Jim asked them, "It seems like we've tried a number of things in the past to improve usability. Why do you think everyone is complaining about the UI? What do you think we can do to improve things?" Jim wasn't surprised when they answered, "The UI is actually pretty good. We can't understand why management felt they needed to hire you." Jim then asked, "I hear that you guys are behind schedule right now. What happened? How do you think we can improve things so you can hit your dates going forward and deliver a more usable product?" They responded, "Management doesn't hire enough developers and give us enough time to do the job right." As he left, Jim thought to himself, "The first step to addressing a problem is recognizing that you have one." There was no evidence of past work on improving the user experience because they hadn't really put any emphasis on making it a formal process.

Some time passed, and Jim was making good progress learning about the organization and its products. But then things took an unexpected turn. The head of sales resigned. During the initial years, sales were good and the sales people were valued. However, when market conditions changed, the rest of the company started to blame the sales team. After all, the engineers believed their technology was the best on the market. Why couldn't the sales team sell it? Key sales staff left for other companies where they could more easily make their commissions. The remaining sales staff, particularly the sales engineers (who supported sales by doing demos), responded to the situation by complaining that the current products were not competitive. They told senior management and Jim that they kept losing deals to competitors who had better UIs (and were easier to demonstrate to prospective customers).

Jim had hoped to meet with the head of sales, but now this opportunity was gone. He wanted to learn more about the "downstream situation." He was curious about what was happening in the field once the product was released for sale. He decided to follow up with the manager responsible for professional services (the team that helps customers install and configure the products) company-wide but found this to be an impossible task. Collaborating with professional services people was difficult because they were always out of the office at customer sites. After some significant effort, Jim managed to meet with some of the long-time staff of professional services at headquarters. They worked with the engineers to find solutions to customer problems with the products. One of the members of this group, Hakim, had been with the company in professional services for many years, helping customers use the products. Hakim said, "I think the products are great, but often the features don't quite work the way you would expect them to. The frustrating thing is that whenever I talk to the engineers about this, they tell me to file a bug, but it seems the bugs I file never get fixed." "So, what do you do about this?" Jim asked. Hakim smiled, shook his head, and said, "Typically, professional services will code up some work-around to the problem and just give it directly to the customer." He noted dryly, "We have some really good engineers in our organization."

Finally, Jim met with Jerry, the head of the support team. Jerry was a strong leader and was highly regarded throughout the company. Jerry explained during his discussion with Jim, "I know from the customer feedback collected by my team that there are issues with the product quality. I'm actively working with Jack to drive initiatives that will improve quality overall." As a very process-oriented guy, Jerry was open to process changes, especially if they had an impact on overall product quality. Jerry explained further, "One of my key initiatives is to help Jack figure out how to reduce the number of patch releases and to figure out why customers won't upgrade to the latest release when it becomes available." Jerry held a lot of power because support was a profit center for the company. JMC charged for support and it was a good business. Ironically, like at many companies, JMC's support organization benefited from the fact that the products they supported were complex and hard to use.

Questions

3. What about the company culture contributed to the problems with the products? How is Jim in a unique situation to help resolve these problems? How might the reward structure of the organization influence attempts to drive UCD efforts?

4. What would you do next if you were Jim? What can he do to get the rest of the company onboard?

The Compromise

After reviewing the products, Jim's initial reaction was to run some usability studies to help him prioritize their problems. While investigating the feasibility of this action he encountered some resistance, particularly from Mark. One day in the cafeteria, Mark cornered Jim. He asked Jim, "Do you really think we need to expend a lot of effort to uncover usability problems? After all, there are some obvious issues with the UIs here. I don't see why we should waste time and resources on formal testing." Jim thought about this and hesitantly agreed. From his initial reviews of the products with the teams, it was clear that there was plenty of "low hanging fruit." He knew that some key projects would only benefit if the problems were addressed very quickly, and none of the infrastructure was in place that would allow him to run usability studies efficiently. In addition, he lacked a budget to hire any type of outside help at this point. But Jim was still hesitant; his biggest concern was that although he might prioritize some changes to the design, everyone had different opinions of how to fix things. Without some type of data, it could be hard to get people to buy off on his expert recommendations. He still only had delegated authority.

Jim did some further investigation into the possibility of running an informal test using the sales engineers or the professional services staff who worked in the field. He knew these people were not the "real end users" but believed they might be detached enough from the current design (which was radically different from previous releases) to get some quick and dirty data. Immediately, he got pushback. Both teams told him they were too busy traveling to customer sites to schedule time at headquarters to be involved with a traditional usability test. When he investigated using remote testing methods, he found that many of the professional services staff lacked the dedicated high-speed internet access that would be required to support such a study.

Jim quickly came to the realization that setting up a traditional usability test was going to be a challenge. When Jim talked to the engineers on Michael's team, they explained, "Many of the features are done, but the product is still very unstable. It crashes a lot. We won't be able to get you a stable copy you can use for usability testing for almost a month. We're short on QA staff, and we're struggling to try and both test the UI and fix the bugs we already have. We're also very concerned that any usability problems you find will just create more work. Every time we modify the code, it requires retesting and we're already well behind schedule."

Jim asked, "Do you have alpha and beta programs?" (Such programs involve releasing an early version of the product to internal users or select customers.) As he expected, the engineers explained, "No, since the product is typically used to develop business systems, we don't really have an alpha or beta program." Jim walked away, wondering what he should do next.

Questions

5. Should Jim try to run a usability test?
6. What other alternatives exist? What else could he do?

Creating Feedback Mechanisms

The next day Jim came up with an idea and discussed it with Michael, the manager in charge of the GUI engineers. Jim suggested, "Why not get the field personnel (sales and professional services) to test the new release? They could help the engineers test the UI so the engineers could spend more time fixing bugs. If the new design is really as good as the engineers think, then it should be obvious to the people in the field. While it wouldn't be the same as customers using the product, it would be close, because the sales team builds demos of the key tasks in the product and the professional services staff helps customers use the broader set of features after the sale."

Michael explained his concerns: "I don't want the team to be bombarded with e-mails on bugs and spending a lot of time explaining the new design." Jim suggested, "What if I get the field to enter their bugs directly into the bug database? I can also collect all the feedback via a survey and summarize it. That way the team would benefit from having a large team of people testing the product who know how customers want to use it." "In addition," Jim explained, "Once the product is released the people in the field will likely find bugs. Wouldn't it be better to give them the chance to provide feedback early while there is still time to fix things?"

Michael thought about this for a while and agreed the idea had some merit. His only objection was that he didn't want the field bothering his team with new feature requests and design changes. Jim suggested that he coordinate this feedback. Michael laughed, "You're asking for trouble." Michael knew that Jim would probably get swamped with feedback via e-mail. Jim explained his plan: "We'll make the prerelease version available only to people who agree to fill out a survey that asks them to rate the ease of use of the design. I've used a similar technique in the past and I know it will scale well and help me prioritize the feedback very efficiently."

With Michael and Jack's agreement, Jim began work on the "internal beta." Jim sent out an e-mail to his contacts in the sales and professional services teams (Figure 1.2).

Jim was very careful to pitch his idea in terms of the benefits to these teams. He knew that many staff members in the field were anxious to get their hands on this software, because they were curious as to what the next

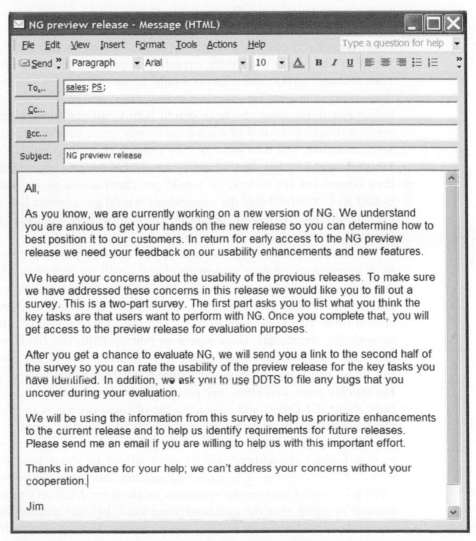

Figure 1.2. E-mail requesting volunteers for the preview evaluation.

release of the product would look like. Jim referred to the comments he heard about the prior releases of the product being of poor quality. Jim tried to tactfully point out that if they weren't willing to volunteer to help out, then they couldn't complain if the next release didn't meet their expectations. In response to his e-mail, Jim got about 20 volunteers.

Soon after, Jim arranged for the volunteers to have access to the development bug database (which was off limits to most staff outside of engineering) so the volunteers could file bugs. He then set up a simple web server and created a short survey that contained questions about software experience (with previous releases and related types of software) and asked for a ranked list of the key tasks users were expected to perform with the product. The tasks and user profile information would be helpful for prioritizing bugs and developing scenarios for usability testing later on. In addition, having the volunteers think about the tasks would help them test more effectively. Jim wrote a simple script that processed the survey form, checked that the answers were complete, and then automatically e-mailed him the results of the survey. He then sent the link to this survey to his volunteers, explaining that once they completed the survey, he would get them access to the software. His e-mail also explained that the respondents would get another link to a survey they could use to provide feedback once they had a chance to use the software.

When the results from the first survey arrived, Jim sent another e-mail with instructions on how to download and install the software. The software was still very unstable, but because Michael's team knew their product was going to be evaluated by the field, they had already fixed some of the more critical bugs. A few days after he sent out the link to the build, Jim checked in with the developers. Bugs started to pile up from the field testers, and a few field testers sent e-mails asking how to use some of the new features. Jim knew this might happen and worried that Michael might get concerned. He quickly tried to address any possible fears. He called Michael: "Michael, how about if I collect and compile a list of these questions so you and your team can review them more efficiently?" Michael didn't believe it was necessary. He explained, "My team has told me that the new version is very easy to use. I don't think there will be many questions about how things work now." A fair number of e-mails flew around, but, strangely enough, there were no complaints from the engineers working on Michael's team. Nobody wanted to admit that the questions were valid, because usually they pointed out some serious flaws in the UI design, so the developers quietly answered the e-mails.

The bug count climbed, but the fix rate improved dramatically as well. Jim joined in on some of the meetings to prioritize the bugs and made an interesting observation. The developers were entering bugs for usability issues that the field testers had raised in e-mails—and they were quietly fixing some of them without any discussion. After some informal discussions, they asked Jim to set up a meeting to discuss solutions to the more difficult design problems raised by some of the bugs, which he gladly did. Jim was surprised that although the engineers were stressed by the work load, they seemed to be motivated by the feedback. He wondered if the feedback was helping them focus. Previously, the engineers worked in a relative vacuum. Now at least they weren't debating what might or might not catch users' attention. Although the feedback was definitely mixed, when the problem was fixed the individual reporting the bug usually responded with an e-mail praising the solution.

Not long after, Jim sent out the second part of the survey asking the volunteers to rate the ease of use of the software. He got a few responses, but not as many as he had expected. Not sure what to do, he decided to call a meeting with some of his key contacts in professional services and sales. Jim also invited product management and members of the product team. On the meeting agenda, he explained they planned to go over the results of the first survey and hoped to go over the results of the second survey. Jim noted that he could only discuss the second survey if more of the volunteers completed it before the meeting. Not long after, he got a phone call from one of his sales contacts asking who hadn't filled the second survey out. Jim listed the names. The next day, the responses from the remaining individuals showed up in his inbox. Jim analyzed the data from the surveys and gathered some statistics about the bugs being filed. Clearly, the field testers found a fair amount of bugs that had usability impact. The rate of bug finding was much higher than when the development team was testing its own code. It was also obvious that the developers had been fixing bugs at a far faster rate than they had previously. At the meeting Jim presented his findings, reviewing the top usability bugs fixed as well as the satisfaction ratings collected. The meeting went fairly well. Everyone was very happy with the progress that had been made. Jim ended the meeting by emphasizing the need to develop prototypes and test them against the key tasks with "real users" before starting UI development in future projects.

After the meeting Jim updated Mark on his progress and went over his high-level plans for the various projects underway. Mark was pleased that Jim had helped them fix many of the UI issues on the project. Mark said, "You know, the field is normally a source of complaints, but this time they've sent me several positive e-mails about how you got them involved. That's a real accomplishment. I'd like for you to make a presentation to the senior staff and engineering managers. Describe to them the changes needed to improve the user experience of our products going forward, and invite Laura, the VP of product management, as well." Mark also asked Jim, "What can we do to ensure that a project to build a new application will be successful?" Jim explained, "We need to build a prototype of the key areas of the application and test the design with end users." Mark agreed but wanted to have his engineers build the prototype. Jim explained, "It would be faster to have a dedicated UI designer do this, so the engineers can focus on back end issues while the UI design work goes on in parallel. Trust me, doing it this way will actually take less time." Mark was intrigued but remained unconvinced.

Jim went off to prepare his presentation. He started to describe what a full UCD process would look like and quickly realized that this would be inappropriate for the situation. He had explained his vision to many of those who would be in the audience during prior meetings and remembered most of them thought he was being unrealistic. He decided instead to focus only on things that the audience members would perceive as directly benefiting them. Jim knew that he should try to summarize his thoughts in less than seven key points (so that the audience could remember them easily).

Questions

7. What problems should Jim identify as key to solving to improve the user experience of the products?
8. What factors should Jim consider when presenting the objectives behind his proposed changes?

The Presentation

To address the problems, Jim included the following actionable recommendations in his presentation:

- Develop UI style guides to drive reuse of code and enable framework development

- Develop a company-wide glossary to reduce terminology changes in products and documentation
- Document use cases to clarify requirements and enable quality assurance to develop tests earlier
- Write user-experience specifications to facilitate remote collaboration and more accurate scheduling
- Prototype all new UIs to ensure the design is complete and understood early on
- Improve tracking of UI bugs so it is easier to understand how they contribute to overall quality
- Review UIs as part of the feature complete process to reduce last minute changes

In reviewing this list he realized something was missing: There were no user research deliverables! That night, Jim reflected on this omission. He realized that, in many cases, other functional teams did a lot of work behind the scenes that people outside of their own group did not appreciate. Do these things matter? Of course they do, but not necessarily to someone indirectly impacted by them.

The next day Jim completed his slide deck. As he did this he paused and then hid the slides describing the user research deliverables. Jim wanted to focus the audience on the key activities that would make the most difference to them. He delivered the presentation that afternoon. He carefully listed all the examples where prior projects at the company had problems that his proposed changes could prevent. Only one person in the room asked him about user research. Jim pointed out that research needs to be done to make sure the use cases are valid and to verify the quality of the UI prototypes and final product designs. Sure enough, there was plenty of debate whether all his suggestions were realistic given the existing resources, but in the end they agreed to the changes in process. More importantly, Jack told them to all support Jim in making these changes—as long as it improved their ability to hit project deadlines. Jim agreed to follow up and work with the managers to get these changes into their plans.

Thank You Mr. Gantt

A few days later Jim met with Mark. Jim explained that he wanted to hire a dedicated user-experience resource to help deliver on the items he listed out during his presentation to Jack's staff. Mark knew this was coming. Jim had discussed his request with him many times before. As they talked, Jim pointed out the efficiencies. They drew some project plans on the whiteboard together and transcribed them into a project management application (Figure 1.3).

Jim pointed out that he could hire a person to support several projects at the same time if they followed a plan like the one described in the Gantt chart. The key would be to make sure the design work was mostly complete before significant development started. That way, he could start the person

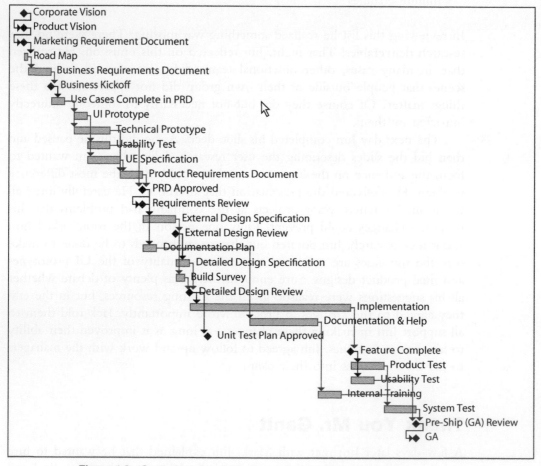

Figure 1.3. Gantt chart describing new product development process.

on the next project during implementation of the first. He could also have this person work on related infrastructure projects, like style guides, between projects. "Developing infrastructure would ultimately make us more efficient on new projects," said Jim. Mark asked, "Would this new hire contribute to writing the GUI code?" "Not directly," said Jim, "but given the new applications would be web-based, the UI prototypes could be done in HTML. This could save the developers a lot of time. During the implementation phase, the developers could copy and paste the HTML from the prototypes into the product code. And, at least the UI code would be stable before integrating it with the server logic code. That way, the back-end code would have fewer changes late in the project to accommodate changes in the UI design. Since the UI and the associated logic often accounts for a large proportion of the overall implementation effort, having the design locked down before committing to the schedule will improve the accuracy of the project plans." (Jim knew that Jack based part of every engineering manager's bonus on meeting deadlines.) Mark was convinced and approved Jim's hiring budget. Shortly thereafter, Jim hired Rick to work on prototypes and design specifications, including style guides.

Doing It Right–Iterative Design Based on User Feedback

Some time later Jim got a call from one of the product managers, Vinesh. Vinesh explained "We want to build a new product based on discussions with an existing customer that uses JMC's back-end software." Vinesh described the functionality at a high level and told Jim, "I want to use your new process of writing use cases as part of the requirements process and I need your advice on how to follow your new method on this project." Jim asked Vinesh, "How much do you know about the targeted end users and their tasks?" Vinesh said, "I have some information, but I admit it's pretty vague. I've been asked to work with the professional services team to do requirements analysis at the customer site. Do you want to get involved?" Jim agreed, "Sure, but only if you get the CTO to request my involvement. I want the CTO to know that product management is requesting my help because they feel they need user-experience expertise to do part of the requirements analysis." Jim knew that to work on a professional service engagement would require Jack's approval. Having the CTO request his involvement would make getting that approval easier. In the past, that was a hard sell because it meant Jim would need to be focused on something not on Jack's scheduled list of deliverables. This time it might be easier to convince Jack—he now had more staff to keep the projects running smoothly while he was out of the office.

With Jack's approval, Jim went to the customer site. He met with the professional services staff to review the requirements work. It was still very much a work in progress. The professional services team was clearly not familiar with doing a project of this type. They were spending all their time with the IT team discussing the technical requirements. Nobody had even talked to an end user yet despite having been onsite for a couple of weeks. Jim met with the manager of the IT project, Mary, and explained, "I'd like to meet directly with the targeted users. I want to make sure the final product is designed to support their needs. I'd also like to see copies of any documentation for the systems the targeted users work with today. This will help me understand how our products need to integrate with the users' existing work environment. They'll accept our products much more quickly if they fit into how they work today."

The next day Jim got the necessary permissions and introductions to go down to the offices where the end users worked. None of the staff really understood why he was there. Jim explained, "Your IT department is working with JMC to improve the software you use." They gave him an amused look and provided him with some good information on workflow and critical incidents that the new software needed to support. Then, Jim gave them the standard pitch, "Go about what you normally do and just let me observe things. I might ask you some questions occasionally, but I really just want to see how you use your existing systems in a normal day." After watching about six different people do their jobs over the course of the next 2 days, Jim believed he had enough information. Given the software would only be used by about 40 users at the company, it was a good starting point. The next day he met with Mary, the IT manager, and reviewed the results. She made a suggestion: "Can you review these findings with my team, including some of the IT staff members who have not yet been involved with the current project?" These meetings were productive. The IT staff members explained how all the things Jim had observed worked together from both a technical and a business process standpoint. Satisfied he understood the environment and the proposed use cases well enough, Jim caught the red-eye flight home so he could be in the office the next day.

Jim worked with Vinesh to incorporate his findings into the draft product requirements document. After a series of conference calls with the professional services team working at the customer site, they got the requirements to a point where it made sense to start the design. At this point Jim called in his newest senior staff member, Rick, to get him up to speed so he could help. Jim and Rick brainstormed about the UI design for the application in a series of meetings, and Rick quickly mocked up some HTML prototypes. In no time at all they had a prototype to show the professional services team and the IT staff via remote collaboration software. The demos of the prototype went so well that the team wanted the IT manager to review them herself in another remote meeting. Everyone was pleased, but Jim used the opportunity to pitch doing an onsite usability test of the prototype. Jim explained, "Until we watch users try to use the prototype, we won't know how good the design really is." The IT manager agreed to arrange this. Jim and Rick booked their flights.

The next week at the customer site, Jim and Rick let the users try out the prototype in a conference room over the course of a couple of days. After testing with a handful of users, they updated the prototype and showed it to the IT manager and her staff. She was impressed enough to ask them to show it to her vice-president. The next day they met with the vice-president and reviewed the prototype. The vice-president had some good suggestions to improve the proposed design, but mostly he was satisfied. The next morning at the airport before they flew home, Rick made minor improvements to the prototype based on the vice-president's suggestions.

Back at the office, Rick started writing the design specifications. Jim arranged some meetings with the engineers who would be building the product in collaboration with the professional services team at the customer site. They had been working with the initial information provided by professional services and struggling to do a technical prototype. Once they saw the UI prototype, they got it. If a picture is worth a thousand words, a prototype is worth a million. The design goals of the application became clear. After a few more days Rick held a review of the detailed user-experience specification that showed all the screen shots from the prototype, illustrating step by step how the proposed design addressed each of the use cases. Unlike past design reviews at JMC, this one went smoothly. Nobody questioned the requirements, and everyone understood the proposed design in detail. Senior management heard about the progress, and Jim got some positive e-mails, which he shared with his boss and staff. During the course of the project, Jim was asked to demo the prototype several times to prospective clients. The sales staff realized that it was much easier to sell an application if they had a professionally designed prototype of the UI.

Summary

Introducing UCD at JMC required changes that crossed the functional boundaries within the organization. To determine the correct tactics to drive the necessary changes, Jim needed to

- Analyze the organization and how its behavior contributed to poor product design
- Understand the agendas of the people involved and what might motivate them to change
- Determine how the problems in the product were related to the operational deficiencies
- Find a way to help create a shared vision about the key user tasks and design problems across the teams

Jim recognized it was important to drive changes incrementally, moving toward the ideal process by engaging the impacted teams and partnering with them so they recognized the benefits through direct experience. He knew to start small and build on the successes to take on bigger initiatives. This is the management philosophy often summarized by the phrase "crawl, walk, run." Organizational change follows the famous psychologist B. F. Skinner's laws of operant conditioning (Schwartz and Reisberg, 1991). Often it isn't possible to get directly "there from here"; change must be introduced in gradual steps, slowly making all the necessary changes to reach the final goal.

One of the major obstacles to achieving a UCD process is convincing people in the existing organization to change how they currently do things. Each of these changes may seem small, but slowly they add up. In negotiating with people over the necessary changes, it is important to take a "win–win" approach (Covey, 1989; Stark and Flaherty, 2003) and consider the perspective of those individuals involved. Individuals and teams tend to focus on what is in it for them rather than considering the benefits for the customer, the end user, or the company.

When dealing with organizations and the individuals they comprise, it is always important to understand why people are behaving in a way that creates unusable products. No individual has the intent of creating an unusable product. Once you analyze the personalities and agendas in an organization, you often find that people are only human, and they naturally make mistakes that lead to unusable products. By helping people understand the implications of their actions and providing them with solutions in a nonthreatening fashion, you can help them change how they look at things. You can change their minds and behaviors so that the organization at a whole can embrace a user-centered approach to product design.

Jim knew that Michael was under pressure to improve the quality of the product and would value having additional resources to help his team test the code. However, Jim's proposal had to align with Michael's goals and provide some benefit other than finding and fixing usability problems. Jim also took Mark's perspective when trying to get the budget to hire additional staff. He knew Mark was looking for a way to improve project planning as Mark's bonus depended on meeting the planned ship dates. Even the selection of the communications medium can be important. When discussing project planning, Jim used Gantt charts rather than bullet points in Power-Point because that was Mark's way of thinking about projects. It is important to keep the other person's perspective in mind.

Jim took a user-centered approach to defining the process changes in the sense that he spent a significant amount of time learning about the problems that impacted the other functional teams before proposing any changes. He knew that selling or marketing UCD is not unlike marketing anything else. That is why he focused on the key changes that would directly benefit the teams during his presentation to the senior managers and staff. A standard "what is UCD?" pitch would have failed. To be successful, one should follow Peter Drucker's (2001) famous advice on marketing anything:

> True marketing starts out . . . with the customer, his demographics, his realities, his needs, his values. It does not ask, what do we want to sell? It asks, what does the customer want to buy?

Jim knew from past experience that every company is different. He had to come up with a long-range plan for how to adopt UCD to JMC's particular situation and then develop a strategy to achieve that goal, step by step.

Further Reading

Christensen, C. (2000). *The innovator's dilemma*. New York: HarperBusiness.

Covey, S. (1989). *The seven habits of highly effective people: restoring the character ethic*. New York: Simon & Shuster.

Drucker, P. (2001). *The essential Drucker.* New York: HarperCollins.

Herbold, R. (2004). *The fiefdom syndrome: turf battles that undermine careers and companies—and how to overcome them. New York,* Currency.

Schwartz, B., and Reisberg, D. (1991). *Learning and memory.* New York: W. W. Norton & Company.

Stark, B., and Flaherty, J. (2003). *The only negotiating guide you'll ever need: 101 ways to win in every time in any situation.* New York: Random House.

Vredenburg, K., Isensee, S., and Righi, C. (2001). *User-centered design: an integrated approach.* Upper Saddle River, NJ: Prentice Hall.

Managing Politics in the Workplace

Elizabeth Rosenzweig, Bubble Mountain Consulting

Soon after Joe's department was established and Linda and Joe learned of each others' existence, a rivalry began to grow between them and their respective groups. Competition between Linda and Joe became so fierce that upper management noticed it, so much so, in fact, that the vice-president of operations delivered an ultimatum to fix the problem. Now Linda and Joe had some real work to do.

The Cleveland Company: Evolving From Old to New Economy

The Cleveland Company is a large old publishing company based in New York City that has been printing large newspapers and magazines for about 100 years. At the turn of the century they were publishing the smart well-designed publications that it seemed everyone was reading. In fact, Cleveland held the largest share of the publishing market in the United States for most of the last century. And because of their corporate culture and success, Cleveland enjoyed great employee loyalty. Most of the employees signed on young and worked there for the duration of their careers.

By the mid-1930s the Cleveland Company had over 500 people working for them in the New York City area. By 1940 they were up to 750 employees. Later, during World War II, Cleveland started branching out to Europe and Japan with publications for American soldiers, medical professionals, and other expatriates. After the war, Europe and Japan were busy rebuilding; they didn't have the resources to create English language publications. Cleveland filled that need.

The lack of external competition created a company culture that was focused on looking inward. During the first years of the company, because they had no competition, the culture created an internal competition for power and money. The larger the corporate structure became, the more the internal power struggles developed. The leaders at Cleveland thought this environment was a good way to keep ahead in the marketplace and spur innovation. But they didn't see the downside: A competitive internal company culture does not encourage collaboration and can impede a realistic approach to the changing marketplace.

Nevertheless, the Cleveland Company enjoyed profits from the traditional printed newspaper business until early in the 21st century. Even up to 2002, Cleveland was making most of its money from its newspapers. However, the market research team believed that trend was going to change and that by 2007 more profit would be coming from digital than from printed newspapers. Even as early as 2004 the annual report showed a trend that would prove them right. The digital online news sites were drawing more readers than printed papers. Because the Internet allowed newspapers to be sent to many more people in shorter time and for lower subscription rates, this challenged the original market for printed newspapers. Consequently, the marketing team started researching innovative ways to make money selling news online.

The only concern regarding these new future strategies came from the research and development group for traditional print technologies. They wanted to spend money to improve their area of the business, to make it more efficient and cost effective, and to salvage their jobs. Meanwhile, the digital print team within the research and development department also wanted a bigger budget so that the Cleveland Company could be prepared to implement newer digital printing solutions. This set up a conflict for research and development funds that led to several power struggles within the company: The research and development team saw that digital was the future and that resources should be focused on creating digital technology and delivery systems for the publications worldwide. But the sales and printing departments did not want to sacrifice their work and subsequent profits for digital research, because the paper publishing business was still producing most of the profit for the company.

Elsewhere in the company, an incident occurred that created a new focus for Cleveland. The company didn't really pay much attention to human factors until a worker on the printing press injured himself and started drawing workmen's compensation. The company vice-president in charge of finance heard of "human factors" and decided to bring a professional in to improve the ergonomics of the pressroom. Before that, workers were getting injured because of the placement of presses and cutting machines in the room. Injuries occurred because the workflow in the press room did not take into account human needs and efficiencies, such as how close cutting machines should be to presses and whether some of the presses needed platforms for the workers to keep them from being too close to the grippers on the press. The new layout of the pressroom not only helped reduce injuries, it also improved performance and output of the presses.

The new focus on human factors affected both the reduction of injuries in the pressroom and increased efficiency in printing production. This impressed the management team at Cleveland. The result was that Cleveland established a world-class human factors lab in the main office in New York City. Linda Wood, a young hardworking front-line manager, was tapped to lead this group. Linda had spent her whole career at Cleveland and approached her work in the formal way that was the Cleveland culture. She felt comfortable with the structure and rules of a large corporation. Linda was proud of her team, especially the guidelines and processes they created for user-centered design within the Cleveland Company.

Linda's group initially focused on workplace issues, but after a few years the management team realized they should be doing research as well. The human factors group was divided into two units. One was placed in charge of workplace issues, whereas the other conducted research. Linda led the research group, whose mission was to find and integrate new technologies and practices for creating a more user-friendly digital layout design publishing system. Linda's group subsequently developed several system solutions and technologies for printing and typesetting. She used traditional development methods and processes that Cleveland had in place for over 30 years.

When the digital revolution hit and the New York City group became interested in digital equipment, Linda's research group knew that it was important to develop electronic information systems with usable user interfaces. However, at the same time new digital research in publishing was taking place in a remote Cleveland office in northern California. This group, largely unknown to Linda, was led by Joe Smith. Joe, who had studied human computer interaction at California Institute of Technology, was very confident of his skills. He enjoyed developing close working relationships with his coworkers, no matter where they worked. Joe was a people person; he always asked his coworkers about their home life and found they were also interested in his.

The company was just beginning to have their main operations decentralized when Joe was hired into the research group in California. Cleveland started this office as a "skunk works" idea factory to generate innovative ideas for their online digital offering, Cleveland.com. The California office had hired all their staff from the Silicon Valley area; they had all worked at various start-ups and other software companies. This group reported to the marketing division at the Cleveland Company but worked on both market needs and the software development together to create the user experience. They were familiar with operating on tight schedules that included integrating new technologies and working with remote teams.

Neither Joe nor his manager, Daniel Sky, knew much about the human factors groups in New York. They knew there was another group within the company doing similar work, but they didn't know where it reported in the organizational structure.

When Joe entered Daniel's office first thing on a Monday morning, Daniel greeted him warmly and wished him a bright future at Cleveland. Joe was encouraged by the greeting and told Daniel that he wanted to contribute to Cleveland's efforts to keep up with current digital technology by creating a strong online presence. Wanting more information, he asked, "Our main office is in New York. What is our relationship to them?" Even though he was usually laid back, Joe wanted to be well prepared with regard to understanding the corporate culture of his new employer.

Daniel smiled and said, "We are absolutely in the midst of a great change. The company is working hard to build on our brand to create a world-class online digital experience. Cleveland.com has a great group of developers and webmasters who create the digital offering. However, there are no interaction designers or even web designers in the group. Unfortunately, the group in New York is really still focused on the traditional analog print technology. Since they are focusing on the printed piece, it will be up to us to lead the way in the digital user experience."

Joe was excited: "I didn't realize that our mission here in California was so clear. It sounds to me like we are supposed to push the digital envelope. But tell me, Daniel, is there anyone in New York I should be checking in with, you know, folks who are playing with digital experience at all?" Daniel replied, "I don't really know anyone in New York City who is charged with improving the digital user experience for the Cleveland Company news outlets. Perhaps I should ask around and find out who the webmasters and developers are in the New York office, and indeed, if headquarters has any there." Joe said, "Wow, I didn't realize there could be so little happening there." Daniel replied, "Well, Cleveland is a large old company. It is possible something is going on somewhere we don't know about, but I believe if there were, I would have heard about it by now. At any rate, I'll do what I can to help with the liaison; welcome to the California development team!"

Joe left that first meeting excited, encouraged, and looking forward to breaking new ground in the digital user experience for online news.

Questions

1. Where should Joe position his department within the Cleveland Company to be more effective? What should Joe be thinking about to make this decision?

Sibling Rivalry

Soon after Joe's department was established and Linda and Joe learned of each others' existence, a rivalry began to grow between them and their respective groups. Even though Linda's team was originally only working on the old press machines and workplace human factors, the fact that her team was at the geographic heart of the company made her feel confidant that her group was secure and powerful. It didn't matter that she was not experienced in user interface design and usability; she had a large staff and they seemed to work well together. Linda ran a tight ship. She prided herself on sticking to deadlines and coming in under budget. She had a lot on her plate and liked things that way: Many products ended up in Linda's lab.

On the other hand, Joe was accustomed to working with small, nimble, remote teams and often didn't meet his coworkers face to face, only on the phone or via a videoconference. Despite this experience Joe really enjoyed socializing with the people he worked with. Joe's group was one of the few in the company that was doing innovative digital product design and was thus a valuable asset for Cleveland Company. Although Joe's group was fast on its feet, it did not always meet delivery schedules. Nevertheless, Joe gave his folks a lot of rope. "After all," he thought, "how can you be innovative if you're not given the freedom to do so?"

Even though they seemed to be working in different areas, the competition between Linda and Joe became so fierce that upper management noticed it. In fact, it was an embarrassment for them. Lyle Cane, the vice president of operations, called a meeting with Joe and Linda, as well as with Sean Green, the director of design, and Kim Lee, director of the website, all based in New York City. Sean and Kim worked quite well together but were affected by the competition between Linda and Joe because they worked closely with them as well. The meeting, they all hoped, would resolve these tensions.

The Team Meeting

The meeting took place in New York City in a conference room at the main printing plant. Joe flew in a day early to have time to rest from his jet lag before the 7:30 a.m. meeting the next morning. He felt somewhat put out and annoyed; he had to take an extra day away from his family, and no one that he worked closely with on a day-to-day basis would be at the meeting. He truly was the "out-of-towner." In addition to the stress of travel and jet lag, Joe had been busy working on his project and taking care of some personal issues in his life, so he hadn't set aside enough time to prepare in a careful way for the meeting. If Joe had more time, he thought he would have called Linda before the meeting to check in and set a more collaborative tone.

Linda, on the other hand, did spend some time preparing for the meeting. At Lyle's request, she had even reserved a conference room in her building and ordered the food. Other staff members from the Cleveland and New York offices had to come to her building for the meeting.

When Joe arrived at 7:25 a.m. to the conference room, he was the last one there. Even though he arrived early to chat and connect with people on a personal level, everyone else, knowing that breakfast was available, was already there, drinking coffee and having donuts. They were making jokes and were clearly quite comfortable with each other. Joe was tired and a little tense. Linda greeted him stiffly and asked him about his flight. When Joe commented that he should have packed a lunch because the airlines no longer serve food, she quickly countered that she always remembered to pack a lunch because of the unreliability of the airlines. Feeling a bit put off by this odd exchange, Joe was relieved to see Kim, who chatted about his children with him. Then, just as Sean Green approached to discuss some technical issues around the graphic design, Linda interrupted and called the meeting to order. Joe thought this was a bit insensitive of Linda. After all, Lyle, vice-president of operations, had called this meeting. Lyle stood quietly behind Linda until she noticed him. Linda finally sat down and Lyle took the helm.

Lyle said, "Okay folks, let's get started." Everyone else immediately sat down and got settled. Joe looked around for an agenda, but it appeared that there wasn't one.

Lyle began, "I know it has been challenging for Cleveland Company to make the change to digital. The big push right now is to balance our print business with our digital online presence. We are exploring how to keep that balance while staying on the bleeding edge. And let's face it; we know it has not been easy for you guys in the trenches. You have had to add new methods to your own bag of tricks, and we are piling more and more on you to do. But make no mistake: Having the California site and the New York headquarters working together is important to our business and will probably lead the way in integrating new technologies to our foundation."

Everyone looked around the room nervously. They all knew the history of Joe and Linda's lack of collaboration.

"I know that change can be challenging," Lyle continued, "but that's no excuse for not working together. Unless you can sort this out, I'm going to find an organizational consultant to come in to help this process along. So here's your agenda for today: I advise you to take this time to put the big issues on the table. Lay the groundwork here if you can. See how far you can go in my absence; I have a meeting with our CTO. I'll be back in an hour."

Needless to say, Lyle's speech was sobering. Joe, Linda, and everyone else in the room didn't have much else to say; they were flabbergasted. Everyone knew what the problems were. Underneath the practical issues that led to some problems, there were also underlying emotional issues. Linda and Joe were very different people. Linda was very structured and liked to work within constraints of the job, the company, and the economy. Joe was more experimental and liked to spend time brainstorming and thinking outside of the box. Linda took a more formal approach to working relation-ships, whereas Joe liked to be more personal with his work colleagues. Linda was a company woman, working for Cleveland her whole career. Joe was very much a California man who loved a laid-back lifestyle, exploring and thinking about new technologies, and not letting the structure of his job get in the way of his creativity.

Lyle left the room and everyone let out a sigh of relief. Linda decided to take the lead. "We might as well put our stuff on the table. I'm wondering why they have to go to an outside consultant to 'fix' this. I don't see *such* a big problem here." But Kim had had enough. "Linda, face the facts. There is a communication problem here as well as a difference about goals. Digital technology will push the conventional print business out. We have to face the fact that the marketplace is changing faster than we are!"

"I agree," Sean piped in. "Hey, look, Kim and I have a great relationship, but honestly, I can't say the same for other departments." He looked at Linda for a long time. Things were getting extremely uncomfortable. "And whose fault is that?" Linda was on the defensive. "It wasn't right for Lyle to dump this on the table at this meeting and leave! I've been working hard at this for a long time. Besides, I'm not convinced of what you said, Kim. I think that paper will never be outdated."

It was finally Joe's turn to speak. He composed himself and said, "That may be, but we have to figure out how to make this work. The company's future is in our hands." Attempting to be positive, Joe offered, "I will try to be more communicative and be proactive. If I need something, then I will ask for it," Joe said. But Linda had no response. She always asked for and got what she needed—in spades. So she didn't know quite what to say. But she searched for words because she began to realize how important this process was. She didn't want to fail. Besides, she'd be humiliated if an outside consultant had to evaluate her.

Looking at Joe, Kim said, "I guess it would help to keep us reminded that you are several time zones away. Look, let's try this: Let's make a list of our strengths and how we can build on them. Then we can tackle the problems more easily."

"Sounds good," Linda concluded. Somehow she seemed momentarily meek. She still hadn't the foggiest idea how to define the issues and how to communicate with someone who used a different style than hers. But she knew she needed to try.

A few more comments were made, and the meeting was finally over. Linda and Joe convinced Lyle that they had made progress on moving forward in a more positive manner. But neither truly believed it.

Joe went back to California and immediately scheduled a meeting through Daniel's online calendar. He had to brainstorm a solution to these problems, and fast.

A New Leader Comes to New York City

Joe returned to California and looked forward to his meeting with Daniel, where he hoped to get some help in navigating through the difficulties with Linda. When Joe got to Daniel's office he didn't wait to sit down before he began. "I was a bit surprised at the outcome of the meeting in New York. Do you know Lyle Cane? He called the meeting, but I couldn't figure out whether he or Linda was running it. Then Lyle gave us an ultimatum, to create a better working relationship or he would bring in a consultant to shake things up. Frankly, it was a bit confusing since I didn't realize there even was such a big problem until I got there. I don't think they have a lot of experience working in remote teams."

"Joe, perhaps I should have had a longer talk with you before you left. I was aware that there was a bit of bad blood coming from Linda's team, but I thought it would blow over. I think they were not happy when we created our positions here. My impression was that they thought they should be doing this work," Daniel said kindly.

A lightbulb went on in Joe's head. "Well, that explains a few things, but I still need to figure out how to bridge this gap. Do you have any ideas?" Joe asked.

"The only thing I can think of is to try to move this away from a personal thing between you and Linda and create a team spirit. Maybe I should get our developers to check in with Linda. In turn, you can call a meeting with their folks and ours and create a plan for integrating some of our research work into their commercialization processes."

Over the next several weeks Joe set up some meetings with Linda and they tried to improve their working relationship. However, it was very challenging. Linda suggested she come out to the west coast to work together with Joe. While he appreciated her taking initiative, it also made him suspicious as to what her real motive was. Perhaps she was looking to take over his group.

Nevertheless, they made some headway in their working relationship when they worked on a project together. They had their teams working on separate parts of an online news service. Typically, the news was laid out on the page physically, copied verbatim from the print version, and then pasted onto the website. But Joe thought that the online experience should be unique and not try to mirror the printed piece. It took quite a while and a good deal of effort on both Joe's and Linda's part for them to reach a compromise. Finally, it seemed they found a solution in which Joe's group would design templates for the news and Linda's group could place the content. It worked for about a week, until Joe looked online and realized that only the first page used the new layout. The rest looked sloppy and formatted incorrectly.

The next year Lyle retired, and Joe and Linda were truly left to their own devices for the next several years. Linda's group was so accustomed to the old technology for developing printed newspapers that they were having a great deal of trouble making the transition to digital. Meanwhile, Joe was so sensitive that everything looked like a direct attack on him. Sometimes it seemed things would improve, only to blow up over a small issue. The struggle was real, even though each believed they were doing their best to be respectful and helpful to the other. They agreed to disagree on several issues, and that became the foundation for their work together.

Finally, dissatisfied with this lack of progress, the Cleveland Company's upper managers decided to reorganize the team. They brought in Tim, a new leader whose mission it was to bring the team together by taking the lead of all groups. Only the upper managers interviewed Tim, and none of his peers or direct reports was involved in the hiring process. This was the traditional way that employees were hired at Cleveland.

Meanwhile, the Cleveland Company managers had been reading about user-centered design (UCD) and wanted to bring it into front and center of the product development life cycle. They decided to put together a central group that pulled together design, human factors, usability, and innovation. This new UCD group, which Tim would lead, would be based at the headquarters in New York City, because all but one of the groups were based there. Before this reorganization, Linda's group had reported to the research labs and Joe's group reported to the marketing division. Now they were part of the same central group. The upper managers hoped this would bring Linda and Joe together, because they were now on the same team and therefore shouldn't have to compete for the same work and resources.

Tim didn't know the history of and the extent to which Linda and Joe had problems. He had worked in other large old economy companies. He knew many of them had an internal competitive environment and had learned that it was wise to get the lay of the land before making any plans. Tim knew that his new UCD group had not worked as a single team before. He also knew he needed to move slowly to make the best progress with a long-lasting solution.

Tim spent his first week getting to know the team in New York City. Linda walked Tim around her world-class human factors lab and introduced him to each team member. She followed the introductions with a meeting between Tim and all members of her team, who presented their work in great detail.

Tim went around and met with managers of the graphics, package, and industrial design groups. Those managers had their staff present their projects to Tim. He spent a lot of time walking around the company, casually meeting with the teams, going through their labs and their projects. Tim also made sure he was in the cafeteria at lunchtime so that he could get to know his staff. Tim even started playing golf at the same clubs where his managers played so he could develop a good team spirit in his division. Tim succeeded in developing a good working relationship with all of the teams in New York City. He created a team where all the members believed they had value and that their work was important.

No, You Come to Me

Because Tim was spending so much time getting the big team together in New York City, he didn't get a chance to meet the team in California. Tim had been working for Cleveland Company for over 2 months and he was still unable to schedule a visit to California, even though Joe reported directly to him. It seemed that every time Tim scheduled a trip to meet with Joe, he canceled it.

Tim set up some division meetings and invited Joe to call in to those. They were usually early in the morning eastern time, so Joe had to get up at 6:00 a.m. his time to call in. Joe was often frustrated because the meetings didn't use the screen-sharing system Cleveland had at its disposal. In addition, the handouts or presentations were not made available ahead of time. Joe couldn't see the presentations or read the handouts the other meeting participants could, and this left him feeling disconnected.

Joe had several one-on-one meetings with Tim over the phone and finally asked him for a face-to-face meeting. "I think it would be helpful if you could come out here and meet the team," Joe said, paying attention to the tense tone of his voice. "I know you are busy getting the large team in New York City together, but we would appreciate meeting you as well," he said evenly.

"I see your point. I wish it were that simple. I have our CTO breathing down my back to put things together quickly in New York City," Tim told him, directly but not unkindly. "Instead, I would appreciate it if you could come out to New York City, Joe. I will make sure we get some time to talk for a one-on-one while you are here. You can catch up with Linda and I know there are other folks here in New York City you can see while you are here," Tim concluded.

Joe was reluctant to go, because he was concerned he might be losing some power. Nevertheless, he believed he had no choice but to accept and made his plans to go to New York City.

Joe decided to compile a slide presentation that included summaries from every member of his usability team. He wanted to make sure that Tim understood the capabilities of his team. Joe also decided to meet with his team right before he left for New York City. He wanted to give everyone a chance to present their work so he would understand it well and in turn would be able to present it to Tim.

When Joe started the meeting with his team, he was wondering whether to let them know he was frustrated with Tim or not. He wanted to be professional, but he knew the team was feeling the same way, and he wanted to make them feel better and allow them to vent if they needed to. Joe asked everyone how they were doing and spent a few minutes on small talk to make everyone relaxed.

Joe exclaimed, "I can't believe I have to fly into New York City in January. It must be 10 below." One of the younger team members, Charley, commented, "Yes, and I guess it is just as 'cold' inside the Cleveland Company office building as outside on the street in New York City." His tone and emphasis of the word "cold" left no one in doubt about his feelings about Linda's team and their treatment of the California team. "Actually, I am happy to have a chance to wear my new ski parka; it's my favorite color." That got a laugh, and everyone felt a little better.

Joe finally decided to just go straight to the heart of the problem. "Folks, I understand you're feeling frustrated and the truth is, I'm also frustrated. I know that we haven't always felt a part of the action at Cleveland. We all think we have great solutions to get the company into the digital world and they are not listening to us, not investing in our work. So my plan is to go to New York City and represent our team in the best light possible. In addition, I want to ask Tim how we fit into his big picture. I was planning to give him plenty of ideas of things we can do, deliverables and processes we can add to his team. So, show me what you have."

Charley went first and presented his work on flash demos for voting technology. Although it was slick and timely and integrated many emerging technologies, it was not directly related to printing and Joe was nervous he would get criticism from Tim for that. Emma showed a demo of a new e-book she was working on that could download 20 daily newspapers and parse them for the reader. Dan showed off his new web design for the San Francisco daily online version of the printed paper.

In spite of some reservations, overall Joe was quite confident his trip to New York City would be productive and time well spent.

Questions

5. What were some of Joe's feelings about having to meet Tim in New York City that would likely impact his attitude during the meeting? How did Joe decide to handle his feelings? What worked and what didn't work?
6. What should Tim to do prepare for the meeting? What should Joe do to prepare for the meeting?
7. Is there a bigger issue here for Joe in terms of his group and their relationship to the New York City group and to Tim in particular?
8. Is there anyone who can help? What is the real issue here for Joe related to Tim and the Cleveland Company?

Balt and Switch

Joe arrived in New York City late in the morning. He was hopeful that he could talk to Tim and make him see how things were going from the California's team point of view. Joe wanted to share some of the team's new technology development with him and show him the great potential of what could be done. Joe was even hoping that this new work would get him a well-deserved promotion. His meeting with Tim was scheduled first thing after lunch. Joe took the time to take care of himself and reduce his stress by getting a nice healthy lunch before the meeting.

But when Joe walked in the room his jaw dropped. He was surprised to find Linda in the meeting, sitting in the one chair left open on Tim's side of the table. Joe sat down in the open chair on the other side of the table. He was trying to control his reactions, because had been told it would be a one-on-one meeting. "What is Linda doing here?" he wondered.

"Hi Linda. I didn't expect to see you today. Good to see you," said Joe, trying to be pleasant. "Are you just finishing up your meeting with Tim?"

"No, I asked her to be here for our meeting," Tim stated, flatly.

"Oh, I was led to believe that this was our one-on-one meeting. I didn't realize we were having a team meeting instead," Joe replied. He felt blind-sided but tried hard to sound calm and even toned. Tim told Joe, "I thought it would be helpful to have Linda here, since she has a better sense of the big picture here in New York City." Joe felt the room spin. He couldn't believe that after all he had been through with Linda, that she would betray him by stepping into his territory. It became painfully clear to Joe that Linda was quickly becoming Tim's right hand and inserting herself between Tim and himself. He had to remember to take some deep breaths and count to 10. Joe knew he was jumping to conclusions and assuming the worst, without any information. The problem was, even after using his stress control technique of counting to 10, he was feeling anxious and even panicky.

Joe composed himself and said, "Well, it does put me in a difficult position, since I am unable to establish a direct relationship with you, Tim. I am a senior professional in my field and it is customary for someone of my status to have one-on-one time with my manager. Perhaps after we cover some general issues with Linda, then we can have our one-on-one meeting."

Tim realized he might have misjudged the situation by bringing in Linda, but at this point he wasn't sure how to undo the situation. Tim wanted to be the one in control, but also realized he was off to a bad start with Joe.

At the same time, Joe knew that what he was saying to Tim didn't sound good. He didn't want to be begging or making himself sound weak. He decided to backpedal a little bit. "Tim, I understand how much you have to integrate. Cleveland is a large company and you are bringing many groups together into one—that is not an easy thing to do. I will try to help in any way that I can," Joe said calmly.

"I appreciate that attitude, Joe." Tim replied. He decided to try a different tack. "Now let's talk about how your group can work with Linda and then you and I can have a one-on-one." Joe, still off guard, but starting to feel better said, "Okay, Tim, that sounds reasonable."

Questions

9. Why had Tim most likely pulled Linda into the meeting?
10. What effects would Linda's presence at the meeting likely have on Joe?

Trench Buddies

Joe returned from New York City feeling defeated. On the plane he reviewed in his mind what had happened at the meeting. Joe remembered how he felt when he saw Linda in the room. He still acutely felt the pain in his gut when he realized that Tim had invited Linda to his meeting. He was unhappy that he was unable to bridge the communication and collaboration gap that he saw. Still, he reminded himself that he still liked the work and was happy to run his group, but he was giving up a little power. Joe decided that if he could still make a difference and get interesting products and services out to customers, he would not fight the folks in New York City quite so much.

Joe hoped that his new that approach would work better for him. He knew that if he could figure out a way to work with Linda and Tim, together, they would be greater than the sum of their parts. In fact, when Joe reviewed the issues, he found that he was usually on the same side of the arguments with Linda and Tim. In fact, they were all on the same side: the side that wants to build more usable technology for everyone.

Joe decided to do some reading about how to improve working relationships. He came across a description of an iterative approach to better working relationships (Figure 2.1) and decided to try this approach. He looked at what he did, and thought about how he could have done things better. He realized that he had to take more initiative in dealing with the people at the home office. He had to remind them to send out agendas and presentations ahead of time. Joe made a note to himself to check in with the people running those remote meetings ahead of time to make sure he would know what to expect.

Joe called Tim and left him a message: "Thanks for the meeting, Tim. I know how challenging it is to pull together such a large and remote group. I will do whatever I can to make this work. I want you to know I'm a team player."

Joe received an e-mail from Tim the next day, thanking him for coming out for the meeting. The next thing Joe did was to forward a joke about

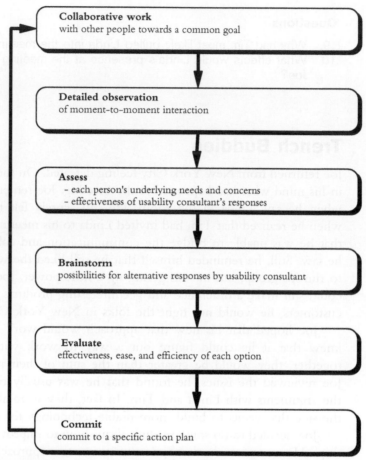

Figure 2.1. Iterative approach to better working relationships. (From Rosenzweig, E., and Ziff, J. (2004). An iterative approach to better working relationship. Presented at the Usability Professionals' Association Annual Conference Proceedings, Tutorial, June 2004.)

human factors consultants to Linda, a joke he believed she would find funny. Within 10 minutes Linda sent a reply: "LOL."

Joe decided that was enough team building for the day. He made a note to himself to try to think of the big picture and not get hung up on details and annoyances. He didn't always find that to be easy, but decided to work hard to keep it in his consciousness. He found it was not always easy to keep from taking things personally but tried to keep looking at the big picture.

Joe worked hard to find a positive angle and appeal to everyone's sense of justice and good design. Joe decided to show Linda the new book he had on better working relationships. He told her that he knows they both have the same goals and he found the book helpful. Joe suggested Linda get a copy of the book. Over time, Joe is finally able to unify the group around the goal of making the product and processes easy to use for the customer.

Finally, Success

Joe decided to be proactive in creating a better working environment. He saw that one of the problems at the Cleveland Company is its inability to collaborate between remote locations. As a means for improving communication between remote groups, Joe formed a committee for remote meeting process improvements. Tim was happy with Joe's initiative to help his division create processes for communicating with remote sites. Joe's team produced process guidelines for remote meetings to better account for diverse work styles and locations. Guidelines included the following:

- Set clear expectations in job descriptions, team deliverables, schedules, and published agendas for meetings.
- Adopt technology and practices that foster remote collaboration, and communicate them to the group and test them before the meetings.
- Send out presentations and materials for the meeting at least 24 hours in advance.

Once the team had a process for remote meetings, things improved. Now, presentations are sent out ahead of time, and voice and online conference sites are set up and used effectively. Eventually, people from the New York City office decided to do some work at home. Soon, the employees were more evenly distributed between those calling in from remote sites and those sitting in the conference room in New York City. The meetings were not just geared for one set of employees, and they started collaborating as a cohesive group. The team felt better and operates more efficiently.

Summary

Creating a good working UCD system within an organization is not a trivial task and is made even harder when some members of the team work remotely. It is helpful to remember the following:

- Define the organizational entities and any cultural differences.
- Create a reporting structure that fosters common goals, not competing ones.
- Consider the personalities and cultures of the key individuals, especially when choosing their managers.
- Arrange for at least occasional face-to-face meetings of people in key positions.
- Regularly communicate status updates of projects between the groups so each is kept abreast of what the other is doing, and who is working on it.

Once external issues such as the stress of communicating between sites are clarified and steps taken to resolve the issues, it is time to look at internal issues. Sometimes, people just have to talk about their feelings; perhaps they feel marginalized and hurt about an interaction they had with a coworker. If this happens, it is helpful is to take a long view. Just because an issue is burning in the moment does not mean it will survive the week. Try to see the forest for the trees.

Many factors come into play when setting up a UCD system within a company. It is helpful to look at the company's social model and interpersonal dynamic. Corporate climate is one of the biggest factors in determining how new ideas are dealt with, how people work together, or whether there is a competitive atmosphere that dominates the culture. The age of the company is often another factor, because older established companies have more administration processes in place, whereas younger companies are often still working out their internal processes.

For a UCD process to be successful, all factors must work together, integrating the best and working out the worst issues. Conflict and struggle are inevitable, so avoidance is usually a longer road than a more direct approach. Sometimes it is better to directly confront an issue; sometimes it is better to be understanding and work in a softer manner to get cooperation. Each situation is not the same and so it is helpful to have choices and many options available in the repertoire of possible responses.

Further Reading

Autry, J. A. (1991). *Love and profit, the art of caring leadership*. New York: Avon Book.

Fisher, R., Ury, W. L., and Patton, B. (1991). *Getting to yes: negotiating agreement without giving in.* New York: Penguin Books.

Rosenzweig, E., and Ziff, J. (2003). Managing interdisciplinary relationships: lessons learned from the field. *ACM Interactions*, November/December, 10; 6:20–27.

Rosenzweig, E., and Ziff, J. (2004). An iterative approach to better working relationship. Presented at the Usability Professionals' Association Annual Conference Proceedings, Tutorial, June 2004.

Rosenzweig, E., and Ziff, J. (2006). The humans in human factors. In Sherman, P. I. (Ed.). *Usability success stories: how organizations improve by making easier-to-use software and websites.* Hampshire, UK: Gower Publishing.

Raising Awareness at the Company Level

Janice Anne Rohn, World Savings Bank

> *Jill was hired into a vice-president position, indicating that the company seemed to realized the importance of user experience. Nevertheless, Jill assumed the company had little understanding of user experience. Jill knew she needed to set a course for making user-centered design happen at Red Fox.*

Introduction

Jill had managed user experience (UE) teams at multiple companies. Like many people who have been in the UE field for over 15 years, Jill went to college while the field was still developing. She applied her background in psychology and biology, along with taking many classes in design, technology, and usability, and on-the-job training to develop expertise in the field. Jill also took classes in economics and management to increase her business knowledge. Jill started as an individual contributor and after a few years was hired as a first-line manager to build a UE team from scratch. Later, she was hired as a director to build an even larger team, including several managers reporting to her. Sometimes she was hired to start UE teams and sometimes to lead existing teams. Regardless of whether she was building the team from scratch or joining an existing UE team, Jill had learned over the years that in either case she had to assume the company had little understanding of UE and its benefits.

Jill had recently joined Red Fox Technologies, an Internet company that had changed its business model to focus on designing and hosting websites and web applications. Red Fox recently started to produce website soft-ware—a full-featured content management system—to enable companies to design and update their own e-commerce websites. The company was founded just over 2 years before Jill joined. The other departments were fairly well staffed, and the company had transitioned from a small start-up to currently just over 1,000 employees.

Jill was impressed with the creativity at Red Fox and the fact that they had acquired a number of good clients and successes over the past year. Although they had been successful, Red Fox could not close many of the deals with Fortune 500 clients. The feedback the executives were receiving was a concern from potential customers, most of which had in-house UE departments, about the lack of a user experience focus at Red Fox; because Red Fox had neither a UE executive nor a real team, these companies weren't confident that Red Fox could deliver a highly usable web solution. Red Fox did have two visual designers on board, but the executives realized they needed to hire someone who knew how to build and manage a fully staffed UE team.

As a result Jill was joining the company at an interesting time when executives knew they needed to make an investment in UE to substantially grow the company. However, there was very little knowledge of what UE was, how it could help the company, and how it integrated with the other departments such as marketing and engineering.

Jill knew from past experience with introducing UE into companies that she had to use multiple strategies and tactics to raise awareness of the benefits of UE and to integrate it at the company level. Although there was currently sufficient executive management team support of user experience to hire Jill into a newly formed vice-president of UE position, she also knew that support could be ephemeral: If key executives left Red Fox or if the company had to reduce staff, any team that Jill built could be at risk. Jill's initial team comprised two designers already on board and nine open positions (head count).

Some of Red Fox's procedures and processes were documented, but predominantly the company ran as a relationship-based company, relying on individuals knowing whom to contact to obtain key information. A reorganization was also just on the horizon, and Jill was given the option of her UE team reporting to the marketing or the engineering department. Jill had interviewed with both Ellen, the senior vice-president of marketing, and Geoff, the senior vice-president of engineering, and she was very comfortable working with both of them.

Questions

1. Jill was hired into a vice-president position, which would seem to indicate that the company realized that UE was important. But why should Jill assume that the company has little understanding of UE?
2. What strategies should Jill use in her first 2 months at the company?
3. Where should Jill report?

Understanding and Integrating Into the Company

To decide whether the UE department should report to engineering or marketing, Jill assessed that within Red Fox Technologies—other than the chief executive officer (CEO) and chief operating officer (COO)—engineering had the most influence on decisions. Before Jill made a final decision, she scheduled a meeting with Allen, the CEO, so she could discuss where the UE department should reside. Although she may not be able to change Allen's decision at this point, at least she could begin the education process that the UE department should be at the same reporting level as engineering and marketing.

"Allen, you obviously recognize the importance of building a UE team in order to grow Red Fox to the next level. I can certainly help you to achieve that goal by providing the confidence to Fortune 500 companies that we can produce world-class user experience in our website designs. In order to do this, UE really needs to have an equal voice with engineering and marketing. An equal voice can only be achieved by an equal seat at the table with you."

"Jill, I'm very glad that you joined us, and I value the contribution that I know you will make. Unfortunately, I already feel like I have too many direct reports and I also don't have the time to properly help integrate you into Red Fox. I have the confidence that either Geoff or Ellen could help you better than I to successfully integrate into our company. In the future, as you and your team gain experience here, I'm certainly open to reexamining this decision."

Jill was unconvinced. "I appreciate the fact that your time is valuable, and I understand your concern regarding increasing your direct reports," she continued, "I just want to maximize the likelihood that we will make optimal decisions by ensuring that UE requirements are considered as strongly as engineering and marketing requirements. I think it is difficult to give UE requirements an equal consideration if they are communicated through another department. As you've seen with many of the deals which Red Fox has not closed, UE requirements can be a deciding factor."

Jill and Allen continued to discuss the reporting structure, but Allen did not change his decision. As they spoke it occurred to Jill that Allen was not very familiar with UE, so that was probably one reason he did not feel comfortable adding her as a direct report at that time. Because Jill was new to the company, she knew there was only a slim chance that this equal reporting structure would be approved. Nevertheless, Jill thought the meeting was a good step because she used it as an opportunity to start the education and awareness process: "UE 101" for executive management.

Allen asked her to choose between the two departments, so she chose to report to Geoff, the head of engineering. Although Jill chose engineering because it appeared to be the stronger driver in Red Fox, she did not disclose her reasoning to the executives, because she determined there might be more bruised egos if it were to get out that she thought the marketing department did not have as much influence.

Understanding the Company

Jill started her research by meeting with stakeholders across the company. Not surprisingly, she found out that the knowledge and perceptions of UE varied widely. Many stakeholders had very little knowledge of what UE actually was. Jill discovered that some stakeholders in the past had a negative experience with the two designers' previous manager, who had been a marketing art director and did not have a background in UE.

During Jill's meeting with Susan, the director of production, Jill found out some interesting perceptions about UE.

"Susan, how have the designers become involved in projects in the past?" Jill asked.

"They typically become involved in the design phase, which follows the requirements phase," Susan replied.

"And how are user requirements incorporated into the requirements phase?"

"Well," said Susan, "we get customer requirements from marketing. Your predecessor, Jim, said that the marketing requirements were sufficient." Jill was surprised and said, "Interesting, from what I've seen these requirements are focused on the stakeholder requests, but not on the end user requirements."

"Yeah," said Susan, "I brought that up to Jim, because I thought there should be usability requirements, but he argued that the marketing requirements were sufficient, so I just dropped it since I have other battles to focus on. He also said that certain design activities required so many weeks of work, and he appeared to have sort of a one-size-fits-all approach. Frankly, I was concerned about encouraging him to become more involved throughout the development life cycle, for fear that it would double or triple the time required to produce a website."

Jill used this meeting as an opportunity to let Susan know that UE can actually reduce the development time and effort by providing data to prioritize requirements, identifying requirements early in the life cycle, and ensuring that better decisions are made based on direct customer data and feedback. Over the next few months, Jill continued to meet with stakeholders within the company to gather perceptions and gauge the levels of knowledge about UE in different departments.

From her meetings and discussions, Jill compiled the following list of observations:

Item 1. Other than offices and cubes, there were no rooms for UE activities, such as usability labs and design rooms, which are great for posting numerous project page designs and competitive website designs.

Item 2. UE was not part of any documented processes, including development processes, which describe the steps for how sites are designed and developed, and project prioritization processes, which determine the projects and features worked on and when.

Item 3. In addition to the two existing designers, Jill had nine additional head count. (During the interview process, Jill made sure there was additional head count allocated before she accepted the position. She had spoken to many companies over the years who claimed to be serious about their investment in UE, while at the same time allocating just a few UE head count for a company of thousands.) The large number of open head count meant that Jill and her small team would be stretched while working to fill these positions, but there would be significantly better coverage of important projects once the head count was filled.

Item 4. There was no plan or model for how project work would be prioritized across the small number of UE resources currently available; the designers were asked to do work not based on the priority of the project but based on who happened to request work when the designers had bandwidth.

Item 5. There was no information about UE available anywhere within the company, including on the company's Intranet and within internal and external publications. All other departments had an area on the company's Intranet site with information about their departments.

Item 6. The designers and their previous managers had not had any direct customer contact. Only sales and marketing had worked directly with customers.

Item 7. No goals at any level (corporate or departmental) included UE-related achievements. There were corporate goals for acquiring more customers, and departmental goals for increasing the efficiency of developing sites, but no goals directly including UE.

Item 8. According to past project documentation and talking to project team members, no UE requirements were included in project requirements. Project requirements were predominantly based on customer stakeholders and not on end users.

Item 9. There was no UE release criteria, such as meeting certain usability goals to declare the site ready for the customer.

Item 10. There were no UE goals included in the set of goals determining executive bonuses. Executives were receiving bonuses for meeting goals that included increasing revenue and the number of customers, but again there were no goals directly including UE.

Jill knew she had a lot of work to do, and she couldn't do it all at once.

Questions

4. What three items from the list above should Jill concentrate on first, and why?
5. Explain why the other items in the list do not take as high priority as the three identified.

Creating a Plan

Jill and her team started to work on hiring, building a usability lab, and gaining direct contact with customers. Jill knew that the more she could demonstrate both the benefits and organizational requirements of UE in quantitative terms, which would demonstrate objectively the impact of UE, the more likely the executive management would understand UE, accept it, and support it. Executive management typically embraces objective measures that help them manage the business. In addition to the objective data, showing highlights videos of actual customers can give faces to the data, just as the news media use personal stories to convey news stories. By benchmarking metrics before and after involvement from the UE department, Jill and her team can demonstrate benefits in terms the executive management can more easily understand and appreciate. By creating an explicit plan of how UE department resources can be allocated across projects, Jill can communicate to executive management what resources are needed and what the impact will be of insufficient resources.

Jill created a UE organization and staffing plan that demonstrated several important facets to executive management:

- A description of the roles that needed to be part of the UE organization, along with their benefits
- The support that could be expected with the current head count plan
- A head count gap analysis, which demonstrated the number of UE people who should be working on projects compared with what the current head count amount would support
- A growth plan for the group, based on the company's expected growth rate for the next several years

To calculate the support needed, Jill used the company's existing categorization for project scope—levels 1 through 5, with level 1 on the small end of the spectrum requiring less than a day's work, and level 5 being a large multiple month project. Jill created a UE staff allocation for each level. She created the staff allocation based on her past experience of which types of resources would be needed and to what extent for different levels of project scope. Because Jill had little knowledge of how Red Fox compared with her previous companies, she created the initial staff allocation knowing that it may need to change as she became more familiar with Red Fox's culture and processes. For example, companies that emphasize input from multiple departments take longer to deliver work and therefore require more resources than companies in which departments have clear responsibility differentiation and are empowered to make decisions in their areas.

Jill included in the UE organization and staffing plan a matrix that showed each project and its impact to the user experience (its level, priority, and head count requirements) for each type of position (Table 3.1). For

Table 3.1. Head Count Project Plan and Gap Analysis

Project Name	Level (1–5)	Priority	Information Architect	Usability Engineer	Content Writer	Visual Designer
Project X	4	H	1	1	0.5	0.75
Project Y	4	H	1	0.75	0.75	0.75
Project Z	4	H	1	0.75	0.75	0.75
Project A	3	M	0.75	0.75	0.5	0.5
Project B	3	M	0.75	0.5	0.5	0.5
Project C	2	M	0.5	0.25	0.5	0.25
Totals			5	4	3.5	3.5
Current head count			0	0	0	2
Gap			5	4	3.5	1.5

H = high level; M = mid level.

example, the largest size project—a level 5—would require one head count for each of the skill sets: information architecture, usability, content, and visual design. She also included the published priority of each project, which was based on several factors, including the expected impact to revenue and alignment with the corporate goals. When Jill had joined Red Fox the projects were already available in a prioritized list, but she planned to work with the executive stakeholders and project leads to update this list as it evolved.

She also calculated and documented that with the current team of two designers, only a small subset of the important projects would receive any visual design, and these projects would not have any significant information architecture or usability performed due to the lack of resources with these skills. Although the two visual designers had some interaction design skills, they did not have strong skills in information architecture or usability. The plan also described the ramifications of not including input from these important functional areas of UE. By explicitly demonstrating how the small number of resources would be allocated, Jill was able to more clearly communicate how most projects would have to do without any UE expertise.

While working on the plan Jill also worked on writing job descriptions for the nine open head count, including information architects, usability engineers, content writers, web metrics, and a participant recruiter/administrator. Jill then worked to start the recruiting and hiring process for the positions.

Questions

6. In addition to justifying additional head count to support existing projects, what other purpose does the UE organization and staffing plan serve?

Building and Launching a Lab

Usability labs are very effective in raising awareness. In addition to the many reasons listed above, executive management can also be invited to observe or participate in usability evaluations. Highlights videos can be shown to executives and at company meetings to help raise awareness of current product issues and personalize the issues.

To get started Jill created a usability lab proposal, which included the specifications and budget for a lab, along with ongoing costs such as participant compensation. As part of the research for the proposal, Jill met with Joan, the COO, to understand more about the budget process and the company culture.

"Joan, I'm going to be creating a proposal to build a usability lab suite, and I'd like to understand how the budget process works at Red Fox, and what types of information you need for this type of proposal," said Jill.

Joan explained, "For projects that have not been included in the annual budget, such as this usability lab, you will need to write a proposal detailing the project, along with the costs and the timeline. Although the official process is that you provide this to the budget committee and they review it with you, I would recommend that you first meet individually with members of the budget committee to get them all on board and incorporate any necessary changes, and then when you have the official meeting, there will be no surprises."

"Thanks for the good advice," said Jill. "From what I've observed, the company does value having areas that are well designed, which is helpful for giving a good impression during customer visits. Well-designed usability labs also help to raise awareness both internally and externally that the company values usability. At most of my previous companies, I've designed the usability lab to be not only functional, but also aesthetically pleasing to create a professional impression to the customer and prospective customer usability participants, and also when providing tours of the lab to customers. I also think when customers and prospects tour the lab, it is a reflection of Red Fox's design capabilities—a well-designed lab implies that we know how to design websites. Of course, the nicer design typically adds cost, and I'm not sure how sensitive Red Fox is to these extra costs."

"I agree with your points regarding what kind of impression the lab design gives to customers and prospects," said Joan, "and I'm a believer in not being penny-wise and pound-foolish. If Red Fox closes even a few extra deals due to customers' good impressions of the lab, the extra cost will be worth it. I'd recommend that you assume a nice professional design, and budget for that. If the budget isn't workable, then we can look at how to reduce costs."

Jill was enjoying being in the "honeymoon" period at Red Fox. She figured that she had approximately 6 months to prove the worth of UE and that she would get the benefit of doubt for about that amount of time. After that, the stakeholders and the company would expect some measurable results for their investment.

"Sounds great, Joan," said Jill. "Thanks for your helpful advice."

With the help of dropping costs for video equipment, software, and hardware, Jill put together a proposal and budget that worked for the budget committee. Thanks to Joan's advice, Jill was able to get the budget approved with minimal changes. The location for the lab wasn't ideal—it was on the second floor rather than on the ground floor, which would have been easier for escorting usability participants, but other than that, the lab was built according to the proposal. When the lab was nearing completion, Jill worked with her growing team to put together a usability lab grand opening. Jill and her team did the following activities to prepare for the event:

- Scheduling the date for executive presentations: Because Jill wanted to involve the executive team in the event, she needed to schedule the grand opening on a date that worked for their schedules. First she worked with the executive management team to put together a set of presenters, including the CEO and the president, and worked with their schedules to set a date.
- Publicity: Jill worked with the public relations department to identify and invite appropriate press to the event. Because she had the

involvement of the CEO and the president, it was easier to garner the interest of the press.

- Live broadcast: Jill used the video cameras in the lab to capture the event and broadcast the grand opening live across the company, including to those at other locations. She worked with the information technology (IT) department to ensure that the bandwidth would be sufficient and there would be no critical and large network needs at the same time. The video would also be uploaded to a server so that it could be viewed by any employee after the live event.

- Event schedule: Jill created a schedule for the event. The grand opening started with presentations by the CEO and the president, followed by a presentation by Jill with her team. The press was invited to the presentations and a VIP tour, which started after the presentations. After the VIP tour, tours for the company were scheduled for the rest of the day, starting every half-hour. The entire event was scheduled for 3 hours, including the tour, starting at 2:00 p.m.

- Food: Jill's team worked on arranging for the snacks and drinks. The snacks were all of the dry type (pretzels, cookies) so that the usability lab wouldn't get any significant stains on its first day.

- Department identification: The UE team's designers created a new logo for the department and combined the company's logo and their department name and logo for use on giveaways and educational collateral.

- Giveaways: Jill's team worked with a vendor to select items to give to anyone attending the grand opening, settling on small flashlights and pens. They arranged for the items to be customized with the new department name and logo well in advance so that they would arrive in time for the event.

- Educational collateral: Jill wrote a set of educational materials to be given away during the grand opening and in future meetings with project teams. The set of materials included an overview of user experience and its benefits, a diagram of methods to use at different times in the project life cycle, and a process to get UE involved, encouraging teams to involve UE early in the requirements phase. She also arranged to have the materials and folders printed with the department name and logo, along with the company name and logo. She included the materials in the professional customized folders, along with her business card.

- Simulating a usability evaluation: Jill and her team scripted a demonstration of a usability evaluation, so that as part of the tour the employees could see an example of a session. In addition to being educational, the simulation allowed the whole UE team to be part of the tours by playing the parts of facilitators, participants, and observers.
- Collecting contacts: Similar to sales lead generation, everyone attending the grand opening was asked to sign in with their name, job title, and internal contact information. This collection enabled the UE team to follow up with employees after the grand opening and was also helpful in tracking attendance so that Jill could report the success of the event.

The day after the event, Jill met with her manager, Geoff. "Jill, you and your team did an excellent job with the grand opening," said Geoff. "I saw that there were also some press in attendance. It looked like you had hundreds of people throughout the day."

"Thanks," said Jill. "Over 600 people attended the event throughout the day, and the broadcast was watched by an additional 200 employees."

"That's over three-quarters of the company," said Geoff. "And I've also heard people talking positively about it afterward. They don't necessarily understand user experience, but at least they're aware it exists."

The UE team generated more than enough business due to this one event. The executive management team was pleased with the positive press that came out of the event. Although the stories about Red Fox's usability lab and the company's investment in UE were small and not headliners, the company still benefited from the good press.

Customer Involvement

Building the usability lab was a good start to creating direct interaction between the UE department and Red Fox's customers. Jill was a firm believer in direct interaction with customers. Any usability method—whether a usability evaluation in the lab, a field study, an interview, or a participatory design session—should always include customers. There is no substitute for feedback from someone who has used your company's products or services—customers can provide much more informed and specific feedback to identify requirements and enhancements. Not only are the data collected from UE methods more reliable, but highlights videos and quotes from customers can be very influential both at a tactical and strategic level. Seeing and hearing customers describe in their own words what their needs are can have a greater impact on project teams and more quickly influence design decisions and can also help to raise awareness of UE by demonstrating the benefits of the UE methods used. Jill also found that customers enjoy the company soliciting their feedback and are eager to participate in future UE activities. After participating in UE activities, customers cite an improved opinion of the company and greater loyalty, which is not surprising from a relationship-building perspective. As with her experience at previous companies, Jill's UE department at Red Fox started to receive positive feedback from internal stakeholders and customers after the UE department was able to involve customers directly in usability evaluations.

Jill also created a "user experience partnership" program at Red Fox, a program she created in previous companies that had successfully increased customer involvement. This program included regular communication and participation between Red Fox and its customers. The customers who became UE partners were able to provide feedback through UE activities such as field studies and usability evaluations in the lab and occasionally could be consulted when quick decisions needed to be made. Jill asked the customers who were UE partners to sign nondisclosure agreements, so they could have more insight into the roadmap of features and improvements as a result of their involvement in the program. From Jill's past experience, these customers were also more likely to praise UE to the other departments within the company, including sales and marketing. Indeed, during the first month of the program, these departments started to receive positive feedback from customers about the UE department.

In the weekly senior management meeting that Jill attended, along with the CEO, vice-president of engineering, vice-president of marketing, and other senior staff, Chuck, the vice-president of sales, said "Jill, I wanted to let you know that we heard some very positive feedback from the account manager over at Synertech. She said that they've enjoyed working with you and your team, and feel like they have a much better handle on which features they want to add."

"Great to hear," said Jill. "When we worked with them during a participatory design session and mapped out some of their current tasks, we realized that there were some additional features they could benefit from. Although their account manager hadn't originally recognized the need for these features, it became clear to their participants during this session as we explained how the features could help them to accomplish their tasks. We not only gathered good input for how to design some of our future features, but we were able to up-sell some current features they needed."

"Great to hear—good job, Jill" said Allen.

"A lot of the credit goes to Denise, our new usability engineer. She did a great job facilitating the session," responded Jill.

In addition, the UE partnership program became a means to attract even more customers for interaction. When customers heard of the program, they perceived it as a benefit and wanted to join the program. There are additional benefits of direct customer interaction, including customer testimonials.

Customer Testimonials

As the discussion at the senior management meeting demonstrated, Jill knew from past experience that one of the greatest ways to raise awareness did not come from within the UE department but from its internal and external customers. She could not have influenced Allen's or Chuck's opinions about the benefits of UE as effectively if she had claimed that UE was beneficial. By the UE department working directly with Synertech, they were able to help increase Red Fox's sales and garnered a positive customer testimonial, both of which raised the awareness of the benefits of UE for Allen and Chuck. Allen was impressed by the positive outcome the UE department had with the external customer—Synertech—and with the internal customer—Chuck. Jill knew that UE methods involving customers, such as participatory design sessions and usability evaluations in the usability lab, enable more direct interaction with customers and therefore more opportunities for customers to understand and even communicate what they see as the benefits of UE. When external customers are happy, they can become strong evangelists for UE.

Jill also knew the importance of capturing positive feedback from customers. By capturing and communicating customer compliments to executive management, whether they occurred during participation in a usability evaluation, a lab tour, a field study, or some other activity, Jill was able to both raise the awareness of UE and demonstrate its positive effect on the organization and on business goals such as increasing revenue and customer retention. For example, like many companies, Red Fox Technologies was performing regular customer satisfaction surveys. Customer satisfaction is important because companies typically obtain more future business with customers than with prospects and spend more money to acquire a new customer than to retain a current customer.

In past companies Jill demonstrated that customers involved with UE had a higher satisfaction rating than those not involved. In some ways this is not surprising: Customers working with UE are provided with regular opportunities to communicate their feedback, they have more visibility into when usability issues might be addressed, and they also realize the focus that is placed on usability, so they have more confidence that the company is most likely aware of and addressing any issues the customer may encounter. Jill was confident that she could demonstrate the same higher customer satisfaction rating at Red Fox. Customer satisfaction is also another reason to avoid spreading UE too thin: By measuring the results of a project with sufficient UE resources versus no resources, often clear differences in the results can be demonstrated.

Next Steps

After the first few months, Jill looked at her original list and was pleased to see the progress that she and her team had made on items 1, 3, 4, 5, and 6 (Table 3.2).

Questions

7. How can Jill and her team raise awareness for UE by working on the second item: incorporating UE into the company's documented development processes?
8. Assuming this is accomplished, would this documented integration be sufficient for ensuring that UE is incorporated into the development processes as part of the daily practice?

Facilitating the Integration of UE

Jill is a proponent of making it easier for product management and development teams to integrate UE activities into the development cycle. Anything the UE department can do to provide project teams with better results and reduced work loads raises the awareness of UE and ensures that the project team benefits. Examples of techniques Jill used to raise awareness and to reduce work are:

- Templates: By creating and providing templates and a design library of approved widgets, such as HTML page templates and buttons, the UE team can increase design consistency, reduce development time, and

Table 3.2. List of Original Observations and Progress States

Item	Description	Status
1	Other than offices and cubes, there were no rooms for UE activities, including usability labs and design rooms	Built a usability lab
2	UE was not part of any documented development process	Not yet addressed
3	In addition to the two existing designers, Jill had nine additional head count	Hired four of nine employees
4	There was no model for how project work would be prioritized across the small number of UE resources currently available	A model was started as part of the UE organization and staffing plan
5	There was no information about UE available across the company, including both on the company's Intranet and publications	Some collateral was created and disseminated as part of the usability lab grand opening
6	UE had not had any direct customer contact	UE worked directly with customers during usability evaluations, participatory design sessions, and as part of the UE partnership program
7	No goals at any level (corporate or departmental) included UE-related achievements	Not yet addressed
8	No UE requirements were included in project requirements	Not yet addressed
9	There were no UE release criteria	Not yet addressed
10	There were no UE goals included in the set of goals determining executive bonuses	Not yet addressed

reduce the number of errors and omissions made both by the UE and development teams. At Red Fox, Jill's team created a set of page templates that could be used both internally for building customers' sites and by customers using Red Fox's custom content management system.

- Guidelines: By creating and publishing design guidelines, the UE group can also increase design consistency, reduce errors and omissions, and raise the awareness of UE. Templates are typically more effective than guidelines, however, in reducing work and enforcing consistency because templates can constrain designers and developers to only develop designs that follow the guidelines, whereas written guidelines depend on the person reading the guidelines, interpreting them correctly, and remembering them.

- Production code: Related to producing HTML page templates, if the UE group creates production-quality HTML code, instead of producing prototypes that need to be re-created by the engineering team, the company can realize a significant increase in efficiency, including a reduction in errors. In the past, Jill saw over a 50% increase in efficiency by hiring designers who were also great coders. Instead of writing HTML twice—once by the UE team as prototypes and another time by the engineering team as production code—the HTML is written only once by the UE team, with engineering adding dynamic code (such as business logic and database calls). Awareness for UE can also increase when the design and code can be optimized, resulting in decreased page download time. For example, Jill's team at Red Fox was able to compress the images used on web pages to improve page performance.

- Requirements: UE awareness can also be accomplished by demonstrating an increase in efficiency through early identification of requirements. For most companies the requirements phase can be protracted, with changing requirements revealed late in the development cycle. Using UE techniques can demonstrate value by helping to identify valid requirements earlier in the process by performing participatory design sessions, field studies, interviews, and other methods focused on user requirements. At Red Fox, after Jill integrated UE into the concept and requirements phases of the development process, her team was able to demonstrate a reduction of time spent in these phases by performing participatory design and field study methods to more efficiently identify requirements. One way Jill gained the acceptance of UE early in the development cycle was to create a baseline measure by tracking the amount of time and resources spent on the requirements phase before the integration of UE techniques. Although additional resources are needed when integrating UE members into this phase, she was able to demonstrate that the number of requirements identified late in the life cycle was significantly reduced (when changes are more costly), therefore resulting in an overall reduction in time and resources.

Creating a Resource Model

Early in Jill's career, before she had ever become a manager, she witnessed how applying limited UE resources could sometimes backfire. For example, in her first UE position she witnessed UE resources being applied too thinly or too late, resulting in minimal changes to the designs. In these cases the executive management often made a false conclusion that UE had little impact, so they wondered why they should invest more heavily in this area. When Jill became a manager, she tried to ensure that the limited resources in her group were allocated either at an ideal level or at least at a sufficient minimum threshold—both with respect to the number of resources and the activities that they performed—that would ensure a more significant impact to the designs. At Red Fox, creating a resource model to allocate limited UE department resources across projects was another way that Jill worked to raise awareness and ensure that management had a positive view of UE.

Jill started her resource model by creating the UE organization and staffing plan. She also worked to change the approach that had been in effect before she joined Red Fox, when the two designers were more often than not used as visual designers to "make pretty icons" and other isolated activities. The designers were typically brought in late in the process, when the key functionality and interaction design were already completed. The designers had also been assigned to not necessarily the most important projects, but to the project teams who were aware of the design resources. In other words, the UE resources were being used reactively rather than proactively.

To establish a proactive plan to allocate the limited UE department resources, Jill created a matrix of three key project attributes for Red Fox's active projects:

1. Priority: How important the project is to the company, including factors such as:
   - What is the potential revenue?
   - How many business goals are supported (such as customer retention)?
   - Is this an area in which the company wants to be a market leader?
2. Scope: How large is the project?
3. Life cycle: Is this project a new product, service, or feature or is it an iteration of a mature product, service, or feature that has already been improved over time with customer input?

Often, scope and life cycle are related in that a large scope project typically involves the development of a new feature, and a small scope project is an iteration of an existing feature. Based on Jill's experience at Red Fox so far, scope and life cycle appeared to be consistently related. To reduce the complexity of the model for Red Fox, Jill combined these two attributes into a single category, called scope. Jill then created a tiered level of UE resource investment based on the priority and scope, proposing full UE support for high-priority and large-scope projects, mid-level support for medium-priority projects, and little to no support for low-priority projects.

After creating the matrix, Jill worked with executive management to categorize the projects by priority and scope. She then created a gap analysis based on the current projects, showing the difference between the UE resources she recommended versus the UE resources the company currently had. Jill knew that one of the keys to raising awareness is to be viewed as credible and business-focused, rather than idealistic. By proposing that some projects receive little or no resources, she helped to give her plan credibility. Both Jill and executive management knew that always having a UE resource would improve a project, but by proposing a proactive allocation of limited resources Jill was able to demonstrate both a business focus as well as an example of how projects would fare with and without UE resources. Jill handed out the matrix at a senior management meeting so that the stakeholders could discuss the allocation.

"This plan is really good," said Allen, "but I'm concerned about all these projects that have no UE resources assigned to them. Can't some of your people work at least a few hours on these other projects?"

"If we pull UE resources off the projects that we've said are the most important to the company, then we'll be putting those projects at risk for the sake of projects that we agreed are not as high priority," replied Jill. "Also, no matter what the original intentions are, projects rarely take just a few hours. What starts as one small thing typically grows into days or weeks. If we're not convinced we have identified the projects that are most important to the company, then we can revisit the priorities. Otherwise, we should keep the allocation as proposed and decide whether we need additional UE resources to cover these lower-priority projects."

"Okay, let's try this and see what kinds of issues arise," consented Allen.

One of the most difficult strategies to adhere to is the application of limited resources. Jill knew she had to diligently apply full resources only to the highest priority projects and be careful not to fall into the trap of spreading her team too thin. This approach to resource allocation demonstrates the significant difference that a properly staffed UE project team can make and also is another great way to demonstrate how projects fare with and without UE resources. By properly staffing some projects and not staffing others, sometimes senior managers can become envious of the UE resources that other teams have and thus ask for more resources for their projects. This request of resources will work as long as the project team is rewarded for releasing a more usable project or if there are project team members who understand the benefits of UE.

Information on UE

When Jill joined Red Fox, there was no information available internally on UE: what it was, its benefits, or how to incorporate it in project plans. After creating the initial set of information for the usability lab grand opening, Jill then worked with her team to create a UE section on Red Fox's Intranet site to post their material. The set of material included an overview of UE and its benefits, a diagram of methods to use at different times in the project life cycle, and a process to get UE involved, encouraging teams to involve UE early in the requirements phase. Jill also added an area for data so that the UE Intranet site could serve as a data resource for the company. Over time, as the UE team produced research, the data on the site included user profiles, top user tasks and task flows, usability evaluation reports and videos, and field study reports and videos. There were also sections for design best practices, style guides, and templates. By creating and consolidating valuable information about UE for the company, again Jill and her team were able to gain some attention and raise the awareness of the value of UE.

Goals

Most companies have goals at several levels, including corporate-level goals and departmental-level goals. Jill knew from experience that incorporating UE activities and achievements into multiple levels of goals was an effective strategy for raising awareness. A few months after joining Red Fox, Jill was able to start this effort because the departments were beginning to develop the next year's goals. Because incorporating UE into corporate-level goals is often a multiple year effort, Jill started by identifying existing corporate goals that would be supported by UE, such as increasing customer acquisition, retention, and loyalty. Jill created departmental goals to align with these corporate goals, such as measurably increasing the usability of clients' websites (task completion rate and time to complete a task), supporting clients' business goals (such as increasing purchases on their websites), and increasing customer subjective satisfaction (both Red Fox's direct clients and the clients' end users). By demonstrating these types of improvements for clients, Jill was confident that Red Fox could demonstrate increased acquisition, retention, and loyalty and thus UE contribution to the corporate goals.

Value System

From Jill's past experience she knew that one of the most effective ways to raise awareness of UE is to understand the value system of the stakeholders and to translate how UE supports their value system. For example, an executive may value customer retention. By demonstrating that UE is actually a customer retention strategy and communicating in terms of customer retention, Jill enables stakeholders to more easily understand how they benefit from UE. Misunderstandings and silos can occur within organizations due to different groups using different terminology. By practicing UE within the organization—understanding the internal customer requirements—improvements can be made in raising awareness. UE has its own set of terms, and Jill found a good balance of communicating UE terms to demonstrate the skill in the field while still translating how UE supports the stakeholders' values.

Sometimes the translation from UE activities to corporate goals requires educating stakeholders on how UE affects the business. At Red Fox, Jill plans to use some recent research from analysts citing how important the usability and design of a site are when consumers are choosing from which website to purchase products. This analyst research on the impact of UE will help Jill to build her case on how UE supports clients' customer acquisition and retention goals.

Bonuses

Related to goals are bonuses. In most of Jill's previous companies, bonuses were awarded based on the achievement of explicit goals. As most people are aware, when employees have too much work and too little time, they typically prioritize the goals connected to their bonus. This is true whether the employee is a COO or an individual contributor. A strategy Jill used for raising awareness in the past was to incorporate UE goals into executive bonuses. This strategy also can take a year or 2 before the goals are embedded. While working on the departmental goals at Red Fox, Jill decided to use this opportunity to propose the idea to her manager and the executives.

"Geoff, in previous companies I've worked with the executive management team to include UE-related goals in their bonuses," said Jill. "This helped to ensure some focus on UE throughout the year. For example, we could have a goal to perform usability benchmarks for the most important projects, to ensure that we have objective usability data of our current designs. This objective snapshot enables us to demonstrate improvements with future designs or to compare our work with other companies' designs. Then the next year's goal could include achieving an improvement over the first year's benchmarks, such as reducing task completion time by 25%."

"Interesting idea," responded Geoff. "Did that help with integrating UE into the company culture?"

"Definitely," said Jill. "As you know, with so many priorities vying for limited resources, having an initiative tied to bonuses can make a big difference by ensuring that attention is paid to these initiatives throughout the year."

UE Requirements

Companies typically focus on features but often not on user requirements. An important strategy for raising awareness and simultaneously raising the quality of products and services is to bring this user focus into the requirements phase. Jill's past companies had addressed requirements in a variety of ways, from informal approaches to detailed requirements documents. Often there were different types of specification documents that related to UE, including an initial description often created by product marketing or product managers (sometimes called a marketing requirements document or a product requirements document) and a document created by the technical analysts or engineering specifying the functionality details (sometimes called a functional design document or a functionality requirements document). In Jill's experience, UE needs to be involved in the creation of both documents to ensure that the project addresses the user requirements from both a design and functionality standpoint. When Jill joined most of her past companies, these important documents typically did not sufficiently address the user requirements.

In the past Jill raised awareness of the benefits of UE by demonstrating the importance of the early identification and incorporation of user requirements. Jill sometimes used outside research for this strategy, such as the CHAOS Report by The Standish Group (1994). This study demonstrated that the number one reason for cost and schedule overruns, canceled projects, and restarts is the lack of user involvement, including user requirements and feedback. Jill also used internal data. For example, Jill's team was able to benchmark the schedule and resources needed for similar projects with and without UE requirements identification methods. They were able to demonstrate a reduction in the requirements phase by using UE methods such as participatory design. By demonstrating cost and schedule savings, while simultaneously combating any misperceptions that UE is "additional" work, Jill and her team were able to raise the awareness of the benefits of UE.

Jill had also successfully raised the awareness of UE in the past by providing data to prioritize project features. Product managers often have more features than engineering can address in any one release. Jill's UE team gathered data on which tasks and features were most important to customers and provided these data during release planning meetings so that the product managers could prioritize their features with the benefit of this additional information. This strategy helped both the product managers and engineering by reducing the amount of work that needed to be done.

At Red Fox, Jill worked with the product managers to ensure that as they were working on the project requirements, they met with the UE team to incorporate any user requirements that had already been identified, before any requirements documents were finalized. As projects progress and more user feedback is available, there are typically more requirements that are identified, but Jill and her team wanted to make sure that any known requirements were already part of the documented requirements and any newly identified requirements were brought to light early in the project. By incorporating the requirements early, the UE team is more likely to ensure that the user requirements are addressed and not viewed as scope creep.

Release Criteria

In Jill's past companies she had great success in raising awareness by influencing the strategy to determine release criteria. Typically, when she examined the release criteria, they focused on bugs and features but not on UE criteria such as usability goals. Jill found that including UE goals in release criteria was one of the most effective strategies in raising awareness, because senior and executive management are focused on successful releases and therefore are typically involved in major release meetings. At Red Fox Jill worked to educate executive management on the need for UE release criteria, including the benchmark usability metrics that had been included in the departmental goals. Through this approach Jill was able to gather objective usability data in support of both the departmental goals and the project releases, thereby ensuring that every major release included UE release criteria.

Jill and her team were able to build awareness for UE by performing comparative studies with Red Fox's competitors, using usability criteria including successful task completion, time to complete a task, errors, assists, and subjective satisfaction. She then met with executive management to decide in which areas they wanted to be market leaders and in which areas they were content to be either on par or not with their competitors. By focusing resources on the areas in which the executives wanted to be market leaders, UE gained a reputation for being a business asset rather than a group of idealists.

Events

The usability lab grand opening was just one type of event to raise awareness. Jill used and participated in a number of events in her past companies:

- Customer meetings: When customers visit the company to meet with other people, it is a great opportunity for UE to make contact with the customers, give them a lab tour, and let them know about opportunities to be involved in UE activities and answer their questions. At Red Fox Jill coordinated with the person in charge of customer visits and the product marketing department to ensure that customers could be offered the opportunity to tour the lab during their visits. She also produced a professional folder of information to hand out so customers could learn more about UE and follow up after their visit if interested. These customer visits were very effective in raising the awareness both internally and externally, because the customers were impressed with the activities and communicated their positive feedback to the other people within the company, who in turn had more positive awareness of UE.

- Company meetings: UE topics can be covered at company meetings to help raise awareness of UE. At Red Fox the UE team gave several presentations at company meetings, including a usability highlights video of a high-profile project, a case study showing significant improvements, and a field-study highlights video demonstrating opportunities for innovation. All three presentations were interesting topics that helped to raise awareness.

- Customer events: Companies often hold events for customers, whether they are fun and networking events such as sports events or more educational events. At Red Fox Jill set up meetings with the various departments responsible for events to propose ways in which UE could be involved, whether it was giving a presentation, staffing a booth at a conference, or creating a collateral.

- Speakers: In the past Jill arranged for presentations on UE from both experts within the company's UE department and outside consultants. Depending on the topic, she had scheduled presentations with different groups within the company. At Red Fox Jill arranged for several outside speakers, including a presentation from a consultant on participatory design techniques. Jill knew that an important consideration is to ensure beforehand that any presentation, whether from an outside consultant or someone within the UE department, is communicating consistent messaging about UE, including the terminology used. Otherwise, the presentations could do more harm than good, ranging from increasing confusion to enabling problematic conclusions to be drawn.

Consistent Messaging

Early in her career, when Jill was an individual contributor, she worked in a UE group that had open meetings for people to come from around the company and get live advice for their interface design issues. Within the first few months of participating in these meetings, the credibility of UE had plummeted. This is because employees heard a wide variety of opinions from the UE community, which was not only ineffective in resolving the issues but detrimental to the credibility of the UE department. The fact that a wide variety of opinions existed is not surprising given how dependent on context design best practices are and the fact that the UE team had little background on the issues being brought to the meetings. This experience did serve as an important lesson to Jill that companies value consistent messaging.

As mentioned above, another example of the need for consistent messaging is in arranging UE professionals from outside of the company to speak to people from departments outside of UE.

"Who do you think would be a good speaker to help educate our internal stakeholders?" Jill asked her team.

"Well, I think that Evan is a fun speaker, but he doesn't practice collecting real customer data, so I'm a bit concerned that he might say something detrimental to our user research efforts," offered Sandy, one of the designers.

"What about Ramone? We all think his approach to information architecture is very effective," suggested Vikram, an information architect.

While Jill was in the middle of justifying a budget for the usability lab, an external speaker might say that labs are unnecessary. Or the speaker might say that she never uses research methods but does create personas. In most of these examples, except for the suggestion of Ramone as a speaker, this messaging from an external speaker could mean unnecessary problems for Jill and her team. Anyone outside of UE could say, "Well, why do you need thousands of dollars for a lab when this expert says a lab is unnecessary?" Jill found that it is better either to have these experts address only the UE team or to ensure their messaging is not in conflict with the goals of the UE team before the speaker addresses people outside of the UE team.

By having debates internal to the UE department, the company benefits from the best solution the UE team can create and also from knowing that regardless of which UE team member they are currently working with, they will have the same high-quality and consistent approach across the UE department. This is even more important in companies that are ISO certified or working to become certified to demonstrate consistent and repeatable processes.

Questions

9. In addition to including UE goals in the set of goals that determine executive bonuses, Jill needed to negotiate additional agreements to ensure the goals were really met. What types of issues might be encountered and what types of agreements should be put in place at the time the goals are agreed upon?

10. Will the existence of UE release criteria ensure that projects meet the criteria?

11. What might be some of the pitfalls of UE release criteria?

12. When raising awareness, why is it important to have consistent messaging from internal and external UE professionals? Why not have different opinions?

Summary

Over the years Jill learned many strategies and tactics for raising the awareness of UE within organizations. Because every company has a unique culture and values, she also learned that although the strategies typically remained the same, the tactics sometimes needed to be adapted to the particular needs of the company's culture. Regardless of the company, she found the following activities to be successful ways to raise awareness:

- Assume there is very little knowledge of UE within most companies—most companies have at best pockets of knowledge. Between misperceptions, reorganizations, and employee turnover, most companies require constant education.
- Understand the company's culture, the business goals, and the values and ensure that the focus of UE supports these goals. By focusing on the business, UE can avoid common misperceptions of being academic or only focusing on the users.
- Practice user experience with internal customers—understand their values, goals, and terminology. Translate how UE activities support stakeholders' terminology and initiatives.
- Understand the development cycle. Integrate UE activities into both documented processes and undocumented daily practices.
- Report to the same level as engineering and marketing if possible. If not, try to report into where most decisions are made.
- Create a plan of how limited resources are applied to clearly communicate how resources are allocated, set expectations, and raise the awareness of resource shortages. Avoid spreading UE resources too thin.
- Build a usability lab. The lab is not only functional, it helps to raise the awareness across the company and with customers.
- Create direct relationships with customers. Customers provide great input and help to raise the awareness by singing the praises of UE to sales, marketing, and executives.
- Create collateral to be handed out as educational material inside and outside the company. Include benefits and testimonials.
- Integrate UE into goals at multiple levels, including corporate and departmental goals.
- Integrate UE into the requirements process, ensuring that user requirements are included in addition to the business requirements.

- Integrate UE into release criteria, which not only helps to ensure that projects are more usable, but raises the awareness because executives are typically part of the process to ensure that release criteria are met.
- Create and participate in events to help educate people inside and outside the company.
- Create a consistent set of terminology and processes to be used by all members of the UE team.
- Create consistent messaging to the company from internal and external UE professionals.

Further Reading

Bias, R., and Mayhew, D. (2005). *Cost-justifying usability: an update for the internet age*. San Francisco: Morgan Kaufmann.

Bodine, K. (2006). The people who make great web sites. (September 13) Forrester Best Practices. Available at http://www.forrester.com

Dorsey, M., and Bodine, K. (2006). Culture and process drive better customer experiences. (March 31) Forrester Best Practices. Available at http://www.forrester.com

Landauer, T. K. (1995). *The trouble with computers: usefulness, usability, and productivity*. Cambridge, MA: MIT Press.

Rummler, G. A., and Brache, A. P. (1990). *Improving performance: how to manage the white space on the organization chart*. San Francisco: Jossey-Bass.

The Standish Group. (1994). *The CHAOS Report*. Available at http://www.standishgroup.com/sample_research/chaos_1994_1.php

Strassmann, P. (1990). *The business value of computers: an executive's guide*. New Canaan, CT: Information Economics Press.

Usability Step by Step: Small Steps to a More Successful Site

Maggie Reilly, Smart Solutions, Inc.

Justifiably proud of the site's success, the team naturally took the many positive visitor comments as a strong endorsement for the site—and as proof that the site needed no improvement. But Sheila was certain the site could be made easier to use. But how could she convince the development team to rethink the site?

The National Vaccines and Immunization Program (NVIP) hired Laura as a content specialist for both its customer-facing website and its Intranet. Although the team needed strong content management and writing skills to produce and manage the complex content for the website, Laura noted the official job description for her new position included references to "user experience" and "usability." During interviews for the job, Laura learned that these terms were important to her new manager, Coral, but largely meaningless to others in the organization. Coral explained to Laura that she hoped to incorporate usability into NVIP web team processes and was depending on Laura to make that happen.

Laura was a good fit for the dual role: She combined commitment to user experience with a love of the web. In fact, Laura was well qualified to oversee both content and user experience for this site. She had a Master's degree in English, a deep background in scientific and technical communication, and plenty of experience designing and conducting usability tests and reviews for websites, software, and mechanical or electronic displays and interfaces. She would be working with a small team that included Coral as webmaster, two software engineers, a part time graphic designer, and a content developer who had been with the agency for over 20 years and had started as an administrative assistant. With the exception of the content developer, all team members, including Coral, had been hired within the past 18 months.

Stealth Usability

Laura quickly discovered that Coral was right. Most NVIP personnel were unaware of usability or user-centered design. Coral made it clear that she expected Laura to come up with her own methods for integrating usability into NVIP development processes. Laura started by asking what her teammates and other colleagues were working on and then commented on their projects from the perspective of the user. She raised issues about multilingual users or those whose first language was not English. At meetings she wondered whether others would make the silly mistakes *she* made when interpreting frequently asked questions and articles. She pointed to obvious errors and instances of poor or insufficient design by citing examples from her own experience and from published research. She shared her reference and text books; recommended articles, books, and websites to her teammates and acquaintances; and persuaded her manager to invest in additions to the web team's reference library.

Soon she was asked to review and comment on web-based programs offered to the public or developed for use by agency personnel. Opportunities to employ a more user-centered approach began to emerge. One afternoon Laura made her way down one flight in a dingy stairwell to a tiny inner corridor office occupied by Sheila, a health program manager who oversaw health education activities at several client websites supported by NVIP. Sheila leaned out of her office doorway and waved Laura inside. Two people made a tight fit in the tiny space, and there was no room for paper notepads or laptop computers. "I really don't want anyone to overhear us," Sheila explained, pushing the door closed. "Things get repeated and blown out of proportion, and I want this to be done right, without a lot of rumors flying." She sighed and then swiveled to face her computer screen. "It's this website," she gestured. "I know you've seen it, but have you really looked at it?"

Laura drew up a chair and turned toward the computer display. Sheila's web browser was filled with the home page for the Alliance for Disease Prevention (ADP). A client organization of NVIP, ADP was a private non-profit group that distributed information about vaccines, immunization, and disease prevention to medical and public health professionals throughout the United States. ADP received much of its funding from NVIP but was independently operated and managed. ADP used its website as its prime channel for communicating information, educating professionals, and distributing materials, including posters, flyers, brochures, newsletters, handbooks, and articles designed for public health education.

Sheila pointed to the top left center of the screen, adorned with hand-drawn images of popular cartoon characters from classic Superhero comics. "What I really hate is the graphics. These things take up space at the top, and the things people really want don't even appear unless you scroll way down—and even then you can't read them. I can't stand it!"

Just one glance helped to explain Sheila's frustration. Only the scroll bar indicated that scrolling might be an important activity for a visitor. The visible part of the long page showed only a brief uninformative welcome message and was followed by swathes of white space. The long columns at either side mixed navigation links and text links, and the link labels were generic and uninformative. And these were just the problems that were immediately visible on the home page.

"It's just not professional looking," Sheila went on. "It doesn't look as if qualified people are running the site. And you can't find anything on the site unless you already know where to look."

Site Structure, Search Engine, and Search Results

When Laura began to explore the site, she realized it consisted of four websites, not one, with four distinct web addresses. Because the "sister sites" were not distinguished in terms of appearance, format, logos, or tag lines, they were effectively hidden from visitors. The prominently placed search box, which indirectly invited visitors to ignore the columns of links, provided search results *only* for the site from which the search was initiated. Thus visitors who searched from the main home page could not see results for relevant materials housed on the sister sites. And if they initiated a search from one of the subsites, they could only see results from that site.

There were problems with the presentation of search results as well. Relevance was determined by the frequency with which the search phrase appeared, but because the search was not an intelligent search, results consisted of a list of phrases and terms identical to elements of the search string, together with a count of the number of times the terms appeared on a particular page. Results included a long complex URL designed to assist the site's programmer rather than visitors to the site.

Value Versus Viewing Success

Most pages and documents at the site were never viewed. In a site with over 5,000 pages, web logs indicated that about 5% were viewed regularly, with about 85% viewed so rarely these views were not counted. Most hits on the site were limited to 20-odd pages that were often cross-referenced in "What's New" or "Hot Topics" categories shown in the left and right columns.

Yet despite these shortcomings, health care professionals and scientists who visited the site believed its content was extremely valuable for both fellow professionals and the public. These visitors had provided testimonials that were available from the home page. Typical comments included such statements as the following:

Your service and information are second to none. Thanks for all your help!

I love you, I love you, I love you and I love all the resources you develop in the fight against disease transmission!!

Your site is great! Thank you for publishing current, accessible, free material!

Thank you for your quick response to my e-mail. I really appreciate it and your help. Your publications couldn't be easier to read and understand.

The site had originally been created 10 years earlier under the direction of Dorothy, a public health researcher and educator. Working with an all-volunteer staff, Dorothy had built a simple website that quickly became known as a comprehensive reliable source of public health materials and information about immunization and disease prevention. The site was so successful that public and private donor organizations offered to help fund its work, and Dorothy and her small staff now dedicated themselves to managing and operating the site and developing new materials for its audiences.

Justifiably proud of the site's success, the ADP staff naturally took the many positive visitor comments as a strong endorsement for the site—and as proof that the site needed no improvement. But Sheila was certain the site could be made easier to use; she wanted to convince the ADP team to rethink the site. "I've got to be able to show that the site needs to be changed," she said, "and I need to be able to tell Dorothy how we'll assess the site. We can't just say 'change this'—we have to do better than that."

Revising Sites and Redeeming Relationships

Laura outlined her ideas for working with the ADP team to Sheila. "First, we can assess the site from the standpoint of accepted web standards. A lot of the problems with the site are obvious—like the huge blank spaces and all the scrolling on the home page and the inconsistent page layouts. We can talk about things like how new visitors don't know where to look for navigation—there's no standard set of links across pages. There's not even a consistent link back to the home page from all the other pages."

"I know what you're saying, Laura, but just pointing out problems—that won't work," Sheila objected. "I've been talking to them since last fall about stuff like this. They just remind me about the award they won 6 years ago as a top information website for health care professionals."

"That's okay," Laura said. "It's actually part of my plan. What we can say then is that the only way to be sure visitors can really use the site the way it's intended to be used is to set up a test. We can create the test together—they can be part of all the team meetings and help us every step of the way." Laura paused. "I know they won't listen if we tell them what *we* think needs to be improved, so we can present this as, here's what comes up when we do a standard evaluation. That doesn't line up with the data and feedback they have. When two sets of observations about the site are in conflict, there's a gap somewhere. To be sure about how things work, we need to watch people using the site. And we can arrange to do that."

"But how?" said Sheila. "You said a test could cost $20,000 or more. They don't have $20,000 for a usability test. In fact, all they have left in their budget from us for this year is about $3,000. I ought to know—I administer all the funds that NVIP gives them, and Dorothy has to show me their full operating budget each year."

"That's where I come in," Laura said. "I've has done this kind of thing before. I can set up and carry out the test as part of my regular job duties—no special fees or charges. You can tell Dorothy and her team they are getting a huge freebie from the agency, just because their site is so popular and important."

"But what about recruiting, renting a lab, and all that? Won't that cost a lot? Like thousands of dollars for a few days?" Sheila asked. "When we worked with you on the flu campaign last year, just the focus groups cost that much. I'd think a usability test would be even more expensive."

"Yes, it would, but we aren't going to use a lab or do a lot of formal recruiting. We can do this at a conference. We'll do what's called 'low-rent usability,'" Laura explained. "We show up at the conference with a computer and ask people to take part in 20- or 30-minute sessions, focusing on just a few quick tasks—the kind of thing they really use the site for, just to look up a specific piece of information or find an article or set of instructions. It really works, too—I've done it before."

"I'm still not sure I get it," Sheila said. "If this is so easy and cheap to do, why does anyone bother doing the expensive kind of usability test?"

"For lots of reasons," Laura said. "This wouldn't work well for a large complex piece of software or a complicated specialized interface like an automobile dashboard. Traditional software applications, like the programs hospitals use to set up, administer, and monitor chemotherapy, are incredibly complex and require detailed task flows and very specialized knowledge to use—and to assess. Even something that most people use all the time, like the dashboard in a car, has so many choices and functions that you can't just ask someone to try one or two things and get an idea of how well it works. But we don't need a fancy lab setup or special equipment. After all, when you look at a website, you're usually just sitting at your desk. So if we want to see how someone looks at a few pages on a website, it's okay to work outside the lab. In fact, small-scale studies are good ways to test the water—they turn a spotlight on big problems and help you decide what changes can be most productive.

"The most important thing we need to do is pick a conference that will be attended by the key audience members, so that we have the best chance of recruiting the right kind of participants." Laura stopped for a moment. "And here's another thought: If it's the right kind of conference, Dorothy and her team will be a lot more interested in attending with us. Then, they can observe the sessions first hand without spending extra money or time, and it gives all of us the chance to meet and talk right after we've seen participants. At the same time, everyone is involved in an educational experience that applies directly to professional health care. It's a win–win situation."

Questions

6. What difficulties might prevent the success of Laura's plan? Which stumbling blocks has Laura overlooked?
7. What obstacles does the team face, and how can Laura's plan help the team overcome these obstacles?

The Plan and How to Work It

Dorothy identified a conference in Philadelphia for health care professionals with an interest in communicable and vaccine-preventable disease, scheduled about 2 months in the future. This conference would attract a variety of health care professionals with an interest in vaccines and immunization and would provide lead time to plan the test and prepare test materials.

Sheila could recruit participants from visitors to the booth, offering the popular color posters and brochures that were in short supply as incentives for prospective participants. Laura could facilitate the sessions, which could be audiotaped, whereas the ADP web team members could also observe and make notes. It would be a tight fit, but Laura and Coral measured the booth size and then tried arranging the tables, chairs, and other furniture that must fit into the booth. Using a tape measure and office furniture, they came up with a layout to allow Laura to run sessions in the booth itself. Best of all, web team members could debrief directly with participants after each session, asking questions about what they'd watched and how the participants felt about using the site.

Laura and Coral were somewhat concerned about the cramped test setup and the lack of recording capabilities, because the hardware and software required for recording were not part of the current NVIP budget. However, they were convinced that testing would produce useful results even if sessions could not be recorded.

Laura also considered analysis of data from the sessions. After the conference she could list critical problems and then meet with Sheila and the ADP team to classify and prioritize these problems. During the final project phase, Laura would prepare a formal report that would include examples of the kinds of changes that could be made—web page mock-ups and a suggested information architecture for the site—as well as a project plan for implementing the changes.

Planning and Preparing the Test

Sheila arranged the first team meeting that, like all team meetings before the conference, was conducted as a phone conference. Laura's services as a user researcher were presented to the team as an opportunity to benefit from expert research with the right price tag—free. However, when Sheila suggested there might be things worth improving at the site, she was met with actual *cries* of disagreement. "Everyone loves our site!" Dorothy exclaimed. "It's been a great success from the beginning. We'd be afraid to change anything."

"That's right." Larry, the site's programmer, was emphatic. "We have thousands of visitors, and they know how the site works. If we changed things, they would have a hard time."

Maxine, the public health educator who coordinated content at the site, added, "I just can't see what you want us to do. Every change we made would lead to more and more changes. It would be a terrific amount of work, and we hardly have time for the work we do now. . . ."

". . . and we don't know that these changes would help anyone," Dorothy finished up. Sheila leaned forward to reply, but Laura cut in quickly. "You're right," Laura said. "It would be a mistake to just try out some changes and then see what happens. That would be making all your visitors act as your test participants—but you wouldn't be there to watch what they did or ask questions. Instead, what we're thinking of is taking the time to ask visitors what *they* think of the site. We'd like to invite people who haven't seen the site to look at it and tell us what they think."

"Why people who don't know the site?" asked Dorothy. "Don't you think the current users are the most important people to test? After all, they already *know* how the site works."

"That's just the point," said Sheila. "You can't learn much from them. They've already trained themselves to use the site. But people who don't know the site. . . ."

"Actually I think Dorothy has a good point," Laura put in. "We'd probably want to invite people who know the site and some who don't, to get a good picture of how both groups use the site and what they like about it. We want to be sure that people who have used the site for a long time are getting the most out of it, and we want to know how the site works for people who've never come to it before. You see," she explained, "a lot of research shows that people leave websites pretty quickly when they can't find what they want right away. But if they have success in the beginning, they'll persist and keep looking for what they want, because they've had an experience that makes them believe the site will work. What we want to do," she summed up, "is make the site work as well as possible for both new visitors and people who use it regularly. And it might be," she added, "that we'll find out we don't need to change a thing."

Sheila looked at Laura in surprise, but Laura kept talking. "And there's another benefit you get out of this," she added. "You are going to get a test that shows the benchmark—the basic service level, usability, and visitor satisfaction at your site, and the only real cost to you is an investment of some of your time. These test results can be compared with results from future tests and assessments. That way you are laying a foundation to accurately measure the value and the success of your site.

"You can use an established research method to show how usage and services at the site have improved and why the site works so well. You can show solid research-based reasons for the changes you make. And if there are any problems, you'll have a much better idea of what they are and how to go about fixing them. You'll have a plan for future development. And you'll get all this for a couple of thousand dollars in expenses for your team. Ordinarily, this would take a much bigger chunk of your budget—up to $25,000 or more. But in this case you only need to spend a tenth of that, and you get something that will help out the site for years to come.

"And there's one more thing—the best thing of all. This is not about someone coming in and saying 'I think you need to fix this.' This kind of test is about real people who visit your site, showing us where they have trouble and where changes could help them most. And it lets you concentrate on getting the site to work well right from the beginning, rather than waiting for visitors to tell you what's not working for them."

There was a moment of silence. "All right," Dorothy said. "As long as any changes are based on what people who use the site tell us, not just someone else's opinion."

Questions

8. How accurate is Laura's picture of the benefits of testing? What, if anything, is she omitting or disguising?
9. What arguments might have been added if this were an e-commerce or commercial site?

Project Logistics

The concept of the project had been approved, thanks to thoughtful lobbying by Laura and (to a lesser extent) by Sheila. Now the real work had to be done. At this point, the team had 6 weeks to:

- Prepare all test materials, including a compact disc with backup of web pages
- Make all arrangements for conducting tests, including permission from conference organizers
- Complete travel arrangements
- Conduct a pilot test
- Revise the test as needed
- Complete plans and arrangements for recruiting at the conference site

Team Structure and Deliverables

Table 4.1 shows team members and the deliverables from each. Note that team members played several roles.

Table 4.1. Team Members and Their Deliverables

Team Member	Role/Responsibilities	Deliverables
Laura	Roles: PM,[1] test designer and facilitator, lead researcher, presenter Activities: Manage project, facilitate team meetings, identify next steps and critical paths, develop all test materials, conduct/facilitate test sessions, manage participant materials and test notes, review notes posttest, analyze results, prepare report	PM deliverables: • Project schedule • Role definition • Role assignments Test deliverables: • Test plan • Screener • Flyers • Schedule sign-up sheet • Test protocol and materials • Top-line test results report • Final report
Sheila	Roles: Coordinator, technical and administrative support Activities: Provide official liaison between agency and website team; reserve room and equipment for team meetings, sending team meeting notices, preparing and distributing notes for team meetings; assisting Laura to manage all participants and test materials Provide administrative support, including negotiating equipment rental from the conference organizers, arranging travel and accommodations for herself and Laura Recruit participants at the conference, administer screenings, and manage sign-up sheet and schedule conflicts	Marked review copies of all deliverables; meeting notes and meeting notices
Dorothy	Role: Client Activities: Approve final for test design; disburse funds for ADP travel and technical equipment costs; maintain site while others attend the conference	No deliverables
Maxine	Roles: Subject matter expert, reviewer, observer	Marked review copies of all deliverables

Table 4.1. *Continued*

Team Member	Role/Responsibilities	Deliverables
	Activities: Codevelop/edit tasks and scenarios; observe test sessions; and assist with post-session debriefings and reviews	
Larry	Roles: Reviewer, observer, and technical support	Marked review copies of all deliverables
	Activities: Assist with computer setup and troubleshooting; provide backup disc with site in case Internet is unavailable; take notes and participate in postsession debriefing and reviews	

[1]PM means Project Manager.

Session Length and Activities

Test sessions were limited to 30 minutes for several reasons:

- Sessions could not be conducted during the plenary and keynote activities or sessions that conference participants were required to attend; test sessions were scheduled between conference sessions, during lunch breaks, and at periods when attendees could choose from optional sessions.
- Attendees had many commitments at the conference, so it was important to keep sessions brief.
- Test conditions could not meet standards of lab facilities. Noise and distractions on the conference floor were other reasons the team decided it was best to keep sessions short.
- The team chose a broad-test strategy rather than a deep-test strategy. They wanted to observe as many participants as possible, completing as many tasks as possible in a short time frame, much like the approach taken by most visitors to the site: reach the site, find the information, print or download, and leave.

Sessions consisted of the following:

- Pre-session questionnaire and instructions (5 minutes)
- Test activities—scenario-based task list (20 minutes)
- Postsession questionnaire and comments (5 to 10 minutes)

Recruiting Participants

Recruiting was brisk. Most visitors to the NVIP booth noticed the large sign at the front of the booth inviting them to "test drive" a disease prevention website. When they asked about the sign, Sheila initiated a conversation about websites that helped them while at work. During the course of her conversation she asked essential screening questions (e.g., "Are you a health professional? Do you provide immunization information to the public or to other professionals?") and then invited qualified visitors to evaluate the ADP website. There was no shortage of participants, and it became clear that incentives or rewards were really not needed. The idea of assisting others was attractive to participants drawn from helping professions. Prospective participants were also eager to share their opinions and believed that participation itself was a reward.

In fact, the popularity of the sessions became a problem. Sheila recruited backup participants to ensure that all sessions could be run. A questionnaire had been prepared as an alternate activity in case both participants for a session showed up. But when backup participants were offered the take-home survey rather than a turn at the computer, all expressed disappointment, and some were annoyed. These participants felt slighted, and the team received only three completed surveys.

The final participant list included participants ranging in age from 25 to over 60. Participants also represented a mix of hospital emergency room personnel, college instructors, military personnel, and public health workers so that they accurately reflected the range of audiences who visit the ADP site. About a third of the participants (7 of 19) stated they were familiar with the ADP site and used it regularly.

Success with Sessions

Participants were cooperative and enthusiastic. Despite the team's concerns about cramped conditions in the booth and distractions from the crowded exhibition floor, none of the participants seemed distracted or disturbed by the noise and the close quarters for testing. Participants were engaged throughout the session, thoughtfully answering the short initial questionnaire, completing tasks with relish, and commenting freely. Even the "think aloud" protocol was readily accepted. Laura facilitated each session, whereas Coral, Larry, and Sheila observed. All team members frantically scribbled notes and, between sessions, discussed the pattern of problems they noted. Much to Laura's disappointment, Maxine and Dorothy were unable to observe sessions. Maxine was busy at the conference, and Dorothy had chosen not to attend so that at least one team member would be "back at the ranch" supporting the ADP site.

To prevent order effects and to ensure that participants did not see themselves as "failing," the task list was divided into two sets of tasks presented on two sheets of paper. Half the participants started with one task set and half with the other. Participants were encouraged to work at a natural pace. If participants worked slowly or struggled with a task, they were sometimes told to move on to the next task, but they were not shown the second task set until they had finished the first. If they had time for only part of the second task set, participants were instructed to "complete as many as you can, but it's not a time test."

Initial Analysis

Each night after the test sessions Laura compared up to four sets of notes (her's, Coral's, Larry's, and intermittent notes from Sheila) for each session, consolidated them into a single record for each session, and then added to a master list of observed problems. Laura recorded which participants demonstrated which problems, how many times problems occurred, pages where problems occurred (if noted), and comments participants made. Laura also noted comments summarizing the overall experience and value for the site. Working with Coral, Laura cross-classified problems in four ways:

1. The design heuristic or standard each identified problem violates
2. What area of the website the problem applies to (navigation, visual presentation, interpretation of language, concept of site structure, etc.)
3. Severity of the problem (high, or prevents use; medium, or causes difficulty; low, or impairs but does not prevent use)
4. Priority for fixing the problems (rating based on severity plus projected effort required to make changes)

Laura was somewhat uneasy about this early analysis. She would have preferred to classify and prioritize problems with the help of the ADP team, but tight time frames made quick work necessary. And both Larry and Maxine made it clear they preferred not to participate without Dorothy, so Coral and Laura chose to go ahead with this step on their own. As she and Coral categorized problems and assigned ratings to them, Laura reflected that they would have to justify their decisions to the ADP team.

Presenting Results

After returning to the office, Laura spent a day or so completing her analysis of the findings and then developed a short PowerPoint presentation to summarize key findings. At a follow-up meeting a week later, Laura began by reviewing the positive findings:

- The ADP website provides essential information for both health care professionals and patients.
- Participants appreciate the wealth of information available in a single location.
- The clean graphically uncluttered look of ADP pages makes them appealing to participants.
- For the most part, participants respond positively or neutrally to the ADP brand (colors, images, and text styles).

Other findings, however, indicated difficulties participants experienced at the site:

- The structure of the ADP website is not clear to most participants.
- The ADP website does not incorporate standard Internet conventions that participants expected
- Participants' strategies for use of the site result in patterns of use that mean much of the site is never explored or viewed.
- Participants were overwhelmed by the amount of information on index and menu pages and were unable to effectively sort and process the information on these pages.

As Laura read the list, the ADP team listened in silence. Laura asked for questions, but no one commented. She had a sense that Dorothy, Maxine, and Larry were all holding their breath.

After a pause, Laura said, "Let's look at the first problem area we noted—that the structure of the site is not clear to visitors." Laura located the slide with a screen capture of the ADP home page (Figure 4.1). "When people came to the site, they actually didn't see the column headings that are supposed to help them understand how the page works," Laura said. "The column headings are centered and larger than the links, but they are in a visual line beneath the site name and signature graphics, and nothing draws the eye to them. What's more, for visitors who suffer from red–green color blindness, both these links and the teal-colored blocks—the dividers for the sets of links—are practically invisible. Look," she said, and clicked to the next slide.

"This slide shows what the page looks like to someone who has the most common kind of color blindness. Also, when you look at the page printed this way, you see the low visibility of the links and column headings. And look here," she went on, pointing to a hand-drawn horizontal red line drawn about a third of the way down the page. "This is where the page cuts off for a 15-inch diagonal monitor, and here—this second red line—is where it cuts off on a 17-inch monitor. You see how little of the page is actually visible on the screen." She looked up at Sheila and then spoke to the ADP team on the phone. "Your visitors aren't getting any orientation to the site.

Alliance for Disease Prevention

- *Needle Tips*   • *IAC Express*
- *Vaccinate Adults*   • *Hep Express*
- *Vaccinate Women* • *VISs*

Home page

Vaccination and Pregnancy

Schedules   Recommendations   Resources   Journal articles

Recommendations

7/05	"Guidelines for Vaccinating Pregnant Women: Recommendations of the Advisory Committee on Immunization Practices (ACIP)" Source: Centers for Disease Control and Prevention www.cdc.gov/nip/publications/preg_guide.htm www.cdc.gov/nip/publications/preg_guide.pdf
7/13/05	"Prevention and Control of Influenza: Recommendations of the Advisory Committee on Immunization Practices (ACIP)" Source: MMWR Recommendations and Reports, July 13, 2005, Vol. 54(Early Release):1-40 www.cdc.gov/mmwr/preview/mmwrhtml/rr54e713a1.htm
1/03	"ACOG Committee Opinion: Immunization During Pregnancy" Source: American College of Obstetricians and Gynecologists www.acog.org/from_home/publications/misc/bco282.pdf www.acog.org/from_home/publications/misc/bco282.cfm
2/08/02	"General Recommendations on Immunization: Recommendations of the Advisory Committee on Immunization Practices (ACIP) and the American Academy of Family Physicians (AAFP)" Source: MMWR, February 8, 2002 Vol. 51(RR-02):1-44 www.cdc.gov/mmwr/PDF/rr/rr5102.pdf (Specific information about vaccination during pregnancy can be found on pages 18-19)
12/14/01	"Revised ACIP Recommendation for Avoiding Pregnancy after Receiving a Rubella-Containing Vaccine" Source: MMWR, December 14, 2001, Vol. 50(49):1117 www.cdc.gov/mmwr/preview/mmwrhtml/mm5049a5.htm

Figure 4.1. A screen capture of the ADP home page.

They just start looking around, without any idea of just what the site offers or how it's set up."

No one responded to her comments. Aware that it was important to engage the ADP team and help them think through solutions, Laura persisted in asking for feedback. "Now, which links would you say are most important to your visitors?"

"That's easy," said Maxine. "They're most interested in links to information about flu and hepatitis B, and all the latest information is there for them right at the top of the right-hand column."

"Okay," said Laura, "what's the first link in that list?"

Maxine sounded puzzled. "The one that says 'CDC Influenza Site.'"

"And what does that link do?" Laura asked.

"Takes them to the CDC flu site," Maxine said, a little impatiently.

"Yes," said Laura, "and right out of your site. To a place that doesn't look anything like your site and isn't set up like yours, doesn't really work the same way, and has a somewhat different focus. Think about it from the perspective of someone who doesn't know what's coming. Do you see how that might be confusing?"

"Well, yes . . . but the CDC site is the best place for current information about influenza," Dorothy said. "That's why that link is at the top of the list."

"But people still come to your site, right?" asked Laura. "And they probably know about the CDC site, correct?"

"Well . . . yes. . . ," said Maxine.

"Then you might consider reorganizing the order of these links to reflect what people want to do at your site, and the sequence of links they want to see. For example, you might list all the flu-related resources that your visitors want from you, and then put the CDC flu link at the end of the list with a label like 'More influenza information at CDC.'"

"I don't agree with you," Dorothy said firmly. "That is not what we want to do. We want the CDC link right where it is."

"Well, maybe it's too soon to talk about how to address these problem areas," Laura said. "Maybe we should just talk about what the findings are, what they mean, rather than what to do about them."

"Well, let's do that," Dorothy said, "because to tell you the truth, this whole list puzzles me. So, you're saying we should move the links around on the home page. What else?"

"It's a little more than that," Laura said. "I think I confused things by getting too specific too fast. Really, what we noticed is that people were unsure where to go next or what link to try out. They didn't really understand what the site offers or—"

"I didn't see that," Larry said. "I didn't notice people being so confused. They mostly found the information they were looking for."

Laura and Sheila exchanged glances, deeply surprised by the gap between Larry's interpretation of visitor behavior and their observations. Laura responded, "Actually, it might have seemed that way, but pretty often people couldn't find the documents, even when we gave them very specific items. When I started looking at how many times people found what they were looking for, I found out the task success rate for all participants was really below 50%. It's a little hard to take in, but the truth is that most of the time people didn't find what they were looking for."

Dorothy cut in rather coldly. "I find that hard to believe," she said. "You yourself said that most participants found the site to be well organized."

"That's true, most participants did agree with that statement," Sheila said, "but questionnaires don't tell the whole story. What you have to pay attention to is what visitors *do* at the site."

"And in this case," Laura added, "when we asked them what they meant by 'well organized,' most people said they meant the long list of links on the home page. But we saw them bypass the links they needed over and over again. The links might *look* well organized, but they don't help people get where they want to go. And there's another thing to consider. People are often reluctant to be openly critical." Laura looked up for a moment. "Most people do look for the sunny side, you could say. They will say the most positive things they can say because they don't want to offend anyone. So to find out how well your site is working, you really need to watch what people do. What people did here was to ignore the long list of links that could help them."

"They didn't know what the newsletters were, and that's one of the most important things on the site," Sheila said. "They looked for contact information and couldn't find it. It's in the center of the home page, and they couldn't see it—because it wasn't where they expected it. They didn't know where they were when they got to the hepatitis part of the site."

"That's right," Laura agreed. "They had to use the back button and start over at the home page every time they looked for anything. Even in the midst of looking for an item, they'd go back to the home page saying, 'I must have made a mistake.' Or they said, 'I know it's here somewhere, I've seen it before, I'm sure.' That indicates a problem."

"But this is just a small group of people," Dorothy said. "We know people use our site all the time without any trouble."

"I want to suggest something," Laura said. "I am sure many people do use the site without trouble—they have taught themselves to move around on it. But the people we saw *all* had difficulty, and about a third of them said they were familiar with the website. Yet they still had problems completing the tasks. In fact, the participants who said they knew the site actually completed fewer tasks successfully than those who said they had never been to the site. It should be possible to make the site work better for everyone—old hands, newcomers, and those who use it once a year and then forget how to do it."

"I don't think you understand our audience," Dorothy began, but Sheila started talking too. "It seems to me that *you* don't understand what Laura is telling you. The site doesn't work that well, and the people in the usability test showed us that."

There was a silence. Laura thought how unfortunate it was they could not afford to videotape the sessions or use a recording tool like Morae. Audiotapes didn't capture the expressions, movements, puzzled glances, and dead ends that she and Sheila had watched. And they couldn't show the screens and mouse movements that went with the audiorecording. There wasn't a simple way to re-create the participants' experience for Dorothy, who had not observed a single test session. And if Dorothy continued to insist that the findings were "wrong," what could they do next?

The meeting continued for another hour or more in the same vein. Listing observed problems and inviting discussion didn't work very well. Laura and Coral were all too familiar with the list and had already come to conclusions about next steps, whereas Dorothy and Larry denied the problems. Maxine seemed somewhat more receptive to the findings but said very little. Laura eventually suggested that the ADP team review the top line findings and then take a careful look at the full report, due in a week's time. She also suggested that the team set a date to discuss the recommendations she had for the site.

Questions

10. How could Laura and Sheila have avoided or dispelled tension, mistrust, and miscommunication that made the post-test sessions so emotional?
11. What is the "root cause" for the ADP team's resistance at this point? How could it have been avoided?
12. What approaches would you recommend for the team at this point?

Recommendations for the ADP Site

To prepare for the final meeting with the ADP team, Laura carefully researched web-based standards, published findings from major Internet research, and best practices from designer, developer, and UEX forums and discussions. Then she brainstormed "fixes" with Coral and Sheila and developed "to-do's" to support each major recommendation.

As Laura completed the final report, she considered her mixed audience, which included health care professionals, a medical researcher, and a web programmer/developer. She had to include findings, recommendations, support for recommendations, and concrete examples of how to carry out recommendations. She distributed the full report the day before the final team meeting, including these sections:

- Executive Summary: Key Findings and Major Recommendations
- Detailed Findings (illustrated with screen captures)
- Detailed Recommendations (illustrated with screen captures from other sites and with wireframes)
- Project Plan (Phased Approach) for Recommendations
    Time Frame
    Milestones
    Key Roles (skill sets) and deliverables
    Range of estimated costs for each project phase

For example, one of the areas where visitors experienced the greatest amount of difficulty had to do with the lack of global navigation. Laura's report stated the following:

> Visitors to a website must be able to easily find content they need and develop a sense of their location in the site. Visitors' greatest frustration involves failure to find the content they need or expect.
>
> *Issue:* The site does not offer consistent global navigation.
>
> *Recommendation:* Provide consistent global navigation. Identify key navigational elements and place them in the same location on almost every page of the site.

When key navigation persists in the same location from page-to-page, visitors learn to look for particular controls, such as a navigation bar on the left, tabs across the top of a content area, utility links at the top or bottom of a page, or a right column area with contextual links of high interest. Consistent global navigation helps orient visitors and makes it easier to use and explore a site. Visitors develop greater confidence in the site and experience more success at the site because they know what to expect and where to find what they need. Success of a site encourages repeat visits—and repeated experiences of success.

To develop global navigation, it is important to think about the elements that each audience uses regularly. The elements common to all or most audiences should be sought and used as a basis for global navigation. For example, the ADP site might offer its visitors the following links on every page: Vaccines, Recent Vaccine Research, Contagious Diseases, Vaccine-preventable Diseases, Vaccination for Children, and Vaccination for Adults. Utility links available in the header and footer could include Home, Publications, FAQs, Glossary, and Site Map.

"Selling" the Recommendations

Sheila and Laura were deeply concerned about the tone and outcome of this second "debrief." However, much to their surprise and relief, discussion with the team at this second meeting was less confrontational. Laura read through the recommendations, answering questions from the ADP team about exactly how the recommendations had emerged, how critical the recommendations were, and what impact they would have. When she had finished reading all 11 recommendations, there was a short silence. Then Larry spoke up. "What if we hired someone to implement these recommendations—what would they charge us?"

Laura and Sheila exchanged glances. Laura spoke up. "Well, it depends on how you go about it. A big-name design firm might want to charge $50,000. But there are lots of ways to avoid that kind of expense. You can work with talented graduate students who would love the chance to show what they can do at a high-profile health care website. And you know," Laura added, "I don't really recommend that you try to make these changes all at once. That used to be what happened—companies would announce a redesign of the site, and actually take the site down to make changes."

"We could never do that!" Dorothy exclaimed. "We just have far too many people who rely on our site. This is not selling shoes—this is life-or-death information about disease prevention."

"Absolutely right," Laura said. "You wouldn't want to take that route. What I'd suggest is a series of changes. Start with things that are most important to fix, things that will make it easier for visitors to find the most important pieces of information—even just one thing that you want to change. Look at the list and see what changes might help your users most. And then work your way down the list as you can afford to." She went on, "I've put together a plan for making changes—let's look at it and see what you think."

The team completed the meeting with 30 minutes of lively discussion of recommendations, who could make the changes, a possible phased approach to the changes, what upfront cost savings and longer term trade-offs could be expected from using current staff members rather than contractors or consultants, and what Laura's involvement would be (very limited) in this project.

The meeting closed with positive feelings and many expressions of thanks from Dorothy and Maxine. "We really appreciate all the time and hard work you put into this," Dorothy assured them. "We want our site to continue to be the best of its kind."

After a round of friendly good-byes and thank-yous, Laura and Sheila were left sitting in the tiny windowless conference room. Sheila spoke first. "So, what do you make of all that?" she asked. "First they seemed so upset, and then they seemed to suddenly get serious about going ahead with the changes to the site. I can't figure out what made them change their minds."

"I don't think we did change their minds," Laura replied. "I have the feeling they agreed before the meeting to 'make nice' and keep their reactions to themselves. I don't think we'll be seeing many changes at the site. But I think we did everything we could," Laura added.

Sheila stood up with a frown. "Well, I'm not giving up yet. They just have a bad case of 'we're perfect-itis.' They might think differently when I tell them their funds are cut if they don't follow through." She gathered up her papers and shrugged. "We'll just have to wait and see what happens. Dorothy is supposed to get back to me in a couple of weeks. So, we'll find out then."

Long-Term Results

Although Laura initially saw no changes to the ADP site—just as she had predicted—she was soon reminded that long-term outcomes are unpredictable. She heard nothing from Sheila in the next few weeks, and after the

New Year she was involved with other projects. She left NVIP within a few months to accept another position; at that time no significant changes had been made to the ADP site, and none of the team's suggestions had been adopted. When, out of curiosity, she revisited the ADP site some 18 months later, she found that changes had been made to the overall structure of the site, its general look and feel, and its search results (Figure 4.2). Although the home page still scrolled on, with long lists of links in both the right and left columns, general navigation and overall readability and legibility had significantly improved.

A global navigation system had been put in place, all sister sites had been subsumed into the main site, the cartoon character visual themes had been removed from the home page and landing pages, and the site's color scheme had been shifted, on these pages, from predominantly red and green to blue and orange. The site now had the "professional" appearance Sheila had been looking for, and the welcoming messages in the center home page could now be read with ease. Laura noted that even a small relatively inexperienced team can apply usability principles and techniques and gradually improve an organization's services and products.

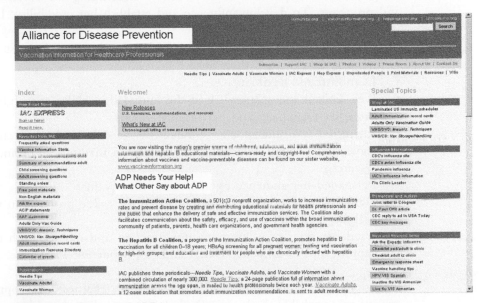

Figure 4.2. The revised ADP home page.

Questions

13. Considering Laura's audience, how might you have structured the report and presentation? What elements were missing? What elements might have been excluded or passed over?
14. At this meeting, what strategies might have been used to increase audience buy-in for conclusions and recommendations?
15. What do you think caused the dramatic change in the tone of this final meeting? Should this turn-around have been a part of the discussion?
16. What do you predict will be the outcome of this meeting?
17. Has the project been successful? Unsuccessful? How so?

Summary

Even with limited time and resources, a small team can plan, design, and conduct an effective usability test and make a real difference to the product being tested. Such a team can have an impact on methods, outlook, and products of an organization. In this case study Laura demonstrated how she played on her personal strengths and leveraged those of her teammates to "infiltrate" the NVIP and introduce concepts of usability and user-centered design and development without formally challenging the current methods and processes. To develop influence and establish her credibility, Laura:

- Began with and maintained an attitude of service and interest in helping others reach their goals
- Demonstrated flexibility
- Recognized and acknowledged the knowledge, skills, and abilities of both her teammates and her internal clients
- Identified and understood the values of the culture she had entered (objectivity, logic, supporting data, accepted methods and standards for research)
- Persuaded her audience by addressing these values
- Demonstrated rather than merely stated the value proposition for usability and user-centered design
- Used her skills as a communicator, teacher, and mentor both to support and to influence others and to present her ideas

Dorothy's initial and continued distance from the test development and process was probably the biggest single failing and the one with most impact. Although Dorothy was the most influential person on the client team, she learned least about usability concepts and methods. She observed none of the test sessions and had to rely on reports of her staff members and the formal report supplied by Laura when sessions were complete. Because her inclination was to question the results and resist the recommendations, her lack of engagement made it simpler for her to dispute or dismiss what others reported. Her skepticism was compounded by her ignorance of usability and user-centered design and the lack of a videotaped record of the sessions.

The findings and patterns from the test sessions clearly supported recommendations developed by Laura, but the audience for these recommendations remained unconvinced. Their interpretation of data and observations did not match those of the NVIP team, and when recommendations were presented, those who supported change for the site were unable to convince those who resisted the changes.

Using her personal strengths, skills, experience, and knowledge, Laura demonstrated ways to bring usability to an organization that did not yet understand the concepts of user-centered design or recognize the value of usability. Although she was not successful in persuading one client, the ADP team, to accept and act on usability-based recommendations to improve their website, she did increase awareness of the concepts of usability, user-centered design, and user experience throughout NVIP. She was also reminded of how important it is to engage with key personnel and win their trust and support.

Finally, Laura was reminded that long-term outcomes are unpredictable. When she revisited the ADP site some 18 months later, she found that changes had been made to the overall structure of the site, its general look and feel, and its search results. A global navigation system had been put in place, all sister sites had been subsumed into the main site, the cartoon character visual themes had been removed from the home page and landing pages, and the site's color scheme had been shifted, on these pages, from red and green to blue and orange. Even a small relatively inexperienced team can apply usability principles and techniques and gradually improve an organization's services and products.

Further Reading

The Usual Suspects: How to Do It

Dumas, J., and Redish, G. (1999). *A practical guide to usability testing.* Revised Edition, Intellect, UK.

Nielsen, J. (December 20, 1999). *Designing web usability: the practice of simplicity*. 1st, edition, Peachpit Press.

Rubin, J. (February 1, 2001). *Handbook of usability testing: how to plan, design, and conduct effective tests*. John Wiley & Sons.

The Philosophy of Usability: Usability Concepts and Principles

Krug, S. *Don't make me think: a commonsense approach to web usability*. New Riders Press; 2nd edition August 18, 2005.

Useful Websites

Colorblind Web Page Filter, http://colorfilter.wickline.org/

Jim.Thatcher.com, http://www.jimthatcher.com/index.htm

Linda.com, http://www.lynda.com/

Usability.gov: your guide for developing usable and useful websites, http://www.usability.gov/

Vischeck: simulate colorblind vision, www.vischeck.com

W3C World Wide Web Consortium, http://www.w3.org/

Zen Garden, http://www.csszengarden.com/

Growing a Business by Meeting (Real) Customer Needs

Marie Tahir, Intuit
Gia Rozells, Intuit

> *Bob just didn't get it. "My engineering team added five new features for the last version. We worked with Johanna's team to update the visual design so that it looks fresher and as catchy as these new products. I don't get it—why aren't customers happy with the product now that it has shipped?"*

Evaluating the Current State of RevPhoto

Sally Amando started the RevLev Company 10 years ago and launched a flagship product called RevPhoto, a photo-editing product, that has been in the marketplace for nearly a decade. Though Sally did not have a background in photography, she recognized that the emerging trend of digital photography would quickly evolve into a large consumer market. High-priced professional photo-editing software existed, but RevPhoto was one of the first editing products targeted toward home users.

As the flood of consumer-priced digital cameras hit the market, RevPhoto flourished and rapidly gained market share. Around the same time graphic design software makers, whose products also targeted home users, began adding photo-editing capabilities to their software. To stay in the race, RevLev added even more graphic editing features to RevPhoto. Sally was proud of how quickly RevPhoto got to par with the leading graphic design package's features.

Sally and her leadership team had noted a slight erosion in market share over time, but in the past 2 years the decline turned into an avalanche. As competitive offerings entered the photo-editing market, existing RevPhoto customers switched products instead of buying RevPhoto's annual upgrade, and new buyers chose the newer less-expensive products. RevLev's mission was clear: They must immediately understand and reverse the flow of customers to their competitors.

Sally called a leadership team meeting to review the state of the company. She asked Carol Deska, head of product management, and Johanna Makina, head of user-centered design (UCD), to present data on why customers are switching to competitors' products.

"Our goal for this meeting is to get a clear picture of how much market share we're losing and determine short-term solutions to reverse the trend," said Sally. "Carol, can you get us started?"

"Okay, let's start with the latest sales data," began Carol. "When we look at unit sales over the last 18 months, there is a clear downward trend, which totals to a decrease of 16% since the beginning of this period."

"Have you figured out why sales have decreased?" asked Bob Nikoursey, head of engineering.

"I have some theories," Carol continued. "First, let me say that I don't think the problem lies in the marketing and sales processes. I've reviewed those with the sales leaders and found no issues. Instead, we need to focus on the product itself.

"You all know that two competitive products have jumped into our market in the past 2 years. They had the advantage of using early versions of RevPhoto, which saved them research time and money, so they can undercut our prices." Carol said.

"It's always easier to follow the leader, isn't it?" Sally lamented. "But have you figured out exactly why our long-time customers are now switching to the new products? Is it purely a price issue?"

"The price difference is an attraction, especially for first-time buyers, but I believe it's secondary. We've surveyed our customers who have not renewed this year," Carol answered, "and many said that they've become frustrated by how hard it is to use our latest versions. They feel that RevPhoto has become overly complex and is more than they need. Here are some customer comments that cover most of the feedback."

> "I'm not a professional photographer. I bought a camera that automatically does all the right settings to make the picture look good. I don't want to be forced to make so many decisions! I don't even know what a 'matte' is! I just want to make my photos better fast."

"Good grief. The main thing I use RevPhoto for is to make sure my subjects don't look like red-eyed devils. When did it get so hard to do that? I can't even find that feature anymore!"

"The last update was so complicated; I was on hold with tech support three times before I figured out how to print my photos. That used to be really easy."

"Sheesh! I'd think you could just move a little lever to make it darker or lighter! You're giving me about five different options for changing color. What the heck is the difference between background brightness and contrast? I just want it darker!"

"I used to enjoy using your product. Photos should be fun! It feels like it's all work now. I feel like I have to learn your product all over again every time you come out with a new release. I'm sorry, but I give up."

"Just help me to print four different pictures on one page with captions. How does that work?"

"Ouch" grimaced Sally. "Is there any good news, Carol?"

"Well," Carol replied, "we do have anecdotal data showing that our brand name is strong and our customers are loyal. Do you want to discuss that, Johanna?"

"Sure," started Johanna. "Our UCD team has done a combination of field research and in-depth interviews with several sets of existing customers. We focused on customers who have been using RevPhoto for 3 to 8 years. They almost consider themselves part of our company because they've been using the product since version 1. Now they feel that we've dropped them and are targeting a professional customer," Johanna stated. "This is because in many cases, our customers use only a portion of RevPhoto's features. There is so much functionality that they simply bypass. Our research suggests that if we can make the product easier to use, customers would prefer to stay with RevPhoto and enjoy the security of our company's brand name and long-term stability."

"Thank you, Johanna. It's hard to hear this, but important that we all have the same realistic perspective on our situation," Sally said. "Bob, what are your thoughts?"

"It's true that RevPhoto has far more functionality now than it did 18 months ago," said Bob, a little miffed by what he'd been hearing. "My engineering team added five new features for the last version. We worked with Johanna's team to update the visual design so that it looks fresher and as catchy as these new products. We even squeezed time into the schedule so that the user researchers could test the usability of each feature. Customers understood them fine. I don't get it—why aren't customers happy with the product now that it has shipped?"

"Good question, Bob," said Johanna. "We ended up using all our design resources to add new features and design a new look and feel for the interface. We didn't have any time to assess some of the core features we've had in the product for many releases. When we ran usability tests, we had only enough time to test the new features. And you're right, customers found them easy to use in that context—that is, when we pulled out those features and pointed them out to the users. However, when those features are mixed in with RevPhoto's 45 other features, they seem difficult to find and use. On top of that, as we've always done, we locked down the requirements for new features before doing any customer research. We had no time on the schedule to respond to feedback beyond making cosmetic changes. Now, this is not the ideal—we all know that. So I have some ideas for how we can improve this process."

"I'm open to hearing anything that might help, Johanna," said Bob. "But this news will really hurt morale. My engineers have been run ragged completing all the new features on time. And they did a great job. But besides doing day-to-day development work, they'd like to train in the latest technologies and implement new architectural changes that could streamline our development processes. They're worried that focusing on our existing technology will make their skills stagnate. And now, after all that hard engineering work, I have to tell them that the sales are still down." Bob had a somewhat disgruntled look on his face.

"I totally understand that, Bob." replied Johanna. "I just had one of my best designers give notice last week. She said she's not having fun here anymore. For all the long hours, she no longer hears raves from our customers. She took a job at another company."

"We've got a lot of unhappy people on our hands. Let's come up with an action plan that will improve life for our employees, our customers, and . . . our balance sheet," concluded Sally.

Questions

1. How do you think the team can get back on track? What type of research plan do you think Johanna will recommend?
2. Given that RevLev has already learned of their ease-of-use problems, why should they consider doing further research rather than just start fixing the problems right away?

Developing an Action Plan

After some discussion, the leadership team agreed to a research plan.

"Johanna, you've given this some thought. Let's hear what you've come up with," asked Sally.

"I have some ideas," said Johanna. "I'd like to work with Carol to create a plan for marketing and UCD research. We should dig into the customer feedback and sales data and then do deeper observational research on key areas of concern. For starters, let's figure out which tasks are critical to our customers' workflow. Once we know that, we can see how well RevPhoto currently helps them to succeed at those tasks."

"Okay," said Carol. "That works for me. And let's not get stuck focusing only on the software. Let's make sure the tech support experience is good as well."

"Great point," said Johanna. "Ease-of-use does not only mean in the product—it's the whole experience with RevPhoto and RevLev. I'll contact the tech support leaders and get their buy-in as well. Bob, can you assign the appropriate engineers to join us on customer visits?"

"Absolutely, Johanna. The engineers love to get out and meet customers. And being part of the research will help them feel excited about the development plans we come up with."

"Alright. We know our immediate marching orders," said Sally. "There's never enough time for all the customer research we'd like to do, but let's learn everything we can in the time we've got. In 3 months we'll finalize our development direction for this release."

Questions

3. What groups should be included in the research?
4. What methods might the team use to determine the tasks critical to the customers' workflow?
5   Do you think the RevLev team is poised for success? Why or why not?

Evaluating the Research Data With the Cross-Functional Leadership Team

Three months later, the entire RevLev leadership team, including product management/marketing, UCD, engineering, technical support, and sales, attended a debriefing to learn what the customer research revealed.

"First, I want to thank all of you for the hard work you've done in the past 3 months," said Sally. "Carol and Johanna are going to summarize the significant findings and offer recommendations for our next development season."

Carol began, "In partnership with Johanna's team, we used a phone survey of 100 customers to begin to understand which tasks they want to do most with RevPhoto. Then, during site visits, we created a list of the tasks our customers were doing with RevPhoto. We then created a web survey that listed the tasks and allowed customers to rank them by importance. Notice that this is pretty different from our past surveys. In the past we listed the features in RevLev (Print Options, Edit Photo, etc.) and asked which customers used most often. This time we listed the tasks we saw people doing (remove red-eye, print photos, etc.) and asked which were most important to them." (Table 5.1 shows the Top 10 task list.)

"You can see how basic the tasks are in the Top 10 list," Carol continued. "We've spent years enhancing our photo editing features, but what we found is that more than anything, people want to do simple things, like changing the brightness, resizing, cropping, and removing red-eye. We also found that things we've ignored since version 1, such as printing and uploading from a camera, are the things that customers value the most. In addition,

Table 5.1. Top 10 Task List

Rank	Task
1	Remove red-eye
2	Print photos
3	Crop photos
4	Darken or lighten photos
5	Change the size of a photo
6	Find photos to organize them into albums
7	Share photos with someone else
8	Delete photos that didn't turn out well
9	Upload photos from digital camera
10	Make a slideshow with music and captions

Table 5.2. Ranking of RevPhoto Planned Enhancements

Ranking	Task
11	Custom photo stationery
12	Make posters
13	Customize my workspace

we discovered that a major customer problem is that they just have too many photos and need a quick way to delete ones they don't like.

"But wait, it gets more interesting," said Carol. "Just as important as what made the Top 10 list is what *didn't* make it. For instance, the three features we planned to enhance in the next version ranked below the Top 10." (See Table 5.2.)

"Are you kidding me?" exclaimed Bob. "We planned to focus 30% of our work on creating the 'custom photo stationery' feature this release. And, it isn't even in the top 10?"

"I know," said Carol, nodding. "I was shocked, too. I was the one that pushed for that as a 'must have' this year. I thought that was going to be our major leg up on the competition."

"Well," Sally said, "looks like we have some interesting new data to digest. How about you, Johanna? Do you have any surprises in store for us? What did the UCD team uncover?"

"I think you'll find some surprises here too," said Johanna. "As most of you know, since you came with us on some visits, we started by going out in the field to see our customers. Our goal was to gather data on key customer problems, especially around the Top 10 tasks that Carol's team identified in the survey. We also wanted to see whether there were any problems customers were having that we hadn't anticipated in our feature plans.

"We wanted to see a mix of experience levels, so we visited both novice and experienced users, which included some of our professional photographer customers. We spent a half day at each site watching the customers do all their work, including things they didn't do at the computer, such as showing photo proof to their customers. We collected data on what tasks they did using RevPhoto and other software programs too. We tried to be inconspicuous while observing so we didn't interfere with their usual workflow. Before we left, we learned more by asking customers about certain things we had seen them do."

Table 5.3. Key Customer Problems

Pain Point	Description	Cause of Problem
Finding a photo	Users couldn't locate photos they knew were on their hard drive.	RevPhoto automatically names files with strings of consecutive numbers during upload. Renaming files is not easy to do, so most users never bother.
Simple editing tasks	Novice and intermediate users struggled to find and use the key functionality they wanted from the product. Users had to wade through a lot of complex editing features. For example, to make an overexposed photo darker took seven steps.	Basic editing features are mixed with advanced editing features. Top 10 tasks require too many steps—better to give users less-precise but simpler controls.
Photo memory cards too expensive and easy to lose	Many customers complained that they needed to buy more memory cards for their cameras and have difficulty keeping track of all the cards. Some of them lost cards full of photos.	Customers don't keep current photos uploaded onto their computers. They have room on their hard drives, but the upload process is cumbersome and time consuming, so they keep photos on memory cards.
Printing too difficult	Customers had great difficulty with our template for 4 × 6 photos, which was by far the most popular size for printing.	The 4 × 6 template was developed many years ago and wasn't updated with the drag-and-drop functionality used in the more complex templates.

Johanna walked the team through the list of key customer problems identified through field research, shown in Table 5.3.

"Our next step," said Johanna, "was to get some task completion data on the critical tasks. We did that in the usability lab. You can see the results in this chart." (See Figure 5.1.)

"This chart shows how many users could successfully complete the Top 10 tasks in our lab testing," Johanna continued. "We'd hope to see at least an 85% success rate here. While we reached that in a few areas, you can see that in some, we fell woefully short of the goal."

"Wow," said Bob. "What's scary is that out of the ones that had such low success rates, we were only planning on touching two of them in this

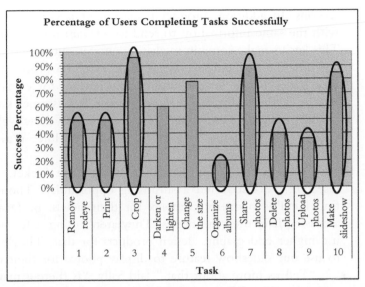

Figure 5.1. Percentage of users completing tasks successfully.

next release, and that was to *extend* their functionality, not work on ease-of-use."

"Also," added Carol, "we *were* planning to update our cropping tool and photo-sharing capabilities, and it looks like our customers did really well using those."

"Exactly!" said Johanna. "We need to rely on these results when we make our recommendations for the next release."

"We have some other interesting data to consider," added Carol. "It relates to technical support. We tallied our technical support logs and verified that the features that scored low on ease of use in usability are also the high call generators. The team then did site visits with our tech support reps and found that because the features were new in the last version, the reps aren't familiar with them. So, when customers call the reps are struggling to answer the questions and the customers are frustrated that the reps can't immediately solve the problems. To make matters worse, we found that we're keeping our customers waiting on the phones for an unacceptable length of time. Just when they need us most, we're leaving them hanging.

"So, working with the support leaders, we've come up with a plan to train the reps in these areas immediately. We've created a team to develop written instructions on how to solve key problems and to train reps in 1-hour sessions. In addition, product management is creating an e-mail newsletter with the same information to send to our customers within the next month. This lets us make some immediate improvements while we fix the real problems for the next release. We also developed a proposal to help reduce the wait times for support, including new options for e-mail and chat support. We think this will make a big difference in customer satisfaction."

"That's great," Sally said. "I'm impressed by how well you've all worked together to get at the cause of our market decline. Was there anything else you wanted to cover?"

"Yes, in fact," said Johanna. "Here's the kicker. In doing our field research, we discovered a surprising opportunity. Though our home users find RevPhoto overly complex for their needs, professional photographers are using it in their businesses. They aren't using it for editing photos—they use higher end graphic design products for that. They're buying RevPhoto to use our slideshow feature to display photos for their clients."

"Tell us more about that," said Sally. "Is there a market opportunity for us in there?"

"We think so," Carol nodded. "For pros, their editing software is great at altering photos. They have an unmet need, though, because the editing software is not good at showing proofs and keeping records of client choices and contact information. They want to be able to show clients the proofs and capture the client's choices, like 'I want four copies of photo number 7, printed at 8 by 11 size.' And our pros would like to do this on the web as well. That way, they can interact with their clients more quickly and easily."

"There is a good chance that by adding the ability to track the client's proof choices, contact information, and web capabilities to RevPhoto's existing slideshow functionality, we could create a product that photographers need and would buy," concluded Johanna. "Before we jump in, we'll do more quantitative and qualitative research and test some paper prototypes with pro customers to validate the idea."

"Looking at our new plans," said Bob, "I think it is possible that focusing on fewer features could free up some engineering time to work on a new product."

"The same might be true for UCD," Johanna responded. "We can verify it as we estimate the resources needed to drive big improvements on the features we are targeting under the new plan."

"In all cases," stated Sally, "we have a strong plan for our current development focus and a potential innovation that meets a need in a market we don't currently sell to. Actually, though our motivation was a painful drop in sales, I feel excited about our new plans, and I'm guessing the rest of the organization will feel the same way."

Questions

6. What recommendations should be made for the next release? Provide a rationale for each recommendation.
7. How did blending quantitative and qualitative research help the team validate their recommendations?
8. How did field research help the team discover the needs of their professional customers?

Summary

One year later RevLev underwent some exciting changes. They'd just released the latest version of RevPhoto, which received best in class awards from numerous magazines and consumer groups. Customers were again raving about how easy it is to use RevPhoto. They especially loved the new automatic red-eye correction feature and the streamlined way the program uploads and organizes photos. There were some complaints on some blogs and user forums about how this release didn't include any cutting-edge new features, but the upward trends in both sales and customer satisfaction showed that these customers were the minority. Johanna's and Bob's teams used an iterative design and development process that incorporated customer feedback every step of the way. Their redesign of the top 10 features that had low task completion ratings really paid off—by release time, the success rates had come up to 90%. Sally was pleased that RevPhoto sales exceeded expectations, and they were rapidly getting market share back.

Sally and her leadership team were also feeling more confident about RevLev's future growth. Their new product for professional photographers, RevView, was garnering great reviews in photographer trade journals, and orders for the product were coming in. Johanna, Bob, and Carol agreed to invest some of their development time in looking at new opportunities each year.

The atmosphere and mood at RevLev also improved. Employees were reenergized by all of the recent success and exciting new product development. They began feeling enthusiastic and inspired at work, and attrition reached a very low level. Word spread quickly that RevLev was the place to be, and resumés from top candidates flowed in steadily.

As Sally and her team evaluated the season in retrospect, they realized that the key change to their process was getting the customer into the loop. By increasing contact with their customers through site visits, surveys, and usability testing, RevLev gained insights that helped them make RevPhoto a product that meets their customers' needs. In the future they plan to always include customer research in their product development process.

Further Reading

Christensen, C., and Raynor, M. (2003). *The innovator's solution: creating and sustaining successful growth*. Boston, MA: Harvard Business Review Press.

Hackos, J., and Redish, J. (1998). *User and task analysis for interface design*. New York: John Wiley & Sons.

Kelley, T. (2001). *The art of innovation: lessons in creativity from ideo, america's leading design firm*. New York: Doubleday Publishers.

Mayhew, D. (1999). *The usability engineering lifecycle: a practitioner's handbook for user interface design*. The Morgan Kaufmann Series in Interactive Technologies. San Francisco, CA: Morgan Kaufmann Publishers.

Nielson, J. (2004). Risks of quantitative studies. *Alertbox*. Available at www.useit.com

Verdenburg, K. (3002). Building ease of use into the IBM user experience. *IBM Systems Journal,* 42. Available at http://www.research.ibm.com/journal/sj/424/vredenburg.html

Vogel, C., and Cagan, J. (2002). *Creating breakthrough products: innovation from product planning to program approval*. Saddle River, NJ: Prentice-Hall.

CASE 6

But the Usability People Said It Was Okay . . . Or, How Not to "Do Usability"

Mary Beth Rettger, The MathWorks

> *Ellen thought she was doing the right thing. Her usability team handled an 11th-hour request for an evaluation. But when the results came back to haunt her, Ellen decided a new strategy was in order.*

Ellen Has a Problem

Ellen, Director of Usability at Fourier Software, walked into her weekly meeting with her boss, expecting a pretty routine half hour. Little did she suspect. . . .

"Ellen, you've got to stop giving out these usability stamps of approval," started Todd, her boss, Vice-President of Development.

"Ummm, excuse me . . . what did you say?" stuttered Ellen.

"You know those horrible stickers the facilities folks put on all the phones? I was just at the executive team meeting, and everyone was complaining about how stupid they were. When we asked Tom about them, he said, 'The usability folks said they were fine,' like that was supposed to end the conversation or something."

"You mean the stickers that instruct you to call 911 in an emergency, not our security?" asked Ellen.

"Yeah, those green things they stuck on everybody's handset. How does that do any good? You pick up the phone in an emergency, and you are never going to see that sticker. Plus, they are so hard to read."

"Well, I know we looked at them, but what do you mean by usability stamp of approval?" asked Ellen.

"This has come up a few times in the last few months. Someone asks you guys to do some work, and then when anybody questions the design, they say 'well, we did usability on it,' and they seem to think that's good enough. People are using you guys like a bat to swat at arguments."

"Okay, but *we* certainly don't represent ourselves that way," replied Ellen.

"Doesn't matter. That's the perception. You have to fix it."

The Usability Group at Fourier Software

Ellen had been with Fourier Software for about 8 years. She started as their second usability person, then grew the group to its current size of 20 people, and was eventually made director of the group. She had learned about user-centered design mostly through on-the-job experience, reading, and taking occasional courses. She'd come to Fourier after building and running a usability group at a more consumer-oriented software company for 6 years. She was professionally active in the usability community and was definitely a practitioner by trade.

Fourier made software for very technical users (e.g., engineers, scientists, etc.); the users valued the power of the computational algorithms in the software and cared less about the user interface. Fourier had "discovered" usability about 10 years earlier, when several of the engineers took a class in paper prototyping. Since then, most of the company had embraced the concepts of user-centered design; it was common for developers to talk about the "user's mental model" when explaining their design.

What set Fourier apart was that it had chosen to provide usability support not just for the products that it sold to customers, but also for applications developed internally for its employees. This concern for the usability of internal applications came directly from Bob, founder and president of the company, whose business philosophy emphasized the need to provide an excellent environment for his employees.

The usability group consisted entirely of usability professionals; individuals on the team had various experience with design, testing, and evaluation. They had a reputation for being professional, adaptable, and savvy about business constraints.

Ellen Remembers How She Got into This Mess

After the meeting, Ellen remembered back to how the usability group had gotten involved with these stickers. One Friday afternoon several weeks ago, when she was already late to pick up her kids, Tom caught her in her office.

"Ellen, I need some help. Bob wants us to get usability done on these new security stickers we want to put on the phones. We need them done by next week."

Tom had made a few of these kinds of requests in the past, most recently to get another pair of eyes on signage planned for the new building. Tom had been a facility manager for about 30 years and did a great job, even if he occasionally found Bob's ideas for the building exasperating (like the time Bob wanted to sit on all the proposed office chairs himself before any were purchased). Because Tom and his folks were always helpful to the usability team, coming through on last-minute meeting requests with users, Ellen really wanted to do what she could this time, too.

"Look, Tom, that's probably not enough time to do much, and all my folks are really overbooked, and I'm running late right now. Here's what I'll do: I'll send a note to the group and ask if anyone has a little time to help to contact you."

"That'd be great Ellen."

"It won't be very thorough. I'm going to tell them not to spend more than an hour or two doing a design review."

"That's fine. Whatever you guys can do would be great."

Ellen dashed off an e-mail to the team, asking if anyone had an hour to spare to look over the text. She suggested that if anyone was interested, they contact Tom directly, and just copy her so she knew someone had gotten back to him. She vaguely remembered that Nancy had responded and followed up a week later saying she did a design review, and everything was all set. Ellen remembered thinking that although Nancy was new to the company (Nancy had only started about 2 weeks before this), she had about 5 years experience working in user-centered design and so had probably done a fine job.

Nancy's Side of the Story

So, Nancy was Ellen's first stop to investigate what happened. As soon as Nancy saw Ellen she began to talk nonstop: "I didn't tell them to print them on green! And I certainly didn't know they were going to use red text to highlight the important parts!"

Ellen saw that Nancy was really flustered: "Slow down Nancy, can you tell me what you did do?"

"Tom e-mailed me some text. He said they needed to get the final text done by Friday. He said they wanted to make up some signs to put around so people would know what to do in an emergency."

Nancy continued, "I told him I didn't have time to do a proper evaluation. I looked at what he sent and gave him a few suggestions. I told him it looked okay to me, but this wasn't my area of expertise, and I suggested that he have one of the editors take a look at it too. I didn't see it again 'til it showed up on my phone."

And, Tom's Version

After talking to Nancy, Ellen went to visit Tom. "Hi Tom, I...."

"Oh, Ellen, did you come to yell at me about those stupid stickers, too?"

"Well, I...."

"Because what got done wasn't what we wanted anyway, and...."

"Okay, Tom, tell me what happened."

Tom explained: "That girl...I mean...woman...from your group contacted me and gave us some suggestions, which we took. She told us to run it by an editor, but we didn't have time. Then, just before we were supposed to get them printed, Bob said he thought they should be colorful and stuck to the phones. So...even though it cost more, and they were a real pain to roll out, we made them colorful and stuck them to the handsets."

"So, the final design wasn't what Nancy reviewed?" Ellen asked.

"Well, no, I guess not, but how much difference does a little color make? I don't get what all the fuss is about."

"Tom, did you know that it's really hard to see red text on green in general and that people who are colorblind have a really really hard time with it?"

"No...."

"And did you know that Bob is colorblind?"

"Oh," sighed Tom.

Questions

1. What could Ellen have done to prevent this situation?
2. What could Nancy have done to prevent this situation?
3. What could Tom have done to prevent this situation?

Fixing the Problem for Good

With the ugly stickers already on the phones and origins of the "stamp of approval" identified, Ellen now had the following issues to resolve:

1. Should she do anything about the stickers?
2. How could she keep this from happening again?
3. Where was this perception of "usability stamp of approval" coming from, and how could she deal with that?

Ellen decided to tackle the last problem first. She started by going back to her boss, Todd, to get more detail about his concerns. Who had he heard talking about usability "okaying" a project? It turned out that all projects where this issue came up were in Tom's group. So, Ellen decided to go back and talk to Tom.

"Tom, you know those stickers?" Ellen began.

"Yeah . . . ?"

"Well, it turns out that the fuss over those has kind of uncovered a more basic problem with how your group and our group work together."

"Really? What's that?" Tom asked.

"The projects that we've worked on with your team? It seems like when you guys roll those out, it ends up sounding like our group blessed them or something."

"Is that a problem? I thought that's what you were supposed to be doing," Tom said.

(Ellen at this point drew on her yoga practice for a few deep cleansing breaths.)

"Well, no. But let's back up a bit. When do you decide to get the usability group involved?" Ellen asked.

Tom described, "Here's what happens. Any time my group is about to do anything that has any words involved in it, Bob asks whether we've 'done usability' on it and whether this matched 'the users mental model,' whatever that means. It's like a check box, and I need to be able to say yes to get the project approved. So, when Bob says that, I call you, and you guys do whatever it is you do, usually make some helpful suggestions, and then I can go back and tell him that the usability folks looked at it and said it was fine."

"Okay, so all you get asked is whether you 'did' usability on it?" Ellen confirmed.

"Yup. Why are you sighing?"

Ellen explained, "Tom, the phrase 'did usability' is the bane of my existence. You can't 'do usability.' The work we do is a collection of methods that can be used to evaluate whether a solution meets the needs of the users for whom it is intended. We can make some suggestions, but we aren't proving anything, and, especially for you, since we are usually borrowing resources to do quick projects for you, our work really should be used to help you shape the design, not 'bless' it like it will never have any other problems."

"Really? I thought you guys were supposed to tell us if it's okay and stuff."

"Tom, do you have a few minutes? I can give you a little more background."

Ellen then proceeded with her 20-minute crash course on user-centered design. She made sure to emphasize these points:

- What her group could help with was evaluating whether a particular solution would work for its intended audience, and then they could provide suggestions to improve the solution.
- The work of the usability group is user-centered design. User-centered design depends on knowing who the users are for a tool, and how they are expected to use it. It was really important to make sure that the developers of the tool weren't designing it just for themselves. And, without this background information, the evaluation her team could do would be incomplete.
- The information her group supplied should be viewed as one more source of data used to make a decision. Design decisions have to be made with the larger business context in mind, taking into account costs, legacy systems, and corporate culture. Usability was never going to supply a go/no-go decision all by itself, and it was important to identify key assumptions or limitations early in the process.
- Finally, designs can be ruined by last-minute tweaks made by someone unaware of all the trade-offs and assumptions that led to a design.

Tom listened carefully and asked some good questions. By the end of the conversation Tom and Ellen agreed that although her group could provide good design advice, Tom needed to stop using them as the last word on any topic. They also agreed that if the team didn't have time to do their jobs right, maybe Ellen should push back on Tom and not take the project on.

"So, Tom, we're straight right? No more 'usability stamp of approval.'"

"Got it," said Tom, "Now what do we do about the stickers?"

Ellen suggested that Tom stop putting the stickers on any new phones, and as soon as it was economical, they consider reprinting the labels and removing the old labels.

Questions

4. Is there anything else Ellen could do to educate Tom?
5. Is there anything Ellen should do with her team?
6. Is there anything Ellen should do with her boss?

Taking on a Project the Right Way

Three days after Ellen's conversation with Tom, Allan appeared in her office. Allan was the audiovisual guy who had helped the usability group lots of times in the past, so Ellen was inclined to try to help him if she possibly could.

"Tom told me to come ask for some help with this project I'm working on."

"Okay, can you tell me a little about it?" Ellen asked.

Allan explained, "We've been having a lot of problems with the equipment in conference rooms because people aren't leaving it right when they leave the room. Like, the new wireless mice that we have in all the rooms? They have to be redocked at the end of meetings so they can recharge or they won't work. And, the data projectors? Those bulbs cost $500 a piece, and if people don't shut those down they burn out way faster than they need to."

"Yikes, I didn't know any of that. What's the project?" Ellen asked.

"We want to create a sign for all the conference rooms that tells people what to do when they leave a meeting."

"Who's involved?"

"Well, it's mostly my idea, but I'm not great with writing instructions, so I know I need help. Also, Bob heard me talking about it, and he has some ideas about what the signs should say, so I need help figuring out how to get him involved, too."

"And when do you need this done?"

Allan said, "There's not a really hard deadline. It's in my objectives to do something about this before the end of the year, so I'd like to get something up in at least some of the rooms by October. It's August 1 . . . is that too soon?"

Ellen replied: "Since you aren't trying to roll it out to the whole company, it seems like we should be able to get you something to try at least by sometime in October."

Ellen offered, "Nobody has a lot of time in the usability group right now, but I think Eric would really like to work on this. We can probably do some simple mock-up and data collection and get a pretty good idea of what's working quickly. Let me check with Eric to see if he has time and I'll get back to you."

"Thanks, that would be great. And I'd love to work with Eric."

Questions

7. Is there anything else Ellen should have asked Allan?
8. What should Ellen do next?
9. What should Eric do first?

How to Say No Gracefully

About 2 weeks after Allan's visit, Tom appeared at Ellen's office again.

"Hi Ellen, I need more help."

"Sure, what can I do?" Ellen asked.

"Well, Bob wants us to come up with a naming scheme for the conference rooms in the new building and asked me to 'do usability' on it."

"What did you tell him?"

Tom reported dutifully, "Well, I said I could get some advice from the usability group, but I wanted to clarify what he thought we'd get from working with you. He said he wanted to make sure that someone with some design instincts thought that the scheme would work before we went with it. He also said he had lots of ideas about what would work . . . like the scheme should convey location but also take into account the history of the company, and that it should be funny."

"Funny?" Ellen asked, "Meaning you need to find something that Bob thinks is funny?"

"Yeah, I guess . . . and . . . he wants to review the scheme at next week's executive team meeting."

"So, what do you want from us?"

"Well . . . help, you know, come up with a list of good names or whatever."

"Tom, this sounds like a potential black hole. You need the information quickly; the criteria are really subjective and probably not possible to meet. I don't think this is a good place for either of us to spend much time."

"But what do I do?" Tom asked.

Ellen said, "Do you have any ideas for the names now? Or do you have any idea if Bob had anything in mind?"

"Well, we were going to go with east and west names, you know, 'East End,' 'West Wing.' I don't know if Bob had any ideas."

Ellen thought and then suggested, "Okay, how about this? If you can write up a little justification for what you think your scheme should be, I'd be happy to do a sanity check to make sure it sounds sensible. I think this is one of those cases where you should just present a straw man and let Bob hack away at it. I don't think it's worth spending a lot of time on this."

"And what do I say when he asks if I 'did usability' on it?" said Tom.

"How about, you asked us, I did a design review, but that I thought it needed more input from him and other people who had ideas about this."

"And I shouldn't say you 'blessed it' right?" added Tom, with a wink.

"Please, no. . . ."

"I'm kidding, I get it. I think that will work fine. I'll get you a draft by tomorrow."

Questions

10. Was it a mistake for Ellen to push back on a project when Bob had specifically asked for usability to be involved?
11. Is there anything else Ellen should do?

Summary

It's sometimes hard to remember to apply usability principles to the work of doing user-centered design. Usability staff members tend to be flexible and have good design skills, so it's pretty common for them to get called in for ad-hoc projects in our companies.

Often, these quick design reviews are great opportunities for us to show the potential benefits of our work and make inroads into new areas of a company. The challenge is to choose these projects wisely and make sure we have asked ourselves the right questions.

Despite our best efforts, the term "usability" is still not as usable as we would like, and people without knowledge of the area do sometimes pigeon-hole usability staff as "the people who police design." This is a very limiting role, and we need to do our best to educate our companies about the full range of our services. The risk in participating in these quick projects is that we skip providing some basic background about the context of user-centered design and leave clients without enough context to understand what we did.

What is the best way to avoid these kinds of problems? We should apply the same techniques we use to evaluate products to make decisions about whether we can really be helpful on a project. Asking the basic questions is critical: Who is this project for, what problem is it going to solve, why are we doing it? In addition, it's important to get a feeling for the real deadlines, potential additional resources, and, especially, any unstated goals or hidden agendas in the project.

Further Reading

Norman, D. (2002). *The design of everyday things*. New York: Basic Books.

PART II

Research, Evaluation, and Design

This part of the book includes case studies that focus on various techniques used to conduct usability research and to design and evaluate a user interface throughout a user-centered design process. Topics covered in this section include accurately scoping a project, conducting heuristic evaluations and card-sorting studies, defining user requirements, developing and using personas, using user-centered design for middleware and hand-held devices, automating summative usability testing, designing for international audiences, conducting remote usability studies, and designing for accessibility.

CASE 7

Estimating a User-Centered Design Effort

Stephanie Rosenbaum, Tec Ed, Inc.
Laurie Kantner, Tec Ed, Inc.

> *Shea submitted yet another iteration of her user-centered design estimate to John, hoping that she accounted for everything this time. "Does your estimate account for the time you'll spend keeping me informed of your progress?" John inquired. Shea wanted to say yes, but she realized she hadn't. Nor had she accounted for the new initiatives John just added to her already heavy work load. Now what?*

Tell Us What You Think It Will Take

Apollo Appraisal Systems has been in the business of developing property appraisal software for 25 years. Apollo's software, XperComp, had increased in complexity over the years with the addition of many specialized functions. A few years ago, responding to a large customer, Apollo Appraisal committed to redesigning the application and transforming it into a web-based service.

XperComp enables appraisers to describe a property by filling in a series of online forms that collect numerous details about the building and parcel, such as dimensions, materials, and zoning. To become competent with Xper-Comp, users are trained for 1 to 3 weeks because the software itself does not include guidance to direct users through their tasks.

Several of Apollo Appraisal's major customers want to reduce training time by having an XperComp user interface that provides task flow guidance. In addition, the customers are eager for more robust reporting capabilities. Apollo Appraisal has also determined that a web version would be highly competitive.

The company gave John Markham, a senior product manager, the assignment to lead the entire redesign effort. John's product team had been responsible for the evolution of the previous client-server versions of XperComp, and they were eager to field a web application. However, John had reservations about whether the company's approach to product development would satisfy their customers' needs.

Historically, XperComp's user interface was the responsibility of Apollo Appraisal's software engineers with input and prioritization of features from the XperComp marketing group. Their typical design process began with a product definition specification, including key screens and forms. As development proceeded, the software engineers consulted the graphic designer in Apollo Appraisal's marketing communications department for cosmetic improvements to the screens.

John was aware that Apollo Appraisal's competitors were receiving high ratings for the usability of their software and that many of the requests from Apollo's large customer base related to ease of use. He wanted to build usability into the redesigned application—and he realized that no one at his company was trained in user-centered design (UCD), although many of his product team members recognized its importance. John decided to hire a usability specialist to join his team and build usability into the XperComp redesign process. To justify adding the new employee, he met with Apollo Appraisal's marketing management and agreed on a corporate goal to build a more usable product than their competitors offered.

Shea Rose had been a usability specialist at a Fortune 500 company for 2 years but had just been laid off. The opening at Apollo Appraisal came at a good time for her. Shea's UCD work had been as a member of a large team, with another person as UCD team lead. She believed she had strong experience with the UCD process although it had been primarily in the role of implementing research plans created by others.

Shea was excited at the prospect of defining a full program of usability research to guide the software engineers in their interaction design for the web application. Shea said to John, "I understand why our users need a lot of training—it's not clear where to start a task or how to move through one. It will take quite a bit of research to define the new reporting features and identify the use scenarios we need to support." John replied, "I'm not setting any limits on the approach you take other than this: We must release the new product in 6 months. I want you to tell us how to make the next version of XperComp competitive in ease of use."

Shea began by thinking of the questions that her research should answer:

- How does XperComp's ease of use compare with its major competitors? What are the major usability drawbacks with the current product? What additional capabilities should XperComp have to meet the requirements of its users?
- What is the best way to organize the functionality in the redesigned application?
- In what ways does XperComp need to change to comply with user interface design standards in general and specifically with web application design standards or guidelines? What features that relied on desktop application functionality must change for an application moving to the web? (These must be noted as soon as possible.)
- How well does the new design, as it evolves, address usability problems with the prior version, user familiarity issues, and issues emerging from new functions and the new web-based service platform?

For each of these research questions, Shea's UCD plan defined a separate "UCD phase." For each UCD phase the plan recommended a methodology and specified parameters. She chose the following UCD components and methodologies:

- UCD phase 1: competitive usability test of the current product, ethnographic interviews
- UCD phase 2: task analysis, interaction design
- UCD phase 3: heuristic evaluation of early prototype, usability testing of early prototype (noncoded) using rapid-iterative techniques, style guide
- UCD phase 4: usability testing of pre-alpha (functional prototype) and alpha version

Shea's rationale was to start the UCD effort by evaluating the existing product (developed without UCD processes). Then she would perform task analysis and interactive design, because the product team had no UCD-trained interaction designer; instead they could use her wireframes as a design skeleton.

In UCD phases 3 and 4 Shea planned appropriate user research activities for each later stage in the development cycle. The phase 3 style guide would also assist the software engineers in implementing—and maintaining—a consistent interface. Shea also recommended conducting competitive usability testing of the new product but didn't include that effort in this UCD plan because it would happen after product release.

Shea's estimates of the working time required for each phase included specifying the parameters for each of the activities (scoping). For example, for UCD phase 1 she identified the following research parameters for the competitive usability testing of the existing product:

- Three products (XperComp and each of two competitors)
- Session length of 2 hours to accommodate tasks with XperComp and one of two competitors per session
- Twenty-four between-subjects usability test sessions (24 total users: 4 user profiles, 6 users per profile, counterbalancing the order of product presentation so that three users per profile start with XperComp and the other three start with the competitor product)

Shea's final step was to calculate how many working weeks she would spend on the usability research work for each UCD phase:

- UCD phase 1: competitive usability test, ethnographic interviews = 7 weeks
- UCD phase 2: task analysis, interaction design = about 10 weeks
- UCD phase 3: heuristic evaluation of early prototype, usability testing of early prototype, style guide = about 7 weeks
- UCD phase 4: usability testing of pre-alpha (functional prototype) and alpha version = about 2 weeks

The activities totaled 26 working weeks, just meeting John Markham's completion deadline of 6 months, so Shea presented her high-level estimates to John. To her surprise, he was dissatisfied.

John said, "I appreciate this first step, but I'm afraid it doesn't really tell me what to expect." She replied, "Well, for example, in 7 weeks I'll have data from the phase 1 research to report to the development team." John shook his head. As XperComp product manager as well as the company's usability advocate, he needed to know

- Exactly when Shea would deliver what UCD inputs to the development team—John needed specific deliverables and dates.
- How much time she would have during those 6 months to contribute her skills to other company development efforts such as internal systems. John wanted to standardize UCD processes across the board, not just for the flagship product.

John wanted enough information to be sure that his developers would stay productive by having usability feedback and design deliverables when needed, instead of having to wait for them or to work ahead and then retrofit.

Questions

1. What should Shea do to satisfy John's need for more detail about project milestones and her availability?
2. What information can Shea draw on to provide that level of detail?

The Detailed Estimate

Once Shea collected information from past projects and consulted colleagues, she identified the following tasks for the competitive usability testing activity in UCD phase 1:

- Create test plan: meet with stakeholders, write/revise plan
- Recruit participants: more than 1 hour per recruited participant
- Create session protocol: write/revise
- Conduct sessions: 24 sessions plus setup (2 hours per session)
- Analyze data: enter data, tabulate, compare
- Report findings and recommendations: write/revise and present

Shea then estimated how many hours these tasks would take, based on the projects she had done in the past, as shown in Table 7.1.

Table 7.1. High-Level Estimates for UCD Activities

Task	Hours Required
Create test plan	20
Recruit participants	30
Create session protocol	25
Conduct sessions	50
Analyze data	60
Report findings and recommendations	30
Total	215 for competitive usability testing

When Shea finished identifying tasks and estimating all activities in the four UCD phases, her draft research plan included the following estimates:

- UCD phase 1: competitive usability test, ethnographic interviews = 300 hours
- UCD phase 2: task analysis, interaction design = 425 hours
- UCD phase 3: heuristic evaluation of early prototype, usability testing of early prototype, style guide = 325 hours
- UCD phase 4: usability testing of pre-alpha (functional prototype) and alpha version = 105 hours

With a total of 1,155 hours in her UCD estimate, Shea acknowledged she would need to work some overtime in the next 6 months to complete the work—not a huge surprise. She did not believe there was enough work to justify adding a second person. She then plotted start and end dates for each activity, based on 45-hour work weeks, as shown in Table 7.2.

In her preliminary scheduling Shea chose to use a basic spreadsheet tool with date calculation ability. If she were managing the whole product devel-

Table 7.2. High-Level Estimates and Schedule for UCD Activities

UCD Phase	Activity	Hours	Hours per Week	Start Date	End Date
1	Competitive usability testing	215	45	7 Jan	11 Feb
	Ethnographic interviews	85	45	11 Feb	25 Feb
2	Task analysis	125	45	25 Feb	17 Mar
	Information architecture	300	45	17 Mar	2 May
3	Heuristic evaluation of early prototype	100	45	2 May	19 May
	Usability testing of early prototype	60	45	19 May	2 Jun
	Style guide	150	45	2 Jun	25 Jun
4	Usability testing of pre-alpha version	75	45	25 Jun	4 Jul
	Usability testing of alpha version	45	45	4 Jul	11 Jul

opment effort, she would probably use a project management tool to keep track of tasks and dependencies.

What About Project Management and External Duties?

Shea brought the new version of her research plan to John Markham.

"Great job! This is getting closer to the level of detail I need," John said. He scanned the plan more slowly. Then he said, "I'm concerned about a couple of things. Does your estimate account for your project management time?"

Shea responded, "If you mean making sure I'm keeping to the schedule, that's my natural way of working."

"What I mean is the time you'll spend helping me stay informed of your progress—including your "plan B" if things get off track. I'm also thinking of the meetings with the design and implementation teams," John explained.

Shea wanted to say yes but realized she had not factored in keeping her schedule updated and attending meetings. "Okay, I can see I need to add time for that. You mentioned two things?"

"There's something I've been meaning to mention. Besides this project, I'd like to see your influence in some new initiatives we're exploring for building usability into our internal systems. I hope you're interested and have time for that work, too."

Questions

3. How should Shea include project management hours in her activities schedule?
4. How can Shea reserve time each week for other work?

It was immediately clear that the result of these changes had an unsatisfactory impact on the schedule. Shea would not finish her activities until well beyond the required 6 months, as shown in Table 7.3.

Table 7.3. Version 2 of High-Level Estimates and Schedule for UCD Activities, Adding Project Management Time and Reducing Weekly Time Investment for Other Activities

UCD Phase	Activity	Hours	Hours per Week	Weeks	Start Date	End Date
1	Competitive usability testing	215	35	6.1	7 Jan	19 Feb
	Ethnographic interviews	85	35	2.4	19 Feb	7 Mar
	Project management of phase 1	43	5		7 Jan	7 Mar
2	Task analysis	125	35	3.6	7 Mar	1 Apr
	Information architecture	300	35	8.6	1 Apr	2 Jun
	Project management of phase 2	61	5		7 Mar	2 Jun
3	Heuristic evaluation of early prototype	100	35	2.9	2 Jun	23 Jun
	Usability testing of early prototype	75	35	2.1	2 Jun	17 Jun
	Style guide	150	35	4.3	23 Jun	23 Jul
	Project management of phase 3	46	5		2 Jun	23 Jul
	Usability testing of pre-alpha version	60	35	1.7	23 Jul	4 Aug
	Usability testing of alpha version	45	35	1.3	4 Aug	13 Aug
	Project management of phase 4	15	5		23 Jul	13 Aug

Shea had already taken a day to perform scheduling and rescheduling. She was tempted just to start working and see whether the work went faster than her estimates indicated.

What About the Development Timeline?

Just as Shea was wrestling with her scheduling problems, John phoned her. "Hi Shea. I have a couple more comments about your XperComp UCD schedule." Shea replied, "Good timing, because I'm having trouble fitting the UCD work into the 6-month development schedule. I need some more time to come up with alternatives."

John gave Shea another problem to consider. "We're going to need the results from your early phases sooner than you had planned, so we can start developing the user interface spec. I think end of February is about as late as we can wait for the early research results. In addition, keep in mind that we'll need all usability test results by the beginning of June to be able to address anything major and still release in early July."

Shea worried that meeting John's end-of-February deadline for requirements research would mean significantly reducing that research: "I'm concerned that we'll miss some important customer requirements if we rush the requirements research and design steps." John agreed, saying "This is our chance to do this right and elevate XperComp above our competitors." Shea offered to work 50 or more hours a week, but John advised her to plan on averaging 45 hours so she could maintain the momentum for the entire 6 months and so that the peak overtime weeks were still physically possible.

Shea said, "Maybe we can bring in an additional researcher to carry out some of the early work. Then, phases 1 and 2 could take place concurrently, and we can deliver the results to the team earlier. It means the work in phase 2 will need to respond to the phase 1 data when it becomes available—not ideal, but we can plan for it." John said, "Sounds good to me. See how that works with your schedule."

Shea planned to solicit proposals from usability vendor firms to handle UCD phase 1. She preferred to handle UCD phase 2 herself. Her rationale was that vendors could provide usability evaluation resources, but she wanted to perform personally the UCD activities most closely tied to the product redesign—the task analysis and interaction design—so that, as a new Apollo Appraisal employee, she could begin building a good working relationship with the software engineers. That division of labor would also result in more objectivity for the evaluation activities.

Shea began by changing some of the assumptions on which the schedule was based, modifying her worksheet accordingly. First, Shea changed the start date for UCD phase 2 to reflect using a vendor for UCD phase 1. She kept 5 hours a week of project management time per phase for phases 1 and 2, because she still needed to manage the vendor's phase 1 work. Now that the phases were concurrent, her project management estimate rose to 10 hours per week for the period covering those phases. These changes produced the schedule in Table 7.4.

Table 7.4. Version 3 of High-Level Estimates and Schedule for UCD Activities: Outsourcing Phase 1

UCD Phase	Who	Activity	Hours	Hours per Week	Weeks	Start Date	End Date
1	Vendor	Competitive usability testing	215	40	5.4	7 Jan	13 Feb
	Vendor	Ethnographic interviews	85	40	2.1	13 Feb	28 Feb
2	Shea	Task analysis	125	30	4.2	7 Jan	5 Feb
	Shea	Interaction design	300	30	10.0	5 Feb	15 Apr
	Shea	*Project management of phases 1 and 2*	75	10		7 Jan	15 Apr
3	Shea	Heuristic evaluation of early prototype	100	35	2.9	29 Apr	19 May
	Shea	Usability testing of early prototype	75	35	2.1	19 May	3 Jun
	Shea	Style guide	150	35	4.3	3 Jun	3 Jul
	Shea	*Project management of phase 3*	46	5		29 Apr	3 Jul
4	Shea	Usability testing of pre-alpha version	60	35	1.7	3 Jul	15 Jul
	Shea	Usability testing of alpha version	45	35	1.3	15 Jul	24 Jul
	Shea	*Project management of phase 4*	15	5		3 Jul	24 Jul
Total time for all phases							
	Shea		992	38	26		
	Vendor		300	40	8		

Shea did not need another meeting with John to see that her end date for UCD phase 2 was later than the end-of-February deadline that John specified, and the completion dates for all phase 4 activities were still unsatisfactory. She looked at the interaction design estimate, which had the largest time investment, to see how she could shorten its schedule. She identified the following tasks for this activity:

- Create task flows: 50 hours
- Create wireframes: 250 hours (including meetings and revisions)

Passing creation of some of the wireframes to the vendor would enable Shea to shorten the timeline for UCD phase 2. However, to continue her collaboration with the software engineers—and to maintain continuity among all the designs—Shea would outsource no more than 50% of the wireframes work. She rescheduled based on these assumptions; her results are in Table 7.5.

Now Shea had to find a vendor who could perform the oursourced activities—competitive testing and ethnographic interviews in UCD phase 1 and half of the wireframes in UCD phase 2—within her timeline. She contacted three usability research firms to discuss the scope parameters for the activities to be outsourced. Table 7.6 shows the parameters she gave the vendor firms.

Shea told the vendor firms her desired timeline for the research activities and gave them a week to provide their proposals. One declined to submit a proposal, saying that their firm could not meet the schedule. The two remaining firms provided proposals that each included longer timelines for the competitive testing and ethnographic interviews than Shea had requested. Shea was dismayed; she wanted to get started doing the work!

Shea studied the proposals to find specifications she could discuss with the firms to negotiate shorter schedules. She compared her estimates against the shortest vendor timeline, as shown in Table 7.7. Vendor timelines stated as elapsed weeks instead of working hours proved a little challenging for Shea's calculations; she had to compare her working time estimates with the vendor's elapsed time schedules.

Questions

5. Why might the usability vendors believe the research would take longer than Shea had thought?
6. What are some possible alternatives to the scope or the schedule that will provide value within the timeframe?
7. Can Shea redefine the work so that the vendors can realistically meet her schedule, or should she alter her schedule?

Table 7.5. Version 4 of High-Level Estimates and Schedule for UCD Activities: Outsourcing Phase 1 and Part of Phase 2

UCD Phase	Who	Activity	Hours	Hours per Week	Weeks	Start Date	End Date
1	Vendor	Competitive usability testing	215	40	5.4	7 Jan	13 Feb
	Vendor	Ethnographic interviews	85	40	2.1	13 Feb	28 Feb
2	Shea	Task analysis	125	30	4.2	7 Jan	5 Feb
	Shea	Interaction design	175	30	5.8	5 Feb	17 Mar
	Vendor	Interaction design	125	40	3.1	28 Feb	21 Mar
	Shea	*Project management of phases 1 and 2*	63	10		7 Jan	21 Mar
3	Shea	Heuristic evaluation of early prototype	100	35	2.9	31 Mar	21 Apr
	Shea	Usability testing of early prototype	75	35	2.1	21 Apr	6 May
	Shea	Style guide	150	35	4.3	6 May	5 Jun
	Shea	*Project management of phase 3*	46	5		31 Mar	5 Jun
4	Shea	Usability testing of pre-alpha version	60	35	1.7	5 Jun	17 Jun
	Shea	Usability testing of alpha version	45	35	1.3	17 Jun	26 Jun
	Shea	*Project management of phase 4*	15	5		5 Jun	26 Jun
Total time for all phases							
	Shea		854	38	22		
	Vendor		425	40	11		

Table 7.6. Research Parameters Given to Outsource Vendors

UCD Activity 1: Competitive Usability Testing	UCD Activity 2: Ethnographic Interviews	UCD Activity 3: Wireframes
Location: Lab Number of products: Three—XperComp and each of two competitors	Location: Homes/offices Number of sites (minimum): Eight—some companies, some individuals	Number of wireframes: 20 to 25
Number of user profiles: Four—two dimensions = residential/commercial, more/less experience	Number of user profiles: Four—one dimension = residential/commercial, one = experience	
Number of sessions: 24—12 sessions for each product pairing, to counterbalance	Number of sessions: 12—three participants × four profiles	
Session length (hours): 2—to accommodate two products	Session length (hours): 1.25	

Let's Redefine and Get Started

Shea looked at her research parameters to identify ways to reduce the scope of work to achieve the timelines she needed from the vendor. She experimented with the following scope reduction ideas:

- UCD activity 1: competitive usability testing. Instead of two competitors, the research would look at just one competitor and XperComp. This change would reduce the number of sessions needed from 24 to 12, which would reduce the timeline by at least a week. The team would need to make the difficult decision of choosing which competitor product would offer the best comparison.
- UCD activity 2: ethnographic interviews. Instead of 12 interviews (3 per profile), Shea decided that 2 interviews per profile, or 8 total interviews, would still yield valuable data. This change would reduce the timeline by at least another week.

Shea requested that the vendors resubmit their proposals for the new scope. The vendors responded within a few days, and Shea selected a preferred

Table 7.7. Comparison of Internal Estimates Against Vendor Timeline

Activity	Shea's Estimate (hours)	Vendor Timeline
Competitive usability test parameters		
Create test plan	20	Week 1
Recruit participants	30	Weeks 2–3
Create session protocol	25	Week 4
Conduct sessions	50	Weeks 5–6
Analyze data	60	Weeks 6–7
Report findings and recommendations	30	Weeks 7–8
Total	5.4 weeks	8 weeks
Ethnographic interviews		
Create the interview protocol	15	Week 1
Recruit participants	15	Weeks 1–2
Conduct interviews	20	Week 3
Analyze data	15	Week 4
Report findings and recommendations	20	Week 4
Total	2.1 weeks	4 weeks

vendor. Now Shea finally had a project plan that met John's schedule needs, as shown in Table 7.8.

Shea was a bit nervous about the outside resources required, but Apollo Appraisal had made a corporate commitment to satisfy its largest customer. John discussed Shea's project plan with his manager, the chief technical officer, showing how vendors were needed to meet the schedule, and the purchase requisitions were approved.

Work began at the beginning of January as planned. Shea was extremely busy managing the vendor's work on the UCD phase 1 activity while she began the UCD phase 2 activity. She needed to review the vendor's work often to make sure the goals of the research were being met and to give her

Table 7.8. Version 5 of High-Level Estimates and Schedule for UCD Activities: Ready for Implementation

UCD Phase	Who	Activity	Hours	Hours per Week	Weeks	Start Date	End Date
1	Vendor	Competitive usability testing	155	30	5.2	7 Jan	12 Feb
	Vendor	Ethnographic interviews	75	30	2.5	12 Feb	29 Feb
2	Shea	Task analysis	125	30	4.2	7 Jan	5 Feb
	Shea	Interaction design	175	30	5.8	5 Feb	17 Mar
	Vendor	Interaction design	125	40	3.1	29 Feb	24 Mar
	Shea	*Project management of phases 1 and 2*	67	10		7 Jan	17 Mar
3	Shea	Heuristic evaluation of early prototype	100	35	2.9	31 Mar	21 Apr
	Shea	Usability testing of early prototype	75	35	2.1	21 Apr	6 May
	Shea	Style guide	150	35	4.3	6 May	5 Jun
	Shea	*Project management of phase 3*	46	5		31 Mar	5 Jun
4	Shea	Usability testing of pre alpha version	60	35	1.7	5 Jun	17 Jun
	Shea	Usability testing of alpha version	45	35	1.3	17 Jun	26 Jun
	Shea	*Project management of phase 4*	15	5		5 Jun	26 Jun
		Total time for all phases					
	Shea		858	39	22		
	Vendor		355	33	11		

a sense of direction for the task analysis. To inform her phase 2 work while phase 1 was still in progress, she also watched some session recordings.

By the middle of February, when she expected to have some wireframes ready to discuss with the development team, she had hardly started them, although the phase 1 deliverables had all stayed on schedule so far. At the next project team meeting, Shea would be empty-handed and behind schedule. She began to fret and took her problem to John. "I'm already behind schedule, and I don't have time to figure out why."

John said, "We have to understand this problem now, so we can learn how long things are really taking and make reasonable adjustments. Please compare your actual time spent against your estimates and forecast the impact on the rest of the schedule."

Shea admitted, "I haven't really been logging my time, just working lots of hours." John asked Shea to keep track of the time she spent on each activity, with enough detail that she could evaluate her actual time spent against her plan. He also suggested that she identify factors between that were responsible for the increased time, so she could revise the estimates for the remaining work and identify the potential impact on the schedule. If further scope reduction would be necessary to meet the deadline, they should make that decision now. (John did not suggest extending his development schedule.)

Now Is the Time for Course Correction

As Shea thought back, she realized her weeks were filled with activities she had not counted in her estimates, primarily for knowledge transfer and project management of early activities. She also looked ahead and realized that she could not accelerate her schedule for wireframes, and in fact she would need to extend it to allow time for meetings with the vendor and for review and input at various stages. She decided to increase her project management budget to 10 hours per week per phase for the early activities and gradually bring it down to 5 hours for the later activities, and see how this change affected the schedule (Table 7.9). With concurrent phases 1 and 2, her project management estimate rose to 20 hours per week for the period covering those phases.

Shea was disappointed to see her end date once again extend past John's deadline, but she knew it was better to find out now rather than later. She thought about what she could eliminate without a serious effect on the quality of the UCD effort. She briefly considered eliminating the style guide, saving

Table 7.9. Version 6 of High-Level Estimates and Schedule for UCD Activities, Showing Increased Project Management Time for Early Activities

UCD Phase	Who	Activity	Hours	Hours per Week	Weeks	Start Date	End Date
1	Vendor	Competitive usability testing	155	30	5.2	7 Jan	12 Feb
	Vendor	Ethnographic interviews	75	30	2.5	12 Feb	29 Feb
2	Shea	Task analysis	125	25	5.0	7 Jan	11 Feb
	Shea	Interaction design	175	25	7.0	11 Feb	31 Mar
	Vendor	Interaction design	125	40	3.1	29 Feb	24 Mar
	Shea	*Project management of phases 1 and 2*	150	20		7 Jan	31 Mar
3	Shea	Heuristic evaluation of early prototype	100	32	3.1	14 Apr	5 May
	Shea	Usability testing of early prototype	75	35	2.1	5 May	20 May
	Shea	Style guide	150	32	4.7	20 May	23 Jun
	Shea	*Project management of phase 3*	80	8		14 Apr	23 Jun
4	Shea	Usability testing of pre-alpha version	60	35	1.7	23 Jun	7 Jul
	Shea	Usability testing of alpha version	45	35	1.3	7 Jul	16 Jul
	Shea	*Project management of phase 4*	15	5		23 Jun	16 Jul
		Total time for all phases					
	Shea		975	39	25		
	Vendor		355	33	11		

it for after the first product release, to guide work on future XperComp versions.

Shea had been working closely with one of the phase 1 vendor researchers, a highly experienced UCD professional named Mary Weiss. She invited Mary to lunch.

"I'm really worried about postponing the style guide, but I can't see what else to do," Shea confided.

Mary replied, "Remember that a style guide is always a 'living document.'"

Questions

8. What is the possible negative impact of eliminating the style guide?
9. What could Shea do instead?

Good Plans Shape Good Decisions

Shea adjusted the hours per week for the prototype usability testing and style guide activities in phase 3 to reflect performing them concurrently. Shea was also fairly comfortable eliminating the phase 4 usability testing of the pre-alpha version, because she would have good user data guiding design of the early prototype and testing of the alpha version would uncover serious problems before release. With these changes, Shea's next schedule achieved her deadline and quality goals while reflecting a more realistic estimate of how she would spend her time (Table 7.10).

Most of the UCD work Shea planned for XperComp took place according to the schedule in Version 7 (Table 7.10), although she continued reviewing her progress against milestones and making adjustments and trade-offs as needed. The development team ultimately delayed the product release date by 2 weeks to fix quality assurance issues, still achieving the company's goal of an August release of a product that reflected user requirements and UCD.

After a much-needed vacation in Switzerland, Shea returned refreshed and ready to start planning the UCD work for a major enhancement to XperComp. She met with John to learn more about the development schedule and corporate goals for the enhancement. Toward the end of the meeting, John asked Shea to revisit the process she used to estimate and schedule the

Table 7.10. Version 7 of High-Level Estimates and Schedule of UCD Activities, Showing Decreased Scope to Achieve Quality and Schedule Goals

UCD Phase	Who	Activity	Hours	Hours per Week	Weeks	Start Date	End Date
1	Vendor	Competitive usability testing	155	30	5.2	7 Jan	12 Feb
	Vendor	Ethnographic interviews	75	30	2.5	12 Feb	29 Feb
2	Shea	Task analysis	125	25	5.0	7 Jan	11 Feb
	Shea	Interaction design	175	25	7.0	11 Feb	31 Mar
	Vendor	Interaction design	125	40	3.1	29 Feb	24 Mar
	Shea	*Project management of phases 1 and 2*	150	20		7 Jan	31 Mar
3	Shea	Heuristic evaluation of early prototype	100	32	3.1	14 Apr	5 May
	Shea	Usability testing of early prototype	75	20	3.8	5 May	2 Jun
	Shea	Style guide	75	15	5.0	5 May	9 Jun
	Shea	*Project management of phase 3*	95	8		14 Apr	9 Jun
	Shea	Usability testing of alpha version	45	35	1.3	16 Jun	25 Jun
	Shea	*Project management of phase 4*	6	5		16 Jun	25 Jun
Total time for all phases							
	Shea		846	34	25		
	Vendor		355	33	11		

previous cycle of XperComp UCD work. He asked what approach she would use now to arrive at a successful estimate and schedule more efficiently.

It was difficult to remember all of her early planning, so Shea looked in the project file on her computer and reviewed the series of estimates and schedules she had created. Comparing the differences and reviewing e-mails, she identified many guidelines for realistic estimating and scheduling of UCD projects, described in the Summary below.

Summary

"The difficult we do immediately. The impossible takes a little longer" (slogan of the U.S. Army Air Forces, after a quotation by Charles Alexandre de Calonne, 1734–1802). Defining a UCD effort is challenging when budget and calendar time are limited. Accurate estimating builds trust and promotes a spirit of creative compromise.

Shea Rose's experience at Apollo Appraisal Systems is typical of many situations in the UCD profession:

- UCD professionals often move during their career growth from a setting where they're part of a supportive group to an organization where they are the primary UCD practitioner.
- UCD professionals usually work in organizations that have a large highly structured engineering group. UCD activities must coordinate with engineering activities and their schedules.
- UCD professionals are strongly motivated to perform high-quality research and design that meet users' needs and goals.
- Therefore UCD professionals must estimate and define UCD activities that satisfy both their own professional goals and the goals—and constraints—of their coworkers and their organization.

Shea's work on the second enhancement to XperComp went much more smoothly because she followed these guidelines:

- Estimate in working hours, not just weeks. Use ranges for hours if you are unsure.
- Allow time for project management.
- Allow time for other responsibilities that are not related to this project.
- Consider the schedules of other contributors to the overall project.
- Allow time for other team members' contribution to the research (reviews, design meetings).
- Be realistic in how much calendar time it will take to recruit participants.

- Be prepared to iterate your estimate and schedule many times, and design an estimating tool that will allow easy iterating.
- Remember that outside vendors can help improve schedules. At the same time, they may create additional review checkpoints to ensure everyone is "on the same page."
- Always add time to your schedule for unplanned events.
- Learn how your estimating process compares with actual results and develop a "fudge factor."

The variables Shea might eventually add to make her estimating process handle more alternative scenarios ("what if-ing") could include the following:

1. Complexity
   - For design activities, number of tasks, functions, and objects, and the fidelity of the mockups/prototypes created
   - For evaluation activities, the number of participant groups, issues to explore, linear or branching use paths to perform tasks, and comparison of products or user profiles
2. Logistics
   - Ease or difficulty of finding participants
   - Travel—time and expenses
   - Number of contributors to manage or confer with
   - Meetings
   - External schedules with which to coordinate

Someday, Shea thought, if she decides to become an independent UCD consultant, her estimating practices will help to ensure that she sets her UCD consulting fees to cover all her working time. Just as they will in her job at Apollo Appraisal, good estimating practices will help her identify "scope creep" sooner rather than later, so she can negotiate a solution. As an external consultant, she will need to determine an hourly rate that covers her overhead, and she will need to estimate her project-specific out-of-pocket expenses such as travel costs and recording media. Shea is on the right path with the lessons she has learned so far and her willingness to continuously improve her estimating process.

The iterative planning, estimating, and scheduling process—and repeating the process at intervals throughout a design and development project—described in this case study is not an exceptional situation. Rather, UCD professionals should expect to revisit their estimates at least monthly during every project. Sometimes we are fortunate and our UCD plan does not need to change, but more often circumstances both within and outside our control require adjusting estimates throughout UCD efforts.

Further Reading

Burstein, D., and Statsiowski, F. (1982). *Project management for the design professional*. London: The Architectural Press Ltd.

Dumas, J. A., and Redish, J. C. (1999). *A practical guide to usability testing*, revised edition. Portland, Oregon: Intellect Ltd.

Hackos, J. T. (1994). *Managing your documentation projects*. John Wiley & Sons, Inc., pp. 145–209.

James, J., and Righi, C. (2005). Sizing and specifying user-centered design projects. *User Experience Magazine, Usability Professionals' Association*, 4, pp. 8–11.

Mayhew, D. (1999). *The usability engineering lifecycle: a practitioner's handbook for user interface design*. Morgan Kaufmann Publishers, Inc., pp. 435–447.

McDaniel, S. M. (2003). "Selling usability: scope and schedule estimates." *Intercom*, December:22–25.

CASE 8

A Case Study in Card Sorting

Carol Righi, Perficient, Inc.
Larry Wood, Parallax Ineraction

> *Loretta's customer service team had been getting more and more calls from customers who were unable to find products on the website. In fact, it got to the point where each time the LANDAU'S team celebrated the launch of a new section of the site, Loretta and her team would cringe and wait for the phone to start ringing. This had to stop.*

Determining the Need for a Card Sort

LANDAU'S Inc. opened its doors in the spring of 1975. Tim Landau, a 28-year-old with a Masters in Business Administration who had a passion for marine sports, set up a small boating shop in his south Florida hometown. Tim prided himself on being a rabid hobbyist as well as a merchant: The store's motto is "If we don't use it, we don't sell it." Tim and his small staff (his two high school buddies, Andy and Rich) pledged to make LANDAU'S the place to go if you were serious about boating.

It wasn't too long before LANDAU'S began to attract a cadre of loyal customers. Within only 2 years word of LANDAU'S had spread; many people were willing to travel a long distance to converse with the salespeople, get expert advice, and shop from a large selection of high-quality goods. The staff had grown to 30. Revenue was increasing annually by significant amounts.

Not resting on his laurels, Tim decided it was time for expansion. The plan was implemented in a blistering 9 months. Building on the strength of his success, Tim quickly secured enough venture capital to build a new store

145

and a warehouse, expand his inventory (including new product lines, such as diving equipment), and create a mail-order business.

Then came the 1990s. Tim had no real love for computers, but he was smart enough to see the writing on the wall. It was time for LANDAU'S, Inc. to become LANDAU'S.COM. He pulled Andy aside and confided in him. "I trust you, Andy. This is potentially a big job. I want you to head up our website development."

So Andy went to work. The first thing he did was hire a lead technologist, someone who not only could build the site but could advise him on how to proceed. Working together, they brought on a team of programmers and a graphic designer, along with several independent consultants.

The first few months of LANDAU'S.COM were exciting. The team worked feverishly to get the catalog online. They scanned photos. They put their heads together and created a navigation bar for the home page that contained 10 categories of LANDAU'S products, plus links to other key areas of the site (Figure 8.1).

After 4 months of heads-down production, LANDAU'S.COM was launched.

Over the next couple of years, LANDAU'S continued to grow. The inventory expanded to include an extensive line of clothing advertised to "complement the lifestyle of the LANDAU'S customer," including a full line of children's clothing and accessories. The LANDAU'S.COM website likewise had grown. Sections were added to provide state-by-state boating regulation information, weather forecasts, stories written by boating and diving experts, "getting started" information for boating and diving beginners, and more (Figure 8.2).

Home
Boats
Motors
Marine Crafts
Jetskis
Accessories
Waterskiing
Diving Equipment
Diving Accessories
Dive Wear
Diving Classes and Trips
Customer Service
Contact Us

Figure 8.1. The home page navigation bar for LANDAU'S.COM.

Figure 8.2. The home page navigation bar for a later version of LANDAU'S.COM.

Things were moving along well. The website—and income from the website—continued to grow. But lately Andy's e-mailbox has been a bit more full than usual. And it seemed that more and more notes were coming from Loretta.

Loretta is the manager of LANDAU'S Inc.'s customer service team. Loretta had led that team since the early days of the catalog. Back then, most of the calls the team handled involved taking orders, shipping problems, and product defects. But now it seems that Loretta's team has been getting more and more calls about the website. Always a team player, Loretta initially encouraged her reps to field the calls. But the reps were starting to balk. Web-related calls were beginning to outnumber all other calls. Overall call volume increased alarmingly. In fact, it got to the point where each time the LANDAU'S team celebrated the launch of a new section of the site, Loretta and her team would cringe and wait for the phone to start ringing.

Loretta called Andy and asked for a meeting. At the meeting Loretta leveled with Andy. "Look, Andy . . . we've been friends a long time, so I can be honest with you. My team is at the end of their rope. For months now, all they seem to do is deal with website problems. Call after call, usually some variation of 'I can't find something or other on the website, so I gave up and called you.' Or the customer will say something like, 'I can't believe you don't sell life jackets.' We look it up on the website, and sure enough, they're there: Personal flotation devices galore, right in the Boating Accessories section. In any case, by the time they get to us, the customers are totally frustrated, irate, and ready to yell at someone. And frankly, we're pretty tired of it."

Andy was puzzled. "But revenue from the website is tremendous! We're getting over 50,000 hits a day! I know for a fact that our testers bang on that site day after day, trying to break it, but it's solid as a rock. I just don't get it."

Loretta responded, "Maybe revenue is up, but do you know how much overtime I've had to approve lately? Plus, I've had two reps quit on me in the last month. Each one of them complained about call volume, and the fact that most of the time, what the customer is looking for is right there on the website."

Confused, Andy left the meeting.

Questions

1. What about the website design has most likely caused service calls to increase?
2. Given that the initial website was a success, why did it become worse over time?
3. What about LANDAU'S history, culture, goals, and development process may have contributed to the problem?
4. What should Andy do next?

Planning the Card Sort

After his meeting with Loretta, Andy hit the books—or more accurately, the Internet. He did a fair number of searches on terms such as "website design" and "ease of use." Andy was a bit surprised to discover an entire profession dedicated to designing ease of use into the user experience of applications and websites. What Andy thought was going to be a quick task of finding a book on the topic and assigning it to one of his folks to read turned out to be an education. Andy quickly realized he needed to bring in someone who already had expertise in the area. Andy found Barry Hood.

Barry Hood had been a user-centered design/usability consultant for several years. He lived in South Florida, contracting for several local companies. Barry prided himself on being well versed in many techniques for performing user research and in being able to identify the right tools for the task at hand. Barry arrived at Andy's office on a Tuesday afternoon and started by asking some questions.

"So, Andy, what are your goals for your website?"

"Well, our essential goals haven't really changed with regard to our ultimate goal of selling merchandise . . . of course, we want to increase revenue, convert more visitors into buyers, and so forth. But the reason I called you is because calls to our support staff have recently increased dramatically. We're losing staff, paying lots for overtime, potentially losing customers because of dissatisfaction, and flat-out losing sales."

Barry asked, "How do you define 'dramatically'? Have you been counting service calls?"

Andy fumbled a bit . . . he thought that Loretta may have those numbers but wasn't sure. "Well, our service manager was pretty upset, so in my book that's enough to warrant concern."

"Okay," said Barry. "Let's assume there have been many more calls than usual. What has accounted for the increase?"

Andy replied, "According to Loretta, people are calling to say they're not finding what they're looking for on the website and are calling to first complain but also to place their orders by phone."

"I see," said Barry. "Have you made any changes to your website recently?"

"In fact, yes, we have," replied Barry. "We just dropped a big chunk of change into redesigning the whole site."

"What do you mean, 'redesigning'?" asked Barry.

Andy was starting to wonder why Barry kept asking him to define so precisely what he was talking about. This seemed a little unusual. "Well, you know . . . redesign . . . they changed the whole look of the thing, added a whole bunch of new links, that sort of thing."

"I see," said Barry, who continued asking several questions, including

- Who created the design? What are their titles and responsibilities?
- What mechanisms for user feedback do you have in place, if any?
- At what point in the process do you gather user feedback?
- Who determines what changes based on the user feedback are integrated into the design?
- How and when is the user feedback integrated back into the design, if at all?
- Who needs to approve an overall website redesign?
- What is your budget for the website, and how is it allocated? Do you have specific funding for user feedback studies?

Next, Barry met with Loretta to get a better feel for the nature of the calls her team were receiving. He noted specific items that seemed to cause the most problems. He also did his own walk-through of the site. He attempted some typical tasks that he, as a customer, might want to perform.

Barry came back to Andy with his assessment and recommendations. "Well," said Barry, "It's pretty clear that the main problem with your website is its information architecture—how it's structured, what the categories are, where the products and content reside. Given this, the first thing you need to do in your redesign is to gather information on how your users expect the products on your site should be organized. The way we find this out is by doing a card sort."

Barry proceeded to explain: "A card sort exercise is a method in which representative users organize the content of a website in a way that makes sense to them. Each piece of content of a website is written on an index card or represented as a 'virtual card' in a card sort application. Users sort the cards into groups based on their similarity with one another. They then name each group. Results can be 'eyeballed' or subjected to a statistical technique called cluster analysis to ultimately help determine the way to organize a new or reorganize an existing site."

This all made sense to Andy, who asked for an estimate on what it would cost to perform a card sort. After reviewing the budget, Andy approved the funds to conduct the exercise.

The first step in performing the card sort was for Barry to perform a content inventory of the site. Barry methodically combed through all the pages of the site, noting each item sold by LANDAU'S. To keep the current organization of the site clear in his mind, he identified the levels of the site, starting with the main categories from the home page at the left and then moving down the hierarchy to the right. Table 8.1 shows a section of Barry's inventory.

When Barry was finished, the first thing he noticed was a fairly large number of content items (232) for users to comfortably sort. A typical card sort usually contains no more than 100 items at a maximum. Asking users to sort many more than 100 items is not advised—people start to fatigue and may not do a good job sorting. Barry has seen people just throw cards into any pile just to finish the exercise and get their incentive for completing the exercise. So Barry had to make some decisions: How would he reduce 232 cards down to 100?

Another issue that arose for Barry was one of terminology. Barry has some familiarity with boating and diving. But as he performed the inventory,

Table 8.1. A Section of the Content Inventory for LANDAU'S.COM

First Level	First-Level Description	Content Items
Trailers and accessories	Boat trailers, guides, tie-downs, tires and wheels, winches, and other accessories	
		Tie-downs for boats
		Boat trailer transom savers
		Boat jackets
		Boat trailers
		Boat bearings, bearings protectors, hubs
		Fenders for boat trailers
		Boat tongue jacks
		Boat winches
		Boat trailer guide-ons and bunks
		Tires and wheels for boat trailers
		Boat trailer dollies
		Tire carriers for boat trailers
		Misc. boat trailer accessories
		Couplers and coupler locks for boat trailers
Trolling accessories	Downrigger weights, dodgers and flashers, planer boards, releases, lures	
		Releases
		Drift socks
		Rigs
		Trolling lures
		Dodgers/flashers
		Planer boards

it occurred to him that the terminology might be getting in the way of a pure conceptual organizational scheme. What if some users didn't understand some of the cards' (products') meanings? If they weren't familiar with the products, how could they sort the cards accurately?

In past studies Barry had also noticed that users often focus on common words used in item names and automatically group those items. For example, in a study he did with household items, users seemed to group all items with the word "door" in them (door mat, door bell, door knob), even though it seemed to him that other groupings would make more sense. Barry wanted to be sure the same thing didn't happen here, so he would take steps to avoid it.

Barry made some other decisions about the nature of the card sort study. Was LANDAU'S willing to move away from its current organizational scheme totally? Or did they want to maintain the current category names? The former approach would call for an "open sort" where users create groups from scratch. The latter approach would give users the existing category names and ask them to sort the content into those categories. LANDAU'S decided they wanted to make no assumptions about the information architecture, so Barry chose an open sort.

Finally, Barry opted to use a remote card sorting tool over a low-tech in-person method. Barry wanted to get a large number of customers from diverse geographies to provide input. Further, Barry believed that a "large n" study that enabled statistical analysis would give him a more solid valid set of data to work from than a small in-person study.

Questions

5. How could Barry reduce the number of items in the card sort study?
6. What should Barry do about items with specialized or unfamiliar names?
7. What else can Barry do in the design and execution of the card sort study to ensure that users sort the items in a way that truly reflects their mental models of the important relationships among the set of LANDAU'S products?

Implementing the Card Sort Study

Barry proceeds with the card sort study. Because the target users of the site are widely distributed geographically, Barry works with LANDAU'S marketing director to recruit a sample of typical users to participate in the study by

Figure 8.3. The user interface for the card sort study.

offering them a $25 LANDAU'S gift certificate. He then arranges to conduct the card sort online through a company that markets a web-based card sort tool. The participants are first sent an e-mail invitation that instructs them to point their browser to a URL where they can participate in the study, by dragging and dropping the content items into folders, which they can name. Figure 8.3 shows the interface.

Each time a participant completed the study, Barry received an e-mail to that effect. To encourage participants to participate in a timely manner, Barry's invitation indicated that the study would only be available for 1 week. At the end of that period 29 participants had completed the study, which Barry knew from his research was sufficient for obtaining reliable results. So, Barry closed the study. Any invitees who attempted to enter the study received a polite "Thank you for your attempt to participant in LANDAU'S card sort study, but it is now closed."

During the study, the card sort application saved the data on how each participant sorted the content items into categories and saved the names the participants assigned to the categories. A portion of the data from one participant is shown in Table 8.2. The data were also saved in a form that could be used in a cluster analysis, which would be used to analyze and interpret the results.

After closing the study with sufficient data with which to work, Barry is anxious to see what the participants have told him regarding new organization for the LANDAU'S website.

First, Barry examines the individual data sets to weed out results from participants who completed the study in a haphazard fashion just to receive a gift certificate. Obviously, this is a judgment call, but it is usually easy to identify such a case. For example, Barry may find that a participant sorted all the items into only one or two groups. Such unreliable data only

Table 8.2. A Sample of Participant Data From the Card Sort

Participant Name	Group Name	Items		
bryan.johnson	Hardware	Miscellaneous boating hardware	Boat docking systems and accessories	Anchors
bryan.johnson	Interior	Boat storage items	Pedestals and bases for boat seats	Cup holders
bryan.johnson	Safety	Life jackets and life vests	Safety items for boating	Towable water items

contaminate the results, making them inconsistent and difficult to interpret. In reviewing the results, Barry found two participants whose data seemed to indicate they hadn't taken the study seriously, so he discarded their data.

Barry then reviews the results from a cluster analysis, because it essentially generates an average of the groups formed by each of the card sort participants. Cluster analysis works on the principle of the similarity of each item to every other item, according to how frequently items were placed in the same group by participants.

When using an automated tool such as WebSort, the results of a cluster analysis are displayed in a hierarchical tree structure like that shown in Figure 8.4 for the LANDAU'S study. The "leaves" (the card sort items) are shown at the left of the diagram, and the bottom of the tree is shown toward the right. Starting at the right (bottom) and moving to the left, the branches divide groups of items that are more and more similar to each other and less similar to items in groups on branches further away from them.

As Barry looks at this particular view of the LANDAU'S tree he sees eight groups, indicated by the alternating red and blue colors. Some of the groups are quite large and some are quite small. Barry first attends to the large groups. Barry notices a large blue group of 25 items in the middle of the diagram—the one that begins with "Life jackets and life vests" at the top and "Boat care items" at the bottom. Barry is concerned that a group of 25 is much too large and contains too many different types of items to be manageable from a website organization standpoint: Will users believe these items all belong to the same category? Probably not. Users probably expect these to be subdivided. So Barry considers how to divide this group into subgroups while still preserving the initial structure of the tree.

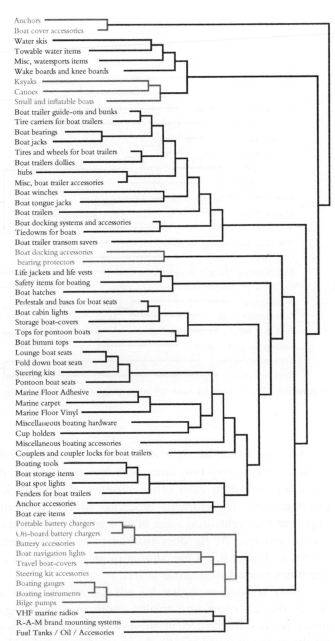

Figure 8.4. A cluster analysis tree.

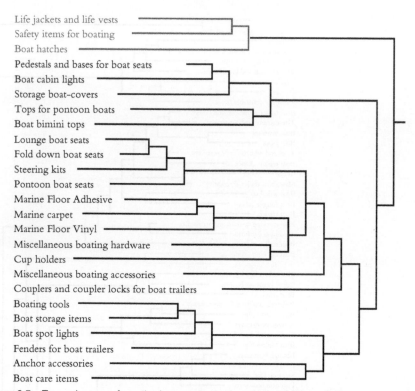

Figure 8.5. Two subgroups from the large group in the middle of Figure 8.4.

Moving from the right of the tree diagram toward the left, the initial branches divide into two more branches, resulting in subgroups of items that are more similar to each other within a group and less similar to those in other groups. Therefore to subdivide the large group of 25 items, Barry begins at the right-most edge of that group and moves left to see what subgroups emerge. As he does that he finds the two branches (subgroups) as shown in Figure 8.5. One, shown in gray, consists of a small group containing items related to boating safety.

Barry is concerned that he still has a very large and varied group. To divide the 22 items into smaller more meaningful groups, Barry needs to move further to the left in the lower part of the tree in Figure 8.5. That results in the two subgroups shown in Figure 8.6. The first subgroup looks "clean"—it consists of boat accessory items. But Barry still has a large and varied subgroup (shown in blue) consisting of 17 items.

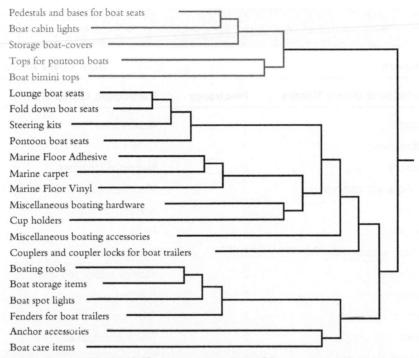

Pedestals and bases for boat seats
Boat cabin lights
Storage boat-covers
Tops for pontoon boats
Boat bimini tops
Lounge boat seats
Fold down boat seats
Steering kits
Pontoon boat seats
Marine Floor Adhesive
Marine carpet
Marine Floor Vinyl
Miscellaneous boating hardware
Cup holders
Miscellaneous boating accessories
Couplers and coupler locks for boat trailers
Boating tools
Boat storage items
Boat spot lights
Fenders for boat trailers
Anchor accessories
Boat care items

Figure 8.6. Two subgroups from the large group in Figure 8.5.

Once again, Barry continues moving to the left in the tree. Barry continues to "drill down" through this group until he feels comfortable he has clean coherent groups of similar items across the entire tree.

Now that Barry has completed his first pass at examining the groups, he is well aware that a limitation of the tree diagram is that it doesn't reveal anything about the names participants assigned to groups they constructed during their individual card sorting activities. So, it's now time for him to make use of those names as he looks forward to developing the site architecture. The method Barry uses to review the participant group names is to first create lists of the group names for each item. Then he can compare the items in the groups from the cluster analysis tree to find a name that seems to fit all the items reasonably.

The first set Barry decides to review is the group of two items at the top of the full tree shown in Figure 8.4 (anchors and boat cover accessories). He notices they formed the last subgroup to be added to make the tree completely connected—they have the longest group "stem" in the tree (that

Table 8.3. Frequency of Participant Group Names for the Items "Anchors" and "Boat Cover Accessories"

Anchors		Boat Cover Accessories	
Participant Group Names	**Frequency**	**Participant Group Names**	**Frequency**
Access	1	Accessories	2
Accessories	3	Covers	6
Anchors	2	Hardware for boats	1
Anchors accessories	1	Miscellaneous items	1
Basics	1	Needs	1
Equipment	1	Parts	1
Fishing accessories	1	Seats, covers, and flooring	1
Hardware	2	Storage equip, and acc.	1
Needs	1	Supplies	1
Parts	1	Tops, covers, etc.	1
Safety	2	Trailer accessories	1
Storage equip and acc.	1	Trailer equipment	1
Supplies	1	Trailering	1
Tools, hardware, anchors and storage items	1		

is, the longest black line connecting that group to the rest of the tree). He understands this is an indication that there was very little agreement among participants about where these items should be placed. Sure enough, as Barry creates the list of group names for the two items, he sees that those two items were placed in 24 different categories and have only three group names in common, confirming his suspicions (Table 8.3). He decides to keep this in mind as he reviews the other items.

Barry then remembers that the second group (in blue) of four items at the top of the tree (water skis, towable water items, misc. watersports items, and wake boards and knee boards) appears to form a reasonably coherent group, so he decides to look at those items to see what group names were given to them by the participants. They are shown in Table 8.4. Barry notes

Table 8.4. Frequency of Participant Group Names for Items "Water Skis," "Towable Water Items," "Misc. Watersports Items," and "Wake Boards and Knee Boards"

Water Skis		Towable Water Items		Misc. Watersports Items		Wake Boards and Knee Boards	
Participant Group Names	Frequency	Participant Group Names	Frequency	Participant Group Names	Frequency	Participant Group Names	Frequency
Accessories	1	Accessories	1	Accessories	1	Accessories	1
Life preservers, watersport items	1	Life preservers, watersport items	1	Life preservers, watersport items	1	Life preservers, watersport items	1
Recreation	1	Recreation	1	Personal watercraft and accessories	1	Recreation	1
Recreational boating	1	Recreational boating	1	Recreation	1	Recreational boating	1
Toys	1	Safety	1	Recreational boating	1	Toys	1
Watersports equip.	12	Toys	1	Toys	1	Trolling supplies	1
Watersports	2	Watersports equip.	12	Watersports equip.	11	Watersports equip.	11
		Watersports	1	Watersports	2	Watersports	2

that there appears to be very good agreement among the participants. Of the 10 different categories in which any of the four items were placed, they share 5, with all being placed in the category "Water Sports Equipment" over half the time. Thus that would appear to be a reasonable name for the group, should Barry decide later that it should be left as a group.

It's important that Barry has a good deal of experience with card sorting because although cluster analysis is a helpful tool, there is still a fair amount of informed judgment that must be applied to the interpretation of results.

Questions

8. What would be Barry's next steps on this project, after he completes his interpretation of the card sort results?

Also, now that the card sort has been performed, Barry should recommend LANDAU'S put some new mechanisms in place to enable the gathering of user research into the future. He might begin by suggesting that LANDAU'S customer service team implement a mechanism for gathering a more accurate count of service calls and logs with descriptions of the problems. And, the service people should ask questions from a user's perspective, for example, "What did you expect to find on the website that you didn't find?"

Summary

LANDAU'S.COM is typical of a website that grew without a well-thought-out expansion plan. As new products were added to the company's inventory, they were haphazardly appended to the site without a concerted effort to fit them in to the user's mental model for where those items should reside. When users started complaining about not finding what they were looking for, LANDAU'S commissioned a card sort study.

The steps involved in performing the card sort are as follows:

- Inventory the content of the site
- Reduce the number of items to a manageable set (typically, under 100)
  - Split the study into multiple studies and then perform a "sort of sorts"
  - Represent like items with a single generic version of the items
  - Eliminate items whose grouping can be determined before the sort study
- Implement the study
  - Recruit, invite, and compensate participants
- Review the results
  - Eliminate invalid data
  - Perform cluster analysis

- ° Split up groups that are too large and too varied to constitute a reasonable category
- ° Assign names to the categories based on user-supplied names
- ° Category names that most users agree on should be assigned to groups

The study provided the data that can be used by an information architect to redesign the site.

Further Reading

Courage, C., and Baxter, K. (2005). *Understanding your users: a practical guide to user requirements*. San Francisco: Elsevier.

Deaton, M. (2002). *Sorting techniques for user-centered information design*. Available at http://www.mmdeaton.com/SortingTechniquesforInformationDesign.doc

Martin, S. (1999). *Cluster analysis for website organization: using cluster analysis to help meet users' expectations in site structure*. Available at http://www.internettg.org/newsletter/dec99/cluster_analysis.html

Maurer, D., and Warfel, T. (2004). *Card sorting: a definitive guide*. Available at http://www.boxesandarrows.com/archives/card_sorting_a_definitive_guide.php

McGovern, G. (2002). *Information architecture: using card sorting for web classification design*. Available at http://www.gerrymcgovern.com/nt/2002/nt_2002_09_23_card_sorting.htm

Robertson, J. (2001). *Information design using card sorting*. Available at http://www.steptwo.com.au/papers/cardsorting/index.html

Tullis, T., and Wood, L. (2004). How many users are enough for a card-sorting study? Presented at the Proceedings of UPA 2004, Minneapolis, Minnesota, June 7–11, 2004.

Wodtke, C. (2003). *Blueprints for the web: organization for the masses*. Available at http://www.informit.com/articles/article.asp?p=30289&redir=1

The HURIE Method: A Case Study Combining Requirements Gathering and User Interface Evaluation

Randolph G. Bias, The University of Texas at Austin
Shannon Lucas, Motive, Inc.
Tammy L. Latham, Benefitfocus.com, Inc.

> *Jake assumed that Maria and Ernie had locked down their user profiles and a set of tasks to investigate. "So tell us, which of the functions currently covered by the user interface prototype do you suppose are the most frequent, the most critical, and the most nettlesome?" Jake asked. Maria replied, "Um, we're not really sure." This is not what Jake expected to hear.*

The Context

The Client: IC² Institute

A humble but energetic usability professional, Jake, returned to academia after over 20 years in industry. Embracing "pure" research but eager to find like-minded researchers with an eye toward the application of their findings, he happened upon the IC² (Innovation, Creativity, and Capital) Institute at the large public university where he was hired. IC² was founded in 1977 to nurture technology education, entrepreneurship, and innovation. Affiliated with The University of Texas at Austin McCombs School of Business, IC² spurs innovations, offers continuing education for high-tech workers, trains new entrepreneurs and managers, and collaborates directly with local businesses.

One of IC^2's projects, "Digital Warrior," is a software application being developed for the U.S. Army to allow battle command training at a distance via a gamelike user interface (UI). At lunch one afternoon Maria, the project manager of the Digital Warrior project, described to Jake the project and showed him the prototype UI that had already been developed. "Why don't I help you ensure that the UI is usable?" asked Jake. "You could perhaps find some funding for some Graduate Research Assistantships, and I could identify one or two excellent students from the School of Information." The project manager liked the idea and found the funding.

Software Development

Jake and Maria informally kicked off their collaboration at a morning meeting with some students who were working on the Digital Warrior team and Jake's two grad students. One of the more intelligent young student programmers, Ernie, was interested in learning more about the field he was studying. He had heard that software development once followed a pattern known as the *waterfall model* and asked Jake and Maria to explain what that meant.

"Well," began Jake, "The waterfall model is based on the classical engineering approach where a project begins with a complete requirements and specification document, followed by a formal design, an implementation, and, finally, testing."

"Right," Maria offered. "This approach is appropriate for building things such as bridges, dams, and airplanes. Software, however, is a mutable medium; a project can begin with the intent to build one thing but that thing can become something very different by the time it is finished. In a cool book called *The Mythical Man-Month* written three decades ago, Brooks wrote that the basic fallacy of the waterfall model is that it assumes a project goes through this process *once* and things go according to the original plan. The lack of feedback from one stage to another can result in errors entering in the early stages of the project but not being discovered until after implementation."

Maria continued, "Creating a computer program's requirements specification can be the most difficult part of software development. Software is created to address a problem within a specific domain such as medical imaging, banking, or airline flight control systems. The people who conceptualize and implement the software are not likely to be doctors, bankers, or flight controllers—in other words, representatives of the target user audience. This introduces the problem of not knowing what the user or customer wants, but asserting—and building—what the product developers think the user or customer needs." Jake jumped in: "Interviewing the users and customers only partially addresses this problem because this method is based on the premise that these requirements can be articulated in a way you software developers can understand. This is not to say that either party is incapable but rather that they often don't have the common knowledge base to make this communication effective."

The morning discussion moved on to the *spiral model* of software development which involves an evolutionary cycle. Project manager Maria took the lead: "In the spiral model, there is a short initial phase of requirements gathering and design, followed by a short implementation phase. The results of that implementation phase are then reviewed with the customer, and this feedback informs the next iteration of the process. This evolutionary approach accommodates the reality that a customer may not be able to completely specify the requirements for the product in the beginning of development."

"'Accommodates the reality'"? asked Ernie. "When did you get so high-falutin'?"

"As I was saying," continued Maria, "In a book on software engineering, Sommerville notes that an evolutionary approach is the most appropriate for interactive systems with a significant UI component, like our own Digital Warrior."

Usability

Jake took over, as he swooped into a discussion of the role of usability engineering in software development. "The modern practice of usability engineering entails collecting user data to inform, early on, and later validate human–computer interfaces. Usability practitioners have fought—and continue to fight—to be integrated into the software development process from the beginning of a project. Mayhew, for example, in her book, *Usability Engineering Life Cycle*, offers an iterative approach to the application of user data to a software development project. This iterative approach assumes a more incremental software development methodology that has a solid product requirements specification in the beginning. The collection of user data begins in the requirements analysis stage and continues throughout product development, with the data possibly changing the design at any stage."

Ernie asked Maria, "Did we involve any users before coming up with the Digital Warrior prototype"? "We'll get to that in a minute," mumbled Maria.

Jake continued, "In a book on interaction design Preece and her colleagues distinguish between *formative* and *summative evaluation.* By itself, summative evaluation, conducted only when the product is complete, still allows for the same type of design flaws that could be introduced in the waterfall model. Formative evaluations, conducted throughout the development process, are used to avoid this. However, even formative evaluations have tended to assume that the product functional requirements were fixed and good."

As an aside, after the meeting, when they were walking toward their cars, one of the School of Information students, Sean, asked his professor, Jake, "Why do usability professionals continually have to struggle to insinuate themselves early into the software product development cycle?" Jake's scholarly reply was, "Perhaps it is because usability doesn't show an immediate and obvious return on investment. Software development managers who are being evaluated only on getting functionality developed on time have a hard time hearing an argument for resources for something that isn't helping them get the product out the door sooner. Usability is often perceived incorrectly as just 'window dressing' among software developers."

The Product: Digital Warrior

Back to the combined team meeting, the team went on to discuss the product. The history of Digital Warrior began when the U.S. Army sought to leverage the potential capabilities of digital distance learning training environments. Distance learning technologies provide new training opportunities that combine the science of human cognition with the computer-based instructional advantages of interactive multimedia, automated assessment, on-demand access to remediation and enrichment materials, and anytime-anywhere availability.

Maria continued with Ernie's education: "Before you came on board we at the IC^2 Institute spent 6 months investigating operational and technological issues, assessing current 'best practices,' and developing and analyzing potential solutions to the application of distance learning to the problem of training the digital force. We made an extensive review of the U.S. Army literature on digital skills and digital transformation, plus information interviews conducted with key personnel at the Battle Command Training Center at Fort Hood, Texas. Soldiers and leaders were observed and interviewed during live, virtual, and constructive—that is, they helped build online training tasks—battle commander training exercises. Based on this research and in coordination with the Institute for Advanced Technology, IC^2 authored three technical papers and developed a training prototype that demonstrates the capabilities and potential effectiveness of distance learning solutions to a common digital skills training need."

The Problem Revealed

Jake then attempted to bring the discussion around to the true purpose of the meeting: the design of the usability evaluation. As is so often the case, necessity was the mother of invention. Jake and his two graduate students had formed what we'll call the "University of Texas Usability Team." The role of the University of Texas Usability Team in support of the Digital Warrior project was to perform a usability evaluation of the prototype UI, gathering data from battle commanders and other representative users. They had access to two groups of representative users, for a small period of time each, and so decided to conduct two pluralistic usability walk-throughs (WT) (Bias, 1994). A pluralistic usability WT is a group exercise that uses representative users in a systematic step-through of the UI design. It is a good candidate method when there is any early design (even paper-and-pencil level) and is particularly valuable in that it gets representative users and product developers into the same room. In a pluralistic usability WT, product designers/developers are prepared in advance *not* to bias the representative users and to give the users' comments unconditional positive regard. Then they, the product designers/developers, are welcomed to participate in the WT.

The method is "pluralistic" because there are three types of participants in the same exercise: representative users, product designers/developers, and usability professionals. A key characteristic of the pluralistic usability WT is collaborative redesign "on the fly" that happens, at the direction of the usability professional/moderator, among all the types of participants. In the pluralistic usability WT, participants are given a description of a task to complete and a packet of screen shots in the order in which the screens would be encountered if carrying out the task online. The participants each write down which action they would take on a screen, then the "correct" answer (given the current design) is announced, and then a discussion ensues about the good and poor features of the design of the UI.

Pluralistic usability WTs also have shortcomings and are often supplemented with later end-user testing, in a complete course of usability engineering. These shortcomings are as follows:

• Participants can't explore the interface, as they might with an actual application.

- There are often multiple correct actions on any particular screen, and each participant has to reset and assume he or she went down the one chosen path for which the screen shots are gathered into the packet.
- Some data (e.g., time on task) are impossible to obtain, given that it is a group paper-and-pencil exercise.

Dutifully preparing for the WTs, Jake started to quiz Maria and Ernie about user profiles and a set of tasks to investigate. "So tell us, which of the functions currently covered by the UI prototype do you suppose are the most frequent, the most critical, and the most nettlesome?" Jake asked.

Maria replied, "Um, we're not really sure. Indeed, we're not even confident that the prototype covers the functionality it needs to cover."

As the session progressed, it quickly became clear to the usability team, as well as to all the other stakeholders, that no one had a crisp idea of the exact set of functions needed in the tool. Despite the earlier literature review, interviews, and observation of live training, the Digital Warrior team was uncertain if the prototype afforded the function needed to allow for game-based distance learning of battle command skills. Faced with this lack of clarity about the product functionality, and also faced with very short and precious windows of time during which the software development team (including the usability team) would have access to the representative users, the usability team needed to come up with a creative solution.

"What about if we discover through the tests that the whole design is bogus?" one of the Information School grad students asked.

Jake cleared his throat. "Well, 'bogus' is a strong word. What I worry about is the possibility that we find that the current UI is, in fact, quite usable but later learn that it doesn't have all the functionality needed to afford successful training. Let me add, Maria, that it is not uncommon to see teams begin prototyping before they have a clear view of what the product will do. There's your 'mutable medium' you mentioned earlier. Here's what I propose. Let's proceed with the evaluation of the existing prototype, *but combine the exercise with a requirements-gathering effort.* These two activities—requirements gathering and UI evaluation—are typically done separately. And you *did* do some requirements gathering. But because you still aren't confident that you have the right functionality set, why don't we use these usability walkthroughs, these early formative usability evaluations as, also, a tool for requirements gathering and validation?"

One of Jake's students spoke up: "But mightn't the results of the usability tests invalidate some of the software's existing design and specification"?

Jake said, "That's a possibility, but given the work the Digital Warrior team did with their literature review and interviews, I doubt that anything we find will invalidate neither Digital Warrior's root concept nor the whole UI design. Now, this might be a serious problem for a product that just emerges from a software developer's imagination, with no user-centered design at all. Given that this is our first involvement on this project, I think it's important to improve the product *this time* but also to demonstrate to the product development team the value of usability engineering, in general. Go read the Wilson and Rosenbaum 2005 chapter on 'social return-on-investment'."

The usability team decided to call this the hybrid user-requirements and interface evaluation (HURIE, pronounced "hurry") method. This method they believed would lead to further integration with the software development process, having the additional beneficial effect of allowing usability to be perceived by the software development team as internal to the team rather than external.

Thus the usability team had the challenge of performing a usability evaluation of an interactive software system that was in its early stages of development. The software would have an initial design as a nonfunctional UI prototype (digitized, but mostly "stubbed out" so that only one path through the UI could be navigated) based on the software designers' understanding of the problem space being addressed. The usability team used this prototype in a pluralistic usability WT with participants from the software's target audience, while at the same time gathering new product requirements. They then planned to use the results of these tests to inform the next iteration of the design cycle by either validating existing requirements or introducing new ones that the software designers had missed. It was also the usability team's hope and belief that involving the end users this early in the process would help build the users' confidence in the result (Wilson and Rosenbaum, 2005); not only would they ask the users for their input in the process, but the users would know that their input could actually result in changes and new product requirements.

One of Jake's students, Sean, offered an example from his reading: "Frustrated that usability evaluations were left at the end of the development process, Siemens Medical Solutions Health Services created a new methodology that combined their software development and usability cycles into one." (See Anderson et al., 2001.) "Based on the rational unified process, it begins with requirements analysis and proceeds to UI design, system design, implementation, and finally deployment. Though the approach calls for iterative testing of the interface design, it does not involve actual user testing of the design to verify or generate requirements. Like earlier methodologies, it is assumed that requirements can be sufficiently gathered through contextual inquiry methods."

Jake's other student, Pam, added, by way of further team building with the software developers, "One of the key issues, however, in integrating usability into any software development process is the different vocabularies and perspectives held by each group. Usability and human–computer interface design groups are generally multidisciplinary and draw from backgrounds in psychology, sociology, and graphic or industrial design. The perspective and vocabulary held by software developers, however, tends to be closer to the engineering fields. Seems to me that the story approach used in some agile development processes may provide a bridge between the two groups. Sean, I'll share with you two articles where I read about this—Agile Alliance, 2005, and Hwong et al., 2004."

Questions

1. Where do usability activities best fit in a spiral model software development cycle?
2. Why did the usability team choose pluralistic usability WT as their product evaluation method?

The Study

A New Method

The team reviewed the goals of the project. The Digital Warrior project intends to allow soldiers to receive training on various pieces of Army command software before being deployed to a combat situation. A secondary goal is to make this training engaging by creating a gamelike interface. The fact of the presence of a UI prototype made this project ideal for testing the feasibility of gathering UI evaluation data and requirements at the same time. The software's design and requirements specifications were based on literature research and some customer interviews. A skeleton of the UI had been constructed in Macromedia Director that allowed minor interaction and allowed a user to follow one usage scenario through the application. The usability team considered a single path sufficient to perform some early UI evaluation and proof-of-concept demonstrations—indeed, one of the advantages of a pluralistic usability WT is the ability to test with just one such path defined. The usability team elucidated the primary goal of the usability testing: identify potential problems with the UI and task flows and propose improvements. A secondary goal was to identify functional requirements for the application itself. These would include features that test participants either expected the application to provide before the WTs or believed that it lacked after completing the WTs. Thus the team was inaugurating the HURIE method; they were explicitly combining requirements gathering with prototype evaluation.

The Procedure

The usability team conducted two pluralistic usability WTs using the extant prototype interface. As is standard with pluralistic usability WTs, some of the project's developers and designers were present in each evaluation. Before each WT started (i.e., before any participant saw any part of the Digital Warrior interface), the usability team invited one of the software developers to describe the purpose of the software and asked the participants to write down what they believed such an application should offer them as users. This was done as part of both WTs as a way to supplement requirements gathering before the participants were biased by seeing the current prototype design. The WT itself was then typical of any pluralistic usability WT:

- The usability team gave all the participants a task to perform and a packet of screen shots, ordered as the screens would be encountered during the successful completion of the prescribed task.
- The WT administrator (a member of the usability team) asked the participants to write on the pages what actions they would take to complete the task and then stepped through the task one screen at a time.
- For these WTs an interactive prototype was projected at the front of the room to illustrate color and cursor placement, but this method could be just as effective with only a paper-and-pencil design.
- At the end of each WT, along with a traditional satisfaction questionnaire, the participants were asked to describe any features they thought were missing or inadequate or to specify any extant features they thought unnecessary or even harmful.

Sean asked, "Won't these 'new'—that is, postevaluation—requirements likely be influenced by the particular design as instantiated in the UI prototype"? To which Jake replied, "Sure, and so we will weight them a bit less heavily than those requirements the test participants mention *before* seeing the prototype."

The Sites and Participants

The first WT was conducted on the property of the University of Texas at Austin. Participants were graduate-level students of the Army War College. These participants were intended to be a surrogate user group to substitute for actual battle captains, none of whom was available for testing. Regarding the 11 participants in the group,

- Only two had served as battle captains.
- Each had attained the rank of major, lieutenant colonel, or colonel.
- They ranged in age from 36 to 55.
- Eight of the 11 were men.
- All had attended graduate school, and only one had not yet completed his degree.

The first WT's participants were all similar in their backgrounds with computers:

- Most had been using Windows-based PCs for 10 years or more.
- Most had never used a Macintosh.
- All had some experience with the Internet, laptops, and pointing devices.
- Most had experience with simulation video games (both battle and nonbattle related).
- Most had no experience at all with training software (either battle or non-battle).

Responses about computer usage indicated the following regarding this group of participants:

- They used their home computers less than 10 hours each week.
- At work, computer usage was more distributed with about half of the participants using computers over 20 hours per week.
- All participants used Windows PCs at home and at work.

The second WT was conducted at Fort Sam Houston in San Antonio, Texas using noncommissioned officers from the Army Medical Command. This group was selected because they represent the users for a potential derivative of Digital Warrior focused on medical command instead of combat command.

Though this group had more participants than the first WT, only nine participants provided feedback because several of the attendees used the pluralistic usability WT as a chance to learn about the product and were not representative of the target user audience. Regarding this group of nine participants:

- This WT group was notably younger; two-thirds were ages 25 to 35.
- Positions held by these participants included small group leader, training manager, and operations noncommissioned officers.
- Only one participant had ever been a brigade battle captain.
- Eight were men.
- Most had attended some college, though only two had completed an undergraduate degree.
- Most had used Windows PCs for at least 6 years, and two-thirds had no experience with Macintosh computers.
- One participant had no experience with the Internet.
- Experience with simulation video games in this group was high with both non-battle and battle simulation games.
- This group also had a higher level of experience with training software, with most having some experience with nonbattle simulation training software and only one participant having no experience with battle simulation training software.

Computer usage was different for this group:

- Almost one-fourth reported that they used their home computers more than 40 hours per week.
- Less than half reported that they used them less than 10 hours per week.
- All participants used Windows computers at work at least 11 hours per week.
- All used PCs at home, and all but one used Windows PCs at work. This user identified his work computer as a non-Windows, non-Macintosh platform.

And so the two pluralistic usability WTs tested 20 participants with a wide breadth of experience. Although the participants in the second WT were less representative of the ultimate battle captain user, their high PC usage and experience and familiarity with the battle command language and environment made their input valuable.

Questions

3. What could the usability team have done had the pluralistic usability WTs invalidated the entire concept of the Digital Warrior project?
4. How might the wording the software developers used to describe the purpose of the software application potentially influence the users as they wrote down "what they believed such an application should offer"?
5. How should new requirements gathered before the WT starts and those gathered as part of the post-WT data collection be balanced in product design decisions?
6. How might the relatively weak connection between the user audience in the second pluralistic usability WT and the ultimate user audience affect the analysis of the results?

The Findings

The HURIE exercises were considered a success by all the stakeholders in the project, including the test participants. As in most usability evaluations, the usability team collected satisfaction data and performance data. Additionally, with the new "hybrid" technique, the usability team gathered a number of new requirements that were considered important to the project's success, and several of these would have been difficult to implement later if they had not been discovered in this early phase. Project manager Marie was particularly happy with the results: "Now I believe we can move forward with confidence that we are building the right product." Software developer Ernie echoed that thought: "In just two 3-hour sessions we got a ton of ideas, ideas that I'm eager to implement." In general, thanks to the HURIE method, the Digital Warrior product was more reflective of the actual battle command situation, afforded the users a chance to take actions before seeing what the correct actions were, and accommodated various skill levels. Jake was happy to report that "this method uncovered requirements that were not discovered through literature research or by interviewing domain experts. It also fine-tuned the existing requirements."

User Acceptance/Satisfaction

Participant feedback about Digital Warrior was very positive. Only a small number, one participant in each WT, said they would not want to use Digital Warrior as a training tool. Participants in the first WT stated that the tool

Table 9.1. Median Responses on the Posttest Questionnaire

Question	Median, WT 1	Median, WT 2
"I found the individual screens intuitive."	5	5.5
"I found the task flows intuitive."	5	6
"I found the interface visually appealing."	5	6

Answers are based on a scale of 1 to 7, where 1 = strongly disagree and 7 = strongly agree.

would provide them with needed training. One participant said, "I learn best hands-on with discussion and lessons associated but not primary." Another said, "See it, touch it, do it." Those in the second WT commented that the tool would give them a better understanding of the Army's command process and thus enable them to better contribute to that process. One participant said, "It is good practice to see if I have the skills and attributes without being in danger or discomfort. Then still need actual practicum at the National Training Center or similar training sites."

There were three attitude questions asked in the posttest questionnaire of both WTs. Responses were relatively high, as can be seen in Table 9.1.

One valuable suggestion that was implemented, offered in response to an open-ended request for comments after these satisfaction questions, was, "Recommend icons reflecting the staff offices the Battle Captain must interact with."

Additional Requirements

As a result of the two HURIE methods the usability team identified 13 new user requirements, with 6 of them at the C3 (major) level and the remaining 7 at the C2 (moderate) level. The new requirements identified from the WTs were assigned a criticality score as shown in Table 9.2. Below are five examples. Each requirement is followed by a rationale.

C3: Delay highlighting to let the user consider his or her course of action. Participants in both WTs recommended that the highlight indicating a correct path through the prototype UI for a particular task should only appear in a tutorial level and only after 10 to 15 seconds to encourage the user to think about the flow rather than just blindly

Table 9.2. Criticality Ratings

Criticality	Label	Definition
C4	Critical	Critical data may be lost.
		The user may not be able to complete the task.
		The user may not want to continue using the application.
C3	Major	Users can accomplish the task but only with considerable frustration and/or performance of unnecessary steps.
		Noncritical data may be lost.
		The user will have great difficulty in circumventing the problem.
		Users can overcome the issue only after they have been shown how to perform the task.
C2	Moderate	The user will be able to complete the task in most cases but will undertake some moderate effort in getting around the problem.
		The user may need to investigate several links or pathways through the system to determine which option will allow them to accomplish the intended task.
		Users will most likely remember how to perform the task on subsequent encounters with the system.
C1	Minor	An irritant.
		A cosmetic problem.
		A typographical error.

clicking the highlighted button. The research literature on learning emphasizes the value of active learning. With the highlighting available immediately, a user could mindlessly step through the interface without considering deeply, and thus learning, the proper steps.

C3: Terminology should be hyperlinked to definitions. Discussions with the participants of this WT revealed that personnel called to duty from reserves or National Guard may not be familiar with current terminology and acronyms, but the personnel would still be put in the field on short notice.

C2: Accommodate varying skill levels. Our participants suggested that the task flow worked and made sense for an experienced battle captain but that it might be difficult for someone without command experience to grasp. Per the above recommendation about delaying the onset of highlighting, this could be a variable, allowing for shorter or longer periods of time for the user to consider next steps before the highlighting occurs.

C2: Include optional tutorials at the beginning of a session with the application. This would assist users unfamiliar with those systems in understanding what their role is in a combat situation.

C2: Allow user to prioritize available courses of action rather than choosing just one. The experienced battle captains reported that a battle captain would not pick a single course fo action to send to command for approval. Command would want to see all courses of action in a prioritized list.

UI Evaluation

As a result of the two HURIEs, the usability team identified 10 usability problems: 1 C4 (critical), 1 C3 (major), 2 C2 (moderate), and 6 C1 (minor). The following are six examples of the problems, chosen here to reflect the variety of problem types:

C4: Identify how restricted fire areas have changed. Participants in both WTs indicated that they were not able to remember how the restricted fire areas had looked before it was changed, and there was no facility to allow them to look at the previous restricted fire areas.

C3: Indicate that the screen shots in the application are zoomable. Participants reported that they had no way of knowing that they could zoom into the screen shots of the prototype by clicking on them. There should be some indication on the screen that this is possible. The application should *not* rely on a cursor change for this indication (i.e., do *not* require that the cursor be in a certain position to indicate this functionality). A cursor change assumes that the user will be moving the cursor over the zoomable object, and this is certainly not guaranteed.

C2: Need a way to exit out of the tutorials that are offered by the mentor and other information that appears in the middle pane. It is always good HCI design practice to allow the user complete control of what he or she is looking at. If the user can close out of these windows, it is not obvious how.

C2: The meaning of the different types of highlighting isn't clear. It is not intuitive what the difference is between a yellow highlight, a yellow or red arc, and a blinking icon in the UI prototype. They all seem to be intended to grab the user's attention, but the reason for offering one way versus another isn't clear.

C1: Staff in the command chain (S3, XO, CMD) have to be briefed individually; implement method to allow multiple staff to be selected and briefed simultaneously. Participants noted that briefing them individually was awkward and probably not realistic.

C1: Reading of English is best when the text flows left-to-right, top-to-bottom. The focus area in the bottom right-hand corner of the DW UI is difficult to read. (See the original screen in Figure 9.1. Note the lower right-hand corner, and the circular interaction widget.) Not only is it a new UI "widget" that users have to learn, but reading the text in a circle takes longer than reading normal text. In response to this, one of the usability team, Sean, prototyped a redesign of the

Figure 9.1. Original screen that later underwent redesign.

Figure 9.2. Focus area proposed redesign.

"focus" area in the bottom right-hand corner of the UI, shown in Figure 9.2. The usability team believed that it would ultimately save screen real estate plus offer a more intuitive interaction design.

An Additional Application Area

The team developing the HURIE method believes it may be particularly applicable to new "agile" software development methods. Agile software development, a new evolutionary approach, made its debut in 2001 (Agile Alliance, 2005). This new model differs from previous models in several ways. Individuals and interactions are preferred to processes and tools, working software is preferred to comprehensive documentation, and customer interaction is preferred to contract negotiation. A number of agile development methods gained popularity, including XP (eXtreme programming), Scrum, and DSDM (dynamic systems development methodology). The key assumption with agile development is that the developers continue to learn more about the system and its operating environment during a project. The requirements freeze, typical of traditional development methodologies, does not occur in agile development methods (Davies, 2005).

User requirements in agile development are often driven through the use of user stories. A story is often defined as one thing the user wants of the system. If a user story cannot be completed in one iteration of development, it must be broken into smaller stories (Davies, 2001). Usability professionals familiar with user profiling, personas, and scenario-based design (Carroll, 1995) will be comfortable with these stories. Davies notes that the difference between stories and use cases from the rational unified process is that stories represent the users' requirements during development, whereas use cases document these requirements from the software's perspective. Stories also focus on verbal communication rather than attempting to capture everything in writing as a use case does (Davies, 2001). Stories describe a user's interaction with the software without providing detail of what's happening "under the hood." A story is closer to a traditional usability scenario in that it may include some sort of persona for the user. A story will be along the lines of, "Bill, a construction worker, needs some cash. The bank is closed so he goes to the ATM. . . ." Use cases tend to contain information about what the software is doing as the user is performing a single activity, not a whole scenario. They are much more from the software's perspective as in how it reacts internally to user interaction. A use case for an ATM would be along the lines of "User inserts ATM card. System reads magnetic stripe. Is stripe valid?" It is also worth noting that in a use case, a "user" can be another piece of software that has to interact with the software being designed.

Given the frequent iterations, and the close integration of requirements and design, in agile software development, the HURIE method might be well suited to support it.

Questions

7. What are the advantages of offering a redesign as part of the usability evaluation?
8. It seems as though it is sometimes hard to distinguish between what is categorized as a "new requirement" (e.g., "Delay highlighting to let the user consider his or her course of action") and a result of the UI evaluation part of the exercise (e.g., "Indicate that the screen shots in the application are zoomable"). How can these two be distinguished?
9. Should all usability professionals ask "what should this product do" before starting any usability evaluation?
10. What external factors might cause user requirements to change during the course of development?

Summary

As the usability team evaluated the emerging UI design for a gamelike tool for teaching battle command software through distance learning, they found themselves in the uneasy position of having started to plan for two pluralistic usability WTs with two different but equally time-constrained user samples *and* a new discovery that even the product development team members (who had already developed a UI prototype) were uncertain as to the product requirements. The team could have postponed the UI evaluations but chose instead to try to take full(er!) advantage of the test participants already scheduled and to conduct a hybrid method wherein they, in parallel, gathered user requirements information *and* evaluated the UI prototype. They selected the pluralistic usability WT as their evaluation method, both because it allowed them to collect data from a number of these valuable and hard-to-schedule users at the same time and because it would allow for a dialogue between these representative users and the product developers, thus speeding up the back-and-forth that was necessary if they were to be engaged in an iterative design process.

The team added a requirements-gathering exercise onto the front of the pluralistic usability WT to collect user requirements data *before* biasing the pluralistic usability WT participants with the (now somewhat suspect) UI prototype. In this way, engaging a total of 20 users (of two different types and representative of the target user audience to different degrees), the team collected about a dozen new product requirements and about a dozen UI design problems. The product development team was extremely pleased with the new empirically based requirements and was sold on the value of usability going forward.

The team did not believe this approach to be a silver bullet for all software projects; they wouldn't recommend building a UI prototype before having a crisper idea of what the product shall do. They do, however, believe that this HURIE method can add value to the development of interactive software. Even in the spiral approach to software development, there has been a tendency to segregate requirements gathering from UI evaluation (Mayhew, 1999). The HURIE method affords HCI designers the chance to gather user feedback on the completeness of a product's (or website's) requirements set in the same session as they're gathering (prototype) UI evaluation data. This method is particularly valuable when the development cycle is necessarily short and access to representative users is difficult. Key components of the method are

- Availability of an early (even paper-and-pencil) design.
- Uncertainty about the completeness of the current product requirements set.
- Access to representative users.
- Addressing of the requirements question *before* biasing the test participants with the prototype design.

Indeed, the team developing this HURIE method might imagine incorporating these preexercise requirement questions into all usability evaluations, routinely, as a quick and frequent check on the (possibly shifting) user requirements.

Based on the usability team's experiences with software development, they believe the HURIE method fits best into an evolutionary development processes and is particularly suited for agile development. The early delivery of a UI prototype for evaluation helps meet the agile principle of early and continuous delivery (Agile Alliance, 2001).

Further Reading

Agile Alliance. (2001). *Manifesto for agile software development*. Retrieved November 21, 2005, from Principles behind the Agile Manifesto website: http://www.agilemanifesto.org/principles.html

Agile Alliance. (2005). *What is agile software development?* Retrieved November 17, 2005, from Agile Alliance website: http://www.agilealliance. org/

Anderson, J., Fleek, F., Garrity, K., and Drake, F. (2001). Integrating usability techniques into software development. *IEEE Software*, 18:46–53.

Bias, R. G. (1994). The pluralistic usability walkthrough: coordinated empathies. In Nielsen, J., and Mack, R. L. (Eds.). *Usability inspection methods*. New York: Wiley.

Brooks, F. (1995). *The mythical man-month: essays on software engineering*. Anniversary edition. Reading, MA: Addison-Wesley.

Carroll, J. M. (Ed.). (1995). *Scenario-based design: envisioning work and technology in system development*. Hoboken, NJ: John Wiley & Sons, Inc.

Davies, R. (2001). *The power of stories*. Retrieved May 30, 2006 from http://www.agilealliance.com/articles/daviesrachelthepowero/file

Davies, R. (2005). Agile requirements. *Methods & Tools*, 13:24–30.

Ferre, X. (2003). Integration of usability techniques into the software development process. Presented at the Proceedings of the Workshop "Bridging the Gaps Between Software Engineering and Human-Computer Interaction" at ICSE 2003, Portland, Oregon, May 28–35.

Gillan, D. J., Breedin, S. D., and Cooke, N. J. (1992). Network and multidimensional representations of the declarative knowledge of human-computer interface design experts. *International Journal of Man-Machine Studies*, 36:587–615.

Hwong, B., Laurance, D., Rudorfer, A., and Song, X. (2004). User-centered design and agile software development processes. Presented at "Identifying Gaps between HCI, Software Engineering and Design, and Boundary Objects to Bridge Them," a workshop held at the Computer-Human Interaction (CHI) 2004 Conference, Vienna, Austria, April.

Karat, C. M. (2005). A business case approach to usability cost justification for the web. In Bias, R. G., and Mayhew, D. J. (Eds.). *Cost-justifying usability: an update for the Internet age*. San Francisco: Morgan Kaufmann.

Mayhew, D. (1999). *The usability engineering life cycle*. San Francisco: Morgan Kaufmann.

Norman, D. A. (1990). *The design of everyday things*. New York: Doubleday.

Preece, J., Rogers, Y., and Sharp, H. (2002). *Interaction design: beyond human computer interaction*. New York: Wiley.

Sommervile, I. (1996). Software process models. *ACM Computing Surveys*, 28:269–271.

Vredenburg, K., Isensee, S., and Righi, C. (2002). *User-centered design: an integrated approach*. Upper Saddle River, NJ: Prentice Hall.

Wilson, C. E., and Rosenbaum, S. (2005). Categories of return on investment and their practical implications. In Bias, R. G., and Mayhew, D. J. (Eds.). *Cost-justifying usability: an update for the Internet age,* 2nd edition. San Francisco: Morgan Kaufmann.

Two Contrasting Case Studies in Integrating Business Analysis with Usability Requirements Analysis and User Interface Design

Deborah J. Mayhew, Deborah J. Mayhew & Associates

> *Elizabeth's unease grew. She had serious doubts that traveling to 6 to 12 cities to conduct task analysis interviews and observations with users would work in either the project budget or the project schedule. This project just did not fit the mold. It was hard to imagine how she would conduct any of her usability requirements analysis tasks in the way to which she was accustomed.*

Case 1: The Thompson Institute: No Business Analysis

Project Planning

Elizabeth, a seasoned usability engineering consultant with an advanced degree in cognitive psychology and 25 years of experience, was developing a growing sense of vague unease as the day progressed. Not much about this project seemed to be very well defined. And the project team seemed to be missing some key skill sets she depended on to do her work and did not feel qualified to provide herself. Finally, she articulated her main concern in the form of a scheduling question to Pamela, the project manager who would

185

ultimately need to approve her proposal for usability engineering support to the project.

"So, when will the detailed functional requirements for this application be complete and documented?" asked Elizabeth.

"Well," Pamela replied, "we have a general idea of the kind of work we want to automate and plan to work out the details as we go along."

"Oh, okay . . . and so, who on the team is responsible for working out those details?" asked Elizabeth, looking around the room at the team she had been introduced to earlier in the day.

"Well, all of us together. Most of us are familiar with the work of the users we are providing this tool for," was Pamela's rather unsatisfactory reply.

Several months earlier Pamela had taken a course from Elizabeth on her approach to usability engineering. The course described a complete usability engineering life cycle, from requirements analysis through iterative design and evaluation, integrated into the underlying software development methodology. A few weeks after that Pamela had invited Elizabeth to prepare a proposal for a usability engineering project plan for her software development project (currently in the early planning stages). Pamela seemed to really appreciate Elizabeth's systematic approach, confiding that her organization's user community had a lot of very bad experiences of late with poorly designed software applications that made their work harder rather than easier and that she had a mandate from her management to do a better job of usability on this latest project. Pamela suggested that before preparing a proposal, Elizabeth first meet with the project team assembled so far to get an overview of the project and to gather information as well as to present her approach to usability engineering to them. Elizabeth had driven into downtown Boston early that morning to spend the day with the project team for that purpose.

Pamela's organization, The Thompson Institute (TTI), was a nonprofit foundation. It conducted a wide variety of projects related to its overall mission, which benefited both the public and other institutions. Its funding came from both grants and private donations. TTI regularly sponsored events to motivate private donations, such as public speeches, dinners, and auctions. It was a very large foundation, with thousands of employees playing a very wide variety of roles.

One of the roles among TTI staff was "publicity manager." This role dealt with the media, planned and implemented publicity to support TTI's mission, and served as contact points for reporters writing news stories involving TTI. Pamela's software development project was aimed at developing a new automated tool to support the work of publicity managers at TTI. The tool was part database and part document management system and would allow publicity managers to keep track of and share all their media communications, press releases, news stories, and details of fundraising events.

Elizabeth was excited about the opportunity to get in on a development project early in the development life cycle. She planned to propose applying the full arsenal of usability engineering techniques from the beginning to the end of this development project, rather than just coming in late and writing a user interface style guide or conducting a usability test. She had had significant success applying this full life cycle approach on past projects and strongly believed that a usability requirements analysis effort more than paid off in efficiency of design and quality of usability.

Elizabeth also planned to cast her role as lead user interface designer so she could directly ensure that all the usability requirements analysis data she hoped to collect would be sure to find their way into the user interface design. Because the project manager had attended her course and then invited her to submit a proposed usability engineering project plan, Elizabeth assumed she already understood and had bought into this approach.

Elizabeth's extensive past experience primarily entailed coming into development projects at the point when detailed business requirements had already been defined and documented. Typically, she relied on several types of business requirements documentation to do her usability work.

High-level business requirements documentation would typically present a high-level conceptual description of the overall functionality of the intended application and include specific business goals that the application was intended to help achieve. Elizabeth relied on this type of documentation to get "the big picture" of the application (i.e., understand the scope of functionality to be implemented), to get a picture of the intended users, and to understand what key business goals usability could help achieve.

Detailed functional requirements documentation typically identified and provided detail on all required functions (e.g., use cases) and sometimes went so far as to define an information architecture for those functions and to identify specific screens and data (both input and output) that would appear on those screens. Elizabeth would use this kind of information to drive specific usability requirements analysis efforts, such as card sorting and the collection of task scenarios, to generate data that would help drive user interface design. The user interface design she ultimately generated based on data from these usability requirements techniques would often depart in significant ways from the information architecture and screens proposed by the business analysts (simply because the business analysts typically had neither any background or expertise in usability engineering nor the usability requirements analysis data to premise their designs on) but did depend heavily on the functional definitions provided in their documentation.

Thus, typically, business requirements documents were generated before Elizabeth's involvement in a project by professionals known as business analysts who specialized in understanding the business and scoping out and documenting the high-level business and detailed functional requirements that would define a software development project. Then, the business analysts were available on an ongoing basis to answer or resolve any functional questions that might arise as design and development proceeded.

Today's day-long planning meeting had started with introductions. Pamela, the project manager, seemed very congenial, moderately technically knowledgeable, and moderately familiar with the intended users and their work. She was a member of TTI's geographically dispersed software development organization based in New York City.

Also at the meeting were three subject matter experts (SMEs) who were publicity managers at TTI and thus themselves potential end users of the application to be developed. All three looked to be in their mid-30s. Sandra had flown in from her home in Minnesota, Sam lived in Boston, and Sean was from Texas. In spite of their different locations, it was clear they all knew each other well and were very comfortable working together.

During the meeting Elizabeth asked a number of "scoping" questions to help her think about how to structure her usability engineering plan. "How many potential end users are there for this application?" she asked the three SMEs at one point. After consulting each other they agreed the number was 35. This was encouraging—it should not be hard to get a representative sample for the purposes of user profiling and a task analysis.

Noting the different locations of the three SMEs present, Elizabeth then asked, "Can you identify one or two cities with the highest concentration of potential end users? I hope," she explained, "to be able to conduct interviews and observations of a representative sample of users in their work environment, and in my experience I can usually find an appropriate sample of 6 to 12 users in one or at most two different cities."

There was a small pause and then a few chuckles from the three SMEs. Sandra then explained, "There is never more than one user in a given city. It takes only one user to cover even a large metropolitan area, given the work that we do. We communicate with each other via phone and e-mail, and we also have a common website that supports collaboration and communication among us. If you wanted to actually visit six users, you would have to travel to six different cities. But this really won't be necessary, because

Sean, Sam, and I can tell you anything you need to know about the work that this project is supporting."

Elizabeth's unease grew. She had serious doubts that traveling to 6 to 12 cities to conduct task analysis interviews and observations with users would work in either the project budget or the project schedule. This project just did not fit the mold. It was hard to imagine how she would conduct any of her usability requirements analysis tasks in the way she was accustomed to doing them. (For further reading on traditional approaches to usability requirements analyses, see Beyer and Holtzblatt, 1998; Hackos and Redish, 1998; Mayhew, 1999, 2001; Wixon and Ramey, 1996.)

The development staff assigned to the project came from a different department within TTI from Pamela, the project manager, located in Washington, DC. Both a lead developer, Larry, and another developer, Dan, were present at the planning meeting. They were pretty quiet during the meeting time, but Larry took Elizabeth aside during lunch hour. "Listen," he confided, "I'm really glad you might be joining this team! I'm really interested in usability! I've read two or three good books on the topic, and I always put a lot of focus on it in my work as a developer."

"That's great," replied Elizabeth. "Have you ever worked with a usability engineer before?"

"No," was Larry's cheerful reply.

During the day-long meeting Elizabeth gave a presentation she had prepared, describing all the usability engineering tasks that she would typically plan to conduct over the life cycle of a development project, including the following usability requirements analysis tasks:

- Gather basic user profile data directly from end users to help her make various kinds of user interface design decisions.
- Conduct a card sorting exercise with end users to generate data to drive her information architecture design (see Righi and Woods in this volume and Tullis and Wood [2004] for further reading on this technique).
- Collect detailed task scenarios from end users to help drive the design of task workflows.
- Conduct a work environment analysis that will also help drive design decisions.

Halfway through her presentation she was dismayed to notice a lot of glassy-eyed looks among the project team—nobody seemed very engaged in her presentation. She finished up in a much less detailed manner than she had planned. She had the uncomfortable feeling that other team members expected her to simply design a user interface and be done with it. It was obvious that other than Pamela's attendance at her class, no one on the team had ever had any experience working with a usability engineer or incorporating user-centered design methods into their development projects.

Driving home after the meeting, Elizabeth felt perplexed and discouraged. It seemed like such a great opportunity to apply usability engineering the way it should be done, that is, over the course of the complete development life cycle and by the lead user interface designer. The project manager seemed to support this approach. But given what she perceived as the missing pieces in the project team (no business analysts) and project plan (no formal business analysis planned) and the lack of any one location with more than one potential end user to visit, it did not look like her tried and true methods of conducting a usability engineering requirements analysis based on business requirements, followed by user interface design, were going to work.

Questions

1. Elizabeth's first step would be to design the tailored materials she would use to conduct the above usability requirements analysis tasks. Given the lack of any business and functional requirements documentation present or planned, how might Elizabeth plan to get the information she needs (i.e., an identification of key user categories and characteristics, an overview of application functionality and a list of all—and key—user tasks, and a sense of the work environment parameters to research) to drive her design of tools to support the usability requirements analysis tasks she wants to conduct?
2. Given that there is never more than a single potential user in a given city, how could Elizabeth plan to conduct a cost- (and time-) effective usability requirements analysis without traveling all over the country?
3. Answer 1 points to some *advantages* of having SMEs on a project team. What are the potential *disadvantages* of having the three dedicated SMEs as a part of this project team, and how can Elizabeth plan to manage those disadvantages?

Project Execution

After the planning meeting, Elizabeth went back to her office and put together a usability engineering project plan based on the two premises that (1) she would draw on the SMEs to help her develop her usability requirements analysis tools and (2) she would administer these tools remotely using the users' shared website and the support of a high-level user manager, as well as the three SMEs, to motivate users' participation.

Given the difficulty and expense of getting multiple users to a single location as well as the usual budget and schedule constraints, and the general lack of understanding of the value of user-centered design techniques on her team, Elizabeth built just one usability test into her overall project plan, which she would plan to conduct in one-on-one face-to-face sessions with users. In her plan, the bulk of her time would be spent doing user interface design. She would rely on whatever data she could generate from her remote usability requirements analysis efforts and the ongoing availability of the three SMEs, plus her general design expertise, to draft a user interface design and hope that a single round of usability testing would be sufficient to refine it.

The remote usability requirements analysis approach succeeded well in generating user profile and work environment data from a good sized sample of the 35 users. About 20 users responded, probably due to the encouragement to do so from their known and fellow SMEs. It succeeded reasonably well in generating card sorting results and tasks scenarios from users, although Elizabeth believed these data were not as high quality and reliable as she would have gotten from in-context observations and interviews with users. She only got about 8 to 10 responses to each of these requests (perhaps because these tasks were more complex than simply filling out a questionnaire), and they did not always seem to follow her written instructions perfectly.

Elizabeth believed nevertheless that given the practical constraints of the project, she had done the best job she could generating valid and useful usability requirements analysis data. She also knew that her project SMEs would be able to help fill in gaps and provide additional insight into her data.

Elizabeth collated all the raw data she collected and then documented an analysis report that drew conclusions from the data in terms of user interface design implications. For example, Figure 10.1 presents an excerpt from her user profile questionnaire, including collated data (percentages of users selecting each multiple choice response).

Figure 10.2 shows some design implications she drew out of the above—and other—user profile data.

The card sorting data, limited though it was, did point toward some particular implications for designing the high-level information architecture for the application. Figure 10.3 presents an excerpt from Elizabeth's summary of her analysis of her card sorting data.

The following questions will tell us things we need to know about *you*:

11.   In particular, how much **experience using Microsoft Office products (i.e., Word, Excel, PowerPoint, and Access)** do you have?

        _____**None** (I have never used any of these particular MS Windows applications)
  4%___**Low** (I have used only 1, and I only use it infrequently)
13%___**Moderately Low** (I have used 2 or more, but I only use them infrequently)
39%___**Moderately High** (I have used 2 or more and I use at least 1 frequently)
43%___**High** (I have used 3 or more and I use at least 2 frequently)
       _____**Other** (please describe)_____
        I would like more computer training

12.   How would you describe your general level of **experience using Web sites and/or Web-based applications at work and/or at home?**

       _____**None** (I have never used any Web sites or Web-based applications)
  9%___**Low** (I have used only 1 or 2 Web sites/applications)
41%___**Moderately Low** (I have used between 3 and 10 different Web sites/applications)
27%___**Moderately High** (I have used between 11 and 20 different Web sites/applications)
23%___**High** (I have used over 20 different Web sites/applications)
       _____**Other** (please describe)_____

Figure 10.1. Excerpt from user profile questionnaire, including collated data (percentages of users selecting each multiple choice response).

DATA: 2/3 require vision correction

IMPLICATIONS: Adequate text and target sizes (at highest resolution anticipated)

DATA: Users are required NOT to be color blind. Most are currently women.

IMPLICATIONS: No special care need be taken in use of red and green.

DATA: Majority use 2 or more MS Office applications, at least 1 frequently, and have for years, and list them as their most commonly used applications. They tend to use them at home as well as at work.

IMPLICATIONS: Build on MS Windows Conceptual Model and/or conventions where applicable (e.g., assume familiarity with GUI widgets; could use a menu-bar like construct.)

DATA: Fully half indicate relatively low Web experience.

IMPLICATIONS: Do not assume familiarity with common Web conventions – make things as intuitive as possible (e.g., don't assume familiarity with Back button, provide comparable control on each page.)

Figure 10.2. Sample of design implications drawn from user profile data.

Four of the seven users used a **Data Type** organization as their top level category.

> Projects
> Events
> Media Contacts
> Documents
> Media Phonebook
> Speeches

Data Type categories can *also be seen as subcategories in two of the other three organizations.* For example, the one **High Level Task** organization (File vs. Retrieve) does make a distinction between Projects and Media Articles/Speeches (Data Types). One of two **Role/User** (Local vs. National) organizations also makes this same distinction.

Thus, probably a high level Task structure based on **Data Type** *would seem natural or at least understandable and usable to most users.*

There was very *little commonality* across the seven respondents in how the *Access [application] Data, Tracking,* and *Discuss/Share* tasks were located, and in many cases the users created *unique categories* for one or all of these tasks.

Thus, probably *these tasks should stand alone as top level categories* and not be grouped with any other tasks.

Figure 10.3. Excerpt from summary of card sorting data.

Finally, the task scenarios Elizabeth collected highlighted some clear implications for design, such as:

- The need to support switching back and forth between multiple ongoing tasks due to uncontrollable and regular interruptions.
- The need for integration of certain tasks (for example, generating an e-mail directly from a search result).
- The need for support for keeping track of ongoing tasks (e.g., "to do" list or calendar functionality), as often users needed to wait for hours or days for some feedback from a colleague or an appointment before being able to continue and complete a given task.

Figure 10.4 presents an excerpt from one task scenario that teases out the general types of subtasks going on in the task as a whole by tagging them with different text characteristics and also includes notes on the design implications of the scenario.

All the usability requirements analysis data collected would be invaluable in the design process, but Elizabeth still lacked a detailed functional specification—and for that matter even a clear overall scope of functionality—to guide her design process. So although she now had a much better understanding of the overall job that the application under development was meant to

Normal = communication
Bold = search/research
Italic = Document creation
ALL CAPS = TRAVEL/MEETINGS

1. After being contacted by the project manager about a fundraising event, **I queried [applications] to review available internal and media publicity. I reviewed the information and also learned that ABC Foundation was also co-sponsoring the event.**

    (Designer Notes: need for quick transition from notification to [application], without loss of view of notification data, and easy input of data from notification to [application] query screens.)

2. **I researched related media publicity** and advised HQ of the pending event and the national publicity implications due to the current national "hot issues" related to the project. **I also researched internal web sites for general information related to the project.**

    (Designer Notes: need for easy transition from database searches to email, without loss of view of database info so can transcribe easily to email.)

3. Upon learning the co-sponsoring foundation was not going to issue a press release, **I SAT IN ON THE EVENT. ALSO WHILE THE EVENT WAS ONGOING,** I informed a national reporter of the event details and progress.

    (Designer Notes: need for easy location of reporter contact info, and get hands quickly back on relevant info researched earlier.)

4. **At the completion of the event, I retrieved and reviewed all related prior press** *to complete a press release after the event.* After approved by co-sponsoring foundation, *made changes to the draft release,* and went directly to my manager for approval. *The release had to be re-typed because I did not have my laptop with me at the time.* At *this time,* I also learned the national reporter was on vacation. I subsequently followed up with a local reporter **and reviewed all the available data that I had gathered while** *preparing talking points for the project manager about the successful outcome of the event.*

    (Designer Notes: need for easy access to all data researched and pulled together on a prior occasion; need for easy location of reporter contact info, and get hands quickly back on relevant info researched earlier.)

Figure 10.4. Excerpt from one task scenario that teases out the general types of subtasks going on in the task as a whole by tagging them with different text characteristics; also includes notes on the design implications of the scenario.

support, she still did not have a very clear picture of which of the many user tasks she had data on would in fact be supported, and any of the details of those tasks.

For example, she knew that one main task would be to search a database for information in a half dozen distinct categories (e.g., projects, events, media contacts, etc.). However, she did not know (and neither did anyone else on the team) what the search criteria for each category of information should be or what data should be returned from a search within a given category.

Elizabeth's plan, however, had in fact cast her in the role of lead user interface designer, and now it was time to start generating a user interface design. Her usual method was to use a top-down approach to user interface design, starting with information architecture design, followed by a conceptual model design to support and present her information architecture, followed by detailed screen/page standards design, followed by complete detailed user interface design.

Questions

4. How can Elizabeth best proceed to conduct the user interface design process given the lack of detailed functional specification (or even high-level functional scoping) available, the lack of experience the development staff have working with a lead user interface designer or usability engineer, and the geographic disbursement of the team?

5. Elizabeth is taking a top-down approach to user interface design, as described in answer 4. She would prefer to conduct usability testing at each stage along the way. However, given that there will be only one opportunity to conduct a formal usability test one-on-one with users, at what point in the design/development process should Elizabeth plan to do this?

Epilogue

Elizabeth next proceeded to conduct the design process more or less as she planned. That is, she used iterative user interface paper prototyping and specification, a highly collaborative multidisciplinary team approach, and a top-down approach to design, to explore, flesh out, refine, and document both business/functional requirements and usability requirements simultaneously. The application turned out to be of only moderate complexity: The final user interface design involved perhaps 75 distinct basic screens, supporting about a dozen or so basic tasks, each with many variations possible. One such screen from a prototype is shown in Figure 10.5.

There were certainly bumps along the way. In the beginning, everyone else believed they too were user interface design experts—the developers because they had been designing user interfaces for all of their development careers and the SMEs because, in fact, they would themselves be users of the planned application and knew the work being automated inside and out. However, as the design process played out over time, everyone became clearer on their particular role on the team and everyone else's particular role and mutual respect and trust grew.

As the project progressed, Elizabeth's respect for her teammates grew considerably. The SMEs obviously represented the most competent of the user population and were a wealth of information and insight. The developers were highly skilled. All were highly motivated to achieve a high-quality outcome and demonstrated excellent team skills that they applied effectively to that purpose. Elizabeth believed she came to be similarly perceived by the

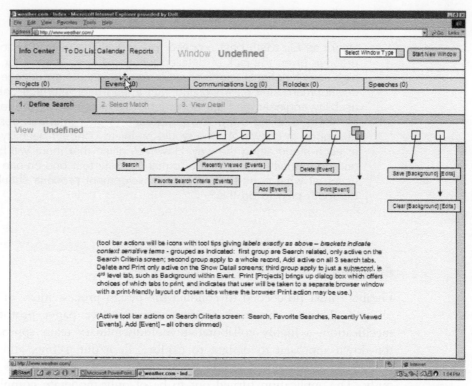

Figure 10.5. Sample final screen. Shown in gray tones: In actuality the darker gray background of the currently active tabs (Info Center, Projects, View Detail, Background) is a medium green, and the darker text in the "Window" and "View" status lines is a dark green.

other team members. The personalities in the overall team mixed well and everyone enjoyed the collaboration.

Initially, no one really understood the need for and value of Elizabeth's usability requirements analysis efforts and only went along with participating in these tasks because Pamela, the project manager, had dictated that these tasks be a part of the overall project plan. However, as the design was iterated on and Elizabeth continually brought discussion of design issues back to what the requirements analysis data pointed to, it became clearer and clearer to other team members what the point, and the value, of those activities—and the data they generated—were.

During the design process Elizabeth picked her battles carefully. She argued hard and drew on the support of the project manager to get acceptance of design decisions that she believed were fundamental to a successful information architecture and conceptual model design (e.g., basic consistency and simplicity), but when there was strong controversy over a design issue that she believed would be relatively easy to "fix" after even relatively late usability testing (e.g., some simple uses of color), she made concessions and let others sway the design decision. This way everyone felt their input was valued and that Elizabeth was a team player who valued others' input and expertise.

In design discussions Elizabeth constantly hammered on the need to maintain a simple and consistent conceptual model. Initially, everyone else tended to come up with design ideas for specific functions that did not take into account the developing overall conceptual model in the design. Their design ideas were often creative but arbitrary and inconsistent with one another. Initially, no one really "got" Elizabeth's obsession with simplicity and consistency. But after awhile the lead developer began to see that not only was this a usability plus, but it would make his life easier as well in terms of reusable code. He began to get invested in the conceptual model and became a strong supporter of Elizabeth's constant focus on making design decisions consistent with the established model.

By the time the team was ready to conduct a usability test, the whole team felt strong ownership of the current design and of the test results, and all attended the testing sessions. When many of Elizabeth's predictions were borne out by the testing results, respect and understanding of usability engineering methods increased even more within this project team.

The project then went into development, during which time Elizabeth was asked to write a user manual and develop a training program for the 35 users that would be taught by the three project SMEs just as the application launched. As she worked with the SMEs developing the training program, it finally began to dawn on them that the consistent and simple conceptual model Elizabeth had designed was going to make it much easier for them to teach users how to use the application as well as much easier for users to learn and remember how to use it.

Sometime later, the training was administered and the application was launched. User reaction was highly enthusiastic, both during training and over the first few months after launch. Because many other applications developed and launched at TTI had met with much less enthusiasm and success, this reaction further reinforced the value of user-centered design methods in TTI's development organization.

Questions

6. This project was a success, and looking back on the anxiety and uncertainty she had experienced when it began made Elizabeth feel especially pleased with its outcome. However, she was not so naive as to assume that her approach to integrating business and functional and usability requirements analyses on this particular project would work as well on any or all other software development projects. What specific aspects of this project, project team, and project approach likely contributed to the success of conducting high-level and detailed business and functional requirements and user interface requirements and design in parallel through an informal, highly iterative, and integrated process?

7. What different project circumstances might make this approach much riskier?

8. What are the particularly desirable aspects of the approach taken on this project (simultaneously iterating on business and functional and usability requirements through iterative user interface paper prototyping)?

Elizabeth looked at the 12 huge volumes Captain Ogden handed her with dismay. They would take her weeks to read and digest, and there might or might not be anything useful in them to guide her usability engineering work. Elizabeth needed a way to move forward.

Case 2: The City Police Department: Business Analysis Already Completed

Project Planning

Some time after her work with TTI, Elizabeth went to work for the police department of a very large city, which was referred to locally as the City Police Department, or CPD. She was hired by a police officer named Captain Ogden. Although CPD had a sizable internal Information Technology (IT) organization, Captain Ogden was not a member of it. He was a police officer with a lot of street experience who was rising through the managerial ranks of the department. Captain Ogden was a very intelligent man who had made it his business to educate himself on technology. He had managed to get support from high-level CPD management to be the project manager of a very large and high profile software development project and had learned much more about software development on the job while managing this project.

The goal of Captain Ogden's project was to build a very complex automated "inventory" system to inventory and track all the property (e.g., guns, drugs, house keys, wallets and their contents, cars) confiscated from prisoners or found and taken as evidence by CPD. The city had eight enormous warehouses that stored such property. All property, from guns and drugs to hair brushes and other personal effects, had to be inventoried and then tracked as it left the possession of prisoners or the sites where it was found, came into the station houses, went to the warehouses for storage, left the warehouses to go to labs for analyses and/or courtrooms as evidence, returned to the warehouses, and was ultimately returned to released prisoners, auctioned off, or disposed of. Currently, all property tracking was managed through a manual paper-based process that suffered from many problems and bottlenecks. Information was routinely captured incorrectly and often lost altogether.

The property inventory application being developed would be highly complex, both functionally and technically. The CPD had hired a well-established, very large, and very successful software development vendor, Software Development, Inc. (SDI), to collaborate with them. CPD would provide project management and business knowledge. SDI would provide technical expertise and actually build the application. The total project team of both CPD and SDI staff currently totaled about 35 people. It was expected to grow significantly larger—and more geographically dispersed—as the project went into the development phase.

During Elizabeth's initial meeting with Captain Ogden, he gave her a candid and detailed history of the project to date.

"We started this project about 5 years ago," said Captain Ogden. "It took us a couple of years just to generate a very high-level project definition, get approval for funding, and go through a bidding process to hire a software development contractor. At this point, we have a very thorough detailed functional specification and system architecture design, represented in these 12 documents here. These took us over 2 years to develop. We spent a lot of time in many of the station houses around the city, observing and interviewing cops and station house chiefs to explore functional requirements for this application." At this point Captain Ogden opened a couple of these huge volumes and fanned through the pages.

"These were prepared by business analysts from SDI working closely with me and others at CPD," said Captain Ogden. Elizabeth looked at the 12 huge volumes with dismay. They would take her weeks to read and digest, and there might or might not be anything useful in them to guide her usability engineering work.

"Is there anything in here that would describe user characteristics to me, like level of computer literacy, attitudes toward technology, educational level, and so on? And any place I can find something like use cases or representative user task descriptions, identifying and describing at a conceptual level some of the key types of tasks users would perform with this application?" she asked. "Also, any information describing the work environment in the station houses?"

"Well, hmm, no I don't think so," replied Captain Ogden with a frown. "But I can probably provide you with some information about the cops. I've been here for many years and I certainly know quite a few. And the types of tasks the application will support. And I can also describe a typical station-house environment to you; I've been in many of them."

"How many cops are there in CPD?" asked Elizabeth.

"About 56,000, located in about 50 precincts throughout the city, each with its own station house," replied Captain Ogden.

"At this point," continued Captain Ogden, "SDI has begun to generate prototypes that not only represent functionality and technical approaches, but also represent user interface design ideas for the application."

Captain Ogden took Elizabeth into another room and showed her several walls plastered with large pieces of paper, on which were recorded highly detailed and complex flowchart-like illustrations of a system-wide information architecture. He also showed her some online user interface prototypes that provided a glimpse into some of the user interface approaches being generated by SDI.

"The reason I want your involvement," said Captain Ogden, pausing to close the door and lowering his voice, "is that I have a very good sense of the cops who will use this application, since I have been one of them for years. I just know instinctively that these user interface designs SDI is developing will simply not be usable to these users. They are not at all self-explanatory, and they assume a lot of general computer literacy, and familiarity with Microsoft Windows in particular, that these users simply do not have. Cops will be using this software very infrequently, under extremely stressful conditions that these software developers just are not tuned in to. I just know if we go with the design that is currently developing, this application, like so many before it, will be a complete failure."

"The other thing I know," he continued, "is that this project is a very, very high-risk one. It will cost CPD millions upon millions of dollars to develop, and I believe a very high degree of usability is absolutely critical to its success. I don't know much about your field of usability engineering, but I have skimmed a book or two on the subject that I happened to find in the computer section of a local bookstore. I know from what little I have read that usability engineering is exactly what I need, and I have funding to support it. I know that usability will make or break this project. That is why I have brought you in."

"Tell me a little about these users, these 56,000 cops, and about the key tasks they do that your application must support, and the work environment they will do them in," said Elizabeth.

Captain Ogden's face brightened. Clearly, he delighted in how well he knew the CPD and enjoyed sharing his knowledge. "Well, in a nutshell," he began, "CPD cops are all over the map in terms of computer literacy. Many have not even used department applications at all and have no computer experience from school, at home, or from any other job. Some may be somewhat computer savvy for whatever reasons, but they did not get it on the job. All 56,000 cops, however, will be expected to use this application.

"The tasks they do that our application will support are primarily inventorying property that they bring in as a part of an arrest. The problem is, the inventory requirements can be extremely complex—it might take 20 different paper forms to document a single gun correctly and completely, for example—and they only do an inventory task very infrequently, say, on average, once every 3 or 4 months.

"In addition, when it comes time to do one of these inventory tasks, it may be 2 a.m. on a Saturday night in August, 90 degrees in the un–air-conditioned station house, and they may have a psychotic prisoner handcuffed to one wrist! The station house is often very noisy, with the public in there with crying babies and boom boxes and lots of other activity going on . . . these guys are often under a great deal of stress, distraction, and interruption when they need to do these tasks.

"And," Captain Ogden continued, "no one taught them how to do inventory tasks correctly in the first place, and they don't do it frequently enough to remember how to do it when they have not done it in several months. They may even have multiple types of property they have never had to inventory before. So, as you can imagine, an intuitive, self-explanatory, and easy-to-remember user interface is key here!"

"Wow!" exclaimed Elizabeth. "If ever there was an application for which usability was critical, this sounds like it!" And, she thought to herself, this project manager is a rare one, who, with minimal exposure to the field of usability engineering, actually "gets it." Next she asked, "Do CPD IT or SDI have any usability engineers on staff?"

"CDP IT certainly doesn't!" exclaimed Captain Ogden with a rueful laugh. "I think SDI might," he continued, "but none is assigned to this project. And I don't think any SDI staff members assigned to my project have ever worked with one. Anyway, I would like to have someone outside SDI, who will be more objective, provide me with user interface design advice."

"I am just curious," said Elizabeth, "how come this project is not being conducted within CPD's IT department?"

Captain Ogden replied again with a rueful laugh. "To be honest," he said, "the CPD, like most large metropolitan police departments, is a pretty peculiar and dysfunctional organization. But our IT department is particularly ineffective. They have a long history of producing very buggy, unreliable, and ineffective software applications. The cops *hate* their software applications. They are expected to learn to use new applications on their own on a moment's notice, with no training provided. The applications—which they are required to use—are totally unusable and regularly crash and fail. It's been a long history of one disaster after another. It really adds to the already stressful life of a cop. CPD IT is also a very political and poorly managed organization. I didn't want to work within that organization, and I managed to get support to lead this project on my own outside of CPD IT. Of course, CPD IT is not happy about this, and would love to see me fail!"

Questions

9. Given:
   - the long history (several years!) of this project before Elizabeth was brought in,
   - the extensive business and functional requirements analysis already complete and extensively documented,
   - the ready availability of experienced business analysts on the project team,
   - the multiple organizations making up the project team,
   - the fact that a fair amount of user interface design has already been generated and prototyped,

- the team's complete lack of experience with and understanding of usability engineering,
- and any other factors that seem relevant,

should Elizabeth include in her usability project plan a set of usability requirements analysis tasks, which are bound to be perceived by many as redundant with the extensive business requirements analyses and user interface design already completed?

10. If Elizabeth decides to include rigorous usability requirements analysis tasks in her usability engineering project plan, how can she best make the case to justify what will likely be perceived by many, including already hostile end users, as redundant with tasks already heavily invested in and completed?

Project Execution

After her initial meeting with Captain Ogden, Elizabeth sat down to generate a high-level plan for the requirements analysis phase of her overall usability engineering project plan to support this project. She did indeed plan to use the most rigorous available techniques for studying users, their tasks, and their work environment.

First, she would develop, distribute, and then collate and analyze data from a user profile questionnaire administered to actual end users to obtain accurate user profile data key to driving her later user interface design efforts. One thing she learned from her conversations with Captain Ogden was that in fact, the users of the new application would not be just police officers working the streets. Users would also include the station-house chiefs (who played the role of overseeing everything that went on in the station houses, including property inventorying), property managers (responsible for actually transporting property out of the station houses to the warehouses and back), and station-house clerks (who would often perform data entry tasks after policemen filled out paperwork manually).

In addition, Elizabeth would visit a number of station houses around the city both to collect representative user task scenarios by observing and interviewing users on the job and to collect data on the range of work environments the new application would be used within.

As Captain Ogden listened to Elizabeth's description of the in-context task analysis observations and interviews she would want to conduct at station houses, he commented, "There is one little problem there. Property inventory tasks occur in an entirely unpredictable way. They don't happen unless there is an arrest or stolen or lost property is found and brought in. We have no control over this and also no control over how much and what type of property might be brought in. So, it's a bit of a crapshoot on what you might get to observe when we visit station houses. This work is simply not scheduled and predictable!"

Elizabeth also planned to spend time with some users in the station-house environments to conduct a card sorting exercise aimed at extracting some application information architecture ideas directly from end users. Now it was time to actually plan in detail and carry out each of these usability requirements analysis techniques.

Questions

11. Given that there are 56,000 potential end users for this application, how should Elizabeth go about obtaining representative *user profile* data from a questionnaire?

12. Given the hostility of end users to any IT efforts based on a long past history, how can Elizabeth ensure a good rate of return on her user profile questionnaire?

13. Given that there are 56,000 potential end users for this application, dozens of user sites (i.e., station houses), and a huge variety of property inventory tasks that occur unpredictably, how should Elizabeth go about conducting a representative *task analysis* and *work environment analysis*?

14. How can Elizabeth address the user hostility to IT staff and efforts to get cooperation and accomplish effective information gathering during her task analysis (and later usability testing) visits to the station houses?

Epilogue

Elizabeth carried out her requirements analysis phase quite successfully. She got a 100% return on her user questionnaire (almost unheard of, but clearly because the request came from the commissioner himself, which in effect made it a direct order). She carried out several rounds of contextual observations and managed in the process to gradually start to win over the hostile user population, who were in fact very receptive to the user-centered approach that was so foreign to them.

Captain Ogden and his management were very happy with the requirements analysis documents Elizabeth wrote up based on an analysis of all her raw data. The SDI staff, although still somewhat threatened, could not help but see the value of this objective and relevant data and, at any rate, reported into CPD and thus had to go along with Captain Ogden's directives.

Thus Elizabeth next went into the design phase of the project. She generated a high-level design that mainly focused on information architecture and conceptual model design (and that was radically different from the user interface designs that had been generated by SDI) and had a prototype built that also incorporated some tentative screen design details. She ran one round of formal usability testing, right in the station houses with the prototype on a laptop, and this further generated positive attitude change within the user population. She redesigned the user interface as indicated by the usability test results, continued to work more on the screen design standards and some detailed design, and was preparing to get a prototype update and planning a second round of usability testing.

All was going well until, most unfortunately, SDI got fired for running way over budget and schedule and ultimately the entire project got canceled.

Summary

The two cases presented in this chapter, TTI and the CPD, represent two extremes of the integration of usability requirements analysis and business and functional requirements analysis.

To sum up the case of TTI:

- No business requirements analysis had been done at the time the usability engineer joined the project.
- The usability engineer was expected to participate heavily in the business requirements analysis, as it unfolded in an unstructured and informal way across the design and development phases of the project.
- No project team members had any particular background in business analysis.
- The project team was small and cohesive.
- Users were available and cooperative.
- Functionality was only moderately complex.
- The two types of requirements analyses were conducted very much in parallel by the same staff members, and this worked rather well in the end on this particular project.

In contrast, to sum up the CPD project:

- A very detailed and thorough business and functional requirements analysis had been invested in and heavily documented well before the usability engineer got involved in the project.
- The usability engineer had to conduct a completely separate and unintegrated usability requirements analysis effort *after* an extensive business and functional requirements analysis was completed.
- Potentially, there would be resistance to conducting a rigorous usability requirements effort, because it likely would be perceived as redundant with and even competitive with the business and functional requirements analysis already heavily invested in.
- The project team was large and divisive.
- The application was extremely complex.
- Users were accessible but hostile.
- On the other hand, given that there were no problematic schedule or budget constraints and there was adequate support from high levels for conducting a rigorous usability requirements analysis, in the end both analyses succeeded in their purposes, although perhaps not as cost and time effectively as might have been possible.

What these two cases represent is a currently unresolved methodologic issue in the field of usability engineering: How can usability requirements analysis techniques be optimally integrated with business and functional requirements analysis techniques, under varying project circumstances such as functional complexity, project team size, overall software development methodology, and so forth so that there is minimal real or perceived redundancy of effort but both usability and business and functional requirements are adequately revealed in a cost- and time-effective manner?

Further Reading

Beyer, H., and Holtzblatt, K. (1998). *Contextual design*. San Francisco: Morgan Kaufmann Publishers.

Hackos, J. T., and Redish, J. C. (1998). *User and task analysis for interface design*. New York: John Wiley & Sons.

Mayhew, D. J. (1999). *The usability engineering lifecycle*. San Francisco: Morgan Kaufmann Publishers.

Mayhew, D. J. (2001). *Investing in requirements analysis*. Available at http://www.taskz.com/ucd_invest_req_analysis_indepth.php

Tullis, T., and Wood, L. E. (2004). *How many users are enough for a card-sorting study?* Poster presented at the Annual Meeting of the Usability Professionals Association, June 10–12, Minneapolis, Minnesota. Available at http://websort.net/articles/Tullis&Wood.pdf

Wixon, D. R., and Ramey, J. (Eds.). (1996). *Field methods casebook for software design*. New York: John Wiley & Sons.

CASE 11

A Case Study in Personas

Robert Barlow-Busch, Quarry Integrated Communications

> *"Do you like going to the movies?" Roberta asked. Joanne nodded. "Okay, in a good movie it doesn't take long before you form an impression of the main character, right? That impression sets expectations of how the character will behave throughout the story." Joanne wondered where Roberta was going with this but hung with her, waiting for an explanation.*

Introducing the Idea of Personas

"I can't believe I did that!"

Joanne March worked hard to suppress a laugh as she watched Mike Rugatino grin sheepishly. After an hour of sitting in the dark and trying to be as quiet as possible, Mike had embarrassingly smacked his head against the observation window when he stood up abruptly for a better look at the focus group on the other side of the glass. Several participants turned at the sudden drum-like noise from the mirror they'd forgotten about until then.

Joanne allowed herself a quiet chuckle. She really couldn't fault Mike for his enthusiasm. The enthusiasm at ClickDox was contagious, and for good reason. They had a team of 25 clever motivated people backed by a healthy bank account thanks to their venture capital investors. Eight months earlier, ClickDox had been established by a group of Information Technology experts who'd worked together in the document management industry. They saw an opportunity to create a new business that focused on exchanging documents over the Internet with complete security. At the time, articles published in business magazines had raised concerns that documents sent online could easily be intercepted or "sniffed" by hackers.

The founders of ClickDox had a very specific plan: within 2 years they wanted to sell the business to a major courier such as FedEx, UPS, or DHL, who would by then be feeling the negative impact on their business of people's changing behaviors. ClickDox was certain that in the Internet age people would no longer ship documents across the country on a truck or an airplane but would do so with the click of a button—and they'd be willing to pay for a private secure service that would do this.

Joanne March was a Director in ClickDox's marketing group. She reported to Mike Rugatino. Mike and Joanne had worked together for several years previously, and when he joined ClickDox it didn't take long before he'd phoned Joanne with an offer she couldn't refuse. "My time is spent working on overall strategy with senior executives. I need someone I can trust to oversee our product and marketing tactics. That's why I'm calling you." Joanne accepted the offer happily.

Joanne chuckled again as Mike rubbed his forehead. On the other side of the glass, the moderator was wrapping up the last of eight focus groups they'd conducted across the country. Today's sessions had echoed much of what she'd heard in the past month. ClickDox's business idea seemed on the mark: Security was a real concern for people, and they seemed willing to pay for a service that lets them send and receive documents through a highly secure website.

That evening, in a taxi en route to the airport, Mike's mobile phone rang. "It's Jason," he told Joanne after glancing at the caller identification.

Jason was a founding partner at ClickDox. He called to inform Mike that he'd hired a consulting company named Blade Technology to advise them on the network infrastructure behind ClickDox's service. From the beginning, the ClickDox founders envisioned a private network of high-speed pipelines and secure data centers across the United States, eventually reaching into Europe and Asia. But Mike knew that ClickDox needed more than technology to succeed. He'd seen enough projects fail to realize that the best technology means nothing if people don't want to use it.

Mike knew it was up to him and Joanne to make sure the market *wanted* their service. Joanne would be in charge of overseeing the design of Click-Dox's website, where customers would upload and download their deliveries, but she needed a team of design experts to pull it off. That meant hiring a consultant, just as Jason had done. And Mike knew who to choose: an agency named Digital Rockit with a team specializing in web design and usability.

Mike had worked with Digital Rockit at his previous job and had been impressed.

He and Joanne discussed this idea and by the time they'd arrived at the airport had already reached Digital Rockit on the phone. They scheduled a few days the following week to kick off the project at ClickDox's offices in San Francisco.

Digital Rockit arrived the next week, fully briefed thanks to several phone calls with Joanne. She was pleased to meet them in person: Greg Bongo, Director of User Experience, and Roberta Meester, their senior designer.

"Mike's mandate to us is pretty clear," Joanne explained. "ClickDox's goal is to be bought by an established courier, so we need to capture market share and showcase a world-class website. The website has to be good enough that FedEx or UPS would be happy to take it over with minimal work aside from rebranding it."

Roberta glanced at Greg before replying. "From what you described last week, it seems like back-end technology is really steering the ship at Click-Dox now. But the front-end website will have a tremendous impact on reaching those goals. FedEx and UPS are mature companies with mature markets. For ClickDox to appeal to them, the technology will have to serve customers—not the other way around."

"That's right," Greg continued. "And given how the market is growing, I suspect it's important for ClickDox to launch with a really solid product. Competitors are showing up already, and you'll get lost in the noise unless it's a stand-out offering from day one."

Joanne was quite aware of that. Over the past couple of months it seemed like electronic delivery companies were appearing every week. There was a rising pressure for ClickDox to get to market soon—very soon.

"Mike and I feel the same way," Joanne confirmed. "We need to be 'best in class' right out of the gate—but we also need to get out the gate right away! That's the challenge." She glanced at her watch and anxiously continued. "We'd better get moving. Our first stakeholder interview is in less than 5 minutes."

Digital Rockit had wanted to kick off the project by interviewing over a dozen stakeholders at ClickDox, from people in senior management to the consultants from Blade. "This really helps us understand what to expect and how our work fits into ClickDox's overall business goals. It's a great way to get everyone's ideas on the table, too, and get them involved in what we're doing," Roberta had explained in their first conference call. Digital Rockit's first day was booked solid with these interviews, which Joanne had managed to schedule.

Greg and Roberta had a few high-level questions that guided each interview:

- Who exactly are ClickDox's customers? What can you tell me about them?
- What activities will customers perform on the ClickDox website? Which are most important?
- What impact will the website have on ClickDox's business?
- What challenges do you expect we'll face in this project?
- How will you know if this project is successful? What can we measure?
- What really excites you about ClickDox overall?

Joanne enjoyed these interviews. They prompted ideas from her coworkers that she'd never heard before. She felt great about everyone's passions for ClickDox's success but was struck by the wide range of answers she'd heard to Digital Rockit's questions. She felt a bit uneasy about that, actually.

"We noticed that too," said Greg. "It's really important to get everyone on the same page. We'll be able to move more quickly if everyone agrees on exactly what we're building and for whom." He hesitated for a moment. "Roberta and I have talked about this and have something we'd like to propose."

Joanne looked at them expectantly.

"We know you've done lots of focus groups already," Roberta explained, "but we'd like to do a bit more research before starting to design." Joanne's dismay must have shown on her face, as Roberta quickly continued. "This will be something entirely different, and we're not talking about month's worth of work. Our suggestion is to go deep with a small set of customers. Instead of getting their reactions to the *idea* of ClickDox—which is what the focus groups have done—we'll collect richer information about their *goals* and actual *behaviors* around exchanging documents."

Joanne still looked concerned as Greg continued. "We'll create models to capture and share what we learn. Here are some examples." Greg gestured to his laptop's screen. "They're called 'personas,' and they actually look like descriptions of real people. But they're composites that represent significant patterns across groups of customers." (See Figure 11.1.)

Joanne was intrigued. These personas contained a lot of information and they seemed so . . . well, so real.

Figure 11.1. The personas that Greg showed to Joanne all have a similar format. They include a name, a photo, a few high-level goals, a representative quote or two, a story that describes the person, and a few short lists with additional facts. (Created by Robert Barlow-Busch and/or Quarry Integrated Communications.)

"It's a neat idea, making up these characters. But why go through the effort? You could present the same information in a simple report."

"Yes, we could. But there's something powerful about personifying customers," Roberta answered. "This format engages people. It helps them to empathize with customers in a way that reports don't."

"There's something else we've noticed too," said Greg. "Reports are collections of facts that tend to stand alone, whereas personas weave those same facts into an actual *character*. When a character is well defined, we're able to predict how that person might behave in new situations. So we get value from personas beyond the plain facts they contain."

"Do you like going to the movies?" Roberta asked. Joanne nodded. "Okay, in a good movie it doesn't take long before you form an impression of the main character, right? That impression sets expectations of how the character will behave throughout the story. Personas take advantage of this effect. They help customers to come alive for the project team."

Joanne considered this. After the interviews they'd just completed, she could imagine the value of having such a clear picture of the potential Click-Dox customer. But more research? She didn't know what to think about that.

Greg cut into her thoughts. "This can do a lot to get everyone at Click-Dox on the same page. And it'll get everyone thinking about *customers* too, instead of just the technology."

Roberta continued. "They'll help to guide us as we design the website. Without understanding customers at this level, we'll make decisions based on how we'd imagine using it ourselves—and we've seen how many opinions people have about that! There's a risk the final website might look like something designed by committee."

This point made sense to Joanne, but she had a few questions. "What information are you looking for that we haven't already heard in the focus groups? And how do you collect it—through surveys or more focus groups?"

Greg started with Joanne's last question. "No, we won't do more focus groups. We'll avoid self-reported data whenever possible, in fact. The idea is to spend time face-to-face with customers in the field, wherever they'd normally use ClickDox. We'll interview them and—most importantly—observe their behaviors related to document exchange. It's a form of ethnographic research. It lets us learn what people *actually* do instead of what they say they do. There's often a surprising difference."

"Okay," Joanne nodded. "What would you hope to learn?"

Greg and Roberta explained that they wanted information on three main areas:

1. What are people's overall job *goals*? By understanding what fundamentally motivates people, we can design ClickDox's website so it helps them achieve something important.
2. What's the *context* in which they'd use ClickDox? By understanding the many factors that influence people on the job, we can design ClickDox so it feels like it was made just for them. For instance, are they interrupted often? Is their environment calm or noisy? Do people work alone or with a tight-knit team?
3. What are their current *behaviors* around document exchange? By understanding how people get things done today, we can design ClickDox to help them do it better.

Joanne paged through the personas that Digital Rockit had created for other clients. She could imagine how these would be useful tools. Mike would be on board too, Joanne suspected, as the personas should help him get the management team talking about customers instead of their network infrastructure. However, the IT folks would be hugely skeptical; they'd already shown little interest in the focus group results, and this would obviously take time to complete—and they were pushing to release something right away. However, with the wide range of opinions she'd heard from her colleagues, Joanne knew they needed to align the team or ClickDox would fall short of its business goals.

"How much time will this take?" she asked.

"That depends on how many people we visit and whether we can find them easily," answered Roberta. "We'll probably need a month from start to finish, though we usually plan on 4 to 6 weeks total. That provides a buffer in case we run into snags."

"Ouch, that's gonna be tough," Joanne winced. "But this is an interesting idea. Let me think about it. I'll talk to Mike, too. I'm meeting him first thing tomorrow morning."

Questions

1. When is it appropriate to create personas for a project?
2. What kind of information should personas contain?
3. How could Joanne, Greg, and Roberta set up this project for success, especially knowing there are skeptics at ClickDox?

Planning the Field Research

"You want the good news or the bad news?" Joanne asked Greg and Roberta the next morning. They glanced at each other warily. "Give us the good news," Roberta decided.

"Okay. Mike loves the idea of these personas," said Joanne with a smile on her face.

"Excellent!" Greg paused. "So . . . what's the bad news?"

"Well," Joanne hesitated. "We're under huge time pressure. We need to wrap this up within 3 weeks. We might be able to stretch it to 4, but I'd rather not."

"Yikes! That could be tough," Greg grimaced. He took a breath and continued. "Let's put a plan together and see how it looks. If we can recruit people quickly, we might be able to do it."

Roberta nodded thoughtfully and then made a suggestion. "We should at least discuss the option of creating assumptive personas," she said carefully. "I don't think it's the best choice here, but if time is really short . . ." she trailed off.

"What are assumptive personas?" Joanne asked.

"They're personas based entirely on information gathered from existing research—and from people's *opinions* inside the organization," Greg explained. "They can be created quickly: Within a week we could hold some workshops to gather the information and then craft some personas to illustrate the results. The drawback is they won't be as rich and may not reflect reality, as we'd be relying on second-hand data instead of observing customers ourselves. I'm pretty sure that assumptive personas would hold little authority with the ClickDox team."

"Yes, that would be a problem," Joanne said. "We've already seen a wide range of opinions across the team. That's what led you to suggest doing personas in the first place!"

Roberta agreed. "I think we need to get into the field. I want customers to show us what they're *really* doing in terms of document exchange; otherwise, any incorrect assumptions will be baked into our work. We need some behavioral data to help validate and enrich your findings from the focus groups."

With that decision made, the trio faced their first challenge in planning the field research: deciding which customers to involve. Joanne scribbled out a short list of industries that seemed the most promising candidates:

- Insurance
- Legal
- Health care
- Civil engineering
- Manufacturing
- Architecture
- Professional services (such as marketing, consulting, real estate, etc.)

"From what we've learned, it seems there are two key groups of people within each of these industries: those who will actually *use* ClickDox and those who will *support* it," Roberta said. "So we're talking about the end users who create and send documents and the IT folks who purchase and support tools such as ClickDox. Is that correct?"

"I'd say so," Joanne confirmed. "The end users are probably more important, as the executives who'd authorize the purchase would be users themselves. But IT can veto the purchase if the system asks too much of them or if they don't trust it."

"We'll need to spend some time with both groups, then." Greg put the finishing touches on a sketch before showing them what he'd drawn. "Here's a matrix of the customers we could potentially visit. Experience tells us that we need to visit between four and six people per cell; after that number we're usually able to identify the core patterns." (See Figure 11.2.)

	End Users	IT Support
Insurance	4–6	4–6
Legal	4–6	4–6
Healthcare	4–6	4–6
Civil Engineering	4–6	4–6
Manufacturing	4–6	4–6
Architecture	4–6	4–6
Professional Services	4–6	4–6

Figure 11.2. Greg's sketch of the potential customer groups to research, showing the number of people to visit in each. There's not enough time to research them all. So how will they decide? (Created by Robert Barlow-Busch.)

Greg gave the others a moment to review the sketch. "Since we have at most 4 weeks to complete our research and create the personas, we don't have time to visit 84 people. Besides, that might be overkill even if we *had* the time. So let's focus our thinking." He elaborated with the following questions:

- Are any of these customers particularly good or bad targets for some business reason?
- Would any of these customers impose requirements that are exceptionally unique to their needs?
- On the other hand, would any of these customers be a strong "proving ground" for the product concept?

Joanne thought for a few moments. "Well, I don't think insurance or legal would be good choices right now. We see these as becoming a huge part of our business in the future, but it'll be a few years before they make the switch. The main reason they send documents is to obtain signatures—but there's no technology or standards in place yet to determine how digital signatures will work. Until a standard emerges, those markets are high risk."

"That makes sense," Greg observed. "For similar reasons, I suspect health care would be a bad choice too. Didn't someone tell us that government regulations have put a big question mark over how patient records will be sent electronically?" Joanne nodded.

"Okay, that narrows the list," remarked Roberta. "We're left with engineering, manufacturing, architecture, and professional services."

Over the next hour the group talked about their choices and got Mike Rugatino on the phone for his input. In the end they decided to focus on two industries: civil engineering and architecture. Everyone believed these choices would be an excellent proving ground for the basic ClickDox concept. They shipped a lot of documents every day, mostly CAD (computer-aided design) drawings of buildings and bridges and such, and security was a big concern according to research. Mike and Joanne were comfortable that a product designed for these industries would lay the groundwork that could help them move into future markets, including legal and insurance.

After some quick calculations, Roberta suggested the following plan:

- One week for planning and recruiting participants.
- One week for conducting the field research.
- One week for analysis and creation of the personas.
- One week contingency in case anything goes wrong.

"It might be hard to finish our recruiting within a week because it's such short notice," warned Roberta. "But we'll give it a shot. We'll get some help from other people at Digital Rockit, and they can continue making calls even when we're in the field—if it comes to that."

A total of 20 participants would be recruited. At four different companies, they would find 12 end users and 8 people from IT support. To save time they would visit only two cities: ClickDox's hometown of San Francisco and Toronto, Ontario, where Digital Rockit had their headquarters. Hopefully their local networks would allow them to recruit participants quickly.

This was a tight schedule but entirely feasible. The key would be sending two research teams into the field, with two people per team. Each team would have to conduct only 10 interviews over the course of a week. Their original idea was to dedicate one team per city, but after talking it over they decided to stick together and set aside one day for traveling between cities. The teams would switch up regularly, giving everyone a chance to work with each other. However, for this plan to succeed, they needed another researcher.

Joanne had an immediate suggestion. "Tell you what. Let me see if Dimitri Ragnus is available. It's important that we work together with him, and you suggested earlier that we get one of the skeptics involved. . . ."

Dimitri was the Chief Technology Officer of Blade Technology, the company hired to consult on ClickDox's network infrastructure. He was a brilliant computer scientist, had the respect of everyone in senior management, and was a very outspoken person. His opinions carried a lot of weight; however, he was of the opinion that ClickDox should be building their website already, because the requirements were obvious. They certainly seemed obvious to him.

"If we get Dimitri on our side, that would be terrific," agreed Greg. "He obviously knows the domain well, so his insights will be useful. And it'll be great for him to 'experience the customer's experience' as we say. He's so focused on technology that it would be a refreshing change of perspective for him. See if you can get him involved, Joanne, and Roberta and I will get some other details in place."

Over the next few days Roberta co-opted a few of her colleagues at Digital Rockit to help recruit participants for the following week. It required a lot of phone calls and sweet-talking past receptionists to find the right people, but once they did a surprising number were happy to participate, even given the short notice. Getting paid $200 for 2 hours of time was definitely an incentive, but Roberta had briefed everyone on how to sell the project. "We're in the early stages of designing a new service for sending and receiving documents over the Internet," they explained on the phone. "It's targeted for people in your industry specifically. Would you be interested in an opportunity to really influence how this product would work?" The secret was in offering an opportunity, not asking for help. Lots of people were interested and by the end of the week nearly all their participants had been lined up.

Meanwhile, Greg had put together a research plan. "These are not highly scripted interviews," he explained to Joanne. "They're more like conversations about a series of topics." Greg's plan identified the topics they wanted to explore and illustrated each with a handful of questions. But the expectation was they'd learn the really interesting stuff on the fly, by asking probing questions in response to what participants said—and especially by asking for demonstrations. "Don't necessarily believe what people *say* they do," reminded Greg. "Our goal is to observe what they *actually* do."

Some of their research topics were general and would apply in almost any project. Others were specific to this particular domain:

Shipping practices
- What are the various means by which you send and receive documents? (*Observe them in action.*)
- How do you decide whether to ship electronically, by mail, by courier, or by some other means?

Electronic file exchange
- What kinds of files do you exchange with other people electronically? (*Obtain samples if possible.*)
- Let's walk through the process of how you send a document electronically. (*You could create a scenario by offering your business card and asking them to send you something.*)

Joanne had been successful in getting Dimitri to join them. The four got together for a morning of orientation, training, and rehearsals. Digital Rockit ran a series of workshop-style exercises to help Joanne and Dimitri understand their roles and learn some basic interviewing and observational skills. Greg and Roberta would each lead one of the teams, so Joanne and Dimitri were to act mostly as note-takers, although they were free to ask questions of the participant if they wanted. Dimitri was certainly an outspoken man—but he was friendly and easygoing and, though quite skeptical of what they'd learn, curious to see how things unfolded. As an outside consultant, he was pleased to be invited to participate.

"I promise to hold back on my own opinions, at least during our interviews," Dimitri assured the group. "But afterward, you'd better believe I'll have something to say!" Everyone chuckled. It was clear you'd always know where Dimitri stood on an issue.

Questions

4. What ideas can you think of for reducing the time or money required to perform this research?
5. Greg identified some research topics that are specific to this project, such as *shipping practices* and *electronic file exchange*. If you were conducting research for personas, what general topics would you explore with participants, regardless of the product domain? Provide some example questions for each.

Conducting the Field Research

Roberta could hardly believe they had completed half the interviews already. Earlier today, they'd flown to Toronto after an exhausting 2 days visiting customers in San Francisco. To her delight things had gone quite well. Joanne was a natural at this sort of work, but even Dimitri found his groove on the second day. The first day was bit rough for Dimitri, as he tended to influence participants with his comments and questions, so Greg had needed to explain.

"When the woman this morning demonstrated her FTP system, you interrupted at one point with a comment like, 'That seems ridiculous! Why would you do it that way?' I'm not sure you noticed, but she seemed kind of embarrassed. It took a while for her to open up again."

"I suppose it seemed like I was accusing her. I wasn't, of course!" Dimitri loudly insisted. "I was just annoyed at the stupid system she was forced to work with."

In the end, because he was so outspoken, Dimitri found it easiest to remain mostly silent, recording notes and snapping photos when appropriate. The team was collecting photos of the people they interviewed and of their environments (Figure 11.3); so far, only a few participants were uncomfortable with the idea. Later, these photos would help everyone to remember their visits much better—and to illustrate their findings for the benefit of people at ClickDox who didn't participate in the field research.

Today, Roberta and Joanne were visiting two people at Laney Architecture. They had two interviews lined up, one with an architect named Yoko Hamachi and one with the IT technician. They had really wanted to meet with Richard Laney, the business owner, but he was already impatient at having them take up several hours of time with two of his employees. "I'll give you 10 minutes before you leave, if I'm not in a meeting. Okay?" They had agreed. Richard didn't give them much of a choice.

Yoko was a terrific person to interview. They knew she would be, as Yoko had participated in one of ClickDox's focus groups last month. Joanne remembered Yoko as an energetic well-spoken woman who'd made some great contributions, so she recruited her for these interviews as well. Roberta agreed that Yoko seemed like a good candidate but had cautioned about doing this too often. "We want to see the broadest possible range of behaviors, so it's generally best to recruit people we haven't seen before," she explained. "But Yoko seems to match our idea of an ideal customer—and it would be interesting to learn more about her. Let's make an exception in her case."

Figure 11.3. After a few days of interviews, it can be difficult to keep them straight in your head. Photos such as these can help to cue your memory, making it easier to remember who you visited, what you observed, and what you learned. (Photos downloaded from www.flickr.com.)

About half an hour into their visit with Yoko, Roberta asked if it would be possible to get a copy of some building plans they'd been discussing. In addition to the photos they were collecting, the team liked to get copies of artifacts such as this to help illustrate the sorts of materials people were actually sending.

"Sure thing!" Yoko agreed. "What's your e-mail address?"

Roberta gave her a business card and watched intently as Yoko opened Microsoft Outlook, created a new message, addressed it to her, and attached a PDF of the building plans. A click later and the document was off to Roberta's inbox.

This was very interesting. And highly representative of a pattern she'd observed with their participants in San Francisco. Although these people were aware that e-mail attachments were completely insecure—and the documents they sent were, technically, supposed to be kept secure—they were casually sending documents as attachments all the time. Yoko was an especially interesting case, because in the focus group she'd been quite clear that attachments were a bad idea.

Roberta broached the subject carefully, because she didn't want to make Yoko feel defensive. She asked a few easy questions about how many e-mails Yoko deals with each day. She then asked how Yoko decides when to send files as attachments versus other options.

In the end, Yoko admitted that she shouldn't be sending files as attachments. But she does, and so does everyone else in the office. Each of their clients has a dedicated, secure FTP server set up for the purpose of exchanging files, but the only times she uses it is when a file is larger than 5 MB, which is their limit for attachments.

"Attachments are so convenient," Yoko explained. "I just create a new e-mail, type a message, attach the file, and it's done. No hassle. And importantly, a copy is automatically kept in my Sent Items folder." She paused for a few moments, staring at her screen. "Now that I'm looking at it, I suppose you could say Outlook serves as an archive and case history for my projects. I hadn't mentioned this before, but I usually copy myself on everything I send; I'll then file that message in my project folder. Everything important goes through here, and it's at my fingertips every moment of the day."

Yoko glanced at her interviewers and gave a conspiratorial grin. "I know security is important, but really . . . it's not like we're building the space shuttle! Does it really matter if someone gets their hands on this plan for a new restaurant? I doubt it. And our clients have never complained. They send us attachments too!"

That night over dinner at a sushi restaurant that Greg had steered them toward, the two interview teams swapped stories of what they'd observed that day. The big news was what everyone perceived as an emerging pattern, with potentially serious ramifications: the fact that people seemed, in reality, to be far less concerned with security than previous research had indicated. Yoko was the shining example, as someone who'd promoted the idea of security during a focus group but turned out, in fact, not really to care—or at least to care about other issues much more.

"This sounds like a textbook example of the difference between what people say and what they do," Greg speculated. "You know, security is something that people aren't going to be *against*. They couldn't be! Especially in a group of their peers. So we set up a focus group around the question of security in exchanging files, and people jump on the bandwagon, agreeing with each other that yes, of course, security is important. What we didn't really appreciate is how much *more* important other issues are to these people, at the end of the day."

The tired group wrapped up their meal with a discussion of some other interesting insights that had begun to emerge:

- People's e-mail clients were a central tool in their jobs. To borrow a term from interaction design, it's a *sovereign application*. It's always open. Many people used it as a repository of project correspondence, as Yoko had.
- Although these architects and engineers used powerful software such as AutoCAD, they were not necessarily sophisticated users. The interviewers were shocked to meet several people who had never encountered "drag and drop" before in Microsoft Windows. Others had never used the right mouse button. This was a big surprise.
- Everyone was struggling with large files. They often had to send PDF files approaching 100 MB in size, which is far too large for an e-mail attachment. In those situations they were forced into using FTP software to transfer the files manually, or they printed and shipped them via courier.

On their way to the hotel after dinner, Dimitri remarked how much he was enjoying this research. "And the participants love it too! Our last guy had totally forgotten he was getting 200 bucks. It was great to see his reaction when we gave him the cash."

"That's for sure," agreed Joanne. "You know that architect who was hesitant to give us even 10 minutes at first? We had to finally excuse ourselves after an hour and a quarter. He didn't want us to leave! He wanted to keep showing us stuff! It was hilarious."

Questions

6. You've just started an interview with a participant. They showed up with a list of wishes and complaints about the product you're working on—and they only want to talk about that. How do you respond?
7. What if you just don't hit it off with a participant and can't seem to establish rapport?
8. The research team feels a pattern is emerging: that people don't care about security as much as they were led to believe. How might they further explore and possibly confirm this in future interviews?

Developing the Personas

After an intense week of interviews, the research team gathered at Digital Rockit's office in Toronto. Their goal was to spend a few days together discussing what they'd learned and sketching out their findings. Digital Rockit would then design and write the final personas in preparation for a presentation at ClickDox the following week.

"How's everyone feel about what we've accomplished so far?" Greg asked.

Joanne was the first to answer. "I'm still shocked at what we saw in the field. And concerned, too. If people don't really care about security—which seems pretty clear from our interviews—then we have to rethink our go-to-market strategy. Security has been the driving concept behind ClickDox from the beginning."

"I have to admit, I'm glad you asked me to participate," Dimitri said. "If I hadn't seen it for myself, there's no way I'd believe that finding. I'm not sure what the implications will be on our technology, but it's obvious you don't want to market ClickDox for its security alone. I mean, security is still really important. But it clearly won't get people excited about Click-Dox, at least not at first."

"I suspect one of the first things to happen after we unveil the personas next week is a strategy discussion with senior management," Greg predicted. "Joanne, you've been keeping Mike informed of our work, right?"

"Yes," she replied. "I summarized my interviews for him at the end of each day, so this won't be a surprise. He's trying to schedule a meeting with management to discuss the personas after we present them."

"That will be an interesting discussion, I'm sure," said Roberta. "Greg, you want to kick off our work for today?"

Greg nodded and waited for everyone to settle into their chairs around the conference table. "We've already talked about our findings a lot, over meals and between interviews last week. So I think we have a good idea of some important insights to capture in our personas," Greg paused to acknowledge people's agreement. "But we need to be careful," he warned. "We could probably find evidence to prove anything we want, or to back up our personal biases. So yeah, we're pretty sure about some key patterns—but let's make sure the data really supports them."

Roberta piped in. "The best way to do that is to follow a process for thinking through what we've learned—or what we *think* we've learned at this point." She turned to her laptop and fired up a presentation on the

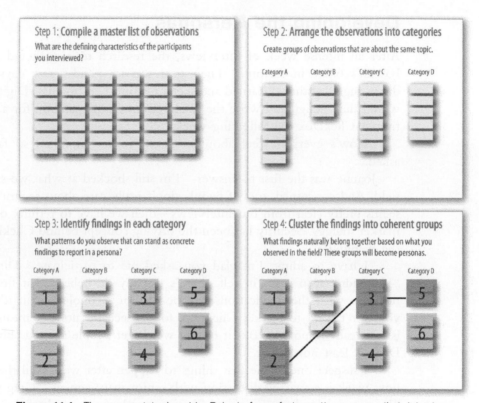

Figure 11.4. The process introduced by Roberta for surfacing patterns across their interviews and identifying their personas. (Created by Robert Barlow-Busch.)

projector (Figure 11.4). "Here's an overview of the process we're going to follow. It starts by sharing highlights from each interview, which is important because we had two teams in the field; we've all seen only half the interviews. Then a few exercises will help to surface key patterns from our notes. That's the main benefit of this process: patterns will emerge from the data itself."

"The steps may not seem too clear at this point, but we'll explain them further as we go along," Greg explained. Their goal was to complete this process by Wednesday, giving them 3 days together. Afterward, Digital Rockit would produce the final personas and share them for review by the end of the week.

"We have 20 interviews to cover," observed Joanne. "I guess we'd better get down to business."

Step 1: Compile a Master List of Observations

Roberta opened Microsoft Word and prepared to act as note-taker for the day. Her job would be to record observations from their interviews; later, these would be printed onto labels for the next step in their process.

Greg offered a few more words of advice. "This step can be approached with different levels of ambition. It's possible to be meticulous and record a great number of observations from each interview. But we're really pressed for time here, so our only choice is to work at a fairly high level. After hearing a summary of each interview, we'll then skim the notes for observations about that person's defining characteristics."

"What do you mean by that?" asked Dimitri.

"It means we'll try to capture only those things that are critical to understanding what makes our participants tick. For example, I propose it's less important to know whether someone uses Outlook or Outlook Express—as opposed to knowing how they decide to send documents via e-mail instead of courier," Greg replied.

"Okay, I think I see what you mean," Dimitri replied. Joanne nodded in agreement.

Dimitri and Greg started the discussion, reviewing the four interviews they'd completed together. Along the way, the group agreed on observations they believed should be captured in a master list. Roberta typed them up, making sure to identify the source of each observation (she numbered the interviews from 1 through 20). Later, this would help them identify patterns across participants.

By the end of the day they managed to review all 20 interviews. A total of 300 observations were compiled in Roberta's Microsoft Word template, an average of 15 unique observations per interview (Figure 11.5).

210. Microsoft Outlook is open all the time. [9]	211. Checks email about every 15 minutes, mostly because she's alerted to a new message. [9]	212. Sends documents as email attachments whenever possible (i.e., recipient has email, file is under 5 MB) [9]
213. Prints files that are too big to email and sends them by courier (next day delivery typical) [9]	214. Has to work at home a couple nights per week to stay caught up. HATES IT. "Work should stay at work" [9]	215. Keeps a copy of all email in a folder in Outlook. This becomes a project record that sometimes gets audited. [9]

Figure 11.5. The group recorded an average of 15 observations from each interview. In this example, the code at the end indicates these observations are about participant no. 9. (Created by Robert Barlow-Busch.)

Step 2: Arrange Observations Into Categories

The next morning Joanne and Dimitri arrived at Digital Rockit's office to find the conference room's whiteboards covered with their observations from the day before. Roberta and Greg had arrived early and printed the observations onto removable labels that they stuck to the walls.

"This part is a nice change from yesterday," she said. "We get to spend some time moving around."

She went on to explain the exercise. "It's quite simple, really. Our objective is to create categories of *observations about the same topic.* For example, observations about the tools people use, or their skills with computers, or the types of documents they're sending. Whatever we feel makes sense."

"One thing we should specifically look for are items that somehow represent people's overall goals," Greg added. "In fact, let's plan on having a category called 'goals' right from the start." He wrote the word Goals on one of the whiteboards.

"Feel free to name the categories as we go. If you believe a name should change, go ahead and change it. If you believe an observation belongs in more than one category, make a copy of it. Also, when a category becomes bloated with a lot of observations, let's take a closer look. Maybe it could be split apart," Roberta advised.

Before getting started, Greg pointed something out. "You'll notice only about 200 of our 300 observations are posted right now. That's because we've split out the observations from our IT participants. Roberta and I talked it over this morning and agreed there's an obvious difference between these two groups. If you agree too, we'll deal with them separately."

Everyone did agree, so they got started. For about 3 hours the group shuffled observations around the walls (Figure 11.6). They formed categories, debated them, split them apart, debated them some more, brought them back together . . . they basically immersed themselves in the data until lunchtime. The momentum slowed noticeably at that point.

"We could debate the fine points of these groupings for another 3 days, I'm sure," Dimitri observed. "But I'm hungry. And I suspect we're satisfied with what's on the walls now. Everyone agree?"

They did. The four sat down with a feeling of satisfaction and began the morning's final debate: where to eat lunch.

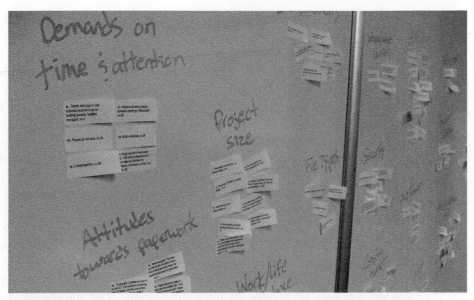

Figure 11.6. At the end of this exercise about 40 different groups had emerged, each representing a different category of observations. (Photographed by Robert Barlow-Busch.)

Step 3: Identify Specific Findings in Each Category

After a quick lunch the team reconvened in Digital Rockit's conference room. Roberta gave them an overview of the next step.

"I really like this step, because we finally get to the meat of the matter: identifying the specific findings that eventually make up our personas. Let me explain a bit further," and she stepped to the nearest whiteboard.

"Here's our collection of observations about the size of projects that people handle. Do we observe any patterns inside this category? Our goal is to distill these observations to a small set of findings that represent what we learned about the size of people's projects. For instance, I'm seeing a number of people here who deal only with projects under $5,000. So 'manages projects under $5,000' could be a key finding that helps to define a persona."

Greg jumped in with another example. "Take a look at our 'Goals' group, too. I'm seeing quite a few observations about people struggling to get their work done each day." He began moving those labels slightly apart from the others. "This might represent an important goal of some customers."

Joanne agreed. "I see that. There's also another pattern in there, something about staying in control of their documents."

That afternoon, the group methodically worked their way through all 40 of the categories they had created. In each one they identified patterns that emerged and captured them in a growing list of findings to potentially report in their personas. Some groups were quite easy, such as "*# documents exchanged per day*": that was a simple range on which each participant could be plotted. In each case they were interested in clusters of observations across several participants, because these represented patterns of behavior. Generally, outliers were ignored as idiosyncratic of a specific person—although Greg took note of a few that seemed interesting in their own right.

"Sometimes it's the outlier, that one thing that doesn't fit with the others, that signals an opportunity to innovate," Greg explained. "I want to think about a couple of these again later. . . ."

The group also tested each finding by asking themselves: Is this really a core finding, or merely an interesting detail? The interesting details would later be included in their personas, but they wouldn't play a role in defining the personas themselves. This was very much a judgment call by the group, but not usually a difficult one. For instance, they identified some good insights into people's behaviors when working at home—but these insights would merely serve to illustrate a persona defined by the finding "works at home for 2 hours every night." This distinction helped keep their list to an easily managed size: By the end of the day they had identified 32 specific findings on which they could base a cast of personas.

"Terrific!" Roberta exclaimed when they had finished. "Tomorrow, we'll arrange this list into groups of findings that belong together, based on what we observed in the field. Those groups will become our personas."

To help with this next step, Roberta had annotated each finding with the participants it had been derived from. For example, here are six of the 32 findings in Roberta's list:

1. Struggles to complete each day's tasks. When work takes longer than expected, there's a domino effect of consequences that may end in them getting blamed for the project not going well. [Participants 4, 6, 9, 12, 13, 16, 17]
2. Wants to know that the documents they send are actually read by the recipient. Worries that documents are ignored, which leads to problems later in the project. [Participants 5, 10, 12, 19, 20]

3. E-mail is a sovereign application. It's always open and visible on their screen, unless they're actively working on something else. [Participants 2, 4, 5, 6, 7, 9, 11, 12, 15, 16, 18, 19, 20]
4. All incoming and outgoing correspondence is stored in a project-specific folder in their e-mail application. It acts as a history of the project. [Participants 4, 5, 6, 9, 12, 16, 19, 20]
5. Although they know their way around AutoCAD and use keyboard shortcuts frequently, they are not sophisticated in the operating system (e.g., don't right-click or drag and drop). [Participants 1, 5, 10, 19]
6. Sending large files is a major frustration they face almost every day. [Participants 1, 2, 4, 6, 7, 8, 10, 14, 18, 20]

Step 4: Cluster the Findings Into Coherent Groups

Today was the last day for the team to analyze their work together. Joanne and Dimitri were scheduled to catch a flight back to San Francisco at 6:30 p.m.

"Today everything comes together," Roberta said. "By the time you guys leave for the airport this afternoon, we'll have sketched out the personas that capture the insights from our research."

Greg gestured to a whiteboard at the front of the room. "Here are the 32 findings we identified yesterday. Somewhere in here are our personas. Our goal is to cluster these findings into groups that we believe belong together, that characterize patterns of goals, of context, and of behavior that we observed in the field. These groups will become our personas."

He then explained that the easiest way to get started was by selecting a finding that represents a high-level goal and then looking for other findings that are also shared by that type of person. He outlined two questions that would guide the exercise:

1. What other findings seem to naturally occur with this?
2. What other findings seem to *not* occur with this?

"That second question will lead us to the different personas in our set," Roberta explained. "For instance, something just caught my eye. Look at finding number 1, 'struggles to complete each day's tasks.' From what I can see, almost none of those people ship documents by courier when they're too big to e-mail. It seems they use tools such as FTP."

Dimitri nodded. "That's interesting. Compare that with finding number 23, 'Is more concerned about quality than deadlines.' It looks like those are the people who ship by courier."

Greg was at the whiteboard. "Okay, so we have two potential personas emerging already. One is a person who is highly motivated by getting things done and who ships large files by FTP instead of courier. Over here is another person who is motivated by doing the best job they can regardless of deadlines and who sends large files by courier. What else do we know about these people?"

The discussion took off from there. In an attempt to wrap up early, they ordered food and worked through lunch and by early afternoon three clusters had emerged, including one for their IT customer. The team felt good about what they'd created; the resulting clusters felt right when they reflected on their week of interviews. The personas built from these clusters wouldn't map *exactly* to any one participant who they'd interviewed, but that was to be expected. What mattered was that they captured key patterns in a representative and realistic way.

Several key attributes of cluster 1 were as follows:

- Wants to get things done. Is highly motivated by finishing the day's work.
- Wants to be in control and confident of what's happening at all times.
- Would be happy with more security, but values convenience more.
- Uses e-mail as a detailed archive of project activity.
- Uses FTP to exchange files too big for e-mail.

Some key attributes of cluster 2 looked like this:

- Strives to be seen as indispensable to customers.
- Is more concerned about quality than deadlines.
- Sends documents by courier when they're too big for e-mail.
- Really doesn't care about security.
- Has limited computer skills outside AutoCAD.

Cluster 3 describes the IT specialist who would support users of ClickDox:

- Strives to save money for the organization.
- Held accountable for downtime due to technical issues.
- Cannot plan ahead. "Fights fires" all day.
- Loves the challenge of juggling priorities.
- Has a dedicated e-mail account for IT emergencies.

"Once we turn these clusters into proper personas, I'm interested in your reactions," Roberta said to Joanne and Dimitri. "They should seem entirely realistic. In fact, they should read like descriptions of actual people who we *might* have interviewed, though of course we didn't."

"I can't wait to see them!" Joanne said enthusiastically as she and Dimitri packed up and prepared to leave. "Thanks for hosting us these 3 days. Let me know when you have drafts for us to review."

Step 5: Develop the Groups Into Full Personas

Roberta and Greg got to work right away by completing a detailed point-form outline of each persona. They agreed on additional insights that should be included based on the results of their exercises that week and from their research notes—such as details about the office environment, common complaints, tools used, and so on. Their initial research plan served as a guide of topics that deserved more elaboration

While Roberta created a template for laying out the personas, Greg got started writing the content. Over the course of 2 days they passed drafts back and forth many times, adding details and tweaking the material. Their early drafts focused entirely on communicating core information. Later, however, they added a few embellishments to make the stories more engaging; they were careful, however, to show restraint and add only enough quirky detail to make the personas come alive. If they went overboard, the personas could be perceived as too "cute" and would lack credibility.

Another important conversation that took place now was about prioritizing the personas. Greg and Roberta believed they had potentially three types of personas in the set:

1. **Primary persona**. Someone who would be unsatisfied with a product designed for anyone but them. The intention would be to design ClickDox first and foremost for this persona.
2. **Secondary persona**. Someone with unique characteristics but who would not be unsatisfied using the primary persona's product. The intention would be to accommodate their needs, but not at the expense of the primary persona.
3. **Supplemental persona**. Someone whose needs deserve consideration but who's not clearly a target.

After some debate the team decided that cluster 1, now known as Timothy Powell, was their primary persona (Figure 11.7). Cluster 2, named Madeline

Timothy Powell

P.Eng., Civil Engineer
GeoLine Engineering
Age 40

"Speed trumps security when it comes to exchanging documents. It's not worth jumping through hoops to protect a document that nobody's interested in but me and the client."

Sends 12 documents/week at nearly 100 MB each **via FTP**

Sends 8 documents/week under 5 MB each **via email**

Receives 15 documents/week under 5 MB each **via email**

Receives 15 hand-edited CAD drawings/week **via fax**

Exchanges primarily PDF and Microsoft Word files

Employs couriers only for shipping physical goods

Internet use is mostly limited to a website that hosts discussion groups for civil engineers. Purchases flights, hotels, and conference registrations twice per year.

Goal: Get everything done before heading home. Timothy has a lot of work to stay on top of and firm deadlines that cannot be missed. Speed is a competitive advantage for GeoLine, so it's essential that delays do not occur. Timothy hates working at night, too, so he makes the most of his hours at the office.

Goal: Cover his back and avoid blame. In Timothy's industry, projects usually go far over budget and are completed late, at which point all the subcontractors involved begin pointing fingers at each other. Tony needs detailed records that prove he completed exactly what was expected of him and his company.

Timothy Powell is famous among his coworkers for once visiting a construction site and remarking to the client, "Look, you may build bridges, but I design them. And that's the most critical part!" He may not have made a friend that day, but Timothy was unconcerned. He doesn't suffer fools, just as he won't put up with anything that stands in the way of getting his job done. Timothy's work is extremely deadline-driven. His clients demand aggressive schedules and expect him to stick to them, as timing is crucial when coordinating subcontractors and suppliers on large construction projects.

"On a great day, I'm able to get everything out the door that needs to get into our client's hands. Never, ever let anything come between you and that door!" This is something Timothy struggles with all the time. With at least three major projects underway, it takes an

ClickDox

Figure 11.7. Timothy Powell, the primary persona that Roberta delivered for final review. (Created by Robert Barlow-Busch.)

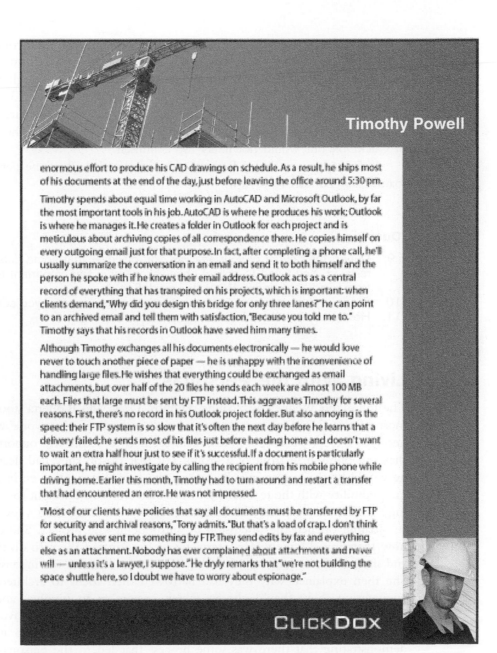

Timothy Powell

enormous effort to produce his CAD drawings on schedule. As a result, he ships most of his documents at the end of the day, just before leaving the office around 5:30 pm.

Timothy spends about equal time working in AutoCAD and Microsoft Outlook, by far the most important tools in his job. AutoCAD is where he produces his work; Outlook is where he manages it. He creates a folder in Outlook for each project and is meticulous about archiving copies of all correspondence there. He copies himself on every outgoing email just for that purpose. In fact, after completing a phone call, he'll usually summarize the conversation in an email and send it to both himself and the person he spoke with if he knows their email address. Outlook acts as a central record of everything that has transpired on his projects, which is important: when clients demand, "Why did you design this bridge for only three lanes?" he can point to an archived email and tell them with satisfaction, "Because you told me to." Timothy says that his records in Outlook have saved him many times.

Although Timothy exchanges all his documents electronically — he would love never to touch another piece of paper — he is unhappy with the inconvenience of handling large files. He wishes that everything could be exchanged as email attachments, but over half of the 20 files he sends each week are almost 100 MB each. Files that large must be sent by FTP instead. This aggravates Timothy for several reasons. First, there's no record in his Outlook project folder. But also annoying is the speed: their FTP system is so slow that it's often the next day before he learns that a delivery failed; he sends most of his files just before heading home and doesn't want to wait an extra half hour just to see if it's successful. If a document is particularly important, he might investigate by calling the recipient from his mobile phone while driving home. Earlier this month, Timothy had to turn around and restart a transfer that had encountered an error. He was not impressed.

"Most of our clients have policies that say all documents must be transferred by FTP for security and archival reasons," Tony admits. "But that's a load of crap. I don't think a client has ever sent me something by FTP. They send edits by fax and everything else as an attachment. Nobody has ever complained about attachments and never will — unless it's a lawyer, I suppose." He dryly remarks that "we're not building the space shuttle here, so I doubt we have to worry about espionage."

CLICKDOX

Figure 11.7. *Continued*

Deville, was a secondary persona. When considering all the attributes that defined these two personas, they had a hard time imagining how Timothy would be happy using a product designed for Madeline—although Madeline could likely be satisfied with a product for Timothy. Cluster 3, their IT specialist, was named Jim Temaki and was classified as a supplemental persona; he would support Timothy and Madeline and would advise on the purchase of ClickDox but would not likely use it himself.

At 5:30 p.m. on Friday Roberta shipped a final draft of the personas for Joanne and Dimitri to review.

Questions

9. During the course of your analysis, you discover that some data are missing. You failed to collect observations about an important topic from every participant. What do you do?
10. Do your personas have to account for every observation you collected?
11. How many primary personas will you have?

Living With the Personas

The following Wednesday, Joanne, Dimitri, Greg, and Roberta stood before most of the ClickDox team to present their findings. Everyone was a bit nervous, except possibly Dimitri, who seemed to relish any opportunity to share an opinion in front of a group. For that reason they had decided that he would be the one to initially present the personas themselves; in addition, his credibility with the technical crowd would lend some weight to their findings, which they expected to be controversial with more than a few people.

Joanne opened the discussion by introducing the project. She described how their initial stakeholder interviews had motivated them to do this work and shared a few of the opinions they'd heard to illustrate the inconsistencies. She then explained why they had narrowed their focus to architecture and engineering, how they'd chosen which customers to involve, and briefly described a typical interview. Greg and Roberta then gave an overview of how they'd analyzed the research, which put the audience more at ease by demonstrating that there was some process that led to the personas. Finally Dimitri took the floor.

"I'd like to introduce Timothy Powell," he began as the others handed out color copies of the personas and placed some large posters at the front of the room. Dimitri proceeded to read the description of Timothy while everyone followed along. Joanne, Greg, and Roberta stole glances at the audience, curious for people's reactions. They noticed a few frowns and several whispered conversations about something on the page, but mostly people were concentrating intently on the information.

Dimitri finished reading. "So, what do you folks think of Timothy?" he asked. Several people spoke at once.

Predictably, the first reaction was to question their finding about Timothy's lack of concern about security. They had prepared for this and spent some time sharing stories from the field to back up that conclusion. People were particularly interested to hear about Yoko, the architect who'd also participated in their focus groups.

Dimitri went on to introduce the other two personas, though he summarized how they differed from Timothy instead of reading them word for word. The presentation continued for another hour after that. They fielded questions, showed photographs from their interviews, and passed around artifacts they had collected such as building plans and shipment invoices.

The meeting wound up when Joanne let Mike Rugatino take the floor for some closing remarks. "I know there are some surprising results in here and some information we'll really have to think about. There's a senior management meeting tomorrow to discuss some of these findings, most notably the question about security. Another big one is the idea that people live in their e-mail application—so what does that mean for our plan to send them to a website? We're not sure yet. But I'm glad we did this research now, because I feel we know something important about the market that our competitors don't. And that's good news."

This presentation marked a change at ClickDox. There was a noticeable shift in perspective in the following weeks, as the personas were an ever-present reminder that ClickDox's passion for technology wasn't necessarily shared by their potential customers—they would be passionate only for what ClickDox could *do* for them. Mike and Joanne led some discussions with management about the requirements for the ClickDox website, and the personas were helpful in getting people to agree with each other; they brought an outside perspective that seemed to allow people to let go of their own personal agendas more easily and come together around a shared vision. Involving Dimitri from the beginning turned out to be one of their better ideas, because he defended the personas to a degree that surprised even Joanne. As a result some key technology decisions were made in favor of the customer instead of by following ClickDox's original intentions.

For instance, the biggest change in strategy was a decision to build a plug-in for Microsoft Outlook that would let people send and receive Click-Dox deliveries right from their inbox. This was technically quite challenging and would be frowned upon by Jim, their IT persona. But Timothy, the primary persona, demonstrated how customers would hate to leave their normal e-mail environment: They wanted all correspondence to flow through Outlook. ClickDox would still create a website for managing deliveries, but it would be considered a secondary resource to the Outlook plug-in. This would be a tremendous advantage for ClickDox, something to really set them apart from every competitor in the market.

"I can imagine shopping this idea to FedEx and showing them all those little FedEx icons inside Microsoft Outlook," Mike liked to say. "They're going to *love* that!"

Joanne, Dimitri, Greg, and Roberta got together 2 months later to reflect on the impact of their work. Digital Rockit had completed several design iterations of both the Outlook plug-in and the ClickDox website, and usability tests indicated that people were happy with the prototypes. There were some challenges still to figure out, especially in making the installation process as simple and friendly as possible while satisfying the demands of an IT department. And Joanne was getting concerned about feedback from some participants that they wouldn't expect to pay *anything* for the service. Clearly, that could be a problem for ClickDox.

"But that's a problem I hope we can deal with through marketing," Joanne said. "Or maybe it won't make a difference to whoever shows an interest in buying ClickDox. If we manage to scoop the most market share, that alone might be worth a fortune."

Greg cleared his throat and grinned. "Speaking of a fortune, perhaps we could talk about the final invoice you need me to send for Digital Rockit's services. . . ." He gave an exaggerated wink. Joanne raised her glass in a toast and smiled.

Questions

12. We've heard how the personas prompted ClickDox to make significant changes to their product's requirements (i.e., producing an Outlook plug-in). In what other ways might the personas make contributions?
13. What ideas could you imagine for helping the people at ClickDox become familiar with the personas and keep them in mind when making decisions?

Summary

- *Describe the problem* that you want personas to help solve. For example, "These personas will help us understand how to design a website where people can send and receive electronic documents."
- *Identify the customers* you need to understand to solve the problem you described.
- *Interview and observe* these customers for about 90 minutes in the environment where they would use your product or service.
- *Compile your observations* from each interview. Focus on observations that in your mind are defining characteristics of that customer. For example, "sends documents only as e-mail attachments."
- *Arrange observations into categories*. The observations in each category should address the same topic or issue. For example: project size, overall goals, volume of e-mail sent, and so on.
- *Identify specific findings in each category*. These represent patterns that you observe across participants inside each category; these patterns will become findings that you report through your personas. For example, in your "project size" category, you may identify a clear group of people who manage projects only under $5,000.
- *Cluster the findings into coherent groups*. Form these groups by looking for findings that naturally belong together based on what you observed in the field. What are the other characteristics of someone who manages projects under $5,000?
- *Develop the groups into full personas*. To each group of findings, add further details as appropriate to create a more complete picture of that person. Assign them an identity and write a narrative to communicate their story.
- *Unveil the personas to your project team*. Describe the scope of your research and the process you followed during analysis. Introduce the personas and be sure to provide everyone with a take-home copy.
- *Put the personas to work*. Help your team understand how personas can play a role in activities such as design, development, and marketing. When people talk about "the user," challenge them to clarify which specific persona they're talking about.

Further Reading

Cooper, A. (1999). *The inmates are running the asylum.* Indianapolis: SAMS.

Cooper, A., and Reimann, R. (2003). *About face 2.0.* Indianapolis: Wiley.

Hackos, J. T., and Redish, J. (1998). *User and task analysis for interface design.* New York: Wiley.

Kuniavsky, M. (2003). *Observing the user experience.* San Francisco: Elsevier Science.

Mulder, S., and Yaar, Z. (2007). *The user is always right: a practical guide to creating and using personas for the web.* Berkely: New Riders.

Pruitt, J., and Adlin, T. (2006). *The persona lifecycle: keeping people in mind throughout product design.* San Francisco: Elsevier Inc.

CASE 12

User–Centered Design for Middleware

Deanna McCusker, VMware, Inc.
Ken Guzik, VMware, Inc.

> *Brian and Carl mulled over the feedback they received from Bob and other users. They invented some of the less useful features because they didn't fully understand what the user might need. Some were designed in response to Bob's requests and may have only fit his situation and not those of other users. They were sensing a growing disconnect between these items and what users actually do in real life. How could Brian and Carl validate these requirements?*

In Need of an Interface

Scientists believe that human beings use only about 5 to 10% of their brain capacity. It is difficult to imagine how smart we would be if we used 90% or more of our ability to perceive, compute, learn, and create. The team at VMware faced a similar difficulty—how to get their customers to see the immense benefits of increased utilization of their server capacity.

Brian, the lead engineer at VMware, tells the history of the VMware products this way: "Most servers today use only about 5 to 10% of their computing capacity, just like the human brain. This is because many server applications are incompatible, and therefore it is best to run only one application on any given server, even though it uses only a small amount of that server's capacity. What if we could make that server 'super smart' by utilizing more than 90% of its power?"

Back in the 1970s IBM developed a technology, called virtual machines, that allowed a single mainframe computer to run multiple operating systems at the same time. Thirty years later, VMware would develop its own virtual machine technology for the PC market and bring it to the general public at a time when the need for computing power was increasing rapidly. The convenience and cost savings of replacing dozens of separate desktop machines with a single computer running virtual machines was compelling indeed.

Brian and his team realized that these same benefits were not lost on the IT (information technology) managers of large companies, where the need to reduce operating costs and squeeze more computing out of existing hardware was critical. The idea was huge, as was the potential market. Brian and Vivek, VMware's marketing specialist, started to imagine how virtual servers might be used in the enterprise.

"You know, a company could easily consolidate all of its server usage with virtual machines," said Brian. "With a set of, say, four physical servers, a company could create 20 to 40 virtual machines, all running different applications with the same level of reliability."

"I think that's exactly the kind of thing many companies need," replied Vivek. "Their resources are often stretched to the limit, and deploying a new server can take weeks."

To meet this demand, the team at VMware created a high-performance server, called ESX Server. With just a few ESX servers, large farms of physical servers could be replaced with the same number of virtual machines running exactly the same applications. This consolidation could easily save not only a tremendous amount of money but also rack space, electricity, and air-conditioning costs.

ESX Server was a breakthrough for virtualization. The users loved it! It saved so much money that many users would have jumped through hoops to use it, and they did. However, ESX Server could not be managed through tools that were currently available for physical servers, and server management tasks had to be done manually. Without tools to help, users wrote their own scripts to perform all these tasks. It soon became clear that VMware needed to develop an interface that allowed users to manage and monitor their virtual machines easily. Thus the idea for VirtualCenter was born.

VirtualCenter 1.0 was designed to address the same needs for virtual machines that users already had with their physical servers—to manage all servers from a single location, monitor the health and performance of the entire system, and adjust configurations remotely. However, virtual machines offer greater flexibility than physical servers in a number of important ways. Virtual machines can be easily moved and copied from one ESX Server to another. Users discovered that many of the labor-intensive tasks of deploying physical servers (also known as "hosts") were very simple with virtual machines. With this in mind, VirtualCenter needed not only to replace existing tools, but also to exploit the added benefits of virtual machines. The possibilities and requirements of such a system were starting to become excitingly clear to Brian and Vivek.

Vivek and the marketing team spent a good deal of time talking with prospective customers to find out why and how they would use a system for managing a virtualized environment. Vivek struck up a strong relationship with Bob, the IT manager of a medium-sized insurance company who was already using ESX servers.

"So, Bob, how is ESX Server working out for you?" asked Vivek.

"Very good," replied Bob. "We're adding new ESX servers every week. But, it's starting to take a lot of time for my IT guys to configure and manage these virtual machines. I saw on the VMware forum that Joe over at SysTec has a script for automatically moving virtual machines from one server to another. But he won't share it. He says it's proprietary."

"Migrating virtual machines across servers seems to be really important to all our customers," agreed Vivek. "Our new product, VirtualCenter, is designed to help you fully manage your virtual machines. You will be able to organize them, control them from this central tool, measure and chart their performance, and move them from server to server. We think it may even be possible to allow you to migrate your virtual machines while they're still running."

"Wow!" said Bob. "You can do that? If you guys can deliver a product like that, I would definitely be interested in investing more in virtualizing my entire environment."

Brian and Vivek realized that the potential for virtual machines was not in competing with physical servers but in going way beyond what was possible in the physical world. Migrating virtual machines while they were running (known as VMotion^{TM}) would eliminate a lot of management downtime. And, with a virtualized environment, the resources for the machines (processor and memory) were not limited to a single physical machine. These resources could be "pooled" together from a group of servers (called "clusters") and shared between virtual machines in ways that could be invisible to the user. This enabled another completely new idea: that virtual machines could be moved, not just when the user wanted to but more or less continuously and automatically as the load on the system required. When the computing demands of the virtual machines on one ESX Server became too great, some of the virtual machines could be moved to a more idle machine, thereby automatically managing the load of the system (called "load balancing").

This was all pretty pie-in-the-sky stuff and completely new to most IT specialists. Although Brian and his engineering team couldn't wait to provide these features to Bob, Vivek began to worry that so many new concepts might be too abstract to grasp. There was a risk that users would not take to virtualization at all. He and the marketing team wanted to highlight the things that make virtual machines compelling to use and ensure that users would be able to use them right away.

In addition, the product needed to address the needs of system administrators at all levels. Senior IT administrators like Bob required full access to maintain complex enterprises, whereas most IT technicians needed access only to basic operations. The VMware executive team realized that they needed to be "best of breed" in usability because they understood that it was not just a "nicety." It was absolutely required for the success of the product. With all these user requirements in mind, the director of engineering decided to hire Carl, an interaction designer.

The Interaction Designer

Because there was no precedent in the marketplace for such a product, it was an important decision to bring in an experienced user interface designer to help make good decisions about what the users would likely need and want in such an interface. Carl had many years of experience designing various types of products. Because he was new to the company, he had to quickly learn all the nuances of virtualization, see the vision that Brian and Vivek had, and draw from his past experience to create an easy-to-use interface.

When Carl, Brian, and Vivek began to work on VirtualCenter 1.0, they designed it largely by intuition. But the concepts were so new that the interface would need to convey these ideas in a simple understandable way. There were many iterations of designs, reviews, and trial ideas. Carl created storyboards (Figure 12.1) to help the team visualize the user experience. Slowly, decisions were made about how the product would present its functions and the overall look and feel, based largely on Vivek's understanding of users' needs, Brian's vision of the coolest technology on the planet, and Carl's expertise with interaction design.

After many design cycles and painstaking evaluation by the whole team, the VirtualCenter design was finally agreed on and built, but there was no time to do a user study. The product was launched, and everyone held their

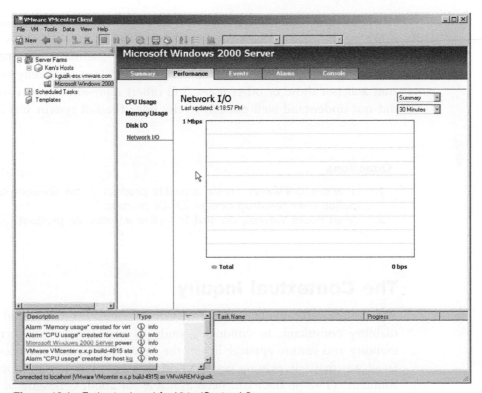

Figure 12.1. Early storyboard for VirtualCenter 1.0.

breath that the users would accept it. VirtualCenter 1.0 met their expectations of both functionality and usability very well, and to the relief of the team, it became popular rather quickly.

When feedback started to come in from Bob and other users, it was mostly positive. Bob liked the models and the metaphors. The inventory model, patterned after the very conventional Windows Explorer user interface, gave the user an easy way to view a list of all virtual machines in a familiar way. The simple drag-and-drop model made it easy for the user to move virtual machines around the inventory and from one ESX host to another. The conventional tabbed-view model provided distinct views for common tasks. The console metaphor, which gave the user a window into the server console along with VCR-style buttons to control the virtual machine power operations, was easy for Bob to understand. However, there were many features Bob didn't use or even see a need for.

Brian and Carl mulled over the feedback they received from Bob and other users. Some of the less useful features had been invented by Brian and Carl because they didn't fully understand what the user might need. Some were designed in response to Bob's requests and may have only fit his situation and not those of other users. Still others represented concepts that Bob did not understand well enough to use once the full system was in place.

Questions

1. How could VMware create a usable product in the absence of an explicit user-centered design (UCD) process?
2. What could VMware do next to further improve its product?

The Contextual Inquiry

About 6 months after the release of VirtualCenter 1.0, Carl hired Pamela, a usability consultant, to conduct a study to evaluate the product for both usability and feature applicability in the field. One of the obstacles VMware faced was that few existing customers used the product in a production environment. (The product had been available for about 8 months at this time, and many customers were still evaluating it.) The year was 2004, the dotcom bubble had burst, and no one on the West Coast was spending money on IT infrastructure.

Carl asked Pamela, "Since I don't have much experience conducting user research, what sort of study will get us the most information? Many of our customers are on the East Coast and not geographically easy to reach."

"Well, there are a few possibilities. You could do phone interviews, a formal usability study, or an on-site contextual inquiry."

"Remember," said Carl, "We're still a very small company on a tight budget."

"On your budget I recommend the contextual inquiry. We could visit three customers on-site," said Pamela. "I think you will get better results by visiting customers on-site because you will learn more from how they are really using this product than by contriving a uniform usability study or from a simple interview. You should carefully choose customers who are the most representative of your customer base and ones that are located near each other. This type of study is called a contextual inquiry."

Carl agreed that the contextual inquiry (CI) would be the best approach. It went as follows:

1. **Develop the protocol:** Carl spent several weeks educating Pamela on the nature of VirtualCenter—the vision and goals as well as how they expected users to use it. Pamela met with Carl and Vivek to discuss the goals of the CI. They wanted to learn who was using VirtualCenter, how it fit into their organization and IT infrastructure, and how well the users were adapting to the new concepts and models.

   Pamela generated a protocol that targeted IT managers and crafted questions to find out specifics about the structure of the IT organization, how VirtualCenter was used day to day, how it fit into the overall business model, and what the users found useful, easy, or difficult about each aspect of the interface. After a few short review cycles, the protocol was approved by the team as the framework for the study.

2. **Choose participants and schedule the interviews:** Vivek sifted through the customer list and found several who were located near each other around the Newark, New Jersey, area. He scheduled three of the most appropriate customers (all were early adopters deploying large numbers of virtual machines) for CI sessions in the same week, and Carl and Pamela made plans for the visit.

3. **Conduct CI sessions:** Carl and Pamela visited each site and spent about 2 hours with each participant. Each one was the top-level technical IT manager for the organization, and all were well versed in the details of setting up ESX servers and the VirtualCenter system.

   Pamela and Carl sat with the users in their work environment. Pamela conducted the CI based on the protocol, whereas Carl listened and provided technical support to Pamela if she or the users got stuck during the session. Pamela tape recorded each session to use as reference for the analysis.

   Of the three visits, two were conducted with two participants who shared technical duties, and they were interviewed jointly. The final CI was conducted with a single user. Interestingly, the best information was gleaned from the two 2-participant interviews. This could be attributed to the individuals involved, but Carl and Pamela thought that the interchange between the participants brought up more interesting information than would have been obtained from either of them individually.

4. **Review the CIs:** Pamela and Carl discussed the points that were revealed in each session—the unique characteristics of the users, their environments, their roles within the organization, and the ways in which they used the VirtualCenter product—and identified some of the important and salient points. These were all noted and represented the starting point for the analysis.

5. **Analyze the data and write a report:** Pamela then went off to analyze the information and write the report. In addition, Pamela came to VMware to present the findings to the entire engineering organization. Both the report and the presentation were very much a success.

The results of the CI were extremely valuable. Generally, the CI revealed two major sentiments from the user:

1. There are a lot of things you did wrong and here is a laundry list of things you need to fix.
2. You gave us a sophisticated yet simple product. We love it! Thank you!

The three things the users (who were system administrators and IT personnel) liked most about VirtualCenter 1.0 were lists, wizards, and the inventory. The list views allowed them to see, in tabular format, what was happening with their hosts, virtual machines, networks, and so on. Bob and his team used these lists to evaluate the state and health of their system. They could, for example, sort a list of virtual machines by status and instantly see the ones that had problems and needed attention. They could sort hosts by load and see which one needed to be relieved. The system administrators mostly lived in these views.

Users liked the wizards for the same reason most people like wizards: They stepped the users through sometimes complex tasks such as creating a new virtual machine and, for the most part, the users didn't have to think too much about what VirtualCenter was doing. They also liked the inventory model that allowed them to navigate through all their servers and virtual machines and group them into folders in ways that made sense to them (Figure 12.2).

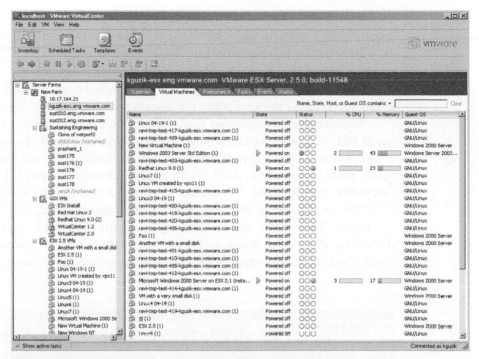

Figure 12.2. VirtualCenter 1.0 inventory and list of virtual machines.

There were, on the other hand, a whole slew of things that turned out to be unusable. Generally, it wasn't the interaction that bothered the users; it was either features they didn't need or features they did need but weren't developed with enough depth or enough support—they liked them, but they needed much more for them to be useful. For example, summary page graphs were unnecessary, the permissions model was necessary but not flexible enough, and "farms" was a concept introduced too early and wasn't fully developed.

Summary Page Charts

Summary page charts were a feature that the engineers had spent a lot of time on but was not so useful to users. These were snazzy charts that showed some interesting statistics of the system, such as resource usage changes and top resources consumed. This idea was presented to users before development. Their responses were something like, "Sure, sounds like a good idea," but they didn't really understand what Carl and Brian had in mind because there was nothing they could see and interact with at the time.

"Bob didn't like the summary page charts as much as we thought he would," reported Carl.

"Why not?" asked Brian, surprised. "I thought he would find them very useful for keeping track of what the system was doing."

"Unfortunately," explained Carl, "they aren't really showing the data he needs and are not understandable at a glance. What he really wants is an alert at the summary level that warns him if something is out of whack. If he needs more information, he'll go to the performance charts." Carl smiled sheepishly and shrugged. "Too bad. They make such great eye candy."

"We spent a lot of time on those charts," Brian sighed.

Figure 12.3 shows the summary page charts. The table in the middle shows the three most active and three least active hosts. However, no one cared about the least active hosts and wanted to see many more than three

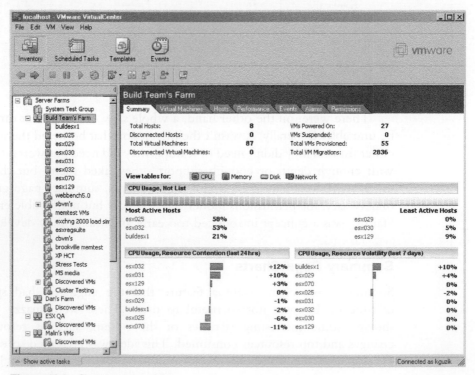

Figure 12.3. Summary page charts.

of the most active ones. The chart on the bottom is visually inconsistent. It was not understood at a glance because the red bars (indicating that something is wrong) extend to the right (the "positive" direction). The information is showing which virtual machines need more resources (red bars = warning) and which have more than they need (green bars = okay). The chart on the right showed the change in memory and CPU usage over time and was not understood at all.

Bob's reaction to the summary page charts in essence was "Wow, what a great idea!" and "Wow, these just don't work." It was a feature Bob wanted, but the presentation was wrong.

This is a common mistake: Vivek and Carl thought they understood Bob's needs from what he *said*. Bob thought he understood what Vivek and Carl *meant*. Bob was agreeable to the idea in general, but because he couldn't interact with the design or see the precise data that would be displayed, his agreement was misleading. Everyone happily went off in the wrong direction. If there had been time to present Bob with a working prototype, or at least the specific data sets for the charts, they might have gotten it right.

Permissions Model

The users liked the permissions model that allowed them to set and restrict access for individual users to the virtual machines (Figure 12.4). For example, Bob needed to ensure that his IT folks had access only to the areas and objects within VirtualCenter for which they were responsible. This is due to both security concerns and the need to mitigate damage that can be caused by mistakes on the part of lower-level IT folks. Bob was accountable for any breaches in security (such as people getting access to virtual machines they shouldn't be able to see) and for keeping the system up and running 24/7. Restricting access to critical machines is the first line of defense when trying to prevent catastrophic failures. VirtualCenter gave Bob only four types of permissions, which were not enough for the granularity of access control that he and his staff needed. Nonetheless, he used those four permissions extensively because he needed them, but he complained because he needed more.

Farms

Farms represented a collection of ESX servers that were "pooled" together so their resources could be shared by all the virtual machines in the farm. The grand plan for VirtualCenter was to manage hosts automatically so that

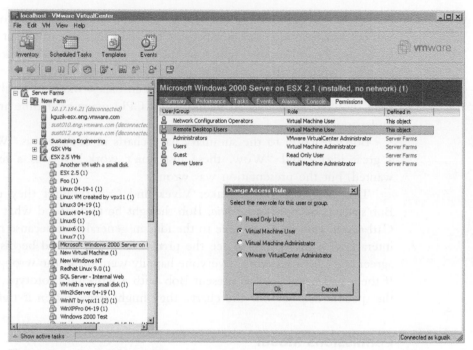

Figure 12.4. Permissions model.

virtual machines could become completely divorced from the hardware on which they ran and the user would never have to know or care which virtual machines lived on which hosts. Unfortunately, there wasn't enough time to implement this concept fully, and this functionality (which would eventually evolve into the cluster and load balancing features for VirtualCenter 2.0) was mostly left out. Because of this, farms in VirtualCenter 1.0 imposed unintended restrictions in the user model that completely separated groups of hosts from each other so that users could not migrate virtual machines across farms, just across hosts within a farm. This made organization of virtual machines more difficult than users wanted.

However, users used them anyway. They learned to use farms as virtual firewalls that prevented interactions between groups of hosts and their virtual machines. When Carl and Brian later designed VirtualCenter 2.0, they augmented permissions to accommodate the need to move virtual machines across groups of servers, but users pointed out that the hard and simple firewall concept was lost when farms were removed. Permissions worked but were far more complicated. Farms had a use after all! It was the users' feedback that saved this concept.

The CI Presentation

A week or so after the CI report was distributed, Carl scheduled a meeting for Pamela to present findings to the entire team: Vivek and the marketing folks, Brian and the engineers, the engineering director, the quality assurance folks and the writers, and anyone else who had an interest or an opinion about the usability of VirtualCenter. By now, the team had read the report, but Carl didn't want to rely on everyone to distill out the important points for themselves; he wanted Pamela to make a professional presentation to give credibility to the findings.

The CI revealed that, overall, VirtualCenter 1.0 worked for users because it gave them something they needed to do their jobs: They could deploy virtual machines much more easily than physical machines and they could clone virtual machines, create new virtual machines, and organize them at a glance. The users had VMotion, which allowed them to move virtual machines, while they were running, from one server to another. This was miraculous technology for many users. Carl had spent a lot of time designing and Brian and the engineers had spent a lot of time implementing these important features that users needed, and it paid off. Those things were easy for the user to use.

The CI also came back with a laundry list of issues and their priority for the users. Carl reviewed the report from Pamela, pulled out the recommendations, and put them into a spreadsheet with a simple priority index. Then he, Vivek, and Brian went through the list, talked about the specific issues, and reprioritized based on importance to the user and difficulty to implement. This list became the task list of enhancements for the next releases. It was a significant list, and VirtualCenter versions 1.1 and 1.2 incorporated about 80% of these enhancements, which were well received by the users.

Although ease of use is the number 1 concern for the UCD specialist, implementation difficulty should not be overlooked. There can be features that are disproportionately difficult to implement for the amount of benefit the users receive. It may be more prudent to spend time on issues that are easier to implement but perhaps less beneficial to the users because more of them can be resolved. These trade-offs must be weighed carefully when deciding which issues to tackle.

Having received validation of the overall concept and armed with specific and well-prioritized issues, Brian and the engineers were eager to start in on the bug-fixing releases.

The CI study and its results were so well received that the management team began to see UCD as a necessary part of the development process.

Marching orders were given to include more formal user testing, more customer interviews, and more CIs. The success of this first study encouraged the management team to push hard to create an entire user experience team to handle the UCD needs of a growing set of product lines.

> **Questions**
>
> 3. Why was the CI successful?
> 4. Why was Brian more engaged in improving the features he developed?
> 5. How are the roles of an interaction designer and a usability engineer different?

Designing VirtualCenter 2.0

After the positive feedback from the CI, Brian was very excited to get started on designing VirtualCenter 2.0, now that the minor releases of VirtualCenter 1.1 and 1.2 had mostly addressed the issues from VirtualCenter 1.0. Virtual-Center 2.0 was finally going to fulfill the grand vision for VirtualCenter. Brian was already brainstorming how to give users more effective management control of their memory and CPU resources and how to harness the power of pooling those resources to an even greater extent. Now that users were able to quickly and easily deploy and migrate virtual machines, they were starting to see the full potential of virtualization and ask for features that Brian and Vivek were already planning, like automatic load balancing and failover, which is the ability to decide what to do in the event that a server with running virtual machines goes down. The team started to think about how to integrate this concept with the current inventory model.

In the fall of 2004, VMware held its first ever user conference, VMworld. The products had become so popular that over 1,600 people from 27 countries attended, which was much larger than anyone had expected. By this time, VirtualCenter was 11 months old and version 1.2 had just been released. The user experience team had grown to four full-time people. Carl attended VMworld to talk with the now experienced users about their usage of VirtualCenter a year after they first started evaluating and using it.

The Case-Study Validation

Several customers gave presentations at the conference telling their stories, such as how they started virtualizing their environment and what it had done for them. Their experiences were very similar, and the stories went something like this:

> I'm Joe from Frobnitz, Inc. We are a $2B company and have a need to maintain large amounts of data. Before virtualization, we had several large servers rooms crammed with hundreds of servers and racks sprawled across the data center. If someone needed a new server, it took weeks to deploy—first, we had to order the new machine, then we had to find space for it, get it installed onto the network properly, and get the necessary applications loaded onto it. The air-conditioning bill alone was huge.
>
> When we heard about VirtualCenter and what it could do for us, we were very intrigued. But we were a little reluctant to start virtualizing our entire infrastructure. What if it didn't deliver on its promise and our processes were disrupted? We started by virtualizing a small part of the business, and it was phenomenal!
>
> Today, we have one-tenth the number of physical servers holding twice as many virtualized servers as we used to use. When someone needs a new server, we find a template virtual machine that contains what they need and clone it. If we don't have one that fits their needs, we create a new one. The whole process takes less than 30 minutes and requires very little effort. The user can call us for a new server and we can deliver it the same day! Now, people are using a lot more servers than they did before because it's so easy to get another one!
>
> Oh, and by the way, we've been able to free up some of the server room space for other uses and our air-conditioning bill has been cut in half! (See Figure 12.5 for an example.)

At the end of a panel discussion Carl went up to the panel table and introduced himself to one of the five customers as the interaction designer for VirtualCenter. Every one of the panelists stopped talking and stared at him. One by one, they got up to shake his hand and pat him on the back. They all said, "Just keep doing this." Carl was shocked. He'd never before had a customer say "I love this interface!" No one ever talks about good user interface. If it's noticeable enough to warrant comment, it's usually bad. Carl realized that the user experience of VirtualCenter extended far beyond the computer screen. The reduction in the amount of physical space needed to house the servers was also a contributor to the positive user experience.

The success of VirtualCenter 1.2 did not mean that the VMware team could rest. On the contrary, the users were beating down the door, and competition was starting to take notice. Now that users had a taste of what

Figure 12.5. From this (left), 300 physical servers, to this (right), a single rack of 8 ESX servers.

could be done in a virtualized environment, they wanted more. Ideas were coming out of the woodwork.

But there was a sense among the engineers that all was not rosy. They were especially concerned about something they discovered during the user conference and through discussions on the Internet user forums. Users were starting to deploy thousands of virtual machines, not the 50 to 100 as the team had originally speculated (Figure 12.6). Virtual machines were so easy to create and deploy that the barrier to usage had been broken. The barriers on physical machines are cost and time to deploy. Virtual machines, in this sense, are basically free, so users are able to create as many as they want.

It seemed that the inventory user interface (a tree list) was woefully inadequate to handle this volume. It was going to need a lot of rework, and the engineers were already brainstorming how to improve it based on feedback from the user conference and the web forum. Perhaps another metaphor was needed—a search mechanism or a way of limiting the inventory through filtering or grouping.

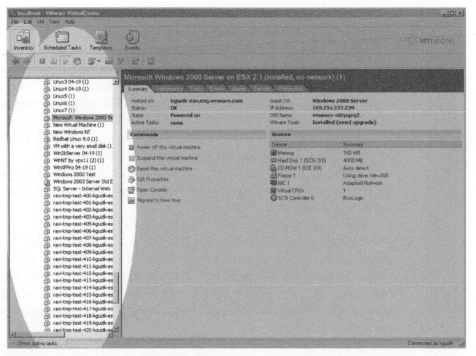

Figure 12.6. Hundreds of virtual machines.

With all the hoopla and kudos and despite the complaints, one message was loud and clear: "Don't change it!" What the users really meant was they liked the interaction and current ease of use of the product. The challenge was clear: Fix it without breaking it.

Questions

6. How can the success of a user interface create problems for the application?
7. How does one go about integrating new features without losing the ease of use of the popular original version?

The Inventory Model

It became clear that the inventory model was not going to scale well from tens of virtual machines and hosts to thousands. The users had initially anticipated their usage based on their current use of physical machines. As it turns out, the use of virtual machines completely changed their methodology. They used more virtual machines because they could. They would have used more physical servers if it were possible, but the cost and space restrictions were too prohibitive to allow it. Like most revolutionary technologies, virtual machines don't just fill an existing need; they create needs people never realized they had.

"Interesting that people are creating so many virtual machines," said Vivek. "Who woulda thunk? But, it makes sense."

"Yeah, it does," agreed Carl. "It reminds me of what happened when the telephone was invented. There was speculation at the time that every town was going to need one."

Vivek raised an eyebrow. "Really? Just one?"

Carl chuckled. "There was a TV show in the 60s called 'Green Acres' about a tiny town named Hooterville," he said. "When the town phone rang, the person who answered it would have to run out to the recipient's house and drag the person back to the post office, the site of the lone telephone. The process could take 20 minutes. The person on the other end of the line just waited!"

When a company creates new needs, the pressure is on to fulfill them. So VMware set to work figuring out how to adapt the existing user interface to manage thousands of virtual machines.

Ultimately, it was decided to work within the framework of the existing inventory model (filtering and grouping rather than a different model of search) because the users liked it and were accustomed to it. They were familiar with tree organizations and found them very easy to use. Other models (search and two-dimensional graphs of object relationships) were explored but in the end were considered too risky for the relatively short development cycle allotted to version 2.0. The team enjoyed the benefits of having such a well-received user interface and did not want to risk that level of satisfaction by changing the basic model. So Carl and Brian explored ways to expand the real estate for the growing number of user objects and to provide additional flexibility in organization to meet a broader set of needs.

Prototyping

VMware was growing almost as fast as its new products were selling. The engineering team was large by now and was experiencing a lot of growing pains. New people were hired every day who had different ideas about how things should work. The good news was that the team was highly motivated, smart, and cared a lot about good design. The bad news was that not everyone had the same idea of what good design was.

There were many ideas on how to manage thousands of hosts and virtual machines. A very logical idea was to filter the inventory, but filtering a tree structure is not an easy task. Reorganizing is another option, but, again, reorganizing a tree is difficult because it disrupts the hierarchical relationships. Searching the tree seemed like a good idea as well, but that would only solve the problem of finding a given virtual machine, not that of maintaining a logical and useful organization.

Half a dozen models were explored and rejected for various reasons, and the team began to split into different camps. Brian and the engineers preferred the filtering option. Vivek thought users would rather use a Windows Explorer model because it was familiar to Windows users. Carl thought a search mechanism would surely be the easiest model to understand. Everybody dug in their heels and became completely paralyzed.

Getting agreement across a large group was difficult. It took several months to decide on the inventory model, and it eventually came down to one of three ideas, so Carl lobbied the engineering director to make a specific call. Looking at this situation, the team realized there was a problem with their process—too many captains, not enough soldiers, and no clear mechanism for breaking deadlocks. No one wanted to organize so that a single person called the shots, but there was clearly a need for a smaller decision-making body.

One idea that started to resonate was to provide different views into the tree and separate the different inventory objects—there were (from top down) server farms, servers, and virtual machines. In addition, new objects were already being designed that would add new functionality to help the user manage their system: clusters (groups of hosts) and resource pools (groups of CPU and memory).

Carl prototyped three different models of separating inventory objects (Figure 12.7) and arranged to interview seven users of VirtualCenter 1.0 and show them the mockups. The first model separated the inventory objects into five discrete views, one for each type of object. The second collected all objects into two views, one for virtual machines and templates and the other for hosts, clusters, networks, and data stores. The third displayed a separate view for each type of object in one panel at the top of the window and showed related objects for each selected item in a panel immediately below.

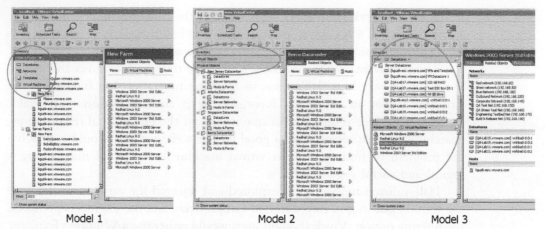

Model 1	Model 2	Model 3

Figure 12.7. The three models for the inventory view.

Carl and Pamela prepared a series of questions to probe the users' understanding of each model. Users were asked to talk about how they thought each model might fit into their organizations and what they saw as its strengths and weaknesses. The responses were recorded and analyzed to find patterns of usage, applicability, and problems. All users indicated that each model was useful to them in one way or another and represented an improvement over the existing inventory model. However, they each had different reasons and there was little agreement on which was the best approach.

Although consensus was not reached, the study highlighted three concepts in the new models that all users found particularly compelling:

1. The ability to see more relationships between objects in the inventory
2. Additional flexibility in organizing these objects
3. The ability to tailor the views for the individual members of their organizations

This last concept was deemed of critical importance because each user should have access only to those virtual machines, hosts, and functionality for which they are directly responsible. Anything else should be hidden to prevent them from making costly mistakes.

"So, you would like to see several different views of varying complexity and depth in the inventory," said Carl. "How would you expect your IT folks to use it?"

"Oh, no, I wouldn't show all of this to them," replied Bob. "*I* need this complexity, but I want *them* to see a simpler model. And I would only want them to see a subset of this inventory for security reasons."

The customer interviews revealed that although the IT managers like Bob wanted ultimate control and flexibility in VirtualCenter, they did not want their junior people to have that kind of access and did not believe technicians could handle the complexity. Bob worried that less experienced people might inadvertently break something if they were allowed full access, so he preferred to limit the view that these people would see.

Ultimately, there wasn't a clear consensus about which model worked best among the users. Everyone had strong opinions except the users. Carl realized that although decisions should be made based on user focus and past experience, the reality was that if engineering didn't buy into the idea, it wouldn't get built. The results of the study helped to sway some opinions, but not everyone agreed. Often, when engineers don't buy into the results of user testing, it is because they believe the users tested were not representative of the "real" users. It seems to be human nature to believe that if we understand the interface, everyone else should understand it too, which is why user testing is so important.

Also, personality issues come into play in the software development world. Very bright, highly motivated, and hard-working engineers can also be very passionate about the look and feel of their work. When there is not a clear design model for a given feature, the interaction designer's expert opinion should take precedent. Often, however, the designer must show that he or she understands the users, the usage patterns, and the application space well enough to gain credibility with the engineers to champion his or her ideas effectively.

The final compromise was to organize the inventory into a couple of different views. This model had been shown to users, and there was evidence from the previous study that it would be acceptable. However, more user testing would be required once the new design was fleshed out to verify that it would work.

Questions

8. What about the makeup of the team led to difficulties coming to a decision about the new interface?
9. How could the team decide whether to keep the successful but inadequate inventory model or risk a new model that might be less effective?

The First Usability Study

While the company was growing, the user experience team was also expanding. Carl hired two summer interns whose help allowed him to do more user testing in the summer of 2005 than would have been possible otherwise.

Besides the inventory, there were several other new features that needed to be tested. The two major and very high-value concepts being introduced in VirtualCenter 2.0 were failover and automatic load balancing. Failover is a concept that allows the system administrator to specify what to do in the event that a server goes down while running virtual machines. This concept was not new to these users. Dealing with server failure is what they do all day, everyday, whether they use virtual machines or physical ones. The expectations for this feature were high, and the interface had to meet all the users' needs.

Automatic load balancing allows the system administrator to group a set of servers into a cluster so they can share resources and, using VMotion, automatically move running virtual machines from an overloaded host to a more idle one. Users do not have this ability at all with physical machines, and with VirtualCenter 1.0 could only migrate virtual machines manually with limited insight into the overall performance of the hosts so they could make load-balancing decisions. Before introducing this new concept, Carl wanted to learn whether users would understand the value of this feature and whether it would integrate well into the existing product.

The Protocol

Carl called Pamela again to help conduct a usability study. Pamela put together a protocol, and it quickly became apparent that it was going to take the user several hours to complete the necessary tasks to get the feedback the team needed. Pamela knew from past experience that users can be expected to be at their best only for about 90 minutes, at most 2 hours before they become fatigued and less effective and focused. Based on her advice the team decided, with much reluctance, that the study would need to be limited in scope and some of the features would need to be left untested. It was a very difficult decision to choose which features to leave out of the test, but ultimately the test included what were perceived to be the two riskiest features—the new inventory model and load balancing.

The Prototype

Carl and the user experience team developed a medium-fidelity prototype by taking screenshots of VirtualCenter 1.2 and modifying them to demonstrate the proposed features. The term "low-fidelity" describes hand-drawn or wireframe static images intended to get feedback on design concepts. Details of the user interface elements are suppressed to remove distraction and provide focus on the concepts being presented. High-fidelity refers to working prototypes or an actual working product where the intent is to get feedback on details such as specific controls and number of steps to complete a task. Medium-fidelity is not a commonly used term but better describes the prototype used here. Static screenshots of the existing product were embellished with the addition of the new concepts. They were put into a PowerPoint deck and grouped together for each of the tasks Pamela had designed for the protocol (Figure 12.8). Each set of tasks contained all the necessary screenshots for the correct actions as well as a few for what were anticipated to be common incorrect actions. Pamela, who was not colocated with Carl or any of the users, conducted a WebEx session with each of them. WebEx (http://www.webex.com) is a technology that allows for remote dial-up of meetings with the ability to view presentation slides in real time on the remote person's computer. As it happens, it also works very well for remote user testing. Pamela was able to walk the users through the slides

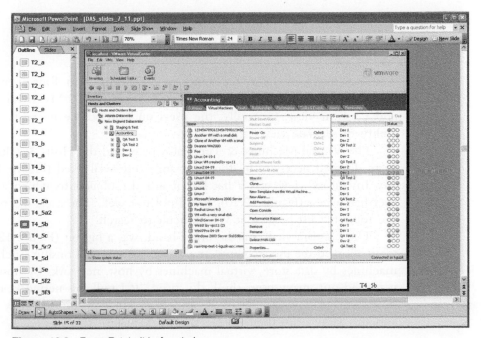

Figure 12.8. PowerPoint slide for study.

while they sat at their own desks using WebEx and the phone. She asked questions at each step of the way about how well these concepts met their needs and how easy or difficult they were to use. The team (Vivek, Brian, and Carl) sat at their own desks and observed the WebEx session with their speaker phones on mute. They could hear Pamela and the study participant, but neither Pamela nor the users could hear the team. The team communicated separately with each other and with Pamela via instant messaging and could answer questions for Pamela when the user asked something she didn't know. This communication allowed a relatively seamless test session and provided Pamela with additional information she could use during her conversations with the users. In many ways this type of interactive remote setup showed definite advantages over the more traditional face-to-face testing session.

Questions

10. What about the use of medium-fidelity prototypes in these studies made testing easier and more cost effective?
11. What about the method of remote testing used in these studies made testing easier and more cost effective?

Test Results

The inventory model tested split the inventory into four views: Virtual Machines & Templates view, Hosts & Clusters view, My Inventory view, and Custom view. Generally, the users understood the necessity and desirability of separate views and liked it.

The Virtual Machines & Templates view and the Hosts & Clusters view were deemed necessary by the users and were well liked (Figure 12.9). The My Inventory view was a flat list of just the objects to which a particular user had access (Figure 12.10). It did not test well. The users did not see any use for a flat list because it was difficult to search.

The Custom view, on the other hand, was a big hit (Figure 12.10). This view allowed the user to show any object by any relationship (such as virtual machines by data store, virtual machines by host, networks by host, etc.). As it turned out, many users think this way: "If I pull this network, how many hosts will go down?" This is an important kind of question they ask often, and this view helps them to see the world in just this way.

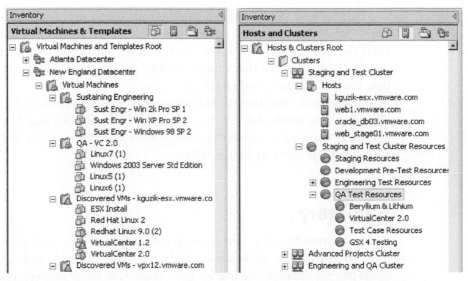

Figure 12.9. Inventory model: Virtual Machines & Templates view and Hosts & Clusters view.

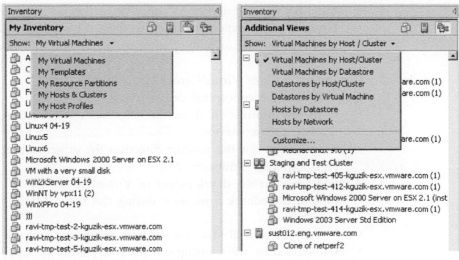

Figure 12.10. My Inventory and Custom views.

As much as the users liked the Custom view, it was decided that again, due to time constraints, the team would defer this feature until a future release even though it would be a very useful view. It is important to prioritize all the desirable features that could possibly go into a product and remember that there is always another release.

In the end, the Virtual Machines & Templates view and the Hosts & Clusters view made the cut, but not the My Inventory and Custom views. This was deemed a reasonable compromise that fit into the timeframe and allowed for growth in future releases.

Summary

VMware introduced a new conceptual design to the market that allowed users to consolidate their servers and save space, money, and time. But this concept of virtualization was so new there was no precedent for how users would interact with such a system. The company did several things to ensure that these new products would be easy for users to learn and use:

1. Hired an interaction designer, who
    *   Used his past experience to conceive of a new conceptual design
    *   Hired the user experience team to keep up with new work
    *   Hired an outside usability consultant to provide unbiased feedback from the user
2. Conducted a CI of VirtualCenter 1.0, which
    *   Validated the conceptual design
    *   Gathered information about the customer's organization, business models, and workflow
    *   Set the stage for the product direction for subsequent releases (1.1, 1.2, and, ultimately, 2.0)
3. Applied UCD to the development of VirtualCenter 2.0:
    *   Obtained feedback from users during the first VMworld User Conference
    *   Prototyped several ideas for the new features
    *   Conducted usability testing on the new feature prototypes

VirtualCenter 2.0 and ESX Server 3.0 were recently released as a combined product called VMware Infrastructure 3 to a very excited customer base. The benefits of this next generation product—automated load balancing, clustering of servers for the purpose of pooling resources, and failover—have been acknowledged as a leap ahead of the prior generation of virtual machine management. The concepts involved are so complex and so new that without an easy-to-use interface the user might not be able to realize the benefits of a virtual infrastructure without a lot of assistance from VMware.

There are, of course, a group of users (often referred to as the "early adopters") who use an important new technology even if it is difficult because they need it. VMware has recognized that to reach the majority user, who will not put up with difficult or fussy products, it needs to invest in usability. The addition of staff (the team is now seven interaction designers and still growing) gave them the ability to spend more time getting user feedback and improving the design concepts. From all appearances, VMware Infrastructure 3 is poised to be an even bigger hit than the revolutionary VirualCenter.

Further Reading

Righi, C., and Clow, A. (February 2004). *Programmers are people too: applying user-centered design to middleware.* TaskZ.com article. Retrieved from http://www.taskz.com/ucd_righi4_indepth.php

Rudd, J., Stern, K., and Isensee, S. (January 1996). *Low- vs. high-fidelity prototyping debate.* ACM/SIGCHI Interactions article. Retrieved from http://delivery.acm.org/10.1145/230000/223514/p76-rudd.pdf?key1=223514&key2=1875646511&coll=&dl=GUIDE&CFID=15151515&CFTOKEN=6184618

Thompson, K., Rozanski, E., and Haake, A. (October 2004). *Here, there, anywhere: remote usability testing that works.* Proceedings of the 5th conference on Information Technology Education. Retrieved from http://delivery.acm.org/10.1145/1030000/1029567/p132-thompson.pdf?key1=1029567&key2=6716646511&coll=portal&dl=ACM&CFID=482409&CFTOKEN=32903881

VMware, Inc. (2006). *What is virtualization?* Retrieved from http://www.vmware.com/virtualization/

VMware, Inc. (2006). *What is virtual infrastructure?* Retrieved from http://www.vmware.com/vinfrastructure/

Isis Mobile: A Case Study in Heuristic Evaluation

Rosemary Pluchino, Texas Instruments

> *"Well, I'd like to be sure that people will not only like how our PDAs look but feel confident in using our products enough to consider us for a future purchase," said James. "I'm confident in the marketing strategy, but I still feel there may be something we're overlooking in terms of what the users need."*

Isis Mobile's History and Direction

Isis Mobile is a successful start-up company involved in the design and production of cordless phones and venturing into the development of handheld cellular devices. James Cartwright, founder and president of the company, saw an opportunity to incorporate cell phones with more elaborate scheduling-type features found in digital organizers. The idea came to him with the surge in cell-phone popularity. If most people were carrying cell phones and depending on them throughout the day and also carrying digital organizers, why not merge the two? This product would be the first of its kind to be developed. The company could even have the first one that hit the market if they played their cards right.

James turned to his development team, which comprised industrial designers, marketing specialists, and mechanical, electrical, audio, and software engineers. He challenged them to create a product that was more than a cell phone and more than an organizer, more like a pocket-sized personal computer capable of placing and receiving calls. The team worked diligently to meet this challenge.

The marketing team was first in line, defining who the target users would be and what features would be vital to the product's success. They began with the assumption that the user base would be likely to consist of "high-end power users." The type of person who would likely benefit from a combined cell phone–digital organizer is someone in a high-profile position, who maintains a demanding schedule, who potentially travels quite a bit, and must be accessible at all times. Doctors, lawyers, and even real-estate agents would fall into their definition of a high-end power user.

Marketing then tested their assumption by hosting a set of focus groups that included a broad range of occupations to see whether the target market they defined would indeed be interested in their proposed product. Of course, people not belonging to the anticipated target market were also included for comparison. Ultimately, the results indicated that the prediction the marketing team made in terms of the target user base was in fact correct.

A few marketing representatives then recruited some participants who fit this user profile for another type of research effort. The marketing reps conducted an ethnographic study, which consisted of observing these people for several days in their work and home environments. In this way marketing learned about the participants' needs in a more contextual and concrete way. The resulting observations were used to make informed decisions about features that would be most appealing to their users and could provide the most benefit to their hectic lives.

The next step was to make a business case for this type of device. Marketing worked with engineering and finance to come up with their best estimate of how much it would cost to make the product. Once this figure was attained, they began researching how much their target users would be willing to pay for this product.

Once again a set of focus groups was run. Marketing discovered that not only were people eager to get their hands on such a device, they were willing to pay more than four times the minimum sales price they needed for a healthy profit. This product would mean absolute success for their company!

Their first concept sketches as well as the flow diagrams of their proposed user interface (UI) were near completion after 4 months. The product team was confident that their designs were well thought out and presented their proposed product line to upper management.

James Cartwright wasn't sold yet on the new concept. He had heard quite a bit on the marketing strategy and positioning of their new line of personal digital assistants (PDAs), but how could they be sure that once people purchased the product they would be satisfied and even consider Isis for future product purchases? With increasing competition and high-profile product reviews available, James knew they ran the risk of flopping with their initial product release—a mistake that would take a huge recovery effort for their brand name.

James met with the product team directors to gain an understanding of what was driving their designs. James found extensive market analysis data but little else to really back how successful these products would be. Sure, the team had nailed down the target users, the features, and the price bracket—but nothing showed whether the design of the UI would be appealing to users, or even usable for that matter. James knew that even if the market accepted the look and cutting-edge features of their product, the new device could be headed for failure if it was too complicated to use.

Determining the Need for a Heuristic Evaluation

James turned to Michael Redding, a highly esteemed human factors engineer for a consulting firm he had read about in a number of online product reviews. He is regarded as one of the industry's best, with a particular focus on small-screen-device usability.

"Michael, how can we be confident that our proposed product strategy will not fail?" James asked.

"There are a number of ways to do that. What exactly are you trying to accomplish?" Michael replied.

"Well, I'd like to be sure that people will not only like how our PDAs look but feel confident in using our products enough to consider us for a future purchase. I am confident in the marketing strategy, but still feel there may be something we're overlooking," James clarified.

"Has there been any work done in terms of usability?" asked Michael.

"Not yet. With our budget limitations we were hoping to be able to bring someone in when our first production model was complete," James confessed.

Michael smiled, "James I'm glad you called me in to discuss this. If you wait until production units are ready, there is little likelihood that anything can be done at that point. Software will have been coded and tools will have been made—it will be very expensive to make any changes and we will be limited as to what can or cannot be improved within your release schedule."

"What do you mean exactly?" James asked.

"Think about it James," Michael continued. "If the first usability study is done with a nearly completed product, you run a high risk of users finding usability issues that will require major design changes. Any benefit that can be realized through their input may not be able to be resolved and implemented by your deadlines or within your budget."

Michael continued. "Look, what I'm about to propose will catch a number of usability issues now, so we can address those before bringing users in. Allocating a portion of your budget for an evaluation at this early stage will ensure we catch these issues before tools are made and before software is coded. This will minimize any rework that needs to be done and save cost and time too. We can still bring users in to validate the changes as we move forward."

"You mean we'd still need budget to run a study later as well? I'm not sure we're quite prepared for that," James looked sullen for a moment. "All the same, I am curious, what do you have in mind?"

"A heuristic evaluation. It's basically a sanity check where usability experts evaluate the product against several well-known design principles. It is a method that was first described by Jakob Nielsen and Robert Mack in 1994. Since then, others have contributed to elaborate on these guidelines, defining them more thoroughly and more specifically to their particular field of use. Bruce Tognazzini, for example, developed a set of heuristics geared toward interaction design of traditional global user interfaces. Think of it like preventative maintenance; typically the most obvious usability problems can be filtered out," Michael explained.

"Well, what exactly are the pros and cons to this type of evaluation?" James inquired.

"The pros of a heuristic evaluation include its cost-effectiveness and its ability to be implemented very early on in the design stages. It can be performed quickly and requires only a small number of evaluators, typically about three to five. It can be performed remotely, so you won't need to provide a lab or incur any cost for recruiting participants. Also, a heuristic evaluation can save you money by identifying and resolving major usability issues very early on in the design process."

"This sounds great so far, but what are the cons?" asked James.

Michael replied, "As for the cons, a heuristic evaluation does not leverage feedback from actual users and is subject to evaluator bias. It is also extremely dependent on the skill level of the people doing the evaluating. The sets of problems found may not have much overlap with those found by user studies, and the same problems may not be rated at the same severity. Heuristic evaluations can produce false positives and, if not well managed, can take as many resources as a usability study. It also does not provide any quantitative data," Michael explained.

"Honestly Michael, the fact that problems found may not line up with those of our target users worries me," James confessed. "However, we are not in a position to take any chances with this release—we need this product to succeed. I am familiar with the work you've done and understand you are one of the leading experts in small-screen-device usability," James seemed torn for a moment as he thought.

"Well, I can see how getting problems out of the way early will help us later on," James agreed. "And we do want to have a usable product. Also, if spending more of our budget now will help us later on, then that makes sense. And you did say we could validate with users later, correct?"

"Yes James, absolutely, a user study can be performed to validate the product. That will provide the quantitative data that is missing from what we'll be doing up front," Michael assured him.

"Okay Michael, you've convinced me that an upfront heuristic evaluation is our best option. When can you start?" James said as he shook Michael's hand.

"Excellent!" said Michael, "I've got a couple of team members finishing up another project this week, and we can get started on Monday."

Questions

1. What factors about this situation made heuristic evaluation a better choice than user testing?

Planning and Performing a Heuristic Evaluation

After getting James' approval of his proposal for the heuristic evaluation, Michael immediately requested copies of the PDA concept sketches and flow diagrams of the proposed UI. He worked with James to identify key features that would be targeted in their marketing campaigns. This would ensure that special attention would be paid to these key features during their evaluation. Michael was eager to begin preparing for the evaluation.

Michael enlisted the help of two of his teammates, Shaun Eaves and Ivy Brenner. He knew that having multiple evaluators working separately would increase the likelihood of capturing a good portion of major usability issues.

"Shaun and Ivy, as you know, we will be performing a heuristic evaluation of Isis Mobile's PDA concept. I stress to you both the importance of not collaborating until all three of us have completed the evaluation," Michael stated as he distributed the copies of Isis Mobile's concept sketches and flow diagrams for their UI.

"Of course, Michael," Shaun interjected. "Ivy and I are aware that not collaborating prior to completing our evaluation will minimize any bias in our independent analysis."

"Also, be sure to review the documents in full before beginning your evaluations, then evaluate on the second pass," added Ivy. "It is vital to familiarize ourselves with the materials and have a good understanding of Isis Mobile's intent prior to commencing the evaluation." Michael and Shaun nodded in agreement.

Michael also distributed copies of the Usability Heuristics (Table 13.1) and the First Principles of Interaction Design (Table 13.2). First, they reviewed the heuristics together. This served to refresh their memories and to answer any questions they might have had.

Michael then reminded Shaun and Ivy to provide a written summary of their findings, including the heuristic that applies to each of the findings. He also reviewed the Severity Rating Scale (Table 13.3) that they should use to classify each issue. This would ensure that each evaluator was using the same criteria in their ratings.

Michael had prepared a list of common cell phone/organizer tasks that users would be likely to perform and key features on which Isis was focusing their market strategy (Table 13.4). He distributed these to Shaun and Ivy as well, so they would be sure to cover these in their evaluation. They reviewed these next for clarity. Michael also encouraged them to provide as many solutions as possible to any design issues they found, to ensure the design team had options from which to choose.

"In a week, we will meet again and compare notes," Michael reminded them. "I will send out an Excel spreadsheet template for you to enter your findings into so it will be easier to compile later."

"Great, that will save us a good deal of time when we meet to review our issues." Shaun was really glad to hear that Michael had already thought of that.

Table 13.1. Usability Heuristics Developed by Jakob Nielsen and Robert Mack

Heuristic	Description
Visibility of system status	The system should always keep users informed about what is going on, through appropriate feedback within reasonable time.
Match between system and the real world	The system should speak the users' language, with words, phrases, and concepts familiar to the user, rather than system-oriented terms. Follow real-world conventions, making information appear in natural and logical order.
User control and freedom	Users often choose system functions by mistake and need a clearly marked "emergency exit" to leave the unwanted state without having to go through an extended dialogue. Support undo and redo.
Consistency and standards	Users should not have to wonder whether different words, situations, or actions mean the same thing. Follow platform conventions.
Error prevention	Even better than good error messages is a careful design that prevents a problem from occurring in the first place.
Recognition rather than recall	Make objects, actions, and options visible. The user should not have to remember information from one part of the dialogue to another. Instructions for use of the system should be visible or easily retrievable whenever appropriate.
Flexibility and efficiency of use	Accelerators—unseen by the novice user—may often speed up the interaction for the expert user to such an extent that the system can cater to both inexperienced and experienced users. Allow users to tailor frequent actions.
Aesthetic and minimalist design	Dialogues should not contain information that is irrelevant or rarely needed. Every extra unit of information in a dialogue competes with the relevant units of information and diminishes their relative visibility.
Help users recognize, diagnose, and recover from errors	Error messages should be expressed in plain language (no codes), precisely indicate the problem, and constructively suggest a solution.
Help and documentation	Even though it is better if the system can be used without documentation, it may be necessary to provide help and documentation. Any such information should be easy to search, focused on the user's task, list concrete steps to be carried out, and not be too large.

From Nielsen, J., and Mack, R. L. (1994). *Usability Inspection methods.* John Wiley & Sons. New York, NY.

Table 13.2. First Principles of Interaction Design Developed by Bruce Tognazzini

Principle	Description
Anticipation	Applications should attempt to anticipate the user's wants and needs. Do not expect users to search for or gather information or evoke necessary tools. Bring to the user all the information and tools needed for each step of the process.
Autonomy	The computer, the interface, and the task environment all "belong" to the user, but user autonomy doesn't mean we abandon rules.
	Use status mechanisms to keep users aware and informed.
	Keep status information up to date and within easy view.
Color blindness	Any time you use color to convey information in the interface, you should also use clear secondary cues to convey the information to those who won't be experiencing any color coding.
Consistency	Levels of consistency: 1. Interpretation of user behavior (e.g., shortcut keys maintain their meanings) 2. Invisible structures 3. Small visible structures 4. The overall "look" of a single application or service (splash screens, design elements) 5. A suite of products 6. In-house consistency 7. Platform consistency
Defaults	Defaults should be easy to "blow away:" Fields containing defaults should come up selected, so users can replace the default contents with new material quickly and easily.
	Defaults should be "intelligent" and responsive.
	Do not use the word "default" in an application or service. Replace with "Standard," "Use Customary Settings," "Restore Initial Settings," or some other more specific terms describing what will actually happen.
Efficiency of the user	Look at the user's productivity, not the computer's.
	Keep the user occupied. Because, typically, the highest expense in a business is labor cost, any time the user must wait for the system to respond before they can proceed, money is being lost.
	To maximize the efficiency of a business or other organization you must maximize everyone's efficiency, not just the efficiency of a single group.
	The great efficiency breakthroughs in software are found in the fundamental architecture of the system, not in the surface design of the interface.

Table 13.2. *Continued*	
Principle	**Description**
	Write help messages tightly and make them responsive to the problem: Good writing pays off big in comprehension and efficiency.
	Menu and button labels should have the key word(s) first.
Explorable interfaces	Give users well-marked roads and landmarks, then let them shift into four-wheel drive.
	Sometimes, however, you have to provide deep ruts. The closer you get to the naive end of the experience curve, the more you have to rein in your users. A single-use application for accomplishing an unknown task requires a far more directive interface than a habitual-use interface for experts.
	Offer users stable perceptual cues for a sense of "home."
	Make actions reversible.
	Always allow "undo."
	Always allow a way out.
	However, make it easier to stay in.
Fitts' law	The time to acquire a target is a function of the distance to and size of the target.
Human interface objects	Human interface objects can be seen, heard, touched, or otherwise perceived.
	Human interface objects that can be seen are quite familiar in graphic user interfaces. Objects that play to another sense such as hearing or touch are less familiar. Good work has been done in developing auditory icons.
	Human interface objects have a standard way of interacting.
	Human interface objects have standard resulting behaviors.
	Human interface objects should be understandable, self-consistent, and stable.
Latency reduction	Wherever possible, use multi-threading to push latency into the background.
	Reduce the user's experience of latency.
	Make it faster.
Learnability; limit trade-offs	Ideally, products would have no learning curve: Users would walk up to them for the very first time and achieve instant mastery. In practice, all applications and services, no matter how simple, display a learning curve.
	Limit the trade-offs. Usability and learnability are not mutually exclusive. First, decide which is the most important, then attack both with vigor. Ease of learning automatically coming at the expense of ease of use is a myth.

Table 13.2. *Continued*

Principle	Description
Metaphors	Choose metaphors well, so they will enable users to instantly grasp the finest details of the conceptual model.
	Bring metaphors alive by appealing to people's perceptions—sight, sound, touch, and kinesthesia—as well as triggering their memories.
Protect the user's work	Ensure that users never lose their work as a result of error on their part, the vagaries of Internet transmission, or any other reason other than the completely unavoidable, such as sudden loss of power to the client computer.
Readability	Text that must be read should have high contrast. Favor black text on white or pale yellow backgrounds. Avoid gray backgrounds.
	Use font sizes that are large enough to be readable on standard monitors. Favor particularly large characters for the actual data you intend to display, as opposed to labels and instructions. For example, the label, "Last Name," can afford to be somewhat small. Habitual users will learn that that two-word gray blob says "Last Name." Even new users, based on the context of the form on which it appears, will have a pretty good guess that it says "Last Name." The actual last name entered/displayed, however, must be clearly readable. This becomes even more important for numbers. Human languages are highly redundant, enabling people to "heal" garbled messages. Numbers, however, unless they follow a very strict protocol, have no redundancy, so people need the ability to examine and comprehend every single character.
	Pay particular attention to the needs of older people. Presbyopia, the condition of hardened less flexible lenses, coupled with reduced light transmission into the eye, affects most people over age 45. Do not trust your young eyes to make size and contrast decisions.
Track state	Because many of our browser-based products exist in a stateless environment, we have the responsibility to track state as needed.
	We may need to know: • Whether this is the first time the user has been in the system • Where the user is • Where the user is going • Where the user has been during this session • Where the user was when they left off in the last session and myriad other details.
Visible interfaces	Avoid invisible navigation. Most users cannot and will not build elaborate mental maps and will become lost or tired if expected to do so.

From Tognazzini, B. First principles of interaction design. Retrieved 8/27/06 from http://www.asktog.com/basics/firstPrinciples.html

Table 13.3. Severity Rating Scale Used by All Three Evaluators for Consistency

Severity Rating	Description
1	Cosmetic problem that does not impact usability; does not need to be fixed unless time permits
2	Minor usability issue; low priority; impedes usability but is easily corrected by user; likely to be a minor annoyance
3	Moderate usability issue; medium priority; impedes usability; requires effort on the part of the user to correct; some users may fail to do so
4	Major usability issue; high priority; impedes usability; limits use of certain features for most users
5	Usability disaster; problem must be fixed before product release

Table 13.4. Tasks and Features to Evaluate in the Heuristic Analysis

Powering the PDA on and off

Placing a call

Receiving a call

Storing a contact into the PDA's memory

Editing contact information

Deleting a contact from the PDA's memory

Downloading multiple contacts from your PC [Outlook] into the
   PDAs memory

Scheduling an appointment reminder

Retrieving a voice mail message

Sending a text message

Changing your ring tone

Setting your PDA to silent mode

Conference calling

Connecting the PDA to a wireless headset

Using speakerphone

"Okay, does anyone have any questions or concerns before we end this meeting?" Michael inquired.

Shaun shook his head no.

"All of my questions have already been answered, so I guess we're ready to go," Ivy commented.

"Great, well thanks for your time," Michael said as he began gathering up his paperwork.

Shaun and Ivy left the meeting eager to begin the evaluation. During the next week, they both worked independently to evaluate the PDA concept. Just as Michael had reminded them, they each reviewed all the documentation they had been provided and became familiar with the operation of the PDA.

Questions

2. Why does Michael have three evaluators assigned to evaluate the PDA concept?
3. Why is it important that the evaluators do not collaborate on the analysis?
4. Why does Michael stress finding as many solutions to problems as possible?

Reviewing, Comparing, and Compiling the Findings

In a week the team met to go over their findings. At this meeting each evaluator discussed each of the issues they identified. They merged the issues and their descriptions when there was more than one evaluator who identified the same problem. This allowed any additional insight into the problem to be captured for a more robust description of the issue that would be shared with Isis Mobile. Each evaluator also provided feedback and severity ratings in real time for issues not identified by one or more of the evaluators to see whether others had different perspectives unseen by the original identifier or alternate solutions.

All three evaluators identified the severity ratings they had assigned to each issue and averaged the severity scores for inclusion in the final report. They also reviewed their solutions to each issue and rank-ordered them in terms of their effectiveness in correcting the problem. The completed list of issues found was sorted by average severity score in descending order. Table 13.5 shows an excerpt of the compiled list.

After compiling their findings, Michael returned to Isis Mobile to give the industrial design team and the engineering team members the evaluation report. He met with the team to review the findings and answer any questions they had about the findings or implementing the recommended changes. He urged them to contact him if any questions arose as they worked through the issues.

In a few weeks a revised copy of Isis Mobile's PDA sketches and UI was sent to Michael, Shaun, and Ivy for review. Isis Mobile had addressed all the findings and recommendations, and these were being coded into the UI software. Tool production had also begun.

Michael was pleased with the progress that had been made at this early stage of the design, and Isis Mobile was confident that some of the obvious design issues had been caught before tooling and coding. The next step would be to bring users in to validate and help further refine their design.

Validating Design Changes

As the engineering team was implementing changes from the heuristic evaluation, Michael had collaborated with one of the marketing leads at Isis to recruit participants for the user study that fit into the PDA target user base. They did this by using a series of questions that could be used to determine whether potential participants fit the particular market segment Isis was focusing on. They used these questions to screen participants and determine which would be the best representatives for the lab study.

Michael recruited 10 participants in total, 5 for each of two major east coast cities where they planned to begin their initial product release. He was sure to get an even split of men and women and an even distribution of ages within Isis's target audience.

Table 13.5. Excerpt of the Compiled List of Usability Issues Found, Listing Applicable Heuristic(s) and Average Severity Scores

| Issue | Description | Heuristic | Severity Ratings | | | | Solutions |
			Michael	Shaun	Ivy	Average	
No tactile indicator on the number 5 key	This is a standard accessibility requirement and must be included on all telecommunication devices.	Consistency and standards	5	5	5	5.00	Add a raised tactile indicator on the 5 key that complies with standard.
Blank screen in battery save mode	After 10 minutes of inactivity, the product enters battery save mode. In this state, any button press would "wake" the PDA. However, there is no indication of the mode on the screen, which may lead users to believe their PDA was powered off by an inadvertent button press or the battery has failed. A user's first instinct may be to press power, which wakes up the PDA, but initiates power down.	Visibility of system status	3	4	4	3.67	1. Allow power key to wake PDA first and then power down if user presses it again. 2. Create a small battery save icon that remains blinking on a corner of the screen.
Ambiguous option labels when entering a contact	After entering a name and number into the address list, the options presented to the user are "Done" on the left and	Consistency and standards	3	3	4	3.33	Change "Done" to "Cancel," "Exit," or something that implies the number

Table 13.5. *Continued*

| Issue | Description | Heuristic | Severity Ratings | | | | Solutions |
			Michael	Shaun	Ivy	Average	
	"Save" on the right. Users read left to right and may not see the "Save" option before selecting "Done." When a user presses "Done," the address list entry is not stored. It seems logical that users, upon completion of the entry, would assume they were done and not expect this choice would exit them without saving.						will not be stored in memory.
Unintuitive error message in calendar	The calendar allows a maximum of 50 appointment reminders. Once this amount is reached, if the user enters another reminder, a pop-up with the following message appears: "Error—Buffer Overload." This is likely to confuse users because it is not plain language, and it does not help users understand how to correct the problem.	Error prevention	3	3	4	3.33	Change error message to say, "Memory full. Delete expired reminders?" Include "Yes" and "No" button options for users to select.

Table 13.5. *Continued*

			Severity Ratings				
Issue	Description	Heuristic	Michael	Shaun	Ivy	Average	Solutions
Unintuitive error message when searching for a contact not listed in phonebook	When searching for a contact in the address list that has not been saved previously, the following error appears: "Error 7x65b; Exit Application and Enter New Information." The error number holds no meaning to users and although some direction is given, it is not clear to users what the problem is. Also, "Enter New Information" is confusing in that it does not specify whether users should search for the contact again or whether they need to add this person to their contact list.	Aesthetic and minimalist design; error prevention	3	4	3	3.33	Reword error message to exclude error number and include clear explanation of problem, consider, "Contact Not Found. Add New Contact?" Have "Yes" and "No" button options for the user to select.
Inconsistent exit labels throughout UI	To exit some menus, the left option reads "back" and for others it reads "cancel," "done," or "exit" but the function is the same.	Consistency and standards	2	3	2	2.33	Choose a term and use it consistently throughout the interface.
No visual indicator for	A press and hold on the number 1	Flexibility and efficiency	3	2	2	2.333333	Add a voice mail icon onto

Table 13.5. *Continued*			Severity Ratings				
Issue	Description	Heuristic	Michael	Shaun	Ivy	Average	Solutions
voice mail shortcut	key automatically dials voice mail as an alternative to accessing it through menus. However, there is no visual cue to this shortcut on the 1 key itself.	of use; recognition rather than recall					the number 1 key.
Multiple labels for calendar feature	In different areas of the User Interface and User Manual, the Calendar feature is referred to as "Calendar," "Date Book," or "Organizer."	Consistency and standards	2	2	3	2.33	Choose one term and use it consistently throughout both the interface and manual.
User manual too wordy and large	Although the information in the manual is thorough, it can be distilled down to contain clear concise steps to accessing features; this reduces the manual size and increase its usefulness.	Help and documentation	2	2	2	2.00	1. Use a bullet format for feature access instructions. 2. Consider providing a separate "quick start" guide that outlines how to get started and two or three major features to get users up and running with their new product.

Michael spent 2 weeks running the test sessions and 1 week preparing the data for the report. He confirmed a high success rate for completing tasks and that the majority of users reported the PDA was extremely intuitive to use. A few minor changes, such as changing some labels, were included as recommendations. Overall, these were easy fixes, and Michael was confident that the PDAs were ready to make their release on schedule.

Isis Mobile benefited from planning and incorporating a heuristic evaluation early on in the design phase of their new product line. They were able to prevent usability problems from entering later phases of the project. They minimized cost in terms of time and rework and validated their design with users before release to ensure their product debut was not greeted with bad press and low sales, thus ensuring that end users would consider Isis Mobile for future purchases.

James Cartwright was not only pleased with the outcome of their initial release, he was also inspired by the possibility of being able to further improve products in a way that would positively impact those who buy and use them. He believed he may have found a way to truly differentiate their brand in the marketplace.

Going forward, as a direct result of the heuristic evaluation, James decided to hire a team of user-centered design personnel as part of the design team to help drive concepts into usable form and provide guidance throughout the product development process—not just at a point when concerns arise. He also mandated that a portion of the product development budget be allocated for usability studies and forward-looking research. He was convinced that the company would flourish because they were focusing on their customer's experience as a top priority.

Summary

The steps involved in planning and performing the heuristic evaluation included the following:

- Identifying the evaluators; three to five is typical for a heuristic evaluation.
- Ensuring that evaluators do not collaborate before completion; this minimizes bias.
- Using a common rating scale for severity of issues; this ensures consistency.

- Reviewing the entire interface at least twice; first to familiarize yourself with it and then to scrub for issues once a good understanding of the design intent has been realized.
- Documenting issues, applicable heuristics, severity, and possible solutions using a common template and/or checklist; this allows for ease of sorting and organizing issues for reporting.
- Comparing findings, severities, and proposed solutions after all evaluators are done with their evaluations; this distills the information into a single report.
- Validating design changes with users and refining the design where necessary.

The major benefits of the heuristic evaluation included the following:

- Can be implemented very early in the design process; it does not require functional products.
- Requires only a small number of evaluators and does not require the additional cost of recruiting participants or booking a lab.
- Can be done in a short amount of time.
- Provides a cost-effective way to prevent major known usability issues from making their way into later stages of the design process.
- Saves both time and money by eliminating problems very early and minimizing any last-minute rework.

A heuristic evaluation does have some shortcomings:

- It does not leverage feedback from actual users.
- It is subject to evaluator bias.
- It is extremely dependent on the skill level of the people doing the evaluating.
- It does not provide any quantitative data.
- A user study is recommended as a follow-up to validate the design.

Conducting up-front heuristic evaluations of design concepts can minimize rework later in the development process. It is a healthy way to validate whether initial designs are on the right track. Following up with user studies is highly recommended. Testing early and often can mean the difference between product success and failure.

Further Reading

Jeffries, R., Miller, J. R., Wharton, C., and Uyeda, K. M. (1991). *User interface evaluation in the real world: a comparison of four techniques.* Presented at CHI '91 Proceedings, (New Orleans, LA, April 28–May 2): pp. 119–124.

John, B. E. (1997). Tracking the effectiveness of usability evaluation methods. *Behavior & Information Technology,* 16:188–202.

Nielsen, J. (1992). *Finding usability problems through heuristic evaluation.* Presented at CHI '92, Proceedings (Monterey, CA, May 3–7), pp. 373–380.

Nielsen, J. (1994). *Enhancing the explanatory power of usability heuristics.* Presented at CHI '94 Proceedings, (Boston, MA, April 24–28), pp. 152–158.

Nielsen, J., and Landauer, T. K. (1993). *A mathematical model of the finding of usability problems.* Presented at INTERCHI '93 Proceedings, Amsterdam, April 1993 pp. 206–213.

Nielsen, J., and Mack, R. L. (1994). *Usability inspection methods.* John Wiley & Sons New York, NY.

Nielsen, J., and Molich, R. (1990). *Heuristic evaluation of user interfaces.* Presented at ACM CHI '90 Proceedings, (Seattle, WA, April 1–5), pp. 249–256.

Tognazzizi, B. *First principles of interaction design.* Retrieved 8/27/06 from http://www.asktog.com/basics/firstPrinciples.html

Vijavan, R. (1997). *CS6751: Topic report, heuristic evaluation.* Retrieved from http://www-static.cc.gatech.edu/classes/cs6751_97_winter/Topics/heur-eval/

CASE 14

Academic Manuscript Submission: A Case Study in Interaction Design

Scott McDaniel, Management Systems Designers, Inc.

> **Dr. Scott started the meeting off. "I'd like to try out this approach of actually designing the interface before we just jump into programming. So, I'm asking Sarah here to work with Rob and Sergei to work out the interface first. I know it's not how we usually do things, but I'm sure you all can figure out how to do this."**

Determining an Approach to Design

In 2004 the U.S. Congress decided that all academic articles funded by the National Institutes of Health (NIH) should be available to the public free of charge. Before then, such papers were only available in academic journals—in other words, by subscription. Taxpayers, who had funded the research to begin with, either had to pay a subscription cost in the hundreds of dollars or find the nearest academic library that had a subscription. Although the NIH examined the directive in detail and worked on setting policies to bring it about, responsibility for putting together a system to accept and display the free articles fell to Dr. Lithgow, director of one of the agency's technology divisions.

Dr. Lithgow went to Dr. Scott. Dr. Scott headed the division's information engineering unit and had led the development of both literature and scientific databases used by scientists the world over. Dr. Lithgow confided to Dr. Scott, "We've got a critical deadline here, and I want to be sure we don't screw this up. I need you to have this manuscript submission system done in 4 months. Congress is going to be watching this, so it's got to be on time and smooth as silk to use. If it's hard to use we'll take the fall for any adoption problems. The problem is, the policy guys are still figuring out all the specifics of how things will work."

Dr. Scott gave the project to Rob, a Ph.D. in biomechanics and upcoming young manager in the group. He also asked for Sarah, an interaction designer, to be part of the project from its inception. He gathered the two of them, plus the development manager, Sergei, and Sarah's supervisor for a kickoff meeting.

Dr. Scott started the meeting off. "I'd like to try out this approach of actually designing the interface before we just jump into programming. So, I'm asking Sarah here to work with Rob and Sergei to work out the interface first. I know it's not how we usually do things, but then we don't normally have projects with actual deadlines." Dr. Scott told Rob, Sarah, and Sergei about some of the policy decisions that had already been made:

- The articles would appear in an existing database of free academic articles that Dr. Scott's group maintained.
- Scientists who had agency grants have to send in their own articles.
- The article submission system would be tied to NIH's grants system such that scientists who followed the policy and submitted their articles would get credit for doing so the next time their grant came up for renewal. Thus their grants would have a greater chance of being renewed.

"The problem is," said Dr. Scott, "that these decisions are still fluid. Not only can they change, but there will be other requirements coming down all the way up through release."

"So, we need a flexible interface that can handle last-minute changes," said Rob.

After identifying this major risk, they moved on to the other one facing the project. "Sergei," said Rob, "who are you going to give the development to?"

Sergei shrugged his shoulders and explained that everyone was busy. "We have a candidate for an open position, so I will give it to him when he starts."

Sarah said, "Do you have someone who can work with us on the design team in the meantime? I think it's important to have a developer's perspective." Sergei shrugged again and said he'd see what he could do.

After the kickoff meeting, Sarah and Rob sat down to work out the project plan. Because Rob had little experience with interface design projects, Sarah proposed a framework based on Cognetics Corporation's LUCID, the Logical User Centered Interaction Design (see Sidebar). Before joining the NIH, Sarah had successfully used the approach on a variety of projects. LUCID divides projects into six stages; Rob and Sarah discussed typical deliverables for each of the stages, deciding which made sense for the academic manuscript submission system. Of particular concern were the design deliverables. Would they do paper prototyping? What kind of wireframes should they produce? How many design and testing iterations did they have time for? What should they produce aside from the wireframes?

> **Sidebar: Logical User-Centered Interaction Design**
>
> *Dr. Charles Kreitzberg, founder of Cognetics Corporation, first developed Logical User Centered Interaction Design (LUCID) to help manage projects and communicate to clients his approach to user interface design. Over the years, Whitney Quesenbery, Laura Snyder, Scott McDaniel, and many others contributed to its evolution. The framework is freely available and is described in Ben Shneiderman's* Designing the User Interface *and on the Cognetics Corporation website (http://www.cognetics.com).*

Rob and Sarah decided that there were two key deliverables to produce for each iteration of the design: a structural diagram of the user interface and wireframe mockups of the screens (devoid of graphic design). Table 14.1 shows all the deliverables they planned (not just the interaction design deliverables) and the time frame they gave themselves for each one.

Gathering User Data

With the completion of the project plan and kickoff meeting, the envision stage of the project was done. Sarah and Rob moved on to the discovery stage, where they intended to analyze their users' needs and set the user interface's requirements. As Sarah and Rob sat down to begin, Sarah asked, "So, how much do we actually know about the scientists who are going to use this? I'm trying to figure out just how much we should do in the discovery stage."

"Well, for the most part we've got principal investigators. The PIs are the heads of the lab and the ones who have the grants. The ones who do most of the research itself, though, are the postdoctoral fellows working in the lab. The postdoc is usually the first author and the PI is usually the last author," answered Rob.

"So who will be submitting it to us?"

"Probably the PI, though not necessarily. Since these are being credited to grants, though, a PI has to at least sign off on each submission."

LUCID Stage	Manager Activities	Designer Activities	Finished When ...
Envision — State and align business, user, and IT goals. Assemble project team. Achieve common understanding of the product concept as well as project objectives and limitations.	Establish project plan, including general strategy for usability activities for each stage. Assign and communicate roles, responsibility, and approval process. Achieve buy-in and common vision from stakeholders, and communicate that to the team.	Identify major user groups. Establish preliminary usability goals. Understand technical, schedule, and resource constraints. Gather high-level design ideas in the form of concept sketches.	All stakeholders and team members understand their roles, and the project vision and roles and vision have been documented.
Discovery — Analyze users, tasks, and information. Develop personas to profile users and scenarios to show their tasks. Derive high-level requirements from personas and scenarios. Revise usability goals.	Determine appropriate user analysis activities. Support designers in executing analysis activities, particularly in the areas of resources and access to users. Coordinate review and approval of personas, scenarios, and requirements.	Assist manager in determining appropriate user analysis activities. Conduct user analysis (interviews, contextual inquiry, usability tests, etc.). Create personas, scenarios, and requirements.	Personas, scenarios, and high-level requirements are approved.
Design Foundation — Establish the basic concept of the user interface, its objects, and its metaphors. Document navigation, basic screen types, and mental model underlying the UI.	Work with designers to plan design activities, usability evaluations, and the number of design iterations. Communicate/coordinate the approval process. Present the key screen prototype to executive management for feedback and approval.	Create the conceptual design, including key screen layouts, graphic design, navigation, and documentation of the target mental model. Conduct high-level usability evaluations. Create a key screen prototype to be tested with users and approved by management.	Executive management approves the design direction, embodied in a key screen prototype.

Design Detail Complete the user interface design, producing specifications for developers. Specifications include UI standards, screen layouts, and element-by-element specifications.	Work with designers to plan usability evaluations and manage their results. Communicate and coordinate the approval process. Coordinate specification handoff to development.	Document UI standards, containing both the graphic design and UI policy decisions. Create detailed layouts for screens and detailed specifications for each element. Conduct usability evaluations of specific screens or workflows.	Specifications are complete, reviewed, and turned over to developers.
Build Support developers and respond to last-minute design issues.	Work with designers to plan usability evaluations and manage their results. Plan and implement change control procedures to document and communicate redesigns.	Answer questions and support developers during coding, redesigning screens if needed. Conduct usability evaluation of critical screens, if necessary.	Development is complete and the product is tested and ready for release.
Release Design and test the out-of-the-box user experience. Measure user satisfaction and usability of the released product.	Plan design of customers' initial user experience. Work with designers to plan and coordinate usability evaluation of the released product. Plan measurement of user satisfaction.	Design and test customers' initial user experience. Conduct usability evaluation to measure the usability of the released product. Measure user satisfaction.	All measurement activities are complete and remaining usability issues have been transitioned to new projects.

Table 14.1. Project Plan for the Academic Manuscript Submission System, Showing the Design Deliverables Selected and the Time Frames for Their Production

Deliverable	Description	Date Due
	Stage: Envision	
Project plan	Establish deliverables and high-level activities for each stage	1 week (after project start date)
Kickoff statement	Document kickoff session and summarize project purpose and assumptions	1 week
Draft personas and scenarios	Early versions of user and task models	1 week
	Stage: Discovery	
Discovery project plan	Revisions to overall project plan and additional detail for the discovery stage	1 week
Personas	User model that presents a composite user, based on the user analysis	2 weeks
Scenarios	Narrative or bullet point summary of the most common or critical tasks involving the user interface	2 weeks
User requirements	Detailed list of each feature that the user interface must support	Draft, 3 weeks Sign-off, 4 weeks
	Stage: Design Foundation	
Design foundation project plan	Revisions to overall project plan and additional detail for the design foundation stage	4 weeks Dec. 30, 2004—shouldn't call out specific date
High-level user interface structural diagram	Graphic navigation map ("site map") that shows screen types and overall user interface structure	7 weeks
Key screen layouts	A mockup or "wireframe" for each of the key screen types identified in the high-level user interface map	Usability test, 1–5 weeks Usability test, 2–6 weeks Approval, 7 weeks
Design patterns	Documentation of basic interaction principles to be used throughout the user interface (how task flows work, how search works, etc.)	7 weeks
User interface design standards	Documentation of layout, HTML, font, and graphic standards	7 weeks

Table 14.1. *Continued*

Deliverable	Description	Date Due
User assistance plan	Determine how documentation and online help will be integrated with the user interface	7 weeks
	Stage: Design Detail and Build	
Design detail project plan	Revisions to overall project plan and additional detail for the design detail stage	TBD
Detailed user interface structural diagram	Graphic navigation map ("site map") that shows all screens and links among them	TBD
Screen-by-screen element specification	Documentation of each field or other element (data type, dimensions, related error messages, etc.)	TBD
User assistance specifications	Research and organize material for documentation (the "Content Specification" from JoAnn Hackos' system)	TBD
Working HTML screens and product	A finished product ready for testing and approval	17 weeks
User assistance	Finished documentation, tool tips, contextual help, FAQs, etc.	17 weeks
	Stage: Release	
Release project plan	Revisions to overall project plan and additional detail for the discover stage	TBD
"Out-of-the-box" usability test results	Usability evaluation of users' first-time experience with a product	18 weeks
Project wrap-up	Documentation of lessons learned and proper archiving of all project deliverables	18 weeks

Rob and Sarah inserted actual dates into their plan, but this one represents times since the project's start. They opted to leave some of the later milestones undefined until they had completed the early design stages. TBD, to be decided.

Sarah continued, "Hmm. That sounds like an approval workflow."

"How many papers do you think they'll submit in a year?"

"I don't know," said Rob. "When I was a postdoc I probably published three or four."

"Okay, we should check that. If it's that infrequent, we'll probably have to assume that they're new to the site each time—it could be months since the last time they submitted anything," said Sarah. "So how do they submit them to journals now? Can we follow something similar to that to build on something they're already familiar with?"

"I hope so. When I did it I'd uploaded a text manuscript file and then each of the figures to the publisher's website. That's what we'll do unless there's some reason not to."

"And if they've already done it for the journal, can't they just send us those files? Should be easy, right? The only thing I guess they wouldn't have is their grant information. How likely are they to know their grant numbers and such?" asked Sarah

"No idea," said Rob. "We should find that out."

Given these and other questions, Sarah suggested that she and Rob interview several PIs and several postdocs, and Rob readily agreed. Meanwhile, Rob began working on the data structures and process requirements. The submission process would involve a submitter providing bibliographic information about the manuscript, entering a grant number, and uploading files. Then, the submission system would create a single PDF document out of all of the files so the submitter could confirm that everything had uploaded properly. After that, a PI would approve the PDF file. After PI confirmation an NIH contractor would convert the submission into an XML web version—a process expected to take 2 weeks. Finally, the submitter and PI would review and approve the web version of the manuscript. After publication, the manuscript would appear in a public database of free journal articles.

Sarah worked on setting up the interviews and coming up with the interview script. Her goal was to create personas—models of the two user types (submitter and PI)—and then to create scenarios or task models based on how they submitted manuscripts to journal publishers. She would use these to work out the users' requirements.

Sarah and Rob conducted the interviews together, with Sarah leading and Rob taking notes. They talked to three PIs and three postdoctoral fellows and asked to see how they submitted manuscripts to journals. Although it turned out that PIs occasionally submitted the manuscripts, they usually had their postdocs do it because the postdocs were typically first author. Consistent with Rob's experience, the scientists Sarah and Rob talked to published two to four papers per year, meaning that they would use the academic manuscript submission system quite infrequently. They had easy access to all the information they needed to submit, such as grant numbers, but they did not necessarily have it all memorized or right on their desks. Sarah and Rob also learned that it typically takes 20 to 30 minutes to upload the files and submit a manuscript to a journal.

After the interviews Sarah produced two personas: Alice was the submitter and Dr. Prescott was the PI. Sarah then produced the scenarios, which often involved both personas. They looked at each of Alice's and Dr. Prescott's steps in the scenarios and wrote down a list of things the user interface should have to support their activities. Thus Sarah and Rob derived a set of user requirements. She also hoped to use the documents to get the developer up to speed quickly once Sergei had selected one. Table 14.2 shows the set of scenarios, and Table 14.3 shows one scenario with its related user requirements. Because manuscripts would go through several stages and approvals, a clear workflow would be a major part of the system. The manuscript's status had to be clear and the next step obvious.

Table 14.2. High-Level Requirements for the Academic Manuscript Submission System

Scenario	Title	Users
1	Submit a manuscript	Submitter
2	Review a manuscript	PI, submitter, author
3	Review/approve web version of manuscript	PI, submitter, author, contractor
4	Register and log in	All
5	Check status of all submissions	PI, submitter, author
6	Access publication history	PI, submitter, author
7	Upload manuscript	Publisher
8	Markup approved manuscript	Contractor
9	Retract a paper	PI

Given their limited resources, Sarah and Rob elected not to maintain this list as further requirements came to light. Instead, it served as a good starting point for the design.

Table 14.3. Scenario 1: Submit a Manuscript

Step	User	Action
1	Alice	Gathers all files needed for submission and all info about authors and journal: • Files (Word, figures, tables, and supplemental data) • Contact info (e-mail address, phone) for authors • Journal name, manuscript title, and abstract • Grant nos. supporting the manuscript • PI identification • Grant-system log-in and account info
2	Alice	Log in (to the grant system) and choose link to go to AMS system
3	Alice	Start manuscript submission
4	Alice	Identify journal publishing the article
5	Alice	Enter title, abstract, author info, grant nos., identify the PI (there may be multiple PIs, but that doesn't happen in this scenario)
6	Alice	Upload files
7	Alice	Review all info and path names, say that this is all info
8	Alice	Create submission proof (PDF confirmation document)
9	Alice	Review submission proof (PDF), notice author misspelling, correct spelling, and produce new submission proof
10	Alice	Approve submission proof

Questions

1. What are the implications of Rob's incorrect assumption that PIs would submit manuscripts as often as postdocs?
2. What requirements are implied by the fact that submitters do not necessarily have all the information they need in immediate reach?
3. Sarah chose to include steps in the scenarios that she did not observe in the interviews. For example, she included a step for users to log in to the system. When would you make scenarios strictly adhere to user observations and when would you insert steps from a projected workflow?

Arriving at a Conceptual Design

Now that Sarah and Rob had requirements, they began the design foundation stage of the project. In this stage they aimed to produce a conceptual design for the interface. That is, they weren't yet interested in every field name or precise button placement. Instead, they focused on the major types of screens and general navigation flow among them. Because ease of learning was paramount, Sarah recommended a wizard approach. She told Rob, "What I'd suggest is a combination of a wizard approach and a hub and spoke approach. This will let us provide a lot of guidance for submitters and also save their progress."

"I've heard of wizards, but what's hub and spoke?" said Rob.

Sarah drew some boxes and arrows on Rob's whiteboard (Figure 14.1). "It's when you have a central read-only page that summarizes an entire document, and users click on a section of that document to go to a separate edit screen where they can edit information from only that section. When they

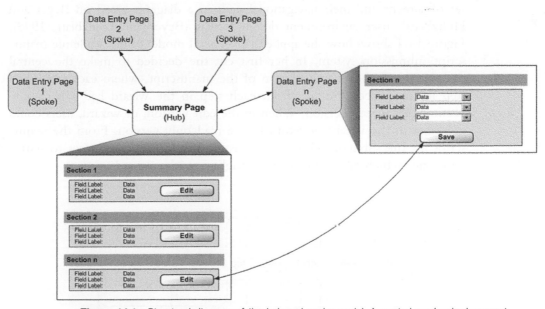

Figure 14.1. Structural diagram of the hub and spoke model. A central read-only document presents all the information entered, and users click on a section to go to an edit screen to change only that information. After saving it, they return to the central screen where they see their edits reflected.

save, the users go back to the central read-only document and see their edits. You don't need confirmation dialog boxes because they can see what was saved and edit the section again if they need to."

Sarah continued by drawing the model for a wizard (Figure 14.2). "See, this shows a typical wizard pattern. Users move from one screen to the next along a process. They can go back one screen at a time, or, if you want, they can go back to any screen they've previously completed."

Finally, she combined the two drawings by showing the wizard pathways through the hub and spoke screens (Figure 14.3). "Rather than starting at an empty read-only document," she explained, "the submitter will start at the first of the edit screens, then continue to the next and the next. After they've done all of them, then we'll take the submitter to the read-only screen with all of the manuscript's information. They can click any section to change the information. Plus, if they save and exit halfway through, we can bring them to the read-only screen to see how far they've gotten. If they go to an edit screen they can keep going on the wizard if they want to."

Before designing specific page layouts, Sarah worked out a preliminary set of screens and their navigational path in a diagram based on Beyer and Holtzblatt's user environment design format (Beyer and Holtzblatt, 1998). Figure 14.4 shows how she applied the general model to the academic manuscript submission system. In her first cut she decided to make the central document a tabbed representation of the manuscript, where each tab was a step in the process. So, in effect, each step in the wizard had a read-only version and an edit version. When in the edit version, or wizard, users could continue in the wizard or return to the read-only version. From the manuscript list the submitter chooses an existing manuscript or chooses to start a new one, which takes him or her straight into the wizard.

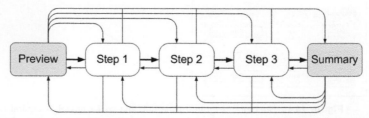

Figure 14.2. Structural diagram of the wizard model. Users move sequentially through the screens and can move back to either the previous screen or, as shown here, any earlier screen they have created. They can also jump forward to screens they have completed if no key data have changed.

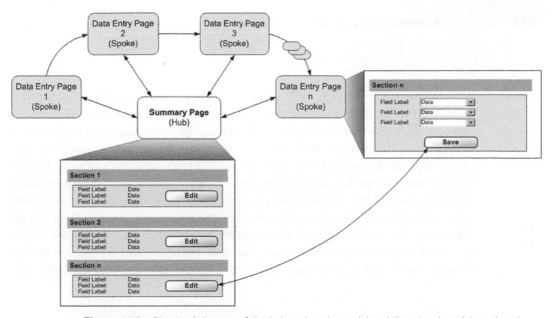

Figure 14.3. Structural diagram of the hub and spoke model and the wizard model combined. Users move through the edit screens in sequence until they save their progress and exit. Later, the users return and see the central document, where they can see their progress. They click on the appropriate section to edit and resume the wizard from that point.

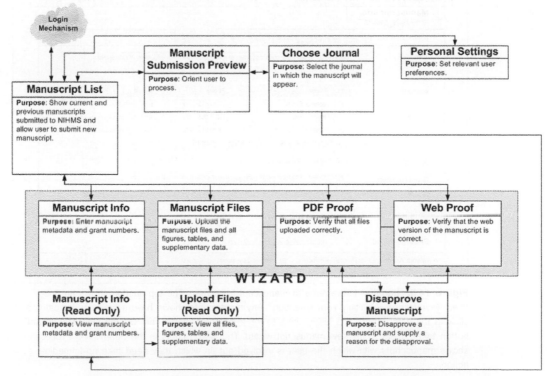

Figure 14.4. Structural diagram for the first-iteration design of the academic manuscript submission system. It reflects a specific implementation of the wizard and the hub and spoke models. Users start at their list of manuscripts and either start the wizard or go to a manuscript page.

Figures 14.5 through 14.7 show the manuscript list screen and both the read-only and edit versions of the manuscript information screen. An indicator on both the manuscript list and manuscript information screens shows progress in the wizard, with the four stages in the indicator matching the four steps in the wizard. Clicking on the "submit new manuscript" button on the manuscript list screen takes users to an orientation page that explains the process and lists all the materials and information they need to complete the submission. (Note that although these pages have a great deal of detail, that was for the benefit of the usability test participants. Sarah and Rob were more concerned with conceptual understanding and navigation at this point.) Sarah and Rob decided this screen would appear every time because

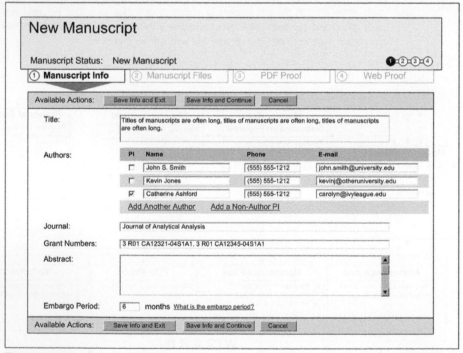

Figure 14.5. Iteration 1 wireframe of manuscript list screen. The top section shows an "Inbox" titled "Manuscripts Awaiting Your Attention." Any manuscripts shown have a progress indicator, and clicking the manuscript's title takes users to the appropriate stage. The "Submit New Manuscript" button takes users to the new manuscript wizard. The "Manuscripts in the Submission Process" shows manuscripts with which the user is involved but on which they need take no immediate action.

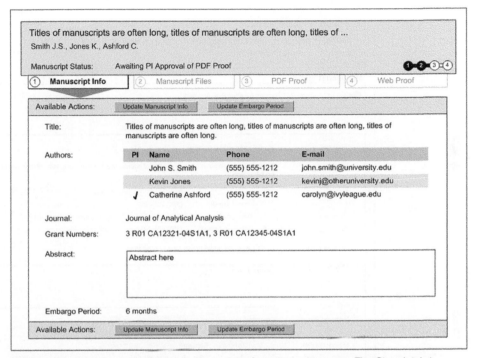

Figure 14.6. Iteration 1 wireframe of manuscript information, edit screen. The Step 1 tab is highlighted, and subsequent tabs are grayed out. After entering the information, the submitter has the option to "Save Info and Exit," which takes users to the read-only version of this screen, or "Save Info and Continue," which goes to the next screen in the wizard.

submitters would use the wizard so infrequently—it wouldn't become an annoyance if they only submit manuscripts four times per year. After that screen, users starting a new submission would see Figure 14.6, and if they stopped the wizard then they would see Figure 14.7.

Questions

4. Sarah split the "hub" screen of the hub and spoke model into four tabs. Why do you think she did that, and what effect would you expect it to have on the design?
5. What is the purpose of usability evaluation in the design foundation stage of a project?
6. What method would you use to evaluate this design's usability?

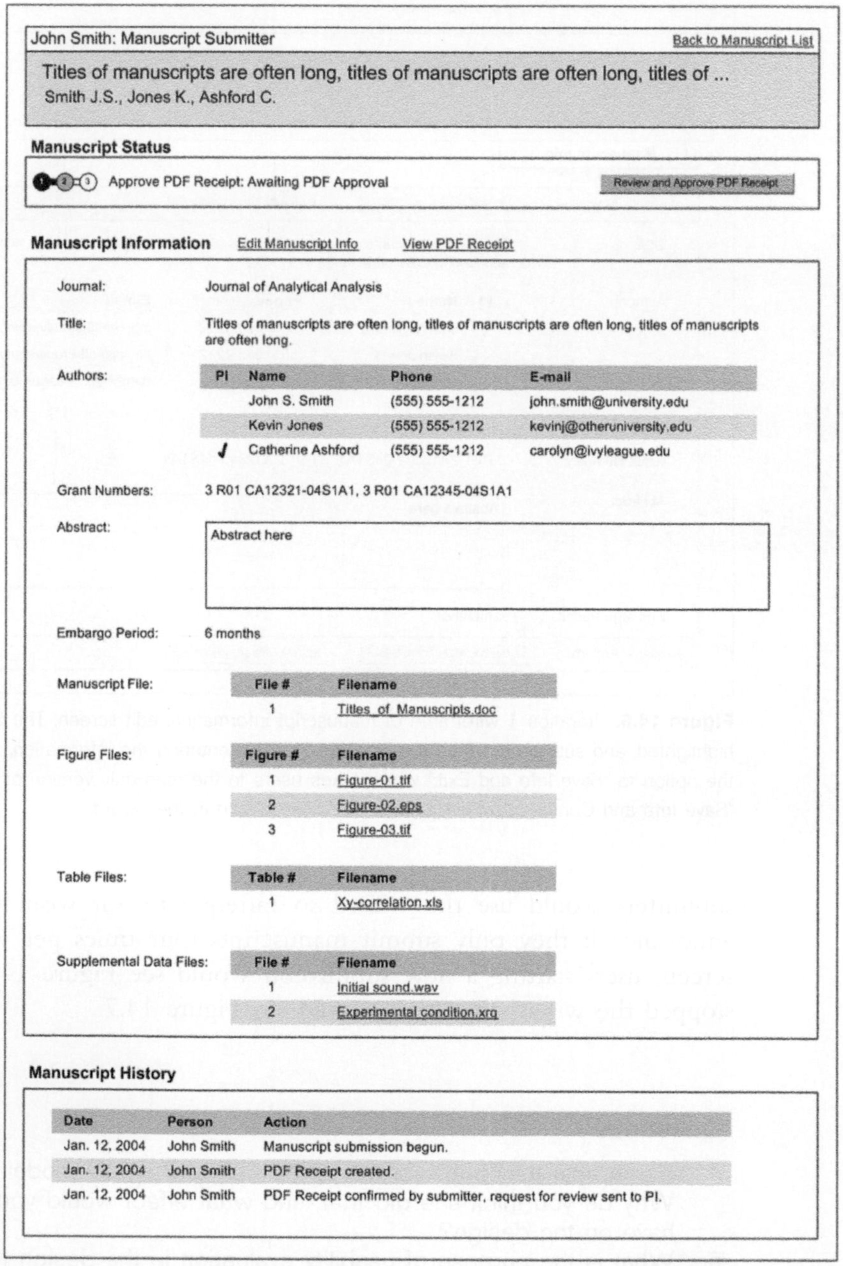

Figure 14.7. Iteration 1 wireframe of manuscript information, read-only. The Step 1 tab is highlighted, and the submitter can choose to update the information on this page.

Evaluating the Conceptual Design

For the first usability evaluation, Sarah recommended the cognitive walk-through and asked Rob who they could find to do the walkthrough with. "It's important to do usability evaluations with actual users if we can," she said, "but at this stage we want to find out if this design makes sense to anyone except us. Do you know people in our group that write and submit papers?"

"Sure, a few," he said. "Aren't we supposed to go outside our own organization, though?"

"That would be best," answered Sarah, "but I'd rather do that starting on the next round. Tracking them down would take longer and we'd probably find out the same things from them that we would from the in-house people. We should do the rest of the testing with external people, though."

Rob then found three people in their group who published in journals. For each wireframe they had, they asked their colleagues to state the purpose of the page. Then, they pointed out various parts of each page and asked what they were for. This process gave them enough usability feedback to move forward with the design. Sarah planned to do a usability test once the "low-hanging fruit" usability issues were solved. The walkthrough revealed several issues, after which Rob and Sarah sat down to do the next round of the conceptual design.

"Well, it looks like I was completely off base about having the read-only screen as tabs. None of them understood what was going on with that. They all saw four separate pages," said Sarah.

"They got the wizard, though. The only problem there was that they didn't always realize they were finished," replied Rob. "But you're right, the tabs were confusing. I think part of it may be that they didn't really look a lot like tabs. They just looked like the wizard screens, but not editable. We could try making them look more like tabs."

"Actually, why don't we go ahead and try putting it all on one page. Yeah, it'll be long, but we can always split it out again if people don't get it. And it will fit the hub and spoke model a little better too. And I'll add a more obvious message that they are done."

Rob agreed, so they moved on to the next issue. "I thought it was interesting that everyone asked which file types they could upload at exactly the same points—on the preview page and then again on the file upload screen. There were a number of other questions that everyone had too."

"I was thinking about that too," said Sarah. "People noticed that 'What is the embargo period?' link and said they'd click it. Why don't we do that with the other questions people had. Since they were always in the same place, we can just put them in those places on the screen." Again, Rob agreed.

Rob then brought up a concern he'd had as his understanding of the process deepened. "Something's bothering me about this wizard. You can't actually complete it at one time. Don't you think that would be frustrating to get to step 3 and then have to wait for your PI to approve things? There's no sense of finishing it. And then, it's going to take 2 weeks before they can approve the web version. I think we should have the wizard end with the submitter sending the manuscript to the PI for approval."

"But what would we do with the rest of the process?" asked Sarah. "It's important for people to be able to see the whole process and where they are in it."

"I don't know exactly. We could have other screens to take care of the approval. Maybe we hang them off the hub, which has an approval button if the manuscript is in the right state."

"I'm not sure, but I'll see what I can come up with," said Sarah. "We can look at it in the next usability test."

In addition to these findings, a new requirement came down from management. Some journals already sent their manuscripts to the agency's free database of articles. If submitters were publishing in one of these journals, they didn't have to fill out most of the information or upload files. All they had to do was enter their grant information and a couple of other fields to get their credit grant review.

To address these issues, Sarah and Rob decided on the following:

- To collapse all read-only pages to a single manuscript-summary screen. The top section of the screen shows the manuscript's status and has a button to take submitters to the next step in the process, whatever that is.
- To have the wizard only go through the PDF file confirmation. The PI's confirmation of the PDF and the approval of the web version of the manuscript would take place in separate stages.
- To show a "what's next" section on most screens below the main context that tells people where they are and what their next step should be. When a user is finished with the relevant portion of the process, the "what's next" section clearly states that they have nothing further to do at that time.

- To place help links on the screens that users had questions about. The text of the link would be the questions that the users had. Clicking the link would pop up a small window that answered the question.
- To make specifying a journal the first step of the wizard. If it turns out to be one already appearing in the database of free articles, the wizard would skip the next several steps.

Figures 14.8 to 14.10 show examples of these changes. The manuscript summary screen in Figure 14.8 shows a button in the manuscript status section labeled "Continue Entering Manuscript." The text of this button would change depending on the manuscript's state, so Rob and Sarah began identifying the manuscript's states and writing button labels for each one. Links next to the manuscript information section take users to the appropriate part of the process and appear only if appropriate to the state and user.

The second wizard step appears in Figure 14.9. Because the submitter specified the journal in the first step, it is read-only here. To change it, users

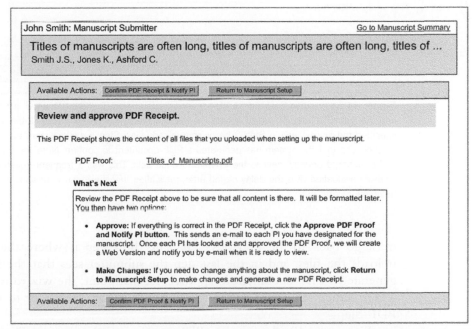

Figure 14.8. Iteration 2 wireframe of manuscript summary. The manuscript status section has a context-specific button that names the next step and takes users to it.

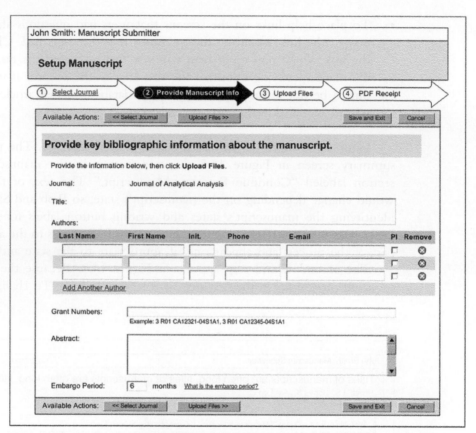

Figure 14.9. Iteration 2 wireframe of manuscript information. The Step 2 arrow is highlighted, and the submitter can choose to update the information on this page. In Step 1 the submitter specified the journal, and in Step 3 he or she uploads files. Step 4 explains that the wizard is finished and that the system has generated a PDF document to confirm. Note the help text "What is the embargo period?" next to the Embargo Period field. This was a frequent question in the first usability evaluation (it is the delay period after publication that the manuscript should appear in the database of articles).

must go back to the previous step. The third step is where the submitter uploads the files, and in the last step the submitter sees that the system has generated a PDF document to approve. At that point, the wizard is complete. Their choices are to go to the manuscript summary screen or to review the PDF file.

Figure 14.10 shows the PDF confirmation screen. The submitter should click the link to see the PDF document and then decide whether it

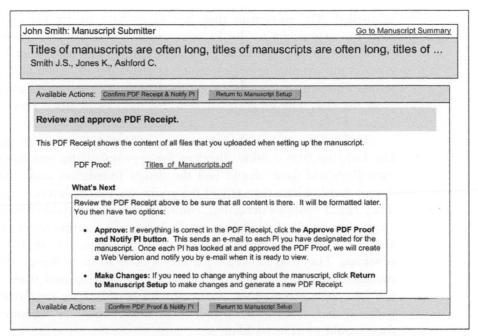

Figure 14.10. Iteration 2 wireframe of PDF confirmation. After finishing the wizard, submitters see this screen. They can go back and make changes or confirm that all files uploaded correctly. The "What's Next" box explains all options and then, after confirmation, clearly states that the submitter has nothing further to do.

is acceptable. The "What's Next" section explains the consequences of approving the manuscript and also explains that the submitter can go back to the wizard and make changes. After confirming the PDF file, the page redisplays with the "What's Next" box displaying the message "As the Manuscript Submitter, you have **nothing further to do** at this time." It also explains that any subsequent modification will reset the process and the submitter will have to confirm the manuscript PDF again.

This time Sarah and Rob conducted a usability test on a paper prototype. Because of time constraints they decided to test with their colleagues again, hoping to test with external users in the next round. They asked test participants to submit a new manuscript and send it to their PI for approval. This would not necessarily involve generating and confirming the PDF document. Then, Rob and Sarah told them that their PI had responded, saying that they had left out a file and that one of the author's names was misspelled. The participant then had to go back in, fix the problems, and send the manuscript to the PI once again. These exercises revealed minor problems that could be fixed in detailed design. The participants successfully entered the manuscript information, sent it to the PI, and edited the manuscript. The participants understood the basic model and could use it to complete the task. The structural diagram for the user interface now looked like Figure 14.11.

The success of the basic model meant that it was time to present it to Dr. Lithgow (the division director) for approval. If he was happy with it, then Rob and Sarah would end the design foundation stage and move to design detail, where they would determine the precise layout of each screen. They could continue designing, confident that they wouldn't have to throw away a great deal of work later on. Rob set up a meeting for the next week, and Sarah created a presentation-worthy prototype out of the wireframe mockups. They also showed what they'd done so far to Sergei, the technical manager, and a couple of other people on his development team. Sergei had just selected a programmer, Andrew, who would create the front end. Rob believed that showing them their work so far would be a courtesy because they would soon be building it.

The day before the approval meeting, Rob stopped by Sarah's cube. "We've got a problem. I just found out that Sergei had Andrew create another design, and he's gotten himself invited to the meeting with Dr. Lithgow. He wants to present it as an alternative to ours."

"That's . . . ," Sarah searched for a professional word, " . . . really annoying. If they didn't like what they saw, why didn't they say something? We could have explained it! Or worked it in!"

"I don't know. I haven't even seen theirs yet. I'm trying to get a peek at it before we go in so we've got some idea what to say. I'm fairly certain that ours is better—we've got the usability data to back it up. What do you think we should do?"

"I'd want to see theirs to know for sure. I think what I'd suggest is that we look for a few things to praise about their design but then make the case that ours is better. If we act threatened or angry, it may hurt us."

Rob and Sarah were both angry. Rather than working with them, Sergei had gone out on his own and directed Andrew to come up with a completely independent design. Rob and Sarah managed to get a look at the competing design that morning (shown in Figures 14.12 and 14.13) to form an initial impression.

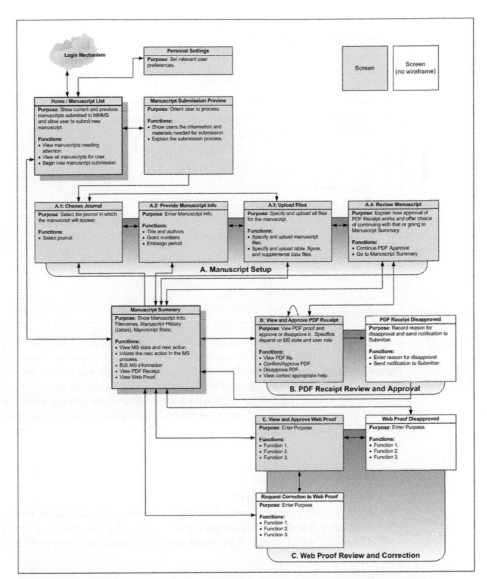

Figure 14.11. Structural diagram after cosmetic touch-ups from the iteration 2 usability test. The two key screens are the manuscript list and the manuscript summary. There are three stages: A. Manuscript Setup, B. PDF Review and Approval, and C. Web Review and Approval. Gray boxes represent screens that Sarah had wireframes for at this point, and white boxes represent screens that had not yet been mocked up.

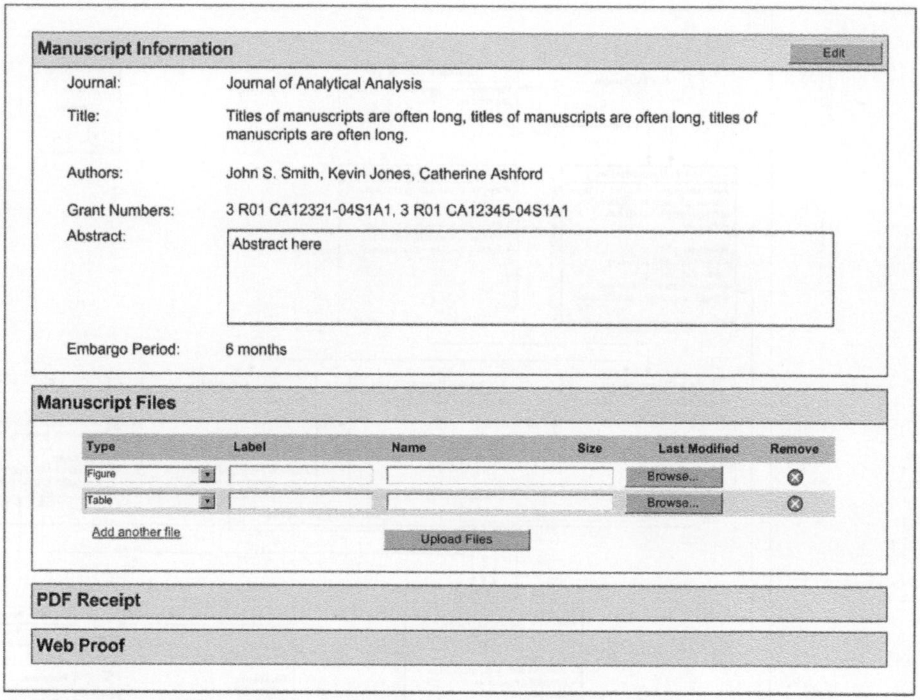

Figure 14.12. Competing design. This design works on a progressive form reveal model, where subsequent sections of a form appear based on what the user filled out earlier. Effectively, each section of the form appears on the page once the user finishes the previous section. It is an alternate to the wizard model that keeps everything on one screen. In this screen, the user is in edit mode for the first section.

Questions

7. Which design is better?
8. How would you persuade Dr. Lithgow that your choice is the right one?
9. Rob and Sarah were annoyed that they had been put in a competition situation. What could they have done to avoid this competition?

Moving to Detailed Design and Project Completion

The reasoning Rob and Sarah used to present their design and critique Andrew's design worked. They were able to deflect several criticisms of their design because they had usability test data to back it up. Dr. Lithgow chose

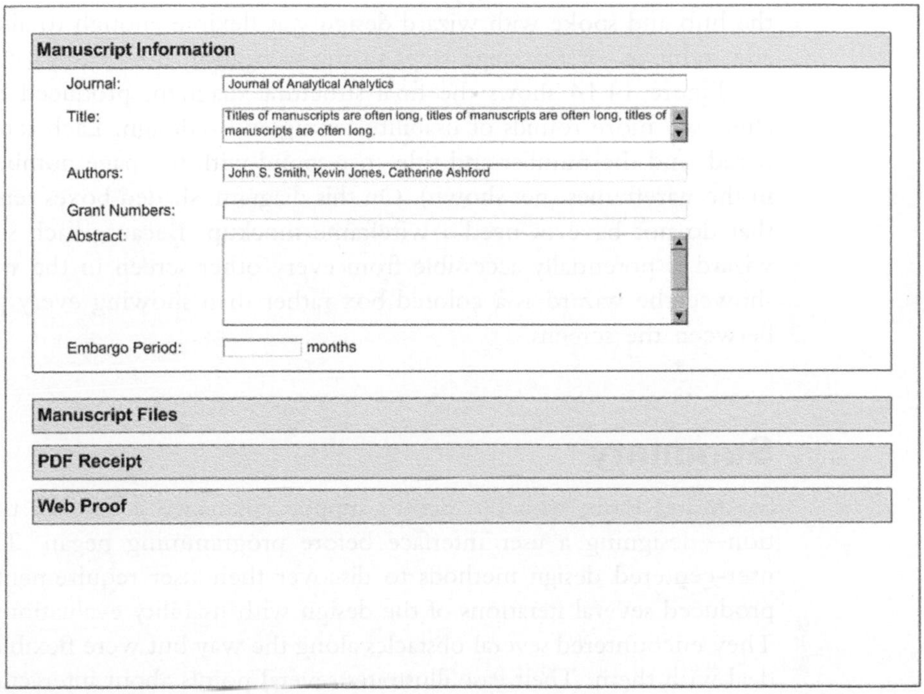

Manuscript Information

Journal:	Journal of Analytical Analytics
Title:	Titles of manuscripts are often long, titles of manuscripts are often long, titles of manuscripts are often long.
Authors:	John S. Smith, Kevin Jones, Catherine Ashford
Grant Numbers:	
Abstract:	
Embargo Period:	___ months

Manuscript Files

PDF Receipt

Web Proof

Figure 14.13. Competing design. After confirming the first section, the user is now in edit mode for the second section and would have to click the "Edit" link on the first section to go back and change anything. Designers can change the content of later sections based on choices made in earlier sections.

the wizard approach and authorized Rob and Sarah to move to the detailed design stage. As Andrew joined the team, the atmosphere shifted to one of wariness. Rob and Sarah had settled into a working relationship that now had to expand to include a person whose design had just been overruled. Fortunately, all parties made an effort to get along and work together. Sarah looked for opportunities to back up Andrew's input while not compromising the overall design, and Andrew accepted Dr. Lithgow's decision and worked to make the wizard approach flow as smoothly as possible. After a couple of weeks, the atmosphere grew less awkward and the three of them formed a cohesive integrated team.

As promised, policy decisions affected the design even as the developers built the system. For example, Dr. Lithgow decided that PIs should approve the PDF document as well as the web version of the manuscript. Fortunately, the hub and spoke with wizard design was flexible enough to allow Sarah to add, remove, or rearrange steps in the navigation flow easily.

Figure 14.14 shows the final structural diagram, produced by the team after two more rounds of usability testing and redesign. Each screen is numbered, and the number and title correspond with the page numbers and titles in the wireframes (not shown). On this diagram, shaded boxes represent those that do not have or need a wireframe mockup. Because each screen in the wizard is potentially accessible from every other screen in the wizard, Sarah showed the wizard as a colored box rather than showing every possible link between the screens.

Summary

Sarah and Rob, with Dr. Scott's support, managed a first for the organization—designing a user interface before programming began. They applied user-centered design methods to discover their user requirements, and they produced several iterations of the design with usability evaluations each time. They encountered several obstacles along the way but were flexible enough to deal with them. Their case illustrates several points about interaction design:

- Using an established framework to plan and guide the project provided a context in which to work.
- Working with actual user data is critical; Sarah and Rob would likely have made inappropriate design decisions if it weren't for the six interviews they conducted.
- Paper prototypes are effective for designing and usability-testing conceptual designs.
- Iterative design results in a superior product. Sarah and Rob saw clear improvements after each round of usability testing.
- Design decisions result not only from usability data but also from management and late-coming changes. Strong conceptual designs, however, can easily incorporate these changes.
- Constant communication is critical. The fact that Rob and Sarah did not stay in close contact with the development team resulted in an uncomfortable situation.

The academic manuscript submission system was released on time and received quite positive comments from both users and policymakers.

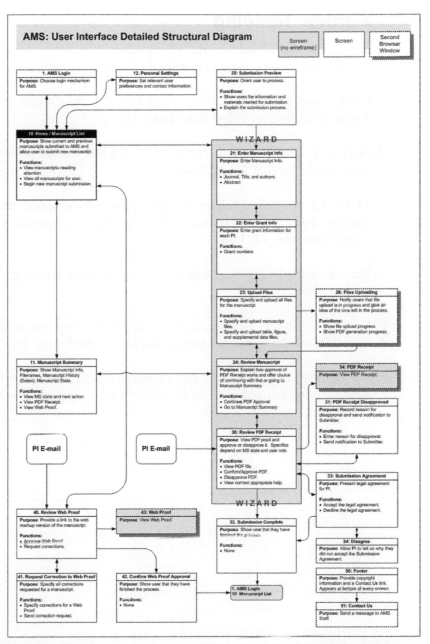

Figure 14.14. Final structural diagram. Submitters see a preview of the process and then move into the wizard. After the submitter completes the wizard, the PI gets an e-mail and comes in to approve the PDF document. After approval, a contractor generates a web version of the manuscript and notifies the submitter, who inspects it. The submitter can either request corrections or approve the web version, thereby finishing the process.

Further Reading

Beyer, H., and Holtzblatt, K. (1998). *Contextual design: defining customer centered systems.* San Francisco: Morgan Kaufmann Publishers, Inc.

Cooper and Reimann. (2003). *About Face 2.0: the essentials of interaction design.* Indianapolis: Wiley Publishing, Inc.

Hackos, J., and Redish, J. (1998). *User and task analysis for interface design.* New York: John Wiley & Sons.

McDaniel, S. (2003). Selling usability: scope and schedule estimates. *Intercom,* pp. 22–25. Retrieved from http://www.cognetics.com/papers/others/intercom_1203.pdf

Shneiderman, B. (1998). *Designing the user interface.* Reading: Addison-Wesley.

Snyder, C. (2003). *Paper prototyping: the fast and easy way to design and refine user interfaces.* New York: Morgan Kaufmann Publishers, Inc.

Van Duyne, D., Landay, J., and Hong, J. (2003). *The design of sites: patterns, principles, and processes for crafting a customer-centered web experience.* New York: Addison-Wesley.

CASE 15

The Mulkey Corporation: A Case Study in Information Architecture

Laconya D. Ruby, IBM

> *Carla expressed her concern during the kickoff meeting. "Normally, the team has access to client executives who identify the business objectives and to real users who identify the user objectives. But, the contract says we'll have no interaction with the users and only direct access to the client executives." Shay replied, "The client is confident that they know their users, and individuals from within the business will explain to us what their users want." Carla's stomach began to churn.*

Gathering Requirements

The Mulkey Corporation is a well-known parent company headquartered in Atlanta, Georgia. The corporation has been in existence since the early 1900s. It has bought and sold many companies of nationally known consumer package products over the past 100 years. These products include such items as cookies, cheeses, condiments, deodorant, mouthwash, and toothpaste.

At any given time, The Mulkey Corporation could be the parent company of anywhere from 5 to 20 subsidiaries. A strong business objective is for their investors to have a clear understanding of the subsidiaries.

Recently, The Mulkey Corporation quickly bought and sold several companies. Vanessa, the Chief Executive Officer, sent the following memo to Alex, the manager of corporate communications:

317

Alex,

We need to immediately update our advertising to reflect our recent acquisitions and spin-offs. The corporate identity may also need to be revised.

Thanks, Vanessa

After reading the e-mail, Alex hired Dorlande, a strategic brand consulting and design firm with which The Mulkey Corporation had previously worked, to focus specifically on this challenge. The new identity concepts and design elements would ultimately impact both The Mulkey Corporation's advertising as well as their website.

Alex worked closely with Dorlande for several months while the new identity and advertising campaign ideas were researched and developed. After the concepts were approved by Alex, Dorlande then scheduled focus groups to get stakeholder feedback. The feedback resulted in some key visual and verbiage alterations.

Alex's team analyzed and documented the impacts to the mulkeycorp .com website based on the new identity. After the focus group feedback was incorporated by Dorlande, Alex's team immediately worked on the changes to the website. Because the changes were front-of-screen (colors, fonts, text, etc.) and did not involve changes to the back-end technology, Alex's team was able to coordinate the website relaunch with the launch of the new identity and ad campaign.

Before the website relaunch, Alex's team had documented through the use of web metrics that 35.5% of the site visitors who hit the mulkeycorp .com Home page immediately left the website with their next click. After the website relaunch, this percentage dropped to 26.9%. The relaunch of the website with the new identity was considered to be a huge success because the numbers indicated that more users were staying on the site once they hit the Home page.

Alex was promoted to director of corporate communications and was relocated to the office in Sedona, Arizona. John, a specialist in corporate communications on Alex's team, was promoted to fill Alex's position of manager of corporate communications. Before Alex left for Arizona, she was in the process of planning and scheduling an upcoming focus group with the senior manager of global user research to evaluate the website relaunch. She gave John her user research files, which included results from past focus groups and her notes for the upcoming focus group.

John had been with the company for 10 years but was not familiar with the day-to-day operations of the company's website. Now that the new identity was online and successful, John was responsible for creating a project plan to expand content, tools, and functionality over the next year. Not wanting to make a mistake on what the next steps should be with the website, John decided to seek advice from industry experts so he put out a request for proposal (RFP) for consulting services to find a strategic partner who would advise on all aspects of the website: strategy, information architecture, graphic design, content creation, and technical development and implementation.

The RFP contained important items such as a list of capabilities they were looking for in a partner, a history of their website development, the website objectives for the upcoming 18-month period, and a list of their website users. It also mentioned that The Mulkey Corporation had used feedback mechanisms such as focus group interviews to inform them of changes needed to their website.

Eager to work with The Mulkey Corporation, many consulting companies replied to the RFP. John whittled the list down and requested in-person presentations from the 4 consulting companies he selected. He specifically asked each company to show their approach, methodology, deliverables, and references to demonstrate how they used strategic input to keep the information architect (IA), graphic designer, content specialist, and technical architect informed and working toward a common goal.

John chose Windy Pine Consulting (Figure 15.1) because he was impressed with their multidisciplinary approach, proven methodologies, and timeline for implementation. Windy Pine Consulting's strategy team recommended starting the engagement by gathering The Mulkey Corporation's business objectives, documenting the website users' objectives, and performing a competitive audit. Based on the output, the strategy team would recommend requirements that would be validated by John's team (see Figure 15.5). Then an IA, the main user advocate on the consulting team, would design the user experience, working with a graphic designer, a content specialist, and a technical architect.

After the consulting company had been selected, John resumed planning the next focus group. John scheduled a meeting with Bianca, the senior manager of global user research, and Ally, the lead user experience researcher. John asked, "Where should we start?" Bianca replied, "We usually start by identifying who we want to participate in the focus group." Ally added, "In the last focus group we included investors, members of the media, and individuals from nongovernmental organizations. We found it difficult to recruit members of the media, so I would recommend one-on-one interviews for this group so that we can get the most out of each session." John agreed to the user types and to the approach.

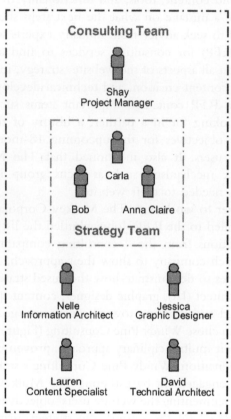

Figure 15.1. The Windy Pine Consulting team.

Bianca said, "Next, we should talk about the objectives. In other words, what do you want to learn from the sessions?" John referred to the notes that Alex had left with him and replied, "I've looked at the suggestions from Alex and at our site metrics. I think we need to ask some fundamental questions: What content is the most important and what tools are the most important. We should also ask what the best name would be for the section of a corporate website that talks about the ways in which a company is responsible. Ally replied, "This gives us enough information to get started. When we finish the detailed discussion guide, we will send you a draft for approval and then we will begin recruiting."

While John was planning the focus group and one-on-one interviews, Shay, the project manager for Windy Pine Consulting, scheduled a kickoff meeting for the consulting team. All the team leads, Carla, Nelle, Jessica, Lauren, and David, were reviewing the contract and the project timeline for the first time. Carla said, "We usually have access to client executives who identify the business objectives and to real users who identify the user objectives. I noticed in the contract that the strategy team will only have direct access to the client executives and that we will not have direct interaction with users. There is also an assumption listed that we will draw from our industry expertise to define user objectives." Shay replied, "Yes, that is correct." Carla seemed concerned. Shay answered, "I understand your concerns, but The Mulkey Corporation is confident that they know their users and they will get individuals from within the business to explain to us what their users want. I realize that this isn't best practice but we have to work within the constraints we've been given."

Realizing the constraints, the Windy Pine Consulting strategy team, Carla, Bob, and Anna Claire, began the strategy engagement by working with John to identify the key executives at The Mulkey Corporation who would have the best insight into the company's business objectives. After the executives were identified, John scheduled one-on-one interviews to be led by Carla with the following people:

- Senior Vice President, Corporate Affairs
- Chief Compliance Officer
- Chief Financial Officer
- Senior Vice President, Human Resources
- Senior Vice President, Mergers and Acquisitions
- Vice President, Public Affairs
- Vice President, Government Affairs
- Associate General Counsel
- Corporate Secretary

Even though Carla had vast industry expertise and could have identified the mulkeycorp.com website users fairly accurately, she still relied on the executive interviews to provide validation. She repeated the same questions with each executive. For example, she began the interview with the Chief Financial Officer (CFO) by asking, "Who are the current users of your website?" The CFO replied, "Investors, current and future, are our primary audience." She continued, "What are your business objectives over the next 6 to 12 months?" The CFO told Carla, "Even though our identity has changed, we need to continue to show our financial strength and we want to reach out to future investors so that they have a clear understanding of who we are."

Carla validated the following types of users during the executive interviews:

- Potential investors
- Current investors
- Opinion leaders
- Potential grant recipients
- Students

Another output of the executive interviews was a list of business objectives. Carla, Bob, and Anna Claire grouped and prioritized the business objectives. The top three business objectives were then translated into website objectives and the two sets of objectives were cross-referenced, as shown in Figure 15.2.

Carla, Bob, and Anna Claire then used their collective industry and personal expertise along with what they had learned during the executive

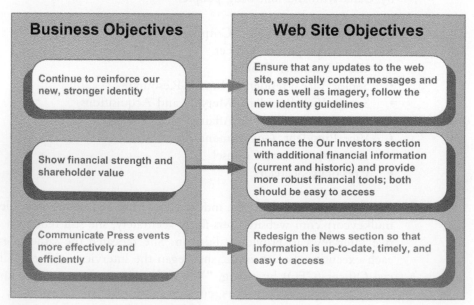

Business Objectives

- Continue to reinforce our new, stronger identity
- Show financial strength and shareholder value
- Communicate Press events more effectively and efficiently

Web Site Objectives

- Ensure that any updates to the web site, especially content messages and tone as well as imagery, follow the new identity guidelines
- Enhance the Our Investors section with additional financial information (current and historic) and provide more robust financial tools; both should be easy to access
- Redesign the News section so that information is up-to-date, timely, and easy to access

Figure 15.2. Business objectives translated into website objectives.

Table 15.1. An Example of Two User Objectives Being Correlated to a Website Objective and a User Type

Website Objective	User Type	User Objectives
Enhance the Our Investors section with additional financial information (current and historic) and provide more robust financial tools; both should be easy to access	Potential investor	• Easy to find, recent company-wide information • Stock quote data

interviews to determine what the objectives would be for each user type. When the team was identifying the investor user objectives, for example, Carla was able to use her investor knowledge to determine the types of content, functionality, and tools an investor would want on a website because she frequently researched companies to buy and sell stock online.

When they started identifying the media user objectives, the strategy team quickly realized that they did not have enough collective expertise, so they scheduled a meeting with the media content owners at The Mulkey Corporation. The media content owners were excellent subject matter experts who were very familiar with the needs of their audience based on previous focus group results and requests for information. After the user objectives were documented, they were then correlated with the website objectives and the user types as shown in Table 15.1.

After defining the business, website, and user objectives, the strategy team moved forward with the final component of the strategy engagement—a competitive audit. The competitive audit gave the strategy team an opportunity to compare The Mulkey Corporation website against other "like company"* websites. The competitive audit is not a formal evaluation by end users but rather a method used to document and compare the types of content, functionality, and tools implemented on a collective set of websites.

Carla, Bob, and Anna Claire used industry research to create an initial list of 17 "like company" websites. They presented the list to John. He liked

---

* A "like company" is either in the same industry, is the same type of company (parent company), or sells the same types of products (consumer goods) as the company to which it is being compared.

the list but remembered there was a list of peer companies identified in the proxy statement that The Mulkey Corporation sent to their shareholders (proxy documents are meant to provide shareholders with the information necessary to make informed votes on issues important to the company's performance*). John provided the peer company list to Carla for her team to review. Based on the strategy team's evaluation of the peer company websites, they took a few companies off the original list and added a few from the proxy peer list. Carla sent the updated list for the competitive audit to John. This time, John signed off on the list of 17 "like companies" so the strategy team was ready to begin the competitive audit.

The Home page and all main sections of the mulkeycorp.com website, such as About Us, Our Investors, News, Citizenship, and Careers, were included in the scope of the competitive audit. The strategy team used the following process for their competitive audit evaluation:

1. Carla, Bob, and Anna Claire each chose specific website sections to evaluate. Carla worked on the Home page and About Us, Bob worked on Our Investors and News, and Anna Claire worked on Citizenship and Careers.
2. They each created a spreadsheet listing all 18 websites along one axis (mulkeycorp.com and the 17 "like companies") and documented all the tools, functionality, and content types on the other axis. Each website that had a tool, type of functionality, or content type got a check in its column. Notations were also added to differentiate the level of functionality offered. For example, almost all the websites might offer an investor calendar, but maybe 6 sites offered the user the ability to be reminded "x" days before a specific event. The notations also included a heuristic point-of-view addressing the usability of the functionality and tools.
3. When all the websites had been evaluated, the number of checkmarks was then analyzed. When 50% or more of the "like company" sites had a specific tool, functionality, or content type, a baseline (bare minimum requirement) was created.
4. After the baseline was created, mulkeycorp.com was then compared against the baseline getting a rating of either equal to, above, or below the baseline. For example, if there was a baseline to show a stock chart on the Home page and mulkeycorp.com didn't have a stock chart on

---

* Part of a definition from Dictionary.com.

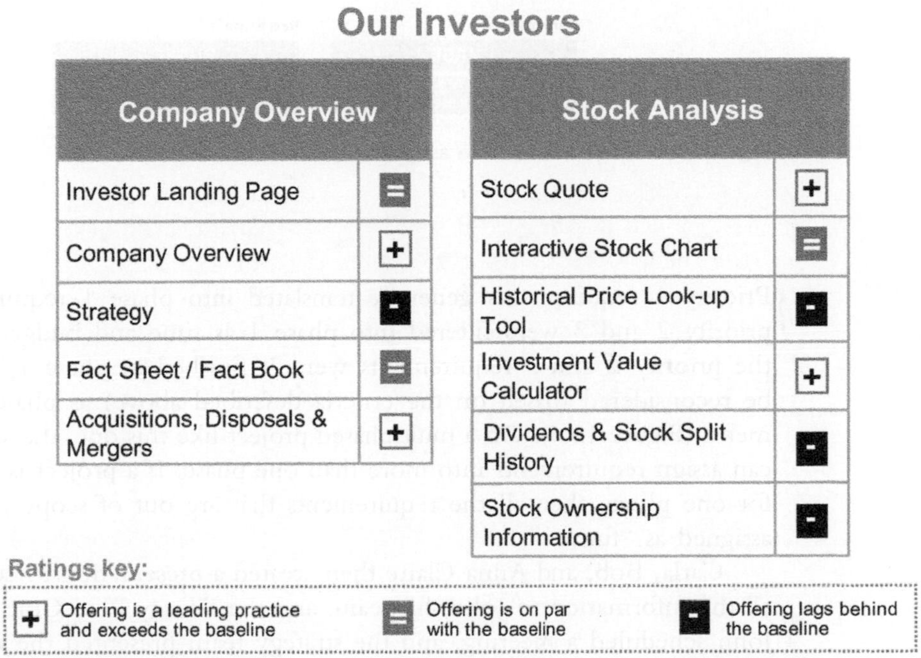

Our Investors

Company Overview		Stock Analysis	
Investor Landing Page	=	Stock Quote	+
Company Overview	+	Interactive Stock Chart	=
Strategy	-	Historical Price Look-up Tool	-
Fact Sheet / Fact Book	=	Investment Value Calculator	+
Acquisitions, Disposals & Mergers	+	Dividends & Stock Split History	-
		Stock Ownership Information	-

Ratings key:

+	Offering is a leading practice and exceeds the baseline	=	Offering is on par with the baseline	-	Offering lags behind the baseline

Figure 15.3. A small sampling of the competitive audit results for the Our Investors section on mulkeycorp.com.

their Home page, mulkeycorp.com would be rated "below the baseline" (see Figure 15.3. for a sample of the mulkeycorp.com ratings for the Our Investors section).

Armed with the business objectives, user objectives, and the competitive audit results, Carla, Bob, and Anna Claire collaborated to identify all the requirements for the website redesign. Keeping in mind the need to get the mulkeycorp.com website at least to the baseline in critical areas for phase 1, they prioritized the requirements based on several factors:

- The triple constraint*: time, cost, and scope
- The benefit and/or risk to The Mulkey Corporation
- The benefit and/or risk to the user

---

* Because these constraints are interrelated, defining two constraints will set the parameters for the third. For example, if Windy Pine Consulting had 6 months and $400,000.00, they must then determine the scope of what they can accomplish in this time period and funding.

Figure 15.4. Requirements were assigned into phases and releases.

Priority 1 requirements generally translated into phase 1 requirements and priority 2 and 3 were filtered into phase 1 as time and budget allowed. If the priority 2 and 3 requirements weren't finished in phase 1, they would be reconsidered (based on the criteria described above) as phase 2 requirements (Figure 15.4). On a multiphased project like this one, the strategy team can assign requirements into more than one phase. If a project is only scoped for one phase, then all the requirements that are out of scope generally get assigned as "future."

Carla, Bob, and Anna Claire then created a presentation to communicate all the information to John, his team, and the Windy Pine Consulting team. John scheduled a meeting, and the strategy team presented the information. After the presentation, everyone in the meeting had a clear understanding of the website and user objectives, what the "like company" websites were doing well, and what mulkeycorp.com needed to do to meet or exceed the baseline.

Questions

1. What were the benefits of the approach that the strategy team brought to the process?
2. What were some of the potential drawbacks that might stem from not using real users to document user objectives? How could the drawbacks be handled?
3. What are some criteria that could have been used by the strategy team in determining which "like company" websites to use for the competitive audit?
4. What is potentially missing or problematic in the competitive analysis as described?
5. What should John do next?

Designing the User Experience Using Information Architecture

After the meeting with the strategy team, John scheduled individual meetings with the main content owners of the website: Corporate Communications, Investors, Media, Contributions, Government Relations, Human Resources, Corporate Citizenship, and Compliance (Figure 15.5). Carla, Bob, and Anna Claire created a section-specific presentation of the strategy results for each content owner meeting.

There were two goals of presenting the information to the content owners. The first goal was to present the details from the strategy engagement so that the content owners would be aware of the recommendations and the proposed requirements. The second goal was to validate the proposed requirements and the timeline for implementation. Because the content owners would ultimately be responsible for approving the updated content in their respective sections, their buy-in was critical.

During the presentation, the content owners looked at the strategy results from several different perspectives. First, they looked at each priority 1 requirement and how it might impact the return on investment and its benefit/value to the business. Second, they evaluated each priority 1 requirement to determine how critical the requirement was to their users. Then, they looked at the priority 2 and 3 requirements to determine whether there were any requirements they should consider implementing sooner based on the business value and user needs.

Even though the strategy team presented a prioritized list of requirements, the content owners' analysis resulted in some of the requirements being reassigned to different priorities. On this project, the content owners were a very reliable source of information about the users of their content because The Mulkey Corporation had frequently inquired about key issues with the website users in the form of focus groups and one-on-one interviews. The content owners were also very clear regarding their business objectives and the best way to achieve those objectives.

At this point in the project, the strategy team had a complete list of validated and prioritized requirements approved by John and the content owners. The strategy team had completed their work, and the requirements were handed over to Nelle, the IA, to start designing the user experience and the new structure for the mulkeycorp.com website. The strategy team was then reassigned to a new project.

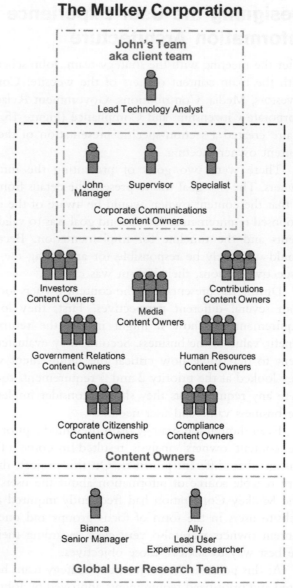

Figure 15.5. John's team, the content owners, and the global user research team at The Mulkey Corporation.

While Carla, Bob, and Anna Claire had been working on the strategy, John had been working with the global user research team to finalize the questions for the focus groups and one-on-one interviews. They were now ready to start the recruiting process. John looked at the calendar and realized that Nelle, the IA, wouldn't have the research data while she was working on the high-level flowcharts* but would have it before she was completely finished with the wireframes. Although there may be some rework needed on the high-level flowcharts and wireframes to account for the user input, it would be beneficial to include it before the recommendations went to graphic design and technical implementation.

Typically, when Nelle joined a project she was given only a requirements document with very little supporting material. This time, however, Nelle not only had the requirements but she also had a lot of additional information to leverage from the strategy documentation. In fact, this was the first time she had been on a project that the client truly understood the value of a thorough strategy engagement during the requirements development and validation phase.

Even though Nelle's title was information architect, she had studied usability methodologies in graduate school. Before joining the team at Windy Pine Consulting, she worked for a usability consulting company where she learned to apply theory to real-life testing situations. Nelle found that listening to users and understanding their needs as well as communicating those needs to the client and consulting teams was one of the most enjoyable aspects of being an IA.

On this project, as with other projects, Nelle represented the voice of the user and was the resource consulted about all usability related issues. Having a user advocate on the project should never replace the actual voice of the user, but sometimes reaching out to users is not possible due to cost or project timeline. In these cases it is helpful to have someone on the team who is well skilled in defining a good and consistent user experience through the use of basic user interface principles as well as someone who has participated in usability testing and can bring that knowledge to any project.

Nelle was already familiar with the current mulkeycorp.com website so she began by validating the global navigation and toolbar. She used the information from the competitive audit to compare the main section names

---

* A high-level flowchart identifies the main sections and subsections of a website and also identifies the terminology used for each section.

Table 15.2. A Sampling of Two Section Names (News and Citizenship) from the Competitive Audit

News Terminology	Number of Instances	Citizenship Terminology	Number of Instances
News	3	Citizenship	3
Media center or Media centre	3	Corporate citizenship	3
Press center or Press centre	3	Corporate responsibility	2
Newsroom or News room	2	Our commitment	2
		Our responsibility	2
Press	2	Responsibility	1
Press room	1	Social responsibility	1
News & media	1	Social commitment	1
Media relations	1	Corporate social responsibility	1
For journalists	1		
		Good works	1

on mulkeycorp.com to the section names used on the "like company" websites (Table 15.2).

Using information from the competitive audit, Nelle started on a high-level flowchart (Figure 15.6). Being an experienced IA she knew that she must consider more than just the information from the competitive audit. She also realized the message and tone of the existing website content must be consistent with the section names.

After Nelle decided what sections would be on the global navigation and toolbar and what each section would be called, she then created high-level flowcharts for each main section identifying all the subsections as shown for About Us in Figure 15.8. Based on the requirement to provide more information on each of the subsidiary companies, Nelle decided to remove the single Acquisitions page, as shown in Figure 15.7, and add a new subsection called Family of Companies in the About Us section, as shown in Figure 15.8. She used the phrase Family of Companies based on the writing style and tone used throughout the mulkeycorp.com website. She also moved Our

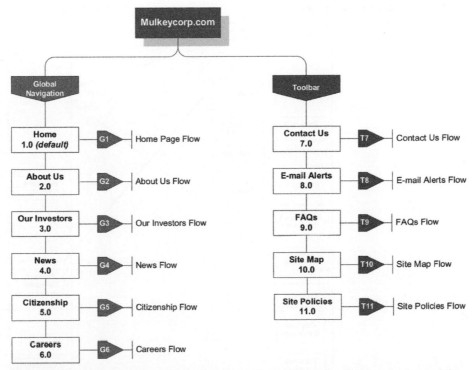

Figure 15.6. A high-level flowchart showing the section names on the global navigation and the toolbar.

Awards & Recognition, Our Advertising, and Our History to be subtopics under the Introduction section.

Redesigning the About Us section was fairly straight-forward. Updating the Citizenship section was much more of a challenge (Figure 15.9). There were requirements for the Citizenship section, but there was also a corporate initiative within the Responsibility department to be more transparent on the website. Because this initiative was currently underway, Nelle worked on a daily basis with the corporate citizenship content owners and Lauren, the content specialist on the Windy Pine consulting team, to draft and refine the high-level flowchart for this section of the website.

Based on her work with the corporate citizenship content owners, Nelle had some concerns about the new user experience for the Citizenship section (Figure 15.10). For example, the corporate citizenship content owners added the word "communities" to the existing Contributions section and moved

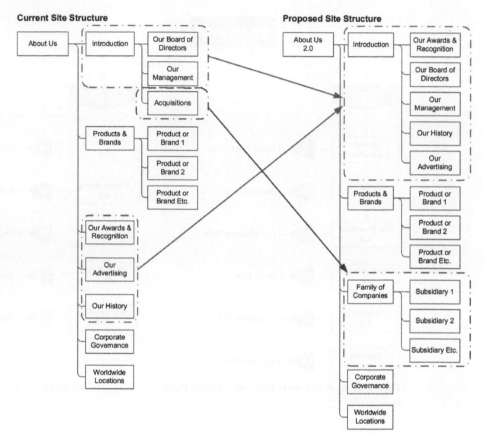

Figure 15.7. High-level flowchart for the *About Us* section of the mulkeycorp.com website.

Figure 15.8. High-level flowchart showing the proposed changes to the *About Us* section.

Our Suppliers into this section. Nelle was doubtful that the users would expect to find Our Suppliers under a section called Contributions & Communities. She also realized that there wasn't a lot of marketing content in the new Products & Marketing section bringing her to the conclusion that the section name was misleading. Although the corporate citizenship content owners took into consideration the recommendations that Nelle made, there were times when they overruled her recommendations. Realizing a usability test that included a card sorting activity was being scheduled right after the initial launch of the revised section, Nelle had a sense of assurance knowing that the decisions being made would be tested by the users. While it is ideal to get the

Current Site Structure

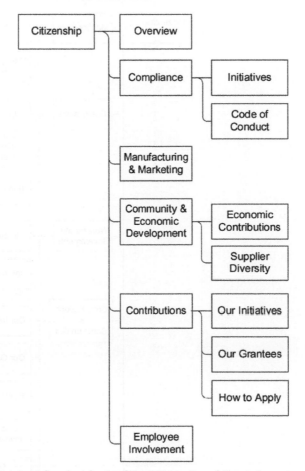

Figure 15.9. High-level flowchart for the Citizenship section of the mulkeycorp.com website.

users' feedback before the launch, getting feedback after the launch would still allow Nelle to make future recommendations based on the usability results.

After documenting all the main sections and subsections of the website in the high-level flowcharts, Nelle scheduled a meeting with the Windy Pine Consulting team to review and discuss the website changes. She started the meeting by stating, "The purpose of today's meeting is to review the proposed changes to the high-level structure of The Mulkey Corporation website. First, I want to point out that based on the requirement to add detailed pages

Proposed Site Structure

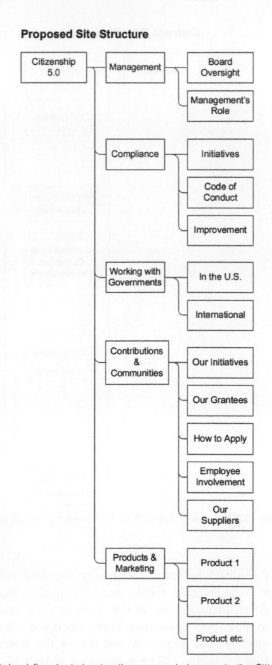

Figure 15.10. High-level flowchart showing the proposed changes to the Citizenship section.

for each of the subsidiaries, I've removed the single Acquisitions page under the Introduction section and added a new main section called Family of Companies. Under the Family of Companies section, there will be one page for each subsidiary. I've also moved the 'Our' topics such as Our Awards & Recognition, Our Advertising, and Our History under the Introduction section."

Jessica said, "Why don't we rename Introduction to Our Company?"

Nelle replied, "I considered that but since the entire About Us section is about the company, I thought Introduction was a better section name."

After the review with the consulting team, Nelle worked with John to get a meeting scheduled with his team. Nelle again covered each page in the high-level flowcharts, pointing out specific changes to the existing website. John's team was very excited about the new Family of Companies section, but John also realized that getting the content approved by each of the subsidiaries and then by their legal team would be challenging.

Nelle made the final changes to the high-level flowcharts and then started documenting the overall user experience in the wireframes, which represent detailed blueprints of each page or type of page as shown in Figure 15.11.

Figure 15.11. An example of one wireframe.

User Behavior Analysis: Our Management

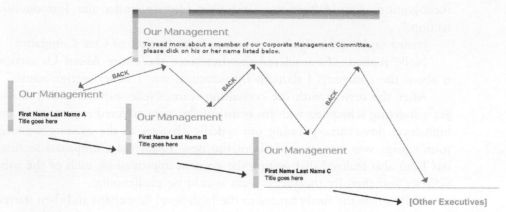

Finding:

Visitors tend to read through Our Management biographies in sequence, but the biography pages are not linked to one another. This creates an awkward "bouncy" user experience.

Recommendation:

Streamline navigation by adding "Next" and "Back" links between these pages.

Figure 15.12. An example of a recommendation based on website analytics.

While working on the wireframes, Nelle not only used the requirements and the high-level flowcharts but also used the user behavior analysis provided from web analytics to help define the navigation from one page to the next.* Web metrics can be provided by software that runs on the website's server. The software provides information such as the number of users coming to the website, where the users come from (countries, regions, and other websites), what pages are viewed, in what order they are viewed, and so on. By analyzing web metrics data, web analytics software detects patterns in users' behavior and suggests ways to streamline navigation based on those patterns.

One example of an analysis with its recommendation is shown in Figure 15.12. From the main Our Management page, users weren't just reading one

---

* The level of detail in high-level flowcharts and wireframes will vary from project to project and from phase to phase on the same project. On this project, the high-level flowcharts only noted main sections, subsections, and main pages. The high-level flowcharts did not note every link from every page. Links were, however, noted on the wireframes.

biography. In fact, they were reading multiple biographies as indicated by the gray lines between the Our Management page and the individual biography pages. Website analytics provided Nelle with insight to the user behavior from the current website so that she could incorporate better navigation between these pages. In this example, the navigation change was very straightforward: Nelle proposed adding "Next" and "Back" links on all the management biography pages. Because navigation is a critical aspect of the user experience and the usability of the entire website, this change was quickly approved and implemented.

Nelle also used information gathered from the annual website survey on mulkeycorp.com to validate information architecture decisions and to determine whether new requirements needed to be surfaced and discussed with the team. The survey was posted for about 2 months and displayed in an automatic pop-up window for all users who visited mulkeycorp.com. The types of feedback from the website survey included the following information:

- Identification of user type
- Reasons the user visited the website
- Satisfaction with the website
- Communication of key messages on the website
- Issues that users would like to have addressed on the website
- Likelihood of return to the website
- Ease of finding information on the website
- Most read, most important, and most satisfying sections of the website
- Opinions about whether specific content or tools would be important to add to the website

The data from the website survey provided important information even though Nelle received the survey information while she was working on the wireframes. For example, Acquisitions was noted as most read, most important, and most satisfying in terms of content. Nelle then looked back at her high-level flowcharts (Figures 15.8 and 15.10) and wireframes (Figure 15.11). She validated that she had expanded the single Acquisitions page into the Family of Companies section. Additionally, the Family of Companies section had individual pages for each subsidiary and was moved out to a more prominent position in the About Us redesign.

It was at this point in the project that the focus group and one-on-one interview results were delivered to John. He scheduled a meeting with his team and the Windy Pine Consulting team so that both teams could attend the results presentation. Of particular interest was the content and tools that the users perceived to have high value versus those perceived to have little or no value. The e-mail alerts functionality was rated as one of the top 3 tools for all user types. Because of its high interest, its priority was moved from a future phase requirement to Phase 1. Online chat was perceived to have low or little value, so it was pushed out to be reconsidered in the future. As for content, the financial information was consistently rated high by the users. This rating was consistent with the focus of Phase 1 being heavily weighted with investor and financial information requirements. When talking about responsibility, the focus groups and one-on-one interviews noted that they liked friendlier words such as community, citizenship, or giving. They did not like words such as corporate or philanthropy. This was good validation for Nelle to keep the section titled Citizenship.

When the wireframes were finished, Nelle followed the same process of review for the wireframes as she had with the high-level flowcharts.

- Nelle led a review with the Windy Pine Consulting team discussing areas of the website where information architecture changes were being proposed—especially in terms of section names, page layout, content, graphics, navigation, and hyperlinks. After some discussion and debate with the team, a few changes were made.
- Nelle worked with John to schedule a wireframe meeting with his team covering the same items she had covered with the Windy Pine Consulting team. John's team had some input, but they were generally very happy with the changes being proposed.

After Nelle made the final edits to the wireframes, she handed the wireframes off to Jessica, the graphic designer, to Lauren, the content specialist, and to David, the technical architect. Jessica worked on all the visual aspects, such as defining the font types and sizes, choosing specific visual imagery from the client's asset library for each page, picking color palettes for use across the entire website, and selecting iconography. Lauren used the wireframes as a guideline to help her create or rewrite content for each page. David used the wireframes to create an architecture to support the user experience. More specifically, he used the wireframes to define the content management templates, to build new functionality for the website, and to develop the back-end infrastructure.

Questions

6. What value did the content owners and John's team bring to the process?
7. What are the benefits that an IA might bring to the process?
8. What might Nelle have noticed about the News section from the competitive audit? The Citizenship section? What might that prompt her to do in the redesign?
9. What might be some drawbacks to a website survey?
10. What should Nelle do next?

Keeping the Integrity of the Information Architecture

Generally, at this point in a project the IA rolls off the project and onto a new one. If questions arise about the information architecture, the project team either tries to contact the IA or they are left to solve the problem on their own.

The website project for The Mulkey Corporation was unique in that they established a 1-year relationship with Windy Pine Consulting. Given this arrangement, Nelle was able to roll right onto the next phase of the project. Because Nelle was still on The Mulkey Corporation project, she was readily available for consultation on Phase 1 issues.

When both the client and consulting teams have technical architects, it is common practice for some of the requirements to be performed by the client's technical team due to skill set or expertise with the client's back-end systems and applications. One of the Phase 1 requirements that The Mulkey Corporation's technology analyst's team worked on was the implementation of the e-mail alerts functionality. Even though the e-mail alerts design (Figure 15.13) was already reviewed and approved by both the Windy Pine Consulting team and John's team, John started getting push-back from his lead technology analyst on the functionality, so John sent an e-mail to Nelle to get her opinion from the users' perspective.

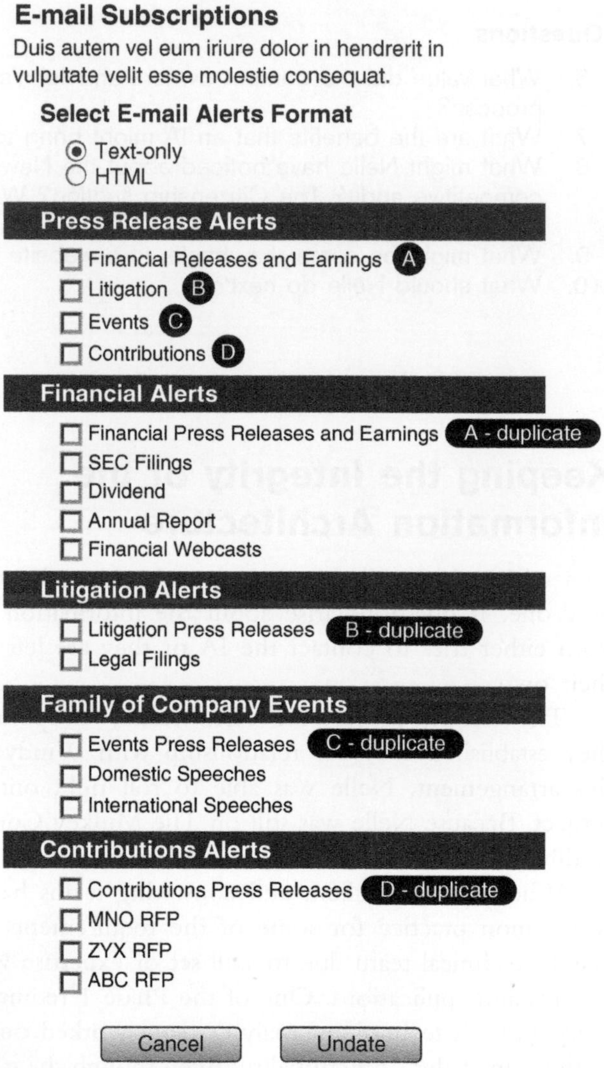

E-mail Subscriptions

Duis autem vel eum iriure dolor in hendrerit in vulputate velit esse molestie consequat.

Select E-mail Alerts Format

◉ Text-only
○ HTML

Press Release Alerts

☐ Financial Releases and Earnings (A)
☐ Litigation (B)
☐ Events (C)
☐ Contributions (D)

Financial Alerts

☐ Financial Press Releases and Earnings A - duplicate
☐ SEC Filings
☐ Dividend
☐ Annual Report
☐ Financial Webcasts

Litigation Alerts

☐ Litigation Press Releases B - duplicate
☐ Legal Filings

Family of Company Events

☐ Events Press Releases C - duplicate
☐ Domestic Speeches
☐ International Speeches

Contributions Alerts

☐ Contributions Press Releases D - duplicate
☐ MNO RFP
☐ ZYX RFP
☐ ABC RFP

[Cancel]   [Undate]

Figure 15.13. Wireframe for e-mail alerts—original design.

To: Nelle

From: John

Re: E-mail Alert Categories

Even though this design has been reviewed and approved, my lead technology analyst is now pushing back on placing duplicate listings for subcategories under two different categories so I need your input. The only subcategories we duplicated were the press releases because we felt, for example, that a user interested in financial news may look first under financial alerts rather than press releases. Thus, we wanted to place the subcategory for financial news under both Press Releases and Financial Information. If you think from a user perspective leaving all the press releases under the Press Releases category is sufficient, then I'll go with that.

During the original discussions on the e-mail alerts functionality, Nelle did not believe the subcategory duplication was necessary but agreed to the design as long as the functionality would work as follows: When a user selected one of the press release options, the second option would also be selected automatically. For example, if the user selected "Litigation" under the Press Release Alerts, then "Litigation Press Releases" would automatically be selected under Litigation Alerts.

Nelle's response to John's e-mail was based on data from web metrics, which showed that the press release pages attracted the highest percentage of users.

To: John
From: Nelle
Re: E-mail Alert Categories

If we can only list the subcategories in one place, I would recommend that since Press Releases is one of the most frequently visited content areas, we would list the subcategories under Press Release Alerts.

John agreed to this approach and approved the change. Nelle quickly updated the wireframes, as shown in Figure 15.14, and redistributed them to the team. John's lead technology analyst then implemented the e-mail alerts page as redesigned.

While advising on the e-mail alerts design, Nelle was also working with the corporate citizenship content team to identify the users and to establish the objective for testing the newly launched Citizenship section. The users would all be corporate social responsibility experts. The objective was to validate the left navigation and the subnavigation of the Citizenship section through a manual card sorting activity.

Nelle interviewed 11 total users: 6 had seen the website before the card sorting activity and 5 had not. Each user was interviewed separately. The first-level navigation was exposed to the users on a whiteboard. Nelle explained that they had come to a website looking for information on citizenship-related topics. They had navigated to a section called Citizenship and were shown the main topics that would appear in that section. Next, Nelle

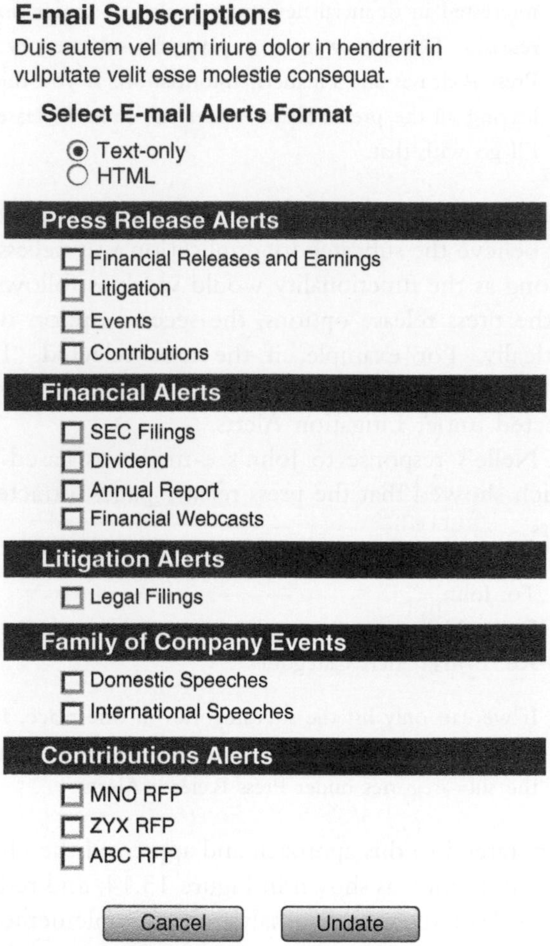

E-mail Subscriptions

Duis autem vel eum iriure dolor in hendrerit in
vulputate velit esse molestie consequat.

Select E-mail Alerts Format

◉ Text-only
◯ HTML

Press Release Alerts

☐ Financial Releases and Earnings
☐ Litigation
☐ Events
☐ Contributions

Financial Alerts

☐ SEC Filings
☐ Dividend
☐ Annual Report
☐ Financial Webcasts

Litigation Alerts

☐ Legal Filings

Family of Company Events

☐ Domestic Speeches
☐ International Speeches

Contributions Alerts

☐ MNO RFP
☐ ZYX RFP
☐ ABC RFP

[Cancel]   [Undate]

Figure 15.14. Wireframe for e-mail alerts—redesign.

asked each user to describe what kinds of information they would expect to
find in each main section. After all the main sections were described, Nelle
gave the user a stack of Post-it® notes. Nelle explained that each Post-it®
contained a subtopic within the Citizenship section and asked each user to
align each subtopic under the main topic where they would expect to find
that kind of information. Each user was then asked if there was any information missing from the Citizenship section, and the users replied that they
expected to find information about people who worked at the company and
other topics such as diversity.

The card sorting activity provided Nelle the user research she needed to validate the recommendations she had previously discussed with the corporate citizenship content owners as well as some new insights that she had not previously expected. For example, the users were unclear about the Management section. Users expected this to be company-wide, not just specific to Citizenship. Compliance contained the types of information users expected and Working with Governments was very clear to all users. Users thought Our Suppliers should be its own section (it didn't live under any of the options presented), and Products & Marketing also made sense to users (because the content was not evaluated in this session, the use of the word "marketing" in Products & Marketing couldn't be validated one way or the other).

Nelle analyzed all the data and prepared a presentation. She shared all the findings and her recommendations (Figure 15.15) with the Corporate Citizenship content owners. Management changed to Responsibility at The Mulkey Corporation and a new section, People, was added to contain subtopics such as Diversity, Work Environment & Locations, and Our Suppliers. The Corporate Citizenship content owners agreed with Nelle's recommendations based on the user research.

About a week later, Jessica (the graphic designer) finished the page design from a Phase 1 requirement: add a stock chart to the Investment Value Calculator page. For this requirement, she had a wireframe to reference (Figure 15.16). Jessica sent the page design, as shown in Figure 15.17, to Nelle via e-mail for her to review.

Due to the page width constraints on the current website page, Jessica did not follow the placement noted on the wireframes and placed the stock chart below the calculator, as shown in Figure 15.17. The problem with this design was that the stock chart fell below the fold line.* In this design, the user would never see the stock chart unless the user scrolled to the bottom of the page (Nelle's usability testing experience has shown that users won't scroll the page if they don't see an indication that there is more information below the fold line). In addition, Nelle knew that investors who were familiar with this page and had scrolled this page in the past would never know that new functionality had been added.

Looking at the page through the eyes of the user, Nelle realized that the stock chart needed to be relocated. She scheduled a meeting with Jessica to discuss the importance of the stock chart position on the page. Nelle brought

---

* The fold line is the invisible line that separates the visible information on a page before a user scrolls from the non-visible information on the page.

Revised Site Structure

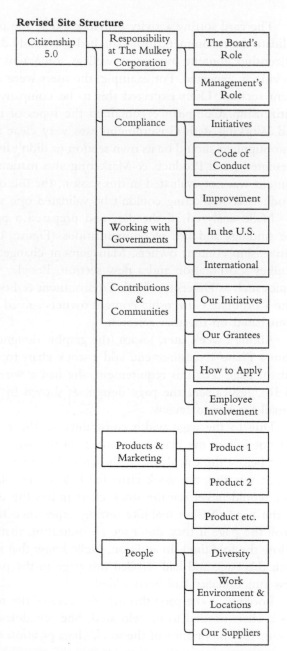

Figure 15.15. High-level flowchart showing the revised changes to the Citizenship section of the mulkeycorp.com website based on the card sorting activity.

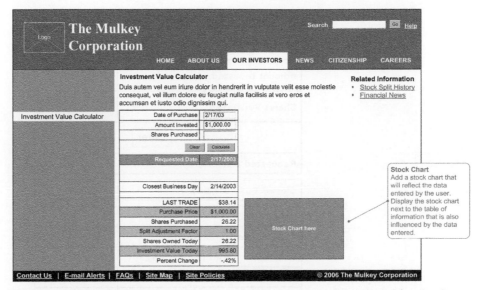

Figure 15.16. Wireframe showing the addition of the stock chart and its intended functionality on the Investment Value Calculator page.

a copy of the wireframe and a copy of the graphic design for the Investment Value Calculator page to the meeting. Nelle began, "Jessica, I wanted to review this page with you—specifically the placement of the stock chart. As I indicated on the wireframe, the information displayed on the stock chart will change based on the data the user enters in the investment value calculator. Adding the stock chart to the page adds no benefit to the user if they don't know it's there! Even if the user learns that the stock chart is on the page, it's equally important that the interaction is seamless to the user. If the user has to constantly scroll down the page to see the results, it'll be cumbersome and they will be less likely to use it. So, it's critical to the user experience that they be able to see the stock chart above the fold."

Jessica thought about what Nelle had said, but she still did not want to redesign the entire page. She later came up with another design (Figure 15.18) where she added a small static graphic of the stock chart with a "View chart" anchor link to the right of the calculator, but she kept the stock chart that showed the interaction with the user data below the fold. In this design, the user would be prompted that a stock chart was available by the static chart graphic and a "View chart" link. When the user clicked the link, the

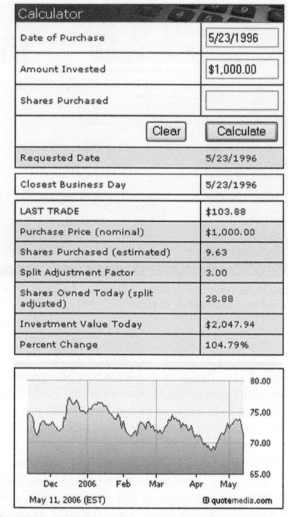

Figure 15.17. The graphic designer added the stock chart below the investment value calculator.

page would scroll down so that the user would see the stock chart based on the user data at the bottom of the page. When Nelle saw the redesign, she realized that Jessica had only solved half the problem.

Another topic that John brought to Nelle's attention was the process for applying for a grant through their website, which was the only way to apply. The Mulkey Corporation had recently gotten feedback from their grant recipients that the process was very confusing. Some steps were online and

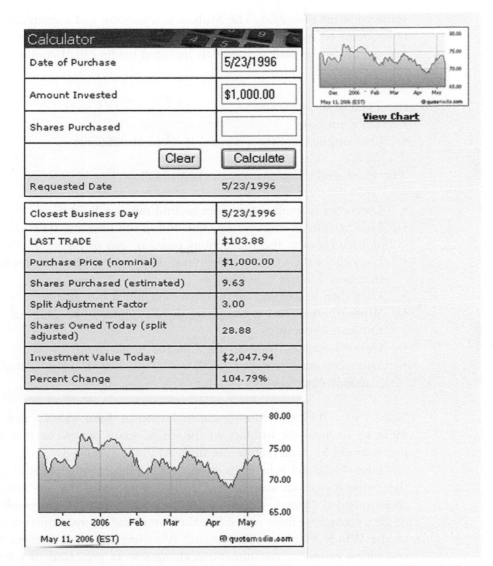

Figure 15.18. Graphic design updated with a stock chart thumbnail image and a "View chart" anchor link.

some were off-line. Also, The Mulkey Corporation had a significant number of incomplete grant applications because the prospective grant recipients did not complete the final step, which included mailing hard copies of the following material:

- Their grant application
- Their proposal
- One original and three copies of seven attachments

The grant application process worked as follows:

- User goes to mulkeycorp.com to find out key RFP dates.
- User returns to mulkeycorp.com during the time the RFP is available and navigates to the Instructions page, as seen in Figure 15.19.
- User clicks the On-line Application link, which opens an application in a new browser window.
- User then downloads the proposal and fills it out off-line.
- When the proposal is complete, the user uploads the proposal into the On-line Application.
- User fills out and submits the On-line Application.
- User then mails the application and proposal with other related materials (attachments).

Since a new RFP was coming out in 2 months, John added a new requirement to evaluate the usability of the online grant process so that improvements could be made before the next RFP was launched.

First, Nelle did a heuristic evaluation of the grant application pages on the mulkeycorp.com website and created wireframes that documented her recommended changes. Next, she worked with Jessica to get graphic screen designs created for these pages. She then presented the recommended changes to the Windy Pine Consulting team. After implementing changes from the consulting team, the recommended changes were presented to John's team. John's team also had a few suggestions. After all the feedback had been implemented, the final changes were re-presented to John and his team. John's team finally approved the new design, and it was time to start planning for the usability test.

Nelle worked with the contributions content owners at The Mulkey Corporation to document usability test objectives. From the objectives, Nelle created a discussion guide for her one-on-one usability interviews. Because

Instructions

In order to apply for funding, organizations are required to:

Step 1

Create an Account.

- You must have an e-mail address in order to create an account.
- You will be asked to create a password of your choice.

Once you've created an account, you will then be able to access the on-line application.

Step 2

Access/Submit the On-line Application (Part A)
The Application includes a Proposal that must be downloaded to your computer. Once completed, you must then upload your proposal to the on-line application.

When you click on **On-line Application**, it will appear in a new window. Click the Proposal link, "Grant Proposal – PART B" (in the upper left corner) to open. Save it to your computer by choosing "File > Save As..." in the menu bar, selecting a location and file name, and clicking "Save." After you've saved the Proposal, you can open it with your word processor to complete it.

To complete the On-line Application, fill in all required fields and as much optional information as possible. Before submitting your application on-line, you must upload your completed Proposal (Part B) using Page 4 of the application. On that page, click the "Browse" button to locate your saved Proposal on your computer. Once you've located your proposal and the file name appears in the box, you then click the "Upload" button. Once uploaded, click "Review and Submit," verify your information, then click "Submit." You will receive an e-mail notification confirming receipt.

Note: You can save your On-Line Application at any time by clicking "Save & Finish Later" at the bottom of any page. If you wish to access your saved or completed applications, you must use this link: **Access My Account**.

Step 3

Mailing Your Complete Application Package

The following **must** be submitted with the application. If the following materials are not received, the Fund's employee committee will be unable to review your application:

- **A hard copy of your grant application (Part A).**
- **A completed proposal (Part B) signed by the Executive Director and Board Chair.**
- **Duis autem vel eum iriure dolor in hendrerit in vulputate velit.**
  Duis autem vel eum iriure.
- **Duis autem vel eum iriure.**
  Duis autem vel eum iriure dolor in hendrerit.
- **Duis autem vel eum iriure dolor in hendrerit in vulputate.**
  Duis autem vel eum iriure dolor in hendrerit in vulputate velit esse.
- **Duis autem vel eum iriure dolor.**
- **Duis autem vel eum iriure dolor in hendrerit in vulputate velit esse.**
- **Duis autem vel eum iriure dolor.**
- **Duis autem vel eum iriure dolor in hendrerit in vulputate velit esse.**

Figure 15.19. Original instructions for submitting a grant application.

the contributions content owners had existing relationships with some of their previous grant recipients, they recruited them for usability testing.

Nelle facilitated the usability test as 7 one-on-one sessions in a conference room at The Mulkey Corporation. At the beginning of each interview, Nelle introduced herself, not as the designer of the application but as part of the client team who was there to listen to their input about what was working and what wasn't working on the online grant application. She explained that she would take each person's feedback to the client team for them to know where improvements were needed to make the online grant application easier to use. Each grant applicant first reviewed the introductory page and commented on what information they would actually read and what information they thought was missing. Because the online grant application was a multiple-step process, the users went through the steps and Nelle documented whether the applicant successfully completed each step.

Next, Nelle reviewed her notes on what the grant applicants told her and what she observed. The feedback was informative and provided Nelle further direction for usability improvements. John and his team reviewed and approved her recommendations, and the changes were live for the launch of the RFP. The number of user complaints dropped considerably and the number of incomplete grant applications dropped from 19% to 5%.

Questions

11. Why do changes happen after designs or concepts are approved?
12. What design problem on the Investment Value Calculator page was not addressed?
13. Could having the IA lead the usability test bias the results?
14. What were some of the problems with the online grant instructions? How might Nelle redesign the online grant submission in response to the users' input?
15. What should the next steps be for this project?

Summary

The Mulkey Corporation project used many critical and valuable inputs for the website redesign:

- Business objectives
- User objectives

- Competitive audit
- Prioritized and approved requirements
- Website survey
- Web metrics
- Heuristic evaluations
- Usability testing

Some of the inputs were available to Nelle when she joined this project. All these inputs allowed Nelle to have sound validation for the information architecture recommendations, and most of the recommendations could be backed up by research.

The steps involved in this project were as follows:

- Document the business objectives and user types through executive one-on-one interviews
- Translate the business objectives into website objectives
- Document the user objectives
- Cross-reference the user objectives with the website objectives
- Perform a competitive audit
- Apply information architecture using the above inputs as well as website analytics, website surveys, heuristic evaluations, and usability testing
  - Create high-level flowcharts
    — Review internally
    — Revise
    — Review with the client
    — Revise
  - Create wireframes
    — Review internally
    — Revise (and revise flowcharts if necessary)
    — Review with the client
    — Revise (and revise flowcharts if necessary)

The information architecture documentation was then used by the graphical designer, content specialist, and technical architect.

Some of the lessons that Nelle learned while working on this project included:

- Although Nelle was using the competitive audit documentation, it was often impossible or it took a significant amount of time to find the exact page referenced on the "like company" website. This was often caused by the website page being moved or completely deleted. Another cause was that the navigation was not shown on the screen shot in the competitive audit documentation. After the first competitive audit, Nelle asked that the URLs be added under each screen shot.

- In Nelle's more than 10 years as an IA, she's learned to not take it personally when the client team doesn't agree with her recommendations. She's come to realize that it is her role to present best practices for the user experience and that, ultimately, the client makes the final decisions—it is their website. Also, the client may have insights into their users and their behaviors that Nelle wouldn't necessarily know or have access to based on past focus groups or other user inputs. These additional insights help inform some of the client's decisions.

- If a client team has legal reviews built into their content approval process, appropriate time should be accounted for in the project timeline. Enough time was not budgeted for the legal reviews, which caused content to launch much later than originally planned.

- Keeping everyone updated on the latest documentation is always challenging. On this project the consulting team created an external website to host all of the documentation. Nelle thought that this would help reduce the problems with team members working from old documents. She soon found that the external site didn't help as much as she had hoped. Team members tend to hold on to the last printed copy that was distributed. The only solution Nelle has is to reprint and redistribute.

- On many occasions Nelle would roll off a project before the technical implementation was complete. She noticed when these websites launched that fine details had been changed in the information architecture. Since she had already left the project, there wasn't an opportunity for her to stand strong representing the voice of the user. On this project, Nelle was involved for multiple releases over two phases and was delighted to be able to routinely perform quality assurance checks to bring the website back into alignment with the original designs. It would be beneficial on future projects to be able to budget time and cost so that the IA could continue to be involved during key project reviews even after the information architecture is complete.

Further Reading

Donoghue, K. (2002). *Built for use: driving profitability through the user experience.* New York: McGraw-Hill.

Fowler, S. (1998). *GUI design handbook.* New York: McGraw-Hill.

Garrett, J. (2003). *The elements of user experience: user-centered design for the web.* New York: American Institute of Graphic Arts, and Berkeley: New Riders Publishing.

Krug, S. (2000). *Don't make me think: a common sense approach to web usability.* Berkeley: New Riders Publishing.

Rosenfeld, L., and Morville, P. (2002). *Information architecture for the World Wide Web*, 2nd edition. Beijing: O'Reilly & Associates.

Saffer, D. (2003). *Writing smart annotations.* Retrieved from http://www.boxesandarrows.com/view/writing_smart_annotations

Stott, L. (2004). *Information architecture: a rose by any other name. . . .* Retrieved from http://www.boxesandarrows.com/view/information_architecture_a_rose_by_any_other_name_

Willis, D. (2004). *Are useful requirements just a fairy tale? (and why an IA should care).* Retrieved from http://www.boxesandarrows.com/view/are_useful_requirements_just_a_fairy_tale_and_why_an_ia_should_care_

Wodtke, C. (2003). *Information architecture: blueprints for the web.* Berkeley: New Riders Publishing.

CASE 16

Incorporating Web Accessibility Into the Design Process

Sarah J. Swierenga, Michigan State University

> *Carmen was in the midst of four projects involving the full complement of design and usability services. Liam, vice president of the product development division, stopped by Carmen's office one day with yet another assignment. He asked, "Could you please figure out the impact, if any, Section 508 accessibility legislation is going to have on our applications and give my team and me a heads up?" Carmen sensed this was going to be bigger—much bigger—than the proverbial bread box.*

Travelers By Design

Carmen works as the senior-level usability specialist for Travelers By Design (TBD), a multinational online travel company. TBD is a premier provider of business travel solutions for corporate travelers and government officials. The company designs and manages e-commerce applications, specializing in travel sites for business professionals booking extended stay, personalized tours, and corporate retreat packages. Carmen has been with the company for about 6 years and is the design and usability lead on several major website releases. Thankfully, her organization has incorporated aspects of user-centered design (UCD) into the standard development process, through usability specialists establishing rapport with product managers who are responsible for user interface functionality on the site. A few successes have demonstrated the value of gathering end user feedback about concept designs. Carmen has performed many concept user evaluations, created wireframe

355

HTML prototypes, written user interface design specifications, and conducted formal one-on-one usability evaluations. She's considered a seasoned UCD professional.

Then along came "Section 508." Section 508 is a U.S. federal law requiring website applications and other electronic and information technologies developed or purchased by the federal government to be accessible for persons with disabilities. Accessible sites allow customers with disabilities to interact effectively with web products using screen readers, voice browsers, TTY, and so on by taking into account their limitations. In an accessible website, for example, users can enlarge text, change the shape of a page, skim through content using headings, see video captions, understand tables and charts, fill out forms, and hear descriptions of images. Without accessibility elements in websites, however, persons with disabilities are unable to take advantage of the web. TBD's customer base includes people who have no significant challenges with vision, hearing, dexterity, or cognition and those who have experienced varying levels of loss (e.g., poor eyesight, low vision or partial blindness, color blindness, complete blindness, hearing loss, deafness, or mobility constraints) that make using the mouse challenging. Also, TBD was bidding on a contract with the U.S. government, meaning that the upcoming legislation had an immediate impact.

Carmen was in the midst of four projects involving the full complement of design and usability services. She was also consulting on a few other projects with colleagues while mentoring three design and usability interns. Then Liam, vice president of the product development division, stopped by Carmen's office one day in mid-December 2000 with yet another assignment. He asked Carmen, "Could you please figure out the impact, if any, that Section 508 accessibility legislation is going to have on our applications and give my team and me a heads up?"

Carmen's first thoughts concerned her already heavy design and usability project work load and learning about a new subject area. Evaluating the code of websites against accessibility standards did not appear to be related to conducting user experience research, which was Carmen's area of expertise.

She said to Liam, "Is this something that a product manager or technical lead could undertake?"

Liam replied, "The reason I came to you to organize this initiative is because no one in the company has the necessary accessibility experience. And, you have the advantage over anyone else of having worked as the internal design and usability consultant on all of the products that might be affected. The product managers and developers know only a few products."

Usability specialists like Carmen had the advantage of working in cross-functional multidisciplinary project teams. Also, Carmen understood the politics of the organizational structure: the players and the relationships among them, their turf, and their agendas. Further, Carmen's research background and product testing experience would also be valuable for approaching this effort systematically. Like it or not, the task to ensure the company's products were "fixed" by June 21, 2001 (the day Section 508 became law), was hers to manage.

Questions

1. What alternatives does Liam have for staffing the accessibility initiative, and what are the pros and cons of the approaches?

Learning About Accessibility

After much deliberation with Carmen and others in the organization, Liam decided the best option was to grow expertise in-house so that the knowledge would remain with the company and the procedures and processes could be developed over time. In this case, Carmen needed to learn the technical aspects of accessible design and set up the program internally. After searching online resources and the few texts available about web accessibility, Carmen concluded that accessibility means enhancing websites to ensure content is understandable and navigable for more users. This includes making the language clear and simple, and simplifying navigation within and between web pages. There is an added advantage to programming sites with accessibility principles in mind: Because the visual design is separated from the content, the underlying code will be cleaner and more browser independent and forward-compatible. It also enables the user interface to render more effectively on emerging technologies, such as mobile phones, personal digital assistants and other small-screen devices, and automobile-based personal computers. Carmen realized that accessibility enhancements are really part of a standards-compliant code development strategy that will result in better products for all users.

Carmen knew she would first need some statistics to make accessibility a priority at TBD. She discovered some interesting and thought-provoking numbers from reading U.S. Census Bureau reports (http://www.census.gov/hhes/www/disability/disability.html, http://www.census.gov/Press-Release/www/2002/cb02ff11.html) and information on the World Health Organization site (http://www.who.int/disabilities/en/):

- Over 54 million Americans (about 19%) have some kind of legal disability.
- There are 600+ million disabled people worldwide.
- One in 10 Americans has a severe disability.
- One in two Americans over 65 has reduced capabilities.

She also found that the number of users affected by accessibility issues is even larger if older online consumers are considered. Carmen realized that people age at differing rates, so that identifying "older" consumers as those over 65, for example, could be misleading. Instead, she decided to think of TBD's customers as representing a continuum, from those without deficits in hearing, vision, dexterity, or cognition to those who had experienced varying levels of loss. In addition to persons traditionally considered to have disabilities, like completely blind or deaf people, this also included persons who had poor eyesight, were hard of hearing, or had difficulty using a mouse. Carmen realized that TBD's customer base of corporate and government travelers was actually quite diverse and could not be easily pigeon-holed. Moreover, because their entire business depended on effective online communication with customers, making its web applications accessible to all users, regardless of disability, rapidly became a high priority within the company. The next step required an organizational strategy for implementing an accessibility compliance program.

Getting Started

Liam and Carmen met to discuss the steps they would need to take to establish the compliance program.

"Carmen, in order to figure out how we should proceed, maybe we should try to identify some questions we need to answer to make this happen," Liam began.

"Yeah, that makes sense," said Carmen. "For instance, I've been thinking about the term 'disabilities.' It's so broad—exactly what disabilities are we talking about? And obviously not all disabilities present the same design issues."

"Right," said Liam. He jotted that down on the board.

"What about scope? Which of our products need to be accessible?"

Liam and Carmen continued their brainstorming. When they were through, they had a list of questions to answer to put a compliance program in place:

- What legal requirements do TBD's products need to meet?
- What are the major design issues for people with different types of disabilities?
- What products will be affected?
- Which key stakeholders and areas of the organization will need to be involved?
- How will the initiative be funded? How will the compliance work be prioritized with the other work?
- How long will it take?
- What resources will be needed to form a core accessibility team?
- How do users with disabilities experience our products?

About Section 508

Now came the hard work: answering these questions. First, Carmen decided to locate and read the legislation, standards, and guidelines relevant to accessibility. Carmen called legal affairs and talked to an attorney, Toni, about the upcoming Section 508 legislation.

"Toni," asked Carmen, "can you give me a quick history of 508?"

"Well," responded Toni, "Section 508 is actually part of the Rehabilitation Act of 1973, but this particular section is going to become effective in June of 2001. Section 508 requires that electronic and information technology developed or purchased by the federal government must be accessible by people with disabilities. That's the essence of it, but there's more."

Toni went on to explain, "Agencies must also purchase the most accessible electronic information technology available commercially to ensure that their employees with disabilities can best perform their duties. To that end, the federal government asks companies to complete a voluntary product accessibility form that describes how their software products, like word processing and web design programs, support accessibility. That way the government can make informed purchasing decisions. Additionally, federal acquisition regulation amendments were passed in 2001 that required agencies to apply Section 508 standards to contracts awarded on or after June 25, 2001. This regulation did a lot to strengthen the impact of the law."

"I always thought the Americans With Disabilities Act, the ADA, would cover all of this. Why do we need Section 508?" asked Carmen.

"Well," said Toni, "sometimes people confuse ADA with Section 508, but they are distinctly different pieces of legislation. The ADA is a civil rights law that was passed in 1990. It prohibits discrimination against people with disabilities. The ADA generally requires employers, state and local governments, and what are called 'places of public accommodation' to offer reasonable services or tools to ensure that people are not discriminated against because of a disability. If you think about it, the web can be considered a place of public accommodation, so ADA could apply to the web in certain situations, for example, when access to the service or product is only available online. What's also interesting is that since Section 508 was enacted, those standards are the minimum requirement for assessing the accessibility of web applications, presumably since the ADA legislation did not provide specific guidelines for digital spaces."

Toni also suggested that Carmen investigate international policies. She told Carmen that several countries had adopted legislation or established policies regarding web accessibility. Carmen immediately understood that because her company's website was also being marketed to governmental agencies around the world, she would also need to pay attention to the World Wide Web Consortium (W3C) Web Accessibility Initiative's (WAI) Web Content Accessibility Guidelines (WCAG). Because the W3C is an international standards body, a number of countries have based their legislation and policies on the WCAG. The conversation was beginning to sound a bit like alphabet soup to Carmen, but she jotted down all the acronyms.

After her conversation with Toni, Carmen began to explore the design issues for people with different types of disabilities. She accessed several online resources to gain a better understanding about the different types of disabilities addressed in the standards. Then she researched what challenges people with disabilities might experience as they interact with the TBD products.

Questions

2. Why would visually impaired users have the most potential problems with web use?
3. What type of problems would users who are deaf or hard of hearing have?
4. What type of problems would users with physical and motor disabilities experience?
5. What type of problems would users with cognitive disabilities have?

Accessibility and the TBD Products

Carmen's research into the company's applications revealed several issues with accessibility. First, the applications required the use of the mouse for interacting with the product, including core functionality such as navigational menus and drop-down lists. Keyboard shortcuts and function keys were not available on most pages, and tabbing through the page would be confusing for screen reader users because the tab order was not clearly defined in the code.

Carmen also noted that in the TBD applications the home pages typically included blinking advertisement images and had many options competing for the user's attention. Also, the primary and most frequently used features, like packaging airfare and hotel accommodations and searching through options for corporate retreats, lacked prominence. TBD also planned to introduce a new section offering discounted vacations that would have to be taken into account.

After Carmen had completed her research, she knew a fair amount about accessibility in general and, more specifically, how TBD products stacked up with regard to accessibility. Next, Carmen needed to understand how to come up with an accessibility compliance plan for the TBD products. She went back to the list that Liam and she put together:

- What legal requirements do TBD's products need to meet?
- What are the major design issues for people with different types of disabilities?
- What products will be affected?
- Which key stakeholders and areas of the organization will need to be involved?
- How will the initiative be funded? How will the accessibility work be prioritized with the other work?
- How long will it take?
- What resources will be needed to form a core accessibility team?
- How do users with disabilities experience our products?

Carmen knew she needed to take a hard look at her own products and thought about a plan. She realized that the only way to know which products might be affected from a legal standpoint was to acquire a list of active products. This was much more difficult than it sounded. There were several products under development, many in the marketplace, and some that were being phased out. Each product involved a different product team, and not many people had knowledge of the bigger picture. Fortunately, Carmen was able to find Louis. Louis was a strategic architecture developer who was working on that very issue. Louis was able to provide Carmen with a high-level list of web and client-side applications. Carmen was then able to use her network of colleagues to find contacts for each product. The sales representatives and marketing managers helped identify which products might be used by the federal government. Finally, Carmen asked the government sales representatives and legal affairs to perform a risk analysis for accessibility compliance for each product, so she could identify those most likely to run afoul of government regulations or agency priorities, trading off the exposure to lawsuits with the costs of enhancing the site to establish priorities for fixing the sites.

Carmen ultimately found over 50 products that needed to be assessed and probably enhanced for accessibility. Although TBD wanted all of its products to be compliant by the deadline, there were simply too many. Carmen had to prioritize the products by exposure to the government market, number of users, and how close the product was "to retirement." The first group targeted by her included TBD's two flagship products as well as several other products heavily used by people in federal government agencies (about 10 total).

Carmen went back to her checklist. She still had a fair amount of work ahead of her. She sat down to strategize how to approach the rest of the questions.

Questions

6. Which key stakeholders and areas of the organization should be involved in an accessibility initiative? How could Carmen get them engaged with the project?
7. What would be some potential funding sources for an accessibility initiative? How can the accessibility work be prioritized with the other work?
8. How long will it take?
9. Who should be involved in a core accessibility team? What characteristics should the team have?
10. How could Carmen understand how users with disabilities experience the targeted products?

Putting the Accessibility Compliance Process in Place

The stakeholders at TBD were concerned about losing significant accounts because of the Section 508 requirements. They now understood that their government sales representatives should work with the legal affairs office to understand the impact of the legislation on future contracts and with the finance office to start prioritizing the revenue implications for fixing or not fixing each product.

Each product team was asked to lend human and financial resources to the accessibility project. Carmen prepared a fact sheet about the new legislation and the potential impact on new and existing contracts. The fact sheet also served as an awareness-raising tool for the many organizations and stakeholders that would eventually need to be involved in the effort. She also dug around on the Internet and found a few videos of people with disabilities interacting with websites, and she shared these with the teams. Fortunately, the executive team was already committed to funding the initiative at an institutional level because of the pending legislation. Across the company, web accessibility became the number 1 priority project. Development work on several new features was placed on hold until accessibility enhancements could be incorporated into the web products; for other products, original schedules were delayed to accommodate the accessibility work.

Carmen recommended to upper management that the team include technical leads for the two largest products, an accessibility specialist (probably a human factors engineer or a usability specialist), a consultant-level customer service representative, and an experienced quality assurance specialist (more toward the middle of the implementation phases of the project). She also proposed assigning a project manager to manage the overall initiative. Finally, she recommended that all the design and usability specialists for the affected products be included in the effort, at least at some point; building internal accessibility expertise would be critical in the long run.

A Blind User Test-Drives the Site

In addition to all the internal preparation for the accessibility initiative, Carmen believed strongly that the team would need to understand how the two largest products were functioning for users with disabilities. Initially, due to the highly visual nature of the web applications, she recruited Robert, a blind professional who was a proficient screen reader user, to review a few of the products using a screen reader. To ensure that the impact of this project was understood by the development side of the house, she asked Sydney and Henry, the technical leads from the two highest-revenue-generating product, to join her in the meeting with the blind professional.

The experience was unforgettable for both of them. It was one of those rare days when they knew their work was going to make a real difference for untold numbers of customers. Sydney asked Robert to bring up the core TBD site and arrange a business trip to New York. Robert was relatively savvy with the JAWS for Windows screen reader (this screen reader enjoys 80% market share), but after listening to part of the home page of the product he already had lots of comments. He found that few of the images made sense because they didn't have alternative text, also known as "hover text." There were at least 50 navigation links clustered at the top and side of the page, and after listening to several of them, Robert wasn't sure where to begin. Unknown to him, the visual interface highlighted the most popular features in the center of the page. Robert then listened to each of the text boxes, assuming there would be a "Going From and To" feature. He found several text boxes but had to change screen reader modes because he could not find their labels. After about 3 minutes, Robert decided that he'd filled in enough information to search for airfares. Of course, the graphic "Go" button wasn't labeled either, but he found it because the file name of the image was "airfaresearch.gif," and screen readers will read the file name if there's no other information available. What a hassle . . . and he was only on the home page!

Robert remained very gracious, patient, and tenacious in completing the task. He said he was accustomed to these issues and that accessing websites with JAWS was a vast improvement over the past. Carmen, Sydney, and Henry, however, were frustrated, aggravated, and even embarrassed about the product after watching him struggle. They left the meeting with a new appreciation of accessible design, a passion for promoting it, and a commitment to repairing the TBD site. Carmen and her team were now ready to launch the accessibility initiative.

Once the accessibility initiative was put into place at TBD, Carmen needed to establish a process for evaluating the products' current compliance with accessibility standards and then implement enhancements. Again, Carmen and Liam met.

"Carmen," said Liam, "I'm extremely impressed with the progress you've made in setting up this compliance program."

"Thanks, Liam," said Carmen, "but I have the sneaking suspicion you're going to remind me of the next chunk of work I have to do."

Liam laughed, "Of course! Now that the program is planned, we need to add two more components. We need to be sure we have a process that can audit our products to be sure they're complying with 508. And of course, we need to be sure that we fix them."

Again, Carmen and Liam brainstormed a list of activities:

- Evaluating compliance
  — Identify website accessibility problems: initial review
  — Establish core team for accessibility enhancements
  — Decide on level of compliance
  — Conduct detailed accessibility compliance inspection
- Implementation
  — Work with developers during implementation
- Verification
  — Verify that site is accessibility compliant
  — Write the VPAT document
- Ongoing compliance
  — Develop an ongoing maintenance program

First, Carmen enlisted her usability intern, Suzanna, to help her look at each product to see how much work might be involved to enhance it. Their initial evaluations focused on several aspects of the web user interface, examining the following areas (from Section 508) for a few main paths through each product:

- Alt text on images and image maps—Does appropriate descriptive text exist for every image?
- Color—Is color only used as a redundant code?
- Style sheets—Does the page still read properly when style sheets are turned off, so that the reading order of the information on the page is still correct?
- Table cell identification—Do data tables include HTML markup to identify row and column headers?
- Frame titling—For the parts of the products that still use frames, have the developers included meaningful name and title attributes for each frame and used descriptive title tags on the pages within each frame?
- JavaScript—Does the page render correctly using a screen reader?

- Search forms—Are field labels adjacent to controls, and does each text box have an ID attribute?
- Skip navigation—Is there a way to skip over repetitive navigation links to get to page content?
- Flicker and timed responses—Do the pages avoid rapidly flickering images, as they can trigger seizures in some individuals? Can users pause timed messages to ask for more time to respond to the information?
- Multimedia—Are video clips captioned for deaf or hearing-impaired users?

During the initial evaluation, Carmen and Suzanna concentrated on the Section 508 requirements because almost all of them were part of the WCAG guidelines, too. The main WCAG item they checked in the initial evaluation was whether or not the page still worked when JavaScript was turned off, because this is a significant issue for most products as so many sites use Java-Script for core functionality, and it is not included in Section 508. Figure 16.1 highlights several accessibility items and provides snippets of example accessibility code, including a skip navigation link, alternative image text, access keys, grouping content within a form, form field labeling, and standard button tags. Note that the page won't look any different, but it will render correctly for people using assistive technologies.

Carmen and Suzanna used Internet Explorer 5.5 to conduct the review. (This version was new at the time and had controls to override style sheets and ignore colors, font sizes, and font styles—but typically evaluators should use the latest version of the browser to conduct evaluations.) They turned off the images so that the image "alt" text (descriptive text coded into the image) was displayed instead, and turned off style sheets for the initial evaluation. Trying out the TBD site in this fashion proved to be an interesting experience. The corporate logo disappeared, as did most of the navigation items and graphic buttons (e.g., Search) because of missing alternative text on those images. (The newly formed corporate branding team lobbied to get this issue addressed immediately.) Thankfully, the pages still read properly with the style sheets turned off because the code was mainly used to add visual font effects rather than to position the information on the pages.

Next, Carmen and Suzanna used JAWS for Windows to evaluate the TBD pages. Using JAWS takes some practice because JAWS does not provide visual feedback indicating what's being read on the page. Some evaluators also use IBM's Home Page Reader, a talking browser designed for people with vision impairments. Home Page Reader allows sighted evaluators to

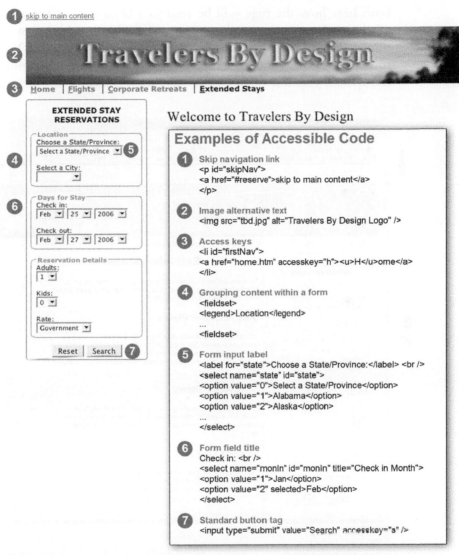

Figure 16.1. Screen shot with accessibility code examples. (1) "Skip navigation" links enable users to quickly get past repetitive navigational links to the page content; (2) screen reader assistive technology vocalizes the alternative text (alt = "Travelers By Design") when images include it; (3) access keys create keyboard shortcuts that enable users to quickly invoke core site functionality; (4) fieldset tags group the information in the specified area of the form and label it (e.g., the gray "Location" box around the state and city drop-downs); (5) form input labels indicate what is included in the drop-down menu list; (6) form field titles associate the text label with the drop-down menu or text box; and (7) standard button tags are read by screen readers (e.g., screen reader would say "Search Button" because the input type was "submit" with a value of "Search"). (Created by Vivek Joshi. Used with permission.)

both hear how the page will be read to a blind user and to see a text view of the web page in another program window, right below its graphical display. Figure 16.2 shows an example of how one of the TBD pages displays in the Home Page Reader program. Being able to track the visual page with the spoken and text output of the application saves a lot of time.

Figure 16.2. Example of a TBD page displayed in the Home Page Reader program. (Created by Michael S. Elledge. Used with permission.)

Carmen and Suzanna also reviewed how the pages would render in a linear manner (i.e., following the order of the underlying code). An easy way to see how a screen reader will interpret your site is to turn off images and style sheets in your browser. This shows how content is read, the relative sizing of headings, and whether your alt tags and link text make sense. Figure 16.3 shows a graphic version and a linearized view of a TBD page. Finally,

A

Figure 16.3. (A) Graphic and (B) linearized versions of the same TBD page. The linearized version reorders the graphical version of the page by following the reading order of the underlying code, reading the page from the top left to the bottom right down the page. Also, note that the screen reader displays (and vocalizes) the descriptive text for each of the images in the linearized version of the page (e.g., "The Four Seasons offers heart-of-everything proximity to all that San Francisco offers . . ."). (Created by Michael S. Elledge. Used with permission.)

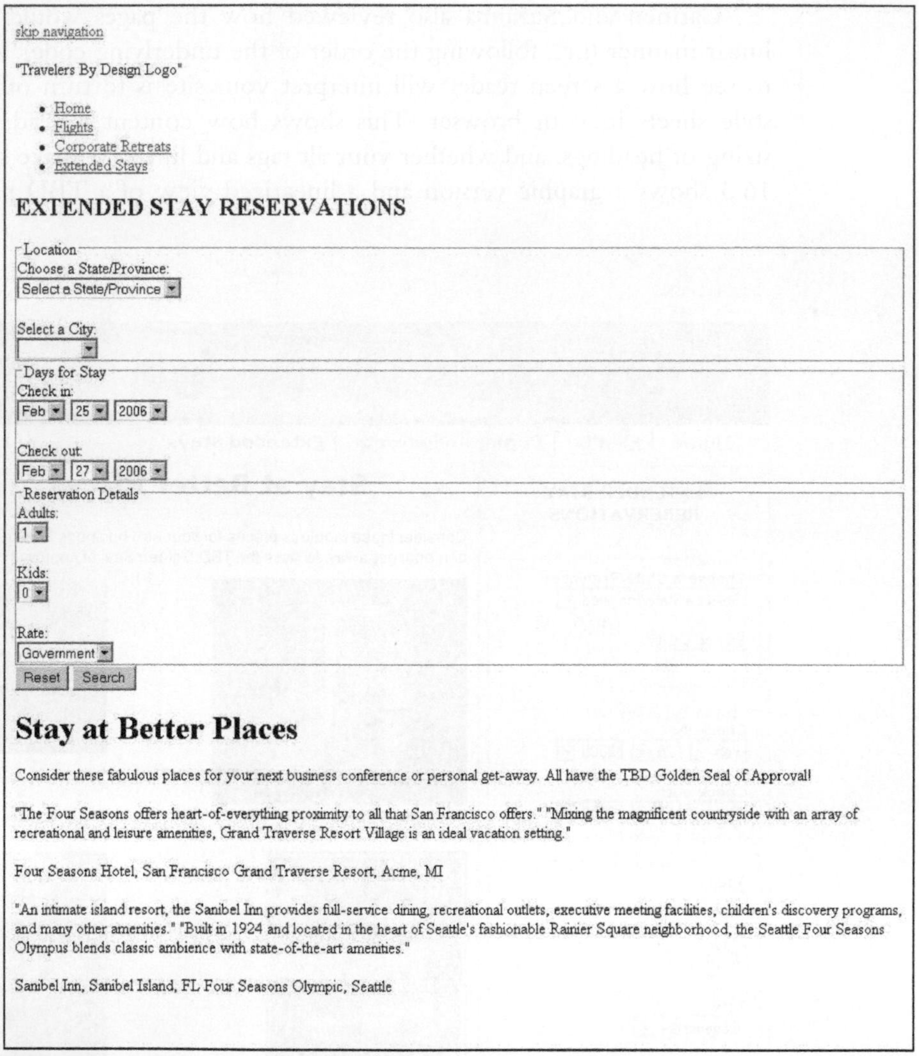

skip navigation

"Travelers By Design Logo"

- Home
- Flights
- Corporate Retreats
- Extended Stays

EXTENDED STAY RESERVATIONS

Location

Choose a State/Province:
Select a State/Province ▾

Select a City:
▾

Days for Stay
Check in:
Feb ▾ 25 ▾ 2006 ▾

Check out:
Feb ▾ 27 ▾ 2006 ▾

Reservation Details
Adults:
1 ▾

Kids:
0 ▾

Rate:
Government ▾

Reset   Search

Stay at Better Places

Consider these fabulous places for your next business conference or personal get-away. All have the TBD Golden Seal of Approval!

"The Four Seasons offers heart-of-everything proximity to all that San Francisco offers." "Mixing the magnificent countryside with an array of recreational and leisure amenities, Grand Traverse Resort Village is an ideal vacation setting."

Four Seasons Hotel, San Francisco Grand Traverse Resort, Acme, MI

"An intimate island resort, the Sanibel Inn provides full-service dining, recreational outlets, executive meeting facilities, children's discovery programs, and many other amenities." "Built in 1924 and located in the heart of Seattle's fashionable Rainier Square neighborhood, the Seattle Four Seasons Olympus blends classic ambience with state-of-the-art amenities."

Sanibel Inn, Sanibel Island, FL Four Seasons Olympic, Seattle

B

Figure 16.3. *Continued*

checking pages in other browsers, such as Opera, Mozilla, or Firefox, gave them an even better idea of how well the pages were coded for browser independence.

As they gained experience conducting initial evaluations on the list of products, Carmen and Suzanna tried a few automated accessibility tools, such as Bobby and Cynthia Says. The results were helpful for identifying places in the code to check for different items, but they generated a lot of output. Also, they could not tell whether the JavaScript was working properly because the automated tools could not test it; that aspect remained a manual task. The general consensus is that evaluators cannot rely on these tools alone.

Questions

11. Do all the pages on a website have to be checked for compliance? What mechanism could Carmen use to track compliance across pages?

Implementing and Verification

Poised to implement the program, Carmen assembled her core team, which consisted of a project manager for the accessibility initiative, the technical leads for the two largest products, and a consulting-level customer service representative.

The technical leads from the two largest products were heavily involved in the accessibility initiative, but the technical leads for the other products were also involved at certain points during the overall effort. Likewise, only a couple of the product managers were closely involved with the accessibility initiative; they relied on the technical leads to ensure that the products would be fixed in a timely manner. A project manager, Kiah, was assigned to the project, which was a great relief to Carmen. Jillanne, the customer service consultant, was excited to be involved in the project and proved to be a valuable advocate for the general users. Unfortunately, the web designers, human factors specialists, and graphics designers from the UCD group who were part of the individual project teams weren't able to participate because of their heavy work load. After some negotiation, Celia, a technical communication specialist, devoted significant time to the effort, assisting the evaluation and modification of the extensive help systems. Additionally, Carmen was able to obtain two more interns from the UCD group. The quality assurance resource worked with the core team more toward the end of the implementation phase. The business and marketing representatives also decided to be involved only on an as-needed basis. They mostly lobbied for organizational approvals and upper-management support. In general, part of the team should focus on lining up resources and funding as well as on obtaining support from other organizations that need to be involved at various times throughout the effort. The technical members of the team should investigate issues uncovered in the initial evaluations.

The accessibility team contacted an outside accessibility technical consultant, Kate, to review how the team was planning to assess the products and to discuss technical challenges revealed in the initial reviews. She concurred with the proposed strategy for assessing the products and was also able to provide technical guidance on a few programming questions that the team had.

Although the team had to comply with all of the Section 508 standards, they weren't sure about being able to achieve full WCAG compliance. Carmen found that most accessibility experts recommended that websites at least satisfy priorities 1 and 2 checkpoints. By comparison, Section 508 focuses primarily on priority 1 checkpoints but also includes some from priorities 2 and 3. Carmen advocated complying with the priorities 1 and 2 checkpoints, but the technical leads recommended holding off on incorporating any of the WCAG guidelines. Kiah, the project manager, agreed with them because of time constraints, so the products were not enhanced to meet the WCAG priorities in the first round. Carmen decided to address this issue in the future.

The product managers identified the three to five main product task paths and some key pages in their respective products. The accessibility evaluation team, consisting of Carmen and the three usability interns, went through the 10 products with JAWS, Home Page Reader, and the Lynx Viewer (displays the page in a linear reading order). They also used Cynthia Says and Bobby (which were free at the time), online accessibility evaluation tools, for automated checking to confirm their manual inspections. It took an enormous amount of time to complete the compliance review—about 5 staff weeks.

Before they began to implement the evaluation, Carmen created an inspection summary template. Carmen, Suzanna, and the two other UCD interns entered the details for each problem in a linked spreadsheet. The project manager used the spreadsheet to track progress. The team added code examples as they worked.

As the team worked through the product evaluations, the word spread about the web accessibility initiative. When the first few accessibility inspection reports were disseminated, the developers began to push back. Carmen overheard an unsettling conversation in the dining hall one day:

"So, as if we didn't have enough to do, I'm hearing we're going to implement a new program for accessibility," said Jake, a mid-level programmer.

"Yeah, I heard about it too," said Trent, Jake's cube-mate. Trent was a programmer who was also trained in visual design. "Well, I'm glad we're going to make our products accessible to disabled users."

"Yeah, that's the good news," said Jake. "But how can they expect us to learn all the new coding conventions and implement them without giving us any more time? I can see it coming—more work for us but no more time in the schedule to do it."

"It's typical," replied Trent. "They're always trying to squeeze a little more out of us. What bothers me is that I hear we're going to have to change the visual design significantly. Remember all those custom buttons I created? I hear most of them are all going to have to go away."

"Why's that?" asked Jake.

"Apparently," replied Trent, "a lot of our visual design can't be read by screen readers. Blind users run into all sorts of problems."

"Oh great," said Jake. "I never thought that was going to be a problem."

"Me neither," said Trent. "I feel like now I'm going to have to either go back to school to figure out how to fix this or just forget about doing visual design altogether. I don't know about you, but I didn't sign up for this."

Carmen realized the programmers' concerns were legitimate and that she needed to do something to allay their fears. So Carmen recommended that the technical leads and the "accessibility early adopter" developers create code examples for common user interface components, for example, using a very small image (with "Skip to main content" as the alternative text) with anchor-link code to enable users to jump to the beginning of page content. She also worked with Sydney, Henry, and technical leads from the other TBD products to raise awareness of web interoperability and device independence among the rest of the development teams, emphasizing that their own content could be rendered more effectively on different devices and operating systems if they designed it according to accessibility principles. Kiah (the accessibility project manager) also had many discussions with the development managers to discuss the overall implementation plan, existing and new functionality programming priorities, and scheduling impacts.

The developers had many questions about how to address the accessibility problems identified in the compliance inspection reports. Carmen and Kiah were not programmers, but they searched online accessibility resources, such as the W3C's site, to find code examples that could be modified for TBD's products. They also hosted a number of meetings to keep communication channels open between the many development teams. Carmen created an accessibility "tips and tricks" manual to help the developers interpret the Section 508 standards within the context of specific TBD products. She also created a small library comprising video clips of people with disabilities using the TBD products to raise awareness about the impact of the accessibility initiative.

Implementation

The most difficult challenge was fitting the accessibility enhancements in with the existing development work. Given the high stakes of not being compliant with Section 508 (due to the size of the contract with the federal government that required compliance), the project was given the highest-priority rating across the company. However, the other functionality under development still needed to be completed in a timely fashion. The technical leads and product managers for the affected projects worked with the executive team to reprioritize the various development efforts; the executive team agreed to place some functionality development on hold and to delay the scheduled release dates on other projects. For the two main products a few of the developers were taken off of their existing work and assigned full time to the accessibility work. As they came up with coding enhancements for specific features within the products, the other developers integrated the code into their specific part of the product. The advantage of this strategy is that a small number of dedicated developers were able to create accessible consistent solutions for the family of products, instead of each developer and/or team creating their own—and likely coming up with multiple solutions that may or may not have been equally effective.

On two other TBD products in a different division the developers were working on site redesign, so they added the accessibility work into the requirements for the redesign. Again, having the accessible code examples that the developers from the other teams had created saved a lot of time and energy. Because the remaining six products that needed to be fixed before the legal deadline were smaller products, the developers were expected to handle the accessibility work in addition to their other assigned work, and release schedules were adjusted according to the amount of enhancement work needed for each product. As for the TBD products that weren't included in the first round, the development teams were required to fix accessibility issues as they worked on modules in the products needing other modifications or improvements.

During the implementation phase Carmen worked with Jillanne (from customer service) to coordinate adding detailed information about accessibility compliance implications for the specific products to the customer service help database that the customer service representatives use when customers call with questions or problems. For example, some JavaScript functionality was particularly challenging to fix and was not going to be completed before the deadline, so the help database provided work-arounds for that functionality or indicated that the customer service representative was going to have to do it for the customer. Because some accessibility issues would take longer to resolve, a plan had to be in place to provide work-arounds for users or, at the very least, the expected release date for fixes. Jillanne had to create new PDF versions of the product training documentation, too, because they were created using older inaccessible versions of the Adobe Acrobat product. She added HTML versions of the content to the site, too.

Joan, the quality assurance specialist, was able to get Perl scripts written by the developers to ensure that every image had alternative text, every form field had an ID attribute, every page had a unique page title, and every frame was labeled. Being able to print off the results was very helpful for Celia (the technical communication specialist) as she reviewed the final text for all of these items.

After a heroic effort on the part of the entire organization, most of the products were ready to be retested in early June, about 5 months into the accessibility initiative. As code freezes for the June and early July releases were upon them, the entire core accessibility team brainstormed the verification process. Time was short, and the reevaluation task was critical but enormous. Because in most cases each project team was responsible for ensuring accessibility compliance, the core accessibility team recommended using the following process:

- The technical lead would be responsible for evaluating his or her product for each of the accessibility items in the comprehensive checklist.
- The technical lead would use a screen reader such as JAWS or Home Page Reader to "listen through" the places in the user interface that used JavaScript to ensure that it was rendering correctly.
- The technical lead would also consult with accessibility compliance specialists for clarification and technical questions.

The core team decided that the technical lead should be responsible for preparing compliance documentation, along with other project documentation. The compliance document should address the changes that were made, assumptions, and known issues. In addition, a document specifying all images and their associated alt text should be generated. The technical lead should also fill out a verification checklist modeled on the original inspection compliance template. The information included within these documents would be used for archival purposes and to create documentation for the customer service department. It would be very helpful for the team to also create an internal website to archive information, so that it could be easily accessed later.

After the technical lead incorporated the provisions of the Section 508 regulation into the product, then he or she would set up a meeting to have a formal accessibility review for the product. The accessibility review team would include an accessibility compliance specialist, the project technical lead developer, product manager, and quality assurance test resource. Others who might be invited to the formal review meeting might include a human factors specialist, usability specialist, web designer, technical writer, and business and/or marketing representative. Meetings were scheduled in a conference room equipped with a computer containing screen reader software, connected to the live version of the product under review.

At each verification meeting, the technical lead would go through the main paths and new functionality using the screen reader to demonstrate the different aspects that were included for compliance. Assuming everything worked as intended, the accessibility review team then decided that the product was compliant (Section 508 for this project, WCAG 1.0 AA for subsequent products). Final documentation (including additional changes resulting from the review meeting) was sent to the project lead, product lead, and the accessibility compliance specialist.

Carmen recognized it was critical to provide accessibility documentation for each product, including the VPAT documentation and customer service information, because teams change and new team members might not be familiar with all of the hard work that had already taken place. Compounding this problem, existing accessibility enhancements could be unintentionally undone when new functionality was added. Fortunately, the technical leads at TBD did an excellent job of documenting the accessibility project, even creating a project website archive. The legal affairs office and marketing team also published an accessibility compliance statement on the corporate site for customers.

Ongoing Compliance

The accessibility team did a terrific job coordinating the company's accessibility effort, meeting the June 2001 deadline. Across the company most of the work was completed in 6 months, including 2 months setting up the project and conducting initial analysis, followed by at least a month for performing detailed analyses, and 3 months for implementing enhancements and retesting the products.

Near the end of the project Liam and Carmen met for an informal postmortem.

"Carmen, you and the team did a phenomenal job on the project," said Liam.

"Thanks, Liam," replied Carmen. "I think we're in good shape now . . . we can actually check the 'Section 508 compliant' box on the Travelers By Design Government project . . . it's up for renewal, and now that we have a process in place for 508 compliance, that's one less hurdle we need to clear."

"Great, Carmen. Now we have one final challenge. Funding is tight, and we're struggling with where to put our resources. Management in the New Product Development Division wants to add a boatload of new features to the corporate and government product site. Unfortunately, this means we won't be able to implement a full ongoing compliance program right now. Still, I'd like to work with you to identify what we'd need to do to get a program in place when funding is available. I'll make a deal with you: I'll keep pursuing funding if you work with me to plan an ongoing compliance process."

"Deal," said Carmen. She set off to prepare the plan.

Questions

12. What potential problems could arise if a compliance program is not put in place?
13. What elements should an ongoing compliance program include?

Summary

Carmen discovered that setting up an accessibility compliance program was challenging but rewarding work. She learned some valuable lessons about handling large-scale accessibility initiatives:

- Get the high-level stakeholders identified and contacted as soon as possible, because gaining their buy-in is critical for the success of the project.
- Conduct a very basic accessibility review of the current products and provide the management team with information they can use for establishing sizings and priorities.
- Get a consultant involved right away to help scope out the effort that will be needed, if you don't have the internal expertise in accessibility.
- Have people with disabilities try out your products early in the process to get a realistic idea of how well the products are currently working; video clips from these sessions are very helpful for raising awareness and generating user requirements for the accessibility effort.
- The accessibility lead needs to stay involved with every stage of the redevelopment process; pull other resources in as needed. An accessibility advocate and champion is important for the success of the project.
- Document the enhancements made to each product; this is critical for maintaining product accessibility, because the composition of design and development teams changes over time.

Usability specialists can play a vital role in promoting the importance of accessible web design. Knowing that the efforts would benefit real people trying to use the TBD sites was gratifying. The organization began to understand in a concrete way that enhancing websites for Section 508 resulted in more accessible and usable products, thereby leading to increased sales of the products and services. TBD beat out the competition and won the government contract! The bottom line is that accessible design benefits the company and its customers.

To create a compliance program, the following steps need to be followed:

1. Gather background information regarding accessibility and how it may affect your products.
   - Review accessibility legal requirements.
   - Decide on whether you will develop in-house expertise, use external consultants, or a combination.
2. Initiate start-up activities.
   - Determine which products will be affected.
   - Locate key stakeholders and areas of the organization that will need to be involved.

- Start figuring out how the initiative will be funded.
- Form a core accessibility team.
- Find out how users with disabilities experience your products.
3. Establish the accessibility compliance process.
    - Evaluate compliance.
        — Identify website accessibility problems: initial review.
        — Establish an accessibility team.
        — Decide on level of compliance.
        — Conduct detailed accessibility compliance inspection.
    - Implementation
        — Work with developers during implementation.
    - Verification
        — Verify that the site is accessibility compliant.
    - Ongoing compliance
        — Develop an ongoing maintenance program.

Further Reading

Accessibility Legislation Websites

- Americans with Disabilities Act: http://www.usdoj.gov/crt/ada/statute.html
- Federal Acquisition Regulation (FAR): http://www.arnet.gov/far/
- Section 508: http://www.access-board.gov/scc508/508standards.htm
- W3C Web Accessibility Initiative (WAI) maintains a listing of web accessibility international policies at http://www.w3.org/WAI/Policy/
- W3C Web Content Accessibility Guidelines 1.0 (WCAG): http://www.w3.org/TR/WAI-WEBCONTENT/

Resources for Getting Started

- The Alexander Graham Bell Association for the Deaf and Hard of Hearing: http://www.agbell.org/
- American Council of the Blind: http://www.acb.org/
- American Foundation for the Blind: http://www.afb.org/
- Attention Deficit Disorder Association: http://www.add.org/
- Autism Resources: http://www.vaporia.com/autism/
- The British Deaf Organization: http://www.britishdeafassociation.org.uk/

- Deaf Blind Information: http://www.lowvision.org/deaf_blind_information.htm
- Dyslexia Adults Link: http://www.dyslexia-adults.com/info.html
- Learning Disabilities Association of America: http://www.ldanatl.org/
- Mental Retardation Fact Sheet: http://www.nichcy.org/pubs/factshe/fs8txt.htm
- Mental Retardation–National Advocacy and Information Resources: http://www.therapistfinder.net/national/menret.html
- National Council on Disability: http://www.ncd.gov/
- National Eye Institute (low vision information): http://www.nei.nih.gov/nehep/what.asp
- National Federation of the Blind: http://www.nfb.org/
- Royal Society of the Blind: http://www.rbs.org.au/

Automated Web Accessibility Tools

- AccVerify from HiSoftware is available at http://www.hisoftware.com/access/
- The Cynthia Says™ Portal can be found at http://www.cynthiasays.com/
- The Evaluation and Repair Working Group of the Web Accessibility Initiative has a list of almost 30 accessibility tools on their site: http://www.w3.org/WAI/ER/existingtools
- LIFT Online from UsableNet can be found at http://UsableNet.com
- Watchfire's Bobby™ can be found at http://bobby.watchfire.com/bobby/html/en/index.jsp

Screen Reader Trial Versions

- A demo version is available on the IBM site at www.ibm.com/able/hpr.html.
- JAWS 7.0 demonstration version: http://www.freedomscientific.com/fs_products/software_jaws70fea.asp
- The Lynx Viewer can be found at http://www.delorie.com/web/lynxview.html
- Window-Eyes demo version: http://www.gwmicro.com/Window-Eyes/

From .com to .com.cn: A Case Study of Website Internationalization

Jianming Dong, PayPal, Inc.

> *Richard was very excited about this new direction. Opening a business in China was a complete mystery. Elaine, the head of the design team, made the decision: "Let's go ahead and have our site translated into Chinese and target to roll out in China. Let's shoot for 2 months." Richard wondered about this estimate—it sounded way off, but how was he to know for sure?*

The Evolution and Expansion of a Website

MediaCentral.com

Richard Hartley was born into a family of journalists in 1972. He traveled with his family to many places while his parents wrote their journal reports. When Richard's parents retired, they settled in a small town close to New York City, where they started to collect all kinds of historical publications memorabilia relating to the places they had visited. Very soon, their house was packed with CDs, magazines, books, and other media they collected.

At the same time, Richard went to a college to study computer programming. In his leisure time he helped his parents with their collections. He often visited a nearby antiques store and a collection store to search for things his parents sought. And one time he was very surprised to find in the corner of the store a record album that his parents had been wanting for years. He thought if he had not seen the album, it would still be sitting there, collecting dust forever.

Over time, Richard became more and more sophisticated in both collecting and computer science. One day, he thought, "How wonderful it would be if these old media items were made available in a computer system to many collectors, so that people could buy them easily." Existing media collection stores operated in a very traditional fashion and were very laid-back with regard to new technologies. Although there were many channels from which store owners could buy the unwanted collection items for decent prices, there were really no other means by which to sell these items, other than in a traditional store.

The Internet provided an excellent opportunity for Richard to realize his dream. As one of the earliest adopters of Internet technologies, Richard founded MediaCentral.com in 1996 jointly with an owner of a collection store and three of his college classmates. Using their connections with journalist friends and colleagues of their parents, they collected historical media in bulk and started to sell them on their website, MediaCentral.com. Shortly after launching their website, their business increased dramatically. It not only survived the dotcom bust, it also increased its size from a 5-person business to a 450-employee e-commerce company by 2002.

Initial Planning for China Launch

Like many small companies, global expansion was a remote thought for Richard for a long time. But one day in June 2002, a phone call changed his mind. Jim Lee, a long-time friend of Richard's parents, called Richard's office from China. Jim Lee was a director of QiLang Inc., one of the most influential media companies in south Asia. Jim had checked out the Media-Central.com website. He told Richard, "You should open up your business to China. There are a large number of media collectors in China, and there are lots of Chinese media items to collect, given China's long history. Media-Central.com should catch the huge business opportunity in China."

Richard was very excited about this new direction. Although he traveled to China several times when he was young, opening a business in China was a complete mystery. Richard called a meeting with his key staff members to discuss the strategy. The team brainstormed the steps to launch MediaCentral.com site in China. Elaine McNeill, the head of the design team, made the call. She said to the team, "Let's go ahead and have our site translated into Chinese and target to roll out in China. Let's shoot for 2 months." Elaine led the team in a brainstorming session and came up with a list of activities they needed to work through for the launch:

- The team needed to come up with a cool translated name for MediaCentral.com in Chinese.
- A translation company needed to be hired to translate all the text on the site into Chinese.
- The legal department needed to work with the Chinese government to have all local legal requirements fulfilled. For instance, the MediaCentral.com website is expected to have financial transactions with its Chinese consumers, so the company needs to be registered as a business unit to fulfill tax obligations. Also, its content will be subject to screening by the local government agencies.
- A Chinese-speaking help line would need to be set up for the Chinese customers.
- The marketing department would need to develop an advertising campaign for the site launch.

"This is certainly very ambitious and enticing," thought Richard. "I sure hope this is a sound plan!"

Questions

1. Is this a plan good enough for rolling out an international site? Has the team missed any critical elements?
2. What types of market research could be conducted to support MediaCentral.com's business decisions?
3. What types of user research could be conducted to support design decisions? What additional considerations would be made if the team decided to add a user research component to their plan?

Tackling Problems in Preparation and Test Launch

Initial Barriers Discovered in the Design Phase

The MediaCentral.com team proceeded to implement their plan as Elaine stated in the kickoff meeting. Because the design team lacked background in Chinese culture and research, they did not anticipate much work beyond translation. The team quickly hired a translation company to translate all site content into Chinese so that they could replace the corresponding English content on the site. Interestingly, the translator, Linda, was originally from

China and also had some experience translating websites. This was very helpful for the design team because Linda could consider lots of issues only native speakers would realize. At the same time, as Linda had been living in the United States for 15 years, she was getting less sensitive to some of the subtle issues of translation. Shortly after Linda started her work, she discovered a long list of potential issues:

- On the website, a link provides users driving directions from any specific location to the physical store of the MediaCentral.com company. This feature should be removed because it does not make sense to drive from China to this office. Assuming there is a need to offer driving directions to a regional office in China, the map in the U.S. site is dynamically generated from a third-party web map supplier, which does not support Chinese addresses. In China, other companies provide such services.
- The shipping calculator was inappropriate for the Chinese market. First, the units of measurements were all in British standard. The item heights were marked in inches, and the weights were all in pounds. Second, the calculator would generate rates based on the formulas from the U.S. Postal Services and in the amount of U.S. dollars. Obviously, this would not work in the Chinese market.
- The only payment method supported by the website is a credit card. However, the credit card is by far not the most popular payment method in China. In physical stores, most transactions are paid in cash or debit card. It was not clear which payment options should be offered for MediaCentral.com as an online store in China.
- Some contents in the account registration form do not fit the convention in China. For example, the default prompting question to backup account password is "What is the name of your pet?" As a matter of fact, having a pet is very rare for families in Chinese cities. Also, there are separate fields for first name, middle name, and last name. Chinese people do not have middle names. Also, they rarely provide their last name and first name separately when filling in any forms.

With Linda's help, the team tested the site on her computer, which had the latest Chinese operating system and the most popular browser installed.

Questions

4. What are the immediate fixes for the issues discovered by Linda?
5. What do these initial findings imply with regard to launching a Chinese version of a website originated from the United States? What other potential problems might or might not be anticipated by not being familiar with the culture?
6. How would Richard and his team address any potential problems related to a China launch that have not yet surfaced?

Design Reviews With a Famous Chinese Collector

As Richard and his team started to realize the importance of involving Chinese customers and advisors in the process, Richard decided to get some feedback on the design from some Chinese collectors who may use the site in the future. He contacted Jim Lee. Jim introduced Richard to one of his best friends, Leo, who retired about 10 years earlier. Leo is a descendant of a Chinese royal family member and has a large collection of imperial antiques and government documents from the Han and Ming Dynasties. Leo went to graduate school in the United States when he was young and then lived in China the rest of the time. He is fluent in English.

Because of the tight schedule, Elaine's team was only able to put together a set of low-fidelity prototypes, in which the Chinese contents and user interface elements were presented in the form of wireframes. Also, the prototype only included static pages, without any interaction. Richard and Elaine, the design manager, spent about 2 hours walking Leo through the translated version of MediaCentral.com over the phone. Leo provided a number of comments and design recommendations:

- There are only a small number of items on the site that might be interesting to the Chinese users. Many merchandise inherited from the U.S. site only appeals to Western culture.
- The site looks too "serious." There is a lot of text. It would be helpful to include more pictures.
- The fonts used in the site are too small to read. Typical Chinese text has more strokes than English words and thus would not display well in the original font size.
- Cash on delivery should be the primary payment method in China.

Richard and his team made immediate changes in the design after this meeting. The changes included

- Adjusting the items to be more aligned with the interest of the Chinese collectors
- Adding some interesting graphics onto the site
- Increasing the font size
- Designing and implementing a task flow to support cash on delivery

They also showed the revised design to Leo two more times before the test launch. Leo was reasonably confident after the second review that the design matched the Chinese audience's needs.

Questions

7. What are the strengths of the approaches Richard and Elaine took to evaluate their design?
8. What are the weaknesses of the approaches Richard and Elaine took to evaluate their design?
9. What could Richard and his team have done better to get more valuable and objective input for design validation?

Customer Support Feedback During Test Launch

Richard and the team did not spend much time conducting more research after their discussions with Leo and Jim. They believed that user research would be very beneficial but were still not convinced that they immediately needed to invest more heavily in this area. Instead, they decided to move forward with the phased roll out.

August 15, 2002 was an exciting date for MediaCentral.com. It was the day that the company test launched the first international site—in China. The address had an exciting ".cn" attached to the legacy name of .com. An invitation was sent to about 2,000 users, who opted to test the new websites, as well as some Chinese users who were enthusiastic about MediaCentral.com.

As Richard and his team expected, the customer support department started getting many phone calls reporting issues with the site. However, very soon they were overwhelmed by the number of problems reported over the phone and through e-mails. After reviewing the issues, Richard decided to shut down the site temporarily. Frustrated, he said, "Apparently the site was not ready for launch yet. Luckily, MediaCentral.com did not rush to do a one-shot complete roll out to the entire public."

Very quickly, the team collected a few hundred issues that the users reported. In general, the surprisingly high number of usability issues was due to insufficient user research before launch. The problems were mostly concentrated in the following areas:

1. *Bugs:* The bugs reported were mostly due to the high variety of computer system variations in China. The MediaCentral.com.cn site was tested on one computer with the latest Chinese operating system and the most popular browser installed. However, most Chinese users have a lower version of the operating system and different browsers from what is installed on the computer tested. Some of these browsers do not even exist in the United States. This complexity causes some user interface element malfunction on the user's computer screen.

2. *Confusing content:* Most of the problematic contents were likely due to inappropriate translation. Although handled by professional translation companies, there were still a number of words and phrases that were not translated correctly or were translated out of context. Linda, the particular translator working on the MediaCentral.com site, had been living in the United States for 15 years and thus was not up to date to the most current Chinese phrases, especially those related to the Internet and IT in general. Because both Leo and the Linda were fluent in English, they most likely overlooked contents that looked a bit odd in the translations.

    Some text content simply did not have good straight translation and thus needed to be rewritten. For instance, there are separate help sections for "novice" and "expert." In the Chinese translations the word "novice" was often understood as "naive," with has a negative connotation. Words like this may need to be translated into phrases or other expressions that are not offensive to their audience.

3. *Inappropriate layout and colors:* Many problems with layout and color existed because the designers did not understand written Chinese and did not have a good feel for readability and aesthetics. For example, they may have designed a block of Chinese text that is too tight or too loose, so Chinese users find it hard to read. Also, the color red is

often used for promotional content in Chinese websites. However, most promotional content on the site was presented in cold color schemes.

Solving the Site-Speed Puzzle

As the company saw more and more product issues related to user research, Richard decided to hire a professional user experience researcher. Shortly thereafter, Sarah Shaw joined the company as the first full-time user researcher. Sarah had gone through systematic training in psychology, experimental design, and user interface evaluations. She was also a native Chinese speaker, which was essential to lead the internationalization efforts in China.

The Puzzle of Site Speed and Initial Analysis

After the successful relaunch of the site, the business volume and popularity of the website increased dramatically. But as the site traffic increased, there seemed to be an increasing number of complaints recorded at the customer service department that the site was too slow to load.

Unlike other usability issues, which are directly tied to page design, site speed is more of a puzzle—it is more complex and involves many departments beyond the design functions of the company. There were a number of controversial opinions about the site speed issue.

Richard met with his team to discuss the issue. He started off the meeting with a straightforward question: "Is site speed really a problem?" he asked.

Jason, the technical lead, told him, "There were a number of users reporting slow loading time. But they reported the problem happening sporadically on a variety of pages. It's not clear to us which pages had the most problems."

"You know, Richard, we have an automatic tracking tool on the server side. The tracking tool records the time for the web pages to be pulled off the server. These data correspond to the actual site download speed. The loading speed recorded by the system didn't show any outstanding issues."

"And, the data we received from customer service is customer self-reported data. We don't know if the Chinese users use the same criteria as we do for site speed. How slow is slow, and how fast is fast? Are there patterns of cultural differences in wait time? We observed some instances of slow download speed in the user study, but the sample size was too low to confirm a system problem."

Richard thought about this for a minute. "Okay," he began, "if speed is a problem, what would be a viable solution to the problem?"

Jason explained, "We anticipated a slower site speed in China. Since we hosted all the pages on servers in the United States, we figured the long distance of data transfer would certainly slow down the speed. And, as you know, as web traffic increases, the download speed drops. Moving the web hosting of the China subsite to China will definitely help the load speed, but it will be very costly."

After a few rounds of discussions, Richard asked Sarah: "What can you recommend to help solve this puzzle?" Given that Sarah is a user researcher, this was a curious question for her.

Questions

11. Can Sarah, in her role as user researcher, help in solving the site speed issue? If yes, how?
12. What are some of the hypothesis Sarah should consider regarding the site speed issue? What are the implications and challenges for her to develop a study plan due to these hypotheses?
13. What should the main attributes of Sarah's study plan be?

Conducting a Site Speed Test

Because of the inconsistent data from automated download tracking tool and customer service report, the team decided to conduct user study to discover more details in this issue. The key to the successful administration of a study is to maintain methodologic consistency across large number of study participants. To accomplish this, Sarah arranged mandatory training on the study procedures for each participant, so that they can fully understand the study instruction in their self-guided sessions. During the training sessions, the study participants also got a chance to practice following study scripts to record data accurately using stop watch.

Sarah also needed to address other issues to derive recommendations to the design team with her study. The main issues follow:

- *System variations causing download fluctuations should be eliminated.* It is hard to determine whether the site has improved in site speed without removing the other factors. For instance, when the user or the service provider upgrades their equipment, the download speed for all sites could become faster for that particular user.
- *The specific reasons for download speed issues of certain pages should be determined.* There are often many elements in a page, including text, images, Flash content, dynamic interactive elements, and others. Stopwatch measurement only provides a single number about the loading of the entire page. It does not tell exactly which part of a page loads slowly.

To address these issues, Sarah added the following steps in the study procedure:

- *Measuring download time of a standard page.* The study administrator sets up a standard page as a reference for each test. The contents of the standard page should be held constant across each study. Before and after each study session, the download speed for the standard page is measured, as a benchmark of system variations. The analysis of download speed for each page is analyzed after the system variation factor is subtracted.
- *Videotaping the study sessions.* Because the stop watch only records the total amount of time for a page to be loaded, it is very hard for the design team to understand which element was the main contributor for the issue. This information is especially critical for the "problematic pages," which have a long overall download time. Having video recordings allows tracing back the stop watch data if necessary.

Sarah conducted the large site speed study successfully. Her study provided answers to the following questions, which were very valuable to the design and implementation team:

- Were there site speed issues for the users? Site speed data showed which pages had long download times.

- Are the site speed issues caused by the MediaCentral.com site or by other factors, such as connection services, firewall, and browser settings? This information is available through detailed analysis of the data after removing the variance from the standard page measures.
- Which pages are most problematic for the users regarding download speed? Which elements in these pages contributed the most to the problem? These data are certainly included in the stopwatch data and the video recordings.

After the first site speed study was completed, discrepancies with the automated tracking method were discovered. For example, download time recorded for some dynamic pages are far longer than the perceived download speed with dial-up connection users. Also, the design of some long pages should be optimized so that the upper portion of the page would be displayed much faster than the portions below the fold. These findings were very valuable for the improvement of overall perceived site speed. Also, this study method was established so that a longitudinal study can be conducted to monitor the improvement of the site speed over time.

Next Steps

To keep improving the business of a site after launch, the following should also be taken into consideration:

1. Working on international sites requires constant learning of the local culture and design trends. The speed of change in the international market is often underestimated. For instance, the rapid growth of Internet technology caused many complex changes in the international market. In the early years, most site users are generally technical with high education. Over time, as the technology becomes easier to use, more and more nontechnical uses will start using the technology and thus change the mix of overall user profiles.

2. It is important to establish local connections to support user research work. Conducting user research and usability testing in foreign countries is often costly, and involves complex logistical planning and coordination. So, getting strong help from local resources is instrumental in the effective administration of projects. These resources may include long-term relationships with high-quality research vendors

or staff researchers in the countries that need significant internationalization efforts.

3. Minor changes in a stable site are often researched via means other than a typical lab study. For instance, comparative testing with the real site is more often used to test minor changes, which provides real data for the business and design teams to make appropriate design decisions.

4. It also helps to establish a system to systematically monitor product and business metrics for the Chinese website. This would provide directions to further user research.

5. As both the U.S. website and the Chinese website evolve simultaneously, there are often opportunities to leverage knowledge and best practices from each other. It is very critical to set up process for collaboration in these aspects.

Summary

MediaCentral.com had a success story in solving lots of unique issues in the process of internationalizing a website. Although their investments were huge in the beginning of the process, it paid off as the China site became one of the most popular e-commerce website in China. Here are some key things that Richard and his team learned from their experience of setting up Media-Central.com in China:

- Before the efforts of launching an international site, significant market research and user experience research is necessary to understand the market and analyze the potential return on investment.
- It is very critical to involve people who are very familiar with the culture and the language of the target market.
- Designing a site for audiences in a different culture always involves much more effort than straight translation. Content and presentation needs to be adjusted according to contexts and local perceptions.
- Many user preferences and conventions should be taken into consideration in the design. Examples include use of color, font, layout, and content density.
- Interviewing a small number of selected people in the target market cannot replace rigorous user studies. Studies have to be conducted with typical users in a real-world environment.

- User research expertise is critical in addressing complicated usability issues. User researchers should work closely with other team members to provide the best decision support.
- Many problems, although seemingly related only to technical setup (such as site speed), can be addressed by qualitative and quantitative user research.
- It is critical to keep an eye toward maintaining and improving site quality after launch by continuing to learn about the local culture, establishing contacts with local members of the community to facilitate ongoing site maintenance, and making incremental changes to the site as needed.

Further Reading

Aykin, N. (Ed.) (2005). *Usability and internationalization of information technology*. Mahwah, NJ: Lawrence Erlbaum Publishers.

CNNIC: http://www.cnnic.net.cn/en/index/index.htm

Dong, J., and Salvendy, G. (1999). Designing menus for Chinese population: horizontal or vertical? In *Behaviour & information technology*, Vol. 18. Abingdon, Oxford, UK: Taylor & Francis, pp. 467–471.

Ehret, B. (2002). Learning where to look: location learning in graphical user interfaces In *CHI 2002 Conference Proceeding*, Vol. 4, Minneapolis, MN: ACM Press, pp. 211–217.

Fernandes, T. (1995). *Global interface design*. San Francisco, CA: Morgan Kaufmann Publishers.

Galdo, E., and Nielsen, J. (Eds.) (1996). *International user interfaces*. New York: John Wiley & Sons.

Hofstede, G. (1997). *Culture and organizations: software of the mind, intercultural cooperation and its importance for survival*. New York: McGraw Hill.

Marcus, A. (2003). Fast forward, user-interface design and China: a great leap forward. *Interactions*, Jan/Feb:21–25.

Mayhew, D. (1999). *The usability engineering life cycle*. San Francisco, CA: Morgan Kaufmann Publishers.

Sacher, H. (1998). Interactions in Chinese: designing interfaces for Asian languages. *Interactions*, Sept/Oct:28–38.

Singh, N., and Pereira, A. (2005). *The culturally customized website: customizing websites for the global marketplace*. Burlington, MA: Elsevier.

Yunker, J. (2003). *Beyond borders: web globalization strategies*. Indianapolis, IN: New Riders Publishing.

Designing for a Worldwide Product

Kate Walton, Amadeus

> *After a reflective moment, Caroline said, "You know how demanding our customers are. They often don't have the same business objectives, and even when they do, they rarely have the same vision for how to achieve them. How are we going to cover the requirements of over 300 customers from all over the world with one source of common code?"*

Flexibility: Too Much of a Good Thing Can Be Bad

Travellers United is a repository of "up to the second" travel inventory data compiled from airlines, hotels, car companies, ferries, cruise lines, buses . . . most anything tied to travel. With these data comes the capability to manage many facets of the travel industry's inventory—from travel reservations to payment transactions to most postpurchase needs such as travel reservation changes. The customers of Travellers United are travel agents who use this repository of information to sell travel reservations to the end traveler.

Traditionally, if travelers wanted to make travel reservations with an airline, hotel, or other service providers, they would contact a travel agency and the sales agents would search through the central reservation system to help the traveler find the most suitable option. Then came the Internet, which introduced a new possibility for distribution of the travel products. The travel agents who were using Travellers United to sell and manage their travel reservations over the phone would then be able to sell their products directly to the end traveler via the Internet.

Caroline Pedreira from marketing and Frederic Lafite from development were charged by Travellers United to create a company division to meet this objective. The "On The Go" division was formed to provide the capability for travel agents to create websites as additional sales channels (see Sidebar). Rather than phoning or visiting a travel office, the end travelers would be able to browse through travel options online and select and purchase the best option themselves.

Sidebar
As with most industries, On The Go has two considerations: its customers and its end users, who are not the same. On The Go builds and maintains travel reservation sites for its customers, the travel agencies. The end users of these travel sites are not the travel agencies but the end consumer, the traveler.

Caroline knew that many of Travellers United customers who were using the central reservation system to manage and sell travel reservations would be keen to invest in this new sales channel. Caroline and Frederic were faced with some important decisions of how to manage the creation and maintenance of Internet sites for 300+ customers based in the United States, Europe, Scandinavia, Africa, and Australasia. They decided to have their first strategy session over lunch. They had worked together in previous projects in their careers at Travellers United and had maintained a friendly work relationship through the years.

After they ordered their main course, Caroline began to sketch out her high-level marketing strategy. Frederic listened and nodded his head from time to time. Caroline then raised her main concern for the scope of the mission. The pitch of her voice grew higher with each comment. "Frederic, how are we going to manage all of these websites? Once the announcement is made, we are going to have hundreds of customers asking us to create websites for them. And you have to consider that most of them serve markets in other parts of the world and they are going to want websites in multiple languages. We are going to need a thousand web developers to create and maintain all of these sites!"

Frederic looked wide-eyed at Caroline and then began to laugh. Caroline was frustrated with his response, but she relaxed enough to laugh with him, although she wasn't sure what was so funny. Their dessert arrived, and while Caroline ate quickly, Frederic introduced his proposal.

"Caroline, I'm far ahead of you. I've been thinking on this subject since we first heard about the new division. You should have more confidence in me," he said with a sly smile. "I believe the best way to manage this is to not invest in the creation of individual sites. Rather, we should invest in a site generation tool that would be able to automatically create a reservation website for each customer who wants to sell travel reservations over the Internet." Caroline responded with a raised eyebrow. Frederic, unfazed by her skepticism, continued, "With one site generation tool, we would create and maintain code that would be common to all the sites. Think of the advantages—if we had to make a change or if we had a new feature that should be reflected in all the sites, we would update the code in one place rather than updating the code in each site independently. Then, when we regenerate the sites, the changes would automatically be included."

After a reflective moment, Caroline said, "Pas mal—not bad. You *have* been thinking. But I see one major problem. You know how demanding our customers are. They often don't have the same business objectives, and even when they do, they rarely have the same vision for how to achieve them. How are we going to cover the requirements of over 300 customers from all over the world with one source of common code?"

Frederic had already considered this. He explained, "The tool we create could include settings that would give a choice to the customer when the common code doesn't suffice. For example, basic user interface components that everyone needs, like destination input fields, could be shared among all the sites. The requirements for these types of items aren't likely to be different for each customer. But we could provide a way to customize certain components which *are* likely to be different—things like background colors and fonts. The site settings could cover choices for many aspects of the site . . . product features, interface appearance, and other settings that tend to change from market to market."

Although Caroline would need some time to consider all implications of Frederic's proposal, she couldn't readily see an alternative to managing hundreds of websites independently. Frederic and Caroline decided they would work on the proposal details in the next 2 weeks and then schedule a formal meeting to present it to the key stakeholders.

At the big meeting with the stakeholders Frederic and Caroline presented the concept, and it was received with little challenge. Everything was fairly peaceful until the end of the meeting when the Vice-President of New Ventures requested that Frederic provide an estimate for budget and resources required to develop the site generation tool. He specifically wanted to have an idea of how much they would need to spend before the first reservations would be coming through. Frederic responded with his rough estimate, and it didn't take Caroline long to do a bit of calculation to realize the impact on her part of the organization. Caroline exclaimed, "That's at least 80% of the yearly budget! We expect to use some part of the budget to perform the research that we need to understand the best way to implement the site setup options. We are going to need to perform some baseline research to ensure that we understand the needs of our customers and their end users. And we are not just talking about end users in our backyard; we're talking about end users from all over the world. You can't expect us to make guesses! Where are we going to get the money to develop both the site generation tool and the research that we need to do?"

Caroline continued her arguments by reminding everyone that building a product and user interface adapted to markets all around the world was a new challenge for Travellers United. The interface of their traditional reservation system was the same for all sales agents throughout the world. A travel sales agent in Brazil would see the same availability display as an agent in London. These agents were well trained to read and understand this interface. But these travel websites would be used by end travelers to make their own reservations. They couldn't force a traveler to use a reservation tool in a foreign language that did not work according to their expectations. And they wouldn't be able to understand what those expectations were without studying how these travelers were working today.

Frederic was able to sway the group to his side by pointing out that they needed to have something up and running as soon as possible, even if "bare bones," to create revenue for further developments and improvements. They needed revenue quickly to demonstrate that the mission was possible and worthwhile. Everyone agreed (including Caroline reluctantly) that they would first focus on getting something working. And this is the direction they followed for the next year and a half. A crude basic version of the site generation tool was built, travel reservation sites were created for the customers, and the travelers were using these sites to make their own reservations over the Internet. No research was conducted, and there was no end user input into the design of neither the site generation tool nor the resulting travel sites. But more and more of their customers, the travel agents, were signing contracts to create new travel reservation sites—success!

And so it seemed for some time. But a year later the customers began to complain that their websites were not adapted well enough to their markets. In addition, money that was supposed to be saved by reducing the number of sales agents was eaten up by having to hire new staff to handle

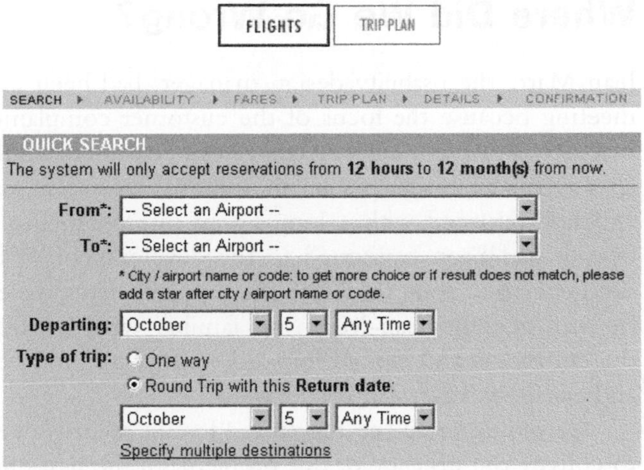

Figure 18.1. Search page with the existing user interface.

help-desk calls. Finally, the customers complained of the quality of their website interfaces, saying that they did not look professional, and it was negatively impacting their end users' (the travelers) perception of their travel agency (Figure 18.1).

After increasing complaints, customers began to migrate to other competitive solutions that had begun to crop up in the market. What had seemed to start so well began to take a steady turn for the worse. The project sponsors requested an emergency assessment of the situation. They wanted answers, and they wanted a plan. Frederic and Caroline would have to urgently rethink their business procedures to put things back on track. They called for an emergency meeting with their key managers to begin to isolate the factors causing the loss of customers and to define corrective actions.

Questions

1. If you were called into this meeting, what would you identify as a key contributor(s) for the customers' rejection of the current solution?
2. On which problem(s) do you believe the On The Go division should focus to create a more marketable solution?

Where Did We Go Wrong?

Jean-Marc, the usability design manager, had been invited to the emergency meeting because the focus of the customer complaints was on the interface, usability, and the mounting costs of the customer's help desks. Jean-Marc had already run usability tests on the product to gather baseline performance data and had returned with a long list of improvements. However, most of the budget had been consigned to the development of the functionality in the site generation tool; therefore the improvements were tabled until prioritized by management. Jean-Marc was familiar with the feedback coming in from the customers and looked forward to providing his perspective of the history and the best way to move forward.

Caroline started the meeting. "I want to first give you some background to convey the urgency of this problem. In the past quarter we have lost three major customers who in combination were bringing around 15,000 reservations per month. We have heard that two other customers have sent out requests for proposals to other providers—it is clear that they are considering leaving us as well. The synopsis of the feedback clearly implicates the poor quality of the user interface. You should have already received a document by e-mail outlining the feedback we have gathered." Caroline then turned to Jean-Marc and asked him to provide his viewpoint of the situation.

Jean-Marc stood. "Well I'm not surprised. The site generation tool is just not capable of producing websites that are tailored enough for our customers in their local markets."

Before Jean-Marc could continue, Frederic exploded, "May I remind everyone that we invested a lot of money to make the site generation tool flexible enough so that it should adapt to *any* user in *any* market!"

Jean-Marc looked flustered, but he stood his ground and cried, "Hold on! Hold on! Please give me a minute to finish my point." He walked to the center of the room and started again. "I agree that the site generation tool is amazingly flexible. There's nothing else in the market to beat it for its flexibility. But, we have to recognize that most of the development has been based on assumptions. We never performed the research needed to validate our assumptions for the customers' requirements. And we don't really have a strong understanding of how those requirements vary as a function of different cultures around the world. This is the root of the problems we are facing today. Without the appropriate research data from the markets, developers often have to make user interface design decisions based on what information they have—their own experience. What we have now is a massive number of site settings that are not always reflective of the true market needs and cultural variances. Because the designers and developers based much of the design on assumptions, many of the site settings they created were unneeded and never used; other site settings which were needed were never developed."

Many people in the room were nodding their heads as Jean-Marc spoke. Encouraged, Jean-Marc went to the whiteboard and began to draw while he spoke. "Let me tell you about a recent problem which demonstrates my point. It's a simple example but a real one. Two weeks ago the developers were asked to develop an interactive calendar where users could select their travel dates. It's a common tool you'll find in most travel reservation sites. The developers were happy to do this, but when they designed it they assumed that everyone in the world used the same calendar. Did anyone here know that there are different versions of the calendar?" No one responded so Jean-Marc continued. "Because the developers assumed that everyone used the same style of calendar, they planned to make only one version and make it common to all of our customers' travel reservation sites. But they didn't realize that the calendar week begins with different days depending on where you are from. The calendar used by Europeans begins with Monday and ends with Sunday. Calendars used in the United States begin with Sunday and end with Saturday." (See Figures 18.2 and 18.3.)

Jean-Marc finished drawing his two versions of the calendar on the board and asked everyone to take a look. "Can anyone tell me why presenting the wrong calendar to a user could present issues?"

Everyone was quiet for a moment, and then Karine from the site setup team bravely responded, "Well, it seems to me if a user didn't pay attention

Figure 18.2. European calendar.

Figure 18.3. U.S. calendar.

to the labels for the day of the week, a user could select an incorrect date."

"Exactly," Jean-Marc replied. He continued, "At a glance, users would immediately recognize the calendar and its purpose. But, as a result, most users would not necessarily expect that they should review the column headers to ensure that the columns match their expectations. A U.S. user could easily assume that the third column indicates Tuesday, whereas a European user would assume Wednesday. The result of an incorrect date selection by an end user at this point could be a travel reservation for the wrong dates. If the user finalizes their reservation without noticing, they may not be able to make a change afterward. And even if they are able to change the reservation, there would most certainly be a charge involved. So this simple tool with all of its good intentions could end up costing the end user time and money if it is not implemented correctly for each market."

Before Jean-Marc could even sit down again, other department managers began to pipe in with additional impacts as a result of the ever-growing site setting choices. Philippe from quality assurance was the first to give vent to his frustrations. "Everyone keeps complaining about how expensive and long the QA cycle is. But you guys have to bear in mind how many configurations and combinations of settings we have to test. If we could reduce the settings, the QA cost would decrease and the quality would improve."

Karine from the site setup team then added her concerns. "Site setup is taking longer and longer. There are so many options, it is hard to remember all the constraints of what settings can be combined. Sometimes, we even forget what site options are possible." Other points were added to the list of arguments for simplifying and validating the site settings, including the difficulties of designing an interface with infinite possibilities of combinations and the risk of only a few people understanding how the entire tool worked to create a website.

The meeting was quite charged while everyone unloaded their grievances. After everyone had finished, the meeting room became silent while Frederic and Caroline took a few moments to gather their thoughts. Finally, Caroline lifted her head and recapped what had become obvious to everyone. She concluded, "There's just no sense in developing and supporting thousands of site setup choices if the sites created don't meet the needs of our customers. And we're never going to be able to produce effective websites to be used worldwide without a strong knowledge of our world markets. It's clear to me what needs to happen now. We are going to have to review the interface and the site generation tool in full, and we are going to have to invest in product changes to not only keep our current customers but to put us back on a path of growth." No one in the room disagreed.

Questions

3. Caroline recognized that they need to redesign to some degree the interface and the site generation tool. What should be Caroline's first step?
4. What should be the objectives of the redesign?
5. What might be some existing sources of information Jean-Marc's project team could use to better understand the market requirements?

Let's Start Again

Caroline believed that the usability team, headed by Jean-Marc, would be the best suited to own the user interface and site generation tool redesign project. They were a small team, but the project was focused on the user interface and the end users' experience so it just seemed to make the most sense. Caroline called Jean-Marc into her office to inform him of her decision. Jean-Marc was very pleased to learn that he had a relatively large budget to undertake this project. He was also promised a lot of autonomy and influence—he would drive all the redesign requirements with the support from the product managers.

But the project was not without its challenges. Jean-Marc could not make any changes that impacted core functionality, and even more alarming was the short timeline to complete the studies and the redesign. But the timeline was something with which Caroline and Frederic could not be flexible. They were losing customers at an increasingly rapid rate. If the trend continued, they would be out of business by the following year. On The Go needed to communicate to its customers that it had a solution, and the customers needed to know that these solutions would be coming within a reasonable time frame. The time taken to improve the product needed to be competitive with the amount of time it would take a customer to build another solution with another provider—about 6 to 9 months.

Jean-Marc set up a series of meetings in the next weeks with various individuals from departments that would be impacted by the project. In the first meetings he focused on investigation of the action plans, timelines, and deliverables. They discussed how they would gather the secondary sources of information for the initial assessments. Different members of the project team would be in charge of gathering the information, analyzing the results, and presenting a summary to the team. From this step the plans for the baseline usability tests would be sketched out. With the review of the data, they could begin to shape some theories and initial research questions.

"I have a question," Philippe said tentatively. "Although it might be too early to discuss now, I am wondering how we are going to choose where we run the baseline tests? And how many countries are we going to allow to include?"

Jean-Marc paused and then responded, "This is actually a bigger question than it would seem. It touches on an important aspect of the project that we might as well discuss now. I need to tell you that our biggest constraint is time, much more so than budget. We have been instructed to roll out at least the major product components to the market within 6 to 9 months. This includes the entire release cycle from the planning until the deployment. We know that we have to deliver the designs 3 months before the code is to be completed, so that leaves us 3 to 6 months to perform the research and redesign the product components."

Some of the team began to laugh nervously, and one of the product managers yelled out, "You must be joking. It already takes us that long today and that's when we don't do any research."

Jean-Marc laughed a bit himself, and continued, "It's true. I know it's tight, but I believe we can manage it. But before we talk about logistical challenges, I would like to focus on the ideal plan. Then we can scope from there." Jean-Marc turned to the whiteboard and began to sketch out a high-level activity plan (Figure 18.4).

Jean-Marc turned from the board and then took the group through it. "We've already discussed how we will gather and review existing informa-

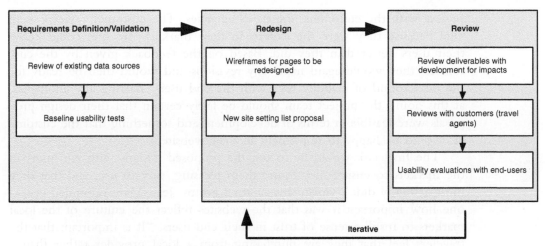

Figure 18.4. High-level activity plan (ideal).

tion. Once we have done that, we would identify the markets and questions where we believe we need additional information in order to make conjectures about the redesign. We would then spend some time conducting baseline tests in a good sampling of markets. From the data that we have and the data that we would gather through the baseline tests, we would be able to have a good assessment of the gap between the existing product and what is required. We could then begin the redesign phase."

Celine, one of Jean–Marc's team members, exclaimed, "Mon dieu! You are talking about at least a year before we even begin discussing the changes to the product!" Jean–Marc shushed Celine, "Again, I want to focus on the ideal plan first. We'll impose realities in a few minutes." Jean–Marc moved ahead with his overview. He explained how they would be able to sketch out wireframes for the pages based on the information they would have gathered in the requirements investigation phase. The deliverables would also include a proposal for the revised list of site settings. Once the initial set of deliverables was stable, they would begin a series of reviews, starting with the development teams. It would be important to involve the developers as early and as often as possible to confirm that their proposed changes would not impact the existing functionality. They had to ensure that their proposals were not headed on a dead-end path.

After the review with development, they would make any necessary revisions to the wireframes and site setting lists and continue with the next review with the customers, the travel agencies. The customer reviews were vital because they were the experts in their markets—no one could know their users better than they did. Based on the feedback given by the customers, they would again make any revisions and would then be ready for the next round of usability tests with the end users. Barring any anomalies, at this point, the project team should be fairly certain that their design proposals were feasible in terms of development and something that the customers would be happy to implement in their websites.

The final task would be to test the proposed designs with end users in the markets to ensure they found them pleasing, easy to use, and that they most certainly didn't violate any cultural norms. Jean-Marc reminded everyone how important it was that the websites reflect the culture of the local markets to instill a sense of trust in their end users. "It is important that the travelers feel that they are purchasing from a local provider rather than a vendor across the world. They need to feel that the vendor is someone who is accessible in case they have problems after their purchase."

Jean-Marc finished his theoretic overview of the plan by pointing to the arrow labeled "iterative." He explained how it could happen that the design phase may have to be repeated depending on the results from the usability tests. In case they found from the usability tests that they had not reached their goals of designing something with which the end users would be happy, they would have to make further changes to the design proposals. If these changes ended up being substantial, they may need to begin the review process again—from the development review to the usability test.

"Now let's switch gears a bit," Jean-Marc said. "Looking at this plan, we could definitely imagine this taking years to complete. In an ideal situation we would want to conduct design reviews with all of our customers and test all of the proposals with end users in all 75 of our markets. But we know this is absolutely incompatible with our directives to release some redesigned components by the end of this year. So now we are back to your original question, Philippe. This is where we need to consider what's possible and how to make it happen. We know that we have to deliver the first redesigned components to development in 3 to 6 months so that they can begin to develop the code. I think we should look at using the first 3 months for the baseline research and then the following 3 months would be dedicated to the redesign of the first phase of product components. It's clear that we are going to have to get creative here. But I've been thinking and I've got some ideas."

Although he tried to appear confident, Jean-Marc was not completely sure himself that his proposal was the way to go. He was depending on the honest feedback from the others to let him know whether he was being realistic. He moved back to the flip chart and began to list some of his ideas.

Questions

6. What would you propose as ways of compromising between the ideal plan and a plan that would allow the team to meet the imposed deadlines?
7. What risks would be introduced by making a compromise in the ideal plan in terms of design, schedule, cost, and so on?

Lessons Shared

Jean-Marc had received management approval for his project plan and had conducted the project in three phases as he had originally proposed. The redesign project was completed on time, and even though they were in the early stages of releasing the redesigned product, all indications suggested that it was going to be a success. The customers who had seen the new user interface were asking to migrate to the new user interface as soon as possible. In addition, the project team had been able to eventually reduce the total number of settings by one-third.

Although generally the results of the project were favorable, the running of the project had been challenging. They had not been able to follow the plans 100% according to what Jean-Marc had presented to his management. For example, there was one case midway through the project where the project team would have preferred to run another iteration of design reviews on one of the key product components but were unable to do so because of their deadline. And as they had approached their deadline for the entire project, they had been forced to move forward with redesign proposals that had not benefitted from *any* usability tests or customer reviews. But thanks to their strategic planning, the components that had not benefitted from the full review process were in fact those that posed the least risk to their overall success. The key product components had been prioritized and redesigned earlier in the project. In all cases when the team could not strictly adhere to the redesign project plans, the project team and their management had to weigh the risk against the cost of a late delivery. But Jean-Marc was positive—he did not believe that all was lost in these cases. The research efforts would continue, and any findings could benefit future versions. It simply meant a reduction in their confidence level as they moved toward the release date.

Caroline and Frederic were pleased with the results of the project. They passed Jean-Marc in the hallway one day after the research had been completed and spoke briefly about the project. Caroline told Jean-Marc, "I think the results of the study really hold a lot of promise in helping us to attract and keep customers." Frederic joined in, "I'm pleased because the results mean a simpler product for us to maintain." Caroline continued, "Jean-Marc, I think it would be great if you could document and present some of your findings to the rest of the team and to the other affected departments. I'm particularly interested in how well you think we'd be able to manage worldwide markets in the future. For example, how much variance do you think there is in the requirements of different markets? Do you think we could truly manage those differences with one product or do we need to investigate different products for different markets?" Jean-Marc put on a brave face and agreed to Caroline's proposal to do the presentation, but he was thinking to himself, "Yikes . . . I don't want to present in front of all those people—there could be hundreds!"

Jean-Marc prepared his findings and sent out a general invitation to the On The Go division. He prepared two formats: a formal presentation in case the audience was large and another more interactive one in case the audience was of a manageable size. On the day of the presentation he waited at the front of the auditorium and assessed the crowd while he attempted to calm himself by practicing his breathing exercises he learned in his yoga courses. When the moment arrived, he made the split decision to roll with the interactive format because the crowd only filled the first third of the auditorium.

Jean-Marc began the presentation by briefly reviewing the project objectives and some of the project milestones. He then introduced the purpose of the presentation: to give a sense of variances in the market requirements and to translate the findings whenever possible into do's and don'ts that his colleagues could carry away with them. Before diving into his specific findings, Jean-Marc was careful to explain that his results should be used as indicators rather than as a doctrine. Although they had been able to conduct a lot of research, it would take much more to answer some of the questions more concretely and confidently. Jean-Marc's long-term plans included research to test the hypotheses he was presenting today.

Jean-Marc first focused on the trends that were shared among the markets. "The information that users need to make decisions in their selection of travel options tends to be the same. They boil down to the same types of product information such as price, travel provider, flight schedules, hotel quality ratings, and purchase conditions. In fact, there was more impact on the information needs from the different types of users, for example, business versus leisure travelers, than from among the markets." He added that they also found very little difference in users' expectations for how the interaction techniques should work. He explained further, "Most users understood how interface widgets such as radio buttons, drop-down lists, scroll bars, and navigational elements worked. Almost all of the users we encountered were somewhat familiar with the Internet, and their expectations appeared to be shaped by their experiences."

Once Jean-Marc had completed his points about the homogeneities among the markets, he steered the presentation toward his findings for the variances in the markets. "Before I present the results, I would like to open the discussion to get a sense of what you, as product providers, would have expected to learn if you had been involved in the research."

A few people raised their hands, and a microphone was passed to Karine from the site setup team. "Because I work with customers from around the world, I've learned that there are quite a lot of differences in how they expect information to be displayed. For example, some countries expect the day to come before the month, but other countries expect the month before the day. And, in some Far Eastern countries the year is often displayed before the month or date. Address formats are often different too. Depending on the country, the zip code may be displayed before or after the city name. Sometimes the country name comes before the city, in other cases the city comes before the country. And then in some countries like the United States and Brazil, you will have to include a state. Oh, and I almost forgot—there are two different ways to display the time of day. For example, in Europe they use the 24-hour clock and in the United States they use the 12-hour clock. So in Spain it's 17:00 and in New York that's 5 p.m."

Jean-Marc had begun to relax now that the presentation was well on its way and the audience appeared to be interested in what he was saying. He thanked Karine and used her comments to launch the presentation on information display and formats. He flipped to a slide in his presentation that showed the list of data format issues of which designers should be aware (Table 18.1).

Table 18.1. Data Format Issues of Which Designers Should Be Aware

A. Date formats	Month/day/year (Sep 23, 2006)	Day/month/year (23 Sep, 2006)	Year/month/day (2006 Sep 23)
Example countries	United States, Canada (English-speaking)	Qatar, Morocco, Singapore, Hong Kong, Canada (French-speaking), Australia, Europe, United Kingdom, Iceland, Brazil, Russia, Thailand, Mexico	People's Republic of China, Taiwan, Japan, Korea,
B. Time formats	12-hour clock (3:00 p.m.)	24-hour clock (15:00)	
Example countries	Singapore, Taiwan, Australia, Canada (English-speaking), United Kingdom, United States, Korea, Mexico	Qatar, Morocco, People's Republic of China, Hong Kong, Canada (French-speaking), Iceland, Japan, Brazil, Russia, Thailand	
C. Calendar formats	Week starting with Sunday	Week starting with Monday	
Example countries	Qatar (weekend: Friday and Saturday), United States, Australia, Brazil, Mexico	Morocco, Europe	
D. Name order	First name/last name	Last name/first name	
Example countries	Qatar, Morocco, Singapore, Hong Kong, Europe, Australia, Canada, United States, Brazil, Russia, Thailand	People's Republic of China, Taiwan, Iceland, Japan, Korea	
E. Address order (not all address components are included for each country)	Name, address, city, state/province, postal code, country*	Name, address, postal code, city, country	Country, postal code, province, city, address, name

Table 18.1. *Continued*

Example countries	Singapore, Belgium, Canada, United Kingdom, United States, Portugal, Russia,* Thailand,* Hong Kong	Qatar, Morocco, Europe (except Portugal), Australia, Iceland, Brazil	People's Republic of China, Japan, Korea, Taiwan
F. Currency symbol placement	Before price ($45,000.00)	After price (45,000.00€)	
Example countries	People's Republic of China, Singapore, Hong Kong, Taiwan, Denmark, Netherlands, Australia, Canada (English-speaking), United Kingdom, United States, Italy (except when price is negative), Japan, Korea, Norway, Brazil, Thailand	Belgium, Finland, Belgium, Canada (French-speaking), France, Germany, Iceland, Poland, Portugal, Russia, Spain, Sweden, Turkey	
G. Decimal/ thousand separator	23,566.00	23.566,00	
Example countries	Qatar, People's Republic of China, Singapore, Hong Kong, Taiwan, Australia, Canada (English-speaking), United Kingdom, United States, Japan, Korea, Thailand	Morocco, Europe, Canada (French-speaking), Iceland, Brazil, Russia	
H. List separators	Comma (item 1, item 2, item 3)	Semicolon (item 1; item 2; item 3)	
Example countries	People's Republic of China, Singapore, Hong Kong, Taiwan, United Kingdom, United States, Canada (English-speaking), Japan, Korea, Thailand, Turkey	Qatar, Morocco, Europe (except Turkey), Finland, Canada (French-speaking), Iceland, Brazil, Russia	

*Postal code comes after country.

Jean-Marc recapped the items that Karine had mentioned and expounded on the date format. "I often see designs where in an attempt to simplify the information display, we present the date in an abbreviated format." Jean-Marc pointed to an example on the slide with the date shown as 3/9/2006. "We have to remember as designers that there is very little information in this case to indicate whether the first or second number is the month. When we show a date in this way, cultural expectations will strongly shape the interpretation of the date. In the United States the user would assume the date to be March 9th, 2006. In Europe, however, the user would understand the date to be September 3rd, 2006."

Jean-Marc then discussed challenges around the display of prices: decimals and the currency symbol. "Do you realize that periods or commas may be used to indicate decimal values depending on where you are in the world? Imagine the two following price formats. 23,566.00 and 23.566,00. In Europe the decimal is indicated by a comma, but in the U.S. they use a period. You might believe that this would be easy to manage, but we had a design challenge some time ago where this distinction narrowed our possibilities for a solution. As you know, we have a feature in our search pages that allows a user to provide a maximum price to shape the search results. The problem we had was that users often entered decimal values, but our back-end system cannot process this information. We tried to provide messages to explain that users should only use whole units when entering this maximum price, but this didn't improve the situation—users didn't take note of the message. One of our designers suggested that we create code that would automatically truncate the value when decimal values were entered. The problem? How do we determine where to truncate? At the comma or at the decimal point? As you can see in the example given here, the values would be drastically different depending on where we truncated. If we decided to truncate at the decimal point, in the United States the value would translate to be 23,566 and in Europe the value would be 23. You can see how it could make a big difference."

He finished his discussion on data formats with the subject of price displays and currency information by posing a question: "Would you expect to place currency information before or after the price? Does it depend on language or on the currency? Any ideas?" Before the microphone could be passed to her, Janine from sales yelled out, "It must be currency. Language shouldn't have anything to do with it." Jean-Marc responded, "You are right for the most part. It most commonly is the currency that drives whether the currency symbol, code, or name would be displayed before or after the price.

But did you know that in the case of the Canadian dollar, the placement of the currency indicator depends on whether it is shown to a French-speaking Canadian or to an English-speaking Canadian? In this case, it depends on the currency as well as the language—it's not always as simple as it seems." Jean-Marc flipped to his next slide to show them an example (Figures 18.5 and 18.6).

Jean-Marc moved ahead to his next subject—information complexity. It was the area he believed had shown the largest variance in results from the different markets. He could only discuss the trends because most of the data were anecdotal and, unfortunately, he had more questions than direction to give. But he still believed it was worth discussing so that the product developers could begin to think about the implications in their work.

Jean-Marc flipped to the next group of slides and began. "In general, the results showed that there was a difference in the way the user responded to the amount of information load on the page. In some markets, such as Scandinavia, the users appear to prefer to see cleaner simpler pages with less information content per page. Other markets such as the United States appear to be completely comfortable with pages highly loaded with content—even when the information was not directly related to the task at hand. But this difference does not only have impact at the page level."

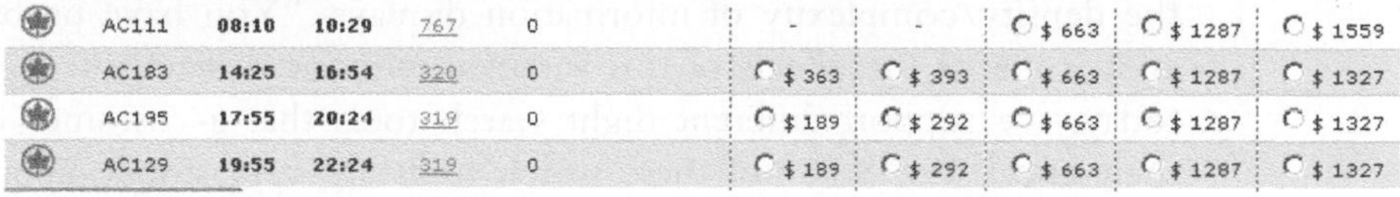

Figure 18.5. Canadian dollars presented in an English language website.

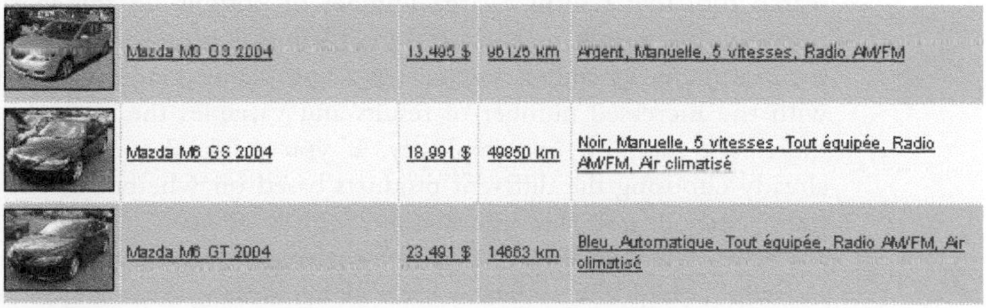

Figure 18.6. Canadian dollars presented in a French language website.

Jean-Marc decided to open the conversation on this point and asked the audience to think about other impacts this variance could have on the product design. Hans from product engineering requested the microphone and replied, "If we have to consider placing less information on each page, we would have to increase the number of pages and steps for a user to complete a reservation. If we do that, I can tell you that we are going to be getting some complaints from some of our current customers."

Jean-Marc agreed with Hans and said, "That is definitely one of the potential impacts for this type of finding. And like you, I believe that although some markets would be okay with the trade-off of increasing the number of steps to reduce the content load on the page, other markets will not so readily accept this." Even though he did not discuss it with his audience, he also knew that if they decided to reduce the content of each page, the impacts would trickle down to other parts of the application as well. In markets where the user would prefer less information on the page, they may have to consider relying more on menu options and links to allow the user to access information rather than presenting it directly at the page. The information architecture and the resulting navigation structure would no doubt have to change as a result. For example, the navigational structure could potentially be shallower (i.e., fewer sublevels) in markets that could support more information on each page.

Jean-Marc continued on the subject of the different markets' reaction to the density/complexity of information displays. "You have probably already seen some of the effects of this variance without realizing it. As you know, today, we support different flight search tools that a customer can offer to their end users. Some of these search tools are very simple in nature. They provide only a few flight options from which the user can select. It is much simpler for the user to operate, but the user has less control over the results and how they are delivered. Alternatively, we have a very powerful flight search tool that returns a large number of options. In this version the user can mix and match to build the ideal solution along a number of variables such as flight schedules, service levels, purchase conditions, and price. But with the increased number of results and variables the user can manipulate, there is a trade-off in complexity. If you think about it, our markets are already choosing the different products based on whether their end users are more open to complex information displays or not."

After finishing the topic of information display complexity, he decided he would draw the audience back in by moving to a subject to which he thought most people could relate—visual design. He again started the subject by mentioning the commonalities among the markets and described how the typical fonts used seemed to be the same for most of the markets and how font size requirements seem to vary more as a function of age rather than of market.

He then jumped to color and asked the audience if anyone had any ideas on how color preferences are impacted by different cultures. As he suspected, quite a few hands went up this time, and the microphone was passed to someone Jean-Marc did not know seated in the front. The man stood and said, "I read a book a couple of years back about the building of Euro Disney. When they first opened, they had designed the street signs to be mostly purple, but they learned that their visitors found this color to be morbid. This of course was the last sentiment that Disney wanted to convey, so they took on the costs to have the signs done again. I think this is an interesting case because the bad choice in color impacted their bottom line." The man sat down and the microphone was passed to Jorgé from marketing strategy. Jean-Marc cringed slightly because he considered Jorgé to be a bit of a know-it-all. He wondered how long they would have to wait for long-winded Jorgé to finish. Jorgé started, "Colors can have different meanings in different cultures. For example, we often take red to imply danger, but in Asia red means happiness and prosperity. And in our culture white is often associated with weddings, but in Asia it is associated with funerals. I could go on and on . . ." Jean-Marc took the opportunity and cut Jorgé off. "Thanks, Jorgé. I'm sure you could. It's a fascinating subject. But in the interest of time, I will recommend for anyone interested that you try an Internet search on the subject to learn more. There is a lot of information available there."

Jean-Marc flipped to his next slide with a couple of examples of travel websites and continued. "In our studies, we also found subtle differences in the reactions to the colors depending on the market. In one of the earlier studies we noticed that quite a few users in France commented that they did not like the appearance of the pages and specifically mentioned the colors. When we investigated further it seemed they found the colors to be too harsh and bold. After this we decided to create two visual concepts for a home page—one with softer pastel colors and another with bolder more primary colors—and show these two concepts to the users. We didn't get a chance to collect a lot of data on this topic, but the results that we do have suggest some difference in how markets respond not only to color, but to the intensity of the colors. For example, in the United States the users preferred the example with the bolder colors; they felt that the option with the pastel colors was washed out. Conversely, end users in Norway preferred the version with softer more pastel colors. They felt that the option with the bold colors was too harsh. We can't draw strong conclusions based on the limited data we have, but it's another theory that we would like to research further as we move forward."

Still on the subject of visual design, Jean–Marc turned the discussion from color to another aspect where he had noticed a pattern. "Interestingly, we found clues that certain cultures such as Europe and Scandinavia seemed to prefer softer more rounded edges and lines, whereas in markets such as the United States they prefer stronger harder lines and right angles." Jean–Marc showed a slide with a European website (Figure 18.7) compared with an American one (Figure 18.8).

While Jean–Marc prepared to move to his next topic, his thoughts drifted to other examples outside of the Internet environment where he thought this same preference could be found. He remembered a British car television program where the announcer proclaimed that American cars appeared to be designed only with a ruler, implying that there were no rounded corners (Figures 18.9 and 18.10).

Jean–Marc also remembered his first impression of city maps in France (Figure 18.11) compared with those in the United States (Figure 18.12). In the United States streets are almost always laid out in a grid pattern. But in

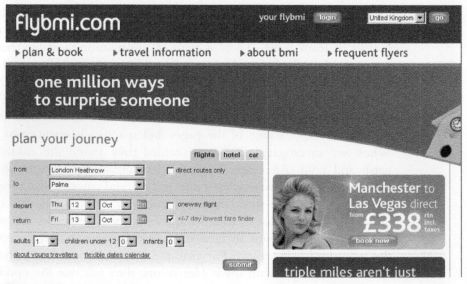

Figure 18.7. U.K. travel site.

Figure 18.8. U.S. travel site.

Figure 18.9. European sedan.

Figure 18.10. U.S. sedan.

France, for example, a right angle for an intersection is a truly rare thing. In the United States red lights and intersections are a defining characteristic of a junction, whereas round-abouts are more suitable to the street layout in Europe.

He didn't have evidence to demonstrate a connection among these things, but he suspected that there might be some correlation.

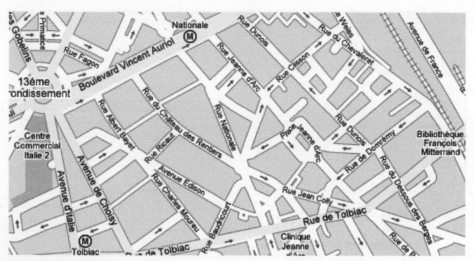

Figure 18.11. French street map.

Figure 18.12. U.S. street map.

Jean-Marc's focus snapped back to his audience, and he moved the presentation to his last topic. It was again what Jean-Marc would call a "soft finding" and would need further investigation before he would ever make any strong conclusions, but he still thought it worthwhile because it was related to users' reaction to Internet security—a hot topic with many of their customers. Jean-Marc introduced the final topic and then said, "But let me first tell you a bit of the background before I discuss the result. When users have concluded a purchase for a travel reservation, we always provide an option to continue shopping for what may result in an additional purchase. Each time the user decides to make a purchase, they need to enter their credit card information. Some of our team members believed that we should default the credit card information from the first purchase in case the user had selected to make an additional purchase within the same browser session. They argued that this could be a real time saver because quite a bit of data entry is required for the credit card information. However, others on our team strongly believed that users would take exception to this default of their credit card information for fear that we were either keeping the information ourselves or that the information might be floating around to be taken by hackers. Both sides felt strongly, so we thought it was worthwhile including a scenario in one of the tests to see how users reacted. Interestingly, we found evidence to support both arguments. Tests with U.S. users showed that they did resent the fact that the credit card information was defaulted. The American users did not believe that the time saved for data entry was worth the perceived risk. Conversely, the Scandinavians appeared to be undisturbed by their credit card information being defaulted. They didn't react negatively during the test session and confirmed through interviews that they appreciated the information being defaulted in the credit card fields—they didn't believe that it was a risk to them." Jean-Marc explained that the European and Scandinavian markets have yet to suffer from the high rate of Internet credit card fraud that the Americans were enduring, and this may be the reason for their higher level of trust with the Internet transactions.

Jean-Marc had reached the end of his presentation, so he looked around the room and asked for any additional questions before continuing to his summary. He began by explaining how strongly he felt that the study had been an imperative step to putting them on track to a profitable future. With the information they had been able to gather, they had a much better understanding of their end users, the travelers. They also had a clearer understanding of how and when the different markets around the world would require variations in their product solutions and the user interface. Although they had found some variance among the markets' expectations, Jean-Marc believed that almost all the differences they had found could be managed with one product and the correct selection of site setting choices. Jean-Marc explained, "Things like visual presentation aspects, product features, and information displays can be managed much as we do today. And with the information we've managed to collect, I believe that we are in much better shape to understand the correct choices to provide. And one last point—we can now provide a better baseline product from which to start, one that offers the best compromise among the different market requirements so that each customer should have fewer customizations to make." Jean-Marc concluded by asking his project team to stand and receive a round of applause from the audience.

Summary

The main objective of this case is to communicate the importance of understanding end users from markets around the world when designing an international product. We ask a lot of our end consumer when we sell our products or services over the Internet. Consider how we require the end consumers to invite us into their lives, from the sharing of their personal information to asking them to provide us access to their bank accounts. It is critical to eliminate reasons for the users to distrust us, the vendors.

One way to build users' trust is to give the sense that the users are dealing with a local provider, a provider closer to home, a provider who understands their needs and is "within reach" after the purchase transaction is concluded. You increase the risk that you will come across as a distant vendor if you ignore the cultural contexts of your end users.

It's a serious but interesting challenge to create a design to accommodate many different markets and cultures. It's not as simple as translating the text in a user interface. There are many design aspects impacted by culture that should be considered. The most tangible design items that should be addressed are data display aspects such as time formats, date formats, and currency formats. Then there are other aspects that are less defined but of which one should be wary, such as complexity of information displays, information load per page, and visual aspects such as color and form.

From experience, it is possible to design a product that is flexible enough to adapt to markets around the world. The challenge is to determine which product aspects can be common to all markets and then to allow for required variances in a manageable way. To achieve this, it is important to know the market requirements and the cultural impacts so that you can effectively cover the customizations that are needed.

To this end, it would be ideal if we were able to perform end user research within the markets before any design began. It would also be great if we could conduct studies in all markets where we plan to distribute the product. But this is rarely the case. It's something that is more realistically achieved through an ongoing iterative process. If you can vary the countries where you perform user research, you will be able to gradually increase your first-hand knowledge of other markets other than your home. But a good understanding of your international market is a strong requirement if you want to penetrate the world market.

Further Reading

Aykin, N. (2004). *Usability and internationalization of information technology.* Mahwah, NJ: Lawrence Erlbaum Associates.

Del Gaddo, E., and Nielsen, J. (Eds.) (1996). International user interfaces. New York: John Wiley & Sons.

Dray, S. (1996). Designing for the rest of the world: a consultant's observations. *Interactions*, 3:15–18.

Fernandes, T. (1995). *Global interface design: a guide to designing international user interfaces.* New York: Academic Press.

Websites

http://www.amanda.com/resources/hfweb2000/AMA_CultDim.pdf

http://www.globalization.com/index.cfm?MycatID=1&MysubCatID=2&pageID=1309

http://molly.com/articles/webdesign/2000-09-colormyworld.php

http://icu.sourceforge.net/userguide/i18n.html

Inspecting a User Interface

Paul Englefield, IBM UK

> *There was good news: Educators "got" the concept and admired the technology. However, by way of bad news, they found the user interface cryptic, ugly, and impractical and saw no way they could ask their students to use it to support their learning objectives. Stuart returned from the trade show with no orders but a determination to find a "fix."*

Prometheus Bound

Stuart Appleby, über-geek and accidental entrepreneur, would rather refactor a class library than make a phone call. Stuart was technical lead for Prometheus, a start-up intending to "bring the fire of learning" to distance-learning science students working with tutors over the Internet. The core Prometheus technology enabled instructional designers to create courseware by embedding extensible standards-based learning objects (IEEE WG12) in a network of modular static topics written to the DITA standard (Oasis). By structuring educational topics as small, independent, context-free resources, Prometheus offered trainers an efficient reuse-based approach to course design. For students, it offered a rich learning environment in which they could explore resources in a nonlinear style.

For example, an instructor might need to construct a course to introduce students to electronic circuit design. To do so, she might combine (1) concept topics introducing ideas such as voltage, current, and resistance; (2) reference topics documenting circuit diagram symbols and units such as volts and amps;

(3) a learning object for visual circuit simulation; and (4) a set of problems to exercise and assess learning. To design materials for more advanced students, she might complement these topics with more rigorous definitions, add a second learning object to enable more mathematical simulations of circuit behavior, and replace the problems with a more challenging assignment.

Prometheus had funding, innovative technology, and a passion for education as an agent of positive social change. Stuart had a strong personal conviction that elegant engineering would necessarily lead to an effective user experience. But, like battle plans, some design philosophies barely survive contact with reality. In this case, Stuart demonstrated a new technology prototype at an educational trade show. Where previous versions of Prometheus relied on authors editing a script, this new version offered an interactive instructional design editor.

There was good news: Educators "got" the concept and admired the technology. However, by way of bad news, they found the user interface cryptic, ugly, and impractical and saw no way they could ask their students to use it to support their learning objectives. In an ironic twist on the myth, the fire of technology was all but extinguished by an unworkable interface. Stuart returned from the show with no orders but a determination to find a "fix."

Stuart called Hannah Sorenson. Hannah, an independent usability consultant and a seasoned veteran of the dot-com bubble, would prefer to calculate a T-interval than enthuse vaguely about an "engaging interactive experience." Stuart shared his vision for empowering trainers and asserted his commitment to "fix" the issues raised by his intended customers. Hannah listened carefully, shaping the dialog by building rapport, asking open questions, and exploring unfamiliar technical and business topics. Most importantly, she deferred diagnosis of the problem, avoiding any responses that could appear critical, judgmental, uninformed, or dogmatic. Stuart quickly decided that Hannah was smart, professional, and a potential partner in solving this problem.

"Okay," said Stuart to Hanna, "Now I can put a name to the problem: It's *usability*. I guess the solution involves a bunch of guys with clipboards working some magic behind a one-way mirror." Hannah grinned. "There's more than one way to skin a Titan" she explained. "Let's design an evaluation that best fits your objectives, timetable, and budget." After a thorough review of Stuart's goals and constraints, it turned out that he needed the answers within 2 weeks to meet an engineering deadline for a product launch.

When Hannah asked him to define "answers," he described a broad range of issues with actionable recommendations. "I'm not looking for irrefutable proof," he said, "but I do need a shopping list of what to go fix."

Questions

1. Why did Hannah put so much care into the conduct of the initial interview?
2. How might Prometheus have avoided usability issues in the first place?
3. Why was Hannah so concerned to get a precise "brief" to shape and scope the evaluation?

Choosing a Method

Hannah and Stuart jointly developed the brief to define the following four goals:

1. Identify the user experience issues in the current design; include accessibility and adoption.
2. Explain those issues and the likely impact on educators and learners.
3. Recommend a prioritized set of actions to address the issues.
4. Complete this work within 2 weeks.

By creating this brief Hannah helped Stuart to articulate the types of data needed to prepare Prometheus for the marketplace. Now they needed to identify an evaluation method that would best match the goals and constraints defined in the brief.

Hannah sensed that Stuart wished to be an active partner in this evaluation. To summarize the tangled academic literature on methods selection, she sketched the simplified model shown in Figure 19.1. She began by explaining, "There are two distinct approaches to evaluation: 'Expert' methods have usability specialists inspect the design against some definition of best practice. These methods, for example, heuristic evaluation or cognitive walkthrough, are top-down, driven by theories of how people interact with systems. On the other hand, 'user' methods, such as usability testing, invite representative users to actually use the design while the experts watch, listen, and measure. These bottom-up methods are data driven; they are closer in spirit

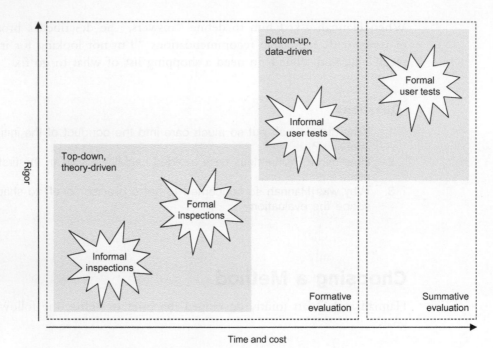

Figure 19.1. Simplified method selection model.

to rigorous defensible scientific approaches to acquiring data and testing hypotheses."

Hannah explained that it was also important to distinguish formative studies from summative evaluation. She said, "You can either look for ways to improve the design or seek reliable evidence of success or failure. Be sure of your priorities; it's hard to reliably achieve both in a single study." Hannah also made a practical distinction between formal and informal evaluation. She observed, "We have to find a principled balance between doing good science and good business. I appreciate that you may care more about turnaround time than formal reporting of results." Informal studies, she explained, represent a simple "health check," whereas formal evaluations involve larger samples, formal test protocols, statistical analysis, and detailed reports. "Time and cost tend to increase with formality and rigor," she continued, "That's why we consider methodology and business together."

Stuart's requirement to identify user experience issues suggested a formative study. Although he had no requirement to rigorously demonstrate compliance with a set of measurable performance criteria, he did need to discover as many of the issues as possible that users might experience. His time constraint, to complete the study within 2 weeks, indicated that a user study would not be practical. He did not have an identified panel of users and, in fact, had no business need for rigorously obtained evidence to persuade stakeholders that changes were necessary. Because he was keen that the evaluation should not only describe issues but should also explain their causes and potential impact, a top-down theory-driven method seemed more suitable than a bottom-up data-driven method. Finally, his desire for broad coverage of potential issues and a prioritized plan for resolutions indicated a more formal study.

Using the model against a review of Stuart's needs, a formal inspection looked like the method that would best meet his needs. A formal inspection invites a panel of experts to predict problems by adopting the role of potential users attempting to satisfy a set of realistic goals. It is formative, fast, top-down, and broad. Hannah and Stuart spent a little more time to scope and shape the proposal, negotiating dates, deliverables, and a commercial framework. As Hannah said, "You need to be confident of a result, and I need to know exactly what to deliver."

Establishing Context

Stuart called Hannah the next day to confirm his agreement to the proposal. He was keen to get started, so they agreed to meet for lunch and refine the approach. They started by talking about how usability had evolved from a reactive test-oriented approach to a broader discipline that incorporated evaluation within a philosophy of user-centered design. Hannah explained that an evaluator needed to thoroughly understand the context in which a design would be used. Together they completed the worksheet shown in Table 19.1.

Finally, Stuart and Hannah deconstructed the design to identify a set of views. A view is an abstract notion for a coherent panel, subpanel, pane, or page. Hannah encouraged Stuart to think in terms of views to focus on the user's perceptions rather than the underlying engineering. These would be used to relate issues to specific parts of the interface to identify hot spots across the design. For example, if many issues turned out to be associated with topic navigation views, Hannah would explore the need for additional design work to enhance this area of the design.

Table 19.1. Design Context Worksheet

Business goals What is the overall value proposition?	Increase the acquisition and retention of knowledge by learners by supporting rich experiential learning. Increase the quality of tutor/student contact time. Minimize the cost of creating course materials.
Usability factors Is the emphasis on efficiency, effectiveness, satisfaction [ISO 9241], or some factors?	The solution should facilitate effective learning and teaching. Efficient setup of courseware requires speed and convenience. A satisfying experience contributes to learner motivation and continued use. A channel for learning must itself be transparently easy to learn.
User roles and goals Who will use this design? What sort of people are they? What do they want to achieve?	Educators are part-time tutors typically educated to postgraduate level and strong advocates of lifelong learning. They may have disabilities. Goal 1: Deliver educationally effective content. Goal 2: Ensure student success through feedback and motivation. Students are adults of all ages, in full- or part-time employment. They may have limited formal education and fragile motivation. They may also have disabilities. Courses define basic computer literacy as a prerequisite skill. Goal 1: Get strong results through understanding and retention. Goal 2: Maintain commitment and motivation. Goal 3: Maximize use of time.
Context of use Where will this design be used? What are the physical, social, and technical considerations?	Using a desktop or laptop at home or in a library. Cached content may also be used from a laptop while traveling. Devices such as PDAs and Smart Phones are explicitly not supported. Study environment may in some cases have limited space and nearby distractions such as family conversation and television. An 18-hour help desk is provided.

Refining the Study Design

As Hannah continued to refine the design of her study, she contemplated the following challenging issues:

- How long should she allow for the evaluation?
- Given the general goals described by Stuart, what specific goals should the evaluators role play to get good coverage in the time available?
- What type of checklist would be appropriate and practical for an experienced panel of evaluators?

Hannah handled these questions by reasoning back from the budget and the research objectives. She had funding to cover 8 evaluator days and a brief to find the majority of errors for two critical user groups. Applying Jakob Nielsen's model that four evaluators would find around 70% of the errors, she chose to have four experts spend 1 day inspecting a broad set of tutor goals and a second day assessing a generous range of student tasks. For each user group she then identified a sample of goals and views, as shown in Table 19.2. She focused on making the definitions thoroughly contextualized and supported by predefined content. In some cases, the scenario contained content that would exercise specific aspects of the design. For example, in Table 19.2 the "Define learning outcomes" goal described a policy of phrasing instructions in the second person. This was intended to lead the evaluator to experiment with formatting options without being explicitly directed to exercise this facility.

Selecting Evaluators

Hannah now needed to recruit the perfect team of evaluators. She applied the following selection criteria:

Table 19.2. Goals and Views Used in the Prometheus Inspection

Role	Goal	Scenario for Goal	Context for Goal
Tutor	Define learning outcomes	You are designing a new course offering. The course is an introduction to contemporary Chinese film aimed at serious movie fans. You have already made some rough notes on outcomes. Your college prefers the form "you" rather than "the student."	College or home office. You often need to fit Prometheus work into short sessions between other commitments.
Student	Register	You are registering for a course on contemporary Chinese film in response to an advertisement in the national press. You suffer from moderate arthritis and qualify for financial assistance as an unemployed student.	You prefer to work in a public library where you have space to spread out study materials. In the evening you work at home; your family and their hobbies can get noisy.

- Strong theoretical knowledge of a relevant area of HCI
- Sufficient familiarity with the domain (in this case computer-mediated learning)
- Professional and articulate writing style
- Considered judgment
- Concentration and attention to detail
- Ability to spot not only surface problems (e.g., errors related to presentation or standards) but also more abstract issues such as mismatch to the user's task model
- Collectively, provide good coverage for the research goals agreed in the brief

Table 19.3 shows the available staff from whom she could recruit a team.
Inspection is both a method and a workflow process for the evaluation team. Figure 19.2 shows the process Hannah chose to follow. The top line shows activities performed by the manager, an experienced practitioner

Table 19.3. Available Staff		
Name	**Specialist Skills**	**Style**
Ronald	Design-related legislation	Incisive, thoughtful
Susan	Visual design, brand, information architecture	Thorough, careful
Michael	HCI, cognitive science	Analytical, applied
Erica	HCI, social psychology, accessibility	Smart, imaginative, funny
Rose	HCI, user interface standards	Brilliant, impatient, caustic
Martin	Instructional design, writing style	Professional, disciplined

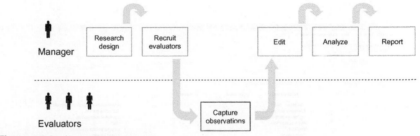

Figure 19.2. Inspection process.

responsible for the overall design, management, and reporting of the study. The bottom line shows the task carried out by the evaluators recruited by the manager. These evaluators take the research design created by the manager, inspect the design, and capture a set of observations to be analyzed by the manager.

The edit step is a preliminary check for correctness. A "correct" observation is clear, grammatical, and professionally phrased. Additionally, it applies HCI theory in an appropriate way and is based on a proper understanding of the problem domain. The analyze step involves systematic qualitative analysis to reveal the big picture. The report step concerns presentation of results in a structure and format helpful to the client.

Questions

7. Who should Hannah pick for the evaluation team from those available to work on the project? What factors might influence her decision?
8. What are the consequences of making the wrong call?
9. Heuristic evaluation recommends a prioritization step in which evaluators vote on the severity of findings. Why might Hannah choose not to follow this advice in this case?

The Inspection

Over the next 2 days the team individually inspected the interface, identifying observations and recording them in a standard form using IBM's Inspection Logger (Figure 19.3), a logger utility optimized for inspections. This tool organizes observation reports as three distinct components: a description, the

Figure 19.3. Inspection Logger.

underlying principle violated (or supported) by the observation, and any recommendations applicable at this level. Additionally, each observation was mapped to one or more goals and views defined in the research design and distinguished as an achievement, comment, or issue. To ensure efficient data entry, the logger provides extensive keyboard enabling, facilities for reusing previously entered data, and tools for finding, managing, and annotating entries.

Editing

When the evaluators had logged their observations, both positive and negative, Hannah performed an initial edit to ensure the quality of the data. Table 19.4 shows examples of poorly written observations selected from several hundred thoughtful entries.

Questions

10. What is the value of recording achievements as well as issues?
11. Why were evaluators asked to record a supporting principle for each finding?
12. What concerns might Hannah have about the style and content of these observations?
13. What consequences would result from ignoring these style and content issues?
14. How might Hannah address her concerns about the quality of these observations to the evaluators?

Table 19.4. Examples of Poorly Written Observations

ID	Issue	Principle	Recommendation
(1)	Too much pink	Aesthetics drive appeal and adoption	Use blue
(2)	More than seven menu entries	Magic number 7 ± 2	Reorganize the menus
(3)	Insufficiant (sic) contrast for legibility. The demon typographer strikes again!	Contrast is a critical factor for readability	

Analysis

The evaluators had now finished their contribution to the study. Armed with a body of reliable data, Hannah's next job was to identify the higher level issues implied by the details. In her daily briefing to Stuart, she explained, "I'm analyzing lots of symptoms to diagnose a few underlying problems. Think of it as the old cliché about not seeing the forest for the trees. So now we need to perform some qualitative analysis in order to classify each observation and then aggregate those classified data points into groups that correspond to findings."

She sketched the examples shown in Table 19.5 to explain the distinction between the two terms "observations" and "findings." Observations are data points that describe individual issues related to specific design

Table 19.5. Observations and Findings

			Findings			
			Generalized analyses derived from observations. Used to describe the underlying problems.			
			Legibility	**Type**	**Graphics**	**Appeal**
Observations	Data points describing individual issues related to specific design features. Used to discover and support findings.	1. Cycling animation on Buy widget makes the text hard to read	✓	✓	✓	
		2. Insufficient contrast impacts reading	✓	✓		
		3. Icons lack refinement and charm			✓	✓
		4. Unattractive typeface compromises user attitude		✓		✓

features. The analyst uses observations initially to identify findings and subsequently to act as evidence to support those findings. Findings, on the other hand, are generalized analyses derived from observations. Each finding is derived from, and supported by, a set of observations that describe similar problems.

Because the data from an inspection are essentially descriptive, Hannah chose to use a qualitative analysis method. Table 19.6 describes a generic approach (Miles and Huberman, 1994) to qualitative analysis, whereas Table 19.7 explains how Hannah adapted this approach to extract findings from observations.

Where it is important to seek "surprises" while avoiding preconceptions, this style of qualitative analysis ensures that an appropriate framework emerges directly from the data. Hannah typically used this generic approach to analyze data from the "discovery" steps of a user-centered design program. For example, she regularly worked this way when analyzing observations of user profiles, environments, and motivation. However, for analyzing inspection

Table 19.6. Standard Steps in Qualitative Analysis

1. SPLIT
Separate raw data into discrete independent elements.
For most qualitative work this involves splitting field notes into self-contained ideas.

2. CODE
Review each data element and assign one or more codes. In methods like Grounded Theory (Glaser and Strauss, 1999), "emergent coding schemes" arise from working with the data.

3. GROUP
Group elements into sets that share a common code. Databases and spreadsheets can be helpful here.

4. REFLECT
Review the patterns formed by each set of elements and refine the coding scheme.

5. ITERATE
Repeat steps 2–5 to refine the coding scheme and associated groupings. Over a series of iterations, the coding scheme should evolve from a loosely organized pool of descriptive codes to a well-structured set of explanatory codes. Analysis stops when the coding scheme provides a satisfactory explanation of the data. The final set of codes typically identifies a set of "Things" and "Relationships" to explain the patterns inherent in the raw data.

6. SUPPORT
Select a subset of the raw data as evidence to support each explanatory code.

Table 19.7. Hannah's Refined Qualitative Approach Using a Predefined Framework

1. SPLIT
Hannah did not need to split the data. For an inspection, the source data are already a discrete set of observations rather than a continuous set of free-form notes.

2. CODE
Hannah used a predefined coding framework in which each code corresponded to a finding. She used the Evaluation Analyzer tool to rapidly assign one or more codes from the framework to each observation.

3. GROUP
The Findings view of the Evaluation Analyzer tool automatically groups observations by finding code.

4. REFLECT
By using a predefined coding scheme, Hannah avoided the need to refine the analytical framework.

5. ITERATE
By using a predefined coding scheme, Hannah avoided the need to iteratively review, refine, and regroup until an appropriate framework emerged.

6. SUPPORT
Hannah used a feature of the Evaluation Analyzer tool to select a subset of the observations for each finding to be used as evidence.

results, she found this iterative strategy to be challenging; it frequently turned out to be time consuming and difficult to do well. Above all, it yielded results in a form that could not easily be compared or aggregated with the results from other studies. For an inspection, the analytical framework is already well established; the types of errors that may or may not be present in the design are not only described by the academic literature but also familiar to experienced practitioners. Consequently, the research goal for an inspection is not to discover a new analytical framework so much as to "slot" observations into an existing framework (e.g., Keenan et al., 1999) to find the subset of predefined issues that are present in the interface.

Hannah used a specialized software tool from IBM, Evaluation Analyzer, to manage the workflow associated with coding and selecting evidence. This tool, shown in Figure 19.4, presents two distinct views on the data, corresponding to the rows and columns in Table 19.5.

The *Observations* view lists the full set of observations aggregated from the logs provided by individual evaluators. It enables an analyst to work systematically through the raw data, assigning a set of codes to each observation from a predefined scheme to define findings.

A *Findings* view lists the set of findings corresponding to the codes assigned in the observations view. It allows the analyst to rapidly review each finding, adding comments and recommendations and then selecting critical evidence from the associated observations.

Hannah worked systematically through the evaluators' logs, using the Evaluation Analyzer to assign one or more codes to each observation. For example, using the screen shown in Figure 19.4 she assigned a set of codes related to understanding user goals to an observation about the need for

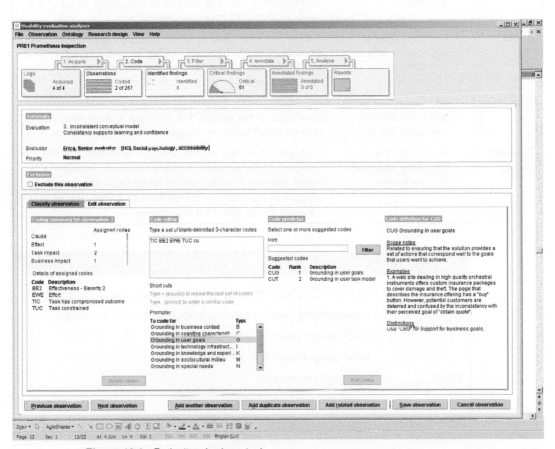

Figure 19.4. Evaluation Analyzer tool.

bookmarking. Hannah used a coding scheme (Table 19.8) with four independent analytical dimensions.

Table 19.9 shows how Hannah used these four dimensions to code an observation that described an "okay" button labeled "Make it so." By using this scheme, she distinguished the problem as perceived by the user

Table 19.8. The Four Dimensions of the Predefined Coding Scheme

Dimension	Has Codes for	Coded Findings Can Be Analyzed to
Cause	Issues in the user-centered design process	Recommend improvements to the design process. For example, a cluster of codes related to understanding user characteristics and the context of use would suggest the need for more rigorous user research.
Effect	Psychological and ergonomic effect on the user	Assess the subjective quality of the user experience. For example, a range of codes related to perception, memory, and attention would imply that the design does not follow best practice for minimizing cognitive load.
Task impact	Impact on the user's ability to correctly complete the task	Predict the user's success in achieving the immediate objectives of the design. For example, a large number of codes related to errors suggest a risk of task failure.
Business impact	Impact on the business objectives for the design	Evaluate the impact on the strategic objectives for the design. A large number of codes related to learnability would indicate potential issues related to training and support costs, whereas a high level of codes related to adoption would predict a low uptake.

Table 19.9. Coding the "Make It So" Observation

Cause	Understanding users/grounding in social and cultural characteristics
	Understanding users/grounding in experience and knowledge
	Initial design/genre
	Initial design/labels and terminology
Effect	Learning/interpretation
	Social and emotional/identity
Task impact	Task underperformed/task initially costly
Business impact	Learnability: severity 3 (low)
	Appeal: severity 2 (medium)

(effect) from the associated methodology issues (cause) and the likely consequences.

By assigning codes from all four observations, Hannah would be able to build up a multidimensional picture of the issues. After completing the coding process, she would be able to analyze a chain of issues for both individual observations and for the set of observations as a whole. Reading the diagram shown in Figure 19.5 from right to left (business impact ← cause), she would be able to predict a business outcome and then trace back to some responsible aspect of the design process. Reading it from left to right (cause → business impact), she would be able to describe a potential issue in the design process and then trace out the consequences to the user, task, and business.

Questions

15. What are the advantages and disadvantages of using a predefined coding scheme?
16. Why might a coding scheme emphasize business outcomes and design process?

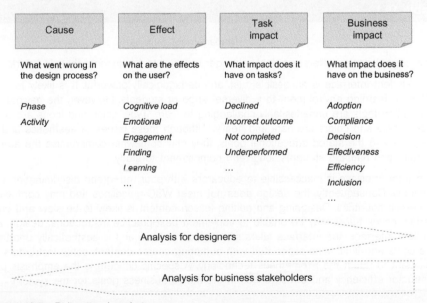

Figure 19.5. Bidirectional analysis.

Reporting

Hannah regularly asked clients to provide feedback on the quality of her reports. One recurrent theme was report structure. Readers made it clear that although detail was important, an incisive high level overview was critical. For example, where technical staff tended to be interested in a listing of issues by page, executives preferred a short summary of the key issues and an overview of the supporting evidence. Consequently, Hannah's team generally wrote reports in an inverted-pyramid style, with the executive summary at the front followed by increasingly more detailed analysis and then presentation of the "raw" observations. This structure allowed a casual reader to skip the detail while enabling more thorough reviewers to study the detail in the context of the big picture.

Table 19.10 shows an extract from the management summary supported by a business score card (Table 19.11) that Hannah includes regularly in her reports. Note the way in which the management summary interprets the score card in business terms. The score card is derived from the findings that are themselves derived from the observations. Together the report forms a pyramid of analysis. It systematically reduces hundreds of individual data points to a few paragraphs of concise guidance.

Table 19.10. Extract from Management Summary

Management Summary

The current design offers a notably stronger experience to students than to tutors.

The student interface is accessible, fast, and pedagogically powerful. It is likely to deliver an effective learning environment to a diverse range of students. However, the navigation scheme and annotation tools are unnecessarily challenging to learn. Type, color, and icons are unrefined and lack appeal and colors are dark and heavy. Although these issues of aesthetics and efficiency are secondary to the stated educational goals, they may somewhat compromise the authority of the content and damage students' long-term commitment to study.

The tutor interface is inaccessible to educators with poor red–green discrimination or limited dexterity. Consequently, the design does not meet W3C guidelines and may contravene legislation in certain countries. Designing and editing lesson content is likely to be slow and challenging. In certain cases tutors may be unable to implement best-practice instructional design. As with the student interface, the interface takes some effort to learn and is aesthetically unattractive. Given the costs and limitations associated with authoring course content, some instructors may be reluctant to adopt the Prometheus technology. A specific concern is the emphasis placed on instructor efficiency and effectiveness in the stated business goals for the system.

Table 19.11. Business Impact Score Card

	Goals					
	Role: Tutor			Role: Student		
Impact	**Define Learning Outcomes**	**Add Lesson Plan**	**Mark Assignment**	**Register**	**Take Lesson**	**Complete Assignment**
Appeal The solution is, to some degree, not appealing to users. It may not adequately attract or engage its intended audience.	☹	☹	☹	☹	☹	☹
Compliance The solution does not comply with applicable laws and codes of practice.	💣	💣	💣	☺	☺	☺
Effectiveness The design does not enable users to work effectively, minimizing errors and maximizing outcomes.	☹	☹	☹	☺	☺	☺
Efficiency The design prevents users from completing their tasks efficiently.	☹	☹	☹	☺	☺	☺
Inclusion The design can not be fully used	💣	💣	💣	☺	☺	☺

Table 19.11. *Continued*

	Goals					
	Role: Tutor			Role: Student		
Impact	Define Learning Outcomes	Add Lesson Plan	Mark Assignment	Register	Take Lesson	Complete Assignment
by a diverse range of users. Examples include users with: disabilities; limited education; and limited access to technology.						
Decision The design may allow or encourage inappropriate decisions by users.			💣			
Learnability The design is hard to learn and may have high learning, training, and support costs.	☺	☺	☺	☺	☺	☺
Safety The design may be physically unsafe for either its operator or others affected by the actions of the operator.						
Credibility The design may				☺	☺	☺

Table 19.11. *Continued*						
	Goals					
	Role: Tutor			**Role: Student**		
Impact	**Define Learning Outcomes**	**Add Lesson Plan**	**Mark Assignment**	**Register**	**Take Lesson**	**Complete Assignment**
have insufficient credibility to achieve its intended purpose.						
Adoption To some extent, the design discourages users from taking up the solution.	☺	☺	☺			

💣, severe impact; 🙁, moderate impact; ☺, slight impact; ☺, achievement.

Table 19.12 shows an extract from the findings section. The description includes both boiler-plate text, taken from the coding scheme, and an extended description added by Hannah to interpret the finding for Prometheus. The report also lists the user goals and views (pages, panes, and dialogs) affected by the finding and the supporting evidence in the form of selected observations.

Table 19.13 shows an extract from the recommendations. Hannah ensured that this material was presented in a concise and action-oriented style.

After Stuart had a few days to review the report, Hannah called him. She was assertive and to the point. "So, you carry the report around for a few days until you forget about it when an interesting engineering problem comes along! You still have a problem. I don't get a satisfied client. There's no happy ending. Let's get together and plan a way forward." They met a few days later. Stuart brought Alex, his business director, and Sam, his project

Table 19.12. Extract from Findings Section

CD11. Design of color

Colors for headings, links, and tints are inconsistent and often do not conform to the brand style. Background colors are generally "heavy" and unrefined. In some cases the low foreground/background contrast compromises legibility. Field highlights are used arbitrarily without explanation.

Recommendations

Use color purposefully to guide attention and convey brand values. Follow the Prometheus brand guidelines for use of color. Select foreground/background combinations for high contrast.

Goals affected

Define learning outcomes, add lesson plan, mark assignment, ...

Views affected

Tutor home page, lesson plan editor, student home page, ...

Selected evidence

Obs.	Observation Description	Design Principles
25	Inconsistent color for headings, links, and tints. The palette is internally inconsistent and incompatible with brand rules.	Visual consistency, brand compliance
165	Light gray on dark gray gives poor legibility.	Ensure contrast for legibility.
201	Dark saturated colors are heavy and unappealing.	Attractiveness bias

Other referenced observations

11, 19, 27, 87, 93, 101, 224, 324, 401

Table 19.13. Extract from Recommendations

1. Engage a graphic designer to define an appropriate visual style. The style should address color, type, layout, and icons to support effective communication and engaging aesthetics. Use this style to review and update the design. Consider using style sheets and templates to simplify the implementation of the presentation layer.

2. Engage a user experience specialist to optimize the instructor task model to create a more efficient effective interaction design. Key areas for improvement include navigation, data entry, and preview.

3. Review the code against W3C guidelines. Use an appropriate mix of automated test tools, code inspections, and disability simulations.

4. ...

manager. Hannah invited her colleague, Val, to join her. As an independent facilitator, Val would manage the agenda to ensure that the process remained on track with a mutually satisfactory conclusion.

After satisfying themselves that the study had been appropriately carried out, Hannah and Stuart's coworkers debated the impact of the findings and the implications of the recommendations. Sam believed that student satisfaction was unimportant; once registered, they would be committed to using Prometheus. Alex, however, argued that course providers needed to encourage students to re-register for follow-on courses. He believed that even a small defection rate could have a serious impact on the business model for education providers, his primary customers. Alex was reluctant to take on an extra staff member to handle the improved visuals recommended by Hannah. However, Sam pointed out that Prometheus had recently hired Merry, an experienced graphic designer. Grinning, he said, "She has just finished doing a nice job on the marketing site—she'll enjoy the creative challenge of applying her skills to the product itself."

Hannah believed that implementing a redesigned task model would help the success of Prometheus. On the other hand, she could see how this might be technically challenging. Stuart agreed but explained to the meeting that the technical architecture of Prometheus enabled easy changes to the dialog structure. He asked Hannah to recommend a designer. Everyone also agreed that accessibility was critical. Stuart then proposed an affordable technical strategy for building the core interface engine around technologies such as W3C, HTML 4, and CSS.

So, the man who adored technology collaborated with the woman who loved precision, and Prometheus was unbound by the application of methods, tools, and expertise. "I brought you a problem," said Stuart, "And you gave me a plan."

Questions

17. Why does the Findings section only list a subset of observations as evidence?
18. Which dimension of the coding scheme predicts the effect of design issues on adoption of Prometheus by learners and trainers?
19. Which dimension of the coding scheme suggests design process recommendations?
20. Hannah had completed her assignment. Why was she so assertive with Stuart about the need to develop an action plan?

Summary

The key elements of a heuristic evaluation include the following:

- Understanding the client's needs is critical to designing a successful evaluation.
- Inspections sit within a spectrum of evaluation methods. They are well suited to formative assessments where a fast turnaround and broad coverage are important.
- An inspection is performed by a panel of evaluators, selected for their collective skills and individual professionalism.
- Each evaluator individually takes on the role of a user attempting to satisfy a goal within a well-defined scenario. While doing so, she uses a checklist to log a set of observations. Observations are mapped to one or more user goals and to a set of implicated views.
- Good observations are clear, specific, and supported by theory. A professional and balanced writing style is important.
- Observations are not findings; they are raw data used as input to qualitative analysis that derives a set of findings.
- Observations can be analyzed by assigning codes from a predefined analytical framework. Each code corresponds to a finding. A single observation may provide evidence for several findings. Likewise, a single finding may be supported by multiple observations.
- One analytical framework uses four dimensions: cause, effect, task impact, and business impact.
- An effective report is structured around the convenience of the reader rather than the intellectual heritage of the analyst. An inverse pyramid style enables readers to stop when they have sufficient information. Business impact and actionable recommendations are both likely to be of interest to a commercial reader.
- A successful evaluation project ends with an agreed action plan.

Further Reading

Butler, J., Holden, K., and Lidwell, W. (2003). *Universal principles of design*, Gloucester, MA: Rockport Publishers, Inc.

Cockton, G., and Woolrych, A. (2001). Understanding inspection methods: lessons from an assessment of heuristic evaluation. Published in *People and*

Computers XV—Interaction Without Frontiers, (2001). Blandford, A., Vanderdonckt, J., & Gray, P. (Eds.), London, UK: Springer-Verlag.

Disability Rights Commission, http://www.drc-gb.org/

Glaser, B.G. and Strauss, A.L. (1967). *Discovery of grounded theory: strategies for qualitative research*, Chicago: Aldine Transaction.

IBM (1993). *Object-oriented interface design: IBM common user access guidelines*, Carmel, Indiana: QUE Pub.

IBM Ease of Use (2003). *User engineering method.* Retrieved from www.ibm.com/easy

IEEE WG12, http://ltsc.ieee.org/wg12/

ISO 9241. *International organization for standardisation. Ergonomic requirements for visual display terminals.* Retrieved from www.iso-org

Jeffries, R., Miller, J, Wharton, C., and Uyeda, K. (1991). User interface evaluation in the real world: a comparison of four techniques. Proceedings of the SIGCHI Conference on Human Factors in Computing Systems 1991, Reaching Through Technology, New Orleans, Louisiana, United States.

Karat, C.-M., Campbell, R., and Fiegel, T. (1992). Comparison of empirical testing and walkthrough methods in user interface evaluation. Proceedings of the SIGCHI Conference on Human Factors in Computing Systems 1992, Monterey, California, United States

Keenan, S., Hartson, H., Kafura, D., and Schulman, R. (1999). The usability problem taxonomy: a framework for classification and analysis. *Empirical Software Engineering*, 4, 71 104

Miles, M., and Huberman, M. (1994). *Qualitative data analysis: an expanded sourcebook,* Thousand Oaks, California: Sage Publications.

Miller, G. (1956). The magical number seven, plus or minus two: some limits on our capacity for processing information. *Psychological Review*, 63:81–97.

Norman, K. (1991). *The psychology of menu selection: designing cognitive control at the human/computer interface,* Norwood, NJ: Ablex Publishing Corporation.

Nielsen, J., and Mack, R. (1994). *Usability inspection methods.* New York: John Wiley & Sons.

Oasis consortium, www.oasis-open.org

Royal National Institute for the Blind, www.rnib.org.uk

World Health Organization, www.who.int/classifications/en/

CASE 20

Billingsly: A Case Study in Managing Project Risks and Client Expectations

Charlotte Schwendeman, Perficient, Inc.

> *"The software did not fare well in our recent usability test," Darla said. "One participant stated he wouldn't use the new software. He'd just turn it over to his assistant and let her deal with it." Sam, a senior vice-president on the business side, didn't know anything about designing and developing software. But he knew he had to act now.*

Dissension in the Ranks

The Problems Mount

Sam woke up that morning with a sick headache. He had been at Billingsly, one of the premier financial services companies in the United States, for 40 years now. He had risen through the ranks and now, as a senior vice-president in the branch office operations division, enjoyed the benefits that come with a long and illustrious career. His current responsibilities included oversight of the thousands of branch offices throughout the United States; he was responsible for their well-being, smooth running, and profitability. In short, he ensured they ran like clockwork, with all the financial consultants selling, opening, and maintaining client accounts and for enabling the success of each branch. He had a great relationship with the branch office managers. Although he managed with a firm hand, he was well liked and respected. Things had been going smoothly for many years now, until recently. Quite honestly, Sam had a hard time remembering anything in his career that had been this devastating.

Less than 6 months ago Billingsly had rolled out a new version of the software that was used by all the financial consultants and branch office managers to open and maintain new client accounts. Since the roll out, Sam's phone had not stopped ringing. Pete, a branch office manager from Tampa, had called just yesterday to let him know he was losing one of his best financial consultants and two of his seasoned financial assistants to a well-known competitor. John in Beverly Hills lambasted him this morning with tales of how his office's productivity had sorely declined as a result of this new application, and sales were off by 10% at his branch. Sam's most recent call was from Don, the branch office manager in one of the most affluent suburbs and highest grossing branches right here in the area. "Somebody should be fired over this," were Don's final words.

In the past Don's financial consultants had no qualms about opening accounts in the presence of their clients using the old InSight software all the financial consultants in recent years were weaned on. Many branches still used the old paper forms to open new accounts. Granted, InSight was a mainframe application, old, and a little "kludgey," but everyone knew the tricks of maneuvering it and how to work around any problems encountered. And the paper forms were easy to complete. Clients expected their financial consultants to pass the paper form across the coffee table for them to sign and the account was opened. But 6 months ago Billingsly rolled out new software, AccountNow, that replaced InSight and the paper forms. The branches were all required to use AccountNow. This application forced them to request information from their clients they never had to before due to new Securities and Exchange Commission and Sarbanes–Oxley regulations, making the whole process take two-to-three times as long as it had before.

The financial consultants felt foolish and embarrassed slogging through the new online account form in front of their clients. As a result, Pete and all the other branch office managers who had been complaining to Sam reported that their financial consultants were instead jotting down notes on scraps of paper or keeping running lists of account information changes and then passing along the scraps and pads of paper to their financial assistants, leaving them to phone the clients to fill in the blanks. The assistants in turn became bottlenecks to opening new accounts. Hence, dissatisfaction and poor morale in the branch offices were rampant. Some of the best financial consultants and assistants were leaving for competitors where, they said, the technology didn't hamper them from closing new business.

Sam knew he couldn't wait any longer. Every new point release his IT (information technology) department pumped out was worse than the one before. For some reason many more government regulatory restrictions that had previously been cleverly disguised in the software were now front and center in the new application and were, in part, responsible for the recent dissatisfaction and dip in productivity at the branches. Sam knew someone from Billingsly's small usability department often attended the frequent meetings at headquarters about the application.

The usability department at Billingsly was so small relative to the size of the IT department and there were so many software projects going on at the same time that they decided some time ago to concentrate on the aspects of usability that they did well. Because they didn't have the time or sheer numbers to be involved in all the software projects throughout the design/ development process that were going on at Billingsly and because their strengths were mostly in the evaluation of solutions and not in design, they decided to concentrate on conducting usability tests of the solutions toward the end of the development process or soon after they were in use.

Sam wondered if anyone in the usability department had anything to say about the new account software. He knew the department was spread too thin across projects, so he didn't know if they had been involved in any of the design decisions in the new account software. The only person he knew in the usability group was Darla. Sam made a quick call.

"The software did not fare well in our recent usability test," Darla replied. "The financial consultants had a hard time finding the portions of the online form that were important to them. They said they had to wade through tons of irrelevant questions they could answer later and not in front of their clients before they got to the parts of the form essential to opening a new account. One test participant stated he wouldn't use the new software. He'd just turn it over to his assistant and let her deal with it." Sam didn't know anything about designing and developing software, but he was beginning to think Billingsly's IT department didn't either. Sam knew he had to act now. But how?

When Sam arrived at Billingsly that morning, he grabbed a cup of coffee and headed straight to Dwight's office. Dwight's people at headquarters used the same software Sam's branches used. Although they used it for a different purpose (primarily to double check and approve the new accounts opened by the branches), Sam needed to know if the productivity of Dwight's people was being affected by the software too. His hunch was right. Dwight reported, "My folks are putting in 20% more overtime than usual. They're asking me what's going on at the branches. They say they have to make corrections all over the place. They're receiving many forms only partially completed. They are forced send things back to the branches to go through the process all over again. This has got to stop!"

Armed with this information, Sam called a meeting of his peers to decide on a course of action. After laying out the problem and much discussion about how this new software was affecting their profit margins, the business owners called a meeting with Vicky, a manager in the IT division responsible for the new account software. Vicky brought several of her best architects and developers to the meeting. When pressed about the problems Sam and his peers were hearing about, Vicky said they were doing the best they could with all the new regulatory rules Billingsly's lawyers were handing them. Vicky stated, "In the old software we could just embed the rules in the coding, but there were so many new rules enacted lately by the government. Legal is forcing us to get all these new rules in there and request lots of additional information. We don't know how to keep them hidden behind the scenes anymore. You know, Sam, our policy has always been to 'buy' software first and only build new software as a last resort. We're much more used to managing package installations than we are developing new ones. We're not miracle workers."

After IT left the room, the business owners conferred. "It's clear that we have a problem that has no easy answer. We gave our IT department a shot at it, but I don't think they know how to fix the problem. I think we need a firm who knows something about our business and who also knows how to design things that are easy to use," Sam said. "Let's go outside Billingsly for help."

After many meetings and phone calls to friends and colleagues at other companies for a referral, Billingsly finally issued a request for proposal (RFP) to a group of consulting firms that knew how to deal with problems like Billingsly's.

Questions

1. What types of problems is the new account software causing at Billingsly?
2. Who is responsible for solving the problems caused by the new account software at Billingsly?
3. What might lead Sam to believe that Billingsly should look outside the company to solve the problem with the new account software?

Selling Paper Prototyping

Monty started his new job as a sales executive at the small but fast-growing consulting firm, 1FineInc, just 3 months ago. He had 10 solid years of successful sales experience at other technology management consulting firms and was excited about this new venture. He was accustomed to selling the kinds of services 1FineInc offered. 1FineInc was a deep technology firm with offices throughout the central corridor of the United States. It was developing a good reputation, and that's what lured Monty to apply. Also, they concentrated on "solutions" selling. At his last company the emphasis was on augmenting a client's IT staff with additional programmers, architects, and developers, something the industry called "staff aug." Well, Monty was done with staff aug. He wanted something more. Although they were known as a technology company, 1FineInc approached projects with the goal in mind of solving other companies' business problems. Now, that excited Monty.

1FineInc usually began a project at a new client account with a small interdisciplinary team comprising a solutions director, a project manager, technology architects and developers, business analysts, and, often, something they called "user experience specialists." In fact, during the interview process he learned that the user experience specialists were often the first ones on the ground on a new project. He knew how to sell the other skill sets, but he needed to get his arms around this user experience stuff. He had heard good things about the national practices during his interview, but he was having trouble getting a meeting with the company's User Experience Practice lead, Sally. He had heard that she was terribly busy, and he knew she had responsibility for this skill set throughout the company, not just here in town.

In an effort to learn something about this field before securing a meeting with Sally, Monty had asked her to send him one of her sales decks so he could come into the meeting at least familiar with the language. As he pored over the material, he learned there was a lot more to this than he thought. He had heard about usability testing. But the materials Sally sent him talked about user-centered design (UCD) with appropriate user input and feedback techniques being a natural part of the development process from beginning to end. He also saw things like interaction design, information architecture, gathering usability requirements through a variety of techniques such as contextual inquiry, and something called iterative prototyping and usability testing. Now what was all this? This intrigued him.

The Information Meeting

At the same time, Monty received a call from Billingsly. From everything Monty knew about 1FineInc's clients, Billingsly would be a potential new client for 1FineInc. Monty chatted for about 15 minutes with a Billingsly project manager. At the end of the call Billingsly requested that 1FineInc come downtown and present a general overview of its usability and design capabilities to a group of Billingsly execs. Monty learned the audience would consist of a couple of IT managers and employees, some members of the usability department at Billingsly, and a large contingent of various business stakeholders, primarily vice-presidents and senior vice-presidents. Monty didn't know if this presentation was linked to a potential project; regardless, Monty wanted to knock it out of the park.

Monty and Sally prepared for the meeting by putting together a slide deck to speak from at the presentation and to illustrate some of 1FineInc's techniques and deliverables. Because the Billingsly usability department would be represented at the meeting, Sally could only surmise that the rest of the audience knew something about usability; however, she didn't know if they knew much about UCD, 1FineInc's approach to creating exceptional user experiences by driving usefulness and usability into solutions. Sally wanted to demonstrate 1FineInc's capabilities in UCD because 1FineInc had strong skills in this area.

Because they only had an hour for the presentation, Monty and Sally collaborated on the agenda. Monty wanted to allow Billingsly time to discuss its needs and pain points, and he knew he needed 10 to 15 minutes to introduce 1FineInc as a company and its overall capabilities. But he also wanted to make sure Sally had enough time to talk about 1FineInc's user-centered approach to design and development. Sally had been in UCD, human factors, and human computer interaction for 20-plus years and was very passionate about her field. Monty knew he would have to rein her in: Sally had a tendency to run over her allotted time in presentations. If he took 15 minutes and Sally took 20 minutes, Monty knew that they had only 25 minutes for Billingsly to speak about their needs in this area and still entertain questions.

Twenty minutes. That wasn't much time, Sally thought. Sally knew she would need to do a good job explaining UCD because Monty told her Billingsly's usability department didn't do design. She pulled in slides about UCD and then wanted to spend the rest of her allotted time talking about some of the techniques 1FineInc used early in the process to understand the users of solutions and their requirements. She pulled together slides on user personas and profiles, contextual inquiry, current solution usability testing, and 1FineInc's 3 × 3 iterative prototyping and usability testing. Sally had so much success in the past 5 years with the 3 × 3 method she considered it to be one of 1FineInc's best practices and differentiators.

Presentation day came, and Monty and Sally headed over to Billingsly. Sally knew Billingsly was formal in their attire, and she and Monty dressed accordingly. As they set up the projector and their laptops for the presentation, they sensed a great deal of tension in the room. Each group sat together and slightly separated from the other groups. IT came in first. They seemed somewhat guarded yet cordial in their demeanor toward 1FineInc. The usability team members knew Sally from local usability interest group meetings. They were friendly but seemed somewhat embarrassed to be there. The business stakeholders trickled in last. They were very formal but very friendly. It seemed to Sally and Monty that the business stakeholders exuded the most interest. Monty and Sally were instructed to wait for Sam, and when he arrived everyone seemed to defer slightly to him.

Monty and Sally thought the presentation went well, even though Sally felt rushed. The business stakeholders and the usability team asked good questions. Sally wasn't sure if the IT team was really interested in what she discussed or even if they understood it. They seemed to be more interested in checking things off a list than in truly listening. That discouraged Sally. Nonetheless, Monty and Sally left feeling as if there were solid potential at Billingsly for 1FineInc to help them out.

The RFP

A few weeks after the presentation an RFP came across Monty's desk. Happily, it was for the high-visibility project Billingsly talked about at the information meeting he and Sally had attended. Monty scheduled a meeting with Sally; Larry, the general manager of the local Chicago office; and Sue, one of the local solutions directors. While they were reviewing the RFP in Larry's office, Larry said, "Hmm. This is odd. I thought you said the business stakeholders at Billingsly were the driving force behind the information meeting. But the RFP was sent by the IT division." The group nodded in unison.

The RFP required the chosen vendor to deliver a working prototype of the "new user interfaces" for an application that let users open and maintain client accounts online. Further, the RFP requested the necessary technical documentation to build and implement the "new user interfaces" for the new account software.

Typically, after an RFP is used the issuer provides a mechanism for the RFP recipients to ask any questions they may have about the RFP and the work described in it. For a very large pool of recipients, the issuer sometimes sets up a meeting for questions to be asked and answered. More often, the issuer schedules a conference call with all the recipients represented on the call, or the issuer may simply collect a list of questions from each recipient, compile the lists, and send out all answers to all recipients electronically. In the midst of the Billingsly proposal work, 1FineInc received a request for RFP questions. From the answers that came back, 1FineInc learned several things that puzzled them. First, Billingsly would neither make the current solution available nor demo it before awarding the contract. The team wondered how they could accurately size the project without clicking through it and at least estimating the number of use cases reflected in the application. When pressed, Billingsly said the current application consisted of 28 use cases and 14 screens. Second, Monty requested copies of results from any usability testing that had been performed on the current solution to date. Billingsly responded they would share the reports after the vendor had been selected. 1FineInc also learned that what Billingsly was really after in the prototype was a demonstration of the new release's screen interaction, navigation, and flow. Finally, 1FineInc learned that Billingsly expected the entire project to take only a few months.

The 1FineInc team forged ahead with their proposal nevertheless. Halfway through their work, a new 1FineInc project manager, Ed, joined the team. The team worked together in a slightly contentious manner: Monty wanted more say in the actual project work the team was proposing than 1FineInc was used to from its sales executives. Ed was new and was trying a little too hard to prove his worth. Consequently, Monty, Sally, Sue, and Ed disagreed and ended up taking turns "controlling" the RFP response document at different times.

Based on what Billingsly wanted coupled with the time frame in which they wanted it and the vagueness of the scope, the 1FineInc team knew they would have to cut some corners. After much discussion the 1FineInc team decided to propose user profiles and personas, contextual inquiry to understand what requirements the users might have, its 3 × 3 iterative paper prototyping, and usability testing technique to come up with the initial high-level design and conceptual model, some detailed design, a final usability test of the working prototype, and, of course, the prototype itself. They knew they would have to take a "light" approach like this to UCD, and they would only be able to prototype selected tasks and not the entire application. The team believed this approach would get Billingsly at least the bones of what they needed to develop and implement their new solution. 1FineInc submitted its RFP response to Billingsly.

Questions

4. What are some of the potential problems the Billingsly RFP could cause for 1FineInc?
5. What are some of the implications of 28 use cases and 14 screens?

The Project Unfolds

Beginnings

After several months of follow-up presentations and reference checking, Billingsly informed 1FineInc they had been awarded the project. Monty and the team prepared the statement of work based on the team's RFP response. It took several more months for 1FineInc's statement of work to go through Billingsly's legal and contracts process. The 1FineInc team had to make many changes to the contract. The team found itself doing work during the contracts process that was typically done during the first weeks of the project. In the end, Billingsly's legal department rewrote the entire contract in a "language" they could understand. 1FineInc had never seen anything quite like this. Monty and Sally feared that if getting through the contracts process with Billingsly was this painful, working with them on the project was probably going to be painful too.

Because so much time had passed since the RFP process began, the 1FineInc team makeup had changed. The solutions director, Sue, was assigned to lead another large project that kicked off in the interim, and Ed, the project manager, left the company. Because all the solutions directors were busy with other clients, the team had to make do without one. They did, however, have a project manager, Paul, who recently came off another project.

Sally's user experience practice was growing by leaps and bounds and, along with it, her work load. Sally hired some senior-level people in the field. One of those was a trusted colleague, Pamela, with whom Sally worked at her previous company. Sally hired Pamela as a user experience director for the Chicago business unit. Although Sally remained in an advisory capacity on the project, allowing her to run the practice and to be involved in other sales pursuits and projects, Pamela led the 1FineInc user experience team on the Billingsly project. The user experience team consisted of Basil and Jean, two senior-level user experience practitioners who were relatively new to 1FineInc.

After the kickoff meeting, Pamela and the team decided the first step was to understand the users and their requirements. To do this, the team conducted contextual inquiry sessions at the branch offices. Billingsly was excited about 1FineInc observing at the branch operations. Sam told them this was the first time in 4 years anyone had gone out to the branches beyond the Chicago area to meet with the financial consultants and assistants.

When the team returned Jean and Basil compiled and analyzed the data and artifacts they had collected and, under Pamela's tutelage, decided on the message they wanted to convey to Billingsly. They then put together a presentation report of the findings.

At the presentation meeting Jean talked about how the problems with InSight were actually "bigger" than InSight, affecting other software and workflows. A major finding from the contextual inquiry sessions was that most of the online applications used at the branches consisted of online forms. But they weren't just in InSight. There were online forms in a variety of applications used by the branches. The project was becoming bigger than just this project. Billingsly needed to study how all the current applications and business processes worked at the branches, and then they needed to work to eliminate the overlap and consolidate the plethora of forms.

The presentation was well received. Sam, the senior vice-president of branch office operations and one of the main sponsors of the project, immediately approved the deliverable.

The 3 × 3

Still pressed to stay on schedule, Pamela, Jean, and Basil didn't waste any time getting prepared for the 3 × 3s. They didn't have a moment to spare. Basil and Jean had done iterative prototyping and usability testing before, but they had not participated on or conducted the 3 × 3. Pamela set about explaining to them that the 3 × 3 was just a specific type of iterative prototyping and usability testing. Pamela borrowed some of Sally's slides and went over them with Jean and Basil.

She told them that in the 3 × 3 human–computer interaction specialists create two to three low-fidelity paper-and-pencil prototypes, each reflecting a unique approach to the solution. Each of the prototypes is approximately three to eight screens deep, hence the name "3 × 3."

The main screen or home page should be as fully fleshed out as possible. Then some number of tasks is decided on to prototype. Typically the three to five or so tasks chosen are identified as a result of a user requirements gathering/identification activity, such as through the contextual inquiry sessions they just conducted at the branches. Sometimes, Pamela explained, when contextual inquiry is not possible, user requirements and functionality are also identified through a usability test of the current solution. Less desirable but often the only alternatives to use to determine user requirements and functionality are focus groups and interviews. The tasks are often determined to be the most important or most frequently performed and are typically a subset of all the tasks available in the solution.

Pamela showed Jean and Basil a sample 3 × 3 (Figure 20.1). For estimating purposes, Pamela explained, it typically takes a team of two HCI (human–computer interaction) specialists 5 to 7 days to brainstorm and draw/design the two to three unique prototypes.

Next, the prototypes are iteratively usability tested and refined over the course of 5 to 10 days, depending on how many user groups have been identified, or until a single model is determined. The result is a single high-level conceptual model of the solution's user interface. Figure 20.2 gives an example of the iteration schedule; however, if the solution is particularly complex and if there are many user profiles, it may take 2 days to test, followed by 1 or 2 days to iterate on the design, followed by 2 more days of testing, and so forth.

Pamela explained that another twist to the 3 × 3, especially for web solutions, is to interject the visual design home page comps in the 3 × 3 testing as well. When this is done, Pamela instructed, each test session comprises two parts—the task-based testing of all three prototypes and preference testing of the home page comps. Jean, the lead user experience practitioner on the team, commented astutely that she didn't believe formative testing like the 3 × 3 was the best venue for preference testing.

"I thought preference testing was more of a market research technique," Jean said.

"It is," Pamela replied, "but used along with the task-based testing of the prototypes, we at least get some direction from users as to whether or not the home or main page is robust enough to include all the main tasks or

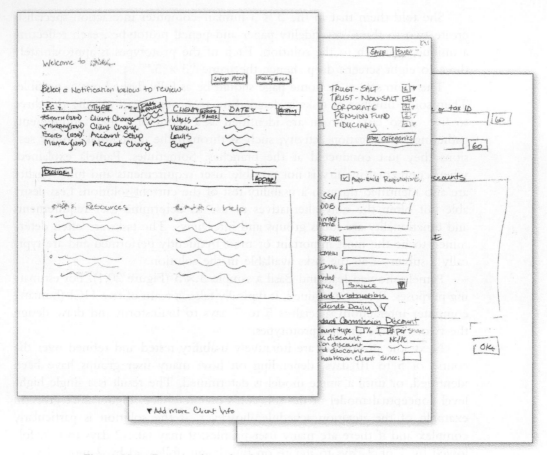

Figure 20.1. Example of one 3 × 3 paper-and-pencil prototype.

pointers to the tasks while, at the same time, is clear enough to support the users in accomplishing their work. In other words, we're trying to find out if it maps to their mental model."

Basil then asked, "When in the design/development process is the 3 × 3 used to its maximum advantage?" Pamela then went on to tutor Jean and Basil in the 3 × 3. She explained that when it's conducted very early in planning and before design, the 3 × 3 can be used to identify the most appropriate conceptual model and high-level navigation. It can also be used in this phase to flesh out user requirements, tasks, and functionality. Often the final activity/deliverable in the planning or discovery phase, it can be

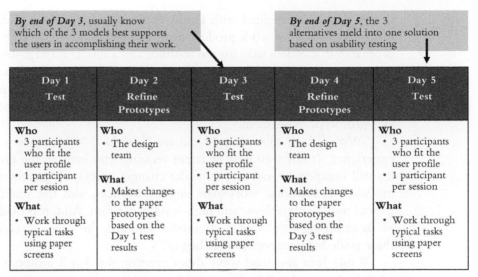

Figure 20.2. Sample schedule for iterative usability testing and prototype refinement.

used to provide a stronger more accurate estimate of both time and cost for designing and developing the entire solution. If used in this phase, it should be fleshed out with additional tasks, paths, and detail followed by further iterative usability testing and prototype refinement. In short, in addition to fleshing out a design, the 3 × 3 can help to manage project risk.

"If it is not done as part of the planning/discovery phase, it should be the first activity in the next phase, the design phase," Pamela asserted. Jean, Basil, and Pamela then went on to discuss how on the very short Billingsly project because the entire project was primarily a combination of the visioning phase and the design phase they would be using the 3 × 3 for a variety of reasons—to further flesh out and validate requirements gathered during contextual inquiry and to come up with a high-level design they felt comfortable moving forward with.

Basil said, "I can certainly see why the 3 × 3 is preferable to traditional iterative prototyping and usability testing. If only one prototype or model is created, you're likely to iterate or improve upon a poor model. By prototyping and iteratively usability testing three unique models, we can explore a variety of design ideas with users in a relatively short time frame with the result being a stronger model that more accurately meets or exceeds the users' mental model for accomplishing their goals. I just want to say that this is awesome!"

Pamela was delighted with Basil's enthusiasm. "Yes," she said. "And the initial deliverable or work product from this technique is the high-level conceptual design of key tasks for the solution and a model for high-level solution navigation. The deliverable is not a prototype of the entire solution, only of key selected tasks. The next steps include mid- and high-fidelity prototyping fleshing in more tasks and more detail, followed by iterative usability testing and prototype refinement."

"Wow," Jean chimed in. "I can see how the 3 × 3 leads to a better user experience. It uncovers new or latent requirements early in the process while it's still inexpensive and easy to make changes quickly. It gauges user mental models, expectations, workflows and preferences, and the usability of the overall model, metaphors, and high-level navigation. And, it provides a means of determining how well each model supports the users in accomplishing their goals before development begins."

While Jean and Basil went about creating the 3 × 3 prototypes over the next 5 days under Pamela's watchful eye, Pamela spent some of her time deflecting requests from Vicky, the Billingsly IT manager, and her team, conveyed through Paul, the 1FineInc team's project manager, to meet to review the 3 × 3s. "Paul, please just go away," Pamela pleaded. She explained that it was going to take her team every minute of the 5 allotted days to finish up the prototypes; however, Vicky and, hence, Paul, persisted. Pamela could see a pattern taking shape: With every deliverable or work product the 1FineInc team created, Billingsly asked to see it or a draft of it before it was complete. If this were a longer project, Pamela could understand their impatience a little better. But this entire project was only 3 months long! Couldn't they wait until the presentations? That's what the presentations were for. Pamela wondered if Billingsly just didn't trust its vendors. Did they believe we were sitting around doing nothing?

Nevertheless, Pamela managed to duck the requests. She and her team set out traveling from branch to branch conducting usability testing interspersed with team sessions spent refining the prototypes.

When they returned to Chicago, the team finalized the resulting prototype and scheduled a presentation with the IT and business stakeholders to show the recommended high-level design they planned to move forward with. Although overall the presentation went well, the team fielded a plethora of questions they weren't expecting. Dick, one of Vicky's programmers, said, "We normally create help and error messages. I don't see those. Where are they?" Other questions included things like, "Well have you thought about what happens when the financial consultant opens an account for multiple clients, like a Saturday morning stock club?" And, "How does the home office approve a joint account with this interface?" Paulette, the Billingsly project manager, concluded the meeting saying, "Now when can we get the final paper prototype?" That left the team even more confused. They didn't have time to wade through the type of detail the IT team was asking about. They needed to move into detailed design and creating the working prototype.

After the presentation Sally walked toward the coffee machine with Sam, the Billingsly senior vice-president of branch office operations. Sam was also one of the project's sponsors and had turned into one of the team's strongest supporters. "What do you think, Sam?" Sally queried. "I'm so damned happy I can't stand it," said Sam. "I don't know why those idiots asked such asinine questions! I don't care whether the home office is happy with it or not. They're not the users!"

Questions

6. What are the implications of "the problems with InSight are bigger than InSight" for 1FineInc? For Billingsly?
7. Why might Billingsly's IT group believe they're getting the entire design of AccountNow in the working prototype?
8. How is the tight schedule impacting both Billingsly and 1FineInc?
9. What are some possible reasons why the IT department wanted to see the 3 × 3s before they went through usability testing at the branches?
10. Why was the 1FineInc team surprised by the questions Vicky's team asked during the 3 × 3 results presentation?

The Farmer and the Cowman Must Be Friends

A Lesson Learned

The 1FineInc team moved quickly into low-level detailed design of the tasks they had prototyped in the 3 × 3. As the user experience team worked through the detail design, the 1FineInc developers began assembling the working prototype.

Meeting with the Billingsly IT team couldn't be deferred any longer. Pamela, Basil, and Jean brought the paper screens and the use case documentation work they had just started to a meeting with a couple members of the

IT team. The purpose of the meeting was to walk through the paper proto-type and the use cases that Basil and Jean had just begun writing to document the design of the working prototype. As the meeting progressed, IT became troubled. 1FineInc's use cases were much more focused than the way Billingsly wrote use cases. Vicky's lead developer, Tim, asked, "Where are the other use cases?" Jean and Basil glanced at each other. "What other use cases are you talking about?" Jean posed.

"All the remaining use cases we'll need to develop AccountNow."

"We are only documenting the use cases that reflect the tasks/scenarios in the working prototype. Those were all we were ever writing."

"No, you're supposed to be writing use cases for the entire solution."

"How can we write those use cases if we haven't designed and usability tested them?"

At that, the two teams began discussing the final deliverables. Pamela was certain her team was supposed to document only the use cases reflected in the working prototype. Tim was just as certain that they had contracted 1FineInc to write all the use cases for the entire solution. They were at an impasse. Finally, it was decided that Pamela's team would bring to a follow-up meeting a list of the remaining use cases they still had to write versus the remainder of the use cases covering the entire solution.

Pamela, Jean, and Basil returned to the 1FineInc office to discuss how they had arrived at this point, how to avoid this predicament on their next project, and their plan for compiling the use case list. In the course of their discussion they realized that the use case list was a new deliverable they would include going forward as a part of the 3 × 3. They could actually begin filling in the template during predesign activities, and by the end of the 3 × 3 they would have the list completed. They decided had they adopted this work product at the beginning of the project, they would have been better pre-pared at all points of the project for discussions with IT.

They decided to use a format that would make it easy to track a variety of criteria for each use case (Figure 20.3). The criteria included in the spread-sheet indicated whether the use case was

- For branch office or home office use
- Selected for UCD
- In scope
- User interface design completed
- Usability test completed

Use Case Matrix - Draft

X = Complete   % = In Progress

High Level Use Case	Task Level Use Case	Branch Office	Home Office	Selected for UCD	In Scope	UI Design Complete	Usability Test Completed	Prototyped	Use Case Defined	Biz Requirements Defined
Setup Account	Setup Single	X	X	X	X	X	X	%	%	%
	Setup Joint	X	X	X	X	X	X	%	%	%
	Setup IRA-Traditional	X	X	X	X	X	X	%	%	%
	Setup Custodian	X	X	X	X	X	X	%	%	%
	Setup Trust - SALT	X	X	X						
	Setup Trust - Non-SALT	X	X	X						
	Setup Institutional	X	X	X						
	Setup Investment Club (????)	X	X	X						
	Setup Corporate	X	X	X						

Figure 20.3. Sample use case list.

- Prototyped
- Use case defined
- Business requirements defined

Pamela, Jean, and Basil attended the follow-up meeting armed with their use case list. The meeting went relatively smoothly considering the two groups still needed to iron out which use cases would get documented and which wouldn't. Pamela's team was prepared. They were crisp in their discussion about the high-level design that resulted from the 3 × 3, and they conversed with IT in a language that made sense to IT. The 1FineInc team learned that they needed to make sure the project stakeholders fully understood the outcome of the 3 × 3 and that UCD wasn't finished at the end of high-level design.

Questions

11. What led up to the impasse at the meeting in which the prototype and use cases were reviewed?
12. What are 1FineInc's next steps?

Fast Forward

One day toward the end of the project Sally and Pamela treated the 1FineInc project team to lunch at one of the local Mexican restaurants. While the team celebrated what had evolved into a very successful project, Sally and Pamela sat across from each other at one end of the table thinking back over the rocky beginnings of the project. They reminisced about lessons learned on this project and throughout their careers and about assessing and managing the various aspects of projects. Sally and Pamela talked about their 40+ collective years of experience in HCI. They both had defined and implemented UCD programs as part of the overall design and development process at a variety of companies. And, they had led teams through countless consulting projects. Why was there so much angst during this project, they pondered.

Sally and Pamela were so passionate about their field they began to think about the pursuit work before winning the engagement. Sally said, "You know, when I talk about our 3 × 3, I get very excited. Probably too excited. I'm always so proud of the successes we've had in driving the three unique approaches to the solution down to one through iterative usability testing and prototype refinement. Sometimes I wonder if my excitement and passion for the process itself gets in the way of my fully articulating what gets delivered, especially when I explain it to people outside of our field."

Summary

As Sally and Pamela began enumerating lessons learned around managing client expectations of conceptual design, they kept coming back to a few critical observations:

- When describing conceptual design using iterative paper prototyping and usability testing, specifically the 3 × 3, during the sales pursuit and during the project kickoff, especially to IT developers, technical architects, and managers, it's important to explain fully what will result from the activity. Often the 3 × 3 is done as the final activity of the first phase of the project ("discovery" or "strategy" or "envision"), primarily for the purpose of scoping, sizing, and pricing the remainder of the project, which will include fully designing and developing the solution. At other times it is used as the first activity of the second phase, typically the "design" phase of the project. In either case it is ideally followed by additional rounds of iterative low-, mid-, and high-fidelity prototyping and usability testing. Therefore the deliverable from the conceptual design phase and the 3 × 3 includes only those screens/pages from the selected tasks that have been prototyped. The deliverable will not include all the screens/pages of all the tasks of the final solution.

- It is helpful to show an example of the deliverable from the various design activities during the sales pursuit and again during the project kickoff and first days of the project so the extent of the deliverable is fully understood by the entire team, especially IT, who will be responsible for developing the solution.

- It is important to make sure HCI terms are defined, understood, and perhaps even illustrated by examples/samples to all. Often, HCI specialists use terms similar to those used by IT, such as "conceptual design," "high-level design," "low-level design," "detail design," "use cases," and so forth, and yet each discipline uses these terms in slightly different ways with slightly different understandings.

Further Reading

Rettig, M. (1994). Prototyping for tiny fingers. *Communications of the ACM,* 37:21–27.

Righi, C. (2001). Building the conceptual model and metaphor: the "3 × 3". In Branaghan, R. (Ed.). *Design for people by people: essay on usability.* Chicago: Usability Professionals' Association, pp. 213–219.

Snyder, C. (2003). *Paper prototyping.* San Francisco: Elsevier Science.

Aikot Corporation: A Case Study in Qualitative/Quantitative Remote Evaluation

Carol Farnsworth, Keynote Systems

> *"Look, here's the thing," said Mark. "Truth is, we focus most of our attention on in-store retail, advertising, and packaging. We only built the website because everyone has one. But now all this troubles me. There is a possibility that our website might not be just increasing market share but may actually be contributing to the decline in our market share."*

Decline of a Strong Brand

Aikot Corporation manufactures and sells electronic products, such as televisions, video cassette recorders, video players, radios, stereos, and mobile phones, which are used by both consumers and businesses. Aikot Corporation grew quickly during the 1980s and 1990s, beginning with thousands of retail stores throughout the United States. In the 1990s Aikot expanded to Canada, Central America, South America, and Europe. During the 1990s Aikot was a popular brand and was ranked in the top 100 Global Brands in 1996 by the Business Week/Interbrand report.

Aikot Corporation was creative about marketing their products and used a variety of marketing strategies. They attempted to establish product branding through a 360-degree strategy that included multimedia advertising (print, television, radio), product packaging, and more.

In the mid-1990s the Internet became a viable marketing channel. As part of the overall corporate marketing strategy, Aikot created an online Internet marketing team whose main mission was to develop the corporate website. The first website was launched for the U.S. market, and within a few years the European and Latin American sites were launched.

For years Aikot Corporation enjoyed continual growth in market share and revenue, which resulted in climbing stock prices. But beginning in the late 1990s and in the early 2000s this growth began to steadily and slowly decline. Market share was falling and the value of the brand decreasing. With the rising anxiety there were threats of layoffs, and the Board of Directors contemplated selling off a portion of the business.

Mark, the chief marketing officer, conducts marketing campaigns that drive consumers to the retail stores and the websites. He always makes sure that the in-store teams know when the campaigns are in progress so they are prepared for customers. He also provides the website teams with the content required for each marketing campaign.

In spite of all the careful planning, Mark did not understand why the company was experiencing the slow, yet steady, decline. During a weekly executive meeting, Mark responded to his peers' questions regarding this issue. "The public perception and feedback we received from our customers is that they recognize Aikot to be a leader in innovative design and that we have competitive pricing."

To try to get a better handle on the declining market share problem, Mark sought guidance from a variety of market and consumer research firms to obtain a better understanding of the purchase decision-making process and the marketplace as a whole.

From this consumer purchase-behavior research, Mark validated his hypothesis that the web is a key channel in the purchase decision process for both consumers and businesses. He knows that if a website does not meet visitors' goals, then the visitors move on to other websites and brands. Visit-and-purchase success on a website increases the likelihood consumers will return to the site, recommend the brand to others, and purchase additional products either online or off-line.

Mark learned of the growing trend for consumers to transact online with suppliers directly rather than with resellers, such as Best Buy and Office Depot. The web is a key online channel for making purchase decisions and transacting, and until recently consumers have been shopping more on reseller sites than on supplier sites. Consumers use online portals and search engine results to find resellers when beginning their product research. The reseller websites are generally comprehensive and convenient one-stop shops with multiple products and suppliers available on one website, making comparison shopping possible and convenient.

Resellers have made it easy for consumers to make the move from off-line to online transactions. They were the first to develop websites with online shopping and purchase transaction functionality. They offer low discount pricing because they buy large quantities from suppliers. Consumers can comparison shop without leaving the website. Resellers have invested in understanding the user experience on their websites and have made continual improvements to the user experience over the years. Generally, consumers find what they are looking for, at a price that is acceptable, and complete the purchase process online.

Mark also learned that consumers are spending more time researching products and looking for information on the web. To keep up, companies need to understand what is driving and influencing the purchase decision process and give consumers what they want—good quality products at a fair price, using a website that is easy to find and purchase products.

Using this research data, Mark began to take a good look at Aikot's online initiatives. Aikot's products are excellent, innovative, and seem to meet customers' needs. They have strong competitors, but Mark believes Aikot's marketing continues to be superior. They have the majority of the market share, although those numbers are decreasing.

Mark understands that competition is tough everywhere and comes from unexpected places. Website visitors researching products can browse products and services from multiple companies at one time by opening multiple web browsers. People will keep looking until they find exactly what they want at the price they are willing to pay. Even auction sites, like eBay, are strong competitors for many businesses. Other websites serve as conduits for many other companies, such as BizRate.com and Buy.com. Through these single websites potential customers can see many companies' products. With stores, customers must travel to get there. So if they don't find the perfect product in the store, sometimes they will take the next best thing. On the web, visitors must be able to find and learn about products. If you provide a way for people to buy products on your site, then you have to make sure people can actually complete the full transaction.

Aikot's website has a pretty good e-commerce application, and most of the customers who do want to purchase online are able to complete the process. However, Mark realizes there may be other difficulties of which he is not aware. For example, he knows that an important aspect of the consumer product research process is finding and comparing prices for products. Some products on the Aikot site do not have prices, and he does not know what impact this has on the customer experience.

Mark reflected that from a business perspective, it is very difficult to provide pricing information for cell phones. Cell phone sales depend on available wireless phone service within the location of the buyer. As a result, cell phones are sold by service providers, such as Sprint and Verizon. The "service package" includes cell phones and, depending on what the current promotion is, the phone unit itself might be free or cost several hundred dollars. Mark knows consumers want to see prices and will continue to go to the site for this purpose.

Aikot doesn't offer pricing on most of their sites because the list price may not be the price available for any given individual consumer. There are so many dependencies based on location alone. Cell phones may not be available for some consumers if wireless providers don't have service in their area. Cell phone units may be free of charge with some service contracts, whereas with others the consumer may have to pay full price. If consumers want to upgrade their phone before the service contract is complete, they may have to pay a penalty fee on top of the cost of the phone unit. For these reasons, Aikot doesn't publish cell phone pricing on the sites that do not have online stores.

Mark realizes that he does not know very much about the experiences visitors have on the Aikot sites. Specifically, he doesn't know if visitors can find what they are looking for on the site or if they are successful and satisfied. He doesn't know if the experience on the website is having a positive or negative impact on the impression of the Aikot brand. He doesn't know when in the purchase process people are visiting the site. He has some assumptions about who the visitors are, but he does not have any data to support his assumptions.

The data Mark currently has available are the traffic pattern data, such as the number of unique visitors to each page, number of pages for an average site visit, and time spent on each page, provided by a product called "Hit Box." To capture the data using the Hit Box application, pages are tagged with code that tracks the number of people who visit that page. For multistep task flows, or process funnels, such as the registration process and online store checkout for purchases, Hit Box provides information about how many people begin the process funnel, from which pages in the process funnel people drop out, and how many people complete the process funnel all the way to the confirmation page. This provides information about conversion rates—the actual number of people completing the checkout process resulting in a purchase divided by the number who begin the checkout process. The fundamental questions for Mark are "why are visitors dropping out of the

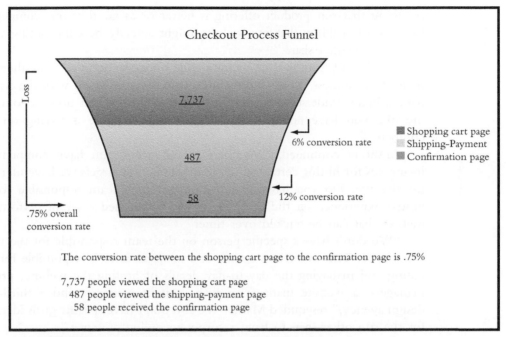

Figure 21.1. A funnel graph depicting the checkout process.

purchase process funnel?" and "why are they not completing the purchase transaction?" (See Figure 21.1.)

At lunch one day with his friend Anthony, whose company does business exclusively on the web selling beauty and cleaning supplies primarily to small businesses with fewer than 200 employees, Mark was talking about the website and what he knows and what he needs to learn about the user experience on the Aikot website. He asked Anthony for suggestions.

"I have several people on my website development team who are responsible for understanding our site visitors," Anthony responded. "The data they collect drives our development efforts. I have learned to pay attention to site visitors. If they are not successful in finding what they want, they will not buy our products, visit the site in the future, or refer the site to their friends. If people don't come back to the site, I lose money."

"Look, here's the thing," said Mark. "Truth is, we focus most of our attention on in-store retail, advertising, and packaging. We only built the website because everyone has one. But now all this troubles me. Based on everything I know and have learned from the consumer research, and assuming that our product offering is better or as good as our competitors, there is a possibility that our website might actually be contributing to the decline in market share."

"Yes!" said Anthony. "A website is almost never 'neutral'—it either helps or hurts a business. You need to find out what's going on with the site and have a better understanding of visitors' experience. Right now, it sounds to me like you have no idea what impact your website is having on your company."

Anthony continued, "Members of our web team have compensation incentives for hitting certain success and satisfaction targets we have identified for the site. Do you have anyone on your web team responsible for the visitor experience on the sites? Have you established a set of performance metrics that can be tracked over time?"

"We don't have a specific person on the team responsible for the visitor experience. The web teams consist of a manager who is responsible for executing and managing the day-to-day details of hosting the website, product managers, a website manager, a web content manager, and a third-party design agency," responded Mark. "We also don't have specific goals identified for the site other than to have a corporate online presence."

"You need to have people on your team who understand the site visitors and the impact the site is having on your brand. You also need to identify the goals and objectives of the site and establish targets for measuring the visitor experience," said Anthony.

The course was clear to Mark: Aikot needed to review and renew their overall marketing plan, establish goals for the site, hire team members who can manage the visitor experience, and understand the experience on the websites from a visitor's point of view.

Questions

1. What types of questions should Mark ask himself about his website to give him clues about how it is affecting sales?
2. What methods of customer feedback does Aikot use today, and why are they not enough?
3. What about the company structure, team makeup, and process contributed to the lack of knowledge about the influence of the website on the company's bottom line?
4. What should Mark do now that he understands the source of the problem may be the website?

The Nature of Quantitative/Qualitative Remote Website Visitor Research

Staffing the Customer Experience Team

Mark knew he had his work cut out for him. Changes would have to be made to the overall marketing plan, recognizing that the website plays a critical role in preserving market share. Aikot's business managers' perceptions of the role of the website in the overall marketing plan will need to change as well. Mark decided to first focus on team development, because any marketing plan needs a strong online marketing team. Anthony had told him about a new role many of his peers in other corporations had created, Director of Customer Experience. Mark decided it was time to hire one for Aikot.

After an intensive search, Mark hired Anne to lead the customer experience team. She has both an MBA and a Master's degree in Human Factors. Throughout her career, Anne has helped software application and website development teams make the experiences of the people who use the applications and visit the websites more enjoyable and successful. In short, she helps teams to focus on the customers' needs. At Aikot, Anne's role would be to listen to the customer and to communicate customer requirements and the strengths and weaknesses of the website to the design and development team.

Anne understands that the Internet plays an important role in the overall customer experience, especially in the purchase decision-making process. Each year, customers spend an increasing amount of time on the Internet researching products, finding information, and making purchases. Success in her new role at Aikot would be accomplished as Anne discovers what drives and influences customers' purchase decision process and decision to make future purchases with the company. She must translate this knowledge into actionable development plans for the web team.

Anne's compensation plan for the next several years is based on improving the online customer experience and increasing brand value. To do this, Anne needs to have information on the current customer purchasing experience on the website. Anne will focus on the prepurchase, purchase, and postpurchase processes on the Aikot website.

To be successful in achieving Aikot's customer experience goals, Anne needs people on her team with usability and user-centered design skills. Anne's team comprises the website managers for three countries: David from Germany, Tomas from Mexico, and Jennifer from the United States.

Anne was concerned she wouldn't be able to do what was needed to manage the customer experience on the websites with the existing team whose primary focus is on executing the day-to-day activities required to manage the websites. Anne believed that having another person design and execute the user research activities was critical to the success of the new plan. Anne called this the "customer experience manager" role. The person hired in this role would have a background in usability and user-centered design.

Anne wanted to hire an external person for the customer experience manager role, but Mark insisted that there could not be any new head count positions this year. He did give Anne the approval to hire a contractor on a part-time basis. So, Anne hired Cynthia Wilson, a user-centered design/usability consultant who has been working with global corporations to improve customer experience on websites. Cynthia has extensive experience conducting U.S. and international focus groups, in-lab, one-on-one usability studies, and remote qualitative/quantitative research.

Reviewing the Consumer Purchase Process

Anne met with her team—David, Tomas, Jennifer, and Cynthia—to review key aspects of the online purchase process and to set goals for improving the online customer experience. The meeting started first with a high-level review of the consumer purchase process.

After introductions, Anne asked David to summarize the consumer pre-purchase process. David explained, "The customer experience during the prepurchase process involves all activities consumers complete before making a decision to buy a product. This stage of the buying process includes

- Receiving communication from the company about their products through multimedia advertising, such as television, radio, newspaper, magazines, billboards, etc.;
- Learning about products from family and friends; and
- Visiting the stores and websites."

Cynthia interjected, "We have to make it easier for visitors to find information in the prepurchase stage since learning about the products is the primary customer goal at this stage. Competitive intelligence research conducted by Keynote Systems, Inc. indicates that good websites typically have visit success rates of 80% or more."

Next, Tomas described the purchase process on the Aikot sites. "Customers are able to purchase products online on the U.S. and Germany websites.

On the Mexico website, visitors are only able to shop for and learn about the products and locate stores to purchase the products. We do not have an online store on this site but plan to add this functionality in the next 6 to 12 months. To add online shopping to the Mexico site we need make sure the site has everything required to make the purchase online, including product displays, product descriptions, shopping baskets, registration, billing, delivery, shipping, payment, and confirmation notifications."

Jennifer cautioned that other considerations would have to be included in the online shopping experience. "Once products are purchased, customers often need additional support, such as learning how to set-up, fix, and/or learn more about how to use the products. The Aikot website has an extensive customer support section and is maintained by the corporate marketing web development team."

Identifying Aikot Website Visitors

"Who visits the website?" Cynthia asked.

Being the most familiar with the web analytics data that reports site traffic, David was quick to respond. "We have 387,328 unique visits per month and, of those, 9.5% are returning visitors."

Cynthia said, "Traffic data do provide important information. But what are the profiles of the people who visit the site?"

"I am sure they are the same people who visit and purchase products in our stores," said Jennifer. "We have four main customer profiles—enthusiasts, conservatives, stylists, and low budget—developed from market research studies conducted for our off-line stores and sales. The enthusiasts are early adopter consumers who like to be the first to have the latest products, and their purchase cycles are somewhat short. Conservatives do everything they can to extend the life of their product, and they spend a very long time in the prepurchase decision phase. The stylists care most about the impressions they make on their friends and would rather have a product with a lot of style instead of one with the most functionality. Finally, the low budget consumer wants the best product for the lowest cost. The low budget consumer buys only products on sale or last year's models. They also purchase refurbished products when we offer them."

"We use content, product messaging, and advertising for the websites similar to what we use in the stores. It makes the production process more efficient," said Tomas.

"Do you have any idea who the actual people are who visit the website?" asked Cynthia.

"Look, Cynthia, the fact is, we have not conducted any research on the sites. For development purposes we have been making the assumption that the people who visit the website are the same as those who visit our stores," replied Anne. "After all, why would we think otherwise? Besides, not all of our websites have online stores, so I would think that the profiles of our brick-and-mortar stores are more important than the website visitor profiles."

Cynthia folded her hands on the table. "This is important because this means that you also do not know why visitors are coming to the site and whether or not they are successful. It also means that we have no idea what impact the website has on visitors' impression of Aikot the company and decisions to purchase Aikot products or not. Do you have key web metrics in place for the website so you know how well the site is performing?"

"No," responded Anne. "We need to develop key web metrics at some point during this year, but in the meantime it sounds like we need to learn more about the visitors of our website. Cynthia, you have conducted research all over the world for large international corporations, what methodologies do you use to learn more about site visitors?"

Cynthia explained, "Quantitative/qualitative online remote research is most effective for answering the types of questions we have for this site. The research I am proposing is quantitative in that we invite a large number of people to participate. Generally, 200 to 400 participants is a good number, but if we want to segment the data by certain criteria such as customer profile or visit purpose, we would want 400 to 800 participants. The research is qualitative in that we capture behavioral data as the participants are navigating the site and we can ask open-ended questions about why they are doing what they are doing. Some of the behavioral data that are captured includes navigation paths, time on each page, time on each task, and number of pages visited."

"I thought six to eight people were enough to obtain insights into the usability of a website or design," interjected Tomas.

Cynthia responded, "Traditional usability studies where we ask six to eight people to interact with an existing website or a new design for a website will not provide us with the necessary visitor data to answer the questions to help us understand who is visiting our website, why they come, and are they successful. Traditional usability studies rely on a handful of people who match a particular user profile to interact with a website, application, or device to help us understand if there are any problems with the design. The usability sessions provide good indications of the problems people may encounter, but they don't tell you how often they happen to real customers and visitors to your website."

"Quantitative research is well suited for answering a number of questions organizations may have about their website and help business managers make decisions regarding development efforts that may cost hundreds of thousands and even millions of dollars to build," continued Cynthia. "Using statistically significant sample sizes of 200 to 400, business managers have more confidence in understanding the strengths and weaknesses of a website than on the responses of six to eight people."

"For the type of exploratory research we need for the Aikot website, we will rely on people naturally visiting the website and in statistically significant quantities—around 200 to 600 completed studies for this type of exploratory research. The more participants we have, the more segmenting we can do and still have large numbers in the sample size. The sample size we need for this study is partly dependent on how many segments we want to analyze after we collect all the data. For a study with no segmentation, 200 participants is a good number and will provide statistically significant data at a high confidence rate. To answer our questions, we need to listen to people who are visiting our websites," replied Cynthia.

"I've seen pop-up surveys on a few of the websites I surf. I completed one survey and they asked a zillion questions about my experience," added Jennifer.

Cynthia replied, "The problem with a 'survey' is that people have to *remember* an experience and self-report data of an event that happened some time in the past. People do not always report information about a past experience accurately. If we conduct quantitative/qualitative studies online, we can obtain both self-reported and behavioral data. We can also capture how long it takes visitors to complete their tasks, how long they spend on each page, and their navigation paths during their visit. It is a known fact that self-reported information does not always match actual behaviors. This is why we need research methodologies that help us gather as much information as possible. The quantitative results give significance to the self-reported information and behaviors, whereas the qualitative observations deliver insights into the visitors' thoughts and actions that help us understand the strengths and weaknesses of the site."

"How can we do that?" asked David.

"With applications that allow us to conduct remote evaluations. Some people call this 'unmoderated' research because the application does it automatically, participants are in their own environment, using any computer available to them at that time, and a researcher is not present during the evaluation. The data analysis from this type of research is much more robust than analysis of pure survey questions as well," responded Cynthia. "We will be able to analyze the navigation path, correlate actions/factors with positive and negative experiences, and segment the data to identify differences between needs of visitors based on what they came to the site to do. We will also be able to conduct an explicit or implicit needs assessment, and . . ."

Tomas interrupted Cynthia. "I don't understand how you are going to get enough data to do all this analysis and what data will be collected."

Cynthia responded, "There are a number of companies, such as Keynote Systems, Inc., with software applications that allow teams like ours to conduct quantitative/qualitative research online with 200, 400, 600, or more website visitors. Since a large number of people naturally visiting the site are invited to participate in the study, we will have confidence in the findings regarding the strengths and weaknesses of the site. In addition, the large sample sizes will help us understand who is visiting the site and provide data to be able to create profiles of these site visitors."

"The remote evaluation applications allow us to ask participants questions while behind the scenes the application captures data, such as time on task, page load time, URLs visited, and words entered in search entry fields," continued Cynthia. "The steps for conducting this type of evaluation include designing the research activities and questions, programming the study using an online remote application, adding code to invite participants to the Aikot website, collecting data, analyzing the data, and reporting findings and recommendations."

Anne nodded her head. "It's pretty clear that we need to first identify our goals for this year. Second, we need to identify key metrics for the website and, finally, learn more about conducting the quantitative/qualitative remote online exploratory research so we can learn more about our visitors."

Questions

5. Based on the discussion of the team members, what should some of the overall goals for the Aikot user experience team be?
6. What are some of the advantages of remote testing that Anne and her team can exploit?
7. What information should the team be able to collect by conducting an online remote research study?
8. Anne and her team want to ensure that the visit experience is as natural and unobtrusive as possible. How could they best invite and entice visitors to participate?
9. How could the team structure the study itself to be as natural and unobtrusive as possible?

Planning and Conducting the Quantitative/ Qualitative Remote Study

"Looks like we are ready to begin planning the study," said Cynthia. "In this quantitative/qualitative remote evaluation, we will invite 200 to 800 website visitors to participate. We will invite people who are naturally visiting the website by intercepting them with a pop-up, or 'floater image,' as they are called today. This floater image contains a link to the research study and is almost like an advertisement asking the visitor to give their opinions and feedback about their experience on the website. This type of evaluation is great because people complete the study using their own computers at home or work or any place they have access to a computer. They can also take as much time as they want to explore your website and answer the questions. Giving people this type of freedom results in a richness of data that we are not always able to get in more traditional user research."

"Aikot has three websites—United States, Germany, and Mexico," Cynthia continued. "Since this is the first user research to be conducted on the site, I recommend that we focus this study on the U.S. site. Later we can have the study script translated into German and Spanish and conduct the study on the other sites independent of the U.S. evaluation."

"I agree," said Anne.

Cynthia worked with Anne and the team to finalize the study questions. In addition, she arranged for a one-time use license for the online remote application for the Aikot U.S. website. Cynthia programmed the study, sent the study URL to the team, and asked the team to review the programmed study and send her feedback.

Here is the flow of the study from the participants' point of view:

- Visitors arrive at the home page of the website.
- Visitors are intercepted with an invitation to participate in the study.
- Participants answer a few key questions before completing their self-directed task.

    How did you hear about Aikot?

    How many times have you visited the Aikot website in the past?

    What is the primary purpose of your visit to the Aikot website today? Please select the most appropriate answer from the list below.

    Which Aikot products are you mainly interested in? Please select one.

    Would you be interested in buying any of the following online? Please select all that apply.

- Before beginning the next part of the study, participants are asked to download a small application. This application collects behavioral data such as URLs visited, time on task, and so on. These data can also be collected through a proxy server if the download option is not desirable.
- For this part of the study, participants interact with the Aikot website, completing the tasks they originally intended to complete when they came to the site. This is the only task in the study, and it is self-directed. As soon as the participant is finished their task, they click on the "answer" button.

  Here's how we phrase the self-directed task: "Now please continue doing what you originally came to the Aikot site to do today. Spend as much time and effort as you typically would on any site visit. When you are finished, please click the 'Answer' button."
- After participants complete the self-directed task, we ask them to answer questions designed to capture the overall experience while completing their intended task.

  Which of the following main content on the Aikot site did you visit today?

  Did you find the information you were looking for?

  How successful were you in achieving your primary goal for today's visit? (This is a rating question followed by free-form questions: Why were you successful? or Why were you not successful?)

  How satisfied are you with the website overall? (This is a rating question followed by free-form questions: Why were you satisfied? or Why were you not satisfied?)

  What, if any, difficulties or frustrations did you encounter? Please select all that apply. (This is a multiple-select question and includes responses that describe common difficulties that might be encountered, no difficulties encountered, and Other—please specify.)
- In the next part of the study, participants answer questions regarding their current Aikot product ownership. This section also includes questions regarding how much influence—positive or negative—the Aikot website had on the previous purchase of the products.
- Next, participants are asked several questions about their future intent to purchase new products and which brand they intend to select for purchase.
- After the current and future purchasing behavior questions, we ask them questions regarding brand value.

For example, we ask, "How did your visit today change your
opinion of Aikot in general? Ratings 1, 2 much worse opinion,
3, 4, 5 no impact to my opinion, and 6, 7 much better opinion.
We also ask participants to rate future calls to action such as
likelihood to return to the site, likelihood to purchase from the
site, likelihood to purchase in a store as a result of this visit, and
likelihood to recommend this site to other people.
When you consider everything surrounding your interaction with
Aikot, what is your overall satisfaction with the company itself?

- In the final section of the study, we ask a variety of demographic
questions targeted to help us understand the profile of the visitors. This
section helps us identify and validate our four main off-line profiles:
enthusiasts, conservatives, stylists, and low budget customers.

"This is great to see the programmed study. Are you sure it is not too long?"
asked Jennifer.

Cynthia shook her head. "I've conducted hundreds of these exploratory
studies and have found that 30 to 40 questions is an acceptable length for a
quantitative/qualitative remote study, especially since we are not going to
give these participants an incentive and that this study should take 15 to 20
minutes longer than the participants' normal visit to the website. If we
planned to conduct a regular directed task-based online study so we can
understand the strengths and weaknesses of the site in more detail, we would
need a longer study. When we ask participants to spend more than 20 to 25
minutes (but never longer than 45 minutes) on a study, we reward their
efforts with a gift certificate."

The team was full of questions. Jennifer wanted to know, now that the
questionnaire was programmed into the application, how to launch the study
and what the next steps were, such as how they'd get participants. David
wondered whether they would be able to see the data while the study was
in progress. Tomas wanted to know how participants in non-English language
tests would be able to see the study in their own language.

Cynthia was glad that the team had a lot of questions about conducting
the research.

"How are we going to get people to participate in this study?" asked
Jennifer.

Cynthia responded, "This is an exploratory study, so we need people
who are naturally visiting our website. Intercepting people from the home
page is the best way to invite people who are visiting a website. We might

use different invitation methods for studies with different goals. For example, if we want to conduct a directed task-based usability study or competitive comparison study, we would use a panel of participants. We would recruit the participants from a market research vendor and invite them through an e-mail invitation. Embedded within the invitation would be a link to our study."

"That makes sense. So we are planning to intercept people on our site for this study. How exactly do we do this?" ask Jennifer.

Cynthia replied, "Potential participants can be recruited using pop-up Javascript code, but with pop-up blockers so prevalent these days, most website visitors won't see the invitation. A more effective alternative is to add layered-based 'floater code' to the home page HTML. This is also Javascript code that is inserted into the header of the home page, but instead of a pop-up an image appears on the page. The image contains an invitation to participate in the study and can be set to appear at specific intervals. For example, if a website has high traffic, the floater image may be set to appear at a frequency of 1 out of every 50 visitors and for a website with very few unique visitors the floater image may be set to appear at frequency of 1 out of every 2 visitors."

David, the team member most familiar with the site traffic, suggested, "We should use floater code and intercept at a rate of one out of three visitors. Here's the message we can present to our visitors. . . ." (See Figure 21.2.)

Before adding the code to the website, everyone reviewed the programmed study and gave approvals for launch. All final modifications were made. The study was ready to be launched. Jennifer, the U.S. website manager, had her web development team add the floater code to the home page header. The floater code is the Javascript code that is added to the home page of the website to intercept people naturally visiting the website. The

> "Aikot wants your feedback!
>
> In an effort to improve our Internet services, we are conducting this survey to gain insights into your views of our web site."
>
> Accept   Thanks, but not now

Figure 21.2. Intercept floater image.

```
<script language="JavaScript1.2"><!--
var InterceptLikelihood = 0.01;
var InterceptTaskKey = 'A1B23C4D5E6F';
var InterceptType = 'Layer';
//Height and Width in pixels
var InterceptWidth = '400';
var InterceptHeight = '450';
function HandleIntercept()
{
 try {
  if (Math.random() >= (InterceptLikelihood*5)) return;
  var s = document.createElement('script');
  s.src = 'http://company.com/applications/intercept/filter_page.asp?inv=' +
InterceptTaskKey + '&type=' + InterceptType + '&rate=' +
InterceptLikelihood + '&max=5' + '&width=' + InterceptWidth + '&height='
+ InterceptHeight;
  document.body.insertBefore(s, document.body.firstChild);
  window.Window = 'primary';
 }
 catch(e){ }
}
if (window.attachEvent) window.attachEvent('onload',HandleIntercept);
 else window.addEventListener('load',HandleIntercept,false);
//--></script>
```

Figure 21.3. Example intercept floater code.

team inserted the code between the <HEAD> and </HEAD> tags on the web page except for the <BODY> tag. The <BODY> code either needs to be combined with the page's <BODY> tag or to replace it. Figure 21.3 shows an example of what the code looked like.

The website managers sent a note to the team letting them know the study had begun. The floater code was removed from the web page as soon as the team's goal of 300 completed studies was met.

Analysis of the Data

As soon as data were collected from the desired number of participants, Cynthia began the analysis of the data, documenting the key findings and recommendations in a report. Cynthia's final report would be in the form of an in-depth PowerPoint presentation that she would deliver to Anne and the rest of the team.

"Cynthia, now that we have all the data collected, what is the next step?" asked Tomas.

"To analyze the data, we use the remote online research application, WebEffective from Keynote Systems, Inc., which collects all the data from the participants," responded Cynthia. "The application makes all the responses to the questions available in percent and number of participants format. We will also be able to segment, or filter, the data by various criteria that are important to us, such as visit intent, success, satisfaction, and other key metrics." (See Figure 21.4.)

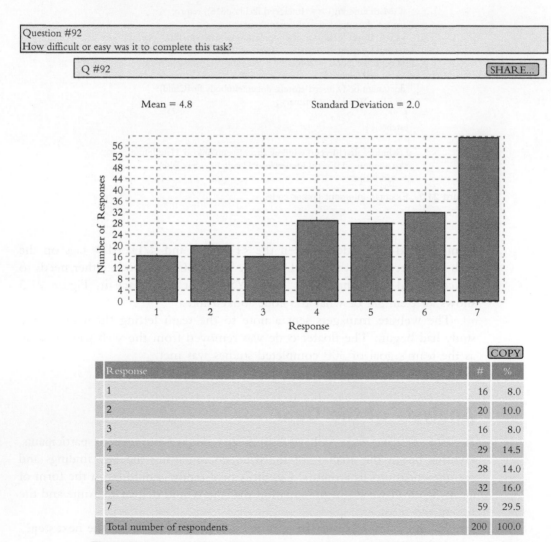

Figure 21.4. Aggregated question responses inside the evaluation tool.

Cynthia continued, "The key aspects of this phase of the project include an analysis of

- Qualitative and quantitative feedback associated with the participant's own task;
- Behavioral data using click streams, which shows the navigational paths visitors took during their visit, the total time taken to complete the primary task, and number of pages visitors viewed during the task completion;
- Visitors' attitudes, preferences, and motivations by key visit intent segments, such as research product information, see what's new, and compare products; and
- Visitors' overall satisfaction, their ratings for site organization, and frustration while completing tasks on the website.

"As I analyze the data, I make recommendations for improving the customer experience based on usability best practices and visitor insights," Cynthia explained.

"Here's a specific analysis example. One of the goals of the study was to understand how successful and satisfied visitors are with their experiences on the website," Cynthia continued. "I want to know if success and satisfaction ratings differ based on the visit intent. Visit intent is the main reason why people come to the website and answers the question 'why did you come here today?'"

"How do we know the main reasons why people come to our site?" asked Jennifer.

Cynthia answered, "The third question in our study asked people about their primary purpose of their visit. Here's the exact question we asked." Why are people coming to the Website?

"When we look at the online report that aggregates all participants' responses, we can see that visitors come to the website primarily to research product information, see what is new, compare products, and look for pricing," continued Cynthia. "Since we cannot predict all of the reasons why visitors come to a website, we include a response called 'Other (Please specify).' This gives the participant an opportunity to tell us what they intend to do on the website if their visit intent is not listed. The 'Other' responses are stored as freeform responses, which we read and categorize. Sometimes the responses are variations of the list of tasks presented in the question. This response type is a great way to learn new reasons why people come to a website as well. For example, in another study I conducted I learned that people came to the website to find the address of local stores. The website did not have this information and it was later added to the website."

"To find out if there is a difference between success, satisfaction, and brand impact ratings based on different reasons why people visit the website, I used the filter tool in the application to look at the data segmented by each of the four main reasons why people visit the site. I found that satisfaction rates varied slightly depending on visit intent. Success and brand impact had higher variances depending on why people are visiting the website. In other words, visitors were least successful when they were researching product information and consequently, their website visit had a lower impact on the 'brand' or their image of Aikot as a company. To measure the brand impact we asked 'How did your visit today change your opinion of Aikot in general?'" (See Figure 21.6.)

"What were the rating questions asked for these three metrics—success, satisfaction, and brand impact," asked Tomas.

Cynthia responded, "Here are the three 7-point rating questions we asked after participants completed their own task on the site. Remember the task they completed was self-directed—it was the task they originally came to the website to complete. Ratings 6 to 7 are the scores we use to determine success, satisfaction, and brand value." (See Sidebar.)

Visit Success

In thinking about your own expectations for the Aikot site how successful were you in achieving your goals for today's visit?

1 = not at all successful

2 3 4 5 6 7 = extremely successful

Satisfaction

Considering your experience today, how satisfied are you with the Aikot website?

1 = not at all satisfied

2 3 4 5 6 7 = extremely satisfied

Brand Impact

How did your visit today change your opinion of Aikot in general?

1 = Much worse opinion of Aikot

2

3

4 = No impact to my opinion of Aikot

5

6

7 = Much better opinion of Aikot

Cynthia continued with the analysis explanation, "Ninety participants' primary visit intent was to research product information. After filtering the data by 'research product information,' we see that 34% of the 90 participants rated their success as a 6 or 7 on a 7-point scale, 48% of the 90 participants rated their satisfaction as a 6 or 7 on a 7-point scale, and 21% of the 90 participants said they had a much better opinion of Aikot as a result of their visit. These scores are low compared with the 59 participants who came to the website to see what's new. The 'see what's new' group reported a success rate of 67%, satisfaction at 53%, and brand impact (influence of the website on the opinion of Aikot, the company) at 58%." (See Figure 21.5.)

"How can we learn more about what's going on for each of these groups of participants," asked Jennifer.

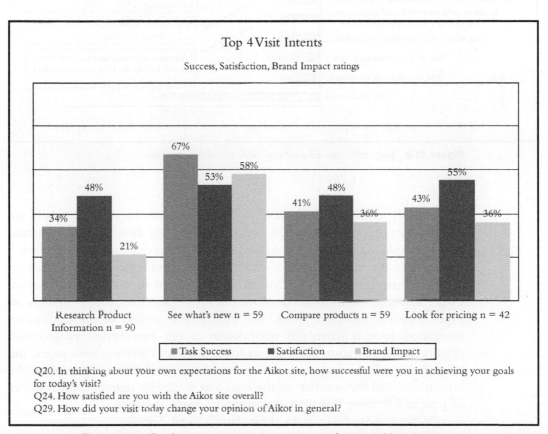

Figure 21.5. Top four visit intents: task success, satisfaction, and brand impact.

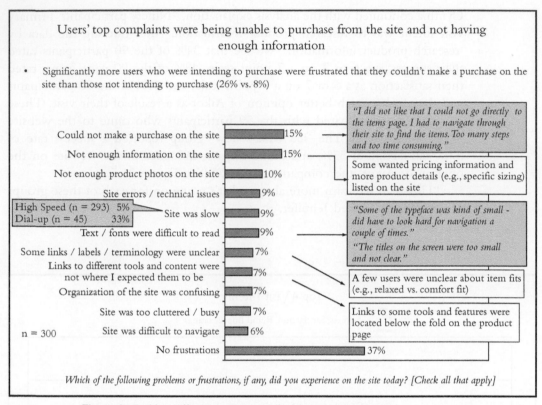

Figure 21.6. Main difficulties encountered while completing the task.

Cynthia responded, "We have to dig deeper into the data, especially the freeform responses from the open-ended questions, the difficulties encountered while completing their own task, and review the navigation paths. Here is a summary of the main difficulties visitors encountered." (See Figure 21.6.)

In the navigation paths, Cynthia was interested in visitors' back-button usage, first-page clicks, time spent on each page, and the average number of pages visited to complete a task. She used a small section of the clickstream navigation to summarize this information in the PowerPoint presentation (Figure 21.7). In Figure 21.7, the yellow rectangles represent web pages, the black lines indicate the navigation paths, the magenta lines represent back-button use, and the number on the lines and rectangles represent the number of people following this path and visiting a particular page.

"What can we learn from these data?" asked Tomas.

Unsuccessful visitors are using the back button extensively for navigation, which may indicate that link labels are not helpful in predicting content location.

- Back button navigation
    - Usually indicates the user does not find what they thought they would find on a given page.
    - This excerpt from the clickstream of unsuccessful visits shows extensive back button navigation.

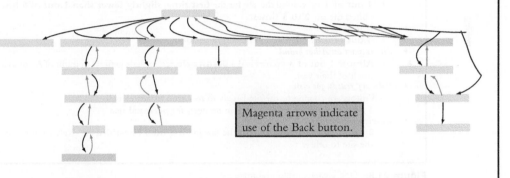

Magenta arrows indicate use of the Back button.

Figure 21.7. Click-stream navigation paths.

Cynthia responded, "We know that Aikot visitors want to be able to view all products within a particular category so they can see the similarities and differences in the products at a glance. They also want help in selecting the right products that meet their needs. Once they own the product, visitors expect help using the product and want to get involved with Aikot."

Jennifer wanted to know more, "What other key findings do you have?"

Cynthia continued, "We learned about who is visiting the website, their profile, reasons for visiting, and impact of the site on their image of the company. I summarized most of this information on one slide." (See Figure 21.8.) "Other slides in the report contain additional information. In summary, visitors had most difficulty with

- Particular products are not available,
- Too many clicks to find something,
- Pricing information not available,

USA Visitor Profile Summary

Aikot's USA site visitors can be described as:

- *Age/gender/household*
  - **67%** of the site visitors are between the ages of **25–49 years**; **71%** are **male**; **28%** live in a **single household with no children**.
- *Brand loyal*
  - **58%** currently own an Aikot product – **Aikot 3329** is one of the **most popular** phone models.
- *New to the Aikot website*
  - **1 out of 4** are visiting the site for the **first time; slightly fewer than 1 out of 6** have visited the site **2 to 5 times**.
- *Likely to shop online*
  - **1 out of 3** are interested in **buying a product online**.
- *Site impact on Aikot brand*
  - **Almost 1 out of 3** visitors had a **positive** change in their general opinion of Aikot as a result of their visit.
- *Primary reason for visit*
  - Visitors are coming to the site largely to **research product info (28%)**.
  - **3 out of 5** visitors are interested in products for **personal use**.
- *Re-visits and referral*
  - **2 out of 5** are likely to **re-visit** the site and **less than one-third** are likely to recommend the site to others.

Figure 21.8. U.S. visitor profile summary.

- Poor search functionality, and
- Information about products was hard to find.

"In addition, visitors had the lowest satisfaction with

- Support area,
- Help choosing a product,
- Look and feel, and
- Finding product information.

"In interpreting the data from this study, we can say that most of the factors causing difficulty related to visitors not easily finding what they were looking for are caused by one or more of the following website design issues:

- Poor site architecture (how the site is organized),
- Lack of pertinent content,
- Poor search functionality, and
- The 'look and feel' of the website was also singled out as a dissatisfier."

"What should we do to improve the website," asked Tomas.

"We should think about rearchitecting the site. To begin this process we should perform a card sort exercise to determine how visitors perceive the site content should be organized, ensure that the main horizontal navigation bar is consistent across the site, and ensure that navigation choices are presented in a way that reflect the way the site is organized," Cynthia answered. "We should also use 'bread crumbs' to show the current path through the site hierarchy, create a site map to depict the site hierarchy, and provide easy-to-understand 'deep links' to popular areas."

Cynthia's complete presentation entailed 63 slides. She was able to develop a story about who is visiting the website, why they are coming to the site, and whether or not they are successful and satisfied—all the goals the team set out to accomplish with the online study. In her executive summary, Cynthia summarized the problems visitors had with the site (Figure 21.9).

The team was surprised at how much they learned about their website visitors. They now have a better understanding of why people come to the website, whether or not they are successful in completing their tasks, what works well on the site, what needs to be improved, and what needs to be added.

Executive Summary

- **Overall: visitors *love* the Aikot brand, and they *tolerate* the Aikot site.**
  - ➢ The site does not have a high influence on visitors because information is buried deep in the site or release dates are inaccurate, but they still come often because they're **eager to find out more about Aikot products**.
    - As a matter of fact, visitors who love the latest technology, come to the web site specifically to find out about products and they are very interested in new products and when they are available
  - ➢ The **main reason** behind visitors' lack of enthusiasm for the Aikot site is the site's poor organization which makes it difficult to find what they are looking for.
    - Visitors wish the site would be much more **structured and organized**, with **better search capabilities**.
    - They also wish that the information about dates for new product releases would be **more accurate** by providing new models when promised.
  - ➢ Visitors don't want to share their experience of the site with others and they are not inspired to purchase an Aikot product based on their site visits. However, they **do** want to revisit the site.
    - They come to the site to try to find information. **They love the Aikot brand regardless of their experience on the site.**

Figure 21.9. Executive summary.

The results of this study were a particular revelation for Mark, the chief marketing officer. He had no idea how influential the website is on consumers' purchase decision behavior. The role of the web is critical during the active decision-making stages in consumers' purchase decision behavior. With this in mind, he also realized that the Aikot websites have some serious problems, especially because fewer than 50% are successful in completing their primary visit task. The Aikot website is not positively impacting visitors' opinion of the brand and, in fact, may be one of the causes of the slow, yet steady, decline in market share.

Mark was grateful for all the work Anne and her team did to conduct this research, and he realized they need to evaluate their websites on an ongoing basis to understand the website's impact and success. As a result of this study, Mark and Anne spearheaded the following customer-centered design plan for the Aikot websites:

- Conduct semiannual exploratory studies where participants are instructed to complete self-directed tasks. Questions should include the following:

    Who is visiting the site?

    Why are they coming to the site?

    Are they successful?

    Are they looking for information that is not available on the site? If yes, what information are they looking for that they cannot find?

    Are they satisfied with the website and with the company?

    What are the trends over time?

- Conduct competitive comparison studies at least once a year to better understand best practices and other competitive information. This research helps answer the question, "How does Aikot stack up against its competitors?"

- Conduct quantitative/qualitative studies during the development cycles for targeted areas of the website. Evaluating prototype designs is more cost effective than evaluating a newly launched website that has no previous user feedback.

Summary

The web is becoming an increasingly important medium for consumer purchase decision-making processes, and customer visits to company websites are steadily increasing. Now more than ever before, websites must provide excellent customer experiences or market share will decline.

Remote online testing can accomplish the following goals:

- Evaluates websites using large sample sizes, giving user experience teams more confidence in the results.
- Large sample sizes also allow the user experience teams to segment the data by criteria of interest to them.
- Participants complete the study when they want to, using their own computers in their own environments.
- During the data collection phase of the project, the user experience team can work on other projects because evaluators are not moderating the study sessions.
- Both self-reported data and behavioral data can be captured about a website experience.
- This methodology combines market research, usability research, and web analytics into one study.

The steps for conducting remote evaluations are as follows:

1. Design the research activities and questions.
2. Program the study using an online remote application such as Keynote Systems's WebEffective application.
3. Add code to invite participants to the website.
4. Collect data.
5. Analyze the data.
6. Report findings and recommendations.

Results from a remote online evaluation include the following:

- Qualitative and quantitative feedback associated with the participant's own task
- Behavioral data using clickstreams (this shows the navigational paths visitors took during their visit), the total time taken to complete the primary task, and number of pages visitors viewed during the task completion
- Visitors' attitudes, preferences, and motivations by key visitor segments, such as frequent visitors versus infrequent visitors
- Visitors' overall satisfaction, their ratings for site organization, and frustrations experienced while completing tasks on the website

Further Reading

Cooper, A. (1999). *The inmates are running the asylum.* Indianapolis, IN: Sams.

Dumas, J., and Redish, J. (1993). *A practical guide to usability testing.* Intellect Books.

Van Duyne, D., Landay, J., and Hong, J. (2002). *The design of sites: patterns, principles, and processes for crafting a customer-centered web experience.* Boston, San Francisco, New York: Addison-Wesley.

Weinstein, A. (2004). *Handbook of market segmentation: strategic targeting for business and technology firms.* Haworth Series in Segmented, Targeted, and Customized Market. New York: The Haworth Press, Inc.

CASE 22

Using Technology to Automate Summative Usability Testing

Charles L. Harrison, Microsoft Corporation

> *Carrie summed everything: "Okay, sounds like we are all on the same page. Our group is looking for a CIF-compliant methodology that can help lead to a repeatable and efficient mechanism to execute summative baselines of our products." Doug smiled to himself. He knew he was being looked to for another project.*

The Call That Started It All

RING, RING!!! Rachael reached for the phone and noticed that the display read Jerry DeSure, her boss' boss' boss. She had met directly with him on this project several times, but he had never called her before.

Rachael hesitated before picking up the handset, as years in the high-tech industry had taught her that often a call from an executive was not good news. In the past it had resulted in a project taking a major turn, causing a significant increase in her work load or, even worse, the cancellation of a project altogether.

The phone rang again and she nervously answered it, "Good morning, Mr. DeSure. How may I help you?"

He excitedly responded, "Wow! I just read your report! This is so cool! Your team pulled it off, came in under budget, finished early, and delivered more than we had initially anticipated! Great job! Come on down to my office so we can talk!"

Rachael quickly put down the phone, took a deep breath, and ran as fast as she could to her boss' boss' boss' office.

A Year Earlier

Rachael Howard had worked in the high-tech industry for over 10 years as a usability specialist. About a year ago she accepted a position at Rational Servers, one of the largest software companies in the world that caters to enterprise class companies. Rachael's design and research group consisted of three smaller teams of product designers and usability engineers, each supporting a different product family.

Rachael supported a product that was basically part of an ogopoly (not quite a monopoly but an area where there are only two or three "key players") in which usability can be just as important as features with regard to a product's differentiation in the marketplace. Rachael supported a product that had been in production for several years, and the difference between this version and the previous one was that it was considered to be more "revolutionary" than "evolutionary." The product itself was huge, had many different target user, and the feature list was in the thousands. Rachael was short staffed and had recently learned that resources were only going to get scarcer.

Rachael reflected back several months to when she received an e-mail from her boss, Carrie:

TO: Rachael Jones (Usability Lead)
FROM: Carrie Sound (Director, User Experience)
SUBJECT: Need to have a simple question answered . . .

Hello,
As you know, the new version of your product is due to hit the market within the next few quarters. This product represents an enormous investment for the company from both a human and financial capital standpoint.

We would like you to lead an effort to determine if the product is "usable" in its current form for all of its many different user types. As you know, time is of the essence and if you want this information to actually have an impact pre-RTM we need to know soon.

BTW—it would also be nice if whatever you decide to do could be scalable to other technologies (both related and widely different). Think of it as a best practice.

Also, it sure would be nice if whatever you decide to do could also be used to compare progress with this product over time and give us information from a competitive analysis point of view.

Sincerely,
Carrie

Because Rachael had been in the industry for a while, she had this type of experience before, and it gave her a mix of dread and excitement because sometimes the "ask" seemed totally impossible but also exciting because:

- Well . . . it seemed impossible, and she'd always lived life on the edge!
- They thought she could pull it off.
- Her discipline, human-computer interaction (HCI), was obviously considered a value add, which was often more than half the battle.

Basically, the director of the design and usability group Rachael worked in was asking her to lead the effort to come up with a proposal of how to best baseline (or benchmark) a family of back office applications from a usability perspective. The method would need to be CIF compliant (common industry format for usability studies) for three reasons:

1. To provide a standardized reporting format for summative usability studies
2. To ensure that efficiency, effectiveness, and subjective satisfaction were measured
3. To be scalable to several technologies that the broader group supported

Over the years Rachael had been involved in many "baseline" projects and knew it was a concept that had different meanings to different people. To make sure she was in agreement with the project's sponsor, she set up a meeting with Carrie to discuss it with her and a usability vendor, Doug, that Carrie had assigned to Rachael to help with the project.

"Okay," Rachael started, "in my opinion, most usability research can be broken down into two basic categories: formative and summative. Over the past few years I've spent a lot of time explaining this to people and have been amazed that such a straightforward concept is so misunderstood in the HCI community."

"I agree," responded Carrie, "that is one of the reasons I am insisting on CIF compliance. The CIF makes a clear distinction between formative and summative usability studies in that formative studies are performed throughout the development of a product to help improve design, can be done in or out of the lab, and the study facilitator and participant interact quite a bit. On the other hand, summative tests are generally performed on fully functioning applications, in a lab, and the participant is interacted with very little. The CIF is specifically geared to summative studies, provides a standard format, and can make it easier to replicate studies over time."

Doug chimed in, "Okay, I guess I see the difference, but it sounds like most lab studies could be considered either summative or formative, depending on how they were described."

"Not really," Rachael explained. "In a nutshell, formative research is what is done by usability professionals 90+% of the time; ethnography, focus groups, heuristic walkthroughs, and most lab studies are examples. The goals are to understand what to build and for whom, how it should be designed, and what usability-related issues the target audience may have and to address them early in the development cycle. For example, the questions might be 'Do users understand the menu system in this prototype?' or 'Are we exposing this new feature at the right time for the user to complete this task?' Formative research can be done throughout the development process, but the earlier the better. If you are running a lab study in which you and the participant are frequently interacting and you are using a think-aloud protocol, or participants are working on a prototype that will likely change significantly over time, you are doing more formative research—which is excellent! It just is not summative."

Carrie continued, "You see, Doug, summative research is really a more performance-based view of a product from a usability perspective. For example, the question may be 'Given this finished, or nearly finished, product, how do our target users perform with the system when attempting the core tasks the system supports using only the resources that the system provides?' Summative and formative research often measures many of the same things, like time on task and pass/fail ratios, but how you measure them and how the data is used is generally very different."

Doug smiled and said, "I can sure see why being CIF compliant is important because from my experience, findings from different usability tests are difficult to compare, and this makes it difficult to track usability issues and improvements or to see how a product compares against an earlier version."

Doug was surprised to learn how much effort had gone into the CIF when Carrie and Rachael told him that the U.S. National Institute of

Standards and Technology initiated the project to define and validate a common industry format for reporting usability tests and their results and that 18 organizations were initially involved—including IBM, Oracle, Microsoft, Hewlett Packard, Sun, and Apple Computer.

Rachael continued. "The CIF is not meant as a visual template to help usability reports look the same, nor does it instruct a usability researcher on how to run a study. Instead, the framework of the report defines a consistent method of carrying out summative usability studies. The American National Standards Institute has published and continues to update a great guide for those wanting to institute CIF in their organization: the ANSI NCITS 354-2001. The publication provides a great overview of the CIF, how and why it was created, and even a check list."

"Sounds like I have some reading to do, and a new language to learn," Doug replied.

Rachael reassured him, saying, "Don't worry, the language and terminology that the CIF uses are basically the same you have learned as a usability professional, but the document does include a comprehensive glossary to help ensure consistency."

Carrie summed everything up: "Okay, sounds like we are all on the same page. Our group is looking for a CIF-compliant methodology that can help lead to a repeatable and efficient mechanism to execute summative baselines of our products. This is to be used in addition to all the formative research we do, not as a replacement for it."

They ended the meeting all agreeing with Carrie's final assessment and to focus on summative research for the project.

Questions

1. Looking at baselines from a purely business perspective, what are the CIF's major advantages?
2. Assume Doug was asked to create a list of positive talking points regarding the CIF. What do you believe he should highlight?

What's Out There?

Rachael was not one to reinvent the wheel, and her company had a lot of experienced usability professionals. Therefore she was hoping to identify an existing usability baseline best practice somewhere in the company and repurpose it.

She had Doug query their various repositories for usability reports containing such key words as "CIF," "summative," "benchmark," and "baseline." They were pleasantly surprised that Doug was able to identify dozens of examples. His next task was to compare those reports with the CIF guidelines to identify candidates that complied with that framework. Unfortunately, there were only a few that met the basic criteria, and none that Rachael believed adequately satisfied all their needs. Therefore Rachael decided to create a new CIF-compliant template. Rachael enjoyed creating methods or trying to improve on existing ones, so for her a benefit about not having a ready-to-consume example was that she actually had the opportunity to create something new.

Carrie had encouraged Rachael to be proactive and build out a small team. She explained, "Rachael, it is always better to assemble a small agile team on this type of effort. It gets more brain power involved and helps to build support for the eventual outcome. The trick is involving the right people and the right number of people. Remember, a two-humped camel is a race horse designed by a committee. I would suggest a three-person team which is adequate during the incubation phase of a project and in case of conflicts; you will always have a tie breaker. Just remember that as the scope of the project grows, so should your virtual team. It is also important not to work in a vacuum apart from the larger organization; keep management and other individual contributors in the loop with regular status and sanity checks."

Because this method was to be adopted by all three "subteams," Rachael recruited usability engineers, Sunil and Mark, from the other two design and usability groups to assist in the definition and execution of the baselining process. Rachael quickly got them up to speed on the various details of the project.

The small team started by having a series of meetings to lay the groundwork. Several important decisions came out of their initial meetings that would influence the entire process:

- They wanted their data to be easily digestible and actionable for the product teams. Common complaints from the teams they supported were that it could take weeks or more to get the data and that expecting them to trudge through a report that closely resembled a ream of paper was unrealistic.
- They wanted the process to be repeatable and as automated as possible.

- They wanted to come up with a process that would allow them to collect baseline data remotely rather than just regionally, because even though Rational Servers was based in a large city, it was often difficult to recruit enough local information technology (IT) professionals to fill out a usability study. Furthermore, Rational Servers provided software to a worldwide market, and the team believed it would be good to explore mechanisms that were not confined by region. This goal would be a stretch.

During an early meeting Sunil said, "One thing that always surprises me is how often we as user researchers do not follow our own guidelines when interacting with product teams. As a user researcher, I firmly believe that we should perform 'research' to better understand what the consumers of our data—the product teams—expect and need."

Mark asked, "I hope you are not implying that we should abandon the concept of standardizing our processes and simply customize our research for individual teams or, worse yet, let the development team drive it—user research is our core competency!"

"Not at all," Sunil responded. "But we should be sensitive to them, set expectations, and deliver data in a way that will best allow them to make more informed decisions."

Rachel smiled. It was at this point she knew she had built the right team.

Scoring System

Rachael considered one of the more novel aspects of their working sessions to be that they developed a proprietary "scoring" system. The goal of the scoring system was to provide a single number that took into account multiple usability related metrics (e.g., time on task, task completion rates, and user satisfaction) that could be objectively collected during a baseline test.

Developing a scoring system was not an easy process, and more often than not the team was mentally spent after their working session. Many of their early equations were incredibly powerful and complex, but they also wanted to easily explain the formula to those consuming the data and other researchers.

With this in mind, and through many iterations, they decided on a fairly simple weighted formula that they believed they could explain within a few minutes. A very simplified example of their formula looked something like this:

(pass/fail ratio) × (.25) + (time on task: goal/median) × (.25) + (click count: goal/median) × (.25) + (user satisfaction: goal/median score) × (.25)

where the usability metrics are ratios:

- Task pass divided by fail
- Goal time on task divided by participants' median time on task
- Goal number of clicks for a task divided by median clicks
- Goal measure of user satisfaction divided by median measure of user satisfaction

Finally, the ".25" indicates how much each metric is weighted in the overall formula, which results in a number between 0 and 1.

If one were to use the formula and plug in numeric ratios, a score would look something like this:

(pass/fail ratio = .68) × (.25) + (time on task: goal/median = .55) × (.25) + (click count: goal/median = .56) × (.25) + (user satisfaction: goal/median score = .75) × (.25) = .635

From a benchmarking perspective, the score of .635 is not intended to be "good" or "bad" but simply a score that can be used for comparative purposes both within a version of a product or across versions of a product. For example, the team could set a goal to achieve a score of .75 for the equivalent task for the next version of the product. In addition, tasks with lower scores (e.g., .40) could be targeted to further exploration in more formative studies.

Some time later, after Rachael and her team had developed their scoring formula, a colleague sent her an example of some similar work done by Jeff Sauro. Jeff had come up with a similar publicly available system called the SUM, for single usability metric, that they found on www.measuringusability .com. Although different in several important aspects, Rachael and her team considered Jeff's system to be well designed.

Rachael shared this news with her manager, and they were pleased that although these two efforts were created totally independently, the simple fact that multiple researchers were working on similar systems, with similar goals, indicated that there was indeed a need for this kind of effort.

Testing Method

Along with the scoring mechanism, Rachael and her team developed and documented a testing method. Their goal was to create a living document that could easily be digested and followed by other full-time researchers as well as usability vendors. This was basically a straightforward "how to" document like many other user researchers have created to facilitate usability testing within their groups. Some of the more important or novel elements of their document were as follows:

- Very clear operational definitions (concisely defining a term by characterizing the functional use of that term) of all metrics, why they were chosen, and how they were to be collected and measured
- A CIF-compliant report template
- A working spreadsheet that researchers could "plug" raw or summary data into to create baseline test scores from the task level to the product level
- A "frequently asked questions" section to answer some of the many questions they struggled with along the way:

    Will a single score mechanism be subject to covariance issues? Covariance should be expected between related metrics because they all measure aspects of usability and therefore should rise and fall together to some degree.

    How important is a consistent participant profile over time in summative studies?

    Participant profiles must be carefully established to ensure a longitudinal comparison between studies can be made. If the first-generation product is baselined with participants who are highly proficient with the product, then the second-generation product needs to use participants with comparable skills for that second-generation product. One approach is to require all participants receive approved certificate training on the product being studied.

    Will the changing performance of the system being baselined impact studies? As systems become ever faster, raw performance time should drop, even if the same participant used the same software longitudinally. This effect is mitigated by the use of experts to establish goal time. The goal time is established using the same system that the participants use, so the ratio should remain constant.

Test Drive

Rachael and the team now had their system ready for review, so they presented it to their management and cohorts. Based on this meeting, they made some adjustments and were ready to pilot their methods on a real product with real users. They selected an existing product with a fairly small feature set to test the new baseline methodology.

From a distance the evaluation appeared to be a typical usability test. It was conducted in a lab, one participant at a time, using a task list and paper surveys. The main differences were that facilitators did not interact with the participants during the study, participants were using a fully functional application, and the team was focused on collecting the metrics that made up the core of their scoring formula. Because this was a summative test, they wanted to know *how* users performed on core tasks; *why* users did certain things was of less importance to Rachael and her team.

Rachael, Mark, and Sunil were relieved that the process worked fairly well, and it was easy to convert the performance-based data into a single score. However, they also learned a few things during their pilot:

- It was difficult for an experienced usability engineer not to focus on the "why."
- Sticking to a very rigid operational definition of a metric was hard, especially across different researchers. For example, if a metric was the severity of an error, one researcher may consider it a "severity 1," whereas another researcher may consider it a "severity 2."
- Conducting baseline studies in a traditional method (e.g., one-on-one lab study) was time consuming and expensive because experiment designers generally want larger numbers of participants.

Now that they had an empirically validated evaluation method and what they considered a novel scoring mechanism, they were ready to put their theory into practice. Based on development schedules, the product Rachael supported (a large back-office application) turned out to be the first candidate to use the new baselining methods. Along the way, Rachael had kept her product teams in the loop with regard to the purpose of the testing, the methods, and the scoring. The first step was simply for her to negotiate with the product team what could and should be tested, what she would require from them (e.g., builds and technical support), and the overall schedule.

As previously mentioned, Rachael's design and usability team was short staffed, and the people hours required to successfully pull off a very large base-lining effort would be significant. There was no way Rachael and her team could possibly complete the project in a timely fashion without additional resources, so she decided that usability vendors would be required. Therefore she created a project plan and budget to pitch to her management.

To complete the project and adequately cover the very large and complex product, she decided that she would need

- Two full-time usability vendors
- Eleven studies
- One hundred thirty-two to 165 participants (12 to 15 per study)
- Five months

She understood that this project would require asking for a fairly significant financial and time commitment. She constructed a schedule showing the many separate and distinct areas of the product, each with a unique user population (Table 22.1). Some of the product areas were too large to adequately cover their core features in a single 2- to 3-hour session, so she would need to run two usability sessions to do so.

Rachael was delighted that Carrie gave her the green light for the project. She told Rachael, "Without your detailed planning and budgeting, management never would have approved such a large and complex project."

After receiving the "go," the hard work really began. Rachael needed to locate and hire two experienced usability vendors who would have the ability to quickly pick up some very technical applications and be able to work relatively autonomously.

Once hired, Rachael placed the usability vendors into a very immersive "boot camp" to adequately learn the aspects of the product they were to test. The usability vendors were also expected to quickly build a rapport with the various development teams, create and validate test plans with the teams, and start the scoping and setup of required hardware.

Table 22.1. Schedule of Product Areas and User Populations

Researcher	Product Area/User Population	Baseline Start	Report Delivered
1	A	Mon 7/26	Fri 8/13
1	B #1	Mon 8/16	Fri 9/3
1	B #2	Mon 9/6	Fri 9/24
1	C #1	Mon 9/27	Fri 10/15
1	C #2	Mon 10/18	Fri 11/5
1	D	Mon 11/8	Fri 11/26
2	E #1	Mon 8/2	Fri 8/20
2	E #2	Mon 8/23	Fri 9/10
2	F #1	Mon 9/13	Fri 10/1
2	F #2	Mon 10/4	Fri 10/22
2	G	Mon 10/25	Fri 11/12

Around this time Carrie, Rachael's direct manager, and a few other members of her team decided to either leave the group or the company. This made her already limited resources even more critical, and she feared that it might derail the entire baselining project. In addition, she was made the acting manager of her group, and the remaining full-time members of her group were stressed and busy.

Rachael and her remaining full-time team members continued with their "day jobs," which now included many more responsibilities. The team was also working with and mentoring the new vendors and engaging with their usability recruiting group to prepare them for the coming study, which would require many hard-to-recruit users.

Questions

6. Why is it important for usability professionals to have business skills?

The Epiphany

Things were moving along relatively well. However, one thing bothering Rachael for some time was that although they had a solid repeatable process and a unique scoring mechanism that made reporting faster and easier, they had not automated the actual data collection process as much as they had hoped, as evidenced by the 5-month schedule. In addition, the current solution was not scalable to their eventual goal of collecting data remotely. Specifically, they had observational-based metrics that required a one-to-one tester-to-participant ratio.

Several weeks before Rachael and her vendors were to begin running participants, she stumbled upon the work of another usability group within the company that had developed some very simple tools to help collect data from multiple participants concurrently. Basically, this group's tools loaded a task list into a simple client-side desktop application that presented individual tasks to a participant. After each task, the tool would ask participants a few questions regarding the task (e.g., "Did you successfully complete the task?"). This allowed the group to run multiple participants through a series of tasks simultaneously in the same room.

Within seconds of seeing this the lights went on in Rachael's head, and she could not believe she and her team had not thought of such an eloquent solution earlier! She believed that if they developed a similar tool (albeit a more powerful and flexible one), they could truly take their baselining efforts to the next level. With such a tool they could collect data rapidly by running multiple participants concurrently, and because they had a formula-based scoring mechanism, they could also generate reports in real time by uploading the raw data into a database and using a report application.

Rachael spent that weekend coming up with a revised project proposal based on these newly discovered tools and a new "task" for development support. In addition, she generated a high-level user interface and functional specification for the applications they would need. During her investigations while "specing" out the tools, Rachael discovered a few somewhat similar publicly available products she could use to give others a good feel for what she was trying to accomplish. For example, SiteUsers.com and Keynote.com both offer automated solutions for the web (but not client-side applications), which was what her team required because their applications were not web based.

Rachael also set up a meeting with Jerry DeSure, her boss' boss' boss, to whom she now reported directly since the two people in the organization above her had recently left and their positions had not been filled. Jerry was the general manager in charge of documentation, localization, regional program managers, design, and usability and other assorted staff in Rachael's division. Jerry epitomized the entrepreneurial spirit and pushed his direct reports and their staff to take calculated risks.

A former mentor of Rachael had once told her, "If you have the opportunity to work for an entrepreneurial type of leader, I implore you to take full advantage of it—push the envelope. Not being afraid to fail is very liberating and may allow you to realize great success both for yourself and your employer." Rachael's opportunity had finally come.

Before Rachael's sit-down with Jerry, she set up a meeting with a senior developer in her organization to go over the specs she had created. The goal was to get a good estimate of the development and test time required to create the proposed applications. Rachael factored those estimates into her overall revised schedule. She also met with Sunil and Mark to discuss the use of the proposed tools, the associated risks versus opportunities, and to ensure she had their full buy-in as partners.

A significant risk facing Rachael, Mark, and Sunil was that the scoring formula they had developed and tested would need to be modified because there were several metrics that could no longer be recorded without direct observation. For example, they wished to track participant errors (e.g., opening the wrong dialog) and assign each error a severity level, and the tool as it was speced could not support such robust tracking of events automatically. These were also the metrics that had the highest possibility of human error and biases. Rachael and her team made some minor tweaks to their scoring mechanism and passed them by some cohorts for a sanity check.

To address the new risks, Rachael revised her project plan and her estimates from those she would have dependencies on, particularly the development resources required. She included a list of risks, as well as ways to mitigate those risks, and the potential benefits of the new plan. In short, she was prepared, confident, and ready to present to Jerry.

Before the meeting Rachael had not gone into too much detail with Jerry regarding the meeting's purpose, just that she needed to discuss the baseline project and to pitch some new ideas. She started the meeting by saying, "I want to start the project 6 weeks late but I'll guarantee that we will finish at least 6 weeks early."

Needless to say, Jerry was skeptical at first because he knew major schedule swings were rarely conducive to a successful project. However, she took Jerry through the plan and as he discovered that she had anticipated and addressed many of his concerns and had engaged other stakeholders before their meeting, he became more and more receptive and excited about the prospects of Rachael's plan. Rachael reiterated that her original plan for the baselining project was very good and that if they decided to continue with it, they would have a lot of excellent data. However, she truly believed they would be missing a great opportunity by not pursuing the new plan.

Rachael summarized, "So what I'm asking for is to push out the project's start date by about 6 weeks but the end date will remain the same. During these 6 weeks I'm also asking for resources to build out an automated usability testing tool. This will not only allow us to still get our easy-to-understand product score cards based on our scoring formula but also to run studies much faster, reduce testing costs, turn around our data faster, and potentially baseline more core tasks."

To Rachael's pleasure, Jerry gave her the go-ahead for her new plan. However, at the conclusion of the meeting he gave Rachael a warning, saying, "I know you are excited about this and I love that you are willing to look at the bigger picture. I think you have a solid plan, but remember: this is a huge risk. If we drop the ball on this, we will hurt our credibility with the product teams. You need to make sure that you do everything possible to rally your staff to ensure the project's success. You have some good people reporting to you, and I'm expecting you to fully utilize and listen to them, just like I'm listening to you now. If this does not work out, it is not the end of the world, but you will likely not get another chance for quite some time."

Questions

7. What were some of the selling points Rachael likely used to convince Jerry to adopt her new plan?
8. What was some of the potential fallout of changing to the new plan?

Execution

During the extra time Rachael's team had while the tools were being developed and tested, she had the opportunity to revise their usability testing plan a bit to take into account the altered process and new tools. For example, they needed to rethink their task list and drop or modify tasks that they believed would not lend themselves well to being tested in a non-observed fashion. The new task lists allowed them to "recombine" testing on some of the larger product areas by running a single 3-hour test rather than two 2-hour tests (which also reduced the total number of participants required). Finally, they were forced to drop two of the product areas from this testing pass because they did not believe they could adequately test them using the new method because the tasks to be tested did not lend themselves well to the more automated testing procedures. Instead, they would test them later in a more traditional way. Table 22.2 shows the revised schedule that Rachael and her team delivered with all these adjustments.

Unlike a traditional usability test, the newly developed tools would allow Rachael's team to run multiple participants at the same time. In addition to multiple people, they could run multiple user profiles concurrently instead of recruiting one profile per testing session, which made recruiting much easier. They could accomplish this because the tools were designed to only expose certain instructions and tasks to certain participants based on a unique identifier. When people arrived, the researcher checked their profile and assigned them a code. When the participants entered their code, they would see only information pertinent to that code. So, in a single testing session, she could have database developers sitting next to database administrators each performing their unique set of tasks. Rachael's team could only seat eight people per testing session. For these logistical reasons, Rachael scheduled three testing sessions per day (8 to 11 a.m., 12 to 3 p.m., and 4 to 7 p.m.) and decided to test over 7 days, creating 168 seats to fill with the 105 participants they needed. Depending on the product area, participants were recruited for either 2 or 3 hours.

Table 22.2. Revised Schedule With Adjustments

Researcher	Product Area/User Population	Baseline Start	Prelim Report
1 and 2	A	Thurs 9/16	Mon 9/27
1 and 2	B	Thurs 9/16	Mon 9/27
1 and 2	C #1	Thurs 9/16	Mon 9/27
1 and 2	C #2	Thurs 9/16	Mon 9/27
1 and 2	E #1	Thurs 9/16	Mon 9/27
1 and 2	E #2	Thurs 9/16	Mon 9/27
1 and 2	F	Thurs 9/16	Mon 9/27

Another attribute of the tools was that the usability engineer became more of a "proctor" during the study because he or she was not directly interacting with any one participant. They instead focused on ensuring that the session ran smoothly (giving breaks, rebooting PCs if necessary, and answering any non-product questions).

Once participants completed all their tasks, the usability vendor would walk them out individually or in small groups. When all participants were gone, the usability vendor would upload each participant's data to the database (it was saved on the client PC's desktop as an XML file) and then reset all the PCs in preparation for the next group of participants (Figure 22.1).

The project was a big success. Rachael collected literally 5 months' worth of data in 7 days and had fairly polished reports in the hands of her product teams within a few days of running the final participants. In addition, several teams around the company (working on divergent technologies) began to use Rachael's, Mark's, and Sunil's tools and methods to save time, money, and other resources.

Questions

9. How would the lab set up for this kind of study look different from a traditional usability study? What logistical issues may arise?
10. How may this type of study affect recruiting participants?

Summary

There are several key guidelines to consider when using summative versus formative research. Summative usability studies:

- Are typically done with completed products
- Observe participants with minimal interaction
- Measure key usability-related performance-based metrics such as time on tasks and task completion rates

Formative usability studies:

- Are typically done on prototypes or early working code
- Use a think-aloud protocol for participants and have moderate interaction between participant and facilitator
- Identify potential usability problems and blocking issues

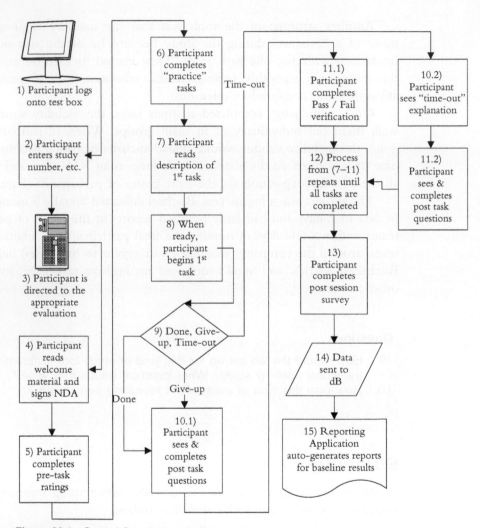

Figure 22.1. General flow during a testing session.

There are many benefits to using an industry standard such as CIF:

*   CIF provides a standardized report for summative usability studies.
*   CIF is designed to ensure efficiency, effectiveness, and subjective satisfaction are measured.
*   CIF allows for easier test procedure replication.
*   CIF can help reduce reporting time for usability staff.

Rachael and her cohorts found many important benefits to automating baseline testing:

- It is far more cost effective and may enable more user research teams to conduct baseline tests for their products because it is not as time consuming or expensive.
- Development engineers, program managers, and other generally "analytical" professionals tend to understand and appreciate a single scoring mechanism.
- User researchers can potentially baseline more areas of a product, thereby making the results of a product-wide baseline effort that much more valid.
- User researchers can easily repurpose studies for longitudinal testing to determine the state of a product's usability over generations.
- Using the automated tools can free up a usability engineer's time at the end of the product cycle, allowing them to concentrate on the next version.

When talking with other usability professionals, Rachael regularly informs them to keep a few things in mind if they are going to build out such a program. For example, summative data is what it is—basically a measure of performance. One will not be able to answer the inevitable "why" questions (unless that capability is built into the tool). The analogy Rachael uses is that when someone goes to the doctor to get their blood pressure taken, the doctor records a score (measure). Depending on that score, the doctor may do nothing or may prescribe additional tests if the results give a cause for concern. The same can be true for summative usability data; if a feature or area of the product scores "poorly," the usability and product teams should perform additional research, knowing they are spending time and effort in the correct areas.

Further Reading

ANSI (2001). *Common industry format for usability test reports (ANSI-NCITS 354-2001)*. Washington, DC: American National Standards Institute.

Bias, R., and Mayhew, D. (1994). *Cost justifying usability*. San Francisco: Morgan Kaufmann.

Hackos, J. T., and Redish J.C. (1998). *User and task analysis for user interface design*. Hoboken, NJ: John Wiley & Sons.

Rubin, J. (1994). *Handbook of usability testing: how to plan, design, and conduct effective tests*. Hoboken, NJ: John Wiley & Sons.

Whiteside, J. (1993). *The Phoenix agenda: power to transform your workplace*. Hoboken, NJ: John Wiley & Sons.

Index

About the Editors

Carol Righi is a Director of User Experience at Perficient. Carol has worked in User-Centered Design for more than 20 years and is widely considered a UCD thought leader. Carol has performed user research, usability evaluation, and interaction design for companies such as IBM, Google, Yahoo, Intuit, A. G. Edwards, Mapquest, Met Life, and many others. She has served as manager for numerous UCD efforts and has helped lead the development of UCD competency in various organizations, including IBM. Carol has also designed and developed many standup and e-learning courses in UCD and has trained thousands of students. She received her undergraduate degree in psychology in 1981 and her Ph.D. in School/Educational Psychology with a concentration in computer Applications to Education in 1988, both from Fordham University in New York City.

Janice James is Director of User Experience for Perficient's Central East Region. She has more than 19 years of experience in the field of human factors, usability and user-centered design and development. Since 1998, as principal of her own consulting firm, Simply Usable through Design, Janice has focused on providing user-centered design consulting services to companies ranging in size from start-ups to Fortune 500s, including CNet, AOL/Netscape, Hewlett Packard, Unisys, Intuit, Humana, BestBuy.com, eBay, AARP and McGraw-Hill, to name a few. Janice's career is highlighted by her leadership in professional associations. In 1990 she recognized the need for a practical-oriented organization dedicated to enhancing the skills and professional success of usability professionals and became the primary founder of the Usability Professionals' Association in 1991. She dedicated ten active years on the Board of Directors and in other capacities for the Association. In 1982, Janice earned undergraduate and graduate degrees in English and Technical Communications, followed by graduate work in Human Factors and HCI.

About the Contributors

Robert Barlow-Busch helps to refine Quarry's methods for design and usability while honing his skills hands-on with projects for clients such as FedEx, RIM, and numerous mid-sized technology companies. Through Robert's advocacy, the Quarry team became early adopters of ethnographic research and personas and has since been recognized by Forrester Research for their expertise. Robert enjoys sharing his 15 years of experience by writing, speaking at conferences, and teaching workshops for practitioners.

Randolph G. Bias is an Associate Professor of the School of Information at the University of Texas at Austin. Randolph worked in industry for 25 years as a usability engineer, at Bell Labs, IBM, and BMC Software, and co-founded an independent usability lab and consultancy. He joined the School of Information in 2003 to research human information processing and human-computer interaction. Randolph has written over 50 articles and recently published a 2nd Edition of Cost-Justifying Usability (R. G. Bias and D. J. Mayhew, Eds.). He is a vigorous advocate for designing technology to fit the user.

Dr. Jianming Dong has 10 years of user research experience at PayPal, eBay and IBM. He directly researched over 1000 users worldwide and provided many critical design recommendations and business insights in his projects. Dr. Dong is now in charge of international research programs at PayPal, based on his ample experience conducting international user studies. Dr. Dong designed and developed EZSort—a card sorting and cluster analysis tool. Jianming had numerous patents and research publications in the HCI field, including a bestselling HCI book in Chinese. Dr. Dong received his Ph.D. from Purdue University.

Paul Englefield joined IBM in 1978 with a Classics degree and a perverse fascination for technology. After working in systems programming, service management and product design, he concluded that designing for users held more appeal than debugging errant pointer chains. He currently works as user experience competency lead for the IBM UK Strategy and Change organization. In this role, he shapes and leads projects to create and evaluate designs for a diverse set of clients in government and industry. His interests include value-driven design, user experience modeling, qualititative analysis, and design rationale—with a common theme of delivering models and methods through tools and resources. Paul is a professional member of the British Computer Society, an active member of its HCI group, and a Chartered IT Practitioner. He holds five patents related to user interface technology, has published on range of usability topics, and is a regular lecturer and collaborator at UK universities. Away from the office, he plays jazz guitar, acts as a role-player for murder mysteries, and makes great black cherry pancakes.

Carol Farnsworth is a Director of Licensing and Partnerships at Keynote. Carol has years of customer experience and usability research both in software application and Web site development. Prior to joining Keynote, Carol taught usability methods and testing courses at Stanford University and served as a faculty member in the university's Information/Web Technology department. She worked for several start-up companies including NetRaker and Noosh after several years leading Stanford University's User Interface and Web site design team. Before the Web became a highly influential medium, Carol developed classroom products for K-12 teachers at CTB McGraw-Hill in Monterey, CA. She holds professional affiliations with the Usability Professionals Association, Bay CHI, and the Society for Technical Communication and the ACM. She holds a B.A. in Sociology and Psychology from Denver University and a Masters in Education from Catholic University in Washington D.C.

Ken Guzik is a user interface designer and software architect who for more than 20 years has designed award-winning software for Xerox, GO Corporation, Sun Microsystems, Motorola, Blue Martini Software and VMware. Ken's professional focus is creating simple to use computer applications and systems, and he holds numerous patents for his work in pen-based computers and television studio applications. Ken has degrees in Biochemistry and Computer Science from UCLA and UC Santa Barbara and currently leads the user experience team at VMware.

Chuck Harrison is a User Researcher for Microsoft Game Studios and works on casual games for Xbox 360's Live Arcade, the MSN Games site, and Microsoft Messenger. Chuck has over ten years of user research experience ranging from consumer products to back office and business applications. Before joining Microsoft, Chuck worked at several other high tech companies such as Siebel, BMC, Intel, & Netscape. Over the years, Chuck has presented research at several HCI related conferences. Chuck has a B.S. in Human Factors from the University of Idaho, an M.A. in Engineering Psychology from New Mexico State University and an M.B.A. from the University of Houston.

Jon Innes is Director of User Experience at Intuit, the company responsible for Quicken, TurboTax, and QuickBooks, where he leads a team working on new product design initiatives. Jon has over a decade of experience, including leadership positions where he has defined and improved user experience processes at some of the world's largest technology companies. He has designed and evaluated user interfaces for SAP, Siebel, Cisco, Oracle, Symantec, and IBM. Jon holds a Masters degree in Engineering Psychology and is a member of UPA, HFES, and ACM CHI/BayCHI.

Laurie Kantner is an experienced usability researcher and project manager, is director of client services for Tec-Ed, Inc. Laurie manages Tec-Ed's staff of interaction designers, usability researchers, and information architects. She is responsible for Tec-Ed's delivery of client work on time, within budget, and at the expected level of quality. Laurie developed and continues to refine Tec-Ed's automated estimating tool for user research projects. She gives presentations at the conferences of the Usability Professionals' Association, ACM SIGCHI, and other forums for professionals in user experience and user assistance.

Tammy L. Latham is a Software Design Consultant in Greenville, SC. For the past nine years, Tammy has been a user advocate on numerous software development teams performing activities such as market research, strategic planning, business process analysis, requirements definition, user research, interaction design, and product training. Her work has focused on web-based software products in a wide variety of industries including benefits enrollment, consumer-driven health care, internet security, billing, transportation logistics, nonprofit accounting, and supply chain management.

Shannon Lucas is a Software Developer for Motive, Inc. Shannon has worked as a software developer for ten years. He has developed interactive software for the defense, airline, and telecommunications industries. He received his M.S. in Information Studies from the University of Texas at Austin in 2006. Shannon currently spends his free time cycling and paragliding.

Dr. Deborah J. Mayhew is an internationally recognized author, teacher, speaker and consultant on software user interface design and usability engineering. She has been Owner and Principal Consultant of Deborah J. Mayhew & Associates, a consulting firm offering a wide variety of services related to usability engineering, since 1986, when she became one of the first independent consultants in her field. Clients have included IBM, AT&T, John Hancock Insurance Co., GE, Hewlett-Packard, Ford Motor Co., GTE, American Express, Apple, American Airlines, Texas Instruments, NASA, the National Cancer Institute, The New York City Police Department, Computer Sciences Corp. (CSC), Cisco Systems, the IRS and many others. Over her 25-plus years in the field of usability engineering, Dr. Mayhew has consulted companies in many diverse industries on the design of products based on a wide range of technology platforms including mainframe computers with "dumb terminals", GUIs, medical technology, manufacturing equipment and Web sites and applications. Dr. Mayhew holds a B.A. in Psychology from Brown University, an M.A. in Experimental Psychology from the University of Denver and a Ph.D. in Cognitive Psychology from Tufts University. Her most recent book is The Usability Engineering Lifecycle (Morgan Kaufmann Publishers, 1999). Another popular book is Cost-Justifying Usability, co-edited with Randolph G. Bias (Academic Press, 1994), which is now out in a second edition, (Morgan Kaufmann Publishers, 2005). Dr. Mayhew has been living and working out of Martha's Vineyard Island (where she also was born and grew up) since 1990. Her website is at http://drdeb.vineyard.net

Deanna McCusker is a user interaction designer and usability specialist with more than 20 years experience designing interfaces and conducting usability evaluations for various companies including Intuit, Symantec, Taligent, HP, and Cadence. She has taught interaction design principles and is an expert in prototyping and testing techniques. Deanna holds a degree in Industrial Design from Carnegie-Mellon University. For the past three years, her award-winning designs have contributed to the outstanding success of VMware's product line.

Scott McDaniel is a user interface designer and usability specialist for the National Center for Biotechnology Information, which is part of the National Library of Medicine. He discovered the field of usability when he joined the Society for Technical Communication in 1994 as a new technical writer. He founded the Washington D.C. chapter's Usability SIG and later served as the Vice-President of the D.C. chapter of the UPA. In 2000, he joined Cognetics Corporation, a usability and user interface design company. Working with Charlie Kreitzberg and Whitney Quesenbery, he helped shape the LUCID Framework™ for interface and usability design. He joined NCBI in late 2004. Scott has a M.A. in Experimental Psychology from the Center for Visual Science at the University of Rochester.

Rosemary Pluchino holds a B.A. in Psychology from Rutgers University. She has 10 years experience in Human Factors working for various companies, including Lucent Technologies, Philips, Motorola, and Intel. She is currently a Senior Interaction Designer at Texas Instruments Educational and Productivity Solutions, working to improve the usability of scientific and graphing calculators.

Marie Tahir has devoted her career to improving the customer experience of software and websites. At Intuit, Marie leads Intuit's whitespace investigations in the Technology Innovation Group. Prior to that, she led the Intuit User Experience Community, including all user research and design functions. Marie has been in the software industry since 1989. Her prior affiliations include Nielsen Norman Group, Lotus Development, Dun & Bradstreet Software, and University of California at Berkeley. She is co-author with Jakob Nielsen of the best-selling 2002 book "Homepage Usability: 50 Websites Deconstructed" and has spoken and taught around the world on customer research methodologies and design, including a course on Field Research. Marie is especially passionate about the importance of learning from customers in their own environment. She has written about the importance of doing site research in PC Magazine, Internet World, and other leading magazines. Marie co-wrote a chapter on Customer Roundtables in Field Methods Casebook for Software Design.

Maggie Reilly is a user-centered design and usability specialist with an extensive background in usability, web design, user interface design, instructional design, and project management. She has worked for firms in the telecommunication, computer, and software industries, including

IBM, BellSouth, Lockheed-Martin, SAIC, and Ceridian, providing public health communications, instructional design, information architecture, and user interface design. She has also taught technical communication at the college level and conducted usability training for corporations and government agencies. In addition, she has written a series of usability and web style manuals, edited public health reference manuals, developed annual reports, and provided models for web-based training and communications in software sales, public health surveillance, and human resource management. She has participated in developing standards for federal websites and in assessing the usability of many publicly supported websites. She currently works as a Design and Usability Consultant for Smart Solutions, Inc.

Mary Beth Rettger is Director of Usability and Development Training at The MathWorks. She is a past president and board member of the Usability Professionals' Association. She has been a frequent presenter and workshop organizer at the annual UPA conference, and has written several articles about low-tech methods of collecting data and involving team members in the user centered design process. She holds an M.B.A. from Northeastern University, and a B.A. from Brown University.

Janice Anne Rohn is Vice President of User Experience at World Savings Bank, where she leads the team responsible for the design and usability of the consumer online banking and other sites. Prior to World Savings, Janice founded and built User Experience groups at Siebel Systems and Sun Microsystems. During her career, Janice has worked in a variety of organizations, hired over 70 UE professionals, and designed and built over 15 usability labs. Janice has also worked at PeopleSoft, Apple, and Stanford University. Janice has been a leader in Strategic User Experience and Cost Justification, researching and utilizing the most effective methods and organizational approaches to ensure optimal decision-making. Janice has authored chapters in both editions of Cost-Justifying Usability. She was President and a founding Board Member of the Usability Professionals' Association (UPA), and was the Usability Chair for two CHI conferences. Janice also founded the Outreach effort, working with the U.S. Congress, the Consumer Protection Agency, and Vice President Gore's office on the benefits of user experience. Janice has over 50 publications, and has delivered many presentations at CHI, UPA, NNG, UIE, Interact, and other conferences, along with keynote speeches and courses at several universities.

Stephanie Rosenbaum is founder and president of Tec Ed, Inc., a 15-person consulting firm specializing in usability research and user-centered design, with offices in California, Michigan, Wisconsin, and New York. A member of ACM SIGCHI, HFES, and a charter member of the Usability Professionals' Association, Stephanie co-chaired the Usability Community for the CHI 2006 Conference. Stephanie's publications include a chapter on "Making User Research Usable" in Software Design and Usability. With Chauncey Wilson, she contributed a chapter to the second edition of Cost-Justifying Usability. Her research background includes Anthropology Studies at Columbia University and Experimental Psychology research for the University of California at Berkeley.

Elizabeth Rosenzweig is currently the Principal Consultant at Bubble Mountain Consulting, where she works with companies and organizations on user-centered design solutions to research and development of technology projects. From 1991 through May 2005, Elizabeth was a Principal Research Scientist at Eastman Kodak Company where she built the Boston Usability Lab—a usability-engineering center of expertise—at the Kodak Boston Software Development Center in Lowell, Massachusetts. In addition Elizabeth has been involved with the Usability Professionals' Association, where she has been on the Board of Directors since 1999, a recent Past President of UPA and the Director of World Usability Day. With 20 years of industry experience, Elizabeth frequently presents at national conferences and has been a contributor to professional journals, among them User Experience and Interactions.

Gia Rozells has been studying how customers use software since 1985. She authored 9 books on early consumer software, including The Power of PC Works, The Lotus Manuscript Book, and Amiga Artist. She currently leads the Online Customer Service team at Intuit supporting products for professional accountants. Previously, she led Intuit's user-centered design group for TurboTax products and created a community for UCD practitioners across all of Intuit's business units.

Laconya Ruby has worked at IBM for more than eleven years. She started working at IBM as an HTML programmer and then became the first Information Architect at the Atlanta Innovation Center. Ms. Ruby is currently a senior IA at the IBM Centers for Solution Innovation. She has led complex interactive design engagements for numerous Fortune 500 companies. Ms. Ruby became interested in usability while she was in graduate school and has had extensive usability testing experience with many customers while working at IBM. She is a member of the Usability Professionals' Association and is quoted in Susan Fowler's GUI Design Handbook. Ms. Ruby was the first graduate to receive a M.S. degree in Information Design and Technology from Georgia Institute of Technology. She has used her education to influence a web-generation of sites and interactive designers.

Charlotte Schwendeman, with more than 20 years of experience in human-computer interaction for hardware, software, Web solutions, handheld devices, and kiosks, she is currently the National Practice Director for User Experience at Perficient, Inc., a leading information technology consulting firm serving Global 2000 and other large enterprise customers throughout the United States. Charlotte defined and implemented Perficient's user-centered approach to design and development in 2000. Since then, it has become a leading differentiator for the company. Prior to this position, Charlotte was an HCI specialist at IBM for 18 years. While there, she consulted for some of IBM's major clients, such as Chrysler, Mercedes-Benz North America, Volvo, Burlington Northern Santa Fe Railroads, MetLife, and the Atlanta Committee for the '96 Olympic Games. Charlotte was a key member of the corporate team that defined, developed, and deployed IBM's user-centered design (UCD) approach throughout IBM's software development labs.

Carolyn Snyder earned her experience in unusable interfaces the hard way—the first 10 years of her career were devoted to creating them, first as a software engineer and then as a project manager. After a decade spent face-down in the code, she discovered that there were real people out there who actually used those interfaces. And thus was a usability specialist born.

In 1993, Carolyn joined User Interface Engineering, a prominent U.S. usability consulting firm founded by Jared Spool. She has worked with dozens of high-tech clients, specializing in paper prototyping and usability testing. She also teaches seminars and writes articles about usability topics. In 1999, she started Snyder Consulting (*www.snyderconsulting. net*) to continue doing the work she loves most—the hands-on involvement with development teams that empowers them make useful and usable interfaces.

Carolyn has a B.S. in Computer Science from the University of Illinois and an M.B.A. from the University of Chicago. She is the author of *Paper Prototyping* and the co-author of two usability books: *Web Site Usability: A Designer's Guide* and *E-commerce User Experience*.

Sarah J. Swierenga, Ph.D., C.P.E. is the director of the Michigan State University Usability & Accessibility Center and Professor by Courtesy in the Department of Telecommunication, Information Studies, and Media. She is responsible for developing and disseminating innovations in theory building, research methodologies, and technologies to enhance usability and accessibility in Web and information technology contexts. The Center serves faculty, students, and organizations at MSU as well as external clients, through consulting, collaborative research, educational programming, publications, and the sponsorship of open houses, workshops, and symposia. A researcher and a practitioner with 20 years of experience in the scientific study of users in commercial, military, and academic environments, Swierenga possesses extensive skills in user interface design, data collection tools, and methodologies including usability tests, accessibility compliance evaluations, questionnaires, interviews, focus groups, and heuristic evaluations. Swierenga also co-authored Constructing Accessible Web Sites (APress, 2003), and has presented widely on accessible website design, usability techniques, health communication technology, and e-learning effectiveness, which comprise her research programs. She is also a Certified Professional Ergonomist (C.P.E.).

Kate Walton has worked as a usability specialist for twelve years in the travel industry. The last eight years were spent working at Amadeus building e-commerce solutions for travel agencies and airlines to help them develop their online markets. Throughout her career, Kate has been fortunate enough to conduct international usability research in the U.S., Canada, South America, and Europe.

Larry Wood is a principle in Parallax Ineraction, a small company dedicated to the development of tools for Web site design and development. One such tool is WebSort, which supports on-line card-sorting. Larry is also a Professor Emeritus of Psychology at Brigham Young University, where he taught HCI and UCD courses for 20 years. In addition, he has published articles on UCD and edited a book on user interface design. He also served on the Board of Directors of UPA from 2000–2003.

Answers

Case 1: Changing Products Means Changing Behaviors

1. To be successful Jim needs to have experience with a wide variety of user-experience techniques so he can select the appropriate design and research methods and develop a process that works within the unique context of JMC's situation. He needs to understand how the functional areas other than user experience influence product design at a software company so he can effectively partner with these teams. He also needs to have enough technical knowledge to gain the respect of the engineers and the founder and CTO. Examples of skills Jim should have include

   - User-centered requirements analysis
   - Contextual inquiry
   - Task analysis
   - Use case development
   - UI design
   - Design specifications and guidelines
   - UI prototyping
   - Heuristic reviews
   - Cognitive walkthroughs and inspection methods
   - Graphic design
   - Usability testing
   - Formative testing of early design concepts and prototypes
   - Summative testing to evaluate products with respect to usability goals
   - Knowledge of other functional areas related to software product development
   - Project planning
   - Marketing research and communication

- Requirements analysis and specification
- Quality-assurance techniques

Jim does not need to be an expert in all these things, but he does need enough understanding of them to develop plans that take into account how they fit together and make the appropriate trade-offs. He also needs to have experience working with teams and persuading them to make significant changes, both in terms of the UI design and their related processes.

2. Jim should begin by examining JMC's existing processes, and the artifacts related to those processes, to understand how products get developed at the company. All companies have processes. Some companies follow formal processes, leveraging things like International Organization for Standardization standards, whereas others are more informal in their practices. Even small start-ups have ad-hoc processes, even if they aren't aware of it on a conscious level. Examples of artifacts related to product development processes include requirements documents, bug databases, design specifications, and project plans.

Then, Jim should talk to the key decision makers and thought leaders to understand their views regarding the organizational needs for user-experience deliverables. Although the people in the company may not be experts in usability or design, they are his clients, and he needs to determine how to best meet their needs and integrate them with their existing processes. One way to determine whom to talk to is to review the organizational chart. Jim should introduce himself to the functional leaders and ask them to explain their roles and identify how their teams impact the user experience. It is also important to consider "thought leaders," individuals who may not be in formal leadership positions but who hold authority due to expertise or tenure. These individuals can typically be identified by analyzing how decisions are made or by informal networking.

Finally, Jim should then examine the products and identify any weaknesses that may relate to functional deficiencies within the organization and determine their root causes. Often, just looking at the UI indicates where problems exist organizationally. For example, if the UI is inconsistent, it often reflects a lack of collaboration and high-level design oversight. If the UI is extremely buggy, it might mean that insufficient time has been allocated to coding or quality activities by the person in charge of project planning. Or, it could mean that the teams are not reusing and refining common UI components

Printed and bound by CPI Group (UK) Ltd, Croydon, CR0 4YY
03/10/2024
01040315-0007

because the technical architects have encouraged custom work. More custom code tends to correlate with more bugs. Keep in mind that the goal of this type of informal review is to determine what functional weaknesses exist in the organization that contribute to poor product design. Jim should conduct more formal studies of how the product is used if he truly wants to learn about the usability of the product. He should also consider reviewing customer support data and how he might get some informal input directly from customers.

3. As is the case at many start-ups, technologists founded the company. Each functional area grew quickly, but the user-experience function was overlooked in the process, because the initial founders and management team were unfamiliar with the concept. They were smart people but tended to ignore the perspectives of others. They never realized that what might be obvious to them might not be so obvious to someone else. As the company grew, management failed to establish clear roles and formal feedback loops, both in general and specifically for user experience. Teams began to try to address related problems independently—they failed to partner effectively with each other and their customers. Unknowingly, many of the teams were working on problems related to user experience. For example, both professional services and the engineering teams were often working on the same problems independently. Jim has the advantage of looking at things not only from a fresh perspective, but also from a cross-functional perspective. Of course, as a user-experience specialist he also has the knowledge of best practices that have worked at other companies that he can apply to the problems at JMC.

Simply having good engineers who can write the code is only a piece of the puzzle. Software product development is a team effort, but teams only work well when everyone knows their role. As the functional teams in JMC struggled to define their roles and integrate into the rest of the organization, they lost focus on the customer. Collaborating with customers and end users was not a priority because the various functional teams were too internally focused. In some cases this was because functional teams defined themselves as competitors instead of partners. All too often individuals or teams may define themselves in ways that can undermine the success of the organization as a whole. Herbold (2004) calls this the "fiefdom syndrome." The fiefdom syndrome is a key problem for most new user-experience initiatives; overcoming it requires breaking down barriers to collaboration by changing processes to reward the correct behaviors. For example, if people are rewarded for making dates without regard to quality or encouraged to define requirements in terms of solutions, then other individuals cannot play their role effectively to create good products for customers.

4. When a person first joins an organization, she or he may have delegated authority but has to work to gain earned authority. Earned authority only comes through trust, and trust only comes with collaboration. There are many possible options here for Jim to get the rest of the company on board. However, Jim needs to identify a relatively low-risk, but visible, quick win to buy him the time and credibility to take on problems that are more substantial. Although there are many possible projects on which to focus, Jim needs to find something to help his initial sponsors. He needs to keep their styles in mind and use tactics that resonate with them. If possible, Jim should define his initial project as something that involves collaborating with the other functional areas so that his work is visible to them and he can gain their trust. He should also choose an area where he can foresee success. It is not the best time to try and choose the most complex problem.

5. It's probably not a good idea in this situation to push ahead and try to run a usability test. Jim could try to run such a test, but he needs to make a decision about the trade-off between spending the time to run a usability study to get data and having enough time to fix what is obviously broken. In an ideal situation he would have enough time to run a study, analyze the results, and then help the team fix the design based on the findings. However, in this situation that might not be realistic. Running a study might take more time than he can afford. Even if testing is feasible, Jim needs to consider the relative amount of effort when weighing alternative options. He also has to consider whether his results will be well received by the team. Given the situation, Jim may find resistance if he runs a study and tries to get the team to make design changes at this point.

6. Jim could do an informal review based on heuristics. However, there are several possible drawbacks to this approach that should be considered. First, unless Jim is a domain expert, his findings may not be as valid as those of a user-experience person who has worked on a product for some time and knows the user profile and use cases well. Second, he has not yet established credibility with the team. They may

argue that the problems he reports are not significant or not agree with his prioritization of the problems. He could try to do a survey (to gather satisfaction measures by feature area) or remote study of users to get their feedback on the existing UI, but there are some logistical issues to consider, including getting a list of users and their contact information (not just the corporate customers who purchased the product, but the actual end users).

Jim could simply sit down with the engineers and try to prioritize the known issues. This might be a viable approach, but it assumes the team will cooperate and the list of issues currently known is relatively complete. It also assumes the team will take time away from their planned development activities to meet with him and they have sufficient time to fix the identified problems.

7. Jim should consider the nature of the problems he has learned about:
   - Inconsistency due to lack of collaboration and shared vision in both layout and terminology
   - Lack of documented user-centered requirements driving product design and project estimates
   - Teams spending a lot of time in meetings debating design details during implementation
   - Quality issues related to lack of formal tracking of UI bugs
   - Last-minute changes related to the informal processes impacting schedule and overall quality

8. Jim needs to make sure his recommendations are actionable. His points must describe observable outcomes that map to the pain points of the audience of his presentation. Jim needs to focus on immediate tactics that might enable slightly different longer term goals as part of his change management strategy. For example, it makes sense to drive thinking about users and use cases before usability testing. Without agreement on whom the product is designed for and what tasks it needs to support, making progress on usability testing is next to impossible.

Case 2: Managing Politics in the Workplace

1. When deciding where to position his company, Joe needs to understand that the Cleveland Company culture has not evolved from printed to online publishing. He is accustomed to working in a newer digital development culture that is more concerned with

software and Internet services than traditional media. To be successful, Joe knows he needs to be working with the researchers who are developing the online newspaper. He therefore needs to position his department in a direct relationship with those who can benefit most from his services, such as the webmasters at the home office and the developers who are creating the online magazine from the printed magazine. Joe needs to work as part of the Cleveland.com team and become an integral part of their development process.

2. It was not clear at the outset who was running the meeting. There was no agenda. Although Lyle called the meeting, he had Linda set up the room and order the food. Linda also kicked off the meeting. This all gave the impression that Linda was going to run the meeting.

3. Lyle should have set the expectations for the meeting long before it began. There was no agenda sent to the participants. Participants can't prepare if they don't know what they're preparing for.

   Further, Lyle didn't facilitate the meeting in a way that encouraged collaboration. He instead set up a contentious atmosphere. It would have been better to have had a dialogue with the key players before the meeting to better understand their individual issues. Then, he could have set an agenda that would have framed the issues in an objective way and worked toward helping them to create a better working relationship.

   Also, because Joe and Linda are both team leaders doing similar work, this problem should have been addressed earlier, and not in such a public forum. Lyle let the problem fester and grow to a point where it was more difficult to resolve.

   Finally, Lyle should not have abandoned the group, leaving them to find their own solutions. Lyle could have considered bringing in an expert in organizational psychology to drive home the point that interpersonal issues ultimately affect the ability of the individuals in the group to influence change and produce a viable product for profit in the marketplace. The expert could have facilitated the meeting, working in time to affect problem solving and team building.

4. Underneath the practical issues that led to problems, there are also underlying emotional issues between Linda and Joe. They should therefore get together and plan how to improve their working relationship. Perhaps they should start out with weekly meetings to review and coordinate the work they are both doing. These meetings could include a discussion of where there might be overlap and

where they might be able to help each other. As time goes on and the working relationship improves, the need for weekly meetings might decrease and they could have more informal means to check in with each other. They should also plan a way for both their teams to work together on a regular basis.

A full team meeting or outing would be a good way to cap off these efforts and ensure that everyone is in fact working together as a team. Especially when teams are geographically separated, there is a great need to have at least one face-to-face meeting so everyone can have a greater familiarity with all the people who are part of the team.

5. Joe had been feeling frustrated with Tim because he never seemed to have enough time for him and his team. Tim had told him that he would come out to California to see the lab and meet the team, but each time he canceled his trip. Joe was traveling to New York City at Tim's suggestion. He was not sure what message Tim was sending by failing to make the trip to California to meet the team there. Joe did try to laugh it off to make light of the situation and develop a thick skin, especially in front of his staff. However, he was not completely successful because he still found himself feeling uneasy and disappointed. Meanwhile, Tim had made an effort to get to know the people on his team. He worked well with the folks in the home office; he just needed to make that connection with the people in the remote office.

6. Tim should be clear about his expectations for Joe and his California team. Because Tim called the meeting, he has a responsibility to Joe to prepare for the meeting and to treat him with respect during the meeting. The best way to do this would be to send Joe a meeting agenda ahead of time so he could see the points Tim wanted to cover in the meeting. He should also ask Joe for his input regarding what he would like to accomplish during the visit. Likewise, Joe should try to understand that Tim is new to his position and needs a little more time to settle in. Tim should also take care to prepare the New York and California teams by making sure he communicates with everyone beforehand so they all come to the meeting with the same expectation. Knowing there has been some difficulty in the past, Tim should know that the meeting might be tense. Tim needs to take leadership by being careful in setting expectations, ensuring there will be no surprises in the meeting that would throw everyone off balance.

7. The bigger problem is the way the Cleveland Company treats its remote employees. Cleveland doesn't understand the importance of getting remote teams to work smoothly together. This is because remote work doesn't fit in their business model. Newspapers are generally written in one location and often printed nearby. The business people all see each other in the course of a day. By contrast, in the digital world people often work together online and in conference calls. It is not uncommon for everyone on the team to be in a different city. The Cleveland Company needs to learn strategies for creating better remote working teams, such as

   - Coordinating calendars, encouraging people to call in from many locations
   - Using technology to enable remote collaboration
   - Sending out agendas ahead of time
   - Preparing for meetings by ensuring their teleconference and web-conference setups are working properly
   - Going around the virtual room to give everyone a chance to talk

8. Tim's manager should help him with various aspects of his job. First, when Tim was interviewing for the position, his manger should have included everyone in the interview process, including, at the very least, Joe and Linda and other direct reports. Tim should also have been briefed on the team dynamics. Once that process was complete, there would have been more buy-in from the employees if they believed they had been a part of the selection process. In addition, Tim's manager should be running the first few meetings between Tim and his team so that everyone is comfortable. Only then should Tim be set off on his own, to forge his own relationships with his team.

9. Tim probably thought Linda could help him find a way to get his new division to work together. Linda had been building a corporate human factors and usability presence for years. Tim is busy focusing on trying to respond quickly to the changes in the economy and wants to move from working on traditional printing to the digital business. He knew Linda would be integral to his goals.

10. Linda's presence at the meeting probably made Joe feel marginalized. As it was, Joe and his team did not feel valued. He knew it was hard to work from a remote location and that he had to work extra hard to communicate and connect with the team in New York. The UCD team in California feels disenfranchised from the rest of the company.

Joe also fears for his job and sees Linda stepping into a position that puts another layer between him and Tim. Also, Joe had thoughts of moving up in the organization and believed himself more qualified than Linda because he has formal training in the field and she didn't. Linda's presence at the meeting added to Joe's feeling that he was not valued by his superiors and that he did not have enough status to have a private meeting with his direct manager. Joe knew he had to come up with a different way of relating to the team in New York.

Case 3: Raising Awareness at the Company Level

1. Jill should assume that Red Fox has little understanding of UE for the following reasons:
    -   Before Jill joined the company there was insufficient investment in UE resources, which is a strong indication that there is a lack of understanding of the benefits of UE within the company.
    -   There was no UE high-level manager, and the two designers probably did not have the opportunity and/or the experience to evangelize UE. With UE so understaffed, the two designers most likely had no time to evangelize because they were working on a large number of projects. Even if the designers had time, they most likely didn't have experience in usability, metrics, and information architecture and would not have been able to paint a complete picture of UE for anyone in the organization.
    -   It only takes one executive to hire a UE vice-president but that doesn't mean there is a pervasive understanding across the company about UE. In the case of Red Fox Technologies there could be more than 1,000 other people who wouldn't know why Jill was hired.
    -   It is possible that a predecessor who did not have a UE background managed some UE people but didn't have the knowledge to either evangelize or to practice solid UE principles and methods. Jill had joined companies in which her predecessors had been a marketing art director and an engineering manager, neither of whom had a strong background in UE.
    Even though a predecessor may have had some positive influence, because of employee turnover many of those people may no longer

be in the same departments or even in the company. From Jill's experience, education and evangelizing are ongoing activities because of employee turnover, growing organizations, and reorganizations. One benefit of reorganizations is that employees who have become aware of the benefits of UE can become distributed throughout the company and help to influence others.

A predecessor might actually have had a negative impact, which could be why there were only two designers in a company of more than 1,000. A predecessor may have spread misinformation, been inflexible in processes and methods, or have considered only the user experience without considering the business needs and trade-offs. If this is the case, not only does Jill need to raise awareness, she also needs to address some misunderstandings.

2. In her first 2 months Jill should use the following strategies:
   - Understand the company: Jill should learn as much as possible about the company, its culture, and the business goals and values. This is critical so that Jill can know how to prioritize work to best support the company to achieve its business goals.
   - Perform a knowledge gap analysis: A gap analysis is performed by comparing the status of different states, often comparing how something currently "is," the current state, with how something "should be," the more ideal state. Jill should assess the current levels of understanding of UE across the company, including any incorrect impressions (the "is" state). She should then compare the levels of understanding (and most likely there will be multiple levels of understanding because different people and different groups will have different sets of knowledge) with what she believes the organization needs to know to make more optimal decisions (the "should" state). The difference between these two states is the gap. By understanding this gap, Jill can then assess what areas she needs to focus on—such as education or introducing and integrating processes—and also determine the priority of addressing these identified issues.
   - Understand the internal customers: Jill should learn as much as possible about the key stakeholders, including their values, goals, and terminology. By aligning with these, Jill can translate UE goals, which are probably not understood by stakeholders, into terms they can understand. For example, if an important goal is to reduce development and quality assurance time, Jill can ensure

that the people she hires and the activities that her team focuses on will address these needs.

- Understand the development cycle: Every company has differences in how it takes an idea and eventually launches it. Sometimes the development cycle is documented as a process, sometimes as multiple processes depending on the type and scope of the project, and sometimes there are no documented processes. Any company that either is trying to obtain International Organization for Standardization (ISO) certification or is ISO certified has documented processes. (Many vendor companies have an interest in becoming ISO certified because the certification often provides the company with an advantage during the vendor-selection process.) Documented processes typically mean higher efficiency and higher quality results because the processes reduce confusion and missed steps. Even with documented processes, more times than not there are at best small differences between what is documented and what is practiced, so it is also critical to assess what is practiced and how much what is practiced varies across the company and from project to project.

3. To optimize decision making, the UE department should actually be at the same reporting level as engineering and marketing. If the UE department is not reporting at the same level, the company is still driven more strongly by these other departments than by UE. This is another clear indication that Red Fox Technologies is not fully educated about user experience and its benefits.

4. The following three items should take the highest priority:

Item 1: Building a usability lab. There are many reasons why building a lab is an important area to focus on early:

- Usability labs are one of the most effective strategies for raising the awareness of UE within companies.
- From a practical standpoint, usability labs can be used for a variety of UE activities, including comparative and benchmark usability evaluations and participatory design sessions.
- With access to a lab with a one-way mirror, stakeholders across the company can watch live evaluations, which increases the likelihood that they will address the issues identified in the usability sessions. Also, web-based applications can enable employees to view sessions from their desks if they aren't able to watch in person.

- Usability labs outfitted with video production and editing tools can also enable the efficient production of video highlights and remote viewing of the usability evaluations if stakeholders are in other geographic locations. These features enable even wider influence of the usability evaluations, allowing stakeholders to watch at other times and locations.

- As Jill knows from past experience, the usability lab can act as a tangible icon of a concept not familiar to stakeholders. People may not understand what UE is, but a first step is to know that there is a lab and that activities occur in the lab.

- Usability labs can help to close important customer deals, thus helping to raise awareness even more. By giving customers tours of the lab, the customers understand the importance the company places on increasing the usability of the products and services. Jill had been able to help close multimillion dollar deals by providing prospective customers with a tour and background of the steps the company takes to increase the usability of their products.

- Jill has also used the completion of usability labs as an opportunity to significantly raise the awareness of UE both within the company and with customers. For example, Jill has had a major usability lab's grand opening event at a previous company. She invited the entire company to come tour throughout the day, had presentations from the CEO and the president both live and broadcast across the company, gave a presentation on the benefits, invited the press and important customers to attend, had the ever-popular free food to lure people, and also had giveaways with the group name on them. Although this event required significant planning and a budget for the food and giveaways, this one event introduced the concept of UE to literally thousands of people in one day. In addition, by working with the CEO and the president on the messaging, they communicated during their presentations the importance of projects using the usability labs. After the grand opening, Jill had people from all over the company contacting her, saying "I don't know exactly what I need to do, but I know I'm supposed to be bringing my projects through that lab." Jill also provided important customers with customized tours over the next few weeks.

Item 3: Hiring. From past experience, Jill knew that hiring was priority one for multiple reasons:

- With more UE professionals, Jill had more people to demonstrate and raise the awareness of the importance of UE.
- From past experience, open head count does not necessarily remain open. Jill wanted to fill the positions before anything could reduce her head count allocation. For example, many companies institute cost-containment measures such as putting open head count on hold after a quarter with flat or reduced revenue.
- Because there were visual designers within her new team but no usability engineers, information architects, and other roles, Jill needed to augment her current team with additional skills.
- One of the reasons Jill accepted the position at Red Fox is that they appeared to be willing to make a significant investment in resources, particularly after she spent some of the interview time educating the executives and communicating that it was a factor in her consideration of the position.

Item 6: Gaining direct contact with customers. To run usability evaluations, along with other reasons, Jill knew that UE needed direct contact with customers.

- Although it's also important to obtain feedback from prospective customers, Jill's perspective has always been that it is a waste of time and resources if a company is not using both real customers and prospects in their usability evaluations.
- Customers can be involved in a wide variety of UE methods in addition to usability evaluations in the lab, including participatory design sessions, interviews, longitudinal studies, and field studies.
- Customers who are involved in UE activities typically have increased satisfaction with the company and often mention their positive experiences with UE team members to the sales or marketing representatives or executive sponsor. One of the most effective ways to raise executives' awareness is for customers to cite the positive influence of their interactions with UE.

5. Although all the items have significant benefits, and progress could be made on any of the items (particularly if an activity involving that item were to start or be underway in some part of the organization),

the three items listed above provide greater leverage for performing the other items:

- Integrating UE into documented processes assumes there are sufficient resources to support the activities.
- If sufficient UE head count has not been allocated and there is no current ability to hire, a plan for project prioritization and resource allocation would be one of the first three activities to perform. This plan would communicate the head count needed and the ramifications of not hiring, such as many or most projects not involving UE. If there is open head count, filling those positions would be the priority (Item 3).
- Information about UE is beneficial but isn't as critical as hiring the resources before the demand for UE increases due to internal communication about UE and its benefits.
- Integrating UE into corporate or departmental goals typically depends on both the time of year and on building some understanding and credibility within the organization. As a result, this is typically one of the later tactics to use.
- Integrating UE into project requirements is also typically performed later because the process for creating requirements needs to be updated and the UE requirements need to be identified.
- UE release criteria have the same considerations as requirements in that both the process and the release criteria need to be identified.
- Integrating UE goals into executive bonuses is often one of the last tactics to use, because typically relationships with the executives need to be established before this can happen. On rare occasions, if a company has a strong initiative to create a culture change, this tactic can be used more quickly.

6. The UE organization and staffing plan also serves to raise the awareness of how UE groups should be staffed and structured. In addition, the plan demonstrates how even nine additional employees do not provide the coverage for all the projects Red Fox had planned for the coming year. By making trade-offs explicit—whether the decision is to do fewer projects or hire more UE people—the UE organization can make executive management more aware of the requirements for a sufficient level of UE resources. To maintain credibility for the UE staffing levels, Jill and her team need to

demonstrate significant added value to projects to justify the head count. Spreading UE resources too thin would not result in significant improvements, so Jill needs to ensure that important projects are properly supported, even if it means other less important projects have no resources. Also, the plan demonstrates Jill's business perspective (her ability to plan and manage against a plan), which increases her credibility among the executives.

7. Companies vary quite widely in which department owns the documentation and oversight of development processes and to what extent the life cycle is documented. For example, some companies have fully specified and detailed processes starting from the conceptual phase to post-deployment. Jill had used different strategies to integrate UE into company processes in the past. In one company the processes were written by the quality officers and maintained by the quality department, so Jill became a quality officer to influence the processes used across the company. At Red Fox Technologies, the production group owned this responsibility. Jill and her team performed the following steps to document and integrate UE into the development processes:

   • Document the UE process: Jill and her team worked with some of the production team to map out the UE activities and deliverables and integrate them into the development process (including the all-important requirements phase at the start of the projects).

   • Integrate UE approval for project milestones: To raise awareness for UE and ensure quality, Jill added approval steps to the process so that projects that affect the UI could not be built and released until approved by UE.

   • Integrate UE approval for prioritizing and activating projects: Jill became a member of the executive team that prioritized the projects so she could ensure that UE issues were brought to light during this important activity. The same team decided when to give projects the green light with resources and a schedule, so Jill could ensure that the UE resources were available and provide input to the other executives regarding any user-experience considerations.

8. Integrating UE into the documented processes is not sufficient for ensuring that UE is incorporated into the development processes as part of the daily practice. Jill knew from experience that most of the

time companies deviated from their documented processes—sometimes they were minor deviations and sometimes they were major. To help raise awareness, UE needs to become integrated into the documented processes *and* into everyday practices.

9.   Embedding UE goals into executive bonuses might seem like a major win for raising the awareness of UE. However, if no one checks with UE to see whether the goals have really been achieved, then all the executives could simply declare victory, thus full bonuses, for the UE-related part of their bonus structure. Jill doesn't want to be naive—when it comes to executive compensation, why wouldn't executives declare full achievement of these goals? Jill needs to make sure that she works in checkpoints so that she can help the executives successfully meet the goals and that she or another UE team member verifies the status to ensure that the goals are truly met.

10.   The existence of UE release criteria will not ensure that projects meet the criteria. As with the goals and bonuses discussed earlier, the UE release criteria must be achievable with the time and resources allocated as well as the technological constraints. Jill and her team needed to actively work with the other project team members throughout the life cycle to maximize the likelihood that the project would meet the UE release criteria. Although theoretically the project could be held up if it didn't meet the criteria, if the effort hadn't been made throughout the life cycle to address the criteria, the project would most likely be released regardless of whether or not the criteria had been met.

11.   Some pitfalls of UE release criteria are as follows:
   •   Unachievable goals: If there are not sufficient resources or time allocated or there are criteria that are not feasible with the technologic constraints, then the goals were not properly planned.
   •   Credibility: When goals aren't properly planned, not only are the UE criteria not met, they lack credibility. If UE goals are disregarded because they are not realistic during one project, they are more likely to be disregarded in other projects in the future.
   •   Setting idealistic goals: Most UE professionals would like to increase the usability of all aspects of all their projects. However, from a business perspective this is not necessarily the best approach for the company given limited time and resources. The more that UE can demonstrate it is focused on what is most important for the business, the greater the awareness will be of the benefits of UE.

12. Jill has seen over the years how differing opinions among UE professionals about methods and approaches, in addition to terminology used, can erode the credibility of the UE group when expressed to the company at large. Jill is a big believer in continual process improvement, including constantly challenging how to improve the efficacy of processes and methods. However, she is also a believer in keeping these debates and conversations within the UE group and practicing consistent messaging outside the group to maintain credibility.

Case 4: Usability Step by Step: Small Steps to a More Successful Site

1. Dorothy, the site's creator, is very attached to the site and far too close to it to assess it objectively. Sheila's reaction to the site is based on a comparison of her experience with this site and others she uses regularly. For Sheila, change is a positive step; for Dorothy, change is an implied criticism and a possible threat.

2. To communicate effectively with Dorothy, it's important to acknowledge her contribution to the site and the value of the site *as it is*. Laura's experience with NVIP so far has taught her that she must be prepared to support any assertions about how the site should look, work, or be structured with references to authoritative sources and data from actual users, which many teams find more compelling than some "expert" from whom they've never heard. She should model effective communication techniques for Sheila and, when the opportunity arises, explain how she plans to approach Dorothy. Finally, she should also provide her with evidence rather than opinion about how to revise the site.

3. Usability testing drives design and redesign. It pinpoints problem areas, helps prioritize trouble spots and gaps, and makes sense of the comments and reaction of users. Usability testing is the first step in a process of analysis that leads to recommendations for better products and services. Usability also helps prevent rework and misdirected efforts by shedding light on what users and visitors *do* rather than what *they believe they do*. In situations where user research has not been part of the initial development cycle, as in this case, later usability testing can provide critical information about user personas, task flows, and preferences.

4. A website redesign involves a reexamination of all elements of the site, from structure and navigation through images, link labels, page types and formats, metatags, style sheets, and content. A good redesign is more than just a renewal—it's a fresh approach to solving the problem of meeting both the audience needs and site owner goals, which have frequently expanded, multiplied, or shifted with time—or were never systematically addressed in the first place. Usability testing is one of the key tools for informing a redesign; it enables a fresh perspective on the use of the site.

5. To avoid disruption of the site, the redesign could be implemented in phases, with each phase concentrating on changes that integrate with one another and naturally cascade to the next set of changes. To reassure an anxious client like Dorothy, Sheila could explain that the changes can be accomplished without taking the site down. For example, she can explain the use of "redirects" for links, when current URLs are replaced with code that automatically sends visitors to corresponding replacement pages in the new site. In this way the ADP team can be assured that the content visitors are accustomed to finding will always be available. In this case Sheila could also point out that at this site only a very small number of documents and pages are consistently used by over 90% of visitors. The rollout of the redesign could be planned to ensure that these most-visited pages are always available and highly visible. Implementing changes in phases also ensures that visitors do not experience "site shock"—reaching a site that has been overhauled and no longer resembles the site they thought they knew.

6. The ADP team is reluctant to consider any changes. They are not convinced that any "outsider" is knowledgeable enough to offer a useful critique of the site, and they secretly believe the site is fine just as it is. A steady diet of praise has made them certain they already do everything right; they have found the magic formula that works. Natural inertia can also be a problem, because change means work—and can be threatening or frightening.

   Sheila's slightly adversarial relationship with Dorothy is another potential barrier; Laura could find that she is tainted by association with Sheila. The small size and tight operating budget for the ADP team means that committing to a website overhaul may be beyond their reach in terms of both personnel and money. Time frames are constraints as well, in two ways: the tests must be conducted during the current fiscal year, which ends shortly, and the recommendations for improvements cannot involve taking the site down for repairs for more than a few hours.

7. This team is not convinced that its website needs help; this is probably the most critical obstacle to the success of the plan. The team also faces constraints of time and money. The ADP team is small and has a limited budget that might not cover the costs of even the modest plan that Laura has suggested. Laura's approach could diminish the team's resistance by appealing to impersonal "data" and "standards"—but it could also backfire. Negative feedback could humiliate the team and make them discount the results of the tests. Laura plans to appeal to the service orientation of the ADP team and its respect for research rather than opinion. She also intends to offer usability services at the lowest possible cost and to include ADP staffers as part of the usability test team.

8. Laura is describing a best-case scenario for conducting and applying the results of a usability test. She is not drawing attention to the inexperience of most of the team members, the investment of time required to plan and prepare, or the possibility that recruiting participants and conducting the sessions may not go smoothly. Also, she is not considering the possibility of any technology problems (although she does plan to prepare a backup disk with site contents for use in case an Internet connection is not available or crashes). Laura is also making the assumption that the experiences of both new and existing visitors will reflect problems at the site and support Sheila's conviction that change is needed. She is repressing the fact that new visitors' needs and preferences might be very different from those of established visitors.

9. For tests of a commercial site, it would be a simple matter to point out that if visitors fail to find products or carry out processes for purchase, the site loses money. Because e-commerce is fiercely competitive, owners of such sites have a compelling reason to watch their competition and keep pace with or overtake the competition. Although owners of such sites must also manage costs, they attract and retain visitors by ensuring high satisfaction with their products and with experience at their sites.

10. Probably most important, Coral and Laura should have insisted that ADP team members be more involved with test sessions and with analyzing the results of the sessions. They could have worked harder

to ensure that Dorothy and Maxine were available to observe some sessions along with Larry. If Maxine and Dorothy had had the opportunity to view some of the sessions and ask questions of the participants directly after the sessions they watched, the test findings might have been more convincing, or at least less surprising. If Larry, Maxine, and Dorothy had taken part in analyzing the results, they might have been more receptive to the findings and more invested in considering changes to the site.

The NVIP team could have helped to dispel tension and build trust by inviting the ADP team members to share more of their plans and aspirations for the website and talking about ways to fulfill those plans. They could also have encouraged more "venting" and expressions of disappointment or disagreement, allowing the ADP team to have their say and believe their ideas and concerns had been fully heard. The NVIP team might also have encouraged ADP personnel to express their fears about the impact of changes to the site, because ADP team members had a gut feeling of "if it ain't broke, don't fix it." Depersonalizing the results and recommendations by referring to other sites and to difficulties and setbacks with the NVIP site might have helped, as well as a more complete acknowledgment of the hard work and success associated with the ADP site. Working to provide a face-to-face meeting might have been worth the cost and effort: Direct communication could have alleviated many of the problems that were exacerbated by lack of eye contact and inability to read body language.

11. The ADP team is resisting recommendations because they don't really believe that visitors to the site experience the difficulties observed by the NVIP team; at heart, they don't believe their site needs improvement, and they fear that changes made by outsiders will "spoil" the site. The ADP team has not really come to trust the NVIP team: They fear losing control of the site, they may believe their work is not valued by the NVIP team, and they believe the NVIP team doesn't understand how visitors use the site. The project goal to improve visitor experience at the site has been obscured by the need for both teams to vindicate their ideas about what's best for the site. Playing up the areas where the ADP team was "right" might have helped, but the root cause goes back to the original lack of commitment to the project. The ADP team also faces constraints with time and money. This small team has its hands full maintaining the

current site. They have neither time to make extensive changes themselves nor money to hire others to overhaul the site.

12. Additional approaches to the ADP team include

    - Asking the ADP team how they plan to reach the goal of improving the site for everyone
    - Inviting everyone to brainstorm what the site could do or offer to work better for visitors
    - Reviewing the test results and ask the ADP team to interpret the results
    - Accepting the fact that it may not be possible to overcome the doubts of this team: They did not initiate the project and did not accept the premise that the site needed to be improved.

    Finally, it is worth noting that Laura should look for a more receptive team with which to work. Coral needs successes to build credibility for usability at NVIP. Resistant teams are not the best place to start, but they are more likely to embrace usability when they see the value other teams place on it or when they observe the successes of others.

13. No matter how receptive the audience, it's a good idea to present positive findings up front and emphasize them. With this particular audience, a segue from "it's very good" to "and here's how it can be even better" might have been more effective. The report neither included quotes or descriptions of user paths nor provided examples of comparable problems (and possible solutions) taken from similar sites. Data and statistics from published research could have been effective in persuading Dorothy and her team. These elements might have helped Dorothy and her team receive the "bad news" with more equanimity.

14. Like other public health researchers and educators, Dorothy, Maxine, and Larry were domain specialists with confidence in their own expertise and a deep respect for formal quantitative research. They could best be persuaded by strong appeals to their commitment to public service, coupled with a wealth of supporting hard data presented in chart or graph form.

15. As Laura and Coral suspected, the change in tone was likely a signal that ADP team members had decided, collectively or otherwise, to "cut their losses" and escape the discussion gracefully. Although Dorothy was constitutionally and by training inclined to argue every point and let no statement or inference go unchallenged, she may also

have been threatened by the clarity and confidence of Coral's team. The ADP team could not concede Laura's points without losing face, and there seemed to be no way to agree to changes without admitting that the site needed improvement—something Dorothy was simply not ready to do. It might have helped if Laura had asked why the tone of their responses and reactions had changed, but unless the subject was raised with great tact, it might also have made ADP team members even more defensive and uncomfortable.

16.   The outcome will most likely be that ADP will appear to accept the findings but refuse to act on the recommendations Laura presented—unless Sheila is able to pressure the ADP team into accepting the recommendations. However, this may result in observance of the letter rather than the spirit of the recommendations, and in the end it may not bring much real improvement.

17.   Laura, Coral, and Sheila have probably not convinced the ADP team that their site has flaws, and they probably have not demonstrated the value of usability to Maxine, Dorothy, and Larry. However, the NVIP team had significant achievements, including designing and delivering a usability test in a short time frame with limited funds. The NVIP team also had experience with both clients and audience members. They apparently mastered "low-rent" usability methods and learned a great deal about how to communicate effectively with a skeptical and strong-minded client. The team successes included

- Rapid test design
- Low-cost test methods
- Effective on-the-spot recruiting
- Operating effectively by leveraging team members' skills: Sheila's communication skills, Coral's ability to organize, and Laura's usability experience and background as a facilitator of sessions and teams

Case 5: Growing a Business by Meeting (Real) Customer Needs

1.   In this situation Johanna might suggest field research and usability tests to learn what RevPhoto's customers need and how well the current product meets those needs. The research will help the team determine which features customers need and which they struggle with or don't

need, as well as whether they have problems that the product is not solving at all.

2. It is well worth the research investment for RevLev to figure out what's broken before launching into a solution. The sales drop has caused them to acknowledge they have been out of touch with customer needs for some time now. This wake-up call should convince them not to rush to code solutions. Because they won't have the resources to fix every problem they learn about, they need to know which areas of the product to focus on most.

3. An optimal research approach includes involving a cross-functional team made up of engineering, product management/marketing, UCD, and technical support in all phases of the research. By watching customers and analyzing the results together, each team member can contribute their unique perspective and have buy-in with the solution.

4. There are many valid ways to gather information on the customer's workflow. A few that are commonly used in software companies are field observations, asking customers to rank a list of tasks on paper or in e-mail, in-depth customer interviews by phone, and online survey tools. Regardless what limitations the team faces in time and costs, they should be able to run some type(s) of effective research that will reveal more of the customer's perspective.

5. The key to success for RevLev—and all software companies—is to design a product that solves their customers' problems. To do that, the team needs to learn from the customers themselves. By doing good field research, RevLev increases the chances of fixing their products the right way—to meet their customers' needs.

   In addition, when time is short and improvements are critical, it will save time in the long run to have buy-in from the cross-functional leaders from the beginning. By being included in the research, each functional group is represented in setting and agreeing on the product direction.

6. The team should explain the need to enact the following three recommendations:

   1. Do not invest further in the features circled in green (Figure 5.1). The task/success data show that these features already successfully meet the customers' needs. The team can invest its resources to improve lower rated features.

   2. Focus heavily on improving success rates for the items circled in red (Figure 5.1). The data show that success rates with these tasks

are below 50% (low ease of use) and rank in the list of Top 10 tasks that users want to do with RevPhoto.

3. Do not invest in the three planned enhancements shown in Table 5.2. Because customers do not value doing these tasks highly, this is not where the team should focus its efforts.

7. Relying too heavily on only quantitative or qualitative data (whether in the lab or the field) does not give a complete view of customers' needs. The team validated the quantitative survey's Top 10 list by going into the field to learn about customers' usage patterns and problem areas.

8. During field research, the team followed a plan to determine which tasks customers did with RevPhoto to validate the Top 10 survey data. By paying attention to other tasks customers performed, the team noticed this "surprise" usage. Though great surprises like this don't happen regularly, without field research, they wouldn't be discovered at all.

Case 6: But the Usability People Said It Was Okay . . . Or, How Not to "Do Usability"

1. Ellen, with 15 years in the usability business under her belt and 5 years of experience at this company, should have known better than to propose a Band-Aid solution without at least a little more information. She should have asked several things:

   - Why does this need to be done so quickly? Chances are she could at least have postponed a discussion with Tom until Monday, to get a little more information about the project.

   - Why was Tom in her office so late on Friday afternoon? It would have been useful to know if he had suddenly been asked to go talk to her or whether he'd forgotten and was making his crisis her problem.

   - Who had asked him to talk to her and why? Understanding whether this was a request from above or if it just came up in a casual conversation in Tom's group would have helped her make a better decision about how to handle the request.

   - What's the usability group's level of responsibility on this project? Specifically, were they being asked to take full responsibility for the design (e.g., they get final say) or to contribute suggestions to influence the design (e.g., their ideas may or may not make it to the final design)? If Ellen had clarified this point with Tom, both would have been better prepared for what followed. Ellen could then have made clear to her team what they should expect, and Tom, when asked later, might have remembered he had specifically told Ellen he wasn't handing her responsibility for the final design.

Any of this information might have suggested to Ellen to either put more resources on the project (if it was really important) or to politely turn it down (if it was a more casual request).

2. Nancy, while new to the company, wasn't new to the usability business either. She should have asked the basic questions that are good background for any project involving a usability evaluation:

   • Who are the users for this information? When would they be using it? Why was this information suddenly being made more widely available?

   • What was the schedule for the project, and was there any wiggle room in the schedule?

   • What stage was the design at? Was this the final version? How was it actually going to be given to users?

   If Tom couldn't answer any of these questions, Nancy could have helped him work through them to resolve some of these open issues. Even in a short conversation, it would have been clear to Nancy whether or not the project was well thought out. If not, and there was no way to get clarification, this probably would have been a good time for Nancy to gracefully exit or to hand the project back to Ellen for resolution.

3. Tom, with 30 years in the facility management business, probably was doing what he thought he should. Educating Tom about the right way to ask for help from the usability team was Ellen's job, and one that she should attend to quickly.

4. In a company where the term "mental model" is used in casual conversation, it might be a good idea for Ellen to lend Tom her copy of *The Design of Everyday Things* and suggest he take a look at the first three chapters so he'll have more background. These first several chapters are accessible for most readers and convey the essential points about user-centered design and can give anyone the vocabulary they need to be more functional in an organization that is using terms like "mental model."

Ellen should probably also spend some time with Tom trying to anticipate what projects the usability group is likely to be called in on. Although his group is not one that she normally supports, she does seem to be asked to find resources for his projects periodically. Understanding what might be coming, and even suggesting where her group would be most or least helpful, could help control the flow of projects into her area.

5. Ellen needs to go back to her team and have a discussion about how the team talks about their work. Using this story as background, they could talk about how to present results and recommendations. Putting their work in the proper context for their clients, especially for people who work with them infrequently, could be really helpful for the clients to understand what work has been done and to ensure the data aren't inadvertently misused. She should also emphasize two other points:

    - Usability team members involved in one-off projects need to be careful to clarify what their roles and responsibilities are on a particular project and scope their language and efforts accordingly. If they are only being asked for recommendations, they need to be very circumspect about presenting these.
    - When working with a team that is relatively inexperienced with user-centered design methods, it's important to take a few minutes to educate them about what the user-centered design process can and can't provide, as well as limitations and appropriate uses of data.

    Although it might seem like overkill, she needs to emphasize to her team the importance of really working to counter this image of their team as an approving body. Most usability teams work as partners with their clients, and any positioning that seems to put them in a position of judgment can be very detrimental to building the necessary working relationships.

6. Ellen also needs to go back and have a chat with her manager, Todd, and enlist his help. She needs to give him the information and language that he needs to use to shape discussions when he hears usability recommendations being misused. If he has a better idea how people can sometimes misinterpret their work, he can help cut off some of these incorrect perceptions earlier by himself. Plus, he needs to be aware that Ellen is going to push back a bit more on projects where she's concerned that their efforts won't be used effectively, and

she needs to get his buy-in that their group shouldn't be used as just a casual set of design reviewers.

7. Ellen could have provided some more background information to Eric by asking Allan a few more questions:

   - Is there anyone else besides Bob who wants to review these signs? Who and why?
   - Have they tried this kind of thing before? What happened if it didn't go well? Why does he believe it will go better this time?
   - What is the usability's group role? How will it be represented?

8. Ellen should do the following things:

   - She should first call Tom and check in with him about his expectations and find out what he knows about the project so far. She can review their recent conversation and confirm that Tom really is looking for design assistance, and he'll be careful not to represent their work as approving the project.
   - Ellen should next check in with Eric to see whether he has time and is interested in the project; then she should probably give him a few words of wisdom:
     - Make sure that Allan knows that Eric is there to help with the design, and the goal is to come up with something they both believe is effective: ideally, a design they've been able to check with users.
     - She needs to remind Eric that this is exactly the kind of situation that she had just discussed with the group. He needs to be careful to represent himself as a partner, not an approver, on the project.
   - Ellen also needs to make Eric aware that Bob wants to review the designs. She should have him talk to someone else who has worked with Bob on a project like this and get some advice about how Bob likes to be involved. For example:
     - Does he like to see early designs, or present early design ideas?
     - Does he prefer to only see almost finished designs? If so, how likely is he to cause significant rework?
     - Does Bob like to see quantitative data to support conclusions, or will convincing qualitative information be more appropriate?

9. Eric should do the following things:

   - Set up a meeting with Allan to review project goals, timing, budget, and so forth. He needs to push Allan a little to find out if there are any underlying agendas that need to be taken into account.

- Because this isn't Allan's usual kind of project, Eric should expect to take Allan through the early steps of deciding who is the target audience and the goal of this project. However, Eric also needs to take into account that Allan may never need to do this kind of work again, and so Eric should scope his efforts to educate Allan accordingly.

- Eric should take Ellen's advice about finding someone who has worked on projects that Bob wanted to review, and get advice. If it turns out Bob can deal with early designs, then make sure to get him involved. If he prefers to see finished designs but is likely to recommend significant changes, then Eric might want to help organize the project to get a reasonably final project to Bob early enough to accommodate any changes that might need to be made.

- Eric finally needs to underline the point with Allan that at the end of the project, Allan will be able to say that he worked with the usability group and that the final design incorporates their recommendations (and carefully repeat, "I'm not approving this, I'm helping you shape the design").

10. Not likely. He only asked that usability be involved, not that a complete user-centered design process should be applied. Given the history to date and Ellen's experience, this seems like a sensible time to test the boundaries of when it's okay to push back on requests that are out of scope.

11. Ellen should, however, go have a chat with her boss, and make sure he's okay that she pushed back on this. She needs his support, just in case Bob asks him about the project.

Case 7: Estimating a User-Centered Design Effort

1. Shea had estimated her activities the way she had always done for her UCD team lead. John had given her free rein to define a UCD process and then map the activities to his development plan. Now she realized she had to define and estimate the work at a more detailed level to do that mapping. She would have to break down the UCD

phases into individual tasks and estimate how many hours each task would take. That way, she could lay out the activities on a timeline and answer John's scheduling and resource questions.

2. To prepare for estimating at this level, Shea recalled how she spent her time on projects for her previous employer, and she sought out experienced colleagues at other companies for their advice. From the information she collected, she created a more detailed UCD plan. She included the parameters for each research component (such as number and length of sessions) and the tasks and intermediate deliverables— such as the test plan, protocol, and report—to carry out each component. She then estimated the hours to perform each of the tasks.

3. Adding up time for meetings and preparing status reports, Shea decided to allocate five hours per week for project management. She multiplied the number of weeks for each activity by five hours per week to calculate the number of project management hours per activity. She then reduced her available UCD hours by five hours per week to allow time for project management. She knew this reduced availability would add more weeks to her schedule, and she needed to see how many more.

4. Shea reduced her available UCD hours per week by yet another five hours per week to reserve time for other company initiatives.

5. Shea discussed the timelines with each vendor and learned that the vendors were allowing time for Apollo Appraisal's review of their deliverables. The vendors also extended the recruiting time to include multiple review checkpoints—review of participant profiles, screening materials, surveys, and final candidate recommendations. Shea had not built these deliverables into her own schedule.

6. An alternative solution is whether a vendor could staff the two Phase 1 research activities to occur concurrently. But then she would not have the data from the competitive testing to inform the design of the ethnographic research; plus the data would be in multiple researchers' heads. Another solution is to hire two firms, each performing one of the activities, again so that the activities could happen concurrently. This approach would pose the same disadvantages as the first solution, plus she would be managing multiple vendors.

7. Her third alternative solution was to reduce the scope of the two Phase 1 research activities so that a single firm could perform them within a shorter timeline. She decided she favored that approach.

8. Shea knew that in a structured work environment like John's department, the style guide would be the UCD specification. Without a style guide, Shea would spend even more time explaining and reexplaining the principles and specifications of the UI design to the engineers. She concluded that lack of a style guide would jeopardize other deadlines and increase the chance of more inconsistencies across the design.

9. Shea decided to start with an abbreviated draft of the style guide and add more information later. She also decided to look at her overall plan again to see whether she could perform some things in parallel or possibly eliminate some activity without major risk. She noticed that she could start usability testing of the prototype at the same time as work on the style guide.

Case 8: A Case Study in Card Sorting

1. The primary problem with the LANDAUS.COM website is that users have difficulty finding specific items. The reasons items are difficult to find relate primarily to weaknesses in the website's organization. The contents of a website should be organized in a way that reflects users' expectations. For example, a user visiting a website that sells boating and diving merchandise would probably expect, at the very least, separate sections for boating and diving equipment. Within each of these main categories, users might expect that contents be further categorized.

    Andy should also explore the possibility that other aspects of the website are contributing to the customers' difficulties. These may include insufficient product information on the site or poor descriptions of customer service policies. But because Landau's has had a successful mail order business for many years and because the website simply used the content from its catalogs, it is unlikely that poor content is the culprit.

2. When a website grows over time, often the information architecture used to initially structure the site may not hold up in the long term. A simple website with only one level of navigation, such as Landau's original site, may be adequate to house all the site's products and content when that universe of content is small. But as the site adds content, a single level of organization may become untenable. The typical response at this point is to add more categories and subdivide

the existing categories. However, if this is done in an ad-hoc fashion, without a true sense of the big picture, a site can quickly sprawl out of control. Categories stop being "clean" and content does not easily fit into a logical location. Consequently, it is difficult to find content once it's categorized.

3. Several aspects of LANDAU'S history, culture, goals, and development process have led to the current problems with the organization of the website:

   - LANDAU'S does not have a multidisciplinary design team in place. Their team consists mostly of programmers and one visual designer. The team apparently has no one with usability, user-centered design, information architecture, or interaction design skills and no one who understands the business of making money on the web.

   - The testers test function and system reliability, not usability.

   - The executive in charge of the website is not a technologist and doesn't have any training in web design, usability, development, and so forth. Although it is not necessary for executives to be experts in the specifics of website design, they should have enough understanding of user-centered design to make personnel, strategy, and resource decisions.

   - LANDAU'S practice of hiring multiple contractors for website development may lead to inconsistency in the product's user experience. If different groups create pieces of the user experience and the efforts of those groups are not coordinated, the result may be an inconsistent user experience.

   - The website was modeled after the catalog, which is a paper document. Creating a successful website is not just a matter of putting a paper document online. A website must take into account the user moving through a virtual information space; organization, navigation, interactivity, and ease of use are critical components of success. In addition, technical considerations such as download speed, performance, forms, shopping carts, search engines, and the checkout process contribute heavily to the user experience with a website.

   - The website was designed without input from the users. LANDAU'S employees provided design input. To successfully design a user-centered product, real representative users must provide input.

- Landau's succeeded as a retail outlet partly because they were "high touch" with customers, providing expert advice and service. That approach typically doesn't translate well to the web. Andy did not spend enough time thinking about how to maintain the approach in Landau's move to the web.
- As Landau's grew and added product lines, they may have moved away from the founders' core competencies. It's possible that Landau's doesn't understand how to sell its products as well as they used to.

4. Andy should educate himself, at least at a basic conceptual level, about website design. Through this education, Andy will likely discover that a well-organized website is not an accident and that there is a body of knowledge and practice that can help him with his user problems.

    Andy should then proceed to address the key problem with the website: its lack of coherent organization. But who decides whether a site is "well organized"? At LANDAUS.COM, the development team "put their heads together" to organize the site. They used the catalog for guidance. Perhaps they looked around at other websites. But they did not go to the users. Andy needs to find a way to involve users in the redesign of the site.

5. First, Barry could group closely related items into a single composite item. For example, LANDAU'S sold seven different brands of boat motors. Instead of listing each motor separately, Barry could choose to create a single item called "boat motors" and in the description refer to the item as follows: "There are seven different brands of boat motors sold. Please sort this item based on where you would put boat motors in general, regardless of brand." Barry realized that this would preclude users from certain sorting schemes. For example, imagine one of the motors was made by a company named AquaTech. Also imagine that AquaTech manufactures other boating supplies. By combining AquaTech motors with all other brands of motors, users would be prevented from creating a category defined by brand. Barry decided to address this concern by discussing with Andy how important brand is to LANDAU'S strategy: Did they want to emphasize vendor brands? Was there a solid business case to do so? And how would this compromise other organizational schemes for items? One way to address this concern is to allow users to shop by brand as well as by category. In essence, this would allow the website to have multiple organizational schemes. Because it is easy to

understand how to organize a website by brand, the card sort exercise could focus on understanding how users sort by concept.

Another way to reduce the number of items in a card sort is to separate out groups of items that obviously seem to fit into different categories. For example, LANDAU'S primarily sells boating equipment but also sells diving equipment and clothing. Barry could make the case that diving equipment, by all reasonable predictions, would likely be sorted into a different category than boating equipment. He could make the same case for clothing.

There is some risk inherent in this approach: By splitting out these items into separate card sort studies, Barry would essentially be making decisions on behalf of the users. This approach sounds contrary to the entire intent of card sorts: to have users sort the items and make the determination of what categories should exist. But holding too closely to this principle may be a case of the perfect being the enemy of the good. The key to making these decisions is to make them based on the lowest possible level of inference, that is, to split out groups that are clearly, conceptually distinct, and perform multiple studies. A "presort" activity, where a small number of users sort a subset of cards before the actual card sort study, may provide some security in making these decisions. If users tend to sort items together in presort exercises, these items should be included together in the same study. If they sort the items into separate categories, then they can comfortably be kept separate in multiple studies. Further, if there is any doubt about whether certain items should be assigned to one study or another because they could exist in more than one category, then the items should be included and repeated across the studies.

Performing multiple studies also requires performing a final "sort of sorts." Once all the "sibling" studies are performed and categories are generated by each, a final study can be performed in which these categories become the items for a new sort study. This final sort "boils up" the results and creates higher level categories. So, for example, Barry can do a study for diving merchandise and one for boating merchandise. Imagine that the diving study generates several categories (e.g., "Masks and Snorkels," "Regulators," "Tanks," "Wet Suits," etc.), and the boating study also generates several categories ("Small Crafts," "Boat Care Accessories," "Trailers," etc.). Once all categories from each study are determined, they become the items in a final study done with a different group of users (e.g., participants will sort "Masks and Snorkels," "Regulators," "Tanks," "Wet Suits," "Small Crafts," "Boat Care Accessories," "Trailers," etc.). The final set of categories will be the highest level categories on the website (e.g., "Diving" and "Boating").

A third way to reduce the number of items from a card sort is to simply eliminate some content items that can be assumed to be sorted together by users. This approach is similar to splitting out obvious groups in that it requires the researcher to make some assumptions about how users will sort the cards. But again, if the alternative is that the study will be compromised by having too many cards to sort, this approach provides a better alternative. Presorting studies can again help provide validation of the researcher's assumptions.

6. Barry should interview content experts, both inside and outside of LANDAU'S. He would be able to learn a great deal about boating and diving. He would understand that the items used while engaging in these hobbies have some very specific names that mean very specific things to those who use them. In such cases, trying to avoid jargon may in fact militate against the accurate placement of the cards. In such cases Barry should not rename those items. It would also be important for Barry to take great care in writing a clear, thorough description of the item that will accompany the item names. When users sort the items, they will see these descriptions, which will help them better understand exactly what the items are. For example, customers familiar with boats might not know that octopus in the world of diving is an apparatus that allows more than one person to have access to the same oxygen tank in case of an emergency. On the other hand, diving customers might not know that a downrigger is a device for a boat that allows one to place a fishing line at a desired depth.

7. To further ensure that users sort cards accurately, Barry can take additional steps:
   - He can review the cards and remove or change words in the item names that might influence users to group them together. In the "door" example earlier, "door mat" might be changed to "floor mat" and "door knob" to "handle."
   - Barry can provide clear instructions to users helping them understand how they are to sort the items. For example, Barry can tell users they are to put items into categories based on where they

would expect to find them on a website. By directing users in this way, they will have a clear context in which to perform the exercise.

- Finally, Barry can recruit carefully, selecting only those users who are truly target audience members. In the case of LANDAU'S, for example, only users who purchase diving equipment should sort the diving items.

8. Barry should proceed to the information architecture phase of the project.

Case 9: The HURIE Method: A Case Study Combining Requirements Gathering and User Interface Evaluation

1. As the catch phrase goes, "early and often." The research shows (e.g., Karat, 2005) that money spent on usability engineering is usually well cost justified, more so early in a software development project. User data can be collected, via a variety of methods, to inform designs early in the cycle and validate them late in the cycle. In the requirements gathering and analysis stages, task analysis and contextual inquiry are valuable methods. During design and early development, prototype testing can provide vital data in this iterative (design–test–redesign–retest) design approach. As the real product takes form, end-user testing is the most common usability evaluation method, and for good reason. Even when the product is shipped (or has "gone live"), surveys and field study continue to bring in user data to drive the designs of subsequent versions.

2. The benefits of a pluralistic usability walkthrough are as follows:
   - It entails real user feedback.
   - It can be carried out very early in the product development cycle.
   - It affords direct contact (and the aforementioned collaborative redesign) between users and developers.
   - It affords some performance data and some satisfaction data.

   The usability team selected this method because, first, it would allow them to collect some user data in the short amount of time that the representative users were available to them and with the nonfunctional prototype UI. In addition, because this evaluation method involves the design and development team directly, during data gathering it is a particularly good method when introducing a product development team to the joys of usability engineering.

3. Of course, it is often the job of a usability professional to convince a team that their "baby is ugly." But what if the usability team has to say, "Your baby is not worth keeping"? (This stretches the metaphor to the breaking point. Perhaps better, "Your product cannot be salvaged.") If the procedure had found a roomful of representative users who were unconvinced of the value of the product concept, the stakeholders would have been happy to learn it sooner rather than later. Luckily, the usability team did not have to address this, because the test participants almost universally found the product to be of potential value. Because the product developers were in the room, hearing the pluralistic usability walkthrough participants' comments just as the usability team heard them, it makes the pluralistic usability walkthrough method particularly useful here; presumably, the product developers would be arriving at the same conclusion and would not tend to question the veracity of the analysis as they might if they were not present during the evaluation. Had the results been different and the entire product called into question, then depending on the amount of market research that had gone before, it might make sense to expect the stakeholders to invest in another evaluation, to corroborate the negative findings, before jettisoning the entire project.

4. The wording used in such a study should be descriptive but not persuasive, more like a product concept description than marketing literature. That is, if a test participant heard, "This is a product that must do X," he or she could scarcely be dissatisfied upon seeing a prototype that reflects X as a product function. Rather, the introductory words should focus on the goals of the product (i.e., "to train battle commanders") and leave it up to the HURIE participants to decide (before they see the UI prototype) what the product requirements should be. In our walkthroughs we asked the product developer not to specify the exact features that were in the prototype or even in the plan.

5. The team should recognize that product requirements mentioned *after* the walkthrough are likely to have been motivated, or at least

influenced, by the pluralistic usability walkthrough exercises. This does not invalidate them. But it does require the product developers to be aware that the stated requirements might well have been different had the UI prototype been different. Those user requirements gathered in the HURIE method *before* the pluralistic usability walkthrough exercise are purer, therefore, at some level. However, the user requirements heard at the end of the exercise might be just as valuable, especially given that the entire HURIE method confirmed the goodness of the general direction of the product. One could even argue that the postprototype requirements are even more valid, because it's much easier for people to think about functional possibilities after seeing a prototype than just in the abstract. As with all usability findings, the product development team, including the usability professionals, should filter the findings through their own design sense, as they build the product.

6. It would have been preferable to have had a large collection of actual battle commanders to test. Times being what they are, these men and women tend to be busy elsewhere and so "help with usability testing of some future training tool" is a task that would most likely struggle to make it to the top of the "to do" list of many of them. The team was grateful for the two populations of users they had access to, and they embraced their comments universally strongly in their presence but in direct proportion to their representativeness to the ultimate user audience once the team analyzed the data. That is, when a comment came from a participant with actual battle commander experience, that comment carried more weight than one coming from a noncommissioned officer from the Army Medical Command, especially if the two comments were contradictory.

7. This is not peculiar to the HURIE method but has general applicability to all usability evaluations. Especially given the tendency for usability professionals to be in the "critique" business, it is imperative to demonstrate that they are *not* simply criticizing. The assumption of an attitude of humility, acknowledging the difficulty of design in the first place, is a good first step. The presentation of a "next turn of the crank" redesign, to address the problems unearthed and to give the whole team a "next" design to work with, is a type of "constructive criticism" that goes a long way toward team building and expedites the speed of iterative design progress. There are various ways to provide this constructive criticism. One way of course is to

do a complete redesign of the UI. But another way is to offer "redesign directions," or some sample ideas that give examples of how certain problems might be solved but that are not meant to be a complete and final redesign spec. An example is the small segment of a redesigned screen in Figure 9.1.

8. This is a difficult distinction, sometimes bordering on arbitrary. It may be more important from a "turf" standpoint ("Does this go into the UI requirements document or the functional requirements document?") than from an actual product standpoint. More substantively, the distinction may lie with who shall address the solution. A UI designer may expect someone else to be more knowledgeable about functional/business requirements but would be more inclined to take the lead on UI redesign issues. Basically, if an item came up in the pre-walkthrough discussion and was associated with new functionality, it qualified here as a "new requirement." If it came up as part of the pluralistic usability walkthrough and was an emendation of some existing functionality, it was a "usability problem." Indeed, they are all part of the same product stew.

9. Why not? If time allows (and it does not take much time), it forces the entire team—including the product developers—to think about the users' goals and couch the product goals in non–design-specific terms. And it provides an opportunity to keep the user in the forefront as the entire product team pursues a user-centered design (e.g., Vrendenburg et al., 2002) approach. If not routinely asked, then at least the usability professionals should determine whether functional requirements were systematically determined through some user-centered research or not. If not, the usability professional would be well advised to include in any UI evaluation some requirements gathering or requirements validation.

10. Imagine you were developing a personal digital music recording and playing device and were about four months from shipping when Apple announced the iPod. Clearly, the success of the iPod would have influenced your potential audience. Their expectations, their mental models (Norman, 1990), would be changed, and so the requirements for your product might change. Even in less dramatic examples, it is easy to imagine ongoing shifting in users' requirements, and so it is theoretically a good idea to repeatedly collect user requirement data to corroborate the current requirements or to fine-tune them.

Case 10: Two Contrasting Case Studies in Integrating Business Analysis With Usability Requirements Analysis and User Interface Design

1. Although the bad news on this project is the inaccessibility of the general population of end users, the good news is the availability of the three dedicated SMEs. Elizabeth could interview them—in person, on the phone, and via e-mail—to get a consensus on what the key user categories are and what the key differences between them might be. This input would then support her development of a user profile questionnaire. She could also rely on the SMEs to give general descriptions of the variety of work environments involved and use this as input to a questionnaire aimed at sampling work environment characteristics. Given the small number of actual end users, this questionnaire could be distributed to them all.

   Whereas no one on the team has a terribly concrete idea yet of the detailed functional scope of the application, the available SMEs could at least provide good descriptions of the overall work of the users as currently performed. Again by phone and e-mail, Elizabeth could guide the SMEs in generating a list of low-level tasks that are at least candidates to be included in the application. This input could then guide her development of materials to support a card sorting exercise (see answer 2 below).

   Once she has had them help her compile a list of candidate user tasks for this application, Elizabeth could provide the SMEs with examples of generic task scenarios to explain what she will ultimately be after from other end users. Then she can ask each SME to generate one or two scenarios from their own experience in the publicity manager role in a similar format. She can then use these more relevant and realistic task scenarios as the basis for explaining to other users what she would like from them.

2. Given the inaccessibility of the end-user population, Elizabeth must conduct all her requirements analysis tasks remotely. She could prepare written instructions and supporting materials for end users to respond to as described in answer 1 above and post them on the common website shared by all the 35 existing users. An e-mail from

an authoritative member of their organization could direct them to the website and request/motivate their participation. One side benefit Elizabeth could hope for from remote administration of her requirements analysis tasks would be larger sample sizes than she could gather through one-on-one in-person sessions.

A user profile questionnaire would be pretty straightforward. It would be easy to design a questionnaire for users to respond to online (see http://info.zoomerang.com/, http://www.surveymonkey .com/, and http://www.websurveyor.com/gateway.asp) or even just download, print out, fill in with pen, and return to her by mail. Questions would relate to such user characteristics as computer literacy, web literacy and Windows literacy, frequency of use of different relevant user tasks, role experience level, typing skill, and so on.

Elizabeth could also incorporate into this questionnaire another group of multiple choice questions aimed at collecting key work environment data. These questions would tap into such things as open/closed office space, level of noise, level of interruptions, and level of cooperation and support across users.

For the card sorting exercise, Elizabeth could create a document containing the list of tasks to be sorted and complete written instructions on how to conduct and document the sort and send back the results. (Card sorting is often used to provide input to organize static content into an information architecture for websites but is just as useful in providing input into how to organize functionality—that is, user tasks—on transactional applications.) Alternatively, there are commercial software tools available to conduct remote card sorting exercises that she could find and use (see Righi and Wood, in this volume).

Using a sample of relevant and concrete task scenario examples generated by the project SMEs (see answer 1 above) as well as the same task list used in the card sorting exercise described above, Elizabeth could similarly create a set of instructions on how to generate and document task scenarios and post it on the common website and ask that users submit documented task scenarios to her via e-mail.

3. One disadvantage of dedicated SMEs (as well as the rest of the team) is that they often believe, as revealed in Sandra's comments, that they represent all the users and are experts in the users' work, so that it is

unnecessary for the team to involve any other users in user-centered design tasks such as usability requirements analyses and usability testing.

To handle this, Elizabeth will have to rely on the support of the project manager to allow her to carry out the usability requirements analysis tasks she wants to conduct and get the SMEs to participate in the way she needs them to (see answer 1 above). Then it will be important to involve both the SMEs and the developers in these tasks and, in spite of the geographic dispersement of the team, to work closely with them all on an ongoing basis to ensure their understanding of the data being gathered and its relevance to the design process, which comes next.

To this end, Elizabeth should be sure to document her analysis of the requirements analysis data she collects and share it with the team and then constantly refer back to it as she embarks on the user interface design process. Seeing data from a representative sample of users will help the SMEs see that their knowledge, preferences, and opinions are not necessarily always perfectly representative of the population at large. If she keeps reinforcing the connection between the data and the design, at least over time the team will start to appreciate the importance and relevance of the requirements analysis data. The biggest mistake she could make would be to fail to ensure that the team comes to understand the connection between the data and the design ideas she based on them. Without that connection being constantly reinforced, even as lead designer she may constantly be challenged on her user interface design proposals, both by the developers and by the SMEs, who believe they are the users.

4. Given the lack of clear functional specs, Elizabeth needs to conduct a highly collaborative design process. Because the team is geographically dispersed, she will need to hold frequent meetings by conference call in which all team members participate. Because the team has no experience working with a lead user interface designer or usability engineer, she will need to manage these meetings very carefully. She will need to establish her authority for making final user interface design decisions (being the author/owner of the design specs makes this easier!) but also successfully solicit useful input from others to help her optimize these decisions.

At the same time she will need to get other team members to make business, functional, and technical decisions that have not yet been made but that the user interface design, as it evolves, must be premised on. She will need to educate all other team members in an ongoing way about the rationale for her user interface design decisions and how the requirements analysis data that she collected support those design decisions. She will need to establish mutual respect and clear roles among the team members, as none of them alone can accomplish the design task and they need to collectively exploit all the skill sets in the team to produce the best possible application for its intended users.

Although she does not yet know for sure what user tasks will and will not be supported by the application, she does have a fairly complete list of possible user tasks and also insight into a logical information architecture for these tasks from her card sorting data. She also has some insight into some very important and specific usability requirements that will impact the design of a high level conceptual model (i.e., navigational structure and the presentation of it).

Elizabeth can start by drafting a user interface design spec that defines a possible overall information architecture and high-level conceptual model (i.e., how the information architecture will be visually presented and interacted with) for the potential set of functionality she has researched. This spec might define how the user would navigate across all potential tasks and what cues and contextual information might be provided to help users keep track of where they are in multiple ongoing tasks but would *not* include the details of how the individual tasks would be carried out once arrived at through the navigational structure. What would and would not be included at this level of design is illustrated in the screen design illustration shown in Figure a.1.

This initial high-level user interface design spec could then be used to drive team discussion that would explore both the technical feasibility and the business utility of supporting each potential task, while at the same time proposing a user interface design for navigating across those tasks that would meet the identified usability requirements. Ongoing team discussion would result in decisions to cut or support identified tasks and with ongoing feedback from SMEs would also provide usability feedback on the high level design.

Then, once the high-level design (functionality plus information architecture and conceptual model design) becomes somewhat

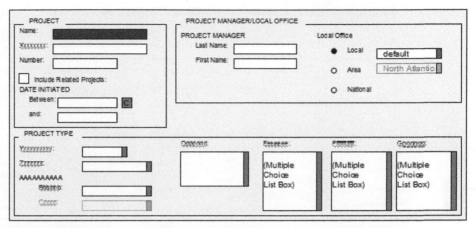

Figure a.1. What would and would not be included in a high-level design.

stabilized, it could be used as the context within which to explore and make decisions regarding lower level functionality and detailed user interface design. For example, once the basic flow and presentation of navigating to any search task was defined through the earlier iterative design discussion, then such within-task details as exactly which search criteria should be offered for each category of search task and how those search criteria should be presented could be drafted and presented for feedback and discussion. An example is given in Figure a.2.

In this top-down fashion, paper specifications of user interface design ideas could be used in an iterative process involving the whole team to iterate toward both functional and user interface design specifications simultaneously. This would require that every design meeting be attended by both the business representatives (the SMEs) and the developers (both project management and staff), so Elizabeth could get both technical and business feedback on the feasibility, utility, and usability of her functional and user interface design ideas all at once.

5. Given that Elizabeth had the opportunity to collect some fairly high-quality usability requirements data up front to drive user interface design and will have ongoing access to the three SMEs to provide regular input and feedback and serve as user interface design walk-through participants as a part of the design process, she concludes she

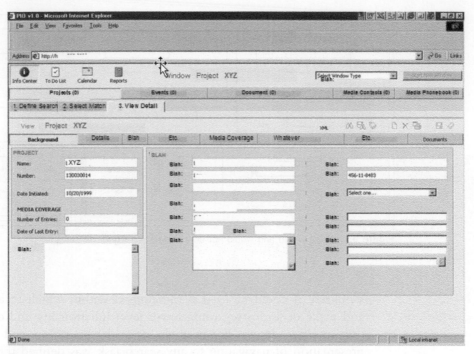

Figure a.2. What would and would not be included at a lower level of design.

will get the most "bang for the buck" from the time and effort to gather enough users together for a formal usability test fairly near the end of the design process, when a live prototype representing not only the information architecture and conceptual model but also the screen/page design standards of a subset of key tasks can be built and tested. She will hope that her usability requirements analysis data and the ongoing feedback and input from the project SME's have provided adequate input to ensure that her information architecture and conceptual model are fundamentally sound. She will rely on this one relatively late formal usability test to help refine all levels of user interface design and serve as validation for the design before development and launch. There is certainly risk in testing so late, but there is also always risk, and one simply must decide how best to spread it out.

6. There were probably a number of factors key to the success of this approach on this particular project.

- First, the *project team was small*, only about a half a dozen key team members. This made the informal collaborative, iterative approach realistic.
- Second, the project manager was a *clear leader dedicated to achieving usability*. Without her unwavering support, as well as her day to day involvement, it would have been harder to establish clear roles and authority early on within the team.
- Third, the *ready availability of three dedicated SMEs* made the relative inaccessibility of the rest of the user population manageable.
- Fourth, *being the author/owner of the user interface design spec* made it much easier for Elizabeth to maintain control of user interface design decisions. Similarly, being lead user interface designer also made it easier for her to ensure that the implications of the usability requirements analysis data she had generated had a direct impact on the user interface design.
- Fifth, this was an *application of only low to moderate functional complexity*, probably making the somewhat informal approach to business requirements analysis and specification workable.
- Sixth, the *particular project team members* contributed significantly to the success of the project. They were motivated team players with good attitudes, good skills, and good interpersonal skills. The team had good chemistry. The impact of this should not be underestimated.
- Finally, the *frequent and very collaborative design meetings* were likely key to success. Especially given the geographic dispersement of team members, without the evolution of buy-in, trust, and mutual respect across team members that the frequent meetings helped build, it is not clear that the necessary communication and team work—undoubted key factors in the success of this project— would have resulted.

7. Any combination of the following circumstances could have made the approach used on this project riskier and might have had an impact on the outcome:
   - A larger project team
   - No clear support for usability in management
   - No dedicated SMEs on the team
   - More complex functionality
   - A different set of team member personalities and motivations

- Usability engineer cast as an advisor to someone else designing the user interface
- A less ongoing and collaborative style of team interaction
- A larger and more diverse user population

8. The approach of developing both business and functional requirements and user interface design in parallel in an iterative fashion based on user interface paper prototypes had at least three very desirable aspects.

- First, there was *no real or perceived redundancy in user research to accomplish both the detailed business and usability requirements.* Often when usability requirements are researched after a rigorous and traditional business requirements analysis has been conducted, this feels to both project management and users like a redundant effort, and to some extent it is. The process is redundant, although the data captured are quite distinct.

- Second, because user interface design and functional design were conducted in parallel in a single process, there was *close involvement of all team members in both.* This was not only more efficient, but also more effective, in that all team members had input to all decisions, accomplishing the important goal of finding good compromises among usability, functional, and technical issues.

- Third, because functional requirements were explored through paper user interface design prototyping, users (in this case, the three SMEs) did not have to learn to interpret any formal but unnatural nonintuitive formats for modeling and specifying functionality. *User interface designs are a completely natural way for users to come to understand proposals for functionality and respond to them.*

9. Absolutely yes! Elizabeth has the complete support of the project manager, Captain Ogden. He believes that usability is absolutely critical on this high-risk project, and he is absolutely right in that assessment. He has adequate funding to support a rigorous usability requirements analysis effort. In addition, the project is moving very slowly and there is time in the schedule to do things right. Elizabeth will simply not be able to deliver a high-quality user interface design without the kind of data she needs (i.e., user profile data, card sorting data, task scenarios, and work environment data) and that is clearly not available from analyses already completed. She should propose a very aggressive, thorough, and detailed usability requirements analysis phase as part of her overall usability engineering project plan.

In spite of the fact that—as in this case—extensive interviews and observations of users in their natural work environment are typically conducted to support business requirements analysis, business requirements analysis documents rarely contain such things as detailed and accurate user profile characteristics, realistic user task scenarios, work environment descriptions, and results of card sorting exercises with users. Business analysts are looking for data to feed into *functional specifications* and *system architecture design*. They are typically not attuned to the kind of data that should drive user interface design and so rarely collect and document it, even though it's often right in front of them as they do their interviews and observations.

In addition, although Captain Ogden himself seems highly knowledgeable regarding the end users, their tasks, and their work environment, it would be very risky to rely on a single person's perception of 56,000 other users and 50 different work environments. He will be a valuable source of information to drive Elizabeth's requirements analysis planning and preparation, but she simply must go into the field and study the users, their tasks, and their work environment herself, in as representative a way as possible, to be an effective user interface designer on this project.

10. Elizabeth does not have to convince Captain Ogden; he is already convinced. But she has a large project team whose cooperation she needs to succeed but who may be hostile given that they have already spent a lot of time generating some user interface design, and she needs to convince them of the value of her requirements analysis work. She also has to make it clear to them that her requirements analyses work is not redundant with—nor does it invalidate—the extensive business requirements analyses they have already conducted over a period of several years. Ultimately, she may also have to explain to already hostile users that she involves in her research that what she is doing is not redundant with what they have already participated in with business analysts in the past.

To convince these potential skeptics, Elizabeth can argue that the "what" (i.e., functionality) but not the "how" (presentation of functionality through a user interface) has been researched to date. Although the process may look similar on the surface (interviews and observations of users in their work environment to understand their tasks), the data captured and documented in the business analysis are simply not the data needed to drive user interface design. Elizabeth can describe user profile data, task scenario data, work environment data, and card sorting data, with a brief explanation of how they are used to drive user interface design, to convince others that the type of data she needs is simply not currently available.

Elizabeth can also argue that this is a very high-risk project (millions of dollars, many years invested, criticality of keeping track of millions of pieces of property, but currently no data available that could drive successful user interface design) and that its level of usability will make or break it. She can also argue that the cost of her usability engineering project plan is literally a drop in the bucket given the overall project budget and will provide some critical and cost-effective insurance on such a high-risk software development project. It will also have little or no impact on the overall project schedule.

The recognized history of abysmal failures in the past due in part to a lack of attention to usability can also be pointed to. Finally, Elizabeth can point to examples of the costs of not getting usability right from her past experience and from the usability engineering literature.

Elizabeth must be careful not to appear hostile to or competitive with the SDI staff responsible for the current user interface design that Captain Ogden is convinced will not work. She will have to work hard to establish credibility with these people and establish a cooperative working relationship with them. Focusing on the data she collects in her requirements analysis—which they did not have access to—as the rationale for her user interface redesign ideas, rather than simply her "expert opinion," will help establish her credibility and avoid hostility and competition.

11. A good rule of thumb for conducting user profile questionnaires is to shoot for an actual sample of responses from 10% of the total population. This in turn requires a distribution to about 33% of the total population, because you can typically only expect to get back about 30% of the questionnaires distributed to internal users. That is, sending out to 33% will yield back 30% of 33% or about 10%.

However, this population is very large—56,000. Elizabeth would have to distribute 18,480 questionnaires to hope for 5,600 (10%) back. This number, 18,480, is too many to distribute and too many, at 5,600, to collate, so this rule of thumb is simply not practical in this case. Instead, Elizabeth will simply have to be practical. In cases such as these, a good general number of questionnaires to base an analysis on is 100. To get 100 back, Elizabeth would have to send out 300 (expecting a 33% return). But, in this case, Elizabeth has identified four distinct categories of users, and she wants to get a good sample of each category. She decides that what is practical is to send out 800 questionnaires, 200 each to the four categories. Her hope is to get back at least 66 or so in each category.

To help ensure representativeness in her final sample, she should draw on Captain Ogden to select individuals to distribute the questionnaire to across the four user categories. She should be sure her target users vary in important ways within categories and are drawn from a good selection of the 50 station houses across the city.

12. Elizabeth should draw on Captain Ogden's standing with higher-ups in the CPD and get the highest possible person in CPD to sign a cover letter to the questionnaire requesting that sample users fill it out and return it by the due date. This may help ensure a good rate of return.

The cover letter should also make it clear that the purpose of the questionnaire is to help ensure that the application being developed is as usable as possible for its end users when it is launched. This is the first step of a "PR" campaign Elizabeth must conduct to overcome end user hostility to IT efforts within the CPD. Figure a.3 presents the cover letter that Elizabeth designed for her user profile questionnaire.

13. The available business requirements documents just seem too big to digest, and Captain Ogden has suggested that it's not likely to be productive for Elizabeth to rely on these documents for orientation information. Instead, she should rely on Captain Ogden and his staff to help her get a sense of the range of property inventory task variations that occur so she has some sense of what to expect—and look for—when she visits station houses to conduct in-context observations and interviews.

She should draw on Captain Ogden's familiarity with the station houses to help her select a representative set to visit and to schedule days and times in which property inventory tasks are most likely to occur and to accompany her and introduce her. Given the known hostility of users to IT, his relative seniority and the fact that he is not a member of CPD IT, is himself a police officer will help ensure some level of user cooperation. Then her own "PR" efforts during

Dear Future Property Inventory Application User:

Inventorying and tracking property in the CPD is currently handled by a complex paper process. The Property Inventory Application, currently being developed by the CPD, will automate all tasks related to inventorying and tracking property. Users will include not only police officers, but also stationhouse chiefs, property managers, and stationhouse clerks.

This questionnaire has been prepared by the Property Inventory Application development team to help us learn more about the future end-users of the application. Your participation is critical to the success of the application, and information that you and other future Property Inventory Application users provide through this questionnaire will help us to design a higher quality application. Your input will help us ensure that the application will be tailored to the needs of you, our users, and thus easy to learn and easy to use.

The questionnaire is anonymous, and we will be summarizing all responses to describe whole groups of users, rather than referring back to any single questionnaire. The more candid and accurate you are in your responses, the more useful the information gathered through this questionnaire will be in helping us to meet your needs. We know the current manual property inventory procedure is tedious and difficult, and we want to make it easier. We can only do this with your input.

It should only take you about 15-20 minutes to fill out this questionnaire (it looks long, but all questions are simple multiple choice). Please return it to your stationhouse chief by [date] if possible, but whenever you can. To insure your anonymity, do not put your name on the questionnaire. Thank you - your participation is greatly appreciated!

Best regards,

_____

Captain Ogden, 33rd Precinct

_____

John A. Doe, CPD Commissioner

Figure a.3. Sample user profile questionnaire cover letter.

her observations and interviews will need to help foster that cooperation (see answer 14).

Given the unscheduled and unpredictable occurrence of the tasks to be observed, she should probably plan to visit a half a dozen station houses for several hours each on an initial round. Depending on how lucky she is in being able to actually observe property inventory tasks while at station houses, she can then schedule additional rounds of visits as needed. She will have to play it by ear. She should aim in the end for visiting a dozen or so station houses that would be expected to show the range of variation in property inventory activity and to end up with a dozen or so task scenarios that represent the range of complexity and frequency described by Captain Ogden.

Elizabeth can plan to use idle time at the station houses (when no property inventory tasks are occurring) to conduct a card sorting exercise with some users. She should aim for a dozen or so users to participate and do the best she can to ensure that they represent at least key variations across and within the four user categories.

Elizabeth understands that a dozen or so task scenarios and a dozen or so users participating in her card sorting exercise is hardly a representative sample of CPD's 56,000 users and highly variable and complex property inventory tasks. However, she also understands that even these little bits of data, which may even be skewed in some ways, are better than no first-hand data at all. She will simply balance scientific validity with engineering practicality and do what's possible. The key to these relatively small samples providing valid and useful information will be in her sampling techniques. Captain Ogden will be able to help ensure and assess representativeness.

If Elizabeth runs out of time and budget to support additional rounds of field visits and still does not have as much data as she would like because her visits simply have not coincided with enough property inventory activity, she will just have to rely on project team staff to fill in her understanding of task variations. Figure a.4 presents one of the task scenarios Elizabeth collected in her visits to the station houses.

Figure a.5 shows a screen shot from one stage in the subsequent design of the property inventory application.

14. As stated in answer 13, the fact that Captain Ogden is himself a relatively high ranking police officer and is *not* from CPD's IT department makes him an ideal person to provide initial introductions at station houses. After Elizabeth is introduced to each user she will observe and interview, she should briefly acknowledge past IT failures (in a professional and diplomatic way) and emphasize that the whole point of her involvement in this project is in fact to ensure that the application being developed is designed to take into account all the demands and difficulties of their job and to support them in carrying

Scenario: Complete Inventory of Property

User: Police Officer (PO)

Description: Domestic dispute - couple filing charges against each other. He beat her with a broomstick, she attacked and cut him with a knife, someone called to report the incident and the PO picked them up and brought them in, with the knife as evidence, a beeper for safekeeping, and a bag of marijuana which was taken at the premises where the arrests were made.

Task Steps:

1. PO goes to desk with perpetrators and shows all property, filling out a summary form for the Stationhouse Chief. Stationhouse Chief makes entry in Command Log.
2. PO secures the prisoners, takes fingerprints, and checks for warrants.
3. PO stores property in her gun locker.
4. PO writes up an Arrest worksheet and Desk Appearance forms, questioning the prisoners to obtain required information.
5. PO enters info into the Arrest System herself and obtains an arrest number, *which she writes on her hand*.
6. PO contacts assistant district attorney (ADA), faxes the Arrest worksheet to ADA office.
7. PO disposes of the prisoners (she must within 2 hours of the arrest, or the Stationhouse Chief will have to file a special report explaining why she did not).
8. PO fills out a worksheet for the Complaint System.
9. PO enters info into the Complaint System herself and obtains complaint numbers.
10. PO retrieves property from her locker.
11. PO returns to the desk, and herself gets inventory forms and bags, for which she signs out on the scratch property index (in other stationhouses, the Stationhouse Chief distributes the bags and inventory forms and keeps the scratch property log).
12. PO bags the property, and enters the relevant inventory number on each bag.
13. PO fills out inventory form worksheets (optional).
14. PO takes bags and inventory form worksheets to Stationhouse Chief for checking (optional).
15. PO types up the inventory forms herself, recording the arrest number and bag numbers, and also types up a letter of transmittal for the narcotics, a Request for Controlled Substance Analysis form, a Domestic Dispute form, and a Prisoner Medical Treatment form (with a great deal of repeated header info on all forms).
16. PO takes all forms to the Stationhouse Chief for approval—he checks especially all the cross-referencing of numbers (arrest #, complaint #s, inventory #s, bag #s), signs off, takes blue copies of inventory forms, and makes entries on scratch property index, and in Command Log.
17. PO seals all bags and attaches inventory forms.
18. PO disposes of all property and inventory forms: narcotics in the Narcotics "Mailbox," other property in Property Room

Task Closure: This scenario took from 1 pm, when the arrests were made, until almost 4 pm to process.

Figure a.4. Sample task scenario.

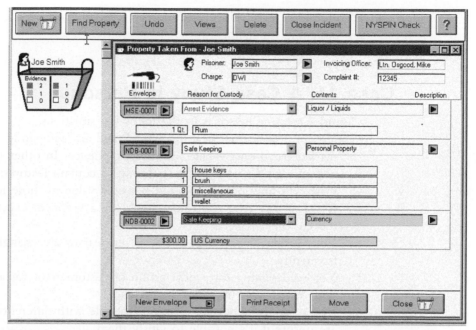

Figure a.5. A screen shot from one stage in the subsequent design of the property inventory application.

out that job. She can give a very brief overview of the field of usability engineering, emphasizing the purpose and importance of user-centered design, which clearly these users have never experienced before. All during her observations and interviews she can present herself as an "apprentice" to the user's masterful expertise and listen closely to and paraphrase back users' frustrations and needs. This will provide stark contrast right off the bat to IT's past approach of zero user input into application design and zero sympathy for their frustration with implemented software applications.

The good news here is that, generally speaking, user-centered design techniques—and in particular usability requirements analysis techniques—sell themselves when done well. It becomes very clear very quickly that it's all about listening to and understanding user needs and then premising a design on those needs. Experience has shown that users respond with a great deal of enthusiasm and cooperation once they understand that someone is actually paying attention to their needs, valuing their expertise, and attempting to accommodate everything about them and their work in the tools they are designing for them.

Case 11: A Case Study in Personas

1. Consider creating personas in the following situations:
    *   You're beyond the "features battle" and are competing in your market based on overall customer experience. In other words, it's not enough for your product simply to contain features: What matters is how people use and perceive value in those features.
    *   It's clear that your team does not share a vision of exactly who the customer is.
    *   Your product's requirements seem unclear or are changing frequently.
    *   You're designing for a new group of customers or for a market with which you have little experience.
    *   You're targeting several groups of people with different needs and are unsure if it's possible to satisfy them all.
    *   Information from existing research doesn't seem helpful when considering how to design your product.
    *   You simply don't know enough about your customers to make good decisions.
2. Personas describe what motivates customers, what behaviors they exhibit, and in what context they function. Typical information includes the following:
    *   **Goals.** What outcome is the person trying to achieve? People have different levels of goals, such as life goals, which help explain a person's overall outlook (e.g., "Make a difference in the world"), and domain goals, which explain what a person is trying to achieve in the context of using your product (e.g., "Finish every project on time"). Personas tend to focus on domain goals, unless your product can actually help people to achieve a life goal. To test if what you've identified is a true goal, ask yourself "Why is that important?" Keep digging until you're no longer describing a task or a process. Goals are outcomes. They generally stay the same regardless of tools or technology. If by introducing a new product you're likely to change someone's goal, then you likely haven't identified a true goal.

- **Tasks and processes.** How is the person trying to achieve their goals? What solutions have they put together, if any? What steps do they take, and why? It's possible—in fact, quite probable—that the product you're designing (or redesigning) will change these tasks and processes.
- **Inputs and outputs.** Information or objects the person requires or provides to other people. For example, a software developer might require business and technical requirements as inputs and would produce various forms of code as outputs.
- **Tools.** What tools does the person use? Tools could be computer hardware or software; paper forms, checklists, or notebooks; communication devices; and so on.
- **Relationships.** Who does this person rely on in the course of their job? Who relies on them? For instance, an x-ray technician in a hospital would rely on the receptionist to schedule patients; various physicians would rely on the technician to produce quality images.
- **Environment.** What factors in the physical environment influence this person and their behaviors? For instance, in many factory settings, workers on the floor can be far from the nearest computer and may avoid using it unless absolutely necessary. Likewise, what factors in the social environment influence them (e.g., social status, group dynamics, and so on)?
- **Past experience.** What past experiences contribute to people's skills or expectations of your product? For instance, consumers switching their home telephones to a new VOIP system may bring some firm ideas on how these phones should work, based on their history with traditional phones.
- **Burning needs.** What does the person find most frustrating, irritating, or annoying? For instance, the shipper at an import/export company might hate how they have to type addresses into their courier's website—when that information already exists in an address book on their computer.
- **Identity.** The finishing touches that bring the persona to life as a character: a name, a photograph, some personal details to make the story engaging.

3. When people are skeptical of personas, it's a signal that they don't believe the effort will produce value. This commonly stems from two fronts: a belief that it's unnecessary to understand customers better or

a lack of clarity around how personas will ultimately be used. For the latter point, kick off the project with a 1- or 2-hour workshop in which you explain how the personas will be created (the observation and analysis process) and give examples of how they can be used (to prioritize features, to set concrete design objectives, and so on). For those who are skeptical about the need to understand customers better, one of the best strategies is to actively involve that person in the process, particularly in the field research; it's rare for someone to spend time on-site with customers and not find the experience valuable. Another smart move is to summarize and share with everyone the main themes from your initial round of interviews with project stakeholders. Once personas are unveiled, it's common for people to forget what they thought originally and say, "Yeah, that's pretty much what we've always known"—even if it's not. A record of those original assumptions can be useful to compare against.

4. The team had already taken a few steps to reduce the time and expense of their research, namely choosing cities that would cut down on the travel required. Other ways of reducing time or costs are as follows:

- **Conduct fewer interviews.** The simplest way to trim the work is to perform less research by recruiting fewer people. However, it's not possible to identify patterns without a large enough sample size, and best practices indicate that you should meet with a minimum of four people per "user type," resulting in at least 15 interviews for a typical small persona project. A large project might include up to 60 participants.

- **Conduct interviews by telephone.** If the project budget or timeline won't allow all interviews to be conducted on-site and in-person, interviews could be conducted by telephone—although the learning experience will be less rich than being in the user's home or work environment. For instance, you'll have such opportunities as observing how people interact, confirming what skills they exhibit while demonstrating a piece of software, and asking about the purpose of those Post-It notes on their computer monitor. Over the phone, you're unlikely to uncover differences in what people say they do versus what they actually do, something Greg has already warned Joanne about several times. Whenever possible, conduct at least some of your interviews in person.

- **Offer less generous incentives or no incentives at all.** Some people are excited to participate regardless of the fact they're getting paid; they just love the idea of being involved. Try recruiting without an incentive and see if you're successful. In some situations employees are prohibited from accepting incentives because of company policy.
- **Have the client handle recruiting.** This won't likely make recruiting go any faster, but if you're a consultant it frees up time for you to spend on research planning—so it saves time (and therefore money) overall. This approach works best when you're attempting to recruit customers of an existing product, as the client should have access to customer lists. They're also more likely to get through to the right people without being turned away.
- **Skip the research entirely.** In this approach you create the assumptive personas that Roberta mentioned briefly. This process usually involves one to three days of a facilitated workshop with representatives from the project team, with perhaps another day or two for writing and designing the personas themselves. This approach is not considered a best practice in persona development, but it's sometimes the only realistic option, especially for shorter term projects and for those on tight budgets. It can help teams to at least agree on a shared vision of the customer, even if that vision is based on flawed or incomplete information.

5. Listed below are some topics and questions that are common to explore in any kind of persona research, regardless of the product domain. Note the question that explores goals: It can be difficult for people to answer direct questions about what their goals are. Instead, you may have to infer their goals from indirect questions such as this.

Goals
   - Think of the last time you had a really great day at work (or at home, if that's the context you're studying). What happened to make you feel that way?

Job responsibilities
   - How would you describe your job here at [company name]?

Tasks
   - What would you say are the five most common activities that you perform on a day-to-day basis?

Habits and routines
- Was yesterday a fairly typical day for you? If yes, tell me about yesterday, starting with the moment you arrived at work. If no, what wasn't typical about yesterday?

Relationships
- Imagine that tomorrow someone inexplicably doesn't show up for work. Whose absence would have the biggest impact on your ability to get things done?

Burning needs
- If you could change one thing about [the study domain], what would it be? What makes you want to change that?

6. This type of research can take participants by surprise, as they expect the conversation to be about product features, not about them. Thank them for their ideas and make sure you either record them or get a copy of their list—then explain candidly that your objective is to learn about the people and the environments in which the product will be used. "Once we understand that, then we'll start thinking more specifically about product features." Most people understand this point and will allow you to shift the conversation accordingly.

7. When you can't establish rapport with a participant, this is when it's great to be part of a small interview team. Switch roles on the fly and let someone else take the lead, someone who seems more likely to connect with the participant. There are other strategies as well:
   - Begin your interviews with very easy questions, such as having people describe their job roles. Save the more difficult or more personal questions for later.
   - Ask open-ended questions that encourage people to elaborate, instead of simple yes or no questions.
   - Ask the participant to demonstrate something. They may be more comfortable explaining a tangible process.

   If nothing makes the interview go smoothly, bring it to an end. There's no point in wasting their time or yours if you're not getting good information. Thank them for the opportunity to get together and then withdraw.

8. It appears that people send documents as e-mail attachments quite often, despite the apparent lack of security. To explore this further, the research team needs to confirm this behavior with their remaining participants, ideally through concrete evidence. Exactly what documents do people send as attachments? How do they deal with

confidential documents in particular? Roberta's strategy of asking Yoko to send her a document was excellent, because it prompted a behavior they could observe. Participants might be persuaded to open their folder of sent e-mails to illustrate what they sent in the past week. Another approach—though use this carefully!—is to deliberately ask a provocative question and see how people respond. For instance: "Wow, this seems like a cumbersome process to follow. Wouldn't it be a lot easier simply to send this as an e-mail attachment?" At that point, people might begin elaborating further on their true feelings and behaviors.

9. This is a common situation. As you conduct interviews and learn more about the domain and the potential customers, you will likely explore new areas of investigation. During analysis, you will have no data on those topics from your earlier interviews. Also, you occasionally may run out of time during an interview or simply forget to ask a key question. This isn't always a problem that needs to be addressed; if you've collected data from enough people to identify it as a pattern, you might feel confident enough to simply move on. If you're not feeling confident, however, you could contact the relevant participants and gather the missing information by e-mail or telephone. Most participants are happy to hear from you afterward—in fact, it's good practice to ask them if you may call if this situation arises. If you're missing some straightforward information across a large number of people, a quick web survey might be the best approach.

10. No. Personas represent major patterns of behavior, goals, and context. Some of your findings won't make it into the personas at all because they were not observed across a significant number of participants— but they may be valuable for other reasons and should be shared accordingly. Consider publishing a point-form report that collects the "Interesting Things We Learned That Aren't Captured in the Personas" (though more appropriately titled, perhaps!). For instance, in this case study the ClickDox research team met two participants whose technology platforms were dictated entirely by their customers. These were consultants who would have liked to upgrade their networking equipment but couldn't; their large client insisted that all vendors use the same setup. This had an impact on their ability to exchange documents electronically. An interesting observation worth sharing— but not indicative of a major pattern nor core to defining the personas.

11. It's impossible to say how many primary personas you will have; in fact, until you complete your analysis, it's difficult to predict how many personas you will have of any type—although experience suggests a range of three to six is quite common. But what should you do if you have more than one primary persona? By definition, each persona would require its own product. Thankfully, in software and on the web, this is sometimes an option. The really hard work in development is usually behind the scenes, in a program's algorithms and data structures; it may be possible to create different interfaces for people to interact with while leaving the background code intact. However, this is often not an option due to project constraints. If you can build only one user interface, then at least you will do so with the explicit knowledge that your design decisions may require tradeoffs in favor of one or the other of your primary personas.

12. Customer insight is valuable to almost everyone in an organization, but personas are purpose-built to inform decisions about product development. Their highest utility is in several activities:

- **Design.** Whether it be interaction design, information architecture, or visual design, the information contained in and empathy generated by personas is inspirational.

- **Usability.** Personas give usability specialists a yardstick against which to judge a product's utility, desirability, and ease of use. They also act as superb profiles of the types of participants to recruit for usability tests.

- **Documentation.** The technical communicator's mantra is, "Know your audience!" Few technical communicators would fail to benefit from the detailed insights into their audience that can be found in personas.

- **Development.** For software developers who have little to no contact with customers, personas do much to illuminate the people who use the products they build—and therefore can have a real impact on what features are implemented and in what manner. Also, personas can help quality assurance teams to write high-level test cases much earlier in development than normal.

- **Marketing.** Personas provide a richer description of customers than traditional market or customer segmentation models. They contain information to help marketers position a product in the marketplace (how will potential customers understand the unique value of our product?) and how to communicate its value (what can we say to make people pay attention to our product?). They also help identify barriers to acceptance (e.g., the need for ClickDox to work with Outlook).

13. Joanne followed some advice from Digital Rockit on how to insinuate the personas into the ClickDox environment:
    - She made sure that everyone received their own set of laminated personas.
    - She hung large 2-foot by 3-foot full-color posters in a prominent hallway near the development team.
    - She occasionally hung pages in public areas that highlighted quick facts about particular personas. For example, one page in the cafeteria advertised that "Timothy hates it when people claim to have read his report but didn't!" These got people talking.
    - The personas were required to attend every meeting. Either the posters or a set of laminated sheets had to be available for reference when discussing items that could impact the customer experience.
    - During design reviews, Joanne sometimes asked people to role-play specific personas when critiquing a design.
    - People were encouraged to avoid talking about "the user"—and pressed to be specific about which user they had in mind.

Case 12: User-Centered Design for Middleware

1. A big factor in the eventual success of the user interface was the foresight of the company to hire an interaction designer. His expertise allowed him to devise a completely new product concept using models and metaphors familiar to the user. The interface worked for many other reasons, not the least of which was a clear marketing vision and a dedicated, passionate engineering team.

   Vivek was so worried that the user wouldn't "get it" that he spent a great deal of time talking with Bob and other potential customers about how they might use such a product. So, although there was not an explicit UCD process used, the company did many of the right things. Vivek and Brian had a very clear vision of what they wanted for the user, and although the situation was not ideal (the complexity of the concepts and the aggressive schedule made it very difficult to get clear feedback from the user), they had a gut feel for the user's reaction. Luckily, their instincts proved right, and they made good design decisions.

2. To improve the product, Carl needed to incorporate the essence of UCD and get feedback from Bob and other customers about how they were really using VirtualCenter 1.0. Carl could talk to Vivek and Brian about doing user studies. Vivek and Brian were largely unfamiliar with UCD, so Carl might write up a small survey of user testing techniques and outline their respective value to the UCD process. Because VMware knew little about how Bob and other customers were actually using the product, contextual inquiry would seem the most logical candidate to apply. Carl could recommend this course of action.

3. The CI study and the report were highly credible with the engineers and the marketing folks because Pamela and Carl talked to experienced representative users and because Pamela presented a well-thought-out and organized report. The recommendations became the cornerstone for improving VirtualCenter. Carl convinced the key managers to embrace the results, and Pamela performed the study in a professional and credible way. The report was essential for gaining acceptance not only of the results but of the process itself. It is likely that the managers at VMware are more willing to accept the costs of user studies and contextual inquiry because of the success of this first study and the good press it received internally.

4. For the most part, the study validated that the key concepts embodied in VirtualCenter 1.0 were correct and well accepted. This made Brian and the engineers eager to address what they saw as the simpler job of fixing individual areas that had no user input when they designed the user interface. If they had missed the mark completely, it would have been a harder blow and would have made the job of deciding how to change things more difficult. Pamela made a point of emphasizing that the overall conceptual model worked. In the end, the report had exactly the right tone of balancing the positive aspects with the need for improvement.

   The work to clean up the user interface was significant and required a lot of redesign and engineering but was viewed as an improvement to the existing application rather than starting from scratch. It is always easier to edit than to stare at a blank piece of paper.

5. The interaction designer, Carl in this case, is the person who creates the interface from his or her understanding of the user's tasks, the engineering schedule, and his or her expertise in user interaction design. The usability engineer, Pamela, is the person who creates a user study that exercises the design to verify its validity to the user. Although the expertise for these two roles overlaps in a big way and many people who call themselves one or the other in fact do both, it is generally preferable that the person who designed a given product is *not* the person who tests it. This is like asking the cook to find out if the guests like the food; they will be biased toward positive feedback.

6. The goal of UCD is to create applicable user interfaces that are easy to use and to provide the right models that allow users to achieve their goals. When a design succeeds, users tend to increase their reliance on the application, and the demands on the feature set can quickly grow beyond the expectations of the original vision. With VirtualCenter 1.2, the system enabled users to easily create large numbers of virtual machines, which swamped an interface that was created to properly accommodate 50 to 100 virtual machines. Engineering and user experience teams must watch carefully for changes in the patterns of use as the market matures and ensure that the product design will evolve over time to maintain its level of quality.

7. How does one go about integrating new features without losing the ease of use of the popular original version? With a lot of user testing. To this end, the team needed to conduct user studies during the course of designing version 2.0. Most of the new concepts (clustering, resource pools, and load balancing) should be run through the usability process. The clustering concept, which is completely new, would have to be studied fairly heavily due to concern that it would not be well understood or would be misunderstood by users of hardware clusters. Some of the concepts with less impact would have to be left out due to time constraints. While Carl and Pamela were studying the new concepts, they had to also keep an eye on how these new concepts "played" with the existing user interface

constructs and planned the testing activities to ensure that the user would not have any trouble transitioning to the new models.

8. The team consisted of lots of creative professionals with strong opinions and a huge passion for creating a great interface. Each person saw the system differently and interpreted the end user's view of the product in his or her own way. Results from the contextual inquiry and the latest round of user testing convinced some folks, but not all. The final form of the interface took quite a bit of time and effort to flesh out and delayed decisions in several key areas (inventory and resource pools being the most important).

    The team discovered that it is not a good idea to get too many people involved in the brainstorming and early decision making. If the group had comprised just Vivek, Brian, and Carl, they could have come to a consensus much sooner and probably chosen something closer to the users' preferences. Because there were about six to eight additional engineers and a few more marketing people involved, the opinions ran in too many directions to make a clear decision. The final decision was one of compromise and was not entirely based on the users' needs.

9. The best way to decide whether a new model will be effective is to get the user to try it out and compare the new model with the way they are accustomed to doing things. The VMware team considered several alternatives (see Figure 12.7), which were presented to users. Unfortunately, there was no clear consensus among the users: Some liked one model, whereas others liked a different model better. In this case, it is up to the design team to select a model. This selection must be based on the designer's expertise and understanding of the various use cases, not his or her own biases or lack of knowledge. An ambivalent user base is not a ticket to take the easy way out. On the contrary, it is the designer's responsibility to implement the best idea without the help of a clear user opinion.

10. The medium-fidelity prototype from modified screenshots of the existing product that Carl and the interns built allowed them to put the new concepts into context with the existing product, helping the user understand its usage. Interestingly, this medium-fidelity prototyping method worked extremely well. The danger of high-fidelity working prototypes or even medium-fidelity static ones such as this is that it is too easy for users to get stuck on issues such as font type, background color, or icon style rather than the more

important conceptual issues of ease of use and navigation. Low-fidelity prototyping is extremely popular because it cannot be mistaken for the real product. The wisdom is that low-fidelity prototypes elicit more honest feedback from users because they can see that it is just a prototype and not a lot of effort has been put into building it yet. Users may be reticent to criticize something they believe is mostly complete because they don't believe their feedback will get implemented. Additionally, low-fidelity prototypes focus the users' attention on the concept behind the design rather than the details of the implementation.

All of this wisdom is true. But medium- and high-fidelity prototypes are useful particularly when the user is already familiar with the product. Showing them a paper prototype at this point would only confuse them because they would lose the context of the application. Carl and his team wanted to learn from the users not only if they understood the new functionality, but if they believed it "played well" with the rest of the application and didn't interfere with the original concept. By seeing static screenshots with the proposed changes rendered to match (using placeholder icons and graphics), the users were able to understand the new functionality within the context of the application they already knew.

11. Using WebEx to display the static prototype remotely, Pamela was free to engage users from any location, including Europe, and to schedule the tests at times when it was most convenient for the user. The users could sit with their current VirtualCenter product and refer to it during the interview. This led to a somewhat more relaxed atmosphere and allowed the user to engage in the test free from additional influences. Furthermore, it was less costly and time consuming than flying to the user's location and was therefore a better value proposition.

During the test session, having Pamela in private communication with Carl and the design team via instant messaging allowed them to confer in real time without disrupting the test. Because the user was not privy to this communication, the flow of thought among Pamela and the team could be very candid and fluid. This helped Pamela not only address the user's questions with greater accuracy than she could normally, but also allowed the team to respond to the user comments with questions of their own that might not occur to Pamela.

Case 13: Isis Mobile: A Case Study in Heuristic Evaluation

1. Heuristic evaluation was a better choice than user testing for the following reasons:
   - No working product samples are available yet.
   - Waiting for functioning samples means added cost and time to change tools and rewrite software and may risk missing a release deadline. It is early enough to implement design changes to prevent major usability issues now, before time is spent implementing commonly known issues that can negatively impact users. Budget constraints likely prevent a larger more in-depth early study to be performed.
   - There do not seem to be any internal usability engineers and no usability input to the products to date. Thus it seems highly likely that evaluations by outside usability professionals will find usability problems that can be addressed now rather than later after a usability test.

2. Increasing the number of expert evaluators helps to ensure most design issues are identified. Different people bring different areas of expertise into the evaluation. They also look at things from their own perspectives and may rate severity of issues differently, which promotes discussion on the range of experiences users can have when they encounter these issues.

3. It is important for evaluators to perform their evaluations separately, so they don't bias each other and so they maintain their own list of issues, severities, and solutions.

4. Finding as many problems as possible allows for the following:
   - It gives the design teams options on how they can effectively address the issues.
   - Different design alternatives allow the design teams to determine other factors that need to be considered when determining which solution to implement, such as corporate goals, user requirements, budget and resources, consistency across other tasks not considered in this evaluation, platform constraints the evaluators are not familiar with, and so on.

5. It is important to get everyone's view on the issues because each evaluator has different experience evaluating other and different types of products. Also, their different skill sets and different backgrounds can

bring different information and perspective to the problem. This also ensures that all evaluators are seeing the whole problem before giving their severity rating, which may be adjusted if a new angle to the problem is brought to the table.

Case 14: Academic Manuscript Submission: A Case Study in Interaction Design

1. Rob thought PIs would submit their manuscripts at least as often as postdocs. In fact, very few PIs would act as submitters. Therefore relatively few submissions would be complete right away. Most submitters would get as far as generating a PDF confirmation file and then have to send it to someone else for approval. Postdocs would probably have to follow up with their PIs to get the submission approved (that is, they'd have to pester their PIs). Had Rob and Sarah skipped the user analysis stage, they would have made a user interface for the wrong audience.

2. Sarah suggested that an initial screen should list all the information and files needed for submission. Because they didn't have all the needed information, it would be easy for a submitter to get halfway through the process and then realize they had to go to their department secretary to pull a file with the grant number. An initial screen would let them gather everything first so submitters could go through the whole process at once and avoid frustration. Additionally, Sarah and Rob decided that submitters should be able to save and exit the wizard at any point along the way.

3. Scenarios are a tool and should be optimized for their intended use. Sarah chose to include steps like entering grant information in their scenarios because they were modeling a specific system with relatively few alternate paths. She knew entering grant numbers would be part of the system, even though nobody did that when submitting papers to journals. If the team had a less clear idea of the final product, she would have written the scenarios to strictly reflect what she observed. Because she and Rob knew the additional steps and roughly where they would happen, Sarah chose to combine the reporting and requirement steps to save time.

4. Sarah divided the hub screen into four tabs to more closely match the wizard and to keep from having a long screen. Her initial concept was

to have a single read-only screen that showed all the manuscript's information. As that screen grew, however, Rob voiced concern that the page would be too long. She therefore split the page into four tabs that were read-only versions of the wizard screens. She wasn't sure about the approach, but figured that usability testing would let them know.

5. A usability evaluation of a conceptual design should show whether users understand the design's approach and navigation. Sarah and Rob had structured the project to use the industry best practice of iterative design. That is, they would repeatedly produce a design, collect usability data, and revise the design. The design foundation stage of a project is the most useful time to follow this strategy because there is still time to make radical changes to the interface if the design has major problems. Sarah wanted to know if users understood what the wizard was for and how it worked. Although she thought that splitting the hub into four tabs would be effective, she wanted to find out if submitters would understand what they were looking at. At this stage she wanted to find out if the progress indicators were useful or not—if so, then she could later work on fine tuning on indicator's exact look and feel. If not, however, she could drop it completely. In other words, Sarah needed to know if the page navigation worked and if the general feature set on each page was understandable. There would be time to work on the details of label names and button placement later.

6. Usability testing, expert review, and cognitive walkthrough each provide good feedback early in the design process. In this case, Sarah chose to do a cognitive walkthrough. She did not have access to another usability professional to do an expert walkthrough (sometimes called a "heuristic review"), and it wasn't practical to review her own design. Sarah knew that first attempts often have usability problems that become obvious once you start the usability evaluation, so she chose to do a cognitive walkthrough because she wouldn't have to prepare as many paper screens. Cognitive walkthroughs are quicker and less labor intensive to conduct than a formal usability test.

7. Both designs have their strong and weak points. Sarah and Rob pointed out that the progressive form reveal design is simple and concise. Yet it does not offer the flexibility in help and guidance that a wizard does. For experienced users, the progressive form reveal model is probably faster. But Rob and Sarah had found that most of their

users only submit two to four papers per year. So, the progressive form reveal model didn't fit the users' needs and habits.

8. Persuading Dr. Lithgow would take both data and tact. Rob and Sarah, having spent a great deal of time and thought on their design, decided that the best strategy would be to look for things to praise in the competing design but argue that the wizard approach should prevail because ease of learning was paramount. Wizards require no learning and give more flexibility to hand-hold new users through a process, whereas progressive form reveal is more efficient for experienced users. They had interview data and usability test data to back them up.

9. Rob and Sarah could have reviewed the design with Sergei until he assigned a developer. Sergei didn't like what he had seen, and he did not express his opinion to Rob and Sarah. Had Rob and Sarah formed a better working relationship with him earlier in the design process, Sergei would probably have been happier with the resulting design. Further, if he did not believe he had the time to review each iteration, he may have been prompted to assign a developer sooner. Andrew was caught in the middle of this situation. His boss had directed him to propose an alternate design, but he would then have to join Rob and Sarah's team with either his design or theirs having "lost."

Case 15: The Mulkey Corporation: A Case Study in Information Architecture

1. Many projects use only one point of view to drive the creation of requirements, but on this project the strategy team collected and analyzed three different points of view: the business executives, the users, and the "like company" websites. The client executives communicated what the business goals were for mulkeycorp.com to be considered successful in the eyes of The Mulkey Corporation. Generally, client executives don't have a detailed understanding of who their website users are and what their needs are, but on this project they did. The strategy team was able to document this perspective during the executive interviews. This was beneficial to the strategy team, allowing them to combine the information from the client executives with their own expertise and experience to determine users' needs and expectations. Another benefit was realized when the

competitive audit validated the kinds of content, functionality, and tools being used on true competitor websites and also on other websites with similar content. By knowing the kind and amount of information and tools available, the competitive audit also helped inform the strategy team what the user expectations would be. The strategy team then analyzed the relationships and interdependencies between these three different points of view to create and prioritize the requirements.

This process also provided invaluable information for the information architect. As you will see in the next section, Nelle used the requirements to make recommendations for the changes that needed to be made to mulkeycorp.com. Nelle created high-level flowcharts and wireframes that were reviewed by the Windy Pine Consulting team and John's team. The competitive audit was especially helpful for Nelle during the reviews to be able to refer to what did and didn't work on the competitive sites to validate the information architecture.

2. Using members of the team to determine user objectives saves time and money; however, there are definite drawbacks. Team members cannot represent all levels of a user type. For example, a team member who is familiar with a process would have a difficult time listing objectives for a novice user (even though they were once novice), and it would be hard for them to document objectives for an expert user because they aren't one. Also, team members do not have the intensive day-to-day experiences that real users have. Furthermore, team members are generally too close to the design and may lose their objectivity.

Depending on the size of the consulting company, the strategy team might be able to find representative users within their company. The strategy team could then interview these users about the kinds of objectives they would have. However, the team must keep in mind the cost, scope, and timeline so that they don't cause a negative impact to the project.

Also, using content owner subject matter experts who have reviewed historical focus group results provided the strategy team with some voice of the user even though it was through several layers of interpretation:

- The interpretation of what the moderator saw during the focus groups (data degradation level 1)

- The interpretation of what the moderator presented to The Mulkey Corporation team (data degradation level 2)
- The interpretation of what the content owner subject matter experts told the Windy Pine Consulting strategy team (data degradation level 3)

  The strategy team could ask to review actual video or audio tapes from previous focus groups. Unless The Mulkey Corporation has a good system for archiving this type of user input, it is likely no one will know where the tapes are. They could also ask to review the original focus group reports. However, every research company presents results and recommendations differently so there is no guarantee about the amount or quality of the information or about the relevance of previous focus group data to a current situation.

3. It was important to look at the websites before nailing down a final "like company" list. Some criteria used by the team included the following:
   - Some of the companies were in the same type of business as The Mulkey Corporation (not all had to be). These companies would be considered true competitors, and it would be easier to compare apples with apples. More specifically, the strategy team could compare the types of overall content displayed and in what order (hierarchy, importance) it was displayed.
   - The website had to have representative content, functionality, and tools. For example, to take an in-depth look at a topic such as "citizenship," there had to be a sampling of websites to compare against that had citizenship type of content. This is an example where the websites in the competitive audit didn't necessarily have to be in the same type of business.
   - Subjective evaluations were also made as to the aesthetic quality of the website, the quality of the information architecture, and the quantity of information available. Ironically, these typically go hand-in-hand; sites with poor aesthetic quality also, generally speaking, have less content. It could be that these companies have little funding for their websites so all aspects of their websites suffer. For example, if there are two sites that the strategy team is trying to choose between and both are in the same type of business as The Mulkey Corporation and both have representative content, a good differentiator is aesthetic and information architecture quality and/or quantity of content to be evaluated.

4. The competitive sites weren't evaluated with real users against real-user objectives so there is no guarantee that the competitive sites provide the content, functionality, and tools that the users need or want. However, if your main user type is an investor and the competitive audit shows that 16 of 17 sites offer a stock quote page full of current data about the daily stock price, it is safe to assume that users will expect to find a stock quote page. If they don't find one, they will be disappointed.

   It is also important to evaluate the content, functionality, and tools from a heuristic point of view. Even though all the competitive websites offer a dividend calculator tool, this doesn't necessarily mean that the calculator tool is usable. On mulkeycorp.com, there was a limitation on how far back data could be provided—data were not available before 1980. Instead of offering a text input field like the competitive sites, the dividend calculator tool on mulkeycorp.com was designed to use drop-down menus that only allow the user to select dates from 1980 forward. Therefore this design prevents the user from entering a date for which data are not available.

5. Ideally, John should get buy-in from the content owners on the information from the strategy presentation, including the business objectives, user objectives, competitive audit results, and requirements. Making the content owners aware of the strategy results would help ensure no big data points were missed or misunderstood. It would also give the content owners an opportunity to participate in the requirements process before seeing the proposed changes and being asked to give their final approval.

6. The content owners at The Mulkey Corporation validated and approved the strategy recommendations, which put the project light years ahead in terms of reaching consensus on a definable, actionable, agreed-upon set of requirements. This was a critical step in preventing scope creep.* Having John's team review and approve the strategy and IA recommendations ensured that the Windy Pine Consulting team maintained a clear understanding of the business objectives and that the requirements and recommendations continued to reflect these objectives.

---

* Scope creep happens when the client or an internal team member asks for content, functionality, tools, etc. that are outside—or above and beyond—the agreed-upon scope of the project.

7. An IA is a critical asset to the team. The IA translates the requirements into tangible visualization through the use of high-level flowcharts and wireframes. High-level flowcharts allow the team to see the proposed skeleton of the website redesign. Once the skeleton is approved the IA creates wireframes, offering the project team a point of clarity—what each page or page type could look like before the pages are graphically designed or programmed. It is the essence of looking into a crystal ball. Titles can be changed, content can be moved around, and new links can be added or removed. All these changes can be done before one line of code is ever written. The IA also maintains consistency of terminology, navigation and navigation models, button names, site functionality, error messages, and so forth. The IA remains focused on the user experience and overall usability of the website from a user advocacy point of view. Although some IAs may have usability expertise and hands-on training, it would not be uncommon for most to not have this background.

8. When Nelle reviewed the competitive audit results (see Table 15.2), she quickly realized that the *News* section was most often called "News," "Media Center," or "Press Center." She also learned that the *Citizenship* section was more commonly called "Citizenship" or "Corporate Citizenship" than variations of "Responsibility" or "Commitment." She used the information from the competitive audit and leveraged the tone on the current mulkeycorp.com website to validate that she did not need to change the section names *News* and *Citizenship*.

9. Two of the challenges with this type of user input are that no one knows, for sure, who these users are (do they fit the profile?) or the specific goals or intentions of these users (what are their objectives?). For example, a noninvestor could be giving feedback about the *Investor* section. One way to keep this from occurring would be to limit the web survey to users who have actually visited certain sections. For example, if a user only visits the *About Us* and *Our Investors* section, offer questions specific to the *About Us* and *Our Investors* sections but not the *Citizenship* section. Still, the users' intentions have to be assumed by a "best-guess" interpretation, and the feedback should be evaluated as a whole. Some could argue that indirect user input is not 100% valid, but others would argue that indirect user input is better than no user input.

10. Nelle started working on the next phase while also participating in graphic design reviews with Jessica to ensure that the information recorded in the wireframes was accurately translated into the graphic designs. Nelle also consulted with David when technical issues arose to ensure that the fine details were not overlooked due to technical constraints and that the user experience was maintained through the relaunch of the website.

11. It seems to be human nature to want to continue to analyze and to perfect. Therefore the longer any team has to review and focus on a page, the more ideas they are likely to come up with to make it "better." Nelle was very familiar with this phenomenon. In fact, she changed her high-level flowchart and wireframe notations from "Final" to "Approved." She'd learned that no design is ever final—even after a design is launched and on the web.

12. When Jessica added the anchor link, she only solved one of the two issues with the original design. The more critical issue was still not addressed. The stock chart, which is updated based on data the user enters into the calculator, needed to be visible above the fold. Jessica, the graphic designer, believed the design options were limited based on the page width and the page width was limited by the template in the content management system. Nelle explained that a new template could be used that would allow more width on the page. After discussing this change with the technical architect, they all agreed that changing the template was the best solution. Jessica came up with the design as seen in Figure a.6. Nelle reviewed and approved this design, as did John.

13. Some might argue that having the IA lead usability discussions would bias the results. In some cases this might be true. However, having an IA who is skilled in usability testing can be an asset. On this particular project, having the IA lead the usability interviews was beneficial. Being familiar with usability testing methodology, the IA asked unbiased questions based on the test objectives that were agreed on by the client's team. Another benefit was that the IA had an investment in the project and was motivated to listen to users' input to make the website experience the best it could be for the target audience.

14. A lot of the problems with the original instructions occurred because the instructions did not do an efficient job explaining what the user would be doing and where the user would be doing it. Step 1 covers

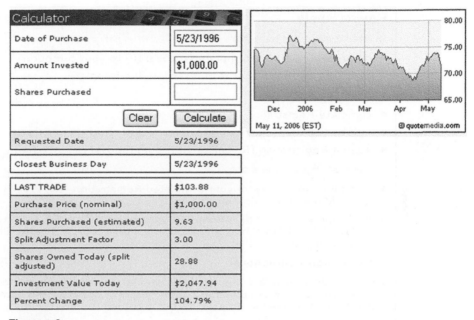

Figure a.6.

"Creating an Account," but there is no link for the user to take action. Step 2 is about "Accessing and Submitting the On-line Application." There is a reference to "part A" in the subtitle, but you have to look really hard (and be paying close attention) to realize that part B is a subpart of part A. That is definitely confusing. It is not clear why step 3 was missed by so many applicants. One explanation might be that this information fell below the fold line and the users simply forgot.

For the redesign, Nelle thought it was important to separate each step and to call attention to them graphically. She also added a *How to Apply* page, which gave an overall summary of what the user would be doing in each step and provided the user with a downloadable set of instructions that the user could print to have available off-line. All three steps are listed at the bottom of the *How to Apply* page, as shown in Figure a.7, with a short description of the task. The tasks are links, and clicking on them will take the user to that page. Steps 1 to 3 are displayed at the top of subsequent pages and the step that the user is on is highlighted.

How to Apply

In Step 1, you will have to:

- download (save) the template Proposal (P) to your computer; and
- complete and save your responses into the template.

In Step 2, you will have to:

- complete Registration (R) online;
- upload (attach) your completed Proposal (P) from Step 1; and
- submit Registration (R) online with your Proposal (P) attached.

In Step 3, you will have to:

- Compile hard copies of your completed Registration (R), Proposal (P), and additional Attachments (A), and
- Mail copies of your Application Package: Registration (R), Proposal (P), and additional Attachments (A) to the address provided in the Step-by-Step Instructions.

Step-by-Step Instructions

We've made available a downloadable and printable version of the full step-by-step instructions to apply for a grant. NOTE: These are the same instructions displayed in Steps 1, 2, and 3 below.

Download Step-by-Step Instructions

Step 1	**Download & Prepare Proposal (P)**
Step 2	**Submit Proposal (P) & Registration (R) Online**
Step 3	**Send Proposal (P), Registration (R), & Attachments (A)**

Figure a.7.

Knowing that users don't like to read a lot of text, Nelle suggested putting the key instructions for each step directly under steps 1 to 3 at the top of each page (see Figures a.8, a.9, and a.10). The key instructions reiterated what the user should do. It was also critical that all the pages use consistent terminology (proposal, registration, attachments).

After the key instructions, a prompt led the user to the next step. Under the prompt to proceed to step 2, "Helpful Hints" were added.

Step 1

Step 1	Download & Prepare Proposal (P)
Step 2	Submit Proposal (P) & Registration (R) Online
Step 3	Send Proposal (P), Registration (R), & Attachments (A)

Proposal Template:

The Proposal Template MUST be downloaded (saved) to your computer so that you can edit and save your information into the template. Your completed Proposal can then be submitted online as directed in Step 2.

Download Proposal Template

Once you have completed your Proposal (P), you can **proceed to Step 2**.

Helpful Hints:

- **How to download (save) the Proposal (P) Template**
- **How to access the Proposal (P) Template**
- **How to complete the Proposal (P) Template (after it has been saved to your computer)**

Figure a.8.

These hints were based on users' input about specific points in the application process that were troublesome.

Step 2 was much more complicated (remember part B was a subpart of part A in the original design). Step 2 still required three actions, so the key instructions listed the three actions. It is also displayed in bold that the users should read all the instructions (see Figure a.9). The three actions are then displayed as subtitles on the page so that if the user only scanned the page, the user would see "First," "Second," "Then," and realize there were multiple actions.

Nelle discovered when she was talking with the contributions content owners at The Mulkey Corporation that the log-in wasn't as simple as entering an ID and password. Nelle learned that there were three different scenarios for log-in:

Figure a.9.

Step 3

Step 1	**Download & Prepare Proposal (P)**
Step 2	**Submit Proposal (P) & Registration (R) Online**
Step 3	**Send Proposal (P), Registration (R), & Attachments (A)**

Before mailing your Application Package, make sure that you have:

- Completed your Proposal (P);
- Completed your Registration (R);
- Attached your completed Proposal (P) to your Registration (R);
- Printed the "Printer Friendly Version" of your Registration (R); and
- Received an email confirmation that your Registration (R) was submitted online.

In addition to electronically submitting the Proposal (P) attached to the Registration (R), applicants must mail a hard copy Application Package containing one (1) original and three (3) copies of the Attachments (A) listed below.

- Attachment 1 - Duis autem vel eum iriure dolor in hendrerit in vulputate velit esse.
- Attachment 2 - Duis autem vel eum iriure dolor.
- Attachment 3 - Duis autem vel eum iriure dolor in hendrerit in vulputate.
- Attachment 4 - Duis autem vel eum.
- Attachment 5 - Duis autem vel eum iriure dolor in hendrerit.
- Attachment 6 - Duis autem vel eum iriure.
- Attachment 7 - Duis autem vel eum iriure dolor in hendrerit in vulputate velit esse.

Figure a.10.

1. User had not applied for a grant with The Mulkey Corporation in the past 12 months.
2. User had applied in the past 12 months.
3. User had applied in the past 12 months and wanted to reaccess a saved application.

Nelle believed that it was important to get the user logged into the correct path. Otherwise, a user with a saved application might not be able to find their application if they logged in as a new user.

Each of the three log-in scenarios is described with its own link into the application.

The content in the second and third parts of step 2 was displayed as a bulleted list (see Figure a.9) instead of paragraphs of information (see Figure 15.19). The bulleted format makes it easier for users to read, especially when there are multiple actions in a step. At the bottom of the page is a link to take the user to the last step (see Figure a.9).

By displaying each step on its own page and by reiterating that there are three steps on every page, the design helps prevent users from missing the last step. On step 3 the key instructions reiterate what the user should have already completed. Step 3 also describes in detail the hard copy requirements for the grant application (see Figure a.10).

15. John's team and the Windy Pine Consulting team should continue to evaluate periodic user feedback received through web surveys, user behavior analysis provided from web analytics, and usability testing. For a multiyear project, The Mulkey Corporation should reengage the strategy consulting team to reassess the business objectives using executive interviews and to reassess the competitive arena by performing a new "like company" audit.

On this project, The Mulkey Corporation decided to reengage the strategy consulting team one year after the original assessment. This provided John's team and the Windy Pine Consulting team with a refreshed perspective. Most "like company" websites had been updated over the year, but a few of the sites were very stagnant and had not changed. The stagnant websites were removed from the list, and new "like company" websites were added in their place.

The results of the second strategy engagement were very fascinating. Some of the baselines had changed and some of the leading practices* were dramatically different. This allowed The Mulkey Corporation to compare their changing business objectives and user objectives with the changes in the competitive arena. Because of these changes and the multiphased approach on this project, John's team and the Windy Pine Consulting team reevaluated the requirements. Some of the requirements were moved up in priority, and others were moved down or removed altogether.

---

* A leading practice is defined when only a few (and sometimes only one) of the "like company" sites have a particular type of content, functionality, or tool.

Case 16: Incorporating Web Accessibility Into the Design Process

1. Because no one in the company has any significant knowledge or experience with accessibility issues, Liam's choices are to develop expertise in-house, hire external accessibility consultants, or some combination of the two.

    Approach 1 is to develop internal expertise to address compliance. Liam could send a few web designers (technical leads, web designers, and usability specialists) to training classes and give them time to learn about accessibility issues. The technical skills that are necessary to successfully address accessibility issues include at least a working knowledge of HTML, CSS, and JavaScript, although designers with programming experience using CSS, dynamic HTML, XML, and other newer technologies would be an advantage. The designers also need to be high enough up in the organization to have the authority to effect change in the development process. The trained resources could serve as accessibility advocates and internal resources, mentoring and training other technical leads, developers, and product managers regarding accessibility design and implementation. The accessibility specialists could also be responsible for working with product teams to ensure product compliance, functioning as "accessibility compliance officers." Additionally, the accessibility experts would be tasked with developing company-specific guidelines and standards. The major drawback to this approach is that developing in-house expertise is time intensive for the technical staff. Ramping up in accessible design practices takes time away from their other job responsibilities. They also have to be interested and willing to change their current design and programming strategies, if needed.

    Approach 2 is to hire outside accessibility consultants. The consultants would conduct accessibility evaluations of the products and recommend solutions to problems. A project manager would be needed to act as the liaison between the consultants and the product manager, technical lead, and usability specialists for each project.

    The advantage of outsourcing the evaluation work would be that the company could benefit from the expertise right away. Experienced accessibility consultants have worked on several projects in a variety of contexts and domains and may well have encountered similar issues in other products. They provide an independent perspective; management may be more receptive to raising the priority to incorporate and fund the accessibility recommendations. However, because accessibility is a relatively new concept for many usability practitioners and other professional technical communicators, few qualified accessibility experts may be available at the time for such a large and intensive project. Consultants would also require a significant amount of time to understand the products and proprietary product code. They face a steep learning curve on the technical side as well as on the organizational/political side of the business.

2. Users who are blind face significant barriers in using websites because many sites are graphics intensive and require the use of a mouse to interact with the site. When the site contains lots of graphics and images interspersed with the text, the pages can be harder to understand because screen readers (and other assistive technology) render the pages in a linear fashion, starting at the top left-most corner of the page and following the order of the underlying code through the rest of the page. Also, many times designers forget to make sure that every graphic has an associated description (alternative text), and when it's missing the screen reader assistive technology reads the file name, which is gibberish a good deal of the time. As for the mouse, users who are blind use keyboard inputs and sites that use certain types of programming options make it impossible to use just the keyboard to interact with the site. Figure a.11 pictures a man

Figure a.11. Song-Jae Jo scans a document using the Kurzweil 1000 software program. He will read the scanned copy using his screen reading software. (Used with permission.)

scanning a document (using the Kurzweil 1000 software program) which will display on the screen in front of him for his screen reader software to read.

Low vision and legally blind users (those who have some vision but whose corrected sight is equal to or less than 20/200) are concerned with being able to see text or images. Text size, color combinations, and color contrast significantly affect legibility for these users. Users need to significantly enlarge the text size of all items on the page, using screen magnification tools such as ZoomText. However, if the text size is fixed in the code, then users can't take advantage of the technology. Additionally, when letters and numbers are included in graphics (e.g., graphic links and buttons), they take on a blurry "pixelated" look when they are magnified, making the text very difficult to discern. Finally, people with partial sight or congenital color deficits, as well as those who are older, find it difficult to distinguish between certain color combinations. It is important to appreciate that it is the contrast of colors one against another that makes them more or less discernible, rather than the individual colors themselves.

Meanwhile, people with anomalous color vision, which is commonly called color blindness, have difficulty distinguishing between combinations and/or pairs of colors, usually red–green combinations or, more rarely, yellow–blue combinations. Using color coding without a redundant way of communicating the information and not providing good color affects not only color blind people but other users as well. However, using Cascading Style Sheets would allow pages to be given an alternative color scheme for color-blind users.

3. Users who are deaf or hard of hearing are primarily concerned with the increasing use of multimedia content that does not include captioning for the audio track and a transcript of the material. The TBD applications included a few virtual tours of corporate retreat locations that would need to be captioned, and a text-based version of the tour should be created. The designers also need to remember not to design interactions that depend on the assumption that users will hear audio information or audible cues. Over time it would be really helpful for the virtual tours to include a version that incorporates American Sign Language wherever possible.

4. Users with physical disabilities and motor impairments typically use an input device other than the mouse. They may also use a nonstandard

keyboard or one-hand devices because they either cannot type two keys simultaneously or they hit multiple keys by accident. Requiring users to enter the same information more than once is not only tedious, it is also prone to additional errors. For users who do use a mouse to interact with the site, if the buttons and "hot spots" on image maps are not large enough and spaced far enough apart, users with hand tremors will have difficulty selecting the item.

5. Users with cognitive impairments can have deficits in memory, perception, problem-solving, conceptualization, and attention. These may result from a range of conditions such as mental retardation, autism, brain injury, Alzheimer's disease, and old age. Similarly, learning disabilities can affect a variety of memory, perception, problem-solving, and conceptualization skills. Learning difficulties include reading problems such as dyslexia; computational, reasoning and organizational deficits; and nonverbal learning disorders. These are sometimes also associated with attention deficit disorder and hyperactivity. Cognitively impaired users need information to be presented in small discrete units without other distractions (such as blinking objects) on the page. Complex inconsistent displays or uncommon word choices also make websites more difficult to understand, as do pages that require people to remember information to interact with the site.

6. To identify the key company stakeholders for this initiative, Carmen would need to ask herself which roles would be affected by Section 508. Carmen should approach nearly every area of the company due to the scope of the effort and the resources she needs to meet the deadline. Figure a.12 shows the affected resources for the two main products by development phase. She should set up informational meetings with several groups within the product development organization, concentrating on the technical leads, development teams, and product managers. She should also meet individually with project managers from the larger products. In these meetings she should play short video clips that showed people with various types of disabilities interacting with websites using assistive technologies to help raise awareness about the value of accessible design for existing and potential customers.

On the business side, Carmen should meet with members of the customer service division because they would be a valuable resource for understanding how people with disabilities might have trouble

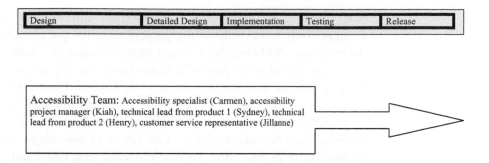

Executive and product team resources were involved at only certain points in the overall

accessibility initiative:

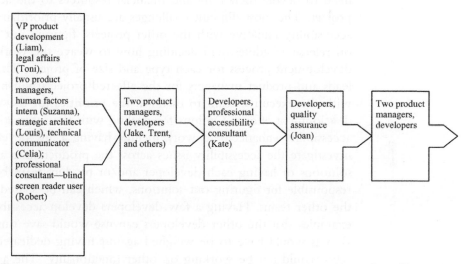

Figure a.12. Travelers By Design—Roles by design phase for the two main products. (Created by Toni A. Dennis. Used with permission.)

with existing products. They would also be responsible for handling calls about accessibility issues after the new law went into effect, so it was important to get early support and buy-in from them. Carmen should meet with the government sales representatives from the marketing and sales organization as well.

Carmen created awareness-raising activities to get everyone excited about and engaged in the accessibility initiative. She provided demonstrations of how pages look from different perspectives (e.g., running the home page through color blindness and color contrast tools to show how the page renders for people with visual deficiencies). Additionally, Carmen could "challenge" stakeholders (even via e-mail or as part of a status report) to try to go to their favorite website and use it with just the keyboard but no mouse. She would also encourage all stakeholders and team members to view the user experience sessions or watch highlight video clips of the key issues as they became available. The key is to encourage stakeholders to participate in this effort so that everyone gets first-hand knowledge of the impact an inaccessible design would have on disabled users.

7. For an accessibility initiative to be successful, all stakeholders would need to devote their time and financial resources to the accessibility project. The most difficult challenges are usually prioritizing the accessibility initiative with the other projects, figuring out the impacts on release schedules, and deciding how to weave the work into the development process for each type and size of project. The technical leads and product managers for the affected projects will need to meet with the executive team to establish the priorities for the various development efforts. Options for dealing with the integration of the accessibility enhancement work include having a few developers investigate the accessibility issues across the product suite and develop solutions or having each developer and/or product team be responsible for figuring out solutions, which can be shared with the other teams. Having a few developers develop accessible code examples that the other developers can use would save time, but that savings would have to be weighed against having dedicated resources who would not be working on other functionality. The advantage of having all the developers trying to generate solutions to accessibility issues is that each developer would come up the learning curve at the same time, leading to more engaged development teams and probably a higher number of viable solutions.

    Across the company most of the work was completed in six months, including two months setting up the project and conducting initial analysis, followed by at least a month for performing detailed analyses, and three months for implementing enhancements and retesting the products.

8. A common question about accessibility initiatives is how long it will take to complete the project. The answer depends on the level of

interactivity, how dynamic it is, the types of JavaScript event handlers used, and number of pages. If the site is an informational website with lots of content, then the accessibility effort would take a few weeks. The sizing would need to include time for adding alternative text to images, adding headers to the content sections, making text versions of PDF pages, ensuring that the menus use non–mouse-based event handlers, and making sure that the text is resizable. For complex interactive web applications, the estimate would probably be from a couple of months to six months, depending on whether or not standards-compliant coding practices were used. If the site complied with W3C standards, then most of the work would involve checking for the same items mentioned above. However, if the site did not adhere to standards, then significant programming changes will be needed, taking several months.

9. In forming a project team, Carmen might find that the most significant challenge would be to create a team small enough to be efficient but large enough to include the key organizations and resources. Key members would include a combination of the following:

- Technical leads: Depending on the number of products affected, the similarity of the products, and work load priorities, one to two technical development leads would be needed for a major accessibility initiative.
- Product managers: Some product managers want to be involved in every aspect of the product design, whereas others depend more on the development team to make sure that accessibility is addressed and incorporated into the product design.
- Customer service representative: One higher level representative is very valuable as he or she is in regular contact with customers calling in about issues with the products.
- Quality assurance specialist: This resource is important during the implementation and testing phases, as he or she can write Perl scripts to automate the testing for some accessibility enhancements (e.g., ensuring that every image tag has an "alt" attribute).
- Accessibility project manager: This person is vital to the success of the project because he or she coordinates and negotiates with all the product teams affected by the accessibility initiative.
- Design and usability specialists: If there is no "Carmen" at your company, then these resources have the interdisciplinary

background and skills needed to ramp up on accessibility, and they likely have already had some exposure to the area.

10. Carmen could recruit users with disabilities to work through the TBD products. Watching users who are blind and/or have visual impairments, particularly those using screen readers and/or screen magnifiers, interact with the major functionality on TBD's sites would yield valuable insights for the team. Because the sites use multimedia or Flash presentations, working with users who are deaf and hard of hearing would be a good idea, too. She could also try out several simulation tools to see how different pages from the TBD sites would look for people who are color blind or have difficulty with color contrast. Using the sites with no mouse would give a quick indication of the sites' usability for assistive technology users. She might try enlarging the text on the screen as much as possible and then try to read it while looking through a straw, somewhat simulating the effect of macular degeneration. Carmen could download a demo version of a talking browser and then try using listening to a few pages with the monitor turned off.

11. To conduct the detailed product inspections, the product managers should identify a few main product task paths in their respective products. The paths should be representative in that they include the entry point to the site (log-in screen), home b (e.g., pages with forms), search and data entry results, price sorting features, and informational pages.

    An inspection summary template (similar to the template in Table a.13) should be created to ensure each of the 16 standards from the Section 508 evaluation would be addressed systematically. The template should include columns for indicating whether the site complied, did not comply with each standard, or did not apply. Another column was used to list specific pages where problems were found during the evaluation (refer to Figure a.13 for a partial listing of a combined Section 508 and WCAG checklist). Another column could be added to track progress. Over time, code examples can also be added to the spreadsheet to document and disseminate repairs to the larger development team.

12. Without an ongoing compliance process in place, products will fall out of compliance relatively quickly. New technologies arise that may pose accessibility problems, new features may be added, and existing features may be modified or enhanced, without being tested or

WCAG /§1194. 22	Section 508/WCAG Priority 1 Checkpoints	Yes	No	N/A	Comments
	In general (Priority 1)				
1.1 (a)	Provide a text equivalent for every nontext element (e.g., via "alt," "longdesc," or in element content). This includes images, graphic representations of text (including symbols), image map regions, animations (e.g., animated GIFs), applets and programmatic objects, ASCII art, frames, scripts, images used as list bullets, spacers, graphic buttons, sounds (played with or without user interaction), stand-alone audio files, audio tracks of video, and video. A text equivalent for every nontext element shall be provided (e.g., via "alt," "longdesc," or in element content).				

Figure a.13. Comprehensive checklist that includes both section 508 and WCAG checklists (partial listing).

retested for accessibility. For example, when new or different developers join the team and they are tasked with maintaining and/or developing new code, they may not be aware of the accessibility aspects of the product and inadvertently undo the completed work. At TBD a new developer took out the alternative text on several

2.1	Ensure that all information conveyed with color is also available without color, for example from context or markup.			
(c)	Web pages shall be designed so that all information conveyed with color is also available without color, for example from context or markup.			
4.1 (no 508)	Clearly identify changes in the natural language of a document's text and any text equivalents (e.g., captions).			
6.1	Organize documents so they may be read without style sheets. For example, when an HTML document is rendered without associated style sheets, it must still be possible to read the document.			
(d)	Documents shall be organized so they are readable without requiring an associated style sheet.			

Figure a.13. *Continued*

images that were used often throughout the site because he wanted to reduce the page size, which rendered the product inaccessible again. Another developer added JavaScript-based menus to the navigation area for a product (rather that using CSS), which meant that screen reader users could only select the first item in the menu.

13. With a project of this scope being completed under fairly severe time constraints, it is inevitable that some aspects of the project are not done. In the case of TBD, the team needed to move on to other projects and they were not able to accomplish several elements of their plan. These elements should be included but were not done for the TBD site:
    - Publish a formal accessibility compliance process.
    - Obtain funding and support for an accessibility compliance specialist position.
    - Establish a training program—including both accessibility concepts and tools—for all developers, product managers, project managers, web designers, usability specialists, etc.
    - Develop in-depth quality assurance test scripts for accessibility—only alternative text on images were tested; nothing else was added to the automated test scripts.
    - Test and enhance the products using the W3C WCAG, which was significant because the products were not accessible at all with JavaScript turned off. Carmen recommended that WCAG priorities 1 and 2 be built into the next round of accessibility testing because many other countries base their accessibility policies on WCAG checkpoints.

    Finally, continued executive level support, awareness raising efforts, and required accessibility compliance training are critical for the long-term success of a compliance process.

Case 17: From .com to .com.cn: A Case Study of Website Internationalization

1. The activities that the meeting attendees outlined are mostly at the operational level, not at the strategic level. The main element they are missing is research, specifically research of the Chinese market and the Chinese user experience:

    First, the approach to developing the Chinese market was merely triggered by a phone call from an executive at a Chinese media company. MediaCentral.com does not have any prior research upon which to base their internationalization strategy. For instance, the company has no information regarding to which countries the investment should go first, or what the return on investment expectation is. Relying on excitement and gut feeling is not enough to support a business decision.

Also, user experience research is not in the roll-out plan. There was an underlying assumption that the user experience with the MediaCentral.com website would be common across countries after the text was translated. However, people living in different countries often have dramatic differences in their needs. For instance, the credit card is the primary payment method in the United States but is far from the most important payment method in China. So, text describing the use of credit cards in the U.S. site would not be applicable to the Chinese consumers.

2. Market research should be conducted to support and verify business decisions. Before the team discussed the roll-out plan and schedule, detailed market research should have been conducted to decide the overall global expansion strategy. Many companies are expanding their business and development globally. Some have the goal of reducing operational costs, but others are intending to increase revenue. For MediaCentral.com, a fast-growing Internet company, going global is definitely a long-term direction, but the company must conduct careful research to determine their approach to expand into China. Some questions for consideration are as follows:

- *What is the prospective profit for doing business in China?* Because China has enjoyed the highest economic growth in the past decade, this market is expected to continue to grow tremendously in the next few years. However, this does not guarantee the same level of financial return for all business investments in China. MediaCentral.com is an online merchant. Online shopping is not a mainstream mode of commerce in China. This implies that MediaCentral.com may expect a lower return on investment in China than in other countries to begin with.

- *Are there other investments that would bring more returns for the company in the short term?* It is true that pioneers have their advantage in a new market. Companies who invest late in the market often need to pay a much higher price to catch up to more established companies. However, because of the drastic differences between the U.S. and the Chinese cultures, adapting a product to the local Chinese market could be very costly. In many cases, improving products in mature markets may bring in more revenue.

- *Should some unique approach be taken for the roll out in China?*
  The differences between Chinese and U.S. culture often have important implications on the business decisions. For instance, there are many ways for promoting products and acquiring users, such as television campaigns, road shows, and giveaways. The effectiveness of each method may be different between the U.S. and Chinese markets. Coupons are very popular in the United States, but this is not the case in China. In contrast, the most popular promotions are combined discounts and gifts in the Chinese consumer market. Also, holidays, fiscal year conventions, and seasonality often have significant impact on business volumes. In the United States the sales of collectable items related to U.S. history are the highest around Memorial Day and National Independence Day. General collectable items sell the most around the Thanksgiving and Christmas season. However, China has a completely different set of holidays than the United States. These differences will consequently generate different sales patterns over the year.

  It is often very hard for people to enumerate cultural differences without sufficient exposure to these cultures. Therefore the team should involve people who are familiar with the culture of the targeted marketplace in the discussions. Jim Lee is an excellent person to start with. Jim may be able to suggest a very specific time frame and the best approaches to launching the site. Jim could also be helpful in creating the initial user base for MediaCentral.com using his connections in China.

3. User research is critical when designing an international site. A site developed from one country or region may encounter a number of problems in another country or region. If user research were included in the process, the following areas would be taken into more consideration:

   - *User profiles:* People with different backgrounds often use websites in different ways. The background characteristics that affect web usage behaviors include age, gender, and years of experience using the web. There are clear differences in user profiles between the U.S. and Chinese users of MediaCentral.com site. For instance, research has shown that Chinese web users are generally younger than the average U.S. web user. Based on statistics from China Internet Network Information Center (CNNIC) in 2006, about

70% of the Chinese Internet users are under 30 years old. However, based on statistics from ClickZ, about 60% of Internet users in the United States are over 30 years old. Therefore a web page design that appeals to middle-aged users may not be satisfying to the majority of Chinese users who, as a group, are younger than the average U.S. web users. Here are some examples of other popular user attributes that caused different behaviors between the U.S. and Chinese web users:

— Typical computer literacy
— Typical web literacy and frequency of use
— Typical typing skills

Demographic data and trends of the Chinese web users are officially surveyed and documented by CNNIC.

- *User preferences and conventions:* Some of the differences in preferences and conventions include aesthetics of layout, font types, density of graphics and animations, and colors. These differences often have direct design implications on a website. For example, Chinese web pages generally have much more information, mixed with extensive use of graphics and animations. Many Chinese users perceive such designs as a reflection of richness in content. However, these designs are generally deemed as bad design for U.S. websites, due to information overload. On the other hand, a web page that is perceived as clean for U.S. users may be perceived as too bland for Chinese users. This difference can be seen by comparing, for example, the home page design of msn.com (Figure a.14) and sina.com.cn (Figure a.15). Both sites are among the most popular portal sites in their markets. It is clear that sina.com has much higher density in content and more extensive use of graphics and animations.

- *Commercial landscape:* It is widely known that China has a very different commercial landscape than the United States. These differences lie in a number of areas, such as market share, business etiquette and policies, and financial transaction processes. For instance, most e-commerce companies in the United States consider other similar e-commerce companies as their competitors. However, in China the competitors of e-commerce companies are largely traditional brick-and-mortar companies.

- *Cultural differences:* Chinese cultural and social context often affects user preference and behavior. For example, many Chinese pay

Figure a.14. Home page design of msn.com: a typical "clean" U.S. design.

great attention to numbers. In Chinese, the number 8 has the same pronunciation as "fortune" and hence is considered a lucky number. By contrast, the number 4 often has a negative connotation. So phone numbers with more "eights" often cost tens or even hundreds of times more than an average or a poor number. Some of the "very best" numbers with a good rhythm may cost up to hundreds of dollars. On the other hand, some of the "very bad" numbers never even sell in the market.

- *Convention and translation issues:* Some of the content on the U.S. site needs to be adjusted based on the Chinese conventions during translation. These conventions include formats of date and time, currency, temperature, icons, and reading direction. For instance, the date in the standard U.S. format is in the form of

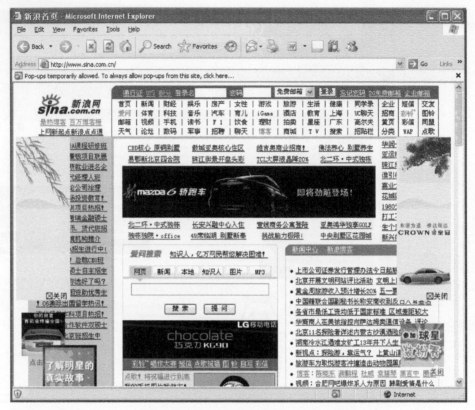

Figure a.15. Home page design of sina.com.cn: A typical "rich" Chinese design.

month/date/year. However, in some other cultures, including Chinese culture, the standard format for dates is year/month/date. Also, the measuring units (inches, pounds, etc.) on the U.S. sites would need to be converted to metric measuring standards (meters, kilograms, etc.) for the Chinese site.

User research should be incorporated in the process from the beginning to the end of the development cycle. In the early design phase, research should be used to collect user requirements and evaluate competition for the specific market. User research should also be conducted to help with design iterations. It should be assumed that adaptation work is needed after a site is translated to another language.

4. The problems illustrated here are attributable to the country-specific website content. Simply translating this content into another language does not make it applicable to the users of that country. Rather, the content should be revised based on local requirements and conventions:

   • In the first example regarding driving directions, if a dynamic map is still necessary for the users, the mapping application that only works for the U.S. addresses should be replaced by the corresponding applications that support mapping in China.

   • To solve the second issue regarding the shipping calculator, further research is necessary to determine how shipping works for China. Popular shipping providers may require users to input information in different ways. For example, the rules of shipping charges against range of weight may differ among shipping companies. This information can only be acquired from local shipping providers in China.

   • The third issue regarding credit card payment should also be addressed by acquiring more information regarding financial transactions in China. Because the existing solutions around credit cards do not work in China, this function should be redesigned around the feasible online transaction methods available in China.

   • To resolve the fourth issue, the form elements should be reevaluated with typical Chinese users. The security questions and the name fields should be redesigned.

5. All four problems are actually examples of many common issues when adapting websites or other product content into another country. For MediaCentral.com, a company that was not experienced in internationalization, these initial findings imply that rolling out a site in China is much more complicated than pure translation. Some of the issues, such as the different use of measurement units or the functionality of certain applications, were relatively obvious. Other issues, such as desirable security questions, are much more subtle. There could very well be other subtle cultural issues, such as connotation of dates and interpretation of rhymes, that could cause design issues. These issues are very hard to tackle by people who do not have sufficient knowledge or background in understanding cultural differences. Thus involving people who live in China to address these problems becomes very essential.

6. After addressing the issues raised by the translator, Richard and his team would most likely realize that the site launch is more complicated than they had originally anticipated. Richard and his team would require more help from people who have a more in-depth understanding of the Chinese culture and business, not to mention some explicit expertise in the localization of websites and user experience in general. Some of the minimal actions they should consider before moving any further are as follows:

- Reviewing page designs with a local Chinese collector who might be a potential user of MediaCentral.com. This collector could be seen as an extension of the design team and provide invaluable information about the Chinese market and typical user needs. This person could also provide some quick feedback on design directions.
- Launching the site in phases instead of all at once.
- Lining up strong Chinese customer support resources during the phased launch to provide on-demand assistance. A large number of problems exposed after the site is first used by real users should be expected. So, having a phased launch with customer support would help avoid problems becoming too big to handle.

7. Richard and his team took their design to a potential user to get feedback. This clearly helped them make a number of design decisions to improve the site. Leo was a very special potential user of the MediaCentral.com website, compared with typical current users. His uniqueness was reflected by the following:

- Expert in the collection of a certain period of Chinese history
- Fluent in English
- Unique personal background as a descendant of a royal family
   These personal attributes definitely helped the design team. Leo was able to provide richer information than typical users due to his superior knowledge in Chinese collections. This helped the team quickly acquire information regarding design considerations, because there were a very limited number of people available to provide specialized feedback such as this.

8. There are a number of weaknesses with the approach Richard and Elaine took:

- Leo has a very unique profile, which isn't typical of most Chinese collectors. His opinion may not represent most intended users. For instance, Leo's fluency in English is helpful in communicating with the design team. However, bilingual people are often more tolerant of translation problems than monolingual Chinese speakers.

- The team got feedback from only one person due to resource limitations. Feedback from one user does not provide any information on how more members of the targeted user group would react to the design. Given Leo's unique background, the findings from talking to Leo could very well be skewed away from the findings if more and typical users were involved in the exercise.

- The study process itself was not rigorous. In the exercise, Richard and Elaine walked through the design for Leo instead of asking Leo to complete certain tasks by himself. Richard and Elaine were likely inclined to take Leo through the typical path they believed most users would take. However, in reality, many users would have their own ways of using the site, which often trigger usability problems beyond the designers' anticipation. It would not be surprising if many potential usability issues did not surface because the user did not get a chance to use the system to accomplish actual tasks. In addition, Richard and Elaine conducted the exercise over the phone, through which they may have unconsciously lost much valuable information than if they conducted the study face to face with Leo. There are many nonverbal cues, such as expressions of confusion, which researchers can capture in a face-to-face study. This is especially important in doing a study in China. Chinese culture emphasizes more implicit nonverbal cues in conversations than does American culture. Chinese people tend to be more reserved in verbal comments, which makes nonverbal cues much more important in revealing issues accurately.

- It is not always a good idea for designers to test their own designs. The designers often form certain expectations during their extensive involvement in the project. These expectations often cause some bias toward certain user reactions. Study participants also tend to intentionally hide their negative opinions when talking directly to the design team or the product owners. These factors would often jeopardize the objectivity of the findings. This is especially important when conducting studies in China, because the Chinese culture highly values courtesy and discourages confrontation. When they know the questions are being asked by the designer, they may become very hesitant to provide any negative comments.

- The walkthrough was done in English. Although Leo is fluent in English, most people articulate things more fully in their native tongue. For a usability study with Chinese users, it would be better to conduct the sessions in Chinese and provide a translator for the English-speaking team.

9. The following points may have improved the study:

- A professional user researcher who speaks Chinese planned and had run the study. A professional researcher would be experienced in generating more rigorous and systematic research plans. They are also trained not to ask any leading questions, which nonprofessionals often make the mistake of doing.

- More participants representing typical users had been included in the study. This may take more time and resources. However, it would ultimately save money if a problem were discovered earlier in the process.

- Participants had been asked to complete key tasks with high-fidelity design prototypes. Low-fidelity prototypes allow testing to happen sooner and thus are often used to collect user comments on design concepts. However, many of the findings from testing low-fidelity prototypes may not apply after many visual and interaction elements are introduced into a high-fidelity prototype or final products. So, more and different usability issues could surface by allowing participants to interact directly with a high-fidelity prototype of the product.

- The exercises had been conducted by an independent researcher at a third-party location in China (not over the phone). This setup would help avoid any concerns participants might have about voicing negative comments. Again, due to the nature of their culture, Chinese people are more aware of context. Their reactions to the product will be more significantly influenced by the protocol used for this evaluation. In this case, if the study had been conducted by an independent researcher, the participants would have been much more comfortable raising controversial comments versus those provided when conducted by the owner of the product. It also would have been good to have had a facilitator from the same culture as the participants. Participants would feel better understood and would consequently be more willing to provide subtle details behind their comments.

10. An action plan should be put in place for the various aspects of the website that were found to be problematic:

1. Action plan for bugs
   - Enumerate the variation of computing environments and dedicate resources to test out implementations more thoroughly. The design team should try to get statistics on what technology is used in China and leverage the problems collected from customer support. This way, they would know which computing environment they should test the site on.
   - Conduct lab-based testing to simulate typical computer and network configurations. After getting information on the main configurations, it would be very efficient to simulate these configurations in the lab and test the site functionality with them. It is often impossible to test all the combinations, but lab testing can find lots of issues, including some serious ones, which may prevent site launch.
   - Test the website in the user's actual environment. There might be many hardware and software configurations in the real world that are very hard to predict or duplicate in the lab environment. So, the team should also sample some real users to test in their own environment. Such tests can be very resource intensive. So, it is good to plan such a study after getting a handle on the resources required for lab-based testing. In-home studies are an important step to verify the testing results in the lab and to be sure that it did not miss any important aspects of the actual user settings.

2. Action plan for confusing content:
   - Conduct heuristic reviews with more language specialists, domain experts (such as media professionals or collectors), and usability specialists. Language specialists are often professionally trained and experienced to write accurately for different types of readers. For instance, they know what words or phrases should be used for the general public and for more specialized user groups. Domain experts would be able to provide more insights on how to accurately express content that is best understood within their field. Chinese usability specialists could be helpful for both content and format. Even if the

team has the resources to go to China, they'd likely need the help of a native firm to conduct testing. Choosing a vendor or two in the early stages means being able to get answers more quickly later on.

- Conduct user studies that focus on the quality of the content. After the content is created by translators and language specialists and reviewed by domain experts, it still needs to be tested by the real users. Real users may not be as professional or sophisticated as content creators with regard to reviewing content, but they may reveal real usability issues that experts do not find. Actual user feedback will almost certainly lead to the discovery of more practical problems than the reviews from a few experts.

3. Action plan for layout and color:
    - Conduct heuristic reviews with native Chinese speakers to fix apparent visual design issues. Similar to asking language experts to review the contents, having Chinese people with a strong user interface design background review the site would be very helpful. These professionals can provide invaluable feedback about site design issues, so that more problems can be fixed before showing the site to users.
    - Research best practices from other site implementations. Good graphic user interface designs have lots of user experience commonalities. Researching designs of other sites will save lots of time for the designers. For instance, the team may not need to conduct separate research with the users to know what the best line spacing should be for a Chinese website. Instead, they can simply collect the line-spacing information from the most popular sites in China and quickly arrive at an answer.

11. Within the first nine months of being hired by MediaCentral.com, Sarah designed and conducted a number of studies, including focus groups, expert reviews, and iterative usability tests. She directly studied more than 100 Chinese users and communicated usability issues efficiently to the design team. In June 2003, the site was launched again successfully. This time customer support received far fewer complaints. Clearly, this success was largely a result of effective user research, which accurately addressed the needs of the Chinese users. Yes, a user researcher can help solve the speed issue.

- The site speed problem seemed to be more of a technical issue than a usability issue. However, site speed relates not only to the performance of the hardware, but also to human perception. People experience site delays in a very subjective manner; the delays can "feel" long or brief without objectively being either. So, a user researcher can provide special input on the human side of the puzzle. They can directly relate user responses to system performance.
- The user researcher has the unique opportunity to collect evidence from real users and delve more deeply into the specific instances of the general problem.

12. Based on knowledge and experience in site speed issues, Sarah might come up with the following speculations and hypotheses to take into account when she developed a research plan:

1. Perceived site speed versus real site speed
   - *Hypothesis:* Depending on the setup of the code on a web page, the site speed perceived by the users can be very different from what is actually recorded by machine. For instance, if the images are all shown as empty squares before they fully appear, then they are perceived as loading faster than in a setup that would not display anything until it is completely received from the client computer.
   - *Implications/challenge:* Perceived site speed, instead of actual site speed, should be measured in the study. However, it is a subjective measurement. This adds some complexities to the measurement. For instance, the user's judgment of what constitutes a complete page load is subjective, and it may be differently perceived among participants, making it difficult to compare across individuals or groups.

2. Above the fold versus below the fold
   - *Hypothesis:* Users care more about how fast they can view the contents above the fold (the area that is viewable without scrolling) than the contents below the fold.
   - *Implications/challenge:* A standard screen resolution for testing should be defined to ensure that roughly the same amount of content is measured across participants.

3. Client side versus server side tracking
   - *Hypothesis:* The data that can be tracked from the server does not necessarily reflect the speed from the client side

because the user-perceived site speed depends a lot on the settings in their own computer. For instance, if some content is cached, it would load much faster than content that is not cached.

- *Implications/challenge:* The tracking on the server side is much lower in cost than discrete user testing from the client side. Once a system is set up, it can collect a lot of data with little effort. There is also a possibility to automatically track downloaded data from the client side, which requires installation of specially designed software. Both methods would show superior scalability, but it is critical to have a solid prediction model for perceived download speed using the automatic tracking data.

4. Potential large variance from many sources
   - *Hypothesis:* Page download speed certainly depends on many factors. Some of the main factors include
     — Connection services: There are a number of Internet connection service providers, and each offers a series of service options and prices.
     — Geographic spread: Internet connection speed relates to the hardware infrastructure of the services. Different cities may have different quality of cable and phone lines, which affects the connection speed.
     — Internet traffic within a day and across days: Within a day, there could be variations in web traffic, and this certainly would affect download speed for individuals. Also, across days, (e.g., working days vs. weekends and holidays), there are also different patterns for download speed.
     — Computer configurations: There is a wide variety of computer brands and level of configurations across different computers. The computational and networking capabilities of each computer would significantly affect the download speed.
   - *Implications/challenge:* In general, a relatively large amount of data needs to be systematically acquired from a number of cities, at certain specific time frames, with certain computer configuration restrictions. The cities should be representative of the location and provider options within the country.

13. Based on her speculations and hypotheses, Sarah should outline the following main attributes for her study plan:
     - It should be a self-guided site test, which requires participants to follow study scripts and conduct the studies individually without moderation by a study administrator. This makes it possible to complete the study with a large sample size in a timely manner.
     - Study participants should use both a stopwatch and software to record load times. This way the data reveal the level of correlation between perceived load time and actual load time.
     - The test should be conducted in multiple cities in China to understand the impact of different network infrastructure across different areas.
     - Broadband and dial-up users should both be tested because both types of network services are popular with Chinese users.
     - Measures should be collected multiple times during a day and across some days, so that the variations of network load due to Chinese users' life-styles can be captured.
     - The measured effect of cached and noncached results should be collected. Once a page is loaded, content may be stored in the cache, which means it will load faster the next time. Capturing both cached and noncached results would reveal this difference.

Case 18: Designing for a Worldwide Product

1. One should consider that much of the development for the site generation tool was not based on requirements stemming from a good understanding of their markets. Caroline had argued that they did not have the knowledge of how the end consumers from around the globe worked and what their expectations would be. The new business division was targeting a new user group, the end traveler, with whom they had little experience. Additionally, they had never built a product that would adapt its user interface as a function of each market's culture. Their traditional product, which targeted the travel agents, had a single user interface—the agents were required to adapt to it. It was critical that the new division take the time to learn about their new

users, the travelers, and the new cultural requirements with which they had not dealt to date.

Caroline's concerns ended up being validated by the customers who complained that their websites were not well adapted to meet their markets' needs. They were doubly disappointed because not only was there little new revenue, they were also losing money for things such as help desk resources.

2. Based on the customer complaints, the On The Go division should determine the gaps between their customers' needs and what they are currently providing. They should review the site generation tool options to ensure that they are providing the right customization possibilities to allow the customers to adapt their websites for their markets. It also appears that they may need to invest in the visual appearance of the user interface to answer criticism such as, "It just doesn't look professional."

3. Caroline had argued unsuccessfully in the early days of the On The Go division that they would need to retain some part of the budget to invest in research to ensure a base understanding of the markets for which they were designing. The decision to move forward without conducting this research was reflected in the poor results they had witnessed.

Caroline recognizes that the lack of knowledge of their markets' needs is the root of the problem. Therefore it makes sense to invest in the research that she would have liked to have done in the very beginning. Caroline would be well served to create a project and find someone to lead the project who will understand the best way to gather the types of data they need. Any redesign should then be premised on these data.

4. There should be two main objectives of a redesign project. The primary objective is to define a site generation tool that can create websites that are well suited for the end users in each market. The sites need to be usable, and they need to make the users feel acclimated—as if it were designed for them. They should review the entire user interface to see what usability improvements could be made universally and to reassess which site components could really be the same for all customers and which ones would have to vary as a function of customers in different markets. The secondary objective of the project is to redesign the site generation tool so that it is easier to maintain and manage. Ideally, they would find that they have fewer numbers of site setup options to manage at the end of the project.

It might appear initially that these two objectives are conflicting. The primary objective would imply that the tool needed to be more flexible to provide more customization possibilities, whereas the secondary objective would require that they reduce the number of options provided for the site setup. However, the two objectives are not necessarily opposing. In the past the designers had often "over-designed" and had created too many options because they were unsure of what customers really needed. The research would be the foundation upon which decisions for the redesign would be made. With a better understanding of their markets' needs, they would be able to reduce most of the guesswork that had taken place to date. They would be able to review across all markets to determine when one solution would truly suffice for everyone and when multiple solutions were absolutely necessary. When they did need to create multiple solutions for a design problem, they would have a better idea of what those solutions needed to be thanks to the research.

5. The ideal approach to the problem would be to conduct primary research with end users around the world. But it would be worthwhile to consider other sources, particularly resources that are already available to the project team. Some of these could include
   - Trends in customer feedback collected during customer meetings, phone calls, or sent by e-mail
   - Usability reports that had been conducted to date
   - Help-desk reports from internal departments as well as from those managed by their customers
   - Independent studies and reports that address cultural differences (general reports and reports specific to e-commerce)
   - Review of the site-settings statistics to see which site settings were being used and which were not

   The advantage of these other types of information is that they are more readily available and can be reviewed before they begin to shape the plans for the international research in the markets. What they learn from these other reports will help them understand and organize the problem patterns, and they will be better able to prioritize their research—in terms of subjects and markets.

6. To perform research on a global basis and to design and deliver a solution (even if only partially) to hundreds of customers within nine months is a tall order. Jean-Marc will most certainly need to look at phasing the project. He should look at listing all the product components/features that need to be redesigned and determine which

components will be included at each phase. To determine this, the team will need to prioritize the user interface components by determining their frequency of use and by defining which components are creating the most difficulties for the customers and end users.

After that, they will need to ensure that grouped product components within each phase can be released as a "stand-alone." In other words, it is necessary that the components within each phase can be released independently from the other product components because they will not be able to release a product that contains a mixture of the old design and the new design. However, they would be able to temporarily maintain two versions of the product—the old version and the new version. The customers would be able to decide whether to publish a site with the old user interface version but which contains all of the product components or a site with the new version of the user interface but which contains only a subset of components.

The second challenge the project team needs to address is their inability to perform design reviews with all their 300+ customers around the world. They should define a subset of travel agencies who are as representative as possible of their global markets. These customers will need to commit to investing their time to review the design proposals that are put forth throughout the project.

Finally, the biggest challenge is to find a way to shorten the timeline required for the end users around the world to evaluate the design proposals. One way to do this is to perform each round of usability evaluations in a different subset of markets. When the project moves to the next phase, previously designed components can be retested along with the new components. In this way the team is able to profit from another iteration of testing on the redesigned components and to gather additional data from the second subset of markets. The team could also consider outsourcing some of the usability tests so that the tests can take place in parallel. The advantage of performing the research themselves is that they can draw directly from their observations rather than relying on someone else's interpretation, but it would mean that they could cover less ground with their current resources. The obvious advantage of outsourcing some of the testing is the ability to increase the rate at which they gather data. Additionally, it could be beneficial to have insights from someone not already embedded in their industry—a fresh perspective.

However, they would need to consider the amount of time it would take to manage an outsourced study (e.g., contract negotiation, training on their business/industry/current product, etc.).

7. The revised/shortened version of the project plan introduces some risks. For the project team to deliver the first part of the redesigned user interface within the seven to nine months, they must assume their findings from the usability tests demonstrate that they have achieved their objectives. If they arrive at the end of the phase and find that they have not succeeded, they will have to consider making further changes to the designs. And if these changes are considerable, they should perform another iteration and cycle through the reviews again. In this case they would not be able to meet the date prescribed for the first deliverable.

It could also happen that they learn things in later phases that would impact the designs completed in the previous phases. If this were to happen, the project team may have to make changes to previously confirmed design solutions—design solutions that may have already been coded and tested. Making changes to code is more expensive and, as a result, less likely to happen unless it is critical to the success of the product.

Case 19: Inspecting a User Interface

1. An effective engagement relies on mutual trust. For the practitioner, an effective interview ensures that the brief is clearly defined in terms of a business and technical context. For the client a well-conducted interview shows that the practitioner is professional and trustworthy and can become an effective partner in solving the problem. Trust is especially critical in a usability inspection; the warrant for the results is the perceived competence and integrity of the evaluator.

2. Stuart did not describe to Hannah any history of user-centered design at Prometheus. However, it is probable that teachers and learners were not actively involved in shaping the usability requirements and user experience design. Prometheus could certainly have reduced risk by evaluating earlier design representations such as low-fidelity prototypes.

3. By fully understanding Stuart's requirements, Hannah could design an evaluation that would deliver the answers Stuart needed, making the

appropriate trade-offs between commercial value and scientific rigor while ensuring a focus on the most relevant set of issues.

4. Inspection methods involve role play. Evaluators adopt the perspective of a specific user role concerned with achieving some realistic goal. By playing the role, they predict both the subjective and objective user experience arising from the characteristics of that role. For example, assumptions about motivation, culture, skills, domain knowledge, and application experience might all be critical in assessing the fit of a solution to its intended audience. For example, knowing that users might include E2L (English as a second language), readers might focus the evaluators' attention on the appropriateness of idiomatic or complex language. On the other hand, awareness of time constraints would encourage evaluators to consider whether the design is sufficiently efficient to satisfy user needs.

5. Good design can be seen as a win–win solution that satisfies both the business goals of the sponsor and the personal goals of the users. An evaluator consequently needs to understand the needs of the organization to assess the fit to strategy. For example, an evaluator should not over-emphasize the lack of walk-up-and-use learnability in a design that has been optimized for efficient use by trained users. Without a good understanding of the business context, evaluators are likely to focus on surface issues such as typography and layout. Business context ensures that the evaluators also consider more abstract issues such as the fit to the user's conceptual model or the adaptation to the context of use.

6. Hannah might use something like the template shown in Figure a.16 to analyze Stuart's input. She could use this analysis as the basis of a formal study design.

7. Susan, Michael, Erica, and Martin would make a good team. Collectively, their skills give good coverage of the areas to be evaluated. Furthermore, they can generally be expected to be professional and insightful. Ronald's skills in design legislation are not strongly relevant to this study. Rose's standards skills are somewhat less critical in web design, and her style may be a liability. Hannah would, of course, need to ensure that Erica restrained her sense of humor when describing observations.

8. If Hannah chose the wrong team members, the team might potentially miss critical issues, overstate problems, or write in an inappropriate style. Although the latter two problems could be

Logistics

    1. When the evaluators should start and complete their inspection

    2. How to install, access, and run the design

    3. Documentation and background reading

    4. Security and confidentiality instructions

    5. Evaluation manager's name and contact details

Goals

    For each user goal:

        Role, context, goal description (as perceived by the user), and scenario

Views

    For each view:

        Name, description, and unique identifier (e.g., URL)

Evaluation checklist

    A checklist to guide the evaluators' attention to areas of interest to the client.

    These might include references to the following resources:

        1. Heuristics (e.g., Nielsen usability heuristics [Nielsen, 1994])

        2. Guidelines (e.g., RNIB guidelines for accessible design)

        3. Principles (e.g., Universal principles of design [Butler et al., 2003])

        4. Standards (e.g., Common User Access [IBM, 1993])

        5. Legislation (e.g., U.K. Disabilities Discrimination Act [Disability Rights Commission])

Figure a.16. Study design template.

addressed by editing, the cost would be high. Because an inspection may generate several hundred individual observations, rewriting for style while maintaining the sense of the original can be time consuming and error prone.

9.   Hannah might be concerned with ensuring that observations are prioritized consistently by an independent analyst who is also thoroughly familiar with the business context and can make an informed judgment on severities. Additionally, she might believe that evaluators can add more value by spending less time "voting" and more time discovering.

10.   Good design should be recognized and acknowledged to encourage best practice and temper criticism. Reporting achievements is an effective technique for building trust by demonstrating a balanced professional perspective.

11.   Asking for a principle encourages practitioners to think analytically within a theoretical framework and tends to discourage "false positives," that is, unsupported opinions that may distort the data. The principle may also subsequently help the study manager to classify the observation against a predefined coding scheme.

12.   Observation 1 ("Too much pink") is a subjective personal opinion. Although the principle seems valid, it does not support the evaluator's opinion. The recommendation is also inappropriately specific. Observation 2 ("More than seven menu entries") is based on a misapplication of a useful principle. The "magic number 7 ± 2" describes Miller's work (Miller, 1956) on empirically determined limits for the number of meaningful chunks that can be held in working memory. Although this research might be helpful for assessing the maximum practical length for a menu readout by an interactive voice system, it does not define the limits for a menu presented visually. Kent Norman's work on menu psychology (Norman, 1991) is probably more relevant here. Although observation 3 ("Insufficient contrast") makes a good point, incorrect spelling and inappropriate humor mar the quality of the report. Furthermore, the issue is identified as legibility rather than readability. Where legibility relates to appropriate use of type and color, readability is a function of style and vocabulary. Finally, this finding also fails to include a recommendation.

13. Observations that are factually or theoretically incorrect are likely to misinform the client and may ultimately lead to inappropriate design changes. Correct but poorly presented observations may not communicate the issues and could, in extreme cases, damage the credibility of the entire evaluation team.

14. Following up observation 1 with the evaluator might uncover a more substantive concern with the branding implications of selecting a color palette. Observation 2 can probably be excluded, and observation 3 should be edited for spelling and style. Hannah might also offer some mentoring to all three authors with a view to improving their reporting style for subsequent studies.

15. A predefined coding scheme has a number of benefits:
    1. It reduces the time and effort required to code raw data by eliminating the need to discover an emergent framework through multiple iterations.
    2. It improves analytical consistency within and across projects by requiring evaluators to use a common model.
    3. It supports meta-analysis such as historical comparisons, trend analysis, and benchmarking.
    4. It can help to shape an analysis to accurately reflect both the business concerns of clients and the scientific models of skilled HCI specialists.

    On the other hand, emergent coding frameworks are powerful tools for finding and communicating the unexpected. Using a predefined scheme establishes an analytical "set"; issues outside the framework may be missed, ignored, or misclassified. Additionally, a predefined framework is only helpful for analyzing issues within its scope. For example, a usability scheme is not helpful for analyzing domains such as safety, accessibility, or branding.

16. Clients are typically more focused on the "bottom line" than the detailed results. Although they may be interested to know that a design makes unreasonable demands on its user's working memory, their primary concerns are more likely to include assessing any resulting risk to their business strategy, mitigating this risk through appropriate design interventions, and avoiding reoccurrence by defining an improved design process.

17. Business readers generally prefer concise pithy reports. Listing all the supporting evidence for each finding would make the report bulky

and repetitive. However, supporting a summary with selected references to the underlying observations both illustrates the overview and demonstrates a rigorous process. Of course, other stakeholders, such as designers and engineers, may wish to review the full set of findings to understand and address the issues described.

18. The "business impact" dimension maps observations to business outcomes. For example, if many observations were coded against Adoption in this dimension, Hannah would predict a risk to uptake by potential users. She might also trace back through the associated "Task impact," "Effect," and "Cause" codes to understand why users might choose not to adopt.

19. The "Cause" dimension of the coding scheme maps observations to phases and activities in the design process. For example, if many observations are coded against the phase Understanding Users, Hannah might recommend more investment in primary user research.

20. Hannah was concerned that Stuart should get the best outcome from his usability investment. In practice, study reports are not always translated into action—often because clients can be daunted by the perceived difficulty of improving the design. However, a joint planning session frequently identifies "quick wins" and affordable follow-up activities.

Case 20: Billingsly: A Case Study in Managing Project Risks and Client Expectations

1. The new account software is causing a variety of problems at Billingsly:
    *   The new account software is difficult to use. It is poorly organized, with the most important parts of the online form interspersed among parts that are not critical for opening and maintaining a new account. Compounding the problems is the fact that more regulatory information is required than in the past.
    *   In the past the financial consultants recorded the information needed to open a new account in the presence of the client by asking the appropriate questions and recording the answers directly onto the paper or online form (the InSight application). Now because the new account software is difficult to use, it makes the financial consultants feel foolish and clumsy in front of

their clients. Consequently, the financial consultants collect the information needed to open a new account by jotting down notes on scraps of paper and passing the notes along to their financial assistants to deal with. Often, the financial assistants have to contact the clients to acquire the remaining information, further stalling the process.

- Because the process takes longer with the new account software, branch offices are not as productive and profitable as they once were.

- The users of the software at Headquarters are forced to work harder and longer to compensate for the problems at the branches. Their morale is also poor.

- The snowball effect (the new account software is more difficult to use, thereby slowing down the process, in turn affecting morale and self-esteem) is causing financial consultants and assistants to leave Billingsly for jobs with competitors.

- Not only was morale low, but branch office managers were angry. Some were calling for those responsible to be fired.

2. Ownership of the problems being caused by the new account software is not clearcut. IT resides in its own division; branch office operations resides in another. IT designed and built the new software; however, the productivity, profitability, and ultimately employee satisfaction at the branch offices come under the purview of the business side of the house. As manager of the IT group that designed and built the software, Vicky believes she owns the problem. Sam, on the other hand, is ultimately accountable for the branch offices and, as such, believes solving the problem is his responsibility. In the end, because of the organizational structure and governance at Billingsly, it is virtually impossible to lay ownership of the problem—and therefore its solution—at any single person's feet.

3. There are many reasons Billingsly might arrive at the conclusion that they should look outside the company for help in solving the problem:
- Most of Billingsly's profits come from opening new client accounts. The software that enables financial consultants and assistants in the completion of this task is, therefore, one of the most important pieces of software that Billingsly can provide its financial consultants and financial assistants. Even though the software is being produced by Vicky's department, it was Sam whose focus was on the overall impact to the business.

- The policy at Billingsly toward new software is to buy first and only secondarily to design and build in-house. This could lead one to the conclusion that Billingsly's IT department has more skill in creating feasibility studies and managing the creation of new software than it does in designing and building it.
- According to Sam, Billingsly's IT department already had a shot at creating the new software and failed.
- Sam knows he has to stem the tide of their best financial consultants and financial assistants leaving for what they perceive to be easier means of closing new accounts. He also knows he has to act fast. He believes that Billingsly's own organizational structure may be a contributing factor to its failure in this area. An outside firm can focus solely on the problem and bring stronger skills to bear.
- Sam knew that Billingsly's technical architects and developers had specified the functionality and designed the current software's user interface. How could that be? They weren't user interface designers.
- Billingsly's usability department is already spread too thin. In addition, they're admittedly not designers. They've made a clear decision to spend their time evaluating solutions.

4. Some potential problems with the RFP 1FineInc could foresee at this point are as follows:

- The RFP is not specific enough about the technical documentation required. Does Billingsly want use cases? A technical spec? A user interface spec? A requirements document? All of these? Some or one of these? Will Billingsly's IT department want to rely most heavily on the working prototype as their "spec," or will they want the documentation to play the stronger role in guiding them in the final design and development of the new solution?
- Although Billingsly states in the RFP that the ultimate deliverable is a working prototype, it appears they are looking for the design of an entire product in a couple of months' time. To get to a working prototype, the team will have to go through many of the same steps they would use to get to a final product, especially in the area of UCD. Just as with a full-blown solution, the UCD team would still need to understand users, their workflows, and

their requirements; understand what's wrong with the current solution; design the high-level conceptual model; iteratively usability test and refine it; design and usability-test detailed design; create the working prototype; and document the requirements and technical specs for implementation purposes. Billingsly seemingly expects more than can be reasonably delivered in a short period of time.

- Although the RFP was written by IT, it appears that there are two sets of strong stakeholders—IT and business, each residing in its own division. And, although the business stakeholders were the most interested in the new project at the information meeting, the RFP was issued by the IT department, which resides in a different division than the business stakeholders do.
- In the information meeting tension existed between IT and business. How would they work together during the project? Would 1FineInc end up being pulled in both directions, thereby satisfying no one? IT would be interested in such things as how they will apply the deliverables to the implementation of the solution. They would want to know how easily the design will be able to be implemented, if it will fit with their software standards, and will they be able to begin their analysis phase in 3 months? In the end, IT wants to get it right, but they also want it to go away. The poor user acceptance of AccountNow diminished them in the eyes of the business. The business stakeholders want the design to be right this time. They want to show the prototype to the branches as soon as possible and then get it released as quickly as they can after that so they can quell the dissension. Even though the RFP was issued by IT, everyone at the information meeting deferred to Sam. Who will lead the project at Billingsly? IT or the business stakeholders?
- Billingsly would be a new client for 1FineInc. Although 1FineInc has successfully designed, developed, and delivered solutions for other financial services companies, Billingsly is the largest one 1FineInc has dealt with. 1FineInc can base its plans and estimations on its experience with similar smaller firms in the same domain, but there are lots of unknowns, including such things as how long it takes deliverables to be approved, is there a formal deliverable approval process, will Billingsly want robust reports and lengthy interim presentations throughout the short

process, or will they more likely want each activity to feed directly into the design of the new prototype?

- Billingsly has a usability department, and, indeed, much of the RFP focused on usability; however, Billingsly was looking for a top-notch usability and design firm to come in and redesign the new account software. The RFP asked 1FineInc to explain how it would work with Billingsly's in-house usability department. 1FineInc was confused. If Billingsly has a usability department, why were they going outside the company? It seemed that 1FineInc had to walk a narrow line in laying out its approach to the problem. It could not offend Billingsly's usability department; at the same time it had to convey to Billingsly that 1FineInc was the best choice for them in the usability arena. No matter how 1FineInc framed it, how was Billingsly's usability department going to react?

- The RFP was vague in its request for a prototype. What did Billingsly mean by "new user interfaces"? Was there more than one? Should the prototype be a redesign of the entire solution? If so, 1FineInc would need more time.

- Because of the problems caused at the branch offices by the first release of the new account software and because of the number of users, divisions, and stakeholders involved, the prototype project will have extremely high visibility in the company. The vendor who wins the contract will be under daily scrutiny by competing groups who want different results from the project. Who will have the final say?

5. Typically, there are more screens than use cases in a software application. Yet Billingsly said AccountNow currently consists of 14 screens driven by 28 use cases. This could have several huge implications for 1FineInc:

   - Because 1FineInc won't have access to the current solution before being selected, the number of screens and use cases are the main contributing factors in estimating the length and, therefore, the cost of the project.

   - This could affect the way 1FineInc estimates the number of user profiles. The number of user profiles is a contributing factor in the planning and execution of the user input and feedback techniques 1FineInc proposes for the project. It determines such things as the number of user types 1FineInc would need to engage in contextual inquiry sessions. It also determines how many participants would need to be scheduled for both the 3 × 3 iterative prototyping and usability test sessions and the final usability test. The number of users engaged in all these activities affects the overall duration of each of the usability techniques and, therefore, of the entire project: the number of sessions to be conducted, the length of time needed to analyze issues and problems found, and the amount of time needed to create and present the findings from each of the techniques. If 1FineInc proposes a set number of techniques and the number of user profiles is greater than expected, 1FineInc won't be able to deliver on time and in budget, ultimately a critical success factor in consulting engagements.

- Because there are few standards in use case writing, 1FineInc may not understand how large the current solution actually is. Does Billingsly include all aspects of a scenario and their exceptions in one use case, or is each exception a separate use case? Is there one major use case for opening a new account, or is each account type documented in its own use case?

6. In addition to the information the team gathered about the users, their tasks, their work, their environment, and their requirements, the 1FineInc team made an important discovery during the contextual inquiry sessions at the branch offices. They learned that InSight is above all else an online form. But they also learned that most of the work the branches did involved forms. InSight was a form, but many of the other applications were forms or collections of forms or containers for forms. Why were the forms spread across so many applications? The team noted inefficiencies in the branch work in general because the users are forced to traverse applications to locate and deal with all the forms they might use in one day, and they are often prompted to gather information for their clients that they already have in another form. The AccountNow prototype project isn't structured to solve this bigger problem. The danger for Billingsly is the AccountNow project solves only part of the problem at the branches. Sam's phone may stop ringing with complaints about the online account software, but it may start ringing with complaints that the forms used on a daily basis at the branches require redundant information to be gathered and the users are forced to go in and out of many different applications to find all the forms they need for the

day. The danger for 1FineInc is that they may be perceived as solving one problem while creating another, which would reduce their chances of winning any new work at Billingsly.

7. Although Billingsly follows a traditional waterfall approach to design and development, 1FineInc's approach is more iterative. At the end of the design phase IT wants something they can use to go off and develop. They want a proscriptive deliverable that they can use as a type of specification. They want the design done. The UCD approach, however, is ongoing with each subsequent iteration building on and adding to the one before. The detailed design phase in UCD actually overlaps the beginning of development. This isn't as cut and dried as Billingsly IT would like it to be and is accustomed to.

   The output of the 3 × 3 is a high-level design—even a conceptual model—to move forward with through detailed design and implementation. But when does "high-level design" end and "low-level or detail design" begin? To human–computer interaction specialists the line between high-level design and detail design is messy. In the 3 × 3 process the home or main page is fully fleshed out; however, the remainder of the pages only exist to illustrate the path through the tasks that were selected to be prototyped. The home/main page, therefore, contains both high-level design and navigation, but because it is as fully fleshed out as it can be in the first round, it's bound to reflect details as well. In fact, if there's time and the designers have ideas about the details of a design, they often end up in the 3 × 3s. There are no hard and fast rules around what goes in and what doesn't go in a low-fidelity paper prototype. The purpose of paper prototyping is, after all, to try out lots of ideas with users while still early in the process. This is definitely one of those areas of HCI and UCD that is more art than science.

8. Because of the tight schedule, made tighter by the delay in the start of the project due to Billingsly's legal and contracts process, the 1FineInc team had to remain very focused on the specific tasks they were doing leading up to the working prototype. They needed every spare minute to complete the work they needed to do before the branch visits, and they needed all the time they could get when they returned from the branches to compile and analyze data and prepare for the next presentation of findings/results. They did not have time to meet regularly with Billingsly's IT group as much as they should

have or would have liked to. Consequently, communication suffered and actions were misconstrued on both sides. Billingsly perceived 1FineInc to be evasive when, in actuality, they were just busy. 1FineInc hadn't been clear on Billingsly's expectations from the beginning of the project and yet they didn't have time to meet to talk things through. In addition, 1FineInc was unaware that Billingsly was trying to begin technical analysis and design during iterative prototyping and usability testing.

9. 1FineInc didn't know why the IT group wanted the paper prototypes at this point in the project. It seemed to the 1FineInc team that Billingsly would want to wait until the prototype was closer to completion. After all, this was a prototype and not a full-blown application. The reasons IT wanted to see the paper prototypes before testing include the following:

   • IT may have wanted to have input to the design. Even though they weren't designers and they had not interacted with the users, they had designed the initial release and might be able to spot potential problems ahead of time.

   • IT wanted to begin sizing the effort so they could begin planning implementation. Were there elements of the interface that would require extra work? Did the workflow and navigation fit with their back end processes and databases?

   • IT feared what the branch offices would see. Would they react negatively? Would they be promised new functionality that the team couldn't deliver? They didn't understand the nature of paper prototyping and hence could have been afraid of over promising, not realizing that UCD practitioners approach this carefully by level setting at the beginning of each user session.

10. The questions Vicky's team asked were either about low-level detailed design or about tasks and paths that weren't the most important and frequently performed; hence, they weren't the tasks/scenarios that had been prototyped. The 1FineInc team knew Sally had explained the 3 × 3 process to IT during the sales pursuit and again at the project kickoff meeting. What was it about high-level design that IT didn't get? Did they not realize that they couldn't prototype three unique approaches to the entire solution in 5 days? Not only was it an impossible task to do, it wasn't part of the purview of the first round of the 3 × 3. In the first round they wanted to learn if they had the "right" conceptual model—a model

that would map to the user's mental model. They wanted to know whether they were *directionally* correct, not that every "i" was dotted and "t" crossed.

11. Due to the aggressive schedule that Pamela's team had to adhere to in order to complete the project on time and in budget, they had deferred important meetings with Billingsly's IT group. When they were finally able to carve time out to have the meeting, they discovered each group had different expectations about the final deliverables. Pamela's team thought they were documenting only the tasks that had been through the UCD process and that they were including in the working prototype. Tim and his team thought that the entire AccountNow solution would be documented in the use cases. How had each team arrived at the conclusion it did? The RFP is vague: It refers to "new user interfaces." Pamela's team was so focused on getting designs and contextual inquiry and test materials ready in time for the next set of branch office visits that it hadn't taken the time to ensure everyone had the same expectations.

12. 1FineInc needs to complete the working prototype and the associated documentation. They need to either create a change order to include prototyping, usability testing, and writing use cases for the remaining tasks or they need with work with Billingsly's IT group to include the work in the next phase of the project. They should work with IT to ensure that several more rounds of iterative prototype and usability testing are conducted during the detailed design phase.

Case 21: Aikot Corporation: A Case Study in Qualitative/Quantitative Remote Evaluation

1. Mark realized that although Aikot has an online presence in a number of countries throughout the world, he has many unanswered questions about the visitors and their experience on the site. Specifically, Mark needs to answer the following questions to help him understand how visitors are using the site:
   - Who is visiting the website?
   - What are they doing when they are there?
   - Are they successful in completing their tasks? If not, why?
   - Why are visitors leaving the shopping cart process?
   - Do the profiles of the online visitors match the profiles of Aikot's off-line visitors?

- How does the website visit impact visitors' impression of the brand?
- How does the website visit impact future calls to action such as returning to the site, purchasing products on the site, and recommending the site to others?

2. Aikot uses Hit Box web analytics on the site to track the number of unique and returning visitors. They have implemented the Hit Box code on all style sheet templates and individual pages of process funnels such as the site registration process. Mark and his team use the Hit Box data at the most basic level to identify traffic flow. These data are not enough because they do not tell why visitors are doing what they are doing. Mark needs to understand why visitors are doing what they are doing in addition to where they are going and dropping off. Mark needs to correlate the web analytics with data from real visitors to have a more complete understanding of the user experience on the website.

3. Several aspects of the development process and team structure may have contributed to the lack of knowledge about the influence of the website on the company's bottom line. The online Internet marketing team consists of product managers, a website manager, a web content manager, and a third-party design agency. There is no multidisciplinary design team in place, and, most importantly, there is no one representing the customer.

    The main goal for this team was to build a website. They did not understand or know that to build a website that is both compelling and easy to use, they need team members with specific usability, user-centered design, market research, information architecture, or interaction design skills.

    In addition, personal performance goals for the product managers on the team are based on product development release schedules rather than how well their products perform in terms of revenue growth or how easy it is to find their product on the website. The result is that product managers focus more on ensuring products are developed on time rather than on how successful website visitors are in finding information and accessories about the product on the website.

4. To be successful, the online team needs customer advocates. Team members designated as customer representatives or advocates often have a background in human factors engineering, usability, psychology, or market research. These team members are the customer advocates who conduct a variety of user research activities to learn more about the

customers and their goals. The customer research informs the design team as they develop the website.

Mark has a lot of work to do, including

- Revamping the marketing plan
- Setting concrete measurable goals for the web channel
- Identifying who is coming to the website, and why
- Learning about visitors' experience on the website
- Understanding what works well and what needs improvement on the website
- Revamping the website based on what he learns from this process
- Hiring personnel or learning enough to do the work himself

5. At the conclusion of their meeting, the Aikot user experience team should have outlined the year's goals for the website, as follows:
- Understand who is visiting the website.
- Identify visitors' goals and activities performed on the site.
- Identify visitors' expectations for the website.
- Understand how successful visitors are in achieving their goals and completing their activities.
- Identify areas of the website that work well and those that need improvement.
- Identify key metrics for the website, obtain baseline measures, and set growth targets (both minimum and maximum).
- Conduct user research to help inform the design and development process.

6. Conducting exploratory quantitative/qualitative online remote research on the Aikot website will allow the team to invite people who are naturally visiting the website. The participants will be able to complete the study in their own environment whether at home, in the office, or somewhere else and will not have to travel to a usability lab or research center. The participants will be able to use a computer they are familiar with and that represents their actual technical work environment. Participants may take as much time completing the study as they want. Anne will have her team add Javascript code to the home page of the website that is used to pop up an image or message inviting people to give us their thoughts about the website experience.

Quantitative/qualitative online remote research is an effective way for Anne and her team to gather customer attitudes, intentions, and behaviors and measure performance directly on a website. This combination of qualitative and quantitative data will help inform

Anne's team about the strengths and weaknesses of the site so they can work on improving the online customer experience. Because a significant number of people naturally visiting the site are invited to participate in the study, Anne and her team will have confidence in the findings regarding what is working well and what needs to be improved on the site. In addition, the large sample sizes will help them understand who is visiting the site and provide data that will enable them to create profiles of these site visitors.

This approach combines the best aspects of market research, usability research, and web analytics. The Aikot team will have data in large quantities to help them understand the behavior of current and potential customers and to provide insight into the attitudes, intentions, behavior, and performance of a statistically significant sample of site visitors attempting real-life tasks on Aikot's websites.

7. By conducting an online remote exploratory research project, the team will be able to collect the following information:
   - Identify who is coming to the website (current customers, potential customers, from which geographic location, compare online visitor profiles with the off-line profiles, etc.)
   - Identify visitors' level of familiarity with Aikot's brand (do they own Aikot's products, how long have they used them, do they intend to purchase more products)
   - Understand visitors' expectations for their visit (find product information quickly, make a purchase online, compare products easily, etc.)
   - Understand what visitors intend to do while visiting the website (find the price, purchase items, find support information, order services, find store locations, etc.)
   - Assess success in completing their tasks on the site (how long did it take to complete the tasks, was the experience difficult or frustrating, why was the task difficult, what helped visitors succeed)
   - Understand how satisfied they are with their visit to the site (did visitors find what they were looking for, did the information meet their expectations, were they able to do what they wanted to easily and quickly)
   - Measure ease of finding information needed (including easy-to-understand language or terms)
   - Compare expectations before and after the website visit
   - Measure visitor success based on personal goals

- Understand the result of their site experience on key calls to action (e.g., likelihood to recommend, likelihood to return, likelihood to purchase)

8. To invite visitors to participate in the study, Ann's team could intercept visitors at each of the designated Aikot home pages (United States, Germany, Mexico) with an invitation in their own language. A welcome message describes the process and the invitation will provide a link to a remote study.

9. Anne's team can set up the study to make the participant's experience as natural as possible in the following ways:

- After participants agree to participate, ask them a few questions regarding their intentions for visiting the website and their mindset at the start of the visit.
- Before participants begin interacting with the website, they will need to download a small application that is used to collect behavioral data such as time on task, URLs visited, and search field entries. Alternatively, the behavioral data can be captured using a proxy server set up by the online research application vendor.
- Next instruct the participants to continue with their visit. During this part of the process, participants will interact with the website completing the activities they originally came to the site to complete.
- To find out whether or not participants were successful, present them with a set of questions designed to elicit feedback regarding their experience.
- Finally, the team can ask other questions they are interested in understanding.

Some remote online research applications will capture other information while the participant interacts with the website, such as how much time it takes to complete the tasks, how much time is spent on each page, the URL of the pages visited, and the navigation paths followed while completing the tasks. Other data captured might include time and date of the study and search terms entered in search fields. This information will help the team understand some of the behavioral aspects of the experience on the website.

Just as with traditional usability studies, Anne and her team can decide whether or not to offer an incentive to the participants of the remote studies for their efforts. If a website has a high daily unique visit rate of 5,000 or more, researchers generally do not have to provide an incentive for this type of evaluation. This research methodology uses self-directed tasks rather than directed tasks for other types of studies. One alternative would be to start the evaluation without offering an incentive and then if the response rate is low, offer an incentive.

Case 22: Using Technology to Automate Summative Usability Testing

1. One major advantage is that the CIF has been developed and adopted by several of the most respected and influential technology companies in the world. A second advantage is that the CIF allows one to measure the "performance" of a product, which could better inform the business of competitive advantages or even risks. The CIF also allows for more direct comparisons across studies over time.

2. There are many things Doug should highlight:
   - CIF provides a standardized report for summative usability studies.
   - CIF is designed to ensure that efficiency, effectiveness, and subjective satisfaction are measured.
   - CIF allows for easier test procedure replication.
   - CIF can help reduce reporting time for usability staff.
   - CIF was created by an international committee of usability professionals and continues to be revised and improved.

3. The biggest benefit regarding a single score is that it can be digested by development teams and executives. If the goal was to achieve a "5" or to increase a previous score by 10%, it is easy for the team to determine a product's standing. In addition, consumers of usability data are often numbers driven (e.g., software engineers or marketing professionals), and providing data to them in their own language can help to ensure that the data are noticed and acted on.

4. The biggest risk in combining related metrics into a single score is ensuring the validity of the "scoring formula," because the output of such a score is only as good as the science used to create it. Therefore it is critical that the scoring mechanism is judiciously reviewed and validated through objective testing and peer reviews.

   Another risk is that the formula is too complex, either in reality or in perception. In general, individuals will not use or trust a new method or concept if they do not fully understand it or at least grasp it conceptually. Rachael's team had a goal of being able to explain and teach their formula to other usability professionals within 10 minutes.

5. When looking at complex concepts with rich sets of data, it is often the goal to have a single score to provide a meaningful summary. Credit report scores, educational scores (such as the MCAT, LSAT, or GRE), and even an IQ score are all examples of the combination of multiple attributes used to determine a single score.

6. Most usability professionals come from a research background, and unless they make a conscious effort to attain rudimentary business skills (i.e., project planning, forecasting, and budgeting) they may struggle when attempting to have a more strategic impact in their business. Leading large and complex projects will tap these skills; without them, the usability professional may be at a significant disadvantage. In addition, having a good grasp of business fundamentals can help a user researcher make more informed decisions regarding user versus business requirements and trade-offs. For example, a system may contain a feature that users find frustrating or too time consuming (e.g., inputting a customer's information into a customer relationship management system). From a user's perspective, this may seem to be a waste of time, because if they were not required to do it they could tackle more customer calls in a day and therefore appear more productive. However, tracking this customer information may be critical to the business and every bit as important as handling customer calls. Therefore user research may focus on how to make this "annoying" but necessary feature as usable and nonintrusive as possible but in no way suggest that it be removed.

7. Based on the proposed tools, method, and scoring mechanism, Rachel's main selling points of the new plan presented to Jerry were as follows:
    - No negative impact on attaining tangible product score cards that key stakeholders could easily internalize or on the single and consistent measure for usability that would afford the ability of user research to track improvements over time and to allocate resources to low scoring areas
    - Ability for user research to execute studies in a fraction of the time because multiple studies could be conducted simultaneously
    - Fewer sessions and therefore reduced study/lab costs and resources

- Ability to turn around data almost instantly via automated reporting
- Potential to "baseline" many more features of a product because more tests could be run in less time with little impact on the development team or user research (economy of scale)

8. There are a few potential problems with the new plan:
   - Rachael now had vendors but no tests for them to run as previously scheduled, so she assigned them other work that was neglected due to staffing constraints.
   - There was also some ill will between Rachael and some other leads in Jerry's organization because the development of her tools required other work in the division to be temporarily paused or deprioritized. To help alleviate this, Rachel scheduled one-on-one meetings with the leads of the groups affected to better explain the project and its strategic importance.
   - The product team was expecting data to flow in, but Rachael had to tell them that the schedule was slipping. However, they appreciated the fact that she promised that her team would deliver the entire data set early.

9. One major difference is that this team needed to set up their lab to run many participants concurrently. Each participant needed their own system, and most traditional labs do not accommodate this type of setup. Therefore one may need to secure a larger room to run the study (e.g., a conference room or a lab designed to run focus groups).

10. A great benefit of this type of study is that it could allow a researcher to run many more participants; however, if the recruiting pool is scarce (e.g., highly technical participants), it may be difficult to recruit enough people, especially if you narrow the study's time frame.